KEY INDICATORS
FOR ASIA AND THE PACIFIC
2020
51ST EDITION

ASIAN DEVELOPMENT BANK

ADB

© 2020 Asian Development Bank
6 ADB Avenue, Mandaluyong City, 1550 Metro Manila, Philippines
Tel +63 2 8632 4444; Fax +63 2 8636 2444
www.adb.org

Some rights reserved. Published in 2020.

ISBN 978-92-9262-358-6 (print); 978-92-9262-359-3 (electronic); 978-92-9262-360-9 (ebook)
ISSN 0116-3000
Publication Stock No. FLS200250-3
DOI: https://dx.doi.org/10.22617/FLS200250-3

Corrigenda to ADB publications may be found at http://www.adb.org/publications/corrigenda.

Notes:
In this publication, "$" refers to US dollars.
ADB recognizes "China" as the People's Republic of China, "Korea" as the Republic of Korea, and "East Timor" as Timor-Leste.

Cover photo:
On the cover: In Viet Nam, the government has applied e-government and started a financial assistance program for the poor via online application and e-payment. In the photo are Mai, an ethnic mother and her child living in Cao Bang, a poor province in the North Viet Nam. The single mother has two children, one of whom is disabled. She and the other child were happy when receiving an SMS informing that money had been transferred successfully to her bank account. They no longer have to travel far and wait in a long line every month. E-payment is more convenient, faster, and safer.

Cover design by Nguyen Thanh Hien.

Contents

Figures

PART III: Global Value Chains

Figures

Tables

Box

Definitions

Foreword

Key Indicators for Asia and the Pacific 2020 is the 51st edition in an annual series that has become a vital reference for policymakers, development practitioners, government officials, researchers, and students around the world.

Covering the 49 Asian Development Bank (ADB) member economies located in Asia and the Pacific, the publication provides statistics on a comprehensive set of economic, financial, social, and environmental measures as well as select indicators for the Sustainable Development Goals (SDGs). This information is also accessible in digitized format via the Key Indicators Database (kidb.adb.org).

Prepared by ADB's Statistics and Data Innovation Unit, *Key Indicators for Asia and the Pacific 2020* highlights the tremendous development progress made throughout the Asia and Pacific region from 2000 to 2019. In that time, our region has become the world's largest contributor to global gross domestic product (in current United States dollars), reaching a 34.9% share in 2019. Value chain statistics also show that changes over time in comparative advantages across economies in Asia and the Pacific reflect their ability to expand their competitiveness in key sectors and strengthen, broaden, and diversify their participation in global production networks. Meanwhile, the region's maternal mortality ratio was more than halved from 2000 to 2017. Perhaps most heartening of all, from 2002 to 2015, almost 850 million people across Asia and the Pacific were raised out of extreme poverty (based on the $ 1.90 a day poverty line).

While the region has done remarkably well, the issues that challenge inclusive and sustainable development remain, and these will likely be amplified by the COVID-19 pandemic and the strategies adopted to mitigate the spread of the virus. The data for SDG indicators to 2019 show that poverty and its associated issues need to be addressed as a priority. The indicators highlight areas in which urgent attention is necessary, in particular, the need to expand provision of safe water and sanitation facilities; improve access to, and the quality of, education and health services; and ensure that all people have safe, nutritious, and sufficient food to eat all year round.

To live up to the "leave no one behind" principle that is inherent in the SDGs, the availability of accurate, granular, and more informative data is crucial. Factors such as location, age, gender, ethnicity, income status, and disability status are needed to identify and address inequitable socioeconomic progress. The special supplement to this year's *Key Indicators for Asia and the Pacific* explores how innovative data sources (such as satellite imagery) and artificial intelligence can complement conventional methods to enhance the granularity of poverty statistics, providing more detailed guidance for policymakers throughout the region.

ADB is indebted to our statistical partners in member economies, who provide us with the most recent data from their official sources. We are also thankful for the contributions of the international agencies that are responsible for the data in many of the publication's tables. We appreciate that many of our friends and colleagues have been working under especially trying circumstances during the COVID-19 pandemic, and we applaud them for their professionalism throughout. At a time when sound evidence for policy design, formulation, and monitoring may be more essential than ever, we hope that *Key Indicators for Asia and the Pacific 2020* will be a valuable resource for data on major development issues. As always, we welcome feedback from our users on both the content and structure of the publication.

Masatsugu Asakawa
President
Asian Development Bank

Acknowledgments

This 51st edition of *Key Indicators for Asia and the Pacific* was prepared by the Statistics and Data Innovation Unit (EROD-SDI) within the Economic Research and Regional Cooperation Department (ERCD) at the Asian Development Bank (ADB). The publication team was led by Stefan Schipper, under the overall direction of Elaine S. Tan. Pamela Lapitan, Melissa Pascua, and Eric Suan provided technical and coordination support in preparing the data and tables.

The statistical tables presenting development indicators for ADB's regional member economies in Parts I and II of the printed publication (and also available online via kidb.adb.org), as well as the 49 tables for individual economies available exclusively online, were prepared by EROD-SDI staff and consultants, under the supervision of Kaushal Joshi, Mahinthan Joseph Mariasingham, Arturo Martinez Jr., Lakshman Nagraj Rao, and Stefan Schipper. The research team included Raymond Adofina, Nalwino Billones, Joseph Albert Nino Bulan, Ephraim Cuya, Criselda De Dios, Madeline Dumaua-Cabauatan, Anna Marie Fernando, Karen Firshan, Pamela Lapitan, Jeffrey Napoles, Asylla Marie Naraga, Melissa Pascua, Lea Rotairo, and Eric Suan. Proofreading of statistical tables was done by Ma. Roselia Babalo, Rose Anne Dumayas, Oth Marulou Gagni, and Aileen Gatson. The analyses of Sustainable Development Goal indicators and regional trends were prepared by Kevin Donahue and Stefan Schipper. The statistical tables and analytical reports for Parts I and II were reviewed by Kaushal Joshi, Mahinthan Joseph Mariasingham, Arturo Martinez Jr., and Stefan Schipper. Mahinthan Joseph Mariasingham led the team that prepared the statistical tables for Part III. This team comprised Julian Alvarez, Gienneen Antonio, Michael Barsabal, John Arvin Bernabe, Rafael Consing, Marc Alvin Ermino, Krizia Anne Garay, Patricia Gonzales, Jahm Guinto, Angeli Juani, Angelo Lumba, Julieta Magallanes, Sarah Mae Manuel, Danileen Parel, Leila Rahnema, Ana Francesca Rosales, Clara Delos Santos, and Jonarie Vergara. Ana Francesca Rosales provided valuable comments on the analysis of Part III, which was prepared by Kristina Baris, Janine De Vera, Reizle Platitas, and Kenneth Reyes, under the guidance of Mahinthan Joseph Mariasingham.

We are very grateful for the contributions of ERCD's statistical partners—ADB regional members and international organizations—who, in spite of the many difficulties presented by the COVID-19 pandemic, still fulfilled their commitment to sharing their data for the statistical tables on Sustainable Development Goal indicators (Part I), regional tables (Part II), global value chains (Part III), and individual economy tables. ADB resident missions in Afghanistan, Armenia, Azerbaijan, Bangladesh, Bhutan, Cambodia, Georgia, India, Indonesia, Kazakhstan, the Kyrgyz Republic, the Lao People's Democratic Republic, Mongolia, Myanmar, Nepal, Pakistan, Papua New Guinea, the People's Republic of China, Sri Lanka, Tajikistan, Thailand, Timor-Leste, Turkmenistan, Uzbekistan, and Viet Nam provided support in compiling the data for their respective economies. ADB Japanese Representative Office, Pacific Liaison and Coordination Office, Philippines Country Office, and Pacific Subregional Office also provided help in data compilation. We greatly appreciate the continuing cooperation of the governments of ADB member economies and other international agencies.

Paul Dent edited *Key Indicators for Asia and the Pacific 2020*. The cover design of Nguyen Thanh Hien was adapted by Rhommell Rico, who also led the typesetting process and provided technical support for the preparation of all promotional and awareness materials. Joseph Manglicmot and Edith Creus assisted in typesetting. Staff from ADB's Information Technology Department provided database management and technology support in coordination with the Key Indicators Database team composed of Raymond Adofina, Nikko Angelo Antonio, Ephraim Cuya, Juan Miguel Olmos De La Cruz, Pamela Lapitan, Albert San Juan, Steve Marrero, and Le Kim Nguyen, under the leadership of Stefan Schipper. The Logistics Management Unit of the Office of Administrative Services facilitated the timely and smooth production of the publication. The publishing team in ADB's Department of Communications provided general guidance on production issues and organized promotional and awareness activities.

Yasuyuki Sawada
Chief Economist and Director General
Asian Development Bank

Statistical Partners

The preparation and publication of *Key Indicators for Asia and the Pacific 2020* would not have been possible without the support, assistance, and cooperation of statistical partners in Asian Development Bank member economies throughout the Asia and Pacific region, along with the invaluable contributions of international, private, and nongovernment organizations. These partners—who shared their data, knowledge, expertise, and other information—help provide the Asian Development Bank, policymakers, and other data users with a better understanding of the performance of economies across the region, encouraging the design, formulation, and monitoring of better policies to improve the quality of life for people in this part of the world.

REGIONAL MEMBERS

Afghanistan	Da Afghanistan Bank (http://dab.gov.af) Ministry of Finance (http://mof.gov.af/en) National Statistics and Information Authority (https://nsia.gov.af/home)
Armenia	Central Bank of Armenia (http://www.cba.am/en) Ministry of Finance (http://www.minfin.am/en) Statistical Committee of the Republic of Armenia (http://www.armstat.am/en)
Australia	Australian Bureau of Statistics (http://www.abs.gov.au) Australian Institute of Petroleum (https://www.aip.com.au/) Department of Industry, Science, Energy and Resources (http://www.industry.gov.au/) Reserve Bank of Australia (http://www.rba.gov.au)
Azerbaijan	Central Bank of the Republic of Azerbaijan (https://www.cbar.az/home?language=en) Ministry of Finance (http://www.maliyye.gov.az/en) State Statistical Committee of the Republic of Azerbaijan (http://www.stat.gov.az/?lang=en)
Bangladesh	Bangladesh Bank (https://www.bb.org.bd) Bangladesh Bureau of Statistics (http://www.bbs.gov.bd) Ministry of Finance (https://mof.gov.bd/)
Bhutan	Ministry of Finance (https://www.mof.gov.bt) Ministry of Labour and Human Resources (https://www.molhr.gov.bt/molhr/) National Statistics Bureau (http://www.nsb.gov.bt/main/main.php) Royal Monetary Authority of Bhutan (https://www.rma.org.bt)
Brunei Darussalam	Autoriti Monetari Brunei Darussalam (https://www.ambd.gov.bn/Home.aspx) Department of Economic Planning and Development (http://www.deps.gov.bn/Theme/Home.aspx) Ministry of Finance and Economy (https://www.mofe.gov.bn/sitepages/home.aspx)

Cambodia	Ministry of Economy and Finance (https://mef.gov.kh/) National Bank of Cambodia (https://www.nbc.org.kh/english/) National Institute of Statistics (https://nis.gov.kh/index.php/km/)
China, People's Republic of	National Bureau of Statistics of China (http://www.stats.gov.cn/english) The People's Bank of China (http://www.pbc.gov.cn) State Administration of Foreign Exchange (http://www.safe.gov.cn)
Cook Islands	Cook Islands Statistics Office (http://www.mfem.gov.ck/statistics)
Fiji	Bureau of Statistics (http://www.statsfiji.gov.fj) Reserve Bank of Fiji (http://www.rbf.gov.fj/) Ministry of Economy (http://www.economy.gov.fj)
Georgia	Ministry of Finance of Georgia (https://mof.ge/en/) National Bank of Georgia (http://www.nbg.gov.ge) National Statistics Office of Georgia (https://www.geostat.ge/en)
Hong Kong, China	Census and Statistics Department (http://www.censtatd.gov.hk) Financial Services and the Treasury Bureau (https://www.fstb.gov.hk/)
India	Central Statistical Office (http://mospi.nic.in) Ministry of Finance (http://finmin.nic.in) Reserve Bank of India (http://www.rbi.org.in)
Indonesia	Bank Indonesia (https://www.bi.go.id/en/Default.aspx) Badan Pusat Statistik-Statistics Indonesia (https://www.bps.go.id/) Ministry of Energy and Mineral Resources (https://www.esdm.go.id/en) Ministry of Finance (https://www.kemenkeu.go.id/en) Pertamina (https://www.pertamina.com/en/home)
Japan	Bank of Japan (http://www.boj.or.jp/en/) Economic and Social Research Institute (http://www.esri.go.jp) Japan Customs (http://www.customs.go.jp/english/) Japan Statistics Bureau (http://www.stat.go.jp/english/) Ministry of Economy, Trade and Industry (http://www.meti.go.jp/english/) Ministry of Finance (http://www.mof.go.jp/english/) The Institute of Energy Economics, Japan (http://oil-info.ieej.or.jp/)
Kazakhstan	Committee on Statistics, Ministry of National Economy of the Republic of Kazakhstan (https://stat.gov.kz) Ministry of Finance of the Republic of Kazakhstan (http://www.minfin.gov.kz) National Bank of Kazakhstan (https://nationalbank.kz)

Kiribati	Kiribati National Statistics Office (https://nso.gov.ki/)
Korea, Republic of	Bank of Korea (https://bok.or.kr) Statistics Korea (http://kostat.go.kr)
Kyrgyz Republic	National Bank of the Kyrgyz Republic (https://www.nbkr.kg) National Statistical Committee of the Kyrgyz Republic (www.stat.kg)
Lao People's Democratic Republic	Bank of the Lao PDR (https://www.bol.gov.la/en/index) Lao Statistics Bureau (https://www.lsb.gov.la/en/home/) Ministry of Finance (https://www.mof.gov.la/index.php/en/home/)
Malaysia	Bank Negara Malaysia (https://www.bnm.gov.my) Department of Statistics Malaysia (https://www.dosm.gov.my) Ministry of Finance Malaysia (https://www.treasury.gov.my/index_en.html)
Maldives	National Bureau of Statistics (statisticsmaldives.gov.mv) Maldives Monetary Authority (mma.gov.mv) Ministry of Finance (https://www.finance.gov.mv)
Marshall Islands	Economic Policy, Planning and Statistics Office (https://www.rmieppso.org/)
Micronesia, Federated States of	Division of Statistics (http://www.fsmstatistics.fm/)
Mongolia	The Bank of Mongolia (https://www.mongolbank.mn/eng) National Statistics Office of Mongolia (https://en.nso.mn)
Myanmar	Central Bank of Myanmar (https://www.cbm.gov.mm) Central Statistical Organization (https://www.csostat.gov.mm/AboutCSO/StatisticalSystem) Ministry of Planning, Finance and Industry (https://www.mopfi.gov.mm/)
Nauru	Ministry of Finance and Economic Planning (http://www.naurugov.nr/) Nauru Bureau of Statistics (https://nauru.prism.spc.int/)
Nepal	Central Bureau of Statistics (https://cbs.gov.np) Ministry of Finance (https://www.mof.gov.np) Nepal Rastra Bank (https://www.nrb.org.np) Water and Energy Commission Secretariat (www.wecs.gov.np) Ministry of Energy, Water Resources and Irrigation (www.moewri.gov.np) Ministry of Industry, Commerce and Supplies (https://moics.gov.np) Ministry of Industry, Department of Mines and Geology (http://www.dmgnepal.gov.np)

New Zealand	Ministry of Business, Innovation and Employment (https://www.mbie.govt.nz)
	Reserve Bank of New Zealand (https://www.rbnz.govt.nz/)
	Stats NZ Tatauranga Aotearoa (https://www.stats.govt.nz/)
Niue	Statistics Niue Office (https://niue.prism.spc.int/)
Pakistan	Ministry of Finance (www.finance.gov.pk)
	Pakistan Bureau of Statistics (www.pbs.gov.pk)
	State Bank of Pakistan (www.sbp.org.pk)
Palau	Bureau of Budget and Planning, Ministry of Finance (http://palaugov.pw/budgetandplanning/)
Papua New Guinea	Bank of Papua New Guinea (https://www.bankpng.gov.pg/)
	Department of Treasury (http://www.treasury.gov.pg/)
	National Statistical Office (https://www.nso.gov.pg/)
Philippines	Bangko Sentral ng Pilipinas (http://www.bsp.gov.ph)
	Bureau of Local Government Finance (https://blgf.gov.ph/)
	Bureau of the Treasury (http://www.treasury.gov.ph)
	Department of Budget and Management (http://www.dbm.gov.ph)
	Department of Energy (https://www.doe.gov.ph)
	Philippine Statistics Authority (http://www.psa.gov.ph)
Samoa	Samoa Bureau of Statistics (http://www.sbs.gov.ws)
	Central Bank of Samoa (https://www.cbs.gov.ws)
Singapore	Department of Statistics (https://www.singstat.gov.sg)
	Enterprise Singapore (formerly International Enterprise Singapore) (https://www.enterprisesg.gov.sg)
	Ministry of Finance (https://www.mof.gov.sg)
	Ministry of Manpower (https://www.mom.gov.sg)
	Ministry of Trade and Industry (https://www.mti.gov.sg)
	Monetary Authority of Singapore (https://www.mas.gov.sg)
Solomon Islands	Central Bank of Solomon Islands (http://www.cbsi.com.sb)
	Solomon Islands National Statistics Office (https://www.statistics.gov.sb)
Sri Lanka	Central Bank of Sri Lanka (https://www.cbsl.gov.lk)
	Department of Census and Statistics (http://www.statistics.gov.lk)

Taipei,China	Central bank of Taipei,China (https://www.cbc.gov.tw) Directorate-General of Budget, Accounting and Statistics (https://eng.dgbas.gov.tw) Ministry of Finance (https://www.mof.gov.tw)
Tajikistan	National Bank of Tajikistan (https:// nbt.tj) Agency on Statistics under President of the Republic of Tajikistan (https://www.stat.tj)
Thailand	Bank of Thailand (https://www.bot.or.th/English/) Ministry of Finance (http://www2.mof.go.th) National Economic and Social Development Council (https://www.nesdc.go.th/nesdb_en/) National Statistical Office (http://www.nso.go.th) Ministry of Energy, Energy Policy and Planning Office (http://www.eppo.go.th/index.php/en/)
Timor-Leste	Central Bank of Timor-Leste (http://www.bancocentral.tl) Ministry of Finance (http://www.mof.gov.tl) General Directorate of Statistics (http://www.statistics.gov.tl)
Tonga	Ministry of Finance and National Planning (http://www.finance.gov.to) National Reserve Bank of Tonga (http://www.reservebank.to) Department of Statistics (http://www.spc.int/prism/tonga)
Turkmenistan	Central Bank of Turkmenistan (http://www.cbt.tm/en/) Ministry of Finance and Economy of Turkmenistan (http://www.minfin.gov.tm/) State Committee of Turkmenistan on Statistics (formerly the National Institute of State Statistics and Information of Turkmenistan) (http://www.stat.gov.tm)
Tuvalu	Central Statistics Division (https://tuvalu.prism.spc.int)
Uzbekistan	Cabinet of Ministers (https://www.gov.uz/en/pages/executive_office) Central Bank of the Republic of Uzbekistan (http://www.cbu.uz/en/) Ministry of Finance of the Republic of Uzbekistan (https://www.mf.uz/en/) State Statistical Committee of the Republic of Uzbekistan (http://www.stat.uz)

Vanuatu	Department of Finance and Treasury (https://doft.gov.vu)
	Reserve Bank of Vanuatu (http://www.rbv.gov.vu)
	Vanuatu National Statistics Office (http://www.vnso.gov.vu)
Viet Nam	General Statistics Office (https://www.gso.gov.vn)
	Ministry of Finance (http://www.mof.gov.vn)
	State Bank of Viet Nam (https://www.sbv.gov.vn)

INTERNATIONAL, PRIVATE, AND NONGOVERNMENT ORGANIZATIONS

Association of Southeast Asian Nations
Food and Agriculture Organization of the United Nations
International Labour Organization
International Monetary Fund
International Telecommunication Union
Interstate Statistical Committee of the Commonwealth of Independent States
Joint United Nations Programme on HIV/AIDS
Organisation for Economic Co-operation and Development
Secretariat of the Pacific Community
Transparency International
UNESCO Institute for Statistics
United Nations Children's Fund
United Nations Conference on Trade and Development
United Nations Department of Economic and Social Affairs
United Nations Development Programme
United Nations Economic and Social Commission for Asia and the Pacific
United Nations Educational, Scientific and Cultural Organization
United Nations Environment Programme
United Nations Human Settlements Programme
United Nations Office on Drugs and Crime
United Nations Population Division
United Nations Statistics Division
United Nations World Tourism Organization
United States Agency for International Development
United States Census Bureau
WHO/UNICEF Joint Monitoring Programme for Water Supply, Sanitation and Hygiene
World Bank
World Health Organization
World Trade Organization

Guide for Users

Key Indicators for Asia and the Pacific 2020 begins with a Highlights section that presents key messages from various parts of the publication.

Part I comprises the data tables and brief analyses of trends of select indicators for the Sustainable Development Goals (SDGs) for which data were available. The indicators are presented according to the United Nations SDG global indicator framework.

Part II explores trends in social, economic, and environmental developments in member economies of the Asian Development Bank (ADB) across Asia and the Pacific. These assessments are grouped into eight themes: People; Economy and Output; Money, Finance, and Prices; Globalization; Transport and Communications; Energy and Electricity; Environment; and Government and Governance. Each theme is further analyzed by specific indicators, which are presented in the 100 regional tables that are incorporated into Part II of the publication.

The SDGs in Part I and the themes in Part II start with a short commentary, complemented by figures and charts describing the status of economies with respect to key trends of select targets and indicators of the 17 SDGs and eight themes. The scales used in some figures and charts are adjusted to show very small numbers. In addition, figures and charts appearing in this publication are also provided with a digital object identifier to facilitate easier access to data. Both Part I and Part II also present discussion boxes on how to approach important measurement issues for select indicators.

The SDGs and regional tables presented in Parts I and II cover 49 national economies across Asia and the Pacific, all of which are members of ADB. The term "country," used interchangeably with "economy", is not intended to make any judgment as to the legal or other status of any territory or area.

The 49 economies have been broadly grouped into developing ADB member economies and developed ADB member economies. The term "developing Asia" refers to the 46 developing member economies of ADB. The developed economies refer to the three economies of Australia, Japan, and New Zealand. Based on ADB's geographic operations, the 46 developing ADB member economies are divided into five subregions within the Asia and Pacific region. These subregions are Central and West Asia, East Asia, South Asia, Southeast Asia, and the Pacific. Economies are listed alphabetically within each subregion. The term "regional members", often used interchangeably with "Asia and the Pacific", refer to all 49 ADB members, both developing and developed. Indicators are shown for the most recent year (usually 2019) or period for which data were available and, in most tables, for a starting year or period (usually 2000). Depending on available data, the starting point may be a year from 2000 to 2009 (usually the year nearest to 2000), and the most recent year may be a year from 2010 to 2019 (usually the year nearest to 2019). There may, however, be some exceptions to these general principles. In the tables, aggregates for regions include economies with available data and are shown if the indicator is available for more than half of the economies and if more than two-thirds of the reference population is represented.

Part III contains select indicators for depicting participation by economies of Asia and the Pacific in global value chains, and the sector-specific comparative advantage of each economy in terms of exports. Typical indicators of international trade, which mainly refer to the value of exports and imports of goods and services, can be traced back to the traditional trading of final goods across borders. Today's globalization has made many economies more open to trade, providing opportunities for firms to scale up production and allocate their resources more efficiently by moving production chains across borders where there is comparative advantage. Analysis of global value chains provides detailed cross-border trading transactions of inputs used in different stages of production—from raw materials, to intermediate inputs, to the final products purchased by the end consumers.

This publication is also available on ADB's website at adb.org/ki-2020, along with individual statistical tables for each of the 49 ADB regional members. The publication's vitally important data and time series are also accessible in digitized format via the Key Indicators Database (kidb.adb.org). Data for the SDG indicators, regional tables, and individual member tables were mainly obtained from two sources: (i) ADB's statistical partners linked to regional member economies, and (ii) international statistical agencies, particularly from the United Nations' Global SDG Indicators Database, a master set of data prepared by the Department of Economic and Social Affairs of the United Nations Secretariat. The term "economy source", cited as a source in some tables, refers to data provided by the statistical partners linked to the ADB regional member economies.

The data presented for indicators in Part I were derived from either official country sources, the Global SDG Indicators Database, or databases maintained by international agencies that, based on their areas of expertise, prepared one or more of the series of statistical indicators included in the Global SDG Indicators Database. The data presented in Part III were mainly drawn from the ADB Multi-Regional Input–Output Tables Database.

Data produced and disseminated by international agencies are generally based on data produced and disseminated by an individual economy (including data adjusted by the economy to meet international standards). However, it should be noted that national data may be compiled using national standards and practices and, as such, international agencies often adjust the data for international comparability. In such cases, data disseminated by the international agencies may differ from data available from national sources. In other cases, when data for a specific year, or set of years, are not available; or they are available from multiple national sources (surveys, administrative data sources, and other sources); or when there are data quality issues; the relevant international agency may estimate the data. Some indicators are regularly produced for the purpose of global monitoring by the designated agency, and there are no corresponding data at the national level (e.g., population living on less than $1.90 at 2011 purchasing power parity). In other cases, the differences between data from national and international agencies may be because the most recent and/or revised data available at the national level are not yet available with the relevant international agency. Some data gaps are filled by supplementing or deriving data collected through sample surveys financed and carried out by international agencies. For example, many of the health indicators are estimated using data from the Multiple Indicator Cluster Surveys and Demographic and Health Surveys.

ADB exercises due care and caution in collecting data before publication. Nevertheless, data from international sources presented in this publication may differ from those available within individual member economies. Thus, for a detailed description of how the indicators are compiled by the international agencies, readers may refer to the metadata available from databases of the individual international agencies, or the Global SDG Indicators Database website for metadata of SDG indicators. Comparable and standardized national data gathered through a robust data-reporting mechanism of the international agencies should be the basis for all data in the global monitoring databases, and global indicators should be produced in full consultation with national statistical agencies.

Data obtained from ADB member economies are comparable to the extent that the ADB members follow standard statistical concepts, definitions, and estimation methods recommended by the United Nations and other applicable international agencies.

Nevertheless, member economies invariably develop and use their own concepts, definitions, and estimation methodologies to suit their individual circumstances, and these may not necessarily comply with recommended international standards. Therefore, even though attempts are made to present the data in a comparable and uniform format, the data are subject to variations in the statistical methods used by individual economies, so full comparability may not be possible. These variations are reflected in the footnotes of the statistical tables or noted in the Data Issues and Comparability sections. Moreover, the aggregates shown in some tables for the developing ADB member economies and ADB regional members are treated as approximations of the actual total or average, or growth rates, due to missing data from the primary source. For a description of the regional aggregation method, the readers may refer to the footnotes presented in the tables and metadata in the Key Indicators Database (kidb.adb.org). Aggregates for the World were sourced from international agencies, and readers may refer to the metadata from the available databases of the individual international agencies.

The data published by ADB do not constitute any form of advice or recommendation. For answers to any questions on the data, users of this publication are requested to seek advice from the relevant data source or organization.

Fiscal Year

There are 24 regional members of the Asian Development Bank with fiscal years that do not coincide with the calendar year. Whenever statistical series (for example, national accounts or government finance) are compiled on the basis of a fiscal year, these series are presented in the column for the single-year during which most of the fiscal year occurred. The 24 fiscal year definitions for 2019 are outlined below.

Regional Member	Fiscal Year	Year Caption
Afghanistan (fiscal year beginning 2012)	21 December 2018 to 20 December 2019	2019
Brunei Darussalam (fiscal year since 2002) Hong Kong, China India Japan New Zealand Singapore	1 April 2019 to 31 March 2020	2019
Fiji	1 August 2018 to 31 July 2019	2019
Australia Bangladesh Bhutan Cook Islands Kiribati Nauru Pakistan Samoa Tonga	1 July 2018 to 30 June 2019	2019
Nepal	16 July 2018 to 15 July 2019	2019
Lao People's Democratic Republic Marshall Islands Micronesia, Federated States of Myanmar Palau Thailand	1 October 2018 to 30 September 2019	2019

Key Symbols

...	data not available
–	magnitude equals zero
(-/+) 0 or 0.0	magnitude is less than half of unit employed
*	provisional/preliminary/estimate/budget figure
|	marks break in series
>	greater than
<	less than
>=	greater than or equal to
<=	less than or equal to
n.a.	not applicable
%	percentage

Units of Measurement

GWh	gigawatt-hour
kg	kilogram
kl	kiloliter
km	kilometer
km^2	square kilometer
kWh	kilowatt-hour
kt	kiloton
ktoe	kiloton of oil equivalent
L	liter
m^3	cubic meter
mj	megajoule
PM	particulate matter
teu	twenty-foot equivalent unit
t	metric ton
$\mu g/m^3$	micrograms per cubic meter

Abbreviations

ADB	Asian Development Bank
BPM5	Balance of Payments Manual (Fifth Edition)
BPM6	Balance of Payments and International Investment Position Manual (Sixth Edition)
BPO	business process outsourcing
CIF	cost, insurance, and freight
CO_2	carbon dioxide
CPI	consumer price index
DHS	Demographic and Health Survey
DVA_F	domestic value-added via forward linkages
FDI	foreign direct investment
FOB	free on board
FVA	foreign value-added
GDP	gross domestic product
GNI	gross national income
GVC	global value chain
HIV	human immunodeficiency virus
IDA	International Development Association
IMF	International Monetary Fund
ISIC	International Standard Industrial Classification
MICS	Multiple Indicator Cluster Survey
MMR	maternal mortality ratio
MOF	Ministry of Finance
MRIOT	multi-region input-output table
NPL	nonperforming loan
NRCA	new revealed comparative advantage
NSO	National Statistics Office; National Statistical Office
ODA	official development assistance
PLI	price level index
PPP	purchasing power parity
RCA	revealed comparative advantage
TRCA	traditional revealed comparative advantage
UN	United Nations
UNDESA	United Nations Department of Economic and Social Affairs
UNICEF	United Nations Children's Fund
UNSD	United Nations Statistics Division
WHO	World Health Organization

Unless otherwise indicated, "$" refers to United States dollars.

HIGHLIGHTS

Part I. Sustainable Development Goals

To be achieved by 2030, the 17 Sustainable Development Goals (SDGs), along with their 231 related indicators, provide a global policy framework for ending all forms of poverty, fighting inequality, and tackling climate change, while ensuring that no person is left behind as economies of the world grow and prosper. A summary of trends for select SDG indicators across economies of Asia and the Pacific is presented here.

- In developing Asia, the number of people living in extreme poverty—as measured by surviving on less than $1.90 per day at 2011 purchasing power parity—has fallen by 846 million (from 1,109 million people in 2002 to 263 million in 2015). However, the achievements in reducing extreme poverty throughout Asia and the Pacific are threatened by the COVID-19 pandemic and ensuing global recession.

- The prevalence of undernourishment across the Asia and Pacific region was significantly reduced from 2001 to 2018. Of the 34 developing ADB member economies with available data, 28 experienced a decline. Furthermore, comparing 2010–2018 to 2000–2009, the prevalence of stunting in children below the age of 5 years (i.e., too short for their age) fell in 25 of the 29 developing member economies with available data.

- Among developing member economies of Asia and the Pacific, the number of women dying during pregnancy, childbirth, or soon after fell from 271 per 100,000 live births in 2000 to 119 per 100,000 live births in 2017. All subregions within developing Asia experienced a reduction in their respective maternal mortality ratio during the review period.

- Early childhood education can lead to improved access to economic opportunities and better income prospects. However, only 13 of the 35 reporting economies throughout Asia and the Pacific had at least 90% of both boys and girls participating in pre-primary education in 2018.

- In the most recent year for which data were available, the percentage of women aged 20–24 years who were married or in a union before the age of 18 exceeded 20% in 11 of the 30 reporting economies.

- The provision of safe water and sanitation services is essential for preventing the spread of disease and for protecting human health during all infectious disease outbreaks, including COVID-19. Since 2000, 21 of the 25 reporting economies have expanded the provision of safely managed drinking water services. Yet, in 2017, the proportion of the population using safely managed drinking water services remained below 50% in nine economies of the Asia and the Pacific region.

- In 2018, more than three-quarters of the region's economies provided access to electricity to at least 95% of their population. Since 2000, 30 of the 47 reporting economies have increased the proportion of the population that has access to clean fuels and technology for cooking, heating, and lighting.

- Unemployment, exacerbated by the COVID-19 pandemic, will challenge many governments around the world in the near future. In 2019 (or the most recent year for which data were available), 36 of the 37 reporting economies from Asia and the Pacific reported higher unemployment rates among people aged 15–24 years than those aged 25 and older.

- During the most recent 5-year period for which data were available, household expenditure (or income per capita) rose for the bottom 40% of the total population in 14 of the 15 developing ADB member economies with available data. However, these gains are at risk of being reversed as migrant workers, both domestic and international, have been forced to leave their jobs and return home as part of COVID-19 containment measures.

- Among the 13 economies with data available for both 2000 and 2018, 12 posted a reduction in the percentage of the urban population living in slums, informal settlements, or inadequate housing.

- The Sendai Framework for Disaster Risk Reduction prioritizes prevention to help governments substantially reduce risk and minimize the loss of lives, livelihoods, and health caused by disasters such as the COVID-19 pandemic. Self-assessments conducted by 24 economies in Asia and the Pacific on the alignment of their national disaster risk reduction strategies with the Sendai Framework showed that, five economies reported comprehensive alignment and 13 reported moderate alignment with the framework.

- Across Asia and the Pacific, forest area covered more than one-half of total land in 18 of the 48 economies with data available for 2019. From 2000 to 2019, 21 of the reporting economies managed to increase their amount of forested land as a percentage of total land, while 9 reported no change, and 18 posted a decline.

- From 2000 to 2019, all 48 reporting economies recorded at least a marginal decline in their Red List Index score, which measures change in aggregate extinction risk across groups of species.

- In the most recent year for which data were available, the percentage of firms indicating that they had been solicited by public officials for gifts or informal payments exceeded 10% in 25 of the 32 reporting economies throughout Asia and the Pacific.

- Comparing 2010–2018 with 2000–2009, the average annual value (in constant 2018 United States dollars) of financial and technical assistance committed to developing economies increased in 35 of the 41 reporting economies from across Asia and the Pacific.

Part II. Region at a Glance

The Regional Trends and Tables section is grouped into eight themes—People; Economy and Output; Money, Finance, and Prices; Globalization; Transport and Communications; Energy and Electricity; Environment; and Government and Governance. Each of these themes has a brief analysis of key trends for select indicators, highlighting important developments across Asia and the Pacific.

People

- The Asian Development Bank (ADB) has 49 member economies that are located across the Asia and Pacific region. The combined population of these members reached 4,207 million in 2019, accounting for more than half of all the people on the planet. Among the world's 10 most populous countries in 2019, there were five located in Asia and the Pacific: the People's Republic of China (PRC) with 1,400 million people, India with 1,343 million, Indonesia with 268 million, Pakistan with 211 million, and Bangladesh with 167 million.

- From 2000 to 2019, of the 22 developing ADB member economies with available data, 19 economies reported an increase in the mean number of years of schooling for both boys and girls. During the review period, one reporting economy posted an increase in the mean number of years of schooling for boys, but a decrease for girls.

- Emergency preparedness, as measured by the number of physicians and hospital beds per 1,000 people, will help health care systems across the Asia and Pacific region respond to the COVID-19 pandemic. In 2018 (or the most recent year for which data were available), the region's three leading economies in terms of physicians per 1,000 people were Georgia, Maldives, and Armenia. In terms of hospital beds per 1,000 people, the leading economies in Asia and the Pacific were Japan, the Republic of Korea, and Mongolia.

Economy and Output

- Asia and the Pacific's share of global gross domestic product (GDP) in current United States (US) dollars increased from 26.3% in 2000 to 34.9% in 2019. Among all regions across the globe, Asia and the Pacific's ranking in terms of its share of global output improved from third in 2000 to first in 2019.

- A majority of reporting economies in the Asia and Pacific region experienced GDP growth of 4.0% or higher in 2019. Only one regional economy contracted during 2019.

- From 2000 to 2019, capital formation—which comprises fixed investment in buildings, civil engineering, machinery, and equipment—increased as a share of GDP in nearly two-thirds of the region's economies for which data were available.

Money, Finance, and Prices

- Comparing 2018 to 2019, consumer price inflation decelerated in 26 economies across Asia and the Pacific, while accelerating in 17 economies. In an additional two economies, which had experienced subdued inflation in 2018, consumer prices fell during 2019. Conversely, in another economy that posted deflation in 2018, inflation returned the following year.

- The 2008–2009 global financial crisis led to a sharp increase in the value of nonperforming bank loans (NPLs) and the percentage of NPLs as a share of total gross loans. From 2010 to 2018, these indicators recovered in the majority of economies across Asia and the Pacific. However, NPLs are expected to rise again in developing Asia as the global economy contracts under the influence of the COVID-19 pandemic.

Globalization

- In 2019, economies of Asia and the Pacific received more than one-third of total global foreign direct investment. The region was also home to five of the world's top 10 recipients of foreign direct investment.

- After falling to $5.8 trillion in 2016, merchandise exports from Asia and the Pacific rose to $6.4 trillion in 2017 and $7.0 trillion in 2018, before dipping slightly to $6.8 trillion in 2019. As a percentage of global merchandise exports, the region's share increased from about 28% in 2000 to about 37% in 2019.

- The aggregate amount of remittances flowing into developing Asia increased for the third consecutive year in 2019, reaching $310.8 billion. The region's top five recipients of remittances in 2019 were India ($83.1 billion), the PRC ($68.4 billion), the Philippines ($35.2 billion), Pakistan

($22.5 billion), and Bangladesh ($18.3 billion). Global remittances are expected to decline in 2020 due to international travel restrictions and economic slowdowns caused by responses to the COVID-19 pandemic.

Transport and Communications

- In 2018, Asia and the Pacific was the busiest region in the world in terms of air carrier departures and passengers carried, accounting for 32.2% and 37.1%, respectively, of the global totals. From 2010 to 2018, an increase in air carrier departures was observed in 30 of the 40 reporting economies.

Energy and Electricity

- From 2000 to 2017, all five of Asia and the Pacific's most populous economies increased their energy efficiency, as measured by the amount of GDP per unit use of energy (i.e., one petajoule). Among this grouping, the largest increase in GDP per petajoule was observed in Bangladesh.

- Asia and the Pacific's energy production as a share of the global total rose from about one-quarter in 2000 to more than one-third in 2017. The increase was mainly driven by expanded energy production in the PRC, which accounted for more than half of all energy production in Asia and the Pacific in 2017.

- In 2017, over two-thirds of reporting economies in Asia and the Pacific remained dependent on energy imports. Ten economies relied on imports to meet more than 90% of their domestic energy demand.

Environment

- In 2017, the total amount of forested land increased in 16 economies of Asia and the Pacific, while decreasing in 15 economies. The region's leaders in terms of reforestation in 2017 were Taipei,China; the Philippines; Azerbaijan; and the Lao People's Democratic Republic.

- Economic growth across Asia and the Pacific has been accompanied by a rise in carbon dioxide emissions. From 2000 to 2016, fewer than one-fifth of the region's economies with available data were successful in reducing their carbon dioxide emissions per capita.

Government and Governance

- Government taxes include value-added tax, sales tax, import duties, income tax, profit tax, property tax, capital gains tax, and compulsory social security charges, among others. In 2019, government taxes were equal to or exceeded 20% of GDP in about half of all reporting economies.

- From 2005 to 2019, 81% of economies in Asia and the Pacific reduced the number of days required to start a business. The largest reductions were achieved in Timor-Leste (154.0 days), Brunei Darussalam (116.0 days), and Azerbaijan (109.5 days).

Part III. Global Value Chains

The Asian Development Bank (ADB) utilizes global value chain (GVC) statistics derived from multi-regional input–output tables to describe Asia and the Pacific's role in global production networks. In 2020, ADB used GVC-adjusted measures of competitiveness to uncover the sectors that Asian economies are specializing in, with the following highlights:

- In 2019, global exports of goods and services reached $25.7 trillion at current prices. However, about 15% of this was value that did not originate from the exporting economy. This share ranges among Asian economies from 10% for Japan, an economy with a large domestic economy, to 44% for the small, highly open Singapore. With the COVID-19 pandemic disrupting supply chains for much of 2020, these segments of global trade have proven particularly vulnerable.

- The revealed comparative advantage (RCA) index, a classic measure in studies of trade, is recalculated to adjust for GVC activity, thereby providing a more accurate picture of specialization in Asia. The traditional RCA and the new RCA sometimes yield contrasting results as the latter nets out foreign value-added content in exports. The difference between the two is particularly evident in industries where fragmentation of production processes is pervasive, such as in manufacturing and business services.

- By convention, an RCA index of over 1 means the economy has a comparative advantage in that sector. In both 2000 and 2019, Bhutan, Cambodia, and Nepal had RCA indices of over 1 for business services using the traditional method, but less than 1 using the new method. This suggests that their exports in the business services sector contain much foreign value-added. Conversely, Bangladesh, India, and Pakistan's comparative disadvantages in the primary sector are reversed under the new RCA in 2000. As developing economies, their agriculture and mining exports have more domestic content than those of the more industrialized economies, boosting their export shares once foreign content is netted out.

- Changes over time in comparative advantage across economies in Asia reflect their ability to expand their competitiveness in key sectors. Southeast Asian economies, such as Viet Nam, show promising patterns in the electrical and optical equipment sector, while others, such as the Philippines, exhibit success in business services.

- RCA measures affirm the potential of "servicification", especially in business services

that are not directly exported but are embodied in physically manufactured goods. Correctly accounting where value-added generated by business services originate, the comparative advantages of some developing economies become much less impressive, while those of high-income countries improve.

- Trends in the competitiveness of Asian economies have been relatively stable since 2000. Central and West Asia remained the most competitive subregion in primary sectors, while Southeast Asia (including Fiji) and South Asia had the most competitive exports of low-technology manufactures. The more developed economies of East Asia continued to specialize in medium- and high-technology manufacturing, while South Asia bested other economies in competitiveness of services sectors.

- The RCA rankings in Asia for two GVC-linked sectors, electricals and business services, reveal both stability and change. From 2000 to 2019, Taipei,China maintained its place as the most competitive economy for electricals, having an unchanged RCA of 3.1. Meanwhile, Viet Nam registered a notable increase in its NRCA, from 0.1 to 0.6, while that of the People's Republic of China climbed from 1.1 to 2.3.

- Among the outstanding performers in business services was the Philippines, whose increase in RCA from 0.6 in 2000 to 1.0 in 2019 catapulted it to fifth place among the Asian economies. This is driven by its business process outsourcing sector, a service-driven industry that provides inputs to international production networks. The giant in this sector, India, registered a stagnant RCA of 1.0 throughout the period under study.

- While increasing the space for international competition, GVCs also expose economies to greater uncertainties. The COVID-19 crisis, for instance, has rattled supply chains around the world. On average, it is found that an increase in GVC participation of 10 percentage points is associated with a 0.06-increase in the standard deviation of the RCA index. To illustrate, the highest RCA volatilities in the electricals sector were seen in Taipei,China and the Philippines at 0.35 and 0.39, respectively. Both of these had average GVC participation rates of over 50%. This relationship points to the need for GVC engagement to be supported by a strong policy framework that maximizes benefits while minimizing risks.

Sustainable Development Goals—Data Stories

The United Nations (UN) Sustainable Development Goals (SDGs) were adopted in September 2015 to set targets for global development that would be achieved within 15 years. Economies in Asia and the Pacific are working toward achieving the 17 goals and 169 targets that comprise the SDG framework. A total of unique 231 statistical indicators are used to track the progress of individual economies toward meeting the SDGs. [1]

Fewer than 10 years remain to achieve the SDGs. At the SDG Summit in September 2019, world leaders pledged to mobilize financing, enhance national implementation, and strengthen institutions to achieve the SDGs by 2030, leaving no one behind (UN 2020a). However, progress made toward achieving many SDGs is being threatened by the COVID-19 pandemic. In addition to the immediate health crisis, lockdowns and travel restrictions have disrupted domestic, regional, and global supply chains; shuttered businesses and left millions unemployed; closed schools and severely curtailed education and job training opportunities for people of all ages; and adversely impacted mental and physical health by restricting access to health care. On 31 July 2020, the Director-General of the World Health Organization described the pandemic as "a once-in-a-century health crisis, the effects of which will be felt for decades to come" (UN News 2020).

Data availability is an area of concern for tracking progress in achieving the SDGs and for the design, implementation, and monitoring of national development plans. A primary constraint to the availability of sufficient data is often a lack of resources devoted to the development of statistics at the economy level (PARIS21 2017). Approved by the UN Statistics Division in March 2017, the Cape Town Global Action Plan for Sustainable Development Data appeals to governments to provide the funding necessary to upgrade national statistical systems, use a combination of traditional and innovative data sources, and harness strategic partnerships with an array of stakeholders (UNSC 2017).

The updated SDG indicator framework comprises a two-tier classification system based on data availability and whether the methodology is well established. Tier I indicators are those with a clearly established methodology and where data are being regularly collected by many economies. Tier II indicators are those with an established methodology, but where data are not regularly collected by many economies. Of the 231 SDG indicators, 123 belong to Tier I, 106 belong to Tier II, and 2 have multiple tiers, i.e., different components of the indicator are classified into different tiers (UNSC 2020).

Part I of *Key Indicators for Asia and the Pacific 2020* provides an SDG status update for ADB's 49 member economies located across Asia and the Pacific, outlining their progress toward achievement of the Sustainable Development Agenda. In addition to the data tables, the discussions for select SDG indicators are accompanied by supporting data stories and charts. Most of the statistics presented in the tables and charts are presented for two data points from 2000 to 2019. Data gaps and other data-related issues are also considered to inform any related policy actions.

---

1 Annual refinements of indicators are included in the indicator framework as they occur. Replacements, revisions, additions, and deletions to the framework were most recently approved by the 51st Statistical Commission in March 2020. For the latest list of indicators, go to https://unstats.un.org/sdgs/indicators/indicators-list/.

SDG 1. End poverty in all its forms everywhere

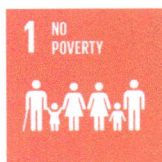

1 NO POVERTY

Much of developing Asia's gains in reducing extreme poverty are at risk of reversal from a global recession in the wake of COVID-19

Those in extreme poverty struggle to meet basic needs and often lack access to healthcare, education, and water and sanitation. The Asia and Pacific region's recent achievements in reducing extreme poverty are threatened by the COVID-19 pandemic and the ensuing global recession caused by measures to contain the virus. The World Bank estimates that between 71 million and 100 million people around the world may be pushed into extreme poverty in 2020 (World Bank 2020).

In developing Asia, the percentage of people living in extreme poverty—as measured by surviving on less than $1.90 per day at 2011 purchasing power parity—fell significantly from 33.5% in 2002 to 6.9% in 2015 (Figure 1.1.1). In absolute terms, this represented a decline from 1,109 million people in extreme poverty to 263 million during the review period. The bulk of this decline occurred in East Asia (from 406 million people in 2002 to 10 million people in 2015) and South Asia (from 505 million people in 2002 to 200 million people in 2015).

As a percentage of the overall population, extreme poverty fell in every subregion in developing Asia and the Pacific from 2002 to 2015: Central and West Asia (from 29.3% in 2002 to 5.8% in 2015), East Asia (from 31.6% to 0.7%), the Pacific (from 46.1% to 24.8%), South Asia (from 39.7% to 13.2%), and Southeast Asia (from 24.8% to 5.4%).

Figure 1.1.1: Proportion and Number of People Living in Extreme Poverty

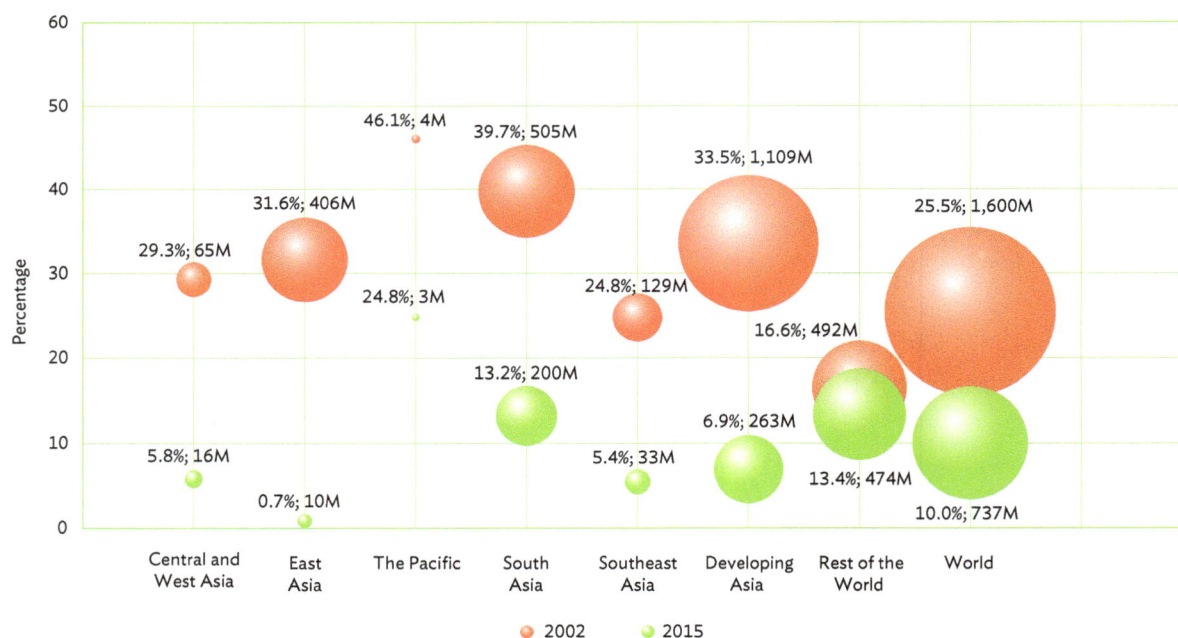

M = million.
Note: The size of the bubbles refers to the number of people living in extreme poverty, and the numbers next to the bubbles indicate the proportion of population in extreme poverty and the number of extreme poor in millions.
Source: Asian Development Bank estimates using World Bank. PovcalNet Database: http://iresearch.worldbank.org/PovcalNet/home.aspx (accessed 27 March 2020).

Click here for figure data

In a majority of the economies reporting for 2019, less than 10% of employed people were living in extreme poverty

The proportion of the employed population living in extreme poverty (i.e., "the working poor") in 2019 was less than 10.0% in 20 of the 26 economies with available data, as shown in Figure 1.1.2. Those economies with a share of the working poor to total population at 0.5% or less were Mongolia with 0.1%; Fiji with 0.2%; Armenia, the Kyrgyz Republic, and Sri Lanka with 0.3% each; and the People's Republic of China (PRC) with 0.5%. The share of the

employed population living in extreme poverty as a percentage of the total population exceeded 15.0% in five economies. The highest shares of the working poor as a percentage of total population in 2019 were observed in Afghanistan (40.1%), Papua New Guinea (21.8%), Timor-Leste (21.8%), Uzbekistan (19.7%), and Solomon Island (17.7%)

From 2000 to 2019, the share of the working poor as a percentage of the total population fell in all 26 reporting economies. The largest declines occurred in Cambodia (62.0 percentage points), Nepal (42.2 percentage points), and Tajikistan (41.9 percentage points).

Figure 1.1.2: Proportion of Employed Population Living below the International Poverty Line
(%)

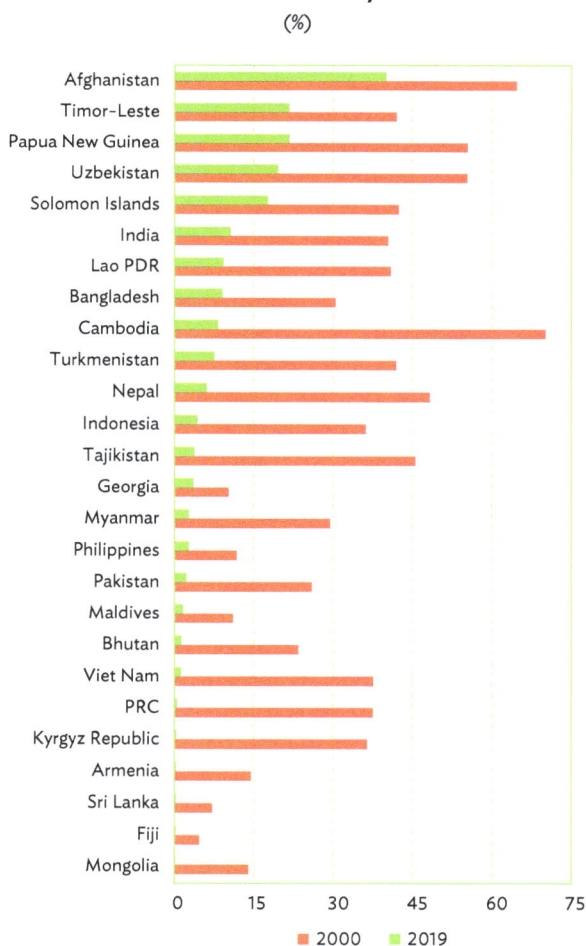

Lao PDR = Lao People's Democratic Republic, PRC= People's Republic of China
Note: Only economies with values greater than zero for both years are included.
Source: Table 1.1.1, Key Indicators for Asia and the Pacific 2020.

Click here for figure data

SDG 2. End hunger, achieve food security and improved nutrition, and promote sustainable agriculture

Undernourishment declined in more than three-quarters of economies from 2001 to 2018

According to the Food and Agriculture Organization of the United Nations, more than 820 million people in the world went hungry in 2018, highlighting the difficulty in achieving the SDG target of eradicating hunger by 2030 (FAO 2019). Furthermore, economic downturns disproportionally undermine food security and nutrition where income inequality is prevalent, especially in low-income economies. This does not bode well for the many economies of the Asia and Pacific region suffering economic shocks caused by measures to combat the COVID-19 pandemic.

Of the region's 37 economies with available data, 28 reported a decline in the prevalence of undernourishment from 2001 to 2018 (Figure 1.2.1). The largest reductions during the review period occurred in Armenia and Myanmar with 23.6 percentage points each, and in the Lao People's Democratic Republic (Lao PDR) with 21.2 percentage points.

Figure 1.2.1: Prevalence of Undernourishment in Select Economies of Asia and the Pacific
(% of total population)

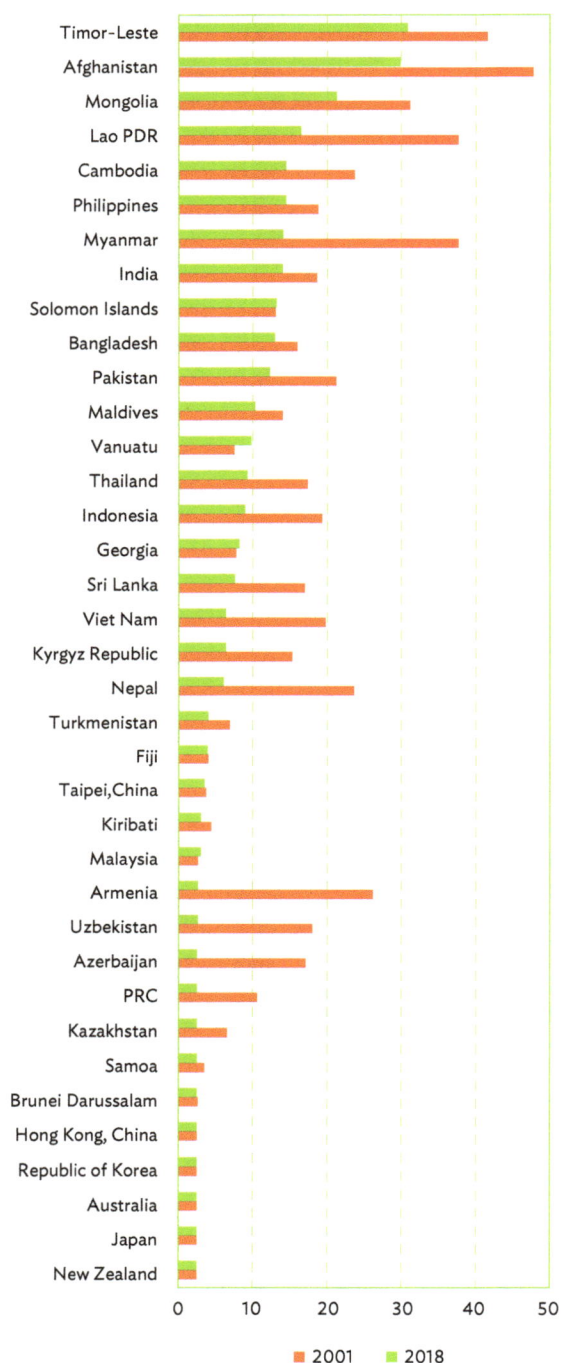

Lao PDR = Lao People's Democratic Republic, PRC = People's Republic of China.
Notes: 2001 values refer to 3-year average for 2000–2002; 2018 values refer to 3-year average for 2017–2019; and data with values smaller than 2.5% are presented as 2.5%. For Hong Kong, China, Lao PDR, and Maldives: earliest year data presented are for 2000, which refer to the 3-year average for 1999–2001; and latest year data presented are for 2017, which refer to the 3-year average for 2016–2018.
Source: Table 1.2.1, Key Indicators for Asia and the Pacific 2020.

Click here for figure data

In 2018, the prevalence of undernourishment was below 10.0% in 25 of the 37 reporting economies, a significant improvement from only 15 of 37 in 2001. The prevalence of undernourishment in 2018 was at a rate of 2.5% or less in Australia; Azerbaijan; Brunei Darussalam; Hong Kong, China; Japan; Kazakhstan; the PRC; the Republic of Korea; New Zealand; and Samoa. The highest rates of undernourishment in 2018 were observed in Timor-Leste (30.9%), Afghanistan (29.9%), and Mongolia (21.3%).

The prevalence of stunting remains an issue in more than half of the reporting economies

In many economies across Asia and the Pacific, poor food security and severe malnutrition have resulted in millions of children being stunted (i.e., too short for their age). In the most recent year for which data were available, the prevalence of stunting in children below the age of 5 years exceeded 20% in 17 of the 29 developing ADB member economies reporting on the indicator. The highest rates were found in Timor-Leste (51.7%), Papua New Guinea (49.5%), and Afghanistan (38.2%) as shown in Figure 1.2.2.

Comparing 2010–2018 to 2000–2009, the prevalence of stunting in children below the age of 5 years fell in 25 of the 29 developing member economies with available data. An increase was observed in three economies during the review period: Papua New Guinea (up 5.6 percentage points), Malaysia (up 3.5 percentage points), and Vanuatu (up 3.2 percentage points). The prevalence of stunting in children below the age of 5 years remained steady in the Republic of Korea from 2003 to 2010, posted at less than 2.5% for both years.

Figure 1.2.2: Prevalence of Stunting among Children under 5 Years of Age

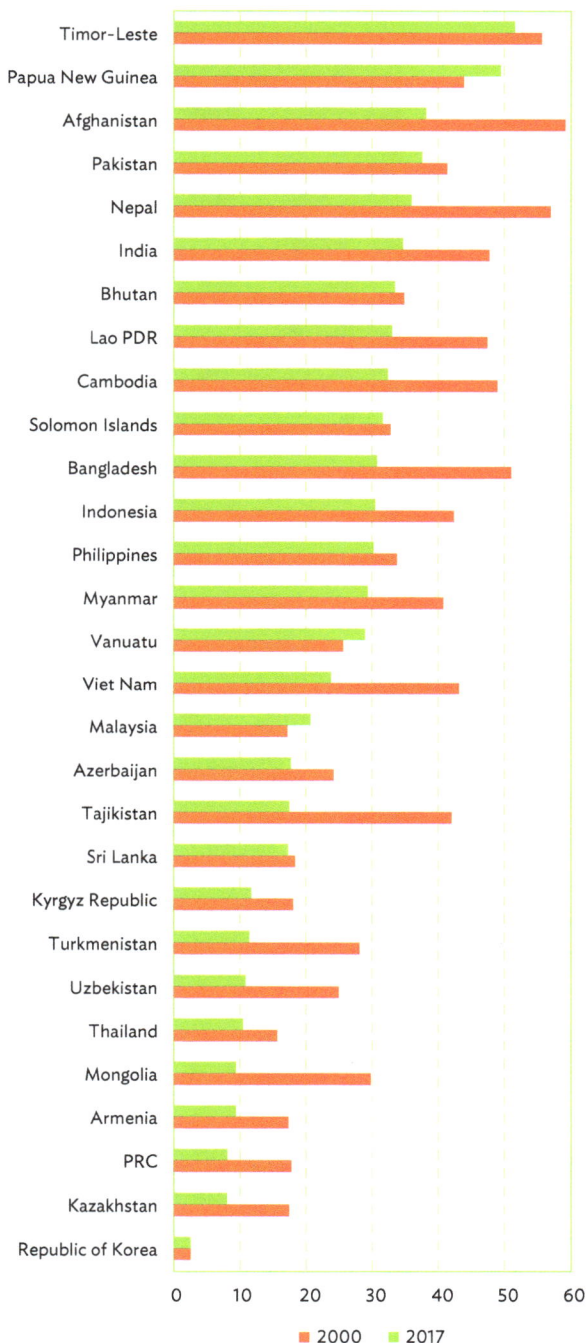

(%)

■ 2000 ■ 2017

Lao PDR = Lao People's Democratic Republic, PRC = People's Republic of China.
Note: 2000 values refer to available data between 2000 and 2009; and 2017 values refer to available data between 2010 and 2018. Only economies with data for both years 2000 and 2017 are included. "Stunting" is when a child is too short compared to the average height for his or her age.
Source: Table 1.2.1, Key Indicators for Asia and the Pacific 2020.

Click here for figure data

SDG 3. Ensure healthy lives and promote well-being for all at all ages

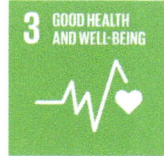

3 GOOD HEALTH AND WELL-BEING

From 2000 to 2017, the maternal mortality ratio fell in almost every developing economy with available data

Among developing member economies in Asia and the Pacific, the number of women dying during pregnancy, childbirth, or soon after fell from 271 deaths per 100,000 live births in 2000 to 119 deaths per 100,000 live births in 2017. This compares with a decline in the world average over the same period from 342 deaths per 100,000 live births to 211 deaths per 100,000 live births.

All subregions within Asia and the Pacific posted a reduction in the maternal mortality ratio (MMR) from 2000 to 2017. During the review period, South Asia reported the largest drop in maternal deaths per 100,000 live births, with a decline of 230 (378 to 148). It was followed by Central and West Asia with a decline of 221[2] (404 to 182), the Pacific with 93 (223 to 130), Southeast Asia with 78 (215 to 137), and East Asia with 29 (58 to 29).

From 2000 to 2017, the MMR decreased in 37 of the 38 developing member economies with available data (Table 1.3.1). The exception was Brunei Darussalam, where the number of maternal deaths per 100,000 live births increased from 28 to 31 during the review period.

Afghanistan experienced the largest decline in its MMR during the review period, with 812 fewer maternal deaths per 100,000 live births in 2017 than in 2000. It was followed by Timor-Leste (603), Nepal (367), the Lao PDR (359), and Cambodia (328). Developing member economies with 10 or fewer maternal deaths per 100,000 live births in 2017 included Kazakhstan (10), Singapore (8), and Turkmenistan (7).

2   For Central and West Asia, rounding affects the observed decline. The precise MMR averages for Central and West Asia are 403.6 in 2000 and 182.2 in 2017 (i.e., 403.6 – 182.2 = 221.4).

Figure 1.3.1: Maternal Mortality Ratios and Proportion of Births Attended by Skilled Health Personnel

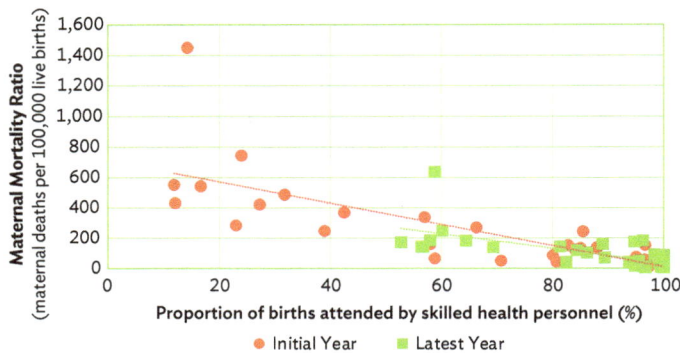

Note: Initial year refers to 2000–2007 and latest year refers to 2009–2019.
Source: Table 1.3.1, Key Indicators for Asia and the Pacific 2020.

Click here for figure data

Economies in which maternal deaths were relatively low tended to be those with a higher proportion of births attended by skilled health personnel, while those economies in which maternal deaths were relatively high had a lower proportion of births attended by medical professionals (Figure 1.3.1). In economies that have imposed restrictions on movement in response to the COVID-19 pandemic, there is the potential for heightened risk of maternal death at births not attended by skilled health personnel.

Economies of Asia and the Pacific have shown strong progress in reducing the under-5 mortality rate

The under-5 mortality rate in Asia and the Pacific declined from 66 deaths per 1,000 live births in 2000 to 30 deaths per 1,000 live births in 2018, as the under-5 mortality rate fell in 45 of the 47 reporting economies during the review period. This compares with world averages of 76 deaths per 1,000 live births in 2000 and 39 deaths per 1,000 live births in 2018.

By subregion, South Asia reported the largest decline with a reduction of 50 deaths per 1,000 live births from 2000 to 2018. It was followed by Central and West Asia (44), East Asia (25), Southeast Asia (22), and the Pacific (17) as outlined in Figure 1.3.2. Among the developed economies, the average decline during the review period was two fewer deaths per 1,000 live births.

Figure 1.3.2: Under-5 Mortality Rate by Region and Subregion of Asia and the Pacific
(per 1,000 live births)

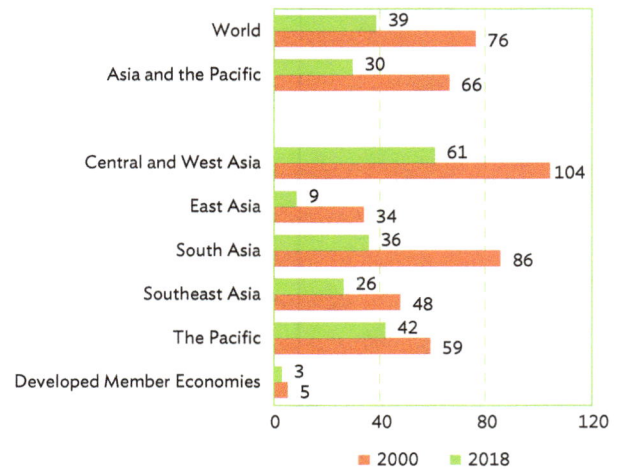

Source: Table 1.3.1, Key Indicators for Asia and the Pacific 2020.

Click here for figure data

By economy, the largest reductions in under-5 mortality rates occurred in Timor-Leste (69 fewer deaths per 1,000 live births), Cambodia (68), Afghanistan (63), the Lao PDR (62), and Azerbaijan (60) as shown in Table 1.3.1.

SDG 4. Ensure inclusive and equitable quality education and promote lifelong learning opportunities for all

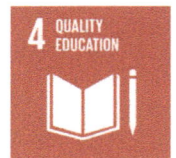

Participation rates in pre-primary education, which are already below 50% for both boys and girls in more than one-fifth of reporting economies, may decline as COVID-19 containment measures restrict access to early childhood education

Early childhood education can lead to improved access to economic opportunities and better income prospects. However, measures to contain COVID-19 are exacerbating challenges to early childhood education in developing economies throughout Asia and the Pacific, which could translate into losses in lifetime opportunities and earnings (Panth and Xu 2020).

In 2018 (or the most recent year for which data were available), 100% participation rates of girls in pre-primary education were observed in the Cook Islands; Hong Kong, China; Indonesia; Malaysia; and Niue. For boys, participation rates of 100% were observed in Pakistan, Palau, Thailand, and Viet Nam (Figure 1.4.1). Only 13 of the 35 economies with available data had at least 90% of both boys and girls participating in organized learning one year before the official entrance age to primary school.

The pre-primary education participation rate for girls lagged behind that of boys in 14 of the 35 reporting economies, with the biggest gaps found in Palau (18.7 percentage points), Pakistan (12.7 percentage points), and the Federated States of Micronesia (9.7 percentage points) as demonstrated in Table 1.4.1.

Participation rates below 50% for both boys and girls were found in eight reporting economies in 2018 (or the most recent year for which data were available): Armenia (45.8% for boys and 49.5% for girls), Bangladesh (36.6% and 36.7%), Bhutan (33.9% and 35.4%), Cambodia (42.4% and 43.6%), Samoa (34.3% and 41.9%), Tajikistan (13.4% and 11.6%), Timor-Leste (43.0% and 42.3%), and Uzbekistan (37.0% and 36.5%).

In over 80% of the region's economies, more than 90% of primary school teachers received the minimum organized training for teaching at the relevant level in 2018

Teachers play a key role in ensuring the quality of children's education. They should therefore receive adequate and relevant training to ensure they can have the appropriate beneficial impact.

As shown in Figure 1.4.2, the percentage of primary school teachers receiving the minimum organized pedagogical training—both pre-service

Figure 1.4.1: Participation Rate in Organized Learning (1 Year before the Official Primary Entry Age), 2018 or Latest Year

(%)

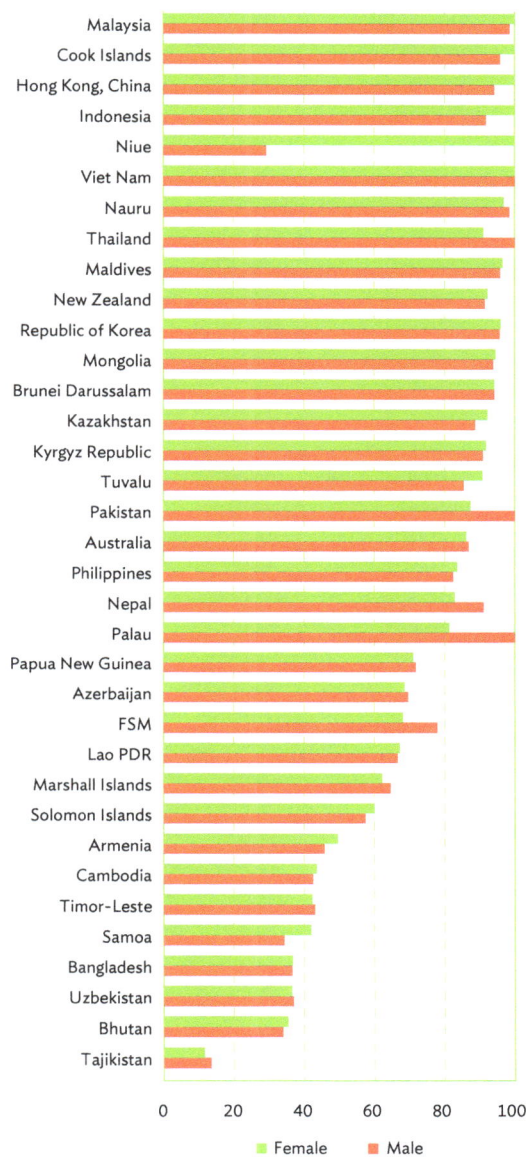

FSM = Federated States of Micronesia, Lao PDR = Lao People's Democratic Republic.

Note:　　For Nepal and Kazakhstan, data refer to 2019; for Tajikistan, the Philippines, Australia, the Republic of Korea, New Zealand, Maldives, and Thailand, data refer to 2017; for the Marshall Islands, Papua New Guinea, Nauru, and the Cook Islands, data refer to 2016; for the FSM, Niue, and Malaysia, data refer to 2015; for Palau, data refer to 2014; for Cambodia, data refer to 2012; and for Bangladesh, data refer to 2010.

Source:　　Table 1.4.1, Key Indicators for Asia and the Pacific 2020.

Click here for figure data

Figure 1.4.2: Proportion of Teachers in Primary Education Who Have Received at Least the Minimum Organized Teacher Training
(% of total teachers)

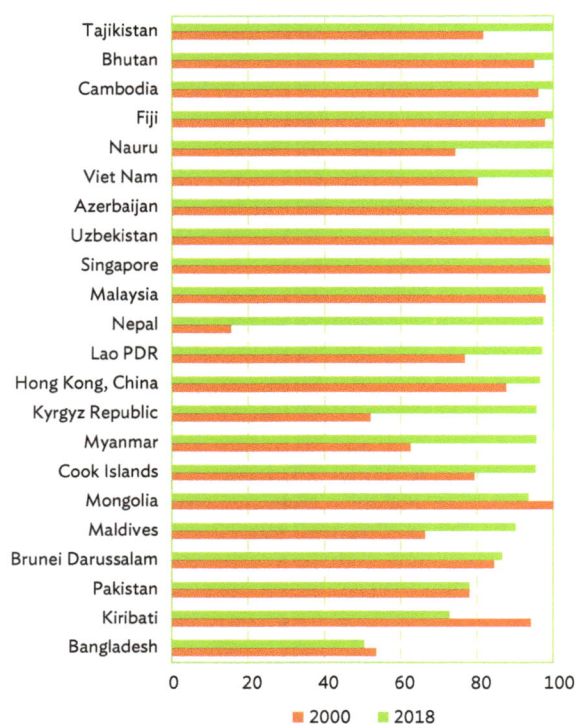

Lao PDR = Lao People's Democratic Republic.
Note: 2000 values refer to data available from 2000 to 2009; and 2018 values refer to data available from 2010 to 2019. Only economies with data for both years 2000 and 2018 are included.
Source: Table 1.4.2, Key Indicators for Asia and the Pacific 2020

Click here for figure data

and in-service training—required to teach at the relevant level exceeded 90% in 18 of the 22 economies reporting for 2018 (or the most recent year for which data were available). In 2000 (or the earliest year for which data were available), only nine of 22 economies with available data met the 90% threshold.

Comparing 2010–2018 to 2000–2009, 14 of the 22 reporting economies from across Asia and the Pacific increased the percentage of primary school teachers receiving the minimum organized training (Table 1.4.2). The largest increases were observed in Nepal (81.9 percentage points), the Kyrgyz Republic (43.4 percentage points), and Myanmar (32.6 percentage points). The largest declines during the review period were noted in Kiribati (–21.2 percentage points), Mongolia (–6.7 percentage points), and Bangladesh (–3.0 percentage points).

SDG 5. Achieve gender equality and empower all women and girls

In more than one-third of the region's economies, at least 20% of women aged 20–24 years old were married or in a union before the age of 18

Early-age marriage or union can limit the education and employment prospects of a girl or young woman, compromising her overall well-being and the health of her offspring (World Bank 2017). The percentage of women aged 20–24 years who were married or in a union before the age of 18 exceeded 20% in 11 of the 30 economies of Asia and the Pacific with available data (Table 1.5.1).

More than a quarter of women aged 20–24 years were married or in a union before the age of 18 in Bangladesh (58.6%), Nepal (39.5%), the Lao PDR (32.7%), Afghanistan (28.3%), India (27.3%), Papua New Guinea (27.3%), and Bhutan (25.8%) as demonstrated in Figure 1.5.1.

Economies in Asia and the Pacific suffer from lack of adequate women's representation in national parliaments

The empowerment of women and their representation in political and economic decision-making can strengthen sustainable development and benefit societies at large. While no economy within Asia and the Pacific achieved gender parity for representation in national parliament in 2019, 16 of the 42 reporting economies had female representation of 20.0% or more (Figure 1.5.2). The regional leaders in this respect were New Zealand (40.0%), Timor-Leste (40.0%), Nepal (32.7%), and Australia (30.0%).

Nine economies failed to meet a minimum threshold of 10.0% of seats in the national parliament held by women (Table 1.5.2). Furthermore, a UN assessment of local governance across Asia and the

Figure 1.5.1: Proportion of Women Who Were Married or in a Union before Age 15 or Age 18

(% of all women aged 20–24 years)

■ Before Age 15   ■ Before Age 18

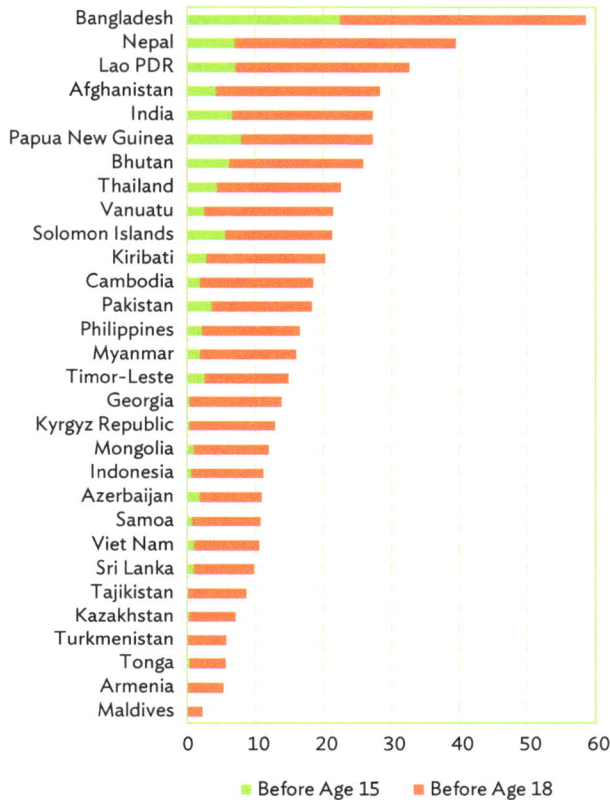

Lao PDR = Lao People's Democratic Republic.
Note: The percentages shown are based on economy data for the most recent year from 2009 to 2019.
Source: Table 1.5.1, Key Indicators for Asia and the Pacific 2020.

Click here for figure data

Figure 1.5.2: Proportion of Seats in National Parliament Held by Women, 2019

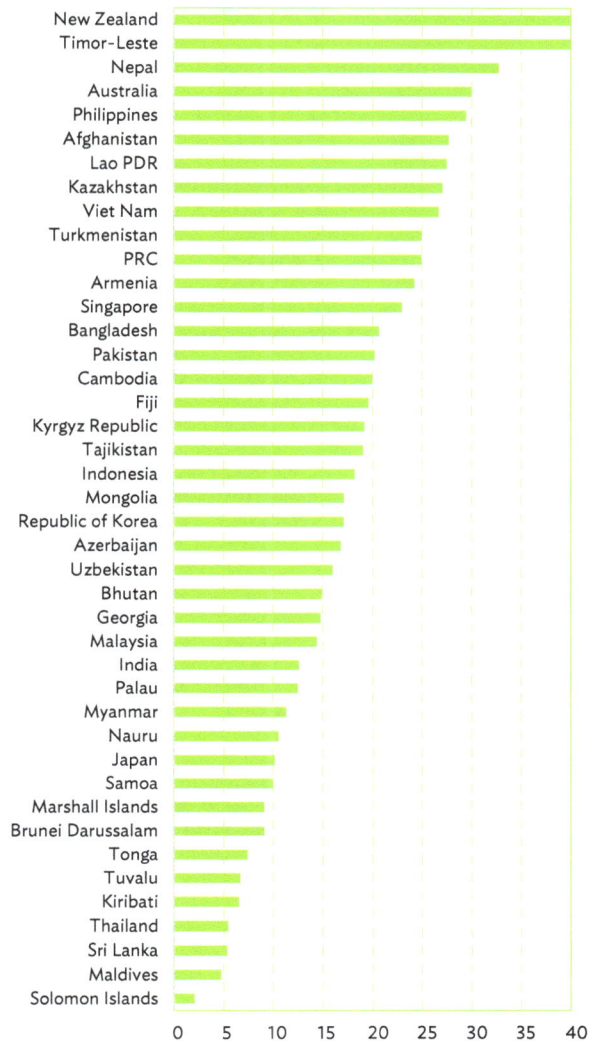

(%)

Lao PDR = Lao People's Democratic Republic, PRC= People's Republic of China.
Note: The Federated States of Micronesia, Papua New Guinea, and Vanuatu have zero representation and are not shown in the figure.
Source: Table 1.5.1, Key Indicators for Asia and the Pacific 2020.

Click here for figure data

Pacific showed that female participation at the local level is far below gender parity levels, which implies that fewer women will continue into higher elected offices (ADB and UN Women 2018).

SDG 6. Ensure availability and sustainable management of water and sanitation for all

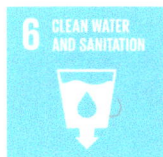

The share of the population benefiting from safely managed drinking water services exceeded 90% in just under one-third of reporting Asia and the Pacific economies in 2017

Sadly, millions of people die every year from diseases associated with inadequate water supply, sanitation, and hygiene (UN 2020b). The provision of safe water, sanitation, and waste management within hygienic conditions is essential for preventing the spread of disease and for protecting human health during all infectious disease outbreaks, including COVID-19. Measures that can improve water safety include protecting the source water; treating water at the point of distribution, collection, or consumption;

and ensuring that treated water is safely stored at home in regularly cleaned and covered containers (WHO 2020).

In 2017, only 8 of the 25 economies with available data had more than 90% of the population using safely managed drinking water services (Table 1.6.1). Meanwhile, the proportion of the population using safely managed drinking water services was below 50% in nine economies (Figure 1.6.1).

Since 2000, 21 of the 25 reporting economies expanded the provision of safely managed drinking water services. The largest increases during the review period were observed in Armenia (56.9 percentage points), Kazakhstan (32.0 percentage points), and Turkmenistan (28.0 percentage points).

For those economies with data disaggregated by location for 2017, use of safely managed drinking water services was higher in urban areas than in rural areas for 9 of 10 economies. The biggest discrepancies

were observed in Uzbekistan (urban coverage 55.0 percentage points higher than rural coverage), Cambodia (urban coverage 39.9 percentage points higher), and the Kyrgyz Republic (urban coverage 39.6 percentage points higher). The exception was Bangladesh, where people in rural areas had greater access to safely managed drinking water services than those in urban areas (by a differential of 16.9 percentage points).

From 2000 to 2017, nearly 80% of reporting economies expanded their coverage of safely managed sanitation services

The spread of many infectious diseases, including COVID-19, can be impeded by safely managing sanitation services and applying good hygiene practices and waste management. Sanitation services and workers are essential for operational support during the COVID-19 pandemic (WHO 2020).

Among the 14 economies of Asia and the Pacific with data available for 2017, the proportion of the population accessing safely managed sanitation services was below 50% in four reporting economies: Samoa (48.5%), Armenia (48.2%), Georgia (27.2%), and Tuvalu (6.3%) (Figure 1.6.2). Conversely, this share exceeded 90% in another four reporting economies: Singapore (100.0%); the Republic of Korea (99.9%); Japan (98.8%); and Hong Kong, China (91.8%).

From 2000 to 2017, the proportion of the population benefiting from safely managed sanitation services increased in 11 of the 14 reporting economies, while declining in two and remaining unchanged in one (Singapore's sanitation coverage was 100.0% in both 2000 and 2017.) The largest increases during the review period were in the PRC (45.5 percentage points), the Lao PDR (36.2 percentage points), and the Republic of Korea (14.0 percentage points).

Among the five economies with data disaggregated by location, three had a higher share of the population

Figure 1.6.1: Proportion of the Population Using Safely Managed Drinking Water Services, 2017

(%)

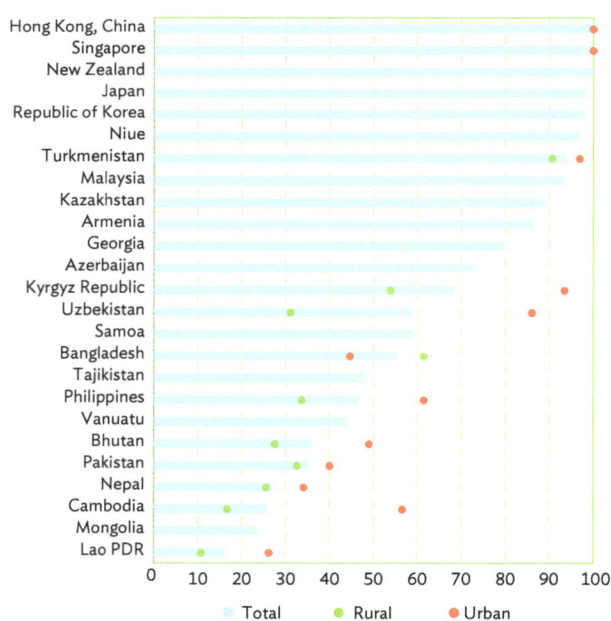

Lao PDR = Lao People's Democratic Republic
Note: This figure excludes economies that provided only urban and/or rural data, with no national totals provided.
Source: Table 1.6.1, Key Indicators for Asia and the Pacific 2020.

Click here for figure data

Figure 1.6.2: Proportion of Population Using Safely Managed Sanitation Services, 2017

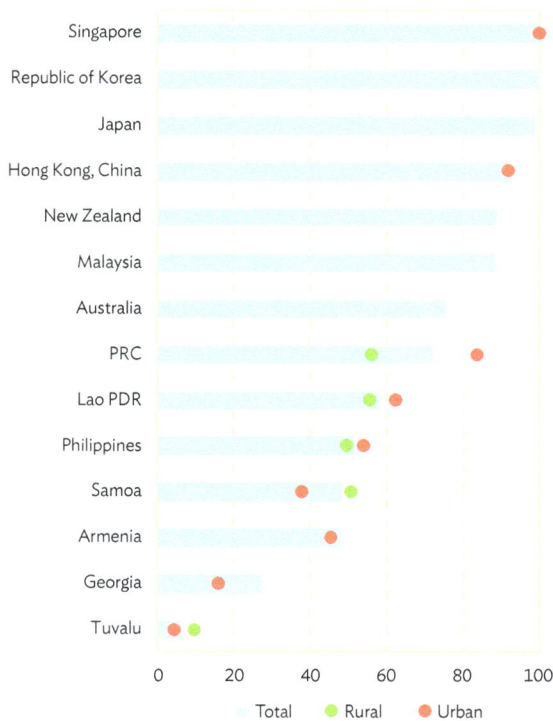

(%)

PRC = People's Republic of China, Lao PDR = Lao People's Democratic Republic.
Note: This figure excludes economies that provided only urban and/or rural data, with no national totals provided.
Source: Table 1.6.1, Key Indicators for Asia and the Pacific 2020.

Click here for figure data

using safely managed sanitation services in urban areas, while two had a higher share in rural areas. The PRC posted the biggest difference in sanitation services coverage in favor of urban areas (27.6 percentage points), while Samoa had the biggest difference in favor of rural areas (13.2 percentage points).

SDG 7. Ensure access to affordable, reliable, sustainable, and modern energy for all

The number of economies providing at least 95% of the population with access to electricity has almost doubled in 18 years.

The development of sustainable communities that have enhanced resilience to climate change and other environmental hazards depends largely on the provision of universal access to energy, improved energy efficiency, and the increased use of renewable energy.

Across Asia and the Pacific, the proportion of the population with access to electricity exceeded 95% in 36 of the 47 economies with data available for 2018 (or another recent year), compared with only 20 of 47 economies in 2000 (or another recent year) as shown in Figure 1.7.1. In 2000, 12 regional economies were providing electricity to less than 50% of the population. There were zero economies with electricity coverage of less than 50% in 2018.

From 2000 to 2018, the largest gains in expanding access to electricity as a share of the population occurred in Afghanistan (75.7 percentage points), Cambodia (75.0 percentage points), and Bhutan (68.9 percentage points) as shown in Figure 1.7.1.

Since 2000, the share of the population with access to clean fuels and technology has risen or held steady at a high level (95%) in more than 80% of economies in Asia and the Pacific

In 2018, 13 of the 47 economies with available data reported that more than 90.0% of the population were already relying on clean fuels and technology for cooking, heating, and lighting—up only marginally from 10 economies in 2000. The share of the population relying on clean energy was below 50.0% in 19 economies in 2018 (Figure 1.7.2).

Comparing 2018 with 2000, 30 of the 47 reporting economies increased the proportion of the population with access to clean fuels and technology, 11 economies maintained the same proportion and six economies posted a decline. The largest increases in access to clean energy from 2000 to 2018 occurred in Indonesia (74.0 percentage points), Viet Nam (51.0 percentage points), and the Marshall Islands (50.0 percentage points).

Figure 1.7.1: Proportion of the Population with Access to Electricity
(%)

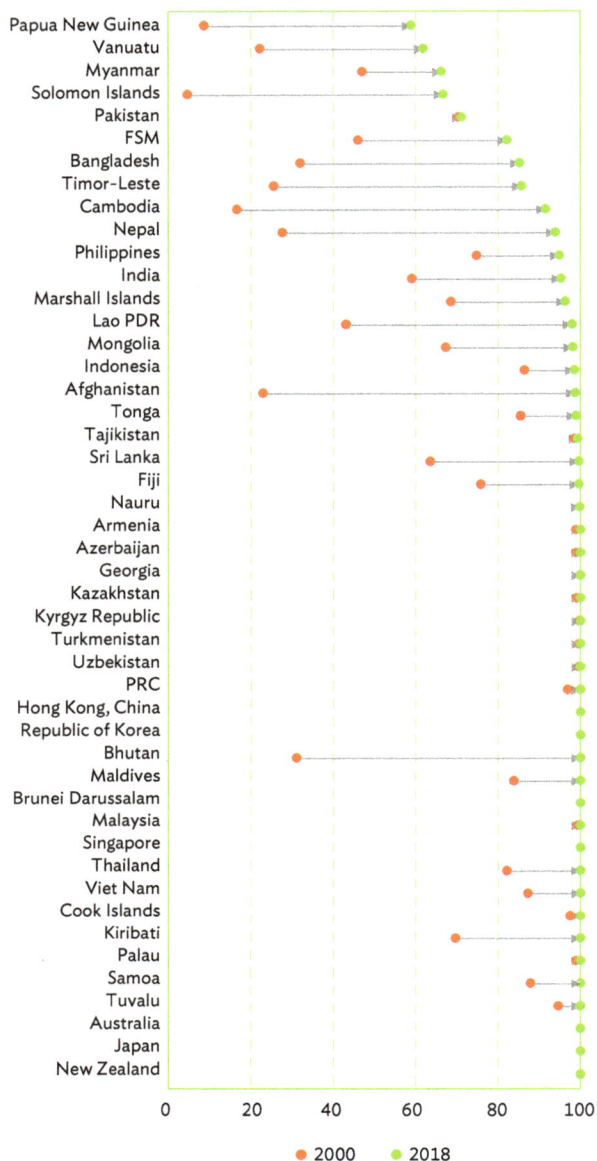

Figure 1.7.2: Proportion of Population with Primary Reliance on Clean Fuels and Technology
(%)

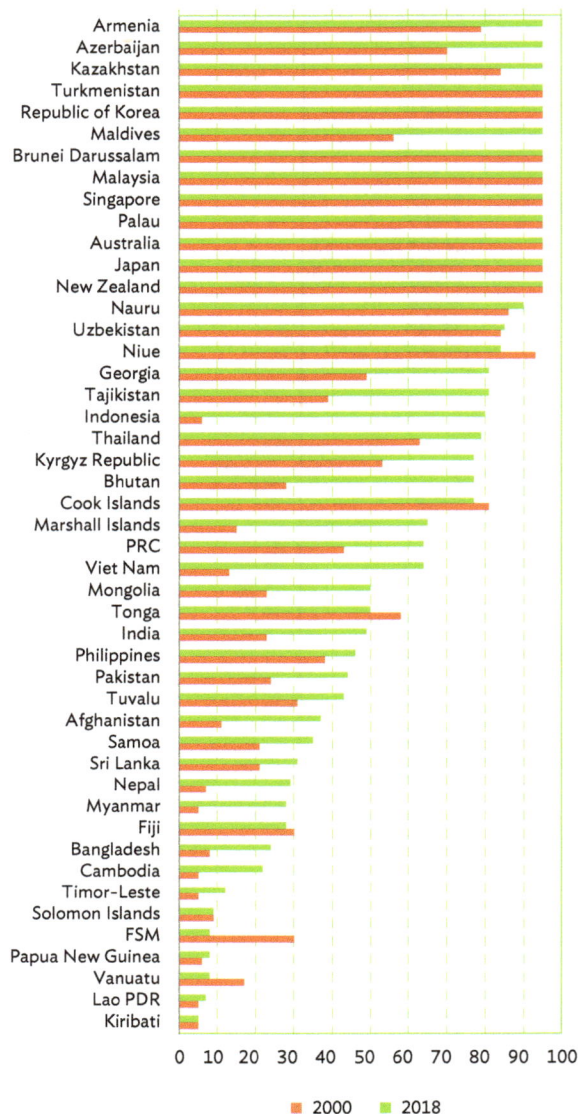

FSM = Federated States of Micronesia, Lao PDR = Lao People's Democratic Republic, PRC = People's Republic of China.
Note: Earliest year refers to the period 2000 to 2009, where data are available. Only economies with available data for both earliest and latest years are included.
Source: Table 1.7.1, Key Indicators for Asia and the Pacific 2020.

Click here for figure data

FSM = Federated States of Micronesia, Lao PDR = Lao People's Democratic Republic, PRC = People's Republic of China.
Note: Data with values greater than 95% are presented as 95% and values smaller than 5% are presented as 5%.
Source: Table 1.7.1, Key Indicators for Asia and the Pacific 2020.

Click here for figure data

SDG 8. Promote sustained, inclusive, and sustainable economic growth; full and productive employment; and decent work for all

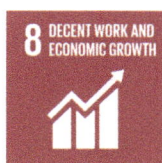

Figure 1.8.1: Unemployment Rate by Age Group, 2019 or Most Recent Year Prior

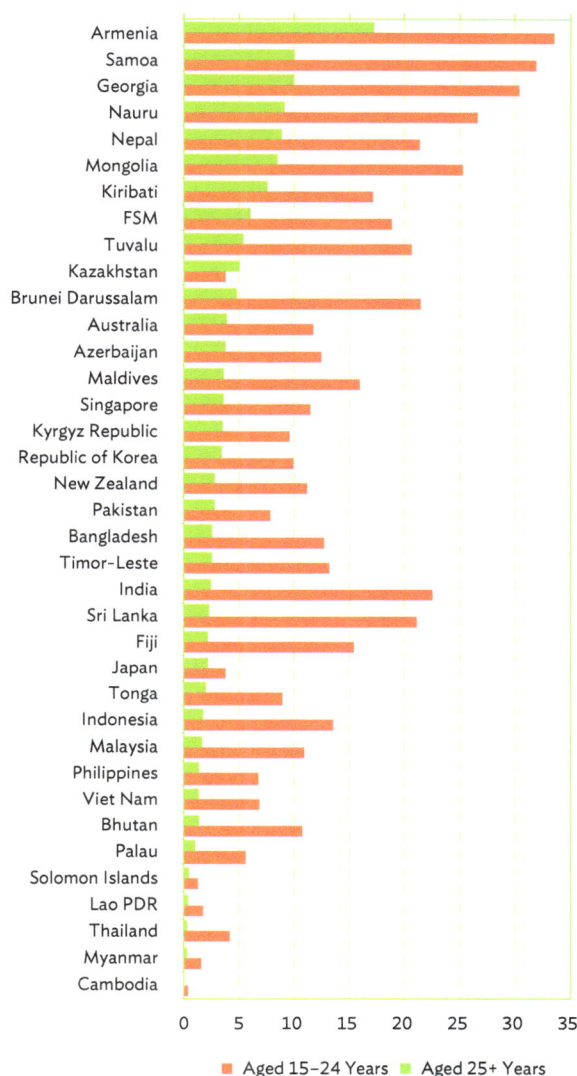

(%)

■ Aged 15–24 Years ■ Aged 25+ Years

FSM = Federated States of Micronesia, Lao PDR = Lao People's Democratic Republic.

Note: For Armenia, India, the Kyrgyz Republic, Malaysia, Pakistan, Sri Lanka, Tonga, data refer to 2018. For Bangladesh, Cambodia, Kazakhstan, the Lao PDR, Nepal, Samoa, data refer to 2017. For the Cook Islands, Fiji, Maldives, Timor-Leste, Tuvalu, data refer to 2016. For Bhutan and Kiribati, data refer to 2015. For the FSM and Palau, data refer to 2014. For Nauru and Solomon Islands, data refer to 2013. For the Lao PDR and Vanuatu, data refer to 2010.

Source: Table 1.8.2, Key Indicators for Asia and the Pacific 2020.

Unemployment, especially among those aged 15–24 years, will continue to be a challenge in many of the region's economies

Employment provides individuals with income. As inequality persists and unemployment spikes due to strategies to mitigate the COVID-19 pandemic, it is increasingly difficult for many people to build better lives through their work (ILO 2020).

In 2019 (or the most recent year for which data were available), Kazakhstan was alone among 37 reporting economies in having a higher unemployment rate for those aged 25 years and older than for those aged 15–24 years (Figure 1.8.1). In Samoa, the unemployment rate for those aged 15–24 years was 21.9 percentage points higher than for those aged 25 years and older. In Georgia, the gap was 20.4 percentage points and in India it was 20.1 percentage points. A total of 16 economies had a gap in the unemployment rate between the two age groups that exceeded 10 percentage points.

Among the population aged 15 years and older, 26 of the 41 economies reporting for 2019 (or the most recent year for which data were available) posted a higher unemployment rate for men than for women (Table 1.8.2). The largest gender gaps in favor of women were all found in the Pacific: Tuvalu (11.6 percentage points), Samoa (10.7 percentage points), and the Federated States of Micronesia (8.5 percentage points). The largest gender gaps in favor of men were in Kiribati (6.2 percentage points), Turkmenistan (3.0 percentage points), and Georgia (2.6 percentage points).

Click here for figure data

SDG 9. Build resilient infrastructure, promote inclusive and sustainable industrialization, and foster innovation

9 INDUSTRY, INNOVATION AND INFRASTRUCTURE

Manufacturing value-added per capita has increased in more than 80% of reporting economies since 2000

The share of manufacturing value-added as a percentage of gross domestic product (GDP) reflects two factors: manufacturing's significance in an economy, and the economy's level of industrialization. An expanding manufacturing sector can support job growth and an economy's overall development.

An increase in manufacturing value-added per capita was observed in 37 of the 46 developing economies with data available for 2000 and 2019 (Figure 1.9.1). The biggest gains in manufacturing value-added (in constant 2015 United States dollars) occurred in the Republic of Korea ($4,732 per capita); Taipei,China ($4,726 per capita); and Singapore ($3,272 per capita). The largest declines during the review period occurred in Australia ($1,160 per capita), Brunei Darussalam ($1,059 per capita), and New Zealand ($409 per capita).

As a share of GDP in 2019, manufacturing value-added was highest in Turkmenistan (45.0%); Taipei,China (31.6%); the PRC (28.8%); the Republic of Korea (27.5%), and Thailand (26.7%) as outlined in Table 1.9.2. Manufacturing value-added as a share of GDP was 1.0% or less in Palau (1.0%); Hong Kong, China (0.9%); the Marshall Islands (0.8%); Tuvalu (0.7%); and Timor-Leste (0.5%).

CO_2 emissions per unit of manufacturing value-added fell in more than two-thirds of reporting economies

The adoption of clean and environmentally sound technologies and industrial processes can reduce CO_2 emissions while promoting efficiency

Figure 1.9.1: Manufacturing Value-Added per Capita
(constant 2015 $)

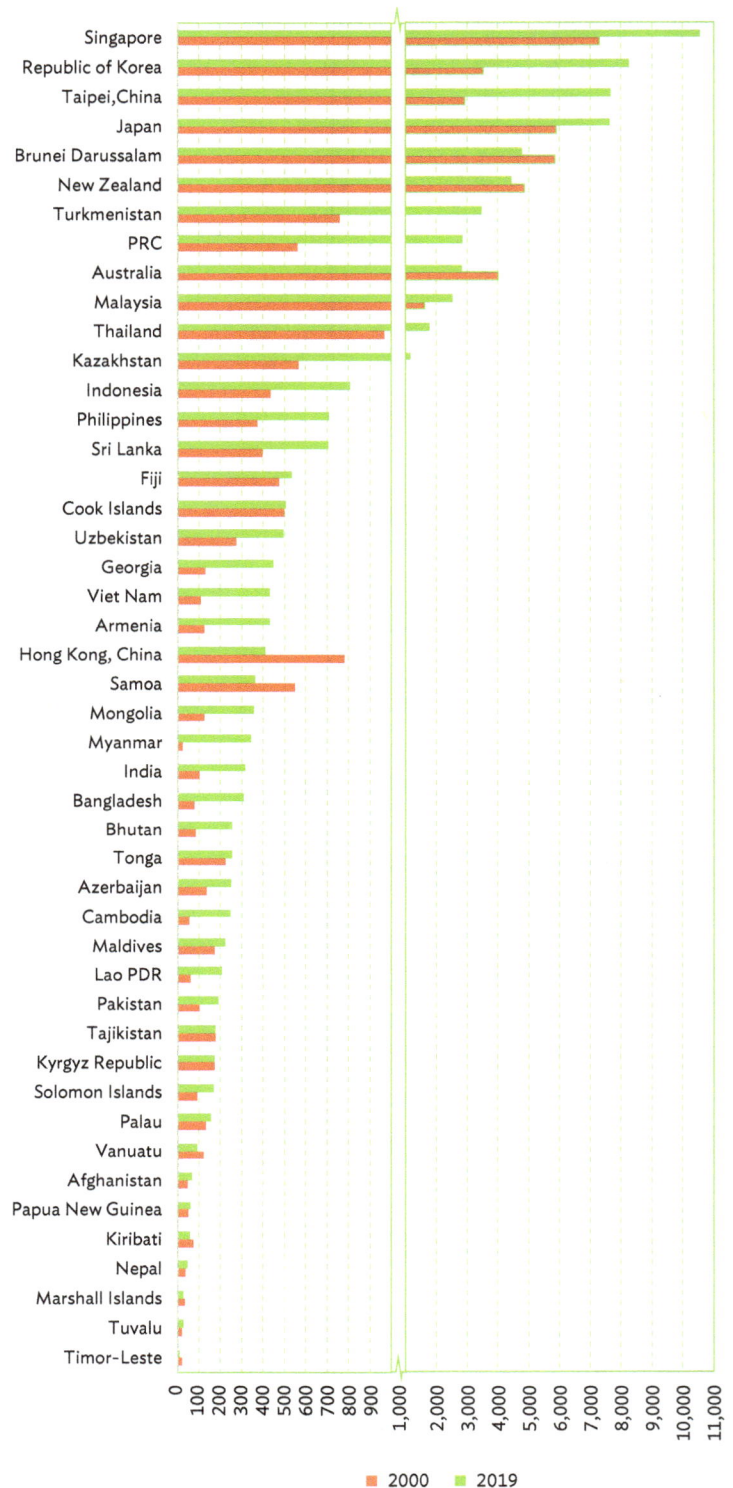

■ 2000 ■ 2019

$ = United States dollars, Lao PDR = Lao People's Democratic Republic, PRC = People's Republic of China.
Note: Only economies with data for both years 2000 and 2019 are included.
Source: Table 1.9.2, Key Indicators for Asia and the Pacific 2020.

Click here for figure data

in the use of resources. From 2000 to 2017, carbon dioxide (CO_2) emissions per unit of manufacturing value-added declined in 21 of the 30 economies with available data (Figure 1.9.2).

During the review period, a decline of 1.0 kilogram (kg) or more of CO_2 equivalent per unit of manufacturing value-added (in constant 2010 United

Figure 1.9.2: Carbon Dioxide Emissions per Unit of Manufacturing Value-Added
(kg of CO_2 per constant 2010 $)

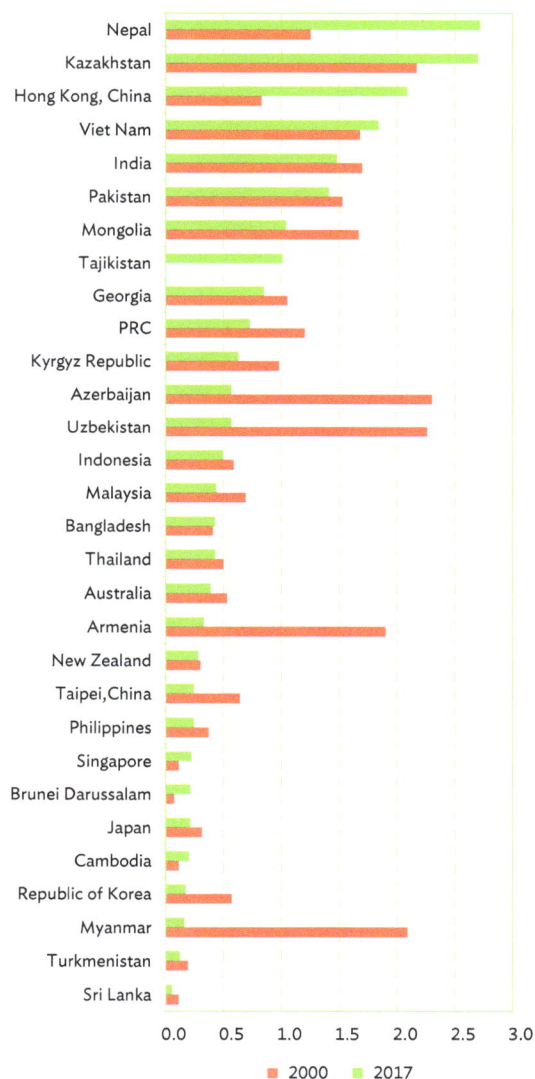

■ 2000 ■ 2017

$ = United States dollars, CO_2 = carbon dioxide, kg = kilogram, PRC = People's Republic of China.
Notes: Only economies with available data for both years 2000 and 2017 are included. For Taipei,China, unit of measure is kg of CO_2 equivalent per constant 2015 $. For 2000, Tajikistan has zero recorded data for the CO_2 emissions per unit of manufacturing value-added.
Source: Table 1.9.3, Key Indicators for Asia and the Pacific 2020.

States dollars) was observed in Myanmar (1.9 kg of CO_2 equivalent), Azerbaijan (1.7 kg), Uzbekistan (1.7 kg), and Armenia (1.6 kg). An increase of 1.0 kg or more of CO_2 equivalent per unit of manufacturing value-added (in constant 2010 United States dollars) occurred in Nepal (1.5 kg of CO_2 equivalent); Hong Kong, China (1.3 kg); and Tajikistan (1.0 kg).

In 2017, the economies with the highest levels of CO_2 emissions per unit of manufacturing value-added were Nepal (2.7 kg of CO_2 equivalent); Kazakhstan (2.7 kg); and Hong Kong, China (2.1 kg). The lowest levels of CO_2 emissions per unit of manufacturing value-added were observed in Sri Lanka and Turkmenistan (0.1 kg each).

SDG 10. Reduce inequality within and among countries

Growth in household expenditure (or income per capita) among the bottom 40% of the population rose in nearly all economies for which data are available; in most cases, this growth was on par with growth in household expenditure (or income per capita) among the general population

During the most recent 5-year period for which data were available, household expenditure or income per capita rose for the bottom 40% of the total population in 14 of the 15 developing member economies with available data (Figure 1.10.1). These gains are at risk of being reversed by the economic fallout from the COVID-19 pandemic. Across Asia and the Pacific, migrant workers, both domestic and international, have been forced to leave their jobs and return home as part of pandemic containment measures. The timing of their return to employment is uncertain in many cases (ADB 2020).

Economies with the highest level of household expenditure growth among the bottom 40% of the population include the PRC and Malaysia at 8.0% each. Kazakhstan was the only economy not to

Click here for figure data

Figure 1.10.1: Growth Rates of Household Expenditure or Income per Capita, 2010–2018

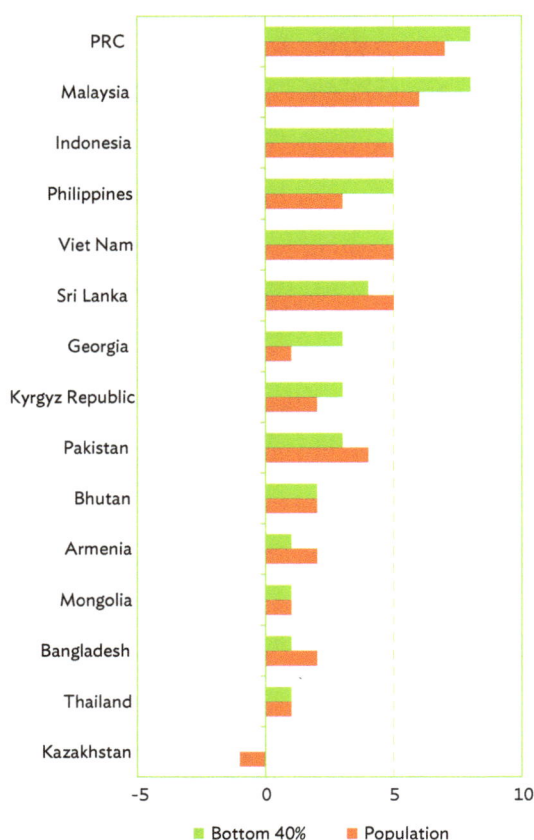

(%)

PRC = People's Republic of China.

Note: Bottom 40% refers to individuals within the lowest 40 percentile band in terms of income. Growth in household expenditure or income per capita is assessed over varying periods for each economy, usually periods of 5 or 6 years falling within 2010 and 2018. Growth rates refer to latest available data for over about a five-year period. Only economies with data for both the bottom 40% and the total population are included.

Source: Table 1.10.1, Key Indicators for Asia and the Pacific 2020.

Click here for figure data

experience growth in household expenditure among the bottom 40% of the population during the most recent 5-year period for which data were available.

Of the 15 reporting economies, average annual growth rates in household expenditure or income per capita among the bottom 40% outpaced growth rates for the total population in six economies during the review period. Growth in household expenditure was the same for both population groups in five economies, and expenditure growth among the entire population outpaced that among the bottom 40% in four economies.

The largest differences in household expenditure or income per capita growth rates in favor of the bottom 40% of the population, occurred in Georgia, Malaysia, and the Philippines at 2.0 percentage points each. The economies in which growth in household expenditure or income per capita lagged behind growth for the total population were Armenia, Bangladesh, Pakistan, and Sri Lanka. In all four cases, the gap was 1 percentage point.

SDG 11. Make cities and human settlements inclusive, safe, resilient, and sustainable

Individual economies have made major gains since 2000 in reducing the share of the urban population living in slums

Lack of access to basic services is pervasive in informal settlements and slums, contributing to the persistence of poverty and undermining attempts at inclusive urbanization. Furthermore, COVID-19 is a largely urban crisis—about 90% of all confirmed COVID-19 cases through the first half of 2020 were reported in cities and towns (UN Habitat 2020)—making the provision of adequate housing and hygienic conditions an even more pressing issue.

Among the 13 reporting economies with data available for both 2000 (or 2005) and 2018, 12 posted a reduction in the percentage of the urban population living in slums, informal settlements, or inadequate housing. The largest declines were observed in the Lao PDR (58.2 percentage points), Viet Nam (35.0 percentage points), and Cambodia (33.8 percentage points) as shown in Figure 1.11.1.

The only reporting economy to experience an increase in the percentage of the urban population living in slums, informal settlements, or inadequate housing during the review period was Myanmar (10.5 percentage points).

Figure 1.11.1: Proportion of Urban Population Living in Slums, 2000 and 2018
(%)

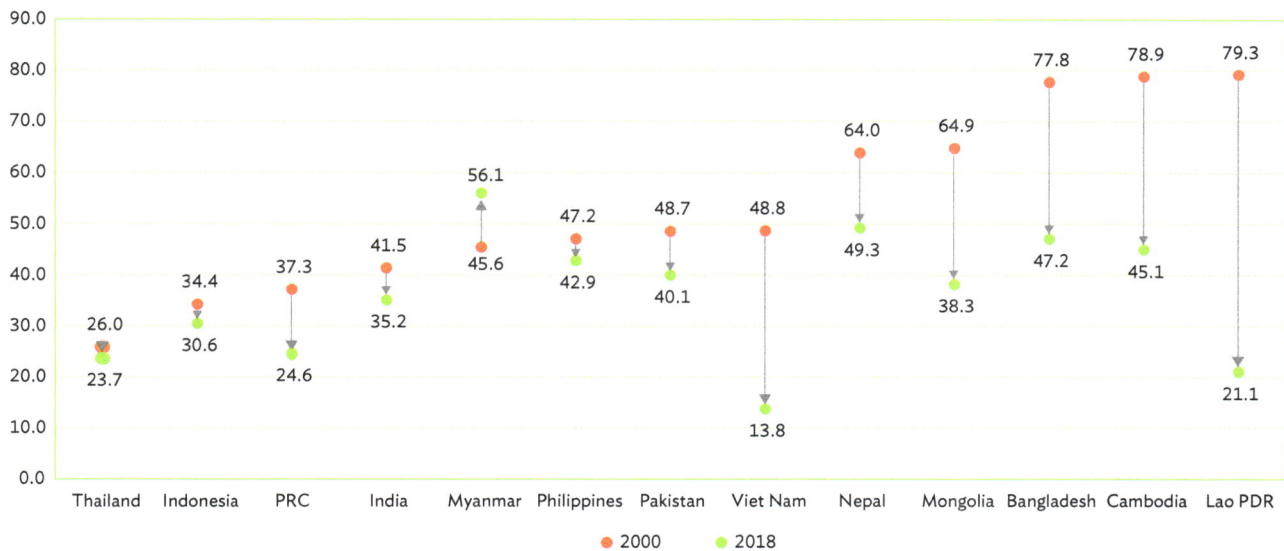

Lao PDR = Lao People's Democratic Republic, PRC = People's Republic of China.
Note: Only economies with available data for both 2000 and 2018 are included. For reference year 2000, data for Cambodia, the Lao PDR, Myanmar, and Thailand refer to 2005.
Source: Table 1.11.1, Key Indicators for Asia and the Pacific 2020.

Click here for figure data

Reporting economies with the highest proportion of the population living in slums, informal settlements, or inadequate housing in 2018 were Myanmar (56.1%), Nepal (49.3%), and Bangladesh (47.2%) as outlined in Table 1.11.1.

Air pollution in urban areas exceeds WHO-recommended maximum levels in more than 90% of the region's economies

The combustion of fossil fuels for industry, transportation, and power generation, as well as household activities such as heating, cooking, and lighting, are the primary sources of particulate matter. Particulate matter with a diameter equal to or less than 2.5 microns ($PM_{2.5}$) is the most commonly used pollutant in studies on the health effects of exposure to air pollution (WHO 2018).

The annual mean of the daily concentrations of PM2.5 in urban areas exceeded 10 micrograms per cubic meter ($\mu g/m^3$)—the maximum value recommended by the World Health Organization

(WHO 2018)—in 39 of the 43 economies of Asia and the Pacific reporting for 2016 (Table 1.11.1). The four economies that fell below this threshold, and their respective annual means, were Brunei Darussalam (5.8 $\mu g/m^3$), New Zealand (5.8 $\mu g/m^3$), Australia (7.3 $\mu g/m^3$), and Maldives (7.7 $\mu g/m^3$). The highest annual means of daily concentrations of $PM_{2.5}$ in urban areas were observed in Nepal (99.5 $\mu g/m^3$), India (68.0 $\mu g/m^3$), and Afghanistan (59.9 $\mu g/m^3$).

In nine of the region's 10 most populous economies, air pollution levels in urban areas exceeded the economy's overall level of air pollution (Figure 1.11.2). The only exception was Myanmar, where the annual mean of daily concentrations of $PM_{2.5}$ in urban areas (34.6 $\mu g/m^3$) was slightly below the economy's overall level (34.7 $\mu g/m^3$). Among the region's most populous economies, the highest annual means of daily concentrations of $PM_{2.5}$ in urban areas in 2016 were found in India (68.0 $\mu g/m^3$), Bangladesh (58.6 $\mu g/m^3$), Pakistan (56.2 $\mu g/m^3$), and the PRC (51.0 $\mu g/m^3$).

Figure 1.11.2: Annual Mean Levels of Fine Particulate Matter in Cities of Asia and the Pacific's Most Populous Economies, 2016
(μg/m³)

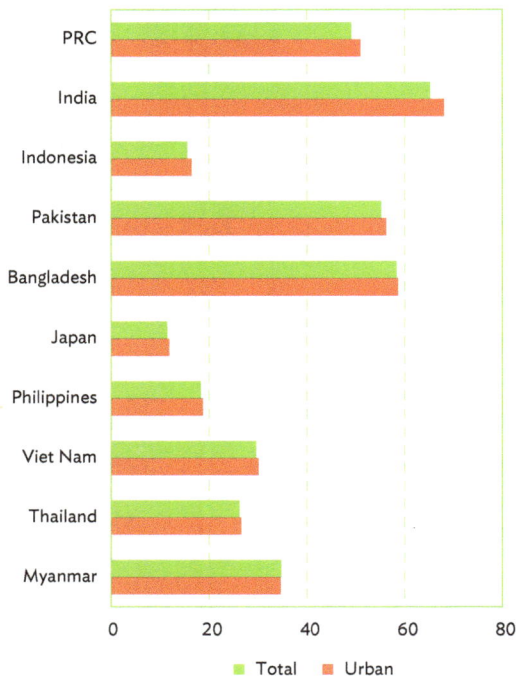

■ Total   ■ Urban

μg = microgram, m³ = cubic meter, PRC = People's Republic of China.
Note: Fine particulate matter is classified as matter with a diameter equal to or less than 2.5 microns in diameter (PM 2.5). The graph covers cities in the 10 most populous economies of Asia and the Pacific.
Sources: Table 1.11.1 and Table 2.1.1, Key Indicators for Asia and the Pacific 2020.

Click here for figure data

SDG 12. Ensure sustainable consumption and production patterns

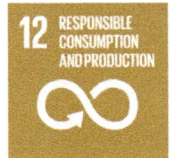

Economies of Asia and the Pacific can do more to reduce material footprint per capita

The quantity of material extraction that is required to meet the consumption of an economy signifies its material footprint. An economy's total material footprint is the sum of the material footprints for biomass, fossil fuels, metal ores, and nonmetal ores. The economies of Asia and the Pacific with the largest material footprints in 2017 were the PRC (29.4 billion metric tons), India (6.2 billion metric tons), and Japan (3.3 billion metric tons) as listed in Table 1.12.1.

Figure 1.12.1 shows a strong correlation between material footprint per capita and GDP per capita across the region's economies in 2017. The largest material footprints per capita were found in the high-income economies of Singapore (76.1

Figure 1.12.1: Material Footprint per Capita and Gross Domestic Product per Capita, 2017

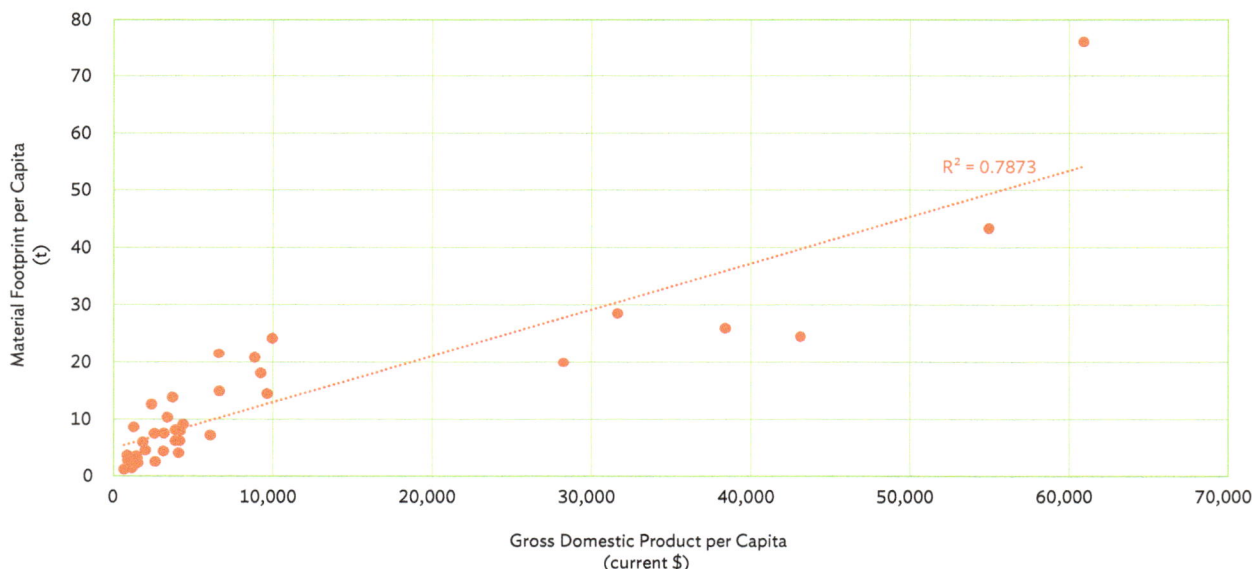

t = metric ton, $ = United States dollars.
Sources: Table 1.12.1 and Table 2.2.5, Key Indicators for Asia and the Pacific 2020.

Click here for figure data

metric tons per capita), Australia (43.3 metric tons), and the Republic of Korea (28.6 metric tons). The economies with the smallest material footprints on a per capita basis in 2017 were Afghanistan (1.2 metric tons per capita), Myanmar (1.4 metric tons), and Bangladesh (2.4 metric tons).

From 2000 to 2017, Japan was the only economy among 36 economies with data available for both years to reduce its material footprint per capita over the review period—from 27.0 metric tons to 25.9 metric tons (Table 1.12.1).

Less than one-fifth of the region's economies have reduced their domestic material consumption on a per capita basis

Domestic material consumption measures the total amount of material directly used in production processes within an economy. As shown in Figure 1.12.2, the region's economies with the highest levels of domestic material consumption per capita in 2017 were Australia (37.9 metric tons per capita), Mongolia (34.5 metric tons), and Singapore (32.6 metric tons). The lowest levels of domestic material consumption per capita were observed in Tuvalu (1.1 metric tons per capita), Palau (1.2 metric tons), and Afghanistan (1.9 metric tons).

In terms of aggregate domestic material consumption in 2017, the region's most populous economy, the PRC, accounted for 35.2 billion metric tons or just under two-thirds of the region's total. The next highest levels were observed in India (7.4 billion metric tons), Indonesia (2.0 billion metric tons), and Viet Nam (1.4 billion metric tons).

From 2000 to 2017, reductions in domestic material consumption per capita were realized in seven of 44 economies, led by Singapore (−33.8 metric tons per capita), Australia (−7.6 metric tons), Fiji and Papua New Guinea (−3.6 metric tons each), and Japan (−3.4 metric tons). During the review period, the largest increases in domestic

Figure 1.12.2: Domestic Material Consumption per Capita
(t)

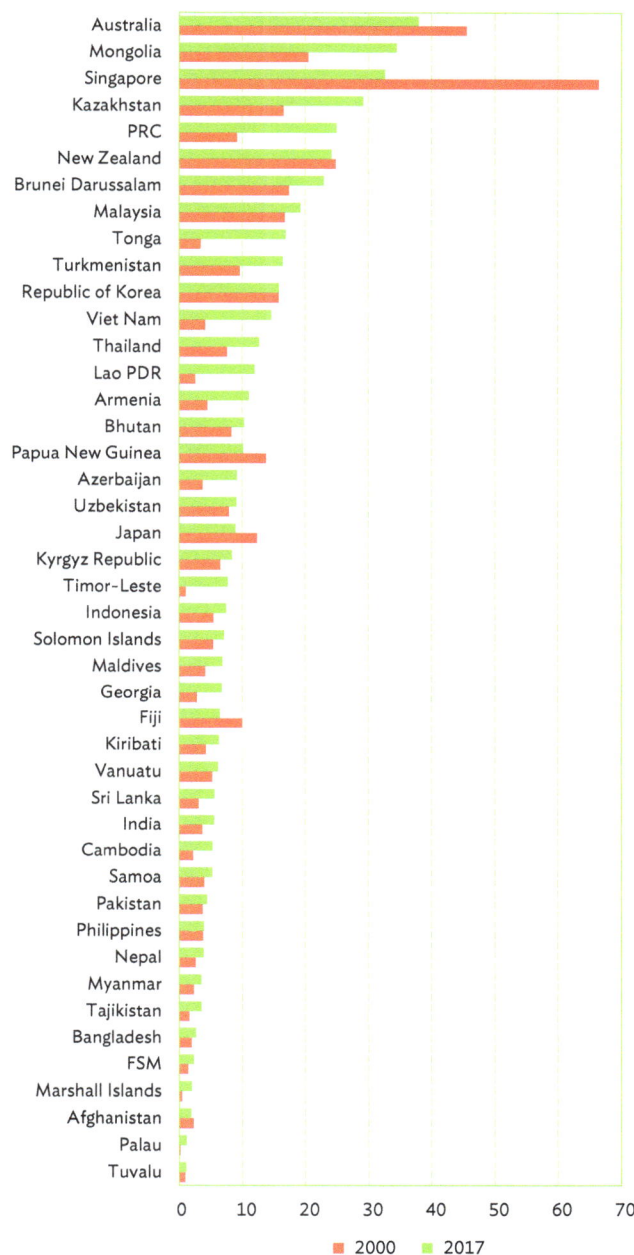

t = metric ton, FSM = Federated States of Micronesia, Lao PDR = Lao People's Democratic Republic, PRC = People's Republic of China.
Source: Table 1.12.1, Key Indicators for Asia and the Pacific 2020.

Click here for figure data

material consumption per capita occurred in the PRC (15.8 metric tons per capita), Mongolia (14.1 metric tons), and Tonga (13.5 metric tons).

SDG 13. Take urgent action to combat climate change and its impacts

13 CLIMATE ACTION

Prior to the COVID-19 pandemic, only five economies of Asia and the Pacific had national disaster risk reduction strategies fully aligned with international standards identified in the Sendai Framework

The Sendai Framework for Disaster Risk Reduction, 2015–2030 assigns primary responsibility for reducing disaster risk to the state (central government), which in turn should share responsibility with provincial and/or local governments, the private sector, and other stakeholders (UNDRR 2020). The COVID-19 pandemic has demonstrated how systemic risk can precipitate a crisis of global magnitude. In such times of crisis, not everyone is affected equally as the elderly, people living with disabilities, workers in the informal economy, and the impoverished and marginalized are usually the most vulnerable. The Sendai Framework prioritizes prevention to help governments substantially reduce risk and minimize the loss of lives, livelihoods, and health caused by disasters such as the COVID-19 pandemic (UNDRR 2019).

Figure 1.13.1 shows the result of self-assessments conducted by 21 economies of Asia and the Pacific on the alignment of their national disaster risk reduction strategies with the Sendai Framework. In 2019 (or the most recent year for which data were available) five economies reported comprehensive alignment with the framework by achieving a score of 1.0. These economies were Georgia, Japan, Mongolia, the Republic of Korea, and Tajikistan. Another 13 economies had a score of 0.5 or higher, reflecting moderate alignment with the framework or better.

Figure 1.13.1: Score Measuring Alignment of National Disaster Risk Strategy with Sendai Framework, 2019

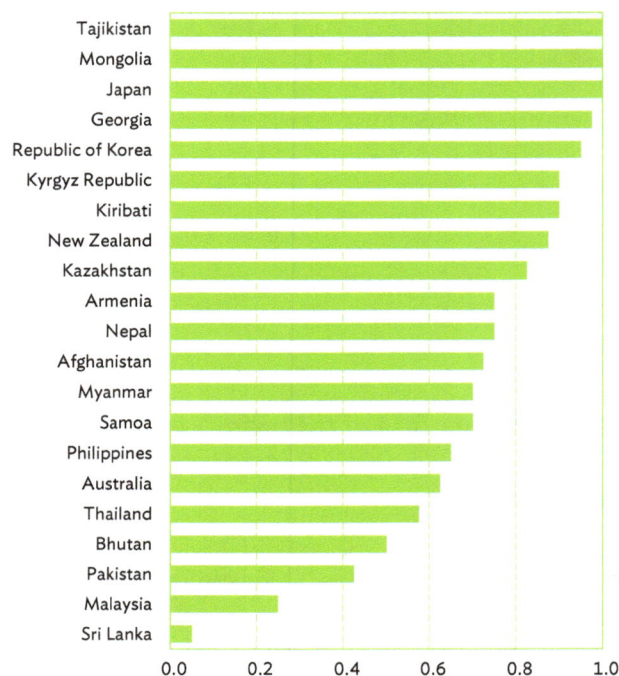

Note: The economies shown have undertaken adoption and implementation of national disaster risk reduction strategies in line with the Sendai Framework. Scores indicate the compliance of alignment with the framework, based on self-assessments of the economy using 10 criteria for monitoring the progress of national disaster risk reduction strategies. The score ranges are as follows 1 = comprehensive alignment, 0.75 = substantial alignment, 0.5 = moderate alignment, 0.25 = limited alignment, 0 = no alignment. Azerbaijan, Maldives, and Indonesia have a score of "0" and are not shown in the figure. For Japan, Georgia, the Republic of Korea, New Zealand, Samoa, Australia, Thailand, Bhutan, and Pakistan, data refer to 2018. For Myanmar, data refer to 2017. For Sri Lanka, data refer to 2016.
Source: Table 1.13.1. Key Indicators for Asia and the Pacific 2020.

Click here for figure data

SDG 14. Conserve and sustainably use the oceans, seas, and marine resources for sustainable development

14 LIFE BELOW WATER

While a few Pacific economies have taken bold actions to protect vital marine resources, most regional economies protect less than 10% of their total marine areas, with more than half protecting less than 1%

Seas and oceans cover nearly 70% of the planet's surface and play a critical role in the provision of vital ecosystems and in our planet's overall health. Their deterioration through overexploitation, pollution, and the impacts of climate change threatens human existence (UN 2020c).

Figure 1.14.1 shows that the proportion of protected marine area to total marine area exceeded 99.0% in Palau (99.4%) and the Cook Islands (99.2%) in 2018. However, after those two marine protection leaders, the drop-off was significant: the next highest shares of protected area to total marine resources were observed in Australia (40.4%), New Zealand (29.8%), and Kiribati (11.8%).

The SDG target of extending protection to 10% of total marine area by 2020 had been met by only five of the 37 reporting economies as of 2018. Of even greater concern, 21 economies reported that protection had been extended to less than 1% of their respective total marine area by 2018.

SDG 15. Protect, restore, and promote sustainable use of terrestrial ecosystems; sustainably manage forests; combat desertification; halt and reverse land degradation; and halt biodiversity loss

While deforestation remains a critical issue, many of the region's economies are making efforts to retain or expand forested areas

Forests cover nearly one-third of the earth's surface and are home to irreplaceable biodiversity. Their absorption and storage of massive amounts of CO_2 is crucial in the fight against climate change (UN-REDD 2020).

Figure 1.14.1: Proportion of Protected Marine Area to Total Marine Area, 2018

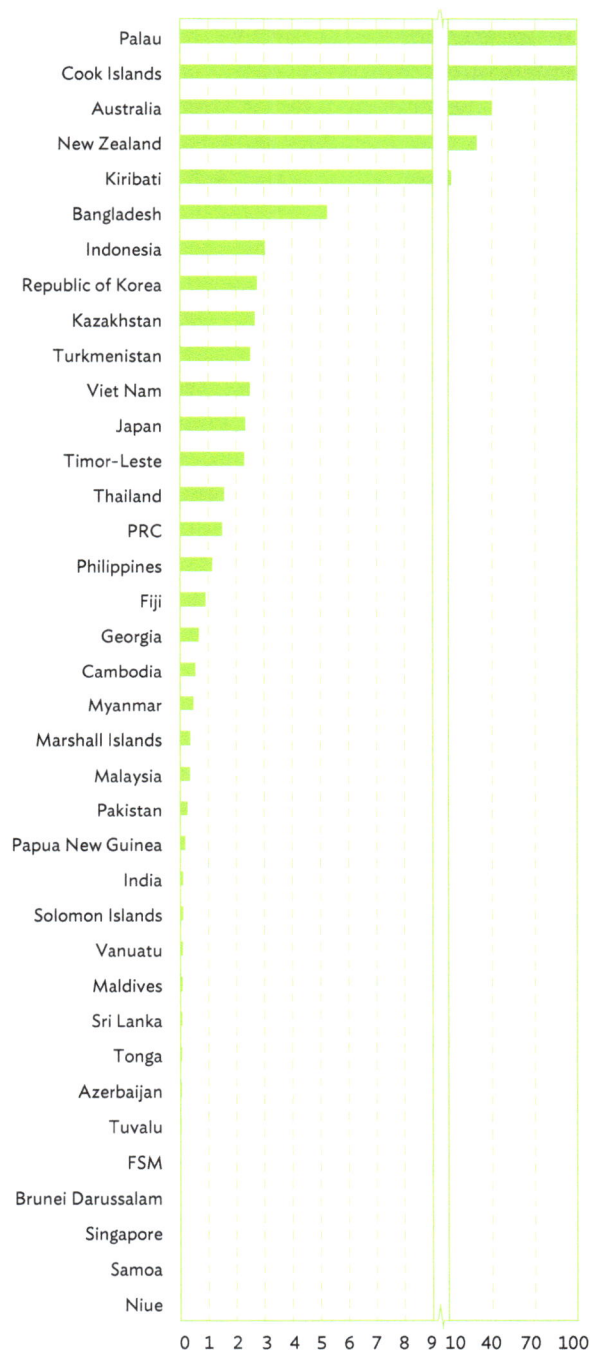

(%)

FSM = Federated States of Micronesia, PRC = People's Republic of China.
Source: Table 1.14.1, Key Indicators for Asia and the Pacific 2020.

Click here for figure data

Forest area covered more than 50% of total land in 18 of the 48 economies of Asia and the Pacific with data available for 2019 (Figure 1.15.1), but the percentage of forested land as a share of an economy's total land varied widely across the region—from 92.0% in the Federated States of Micronesia to 1.3% in Kazakhstan (not including the island economy of Nauru, which has no forested areas).

By subregion, the average share of forested land as a percentage of total land was highest in the Pacific (77.9%) and lowest in Central and West Asia (4.0%). Other subregions posted average proportions of forested land to total land as follows: Southeast Asia (48.0%), South Asia (25.3%), and East Asia (21.7%). For the developed ADB member economies, the average share of forested land to total land was 20.3%.

From 2000 to 2019, 21 of the 48 reporting economies managed to increase their amount of forested land as a percentage of total land, while 9 economies reported no change, and 18 posted a decline. The biggest increases in the share of forested land occurred in Viet Nam (9.0 percentage points), Fiji (6.9 percentage points), and the PRC (4.4 percentage points). The biggest decreases occurred in Cambodia (–14.5 percentage points), Myanmar (–9.2 percentage points), and Indonesia (–4.7 percentage points).

From 2000 to 2019, the risk of extinction across groups of species increased in all 48 reporting economies

The Red List Index is a composite measure representing aggregate survival probability (the inverse of extinction risk) for all birds, mammals, amphibians, corals, and cycads occurring within an economy, weighted by the fraction of each species' distribution occurring within that economy. Index values can range from 0.0 (indicating all species are categorized as "extinct") to 1.0 (indicating all species are categorized as "least concern").

Figure 1.15.1: Proportion of Forested Area to Total Land Area, 2019
(%)

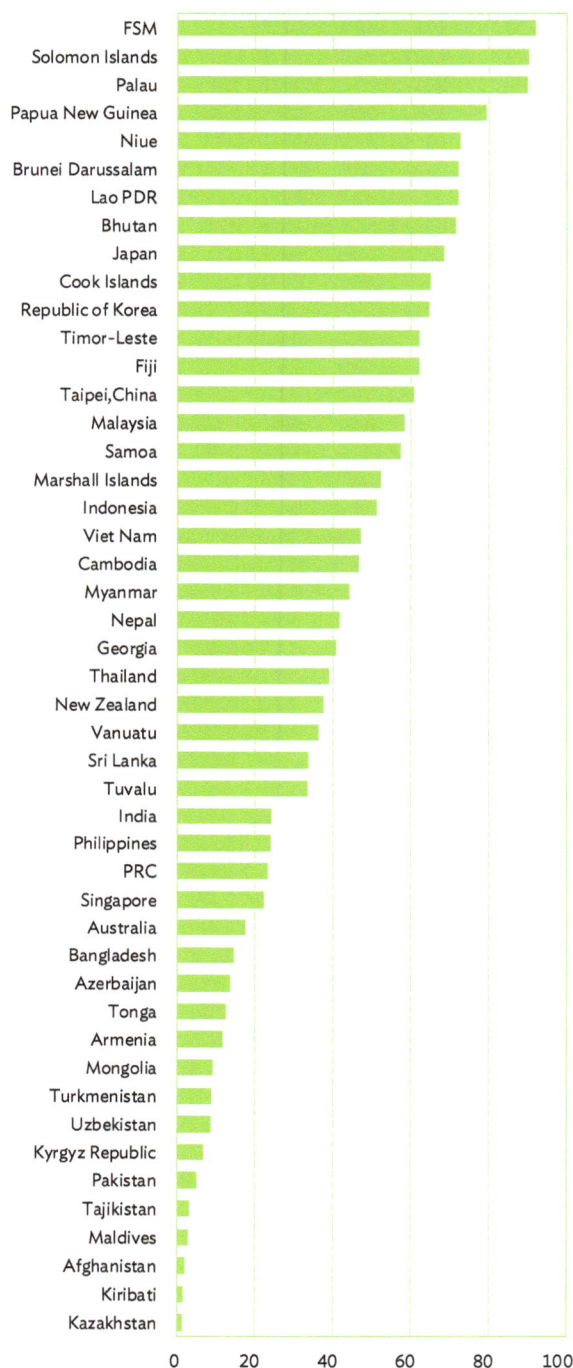

FSM = Federated States of Micronesia, Lao PDR = Lao People's Democratic Republic, PRC = People's Republic of China.
Note: Nauru has 0 forest area and is not included in the figure.
         For Taipei,China data refer to 2018.
Source: Table 1.15.1, Key Indicators for Asia and the Pacific 2020.

Click here for figure data

Figure 1.15.2: Red List Index Scores for Select Economies of Asia and the Pacific

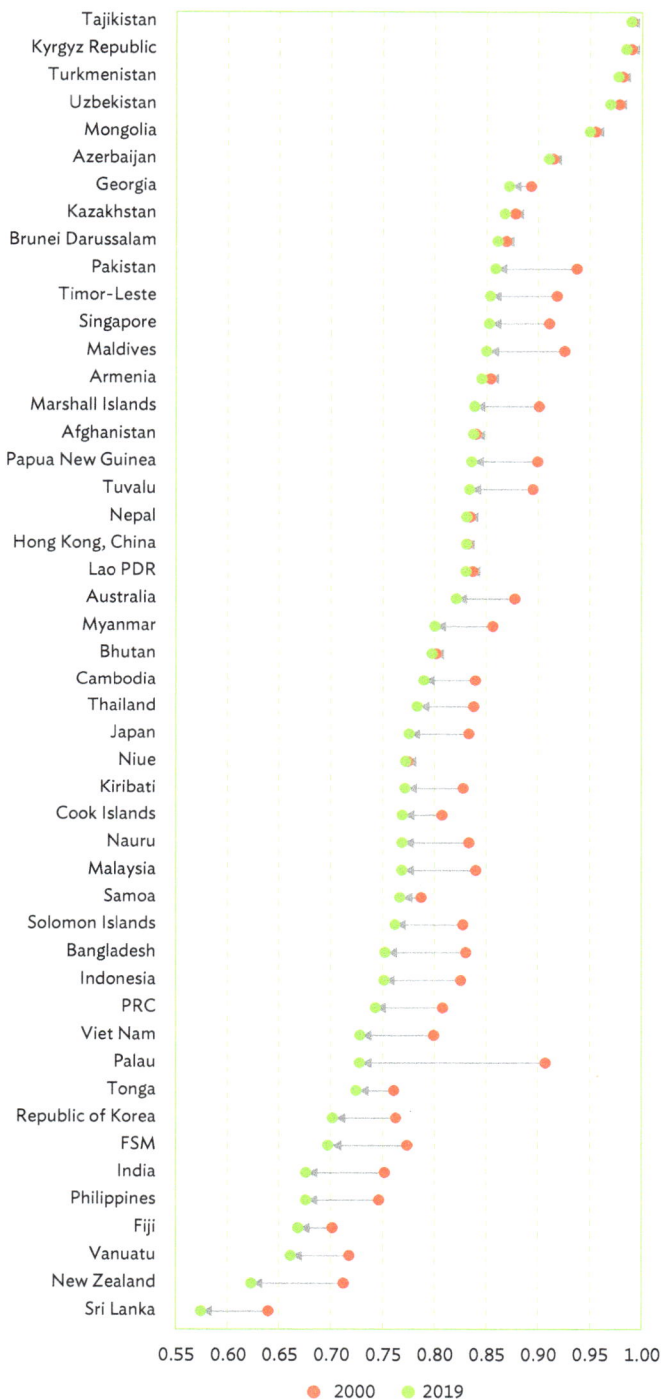

FSM = Federated States of Micronesia, Lao PDR = Lao People's Democratic Republic, PRC = People's Republic of China.
Note: Index values range from 0 (indicating all species are categorized as "extinct") to 1.0 (indicating all species are categorized as "least concern").
Source: Table 1.15.1, Key Indicators for Asia and the Pacific 2020.

Click here for figure data

In 2019, only 24 of 48 economies had a score of 0.8 or higher on the Red List Index, down from 37 economies in 2000 (Figure 1.15.2). The highest Red List Index scores in 2019 were observed in Tajikistan (0.99), the Kyrgyz Republic (0.98), Turkmenistan (0.98), and Uzbekistan (0.97). Six economies scored lower than 0.7 in 2019: India (0.68), the Philippines (0.68), Fiji (0.67), Vanuatu (0.66), New Zealand (0.62), and Sri Lanka (0.57).

Moreover, from 2000 to 2019, all 48 reporting economies recorded a decline in their Red List Index score, indicating greater extinction risk. The largest declines during the review period were noted in Palau (down from 0.91 in 2000 to 0.73 in 2019), New Zealand (0.71 to 0.62), and Pakistan (0.94 to 0.86).

SDG 16. Promote peaceful and inclusive societies for sustainable development; provide access to justice for all; and build effective, accountable, and inclusive institutions at all levels

The incidence of intentional homicide has declined in about 80% of Asia and Pacific economies

Effective, transparent, and accountable institutions are needed at all levels to promote peaceful and inclusive societies, including the reduction of intentional homicides. Comparing 2010–2018 with 2000–2009, the number of victims of intentional homicide per 100,000 people fell in 31 of the 39 economies with available data (Figure 1.16.1). The largest declines in the intentional homicide rate during the review period occurred in Kazakhstan (–10.5), Mongolia (–7.7), and the Kyrgyz Republic (–6.5). The largest increases were observed in Tuvalu (18.6), Kiribati (4.0), Afghanistan (2.7), and Papua New Guinea (1.8).

Figure 1.16.1: Number of Victims of Intentional Homicide
(per 100,000 Population)

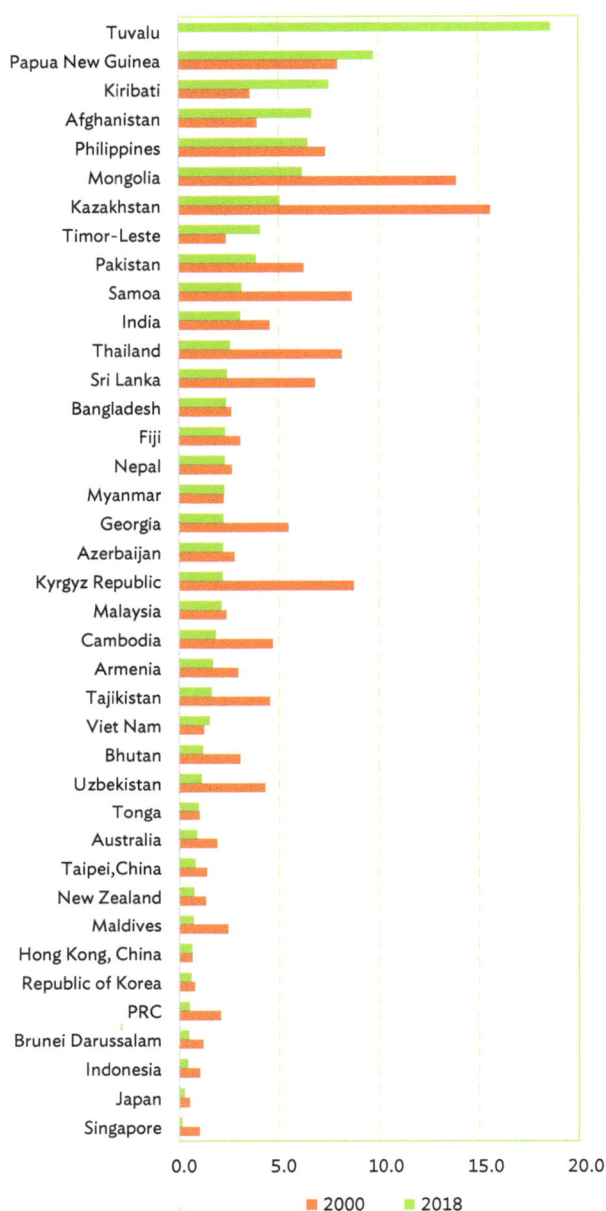

PRC = People's Republic of China.
Note: This chart includes economies with available data for both 2000
           and 2018. For 2000, data included are for 2000 to 2009. For 2018,
           data included are for 2010 to 2018. For 2000, Tuvalu has zero
           recorded data for the number of victims of intentional homicide.
Source: Table 1.16.1, Key Indicators for Asia and the Pacific 2020.

Click here for figure data

In 2018 (or the most recent year for which data were available), the lowest rates of intentional homicide per 100,000 people were in Singapore (0.2), Japan (0.3), and Indonesia (0.4). The highest rates were in Tuvalu (18.6), Papua New Guinea (9.8), Kiribati (7.5), and Afghanistan (6.7).

Firms surveyed in only 7 of 32 developing member economies reported a bribery solicitation rate of 10.0% or less in dealings with public officials within the most recent year for which data are available

While corruption can be challenging to quantify, one measure to determine the bribery prevalence rate in an economy is a World Bank survey that asks firms if they have been solicited by public officials for gifts or informal payments.

In the most recent year for which data were available (2009–2019), the lowest levels of firms reporting bribery solicitations occurred in Bhutan (0.9%), Georgia (1.3%), and the Federated States of Micronesia (4.5%). The percentage of firms reporting that they had been solicited by public officials for gifts or informal payments was 10.0% or less in only seven of 32 reporting economies across Asia and the Pacific (Figure 1.16.2).

Figure 1.16.2: Proportion of Firms Experiencing at least One Bribe Payment Request, Latest Year
(%)

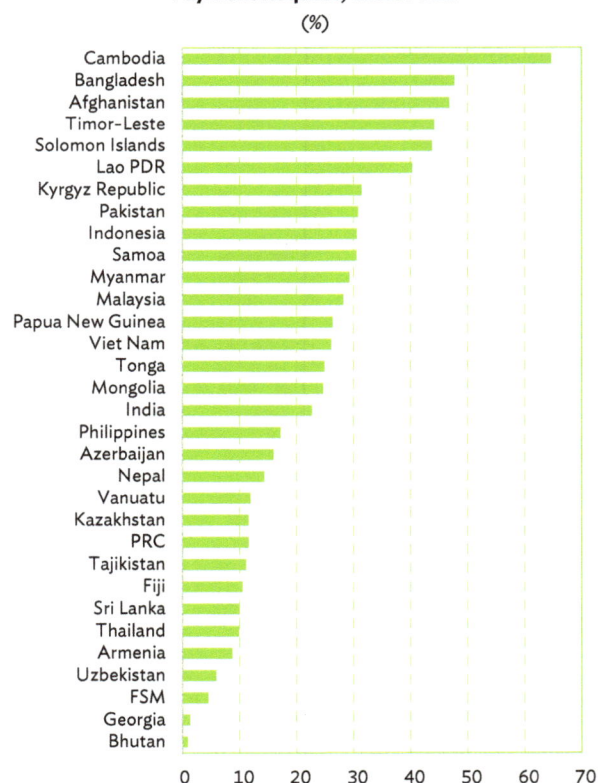

FSM = Federated States of Micronesia, Lao PDR = Lao People's Democratic Republic, PRC = People's Republic of China.
Note: Latest Year refers to 2009-2019.
Source: Table 1.16.1, Key Indicators for Asia and the Pacific 2020.

Click here for figure data

SDG 17. Strengthen the means of implementation and revitalize the Global Partnership for Sustainable Development

17 PARTNERSHIPS FOR THE GOALS

Over 85% of developing economies reported receiving greater financial and technical assistance.

Governments, the private sector, and civil society can collaborate to efficiently mobilize and redirect public and private resources toward sustainable development projects that will help the most vulnerable within each society.

Comparing 2010–2018 to 2000–2009, the average annual value (in constant 2018 United States dollars) of financial and technical assistance committed to developing economies increased in 35 of the 41 economies of Asia and the Pacific with available data (Figure 1.17.1). Indonesia ($1,443 million), Afghanistan ($1,302 million), and Pakistan ($938 million) received the largest average amounts of annual financial and technical assistance during 2010–2018.

As a percentage of an economy's 2000–2009 annual average financial and technical assistance, the largest increases during 2010–2018 occurred in Myanmar (1,231.7%), Kazakhstan (494.8%), and Uzbekistan (469.9%). The largest decreases occurred in the Marshall Islands (–63.5%), the Federated States of Micronesia (–61.4%), and Solomon Islands (–29.3%).

In absolute terms (in constant 2018 United States dollars), Indonesia ($708.6 million), Afghanistan ($572.9 million), and Pakistan ($555.4 million) received the largest increases in financial and technical assistance from 2000–2009 to 2010–2018. The largest absolute declines were in

Figure 1.17.1: Value of Financial and Technical Assistance Committed to Developing Economies
(constant 2018 $ million)

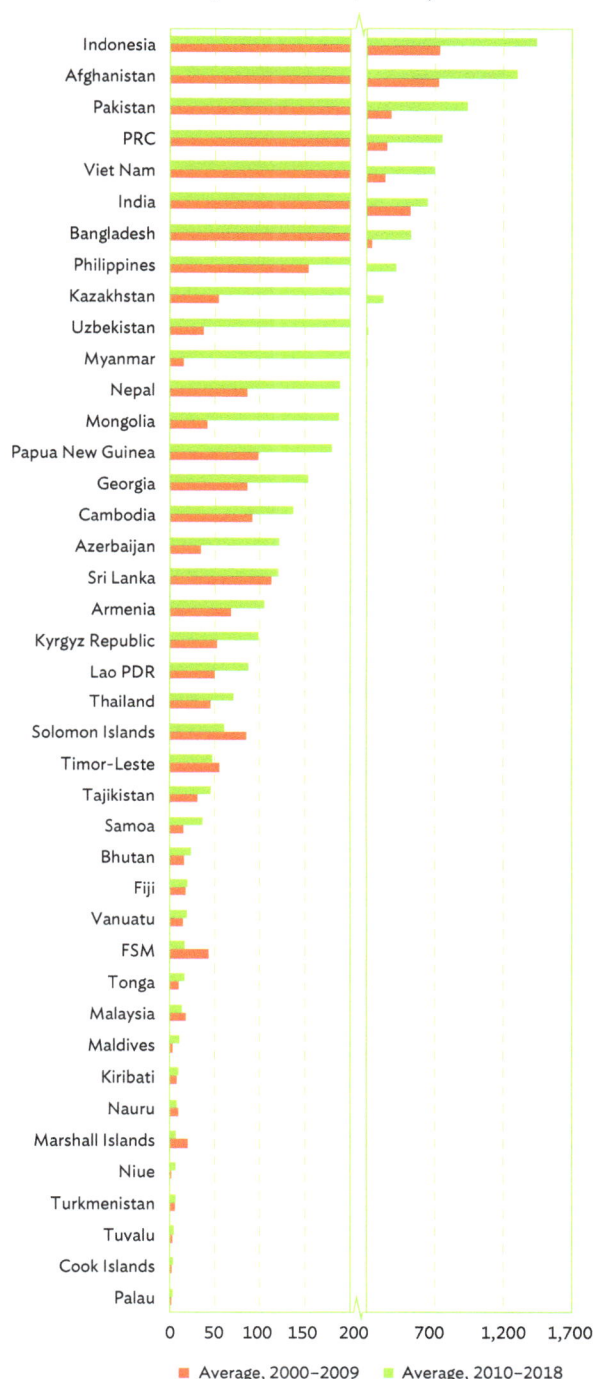

■ Average, 2000–2009 ■ Average, 2010–2018

$ = United States dollars, FSM = Federated States of Micronesia,
Lao PDR = Lao People's Democratic Republic, PRC = People's Republic of China.
Note: Totals include assistance through North-South, South-South, and
         triangular cooperation.
Source: Table 1.17.1, Key Indicators for Asia and the Pacific 2020.

Click here for figure data

the Federated States of Micronesia ($26.6 million), the Solomon Islands ($25.0 million), and the Marshall Islands ($12.7 million).

Only six developing economies of Asia and the Pacific spent more than $1 million to improve their statistical capacity

To improve their development effectiveness, governments throughout Asia and the Pacific must finance better-quality statistical data and increase transparency in monitoring and accountability. At the same time, many of these governments need support from international partners to strengthen capacity building and data collection activities.

In 2017, those economies dedicating more than $1 million (in current United States dollars) to building public sector statistical capacity were Pakistan ($3.68 million), the Kyrgyz Republic ($3.04 million), India ($2.98 million), Myanmar ($2.78 million), Nepal ($2.27 million), and Timor-Leste ($1.03 million) as shown in Figure 1.17.2.[3]

Figure 1.17.2: Value of All Resources Made Available to Strengthen Statistical Capacity in Developing Economies, 2017
(current $)

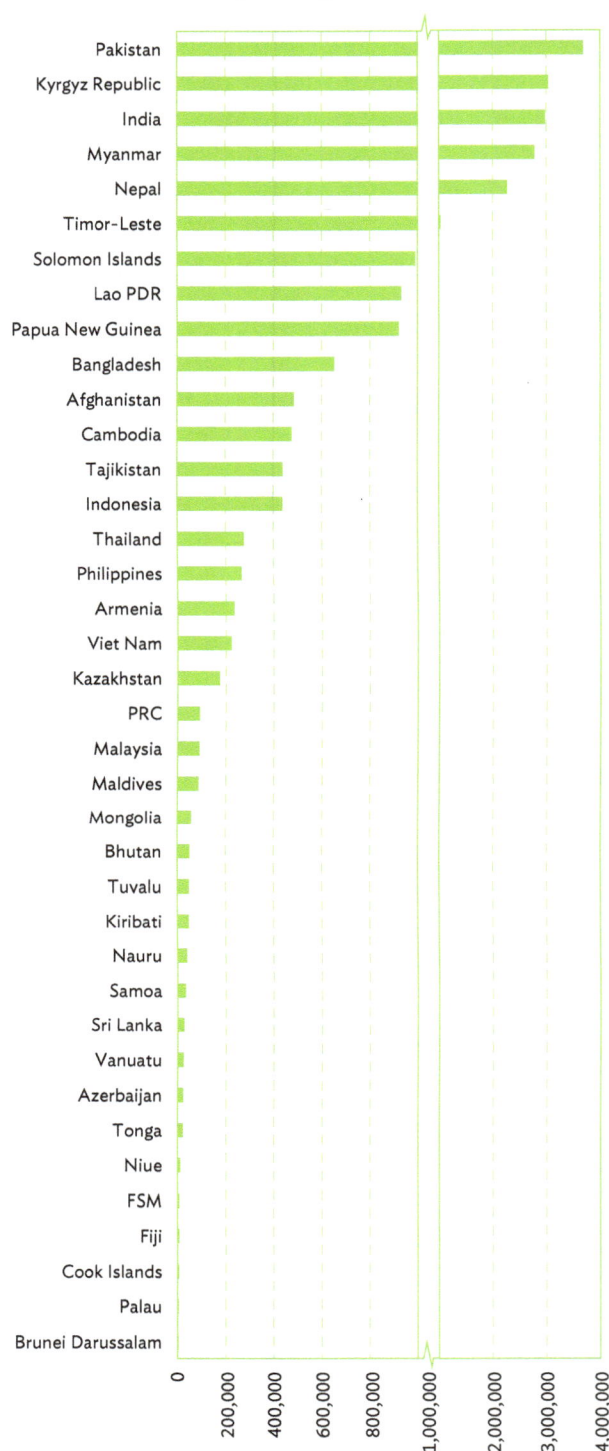

$ = United States Dollars, FSM = Federated States of Micronesia, Lao PDR = Lao People's Democratic Republic, PRC = People's Republic of China.
Source: Table 1.17.2, Key Indicators for Asia and the Pacific 2020.

Click here for figure data

3   The indicator dollar value of all resources made available to strengthen statistical capacity in developing countries is based on the Partner Report on Support to Statistics (PRESS) that is designed and administered by PARIS21 to provide a snapshot of the United States dollar value of ongoing statistical support in developing countries.

Data Gaps and Other Data-Related Issues

New and huge data demands. The approved global framework for monitoring the SDGs consists of 231 indicators with greater disaggregation and across a wider spectrum of topics than the Millennium Development Goals. With international development support, governments are strengthening their national statistical systems to address data demands across all SDG indicators.

Limited data availability for Sustainable Development Goal indicators. While there have been many improvements to data availability and timeliness since the launch of the SDGs in 2015, there is more to be done. While only 25% of SDG indicators had enough data for progress assessment in 2017, sufficient data availability had increased to 42% of indicators by 2019. At the same time, the number of indicators without any data availability stood at over 30%. The importance of data collection is reflected in the fact that the most progress in achieving SDGs has been made for those indicators with relatively high data availability (UNESCAP 2020).

Differing priorities among national statistics offices with regard to economic data production result in disparities in data availability. Most national statistics offices across Asia and the Pacific conduct population and housing censuses every decade. Such sources provide baseline socioeconomic data that overlap SDG indicators with economic and social dimensions. Depending on the frequency of data collection, administrative reporting systems and household surveys—such as labor force surveys, household income and expenditure surveys, demographic and health surveys, establishment surveys, and agriculture surveys—can be other good sources of data for SDG indicators.

Gaps in data granularity. Many SDG indicators require disaggregation by location, sex, gender, age, income, ethnicity, migration status, disability status, and other relevant dimensions. Granular data can illustrate disparities within and across economies.

However, the extent to which specific groups are disproportionately at risk is difficult to decipher given the lack of data disaggregation and interlinkages across indicators. Sex disaggregations, even for basic indicators such as extreme poverty rates based on the $1.90 a day (at 2011 purchasing power parity) level, are not currently available. Similarly, poverty numbers are currently unavailable for vulnerable groups, such as people with disabilities or indigenous peoples, since the sample surveys these poverty calculations are based on are designed to obtain an overview of welfare conditions. Investments are needed (e.g., in special surveys) to obtain poverty data for vulnerable groups that make up only a small proportion of the total population.

Innovative data sources, such as big data and crowdsourced data, can potentially address these data gaps and strengthen the monitoring of SDG indicators. However, some types of big data may not represent the underlying groups of interest. Therefore, it is necessary to ensure that reliable statistical inferences can be made when complementing surveys and other conventional data sources with big data (Cox, Kartsonaki, and Keogh 2018).

Lack of data comparability. Differences in definitions mean that SDG indicators, such as the proportion of the population with access to safely managed drinking water services, rely on data related to housing conditions, which may not be fully comparable across economies. Likewise, comparisons of SDG indicators across economies are difficult for urban–rural disaggregation due to various definitions of "urban" and "rural" across time and economies.

Sparse data and irregular frequency. Some indicators that provide a useful description of income inequality—such as the growth in household expenditure among those in an economy's bottom 40th percentile of income distribution in relation to national averages are only currently available for a few economies. In another example, data on progress made toward addressing climate change are sparse.

Frequency is also of concern as some indicators, such as the coverage of protected areas in relation to marine areas, are not regularly collected. Indicators on material footprint and domestic material consumption, which are widely accepted as strategic sustainability indicators of production and consumption, are not produced annually.

Further, some protected areas are not assigned management categories. While access to remote sensing data has improved in recent years, forest regrowth cannot easily be detected with remote-sensing techniques.

Data limitations. The indicators included in the framework for monitoring the SDGs, while carefully chosen, may have some limitations. For example, the labor share in GDP does not include the income of the self-employed, even though a sizeable proportion of the employed population in developing Asia comprises people who are self-employed. Current measures of poverty used by economies are largely based on income or consumption data, while the SDG indicators include a multidimensional poverty measure that has yet to be tested on a wider scale.

The many challenges facing cities—pollution, traffic congestion, and inadequate housing for the poor—can be exacerbated by migration and population growth, changes in family structures, inequality of opportunity for excluded groups, and rising insecurity. Currently available data do not allow for a simple assessment of these issues.

The Red List Index is a composite index aggregated across multiple taxonomic groups. While it can be updated annually, the index does not adequately capture the deteriorating status of common species that are abundant and widespread yet declining gradually. Data on other indicators for monitoring many targets under SDG 15 are also sparsely available. The absence of a framework for monitoring terrestrial ecosystems,

low data availability, and the lack of good-quality data must be carefully addressed.

Measurement errors. The quality of data for all SDG indicators needs to be considered when identifying trends and drawing inferences. For example, self-reporting of land area and production by farmers is known to have significant biases (Dillon and Rao 2018). The calculation of under-5 mortality rates requires complete counts of live births and child deaths by a precise age, which are not always available in economies of Asia and the Pacific that lack civil registration systems. Maternal deaths are likewise not always accounted for, given incomplete or inaccurate records on causes of death. The measurement of quality education across economies is hampered by the lack of standard definitions for minimum competency. Anthropometric measures of malnutrition (including stunted heights) are subject to measurement errors and issues around reference standards (i.e., local versus international standards). Access to safely managed drinking water and sanitation services, and information on hygiene all depend on more and better data, particularly administrative data sources (WHO and UNICEF 2017).

A complete stocktaking of all statistical capacity development programs cannot be guaranteed in the data compiled by PARIS21 for measuring the dollar-value support for statistics development. Double counting of projects can occur or the data may also be inflated by the inaccurate inclusion of multisector projects. Further, donor commitments do not always lead to actual disbursements to recipient economies.

Ultimately, the reliability of data on SDG indicators depends on the quality of the underlying data sources. Governments across Asia and the Pacific need to increase investment, look for innovative data sources, and form strategic partnerships with a range of stakeholders to enhance data quality, comparability, measurement, and timeliness. Reliable and comprehensive data supports evidence-based policymaking that leads to better development outcomes.

References

Asian Development Bank (ADB). 2020. Asian Development Outlook Supplement 2020. https://www.adb.org/publications/ado-supplement-june-2020.

Asian Development Bank (ADB) and United Nations (UN) Women. 2018. *Gender Equality and the Sustainable Development Goals in Asia and the Pacific: Baseline and Pathways for Transformative Change by 2030*. Bangkok.

D.R. Cox, C. Kartsonaki, and R. H.Keogh. 2018. Big Data: Some Statistical Issues. Statistics & Probability Letters. 136 (5). pp. 111–15.

A. Dillon and L.N. Rao. 2018. Land Measurement Bias: Comparisons from Global Positioning System, Self-Reports, and Satellite Data. *Asian Development Bank, Economics Working Paper Series. No. 540.*

Food and Agriculture Organization of the United Nations (FAO). 2019. *The State of Food Security and Nutrition in the World*. Rome.

International Labour Organization (ILO). 2020. World Employment Social Outlook: Trends 2020. https://www.ilo.org/global/research/global-reports/weso/2020/lang--en/index.htm.

B. Panth and J. J. Xu. 2020. Blending Education and Technology to Help Schools through the Pandemic. *Asian Development Blog*. 18 June. https://blogs.adb.org/blog/blending-education-and-technology-to-help-schools-through-the-pandemic.

United Nations (UN). 2020a. The Sustainable Development Agenda: A Decade of Action. https://www.un.org/sustainabledevelopment/development-agenda/.

UN. 2020b. Sustainable Development Goals—Water and Sanitation. https://www.un.org/sustainabledevelopment/water-and-sanitation/.

UN. 2020c. Sustainable Development Goals—Oceans. https://www.un.org/sustainabledevelopment/oceans/.

UN Collaborative Programme on Reducing Emissions from Deforestation and forest Degradation (UN-REDD). 2020. Forest Facts. https://www.un-redd.org/forest-facts.

UN Economic and Social Commission for Asia and the Pacific (UNESCAP). 2020. Asia and the Pacific SDG Progress Report: Highlights. https://www.unescap.org/sites/default/files/Asia-Pacific_SDG2020_Highlights.pdf.

UN Habitat. 2020. Policy Brief: COVID-19 in an Urban World. https://www.un.org/sites/un2.un.org/files/sg_policy_brief_covid_urban_world_july_2020.pdf.

UN News. 2020. No End in Sight to COVID Crisis. 1 August. https://news.un.org/en/story/2020/08/1069392.

UN Office for Disaster Risk Reduction (UNDRR). 2019. Global Assessment Report on Disaster Risk Reduction 2019. https://www.undrr.org/publication/global-assessment-report-disaster-risk-reduction-2019.

UN Office for Disaster Risk Reduction (UNDRR). 2020. Sendai Framework for Disaster Risk Reduction. https://www.unisdr.org/we/coordinate/sendai-framework.

UN Statistical Commission (UNSC). 2017. Cape Town Global Action Plan for Sustainable Development Data. https://unstats.un.org/sdgs/hlg/Cape_Town_Global_Action_Plan_for_Sustainable_Development_Data.pdf.

UN Statistical Commission (UNSC). 2020. Tier Classification for Global SDG Indicators. https://unstats.un.org/sdgs/iaeg-sdgs/tier-classification.

World Health Organization (WHO). 2018. Ambient (Outdoor) Air Quality and Health. https://www.who.int/news-room/fact-sheets/detail/ambient-(outdoor)-air-quality-and-health.

WHO. 2020. Interim Guidance: Water, Sanitation, Hygiene, and Waste Management for SARS-COV-2. https://www.who.int/publications/i/item/water-sanitation-hygiene-and-waste-management-for-covid-19.

WHO and United Nations Children's Fund (UNICEF). 2017. Progress on Drinking Water, Sanitation and Hygiene: 2017 Update and SDG Baselines. (location and/or publisher).

World Bank. 2017. Educating Girls, Ending Child Marriage. 24 August. https://www.worldbank.org/en/news/immersive-story/2017/08/22/educating-girls-ending-child-marriage.

World Bank. 2020. Global Economic Prospects June 2020. https://www.worldbank.org/en/publication/global-economic-prospects#overview.

Goal 1. End poverty in all its forms everywhere

Table 1.1.1: Selected Indicators for Sustainable Development Goal 1—No Poverty

ADB Regional Member	Target 1.1: By 2030, eradicate extreme poverty for all people everywhere, measured as people living below the international poverty line of $1.90 a day (2011 PPP)							
	1.1.1.a: Proportion of Population Living below the $1.90 a Day (2011 PPP) Poverty Line[a,b] (%)			1.1.1.b: Proportion of Employed Population Living below the International Poverty Line, by Age Group and Sex[b,c] (%)				
				2019				
					Age Group			
					15+		15–24	25+
	2000		2018		Total	Female	Male		
Developing ADB Member Economies									
Central and West Asia									
Afghanistan	...		...		40.1	53.1	36.7	48.4	36.7
Armenia	19.3	(2001)	2.1		0.3	0.3	0.3	0.4	0.3
Azerbaijan[d]	2.7	(2001)	...		0.0	0.0	0.0	0.0	0.0
Georgia	19.4		4.5		3.6	3.0	4.1	4.4	3.6
Kazakhstan	10.3	(2001)	0.0	(2017)	0.0	0.0	0.0	0.0	0.0
Kyrgyz Republic	42.1		0.9		0.3	0.2	0.4	0.3	0.3
Pakistan	28.6	(2001)	3.9	(2015)	2.3	2.7	2.2	2.5	2.2
Tajikistan	30.8	(2003)	4.8	(2015)	3.8	4.4	3.4	4.3	3.7
Turkmenistan	...		...		7.6	5.4	9.2	9.1	7.4
Uzbekistan[d]	62.0		...		19.7	16.0	22.2	21.7	19.3
East Asia									
China, People's Republic of	31.7	(2002)	0.5	(2016)	0.5	0.6	0.4	0.8	0.5
Hong Kong, China[f]	...		...		0.0	0.0	0.0	0.0	0.0
Korea, Republic of[f]	0.2	(2006)	0.2	(2012)	0.0	0.0	0.0	0.0	0.0
Mongolia	9.7	(2002)	0.5		0.1	0.1	0.1	0.2	0.1
Taipei,China	0.0	(2002)	0.0		0.0	0.1	0.0	0.1	0.0
South Asia									
Bangladesh	34.8		14.8	(2016)	9.2	10.3	8.7	10.3	8.9
Bhutan	17.6	(2003)	1.5	(2017)	1.3	1.6	1.1	2.4	1.2
India	38.2	(2004)	21.2	(2011)	10.7	12.5	10.2	14.6	10.2
Maldives	10.0	(2002)	0.0	(2016)	1.7	2.2	1.5	2.0	1.6
Nepal	49.9	(2003)	15.0	(2010)	6.1	6.1	6.1	6.1	6.1
Sri Lanka	8.3	(2002)	0.8	(2016)	0.3	0.2	0.3	0.3	0.3
Southeast Asia									
Brunei Darussalam	...		...		0.0	0.0	0.0	0.0	0.0
Cambodia	...		...		8.3	7.7	8.8	9.7	7.8
Indonesia	39.3		4.6		4.3	4.5	4.2	4.5	4.3
Lao People's Democratic Republic	33.8	(2002)	22.7	(2012)	9.3	8.8	9.8	12.7	8.4
Malaysia	0.4	(2004)	0.0	(2015)	0.0	0.0	0.0	0.0	0.0
Myanmar	...		2.0	(2017)	2.7	2.9	2.6	3.6	2.5
Philippines	14.5		7.8	(2015)	2.7	2.2	3.0	3.5	2.6
Singapore	...		...		0.0	0.0	0.0	0.0	0.0
Thailand	2.5		0.0		0.0	0.0	0.0	0.0	0.0
Timor-Leste	46.0	(2001)	30.7	(2014)	21.8	20.6	22.8	27.0	20.6
Viet Nam	38.0	(2002)	1.9		1.2	1.3	1.1	2.3	1.1
The Pacific									
Cook Islands	...		...		...	...	...	...	...
Fiji	4.9	(2002)	1.4	(2013)	0.2	0.3	0.2	0.3	0.2
Kiribati	12.9	(2006)	...		...	...	...	...	...
Marshall Islands	...		...		...	...	...	...	...
Micronesia, Federated States of	8.1	(2005)	15.4	(2013)	...	...	...	...	...
Nauru	...		...		...	...	...	...	...
Niue	...		...		...	...	...	...	...
Palau	...		...		...	...	...	...	...
Papua New Guinea	...		38.0	(2009)	21.8	28.1	15.7	30.4	19.3
Samoa	2.0	(2002)	1.1	(2013)	...	...	...	...	...
Solomon Islands	45.6	(2005)	25.1	(2013)	17.7	16.2	19.2	22.5	16.0
Tonga	2.8	(2001)	1.0	(2015)	...	...	...	...	...
Tuvalu	...		3.3	(2010)	...	...	...	...	...
Vanuatu	...		13.2	(2010)	...	...	...	...	...
Developed ADB Member Economies									
Australia	...		...		...	...	...	...	...
Japan	...		...		...	...	...	...	...
New Zealand	...		...		...	...	...	...	...

Click on the indictor name in the table header to access the time series in the Key Indicators Database.

Table 1.1.1: Selected Indicators for Sustainable Development Goal 1—No Poverty (continued)

ADB Regional Member	Target 1.2: By 2030, reduce at least by half the proportion of men, women, and children of all ages living in poverty in all its dimensions according to national definitions 1.2.1: Proportion of Population Living below the National Poverty Line, by Urban–Rural Location[a] (%)					
	2000			**2017**		
	Total	**Urban**	**Rural**	**Total**	**Urban**	**Rural**
Developing ADB Member Economies						
Central and West Asia						
Afghanistan	33.7 (2007)	25.7 (2007)	35.7 (2007)	54.5 (2016)	41.6 (2016)	58.6 (2016)
Armenia	53.5 (2004)	...	...	23.5 (2018)	24.9 (2018)	21.3 (2018)
Azerbaijan[d]	49.6 (2001)	55.7 (2001)	42.5 (2001)	5.1 (2018)	...	...
Georgia	34.3 [e] (2004)	34.4 [e] (2004)	34.1 [e] (2004)	20.1 [e] (2018)	18.0 [e] (2018)	23.1 [e] (2018)
Kazakhstan	46.7 (2001)	36.0 (2001)	59.4 (2001)	4.3 (2018)	1.3 (2015)	4.4 (2015)
Kyrgyz Republic	62.6	53.3	67.6	22.4 (2018)	29.3 (2015)	33.6 (2015)
Pakistan	64.3 (2001)	50.0 (2001)	70.2 (2001)	24.3 * (2015)	12.5 * (2015)	30.7 * (2015)
Tajikistan	72.4 (2003)	68.8 (2003)	73.8 (2003)	27.4 (2018)	...	...
Turkmenistan	...	...	...	...	...	...
Uzbekistan[d]	...	...	...	11.0 (2019)	...	...
East Asia						
China, People's Republic of	...	...	49.8	...	...	1.7 (2018)
Hong Kong, China[f]	...	...	...	14.9 (2018)	...	...
Korea, Republic of[f]	...	...	...	16.7 (2018)	...	...
Mongolia	36.1 (2003)	30.3 (2003)	43.4 (2003)	28.4 (2018)	27.2 (2018)	30.8 (2018)
Taipei,China	0.7 [g]	...	...	1.3 [g] (2018)	...	...
South Asia						
Bangladesh	48.9	35.2	52.3	21.8 (2018)	21.3 (2010)	35.2 (2010)
Bhutan	23.2 (2007)	1.7 (2007)	30.9 (2007)	8.2	0.8	11.9
India	37.2 [h] (2004)	25.7 [h] (2004)	41.8 [h] (2004)	21.9 [h] (2011)	13.7 [h] (2011)	25.7 [h] (2011)
Maldives	21.0 (2002)	...	...	8.2 [i] (2016)	...	...
Nepal	30.9 (2003)	9.6 (2003)	34.6 (2003)	25.2 (2010)	15.5 (2010)	27.4 (2010)
Sri Lanka	22.7 (2002)	7.9 (2002)	24.7 (2002)	4.1 (2016)	1.9 (2016)	4.3 (2016)
Southeast Asia						
Brunei Darussalam	...	...	...	...	...	...
Cambodia	50.2 (2003)	...	54.2 (2003)	12.9 (2018)	...	14.0 (2018)
Indonesia	19.1 [j]	14.6 [j]	22.4 [j]	9.4 [k] (2019)	6.7 [k] (2019)	12.9 [k] (2019)
Lao People's Democratic Republic	33.5 (2002)	19.7 (2002)	37.6 (2002)	23.2 (2012)	10.0 (2012)	28.6 (2012)
Malaysia	5.1 (2002)	2.0 (2002)	11.4 (2002)	0.4 (2016)	0.2 (2016)	1.0 (2016)
Myanmar	48.2 (2005)	32.2 (2005)	53.9 (2005)	24.8	11.3	30.2
Philippines	26.6 (2006)	12.6 (2006)	...	16.7 (2018)	9.3 (2018)	24.5 (2018)
Singapore	...	...	...	...	...	...
Thailand	42.3	22.2	51.4	9.9 (2018)	...	...
Timor-Leste	36.3 (2001)	25.2 (2001)	39.7 (2001)	41.8 (2014)	28.3 (2014)	47.1 (2014)
Viet Nam	28.9 (2002)	6.6 (2002)	35.6 (2002)	5.8 (2016)	2.0 (2016)	7.5 (2016)
The Pacific						
Cook Islands	28.4 [l] (2006)	...	...	...	...	...
Fiji	35.0 [l] (2002)	28.0 [l] (2002)	40.0 [l] (2002)	28.1 [l] (2013)	19.8 [l] (2013)	36.7 [l] (2013)
Kiribati	21.8 [l] (2006)	...	...	...	...	...
Marshall Islands	52.7 [l] (2002)	...	...	...	...	...
Micronesia, Federated States of	29.9 [l] (2005)	...	...	41.2 [l] (2013)	...	...
Nauru	25.1 [l] (2006)	...	...	24.0 [l] (2013)	...	...
Niue	13.0 [l] (2002)	...	...	...	...	...
Palau	24.9 [l] (2006)	...	...	...	...	...
Papua New Guinea	...	...	...	37.5 *	...	...
Samoa	22.9 [l] (2002)	...	...	18.8 [l] (2013)	...	...
Solomon Islands	22.7 [m] (2005)	...	...	12.7 [m] (2013)	9.1 [m] (2012)	13.6 [m] (2012)
Tonga	16.2 [l] (2001)	...	...	22.1 [l,*] (2015)	...	...
Tuvalu	21.2 [l] (2004)	...	...	26.3 [l] (2010)	24.8 [l] (2010)	27.5 [l] (2010)
Vanuatu	13.0 [l] (2006)	...	11.5 (2006)	12.7 [l] (2010)	...	10.0 [l] (2010)
Developed ADB Member Economies						
Australia	...	...	...	...	...	...
Japan	...	...	...	...	...	...
New Zealand	...	...	...	...	...	...

... = data not available, * = provisional/preliminary/estimate/budget figure, 0.0 = magnitude is less than half of unit employed or true zero, $ = United States dollars, ADB = Asian Development Bank, PPP = purchasing power parity.

a For indicator 1.1.1.a and indicator 1.2.1, the year indicated in the table refers to the year when the household survey data were collected. For economies in which the household survey data collection period bridged 2 calendar years, the table reports the first year.

b For indicator 1.1.1.a, data are consumption-based, except for Malaysia and the Republic of Korea, where data are income-based. For indicator 1.1.1.a and indicator 1.1.1.b, the estimates are based on the international poverty line of $1.90 a day (2011 PPP).

c Data are taken from International Labour Organization modelled estimates and projections.

d For Indicator 1.1.1.a, the latest available estimate for Azerbaijan is for 2005: 0.0%. For Uzbekistan, the latest available estimate is for 2003: 62.1%.

e Refers to absolute poverty or the share of the population under the absolute poverty line.

f For indicator 1.2.1, the earliest available estimate for Hong Kong, China is for 2009: 16.0%. For the Republic of Korea, the earliest available estimate is for 2012: 18.6%. For Hong Kong, China, data refer to the poverty rate after policy intervention (recurrent cash). For the Republic of Korea, data refer to the relative poverty rate.

g Refers to the percentage of the low-income population to the total population.

h Based on the Tendulkar methodology, using mixed reference period.

i Based on half the median of total consumption expenditure equivalent to Maldivian Rufiyaa 74.

j Reference period is February 2000.

k Reference period is March 2019.

l Data refer to the percentage of the population living below the basic-needs poverty line.

m Refers to the poverty headcount ratio using the upper poverty line, which serves as spatial deflator with respect to Honiara (the Solomon Islands capital).

Sources: For indicator 1.1.1.a: World Bank. PovcalNet Database. http://iresearch.worldbank.org/PovcalNet/povDuplicateWB.aspx (accessed 13 July 2020); and United Nations Statistics Division. Global SDG Indicators Database. http://unstats.un.org/sdgs/indicators/database/ (accessed 16 July 2020). For indicator 1.1.1.b: International Labour Organization. ILOSTAT Database. http://www.ilo.org/ilostat (accessed 16 July 2020). For indicator 1.2.1: Economy sources; United Nations Statistics Division. Global SDG Indicators Database. http://unstats.un.org/sdgs/indicators/database/ (accessed 16 July 2020); and Secretariat of the Pacific Community. National Minimum Development Indicators Database. https://www.spc.int/nmdi/ (accessed 16 July 2020).

Click on the indictor name in the table header to access the time series in the Key Indicators Database.

Goal 1. End poverty in all its forms everywhere

Table 1.1.2: Selected Indicators for Sustainable Development Goal 1—Social Protection[a]

ADB Regional Member	Target 1.3: Implement nationally appropriate social protection systems and measures for all, including floors, and by 2030 achieve substantial coverage of the poor and the vulnerable									
	1.3.1a: Proportion of Population Covered by at least One Social Protection Benefit (%)		1.3.1b: Proportion of Population above Statutory Pensionable Age Receiving a Pension (%)		1.3.1c: Proportion of Poor Population Receiving Social Assistance Cash Benefit (%)		1.3.1d: Proportion of Vulnerable Population Receiving Social Assistance Cash Benefit (%)		1.3.1e: Proportion of Children/ Households Receiving Child/ Family Cash Benefit (%)	
	2019		2019		2018		2019		2019	
Developing ADB Member Economies										
Central and West Asia										
Afghanistan	...		...		...		...		...	
Armenia	47.0		100.0		100.0		34.3		36.5	
Azerbaijan	31.5		100.0		100.0		17.8		4.4	
Georgia	39.9		100.0		100.0		25.8		0.4	
Kazakhstan	100.0	(2016)	82.6	(2016)	28.9	(2016)	100.0	(2016)	100.0	(2016)
Kyrgyz Republic	32.7		100.0	(2018)	89.4		25.4		30.5	
Pakistan	8.0		3.0		69.2		4.0		4.0	
Tajikistan	16.8		100.0		28.1		9.6		5.6	
Turkmenistan	...		...		...		...		...	
Uzbekistan	20.9		100.0	(2018)	82.5		12.8		29.2	
East Asia										
China, People's Republic of	78.5		100.0	(2017)	51.6	(2016)	31.0	(2017)	2.2	(2016)
Hong Kong, China	...		...		...		...		...	
Korea, Republic of	67.0		100.0	(2018)	21.4	(2016)	26.3	(2018)	22.9	
Mongolia	85.0		100.0	(2018)	100.0		81.8		100.0	(2018)
Taipei,China	...		...		...		...		...	
South Asia										
Bangladesh	15.1		38.0		61.0		14.9		24.0	
Bhutan	5.8		18.8		60.2		5.0		18.5	
India	22.0	(2016)	25.2	(2016)	...		10.4	(2016)	8.2	
Maldives	14.3		100.0		100.0		14.0		8.2	
Nepal	21.0		66.1		70.1		18.3		39.3	
Sri Lanka	31.0		38.4		100.0		4.4	(2018)	100.0	
Southeast Asia										
Brunei Darussalam	...		90.9		...		...		...	
Cambodia	16.4		6.6		48.4		9.3		10.4	
Indonesia	54.0		14.1		100.0		42.5		91.2	
Lao People's Democratic Republic	0.4		10.1		0.1		–	(2018)	...	
Malaysia	8.4		19.8	(2018)	100.0		3.0		1.4	
Myanmar	1.6		19.3		0.8		0.3		1.0	
Philippines	44.1		64.0		100.0		8.0		13.6	(2018)
Singapore	19.9		48.9	(2018)	...		13.5		...	
Thailand	76.0		82.0		100.0	(2019)	62.0		15.0	
Timor-Leste	39.7		100.0		94.9		39.7		59.5	
Viet Nam	38.0		39.9	(2018)	100.0		12.6		1.0	
The Pacific										
Cook Islands	86.3		100.0		...		85.8		100.0	
Fiji	30.5		87.3		68.0		25.0		1.2	
Kiribati	4.3		12.8		15.9		3.5		1.3	
Marshall Islands	7.3		81.0		...		1.1		...	
Micronesia, Federated States of	8.2		100.0		...		2.2		6.8	
Nauru	45.4		100.0		...		45.4		...	
Niue	...		...		...		...		...	
Palau	35.8		100.0		56.0		17.8		60.0	
Papua New Guinea	0.2	(2018)	4.9		...		...		...	
Samoa	16.3		100.0		69.2		14.4		–	(2018)
Solomon Islands	1.1		20.5		2.9		0.4		...	
Tonga	4.0		73.3	(2018)	16.7		3.8		0.3	
Tuvalu	...		...		...		...		...	
Vanuatu	58.3		8.5		100.0		58.1		12.9	
Developed ADB Member Economies										
Australia	82.0	(2016)	71.3	(2014)	100.0	(2016)	53.0	(2016)	100.0	(2016)
Japan	76.0		100.0	(2018)	...		21.3		85.4	
New Zealand	67.0		100.0	(2014)	37.4	(2016)	9.7	(2016)	...	

... = data not available, – = magnitude equals zero, ADB = Asian Development Bank.

a   The population covered by at least one social protection benefit (effective coverage) refers to the proportion of the total population receiving at least one contributory or noncontributory cash benefit, or actively contributing to at least one social security scheme. For children, older persons, and the poor and the vulnerable, effective coverage is expressed as a share of the respective population.

Source: United Nations Statistics Division. Global SDG Indicators Database. https://unstats.un.org/sdgs/indicators/database/ (accessed 20 July 2020).

Click on the indictor name in the table header to access the time series in the Key Indicators Database.

Goal 2. End hunger, achieve food security and improved nutrition, and promote sustainable agriculture

Table 1.2.1: Selected Indicators for Sustainable Development Goal 2—Zero Hunger

ADB Regional Member	Target 2.1: By 2030, end hunger and ensure access by all people, in particular the poor and people in vulnerable situations, including infants, to safe, nutritious, and sufficient food all year round		Target 2.2: By 2030, end all forms of malnutrition, including achieving, by 2025, the internationally agreed targets on stunting and wasting in children under 5 years of age, and address the nutritional needs of adolescent girls, pregnant and lactating women, and older persons					
	2.1.1: Prevalence of Undernourishment (%)		2.2.1: Prevalence of Stunting among Children under 5 Years of Age[a] (%)		2.2.2c: Prevalence of Malnutrition (Overweight) among Children under 5 Years of Age[a] (%)		2.2.2d: Prevalence of Malnutrition (Wasting) among Children under 5 Years of Age[a] (%)	
	2001[b]	2018[c]	2000	2017	2000	2017	2000	2017
Developing ADB Member Economies								
Central and West Asia								
Afghanistan	47.8	29.9	59.3 (2004)	38.2 (2018)	4.6 (2004)	4.1 (2018)	8.6 (2004)	5.1 (2018)
Armenia	26.2	2.6	17.3	9.4 (2016)	15.7	13.7 (2016)	2.5	4.4 (2016)
Azerbaijan	17.1	<2.5	24.2	17.8 (2013)	6.2	14.1 (2013)	9.0	3.2 (2013)
Georgia	7.8	8.2	14.6 (2005)	...	20.8 (2005)	...	3.0 (2005)	...
Kazakhstan	6.6	<2.5	17.5 (2006)	8.0 (2015)	16.9 (2006)	9.3 (2015)	4.9 (2006)	3.1 (2015)
Kyrgyz Republic	15.3	6.4	18.1 (2006)	11.8 (2018)	10.7 (2006)	6.9 (2018)	3.4 (2006)	2.0 (2018)
Pakistan	21.2	12.3	41.4 (2001)	37.6 (2018)	4.8 (2001)	2.5 (2018)	14.1 (2001)	7.1 (2018)
Tajikistan	...	...	42.1	17.5	6.8 (2005)	3.3	9.4	5.6
Turkmenistan	6.9	4.0	28.1	11.5 (2015)	4.5 (2005)	5.9 (2015)	7.1	4.2 (2015)
Uzbekistan	18.0	2.6	24.9 (2002)	10.8	11.0 (2002)	4.6	9.0 (2002)	1.8
East Asia								
China, People's Republic of	10.6	<2.5	17.8	8.1 (2013)	3.4	9.1 (2013)	2.5	1.9 (2013)
Hong Kong, China	<2.5 [d] (2000)	<2.5 [e] (2017)	...	...	...	...	...	...
Korea, Republic of	<2.5	<2.5	2.5 (2003)	2.5 (2010)	6.2 (2003)	7.3 (2010)	0.9 (2003)	1.2 (2010)
Mongolia	31.2	21.3	29.8	9.4 (2018)	12.7	10.5 (2018)	7.1	0.9 (2018)
Taipei,China	3.7	3.5	...	...	...	...	...	...
South Asia								
Bangladesh	16.0	13.0	51.1	30.8 (2018)	0.9	2.2 (2018)	12.5	8.4 (2018)
Bhutan	...	...	34.9 (2008)	33.5 (2010)	5.4 (2008)	7.6 (2010)	4.5 (2008)	5.9 (2010)
India	18.6	14.0	47.8 (2006)	34.7	1.9 (2006)	1.6	20.0 (2006)	17.3
Maldives	14.0 [d] (2000)	10.3 [e] (2017)	31.9 (2001)	...	3.9 (2001)	...	13.4 (2001)	...
Nepal	23.6	6.1	57.1 (2001)	36.0 (2016)	0.7 (2001)	1.2 (2016)	11.3 (2001)	9.6 (2016)
Sri Lanka	17.0	7.6	18.4	17.3 (2016)	1.0	2.0 (2016)	15.5	15.1 (2016)
Southeast Asia								
Brunei Darussalam	2.6	<2.5	19.7 (2009)	...	8.3 (2009)	...	2.9 (2009)	...
Cambodia	23.7	14.5	49.0	32.4 (2014)	4.0	2.2 (2014)	17.1	9.7 (2014)
Indonesia	19.3	9.0	42.4	30.5 (2018)	1.5	8.0 (2018)	5.5	10.2 (2018)
Lao People's Democratic Republic	37.7 [d] (2000)	16.5 [e] (2017)	47.5	33.1	2.7	3.5	17.5	9.0
Malaysia	2.6	3.0	17.2 (2006)	20.7 (2016)	...	6.0 (2016)	...	11.5 (2016)
Myanmar	37.7	14.1	40.8	29.4 (2016)	2.4	1.5 (2016)	10.7	6.6 (2016)
Philippines	18.8	14.5	33.8 (2003)	30.3 (2018)	2.4 (2003)	4.0 (2018)	6.0 (2003)	5.6 (2018)
Singapore	...	...	4.4	...	2.6	...	3.6	...
Thailand	17.4	9.3	15.7 (2006)	10.5 (2016)	8.0 (2006)	8.2 (2016)	4.7 (2006)	5.4 (2016)
Timor-Leste	41.6	30.9	55.7 (2002)	51.7 (2013)	5.7 (2002)	1.6 (2013)	13.7 (2002)	9.9 (2013)
Viet Nam	19.8	6.4	43.2	23.8	2.6	5.9	6.1	5.8
The Pacific								
Cook Islands	...	...	...	...	...	...	...	...
Fiji	4.0	3.9	7.5 (2004)	...	5.1 (2004)	...	6.3 (2004)	...
Kiribati	4.4	3.0	...	...	...	...	...	...
Marshall Islands	...	...	...	34.8	...	4.1	...	3.5
Micronesia, Federated States of	...	...	...	...	...	...	...	...
Nauru	...	...	24.0 (2007)	...	2.8 (2007)	...	1.0 (2007)	...
Niue	...	...	...	...	...	...	...	...
Palau	...	...	...	...	...	...	...	...
Papua New Guinea	...	...	43.9 (2005)	49.5 (2010)	3.4 (2005)	13.7 (2010)	4.4 (2005)	14.1 (2010)
Samoa	3.5	<2.5	...	4.9 (2014)	...	5.3 (2014)	...	3.9 (2014)
Solomon Islands	13.1	13.2	32.8 (2007)	31.7 (2015)	2.5 (2007)	4.5 (2015)	4.3 (2007)	8.5 (2015)
Tonga	...	...	...	8.1 (2012)	...	17.3 (2012)	...	5.2 (2012)
Tuvalu	...	...	10.0 (2007)	...	6.3 (2007)	...	3.3 (2007)	...
Vanuatu	7.5	9.8	25.7 (2007)	28.9 (2013)	4.7 (2007)	4.9 (2013)	5.9 (2007)	4.7 (2013)
Developed ADB Member Economies								
Australia	<2.5	<2.5	2.0 (2007)	...	7.7 (2007)	22.0	– (2007)	...
Japan	<2.5	<2.5	...	7.1 (2010)	...	1.5 (2010)	...	2.3 (2010)
New Zealand	<2.5	<2.5	...	...	...	...	...	...

... = data not available, < = less than, – = magnitude equals zero, ADB = Asian Development Bank.

a According to the World Health Organization (WHO), the estimates for some economies were adjusted where necessary to be nationally representative and to cover the age range 0–5 years, which might result in slight differences in prevalence from the results reported in the original WHO survey. Estimates for some economies are also pending reanalysis by WHO. Details can be found in the "Notes" column of the joint child malnutrition dataset.
b Data refer to 3-year average for 2000–2002.
c Data refer to 3-year average for 2017–2019.
d Data refer to 3-year average for 1999–2001.
e Data refer to 3-year average for 2016–2018.

Sources: For Indicator 2.1.1: Food and Agriculture Organization of the United Nations. FAOSTAT Database. http://www.fao.org/faostat/ (accessed 15 July 2020). For Hong Kong, China; the Lao People's Democratic Republic; and Maldives: United Nations Statistics Division. Global SDG Indicators Database. https://unstats.un.org/sdgs/indicators/database/ (accessed 15 July 2020). For Indicators 2.2.1, 2.2.2c, and 2.2.2d: United Nations Statistics Division. Global SDG Indicators Database. https://unstats.un.org/sdgs/indicators/database/ (accessed 15 July 2020).

Click on the indictor name in the table header to access the time series in the Key Indicators Database.

Goal 2. End hunger, achieve food security and improved nutrition, and promote sustainable agriculture

Table 1.2.2: Selected Indicators for Sustainable Development Goal 2—Improved Agricultural Investment

ADB Regional Member	Target 2.a: Increase investment, including through enhanced international cooperation, in rural infrastructure, agricultural research and extension services, technology development, and plant and livestock gene banks in order to enhance agricultural productive capacity in developing countries, in particular least developed countries			
	2.a.1: The Agriculture Orientation Index for Government Expenditures		2.a.2: Total Official Flows to the Agriculture Sector[a] (constant 2018 $ million)	
	2001	2018	2000	2018
Developing ADB Member Economies				
Central and West Asia	...	...	307.8	1,265.8
Afghanistan	0.1 (2003)	0.2	4.6	265.1
Armenia	0.2 (2009)	0.1	15.5	55.7
Azerbaijan	0.4 (2008)	0.5	77.1	6.8
Georgia	0.0 (2003)	0.3	37.9	45.2
Kazakhstan	0.4	0.4	3.7	15.6
Kyrgyz Republic	0.1	0.1	83.9	21.8
Pakistan	0.0	0.0	60.8	271.2
Tajikistan	...	...	24.1	32.0
Turkmenistan	...	...	0.0	1.6
Uzbekistan	...	0.3	0.2	550.9
East Asia	...	...	341.2	533.4
China, People's Republic of	0.3 (2007)	0.3	336.8	515.1
Hong Kong, China	...	...	...	...
Korea, Republic of	1.6	0.7	...	...
Mongolia	0.2	0.1 (2015)	4.4	18.2
Taipei,China	...	...	...	...
South Asia	...	...	712.0	1,046.6
Bangladesh	0.2	0.4 (2016)	349.3	256.5
Bhutan	0.3	0.8	6.1	9.5
India	0.2	0.4	230.1	609.6
Maldives	0.2	0.1	0.0	4.9
Nepal	0.2 (2002)	0.3	72.8	90.7
Sri Lanka	0.4	0.6	53.7	75.4
Southeast Asia	...	...	920.5	1,241.1
Brunei Darussalam	...	...	...	...
Cambodia	...	...	164.1	114.4
Indonesia	0.2 (2004)	0.1 (2013)	203.4	222.9
Lao People's Democratic Republic	...	...	28.5	100.4
Malaysia	0.4	0.3	8.8	2.7
Myanmar	...	0.1	2.1	219.9
Philippines	0.3	0.3	367.4	221.7
Singapore	2.0	12.8	...	...
Thailand	0.9	0.7	29.4	8.5
Timor-Leste	1.2 (2008)	0.2 (2015)	8.8	28.2
Viet Nam	0.1 (2006)	0.2 (2014)	108.0	322.4
The Pacific[b]	...	...	100.3	95.3
Cook Islands	0.7 (2005)	0.9 (2013)	0.0	0.0
Fiji	0.3 (2005)	0.4	1.0	14.1
Kiribati	...	...	7.9	3.4
Marshall Islands	0.1 (2008)	0.1	3.3	1.5
Micronesia, Federated States of	...	0.2	9.8	1.9
Nauru	...	...	0.2 (2003)	0.3
Niue	...	...	0.0 (2002)	0.0
Palau	0.1 (2008)	0.2	0.2	5.8
Papua New Guinea	0.1	...	60.1	44.6
Samoa	...	0.4	2.7	2.8
Solomon Islands	...	0.1 (2015)	3.6	8.3
Tonga	...	...	0.2	1.9
Tuvalu	...	...	7.4 (2001)	2.0
Vanuatu	0.1 (2005)	0.2 (2012)	3.9	8.8
Developed ADB Member Economies	...	...	...	...
Australia	0.2	0.2	...	...
Japan	...	...	...	...
New Zealand	0.3 (2004)	...	...	...
DEVELOPING ADB MEMBER ECONOMIES[b]	...	...	2,381.7	4,182.2

... = data not available, 0.0 = magnitude is less than half of unit employed, $ = United States dollars, ADB = Asian Development Bank.

a Total official flows refer to official development assistance plus other official flows. Data refer to gross disbursements.
b For reporting economies only.

Source: United Nations Statistics Division. Global SDG Indicators Database. https://unstats.un.org/sdgs/indicators/database/ (accessed 20 July 2020).

Click on the indictor name in the table header to access the time series in the Key Indicators Database.

Goal 3. Ensure healthy lives and promote well-being for all at all ages

Table 1.3.1: Selected Indicators for Sustainable Development Goal 3—Maternal and Child Health

ADB Regional Member	Target 3.1: By 2030, reduce the global maternal mortality ratio to less than 70 per 100,000 live births				Target 3.2: By 2030, end preventable deaths of newborns and children under 5 years of age, with all countries aiming to reduce neonatal mortality to at least as low as 12 per 1,000 live births and under-5 mortality to at least as low as 25 per 1,000 live births			
	3.1.1: Maternal Mortality Ratio[a] (per 100,000 live births)		3.1.2: Proportion of Births Attended by Skilled Health Personnel[b] (%)		3.2.1: Under-5 Mortality Rate[a] (per 1,000 live births)		3.2.2: Neonatal Mortality Rate[a] (per 1,000 live births)	
	2000	2017	2000	2018	2000	2018	2000	2018
Developing ADB Member Economies								
Central and West Asia	**404**	**182**	...	...	**104**	**61**	**54**	**35**
Afghanistan	1,450	638	14.3 c (2003)	58.8 c	125	62	61	37
Armenia	43	26	96.8 c	99.8 d (2016)	31	11	16	7
Azerbaijan	47	26	80.7 c	99.4 e	80	19	34	11
Georgia	31	25	95.5 e	99.4 f	32	9	23	6
Kazakhstan	61	10	98.3 e	99.9 f	37	10	21	6
Kyrgyz Republic	79	60	98.6 e	99.8 c	44	19	20	13
Pakistan	286	140	23.0 c (2002)	69.3 c	116	74	60	42
Tajikistan	53	17	70.7 c	94.8 c (2017)	84	35	29	15
Turkmenistan	29	7	97.2 c	100.0 c (2016)	90	40	30	21
Uzbekistan	41	29	94.9 c	100.0 d	55	24	29	12
East Asia	**58**	**29**	...	...	**34**	**9**	**21**	**4**
China, People's Republic of	59	29	96.6 e	99.9 e (2016)	35	9	21	4
Hong Kong, China	6	-* (2019)	...	...	...	...	2 g	1* g
Korea, Republic of	17	11	99.9 f	100.0 f (2015)	8	3	3	2
Mongolia	155	45	96.6 d	99.3 d	73	19	25	9
Taipei,China	8	12 (2018)	...	...	...	...	3	3
South Asia	**378**	**148**	...	...	**86**	**36**	**44**	**22**
Bangladesh	434	173	12.1 d	52.7 d	84	28	42	17
Bhutan	423	183	27.3 e	96.2 e	82	27	32	16
India	370	145	42.5 e (2004)	81.4 d (2016)	87	37	45	23
Maldives	125	53	84.0 c (2004)	99.5 c (2017)	35	9	22	5
Nepal	553	186	11.9 e	58.0 d (2016)	83	34	40	20
Sri Lanka	56	36	96.0 d	99.5 c (2016)	17	7	10	5
Southeast Asia	**215**	**137**	...	...	**48**	**26**	**21**	**13**
Brunei Darussalam	28	31	99.2 e	99.8 e (2017)	11	12	5	6
Cambodia	488	160	31.8 c	89.0 d (2014)	99	31	35	14
Indonesia	272	177	66.3 d (2003)	94.7 c (2019)	48	28	23	13
Lao People's Democratic Republic	544	185	16.7 c	64.4 c (2017)	114	52	38	23
Malaysia	38	29	96.6 e	99.6 e (2017)	9	7	5	4
Myanmar	340	250	57.0 c (2001)	60.2 d (2016)	82	46	37	23
Philippines	160	121	58.0 c	84.4 c (2017)	42	31	17	14
Singapore	13	8	99.7 f	99.5 f	4	3	2	1
Thailand	43	37	99.3 d	99.1 d (2016)	24	10	12	5
Timor-Leste	745	142	24.0 d (2002)	56.7 d (2016)	114	46	37	20
Viet Nam	68	43	58.8 c	93.8 c (2014)	35	17	15	11
The Pacific	**223**	**130**	...	...	**59**	**42**	**25**	**20**
Cook Islands	...	...	98.0 d	100.0 e (2009)	18	7	10	4
Fiji	51	34	96.9 f	99.8 e (2016)	23	23	9	11
Kiribati	136	92	85.0 d	98.3 e (2010)	77	57	29	23
Marshall Islands	...	...	86.2 c (2007)	92.4 c (2017)	45	37	19	16
Micronesia, Federated States of	154	88	82.8 c	100.0 e (2009)	54	34	25	16
Nauru	...	...	97.4 d (2007)	...	46	29	25	20
Niue	...	...	100.0 d	100.0 e (2011)	24	21	13	13
Palau	...	...	100.0 e	100.0 c	32	16	15	9
Papua New Guinea	249	145	39.0 e (2004)	56.4 d	67	48	29	22
Samoa	88	43	80.0 d	82.5 d (2014)	19	17	11	8
Solomon Islands	245	104	85.5 d (2007)	86.2 d (2015)	30	18	13	8
Tonga	77	52	95.0 d	95.5 c (2012)	20	17	8	7
Tuvalu	...	...	100.0 d	...	45	27	25	16
Vanuatu	140	72	88.0 d	89.4 d (2013)	29	24	13	12
Developed ADB Member Economies	**9**	**5**	...	...	**5**	**3**	**2**	**1**
Australia	7	6	99.3 f	96.7 f (2017)	6	3	4	2
Japan	9	5	99.8 f	99.9 f	5	3	2	1
New Zealand	12	9	97.3 f	96.6 f (2017)	7	5	4	4
DEVELOPING ADB MEMBER ECONOMIES	**271**	**119**	...	...	**68**	**30**	**35**	**17**
ALL ADB REGIONAL MEMBERS	**266**	**117**	...	...	**66**	**30**	**35**	**17**
WORLD	**342**	**211**	...	...	**76**	**39**	**31**	**18**

... = data not available, * = provisional or preliminary, ADB = Asian Development Bank.

a Regional aggregates are weighted averages estimated using population of annual live births for the respective year headings. The data for maternal, under-5, and neonatal deaths are from United Nations Statistics Division databases. Aggregates are derived for reporting economies only. Aggregates for East Asia exclude Hong Kong, China and Taipei,China.
b Based on national household survey data and routine health systems.
c Estimate aligned with the standard definitions of doctor, nurse, and/or midwife.
d Includes other health personnel not in alignment with standard definitions.
e Estimate provided with no clear definition of health personnel.
f Refers to institutional births, including all deliveries that occurred at a health facility.
g Calculated based on known births and deaths.

Sources: For Indicator 3.1.1: United Nations Statistics Division. Global SDG Indicators Database. https://unstats.un.org/sdgs/indicators/database/ (accessed 8 July 2020). For Hong Kong, China: Government of the Hong Kong Special Administrative Region of the People's Republic of China. Centre for Health Protection Statistics. https://www.chp.gov.hk/en/statistics/data/10/27/110.html (accessed 9 July 2020). For Taipei,China: Government of Taipei,China, Directorate-General of Budget, Accounting and Statistics. National Statistics. https://eng.stat.gov.tw/mp.asp?mp=5 (accessed 9 July 2020). For Indicators 3.1.2, 3.2.1, and 3.2.2: United Nations Statistics Division. Global SDG Indicators Database. https://unstats.un.org/sdgs/indicators/database/ (accessed 8 July 2020). For Hong Kong, China: Government of the Hong Kong Special Administrative Region of the People's Republic of China, Department of Health. Health Facts of Hong Kong 2019 Edition; past editions. https://www.dh.gov.hk/english/statistics/statistics_hs/files/Health_Statistics_pamphlet_E.pdf (accessed 9 July 2020); and Annual Report 2014/2015. https://www.dh.gov.hk/english/pub_rec/pub_rec_ar/pub_rec_arpis_1415_html.html (accessed 9 July 2020). For Taipei,China: Government of Taipei,China, Ministry of Health and Welfare. Cause of Death Statistics 2018. https://www.mohw.gov.tw/lp-4650-2.html (accessed 9 July 2020).

Click on the indictor name in the table header to access the time series in the Key Indicators Database.

Goal 3. Ensure healthy lives and promote well–being for all at all ages

Table 1.3.2: Selected Indicators for Sustainable Development Goal 3—Incidence of Communicable Diseases

ADB Regional Member	Target 3.3: By 2030, end the epidemics of AIDS, tuberculosis, malaria, and neglected tropical diseases; and combat hepatitis, water-borne diseases, and other communicable diseases					
	3.3.1: Number of New HIV Infections (per 1,000 uninfected population)		3.3.2: Tuberculosis Incidence (per 100,000 population)		3.3.3: Malaria Incidence (per 1,000 population)	
	2000	2019	2000	2018	2000	2018
Developing ADB Member Economies						
Central and West Asia						
Afghanistan	0.01	0.04	190.0	189.0	95.5	29.0
Armenia	0.11	0.05	54.0	31.0	0.0	–
Azerbaijan	0.17	0.06	80.0	63.0	8.2	–
Georgia	0.06	0.18 (2018)	254.0	80.0	5.6	–
Kazakhstan	0.04	0.20	169.0	68.0	–	–
Kyrgyz Republic	0.03	0.14	145.0	116.0	0.0	–
Pakistan	<0.01	0.12	275.0	265.0	7.3	3.4
Tajikistan	<0.01	0.17	219.0	84.0	9.2	–
Turkmenistan	...	...	112.0	46.0	0.0	–
Uzbekistan	0.03	0.13	99.0	70.0	0.1	–
East Asia						
China, People's Republic of	...	...	107.0	61.0	0.0	–
Hong Kong, China	...	...	105.0	67.0	...	...
Korea, Republic of	...	...	49.0	66.0	1.3	0.1
Mongolia	<0.01	0.01	428.0	428.0	...	...
Taipei,China	...	...	...	...	...	...
South Asia						
Bangladesh	–	0.01 (2018)	221.0	221.0	7.2	0.7
Bhutan	0.25	0.11 (2018)	241.0	149.0	13.6	0.0
India	...	0.07 (2017)	289.0	199.0	19.9	5.3
Maldives	...	...	59.0	33.0	...	...
Nepal	0.20	0.03	163.0	151.0	7.2	0.4
Sri Lanka	0.02	<0.01	66.0	64.0	48.6	–
Southeast Asia						
Brunei Darussalam	...	...	106.0	68.0	...	...
Cambodia	0.89	0.05	578.0	302.0	77.8	23.7
Indonesia	0.11	0.17 (2018)	370.0	316.0	9.3	3.9
Lao People's Democratic Republic	0.11	0.11	330.0	162.0	62.7	4.2
Malaysia	0.26	0.20	75.0	92.0	13.7	–
Myanmar	0.58	0.19	555.0	338.0	55.8	3.4
Philippines	<0.01	0.14	590.0	554.0	2.6	0.2
Singapore	0.11	0.03	49.0	47.0	...	...
Thailand	0.66	0.08	241.0	153.0	6.6	0.4
Timor-Leste	0.03	0.15	498.0 (2002)	498.0	122.5	–
Viet Nam	0.30	0.05	296.0	182.0	3.4	0.1
The Pacific						
Cook Islands	...	...	6.4	–	...	...
Fiji	0.03	0.14	22.0	54.0	...	...
Kiribati	...	...	373.0	349.0	...	...
Marshall Islands	...	...	84.0	434.0	...	...
Micronesia, Federated States of	...	...	106.0	108.0	...	...
Nauru	...	...	45.0	54.0	...	...
Niue	...	...	–	71.0	...	...
Palau	...	...	64.0	109.0	...	...
Papua New Guinea	0.57	0.38	432.0	432.0	260.6	184.5
Samoa	...	...	28.0	6.4	...	...
Solomon Islands	...	...	91.0	74.0	623.2	133.6
Tonga	...	...	28.0	10.0	...	...
Tuvalu	...	...	196.0	270.0	...	...
Vanuatu	...	...	110.0	46.0	125.3	4.0
Developed ADB Member Economies						
Australia	0.03	0.03	6.3	6.6	...	...
Japan	0.01	0.01 (2018)	36.0	14.0	...	...
New Zealand	0.02	0.03	10.0	7.3	...	...

... = data not available, < = less than, – = magnitude equals zero, 0.0 = magnitude is less than half of unit employed, ADB = Asian Development Bank.

Sources: For Indicator 3.3.1: The Joint United Nations Programme on HIV/AIDS. Trends of New HIV Infections. http://aidsinfo.unaids.org/ (accessed 10 July 2020). For Georgia, Bangladesh, Bhutan, Indonesia, and Japan: United Nations Statistics Division. Global SDG Indicators Database. http://unstats.un.org/sdgs/indicators/database/ (accessed 10 July 2020). For India: Government of India, Ministry of Statistics and Programme Implementation. India SDG Dashboard. http://www.sdgindia2030.mospi.gov.in/dashboard/ (accessed 27 July 2020). For Indicators 3.3.2 and 3.3.3: United Nations Statistics Division. Global SDG Indicators Database. http://unstats.un.org/sdgs/indicators/database/ (accessed 8 July 2020).

Click on the indictor name in the table header to access the time series in the Key Indicators Database.

Goal 3. Ensure healthy lives and promote well-being for all at all ages

Table 1.3.3: Selected Indicators for Sustainable Development Goal 3—Mortality Rates, Reproductive Health

ADB Regional Member	Target 3.4: By 2030, reduce by one-third premature mortality from noncommunicable diseases through prevention and treatment, and promote mental health and well-being					Target 3.6: By 2020, halve the number of global deaths and injuries from road traffic accidents	
	3.4.1: Mortality Rate Attributed to Cardiovascular Disease, Cancer, Diabetes, or Chronic Respiratory Disease (%)		3.4.2: Suicide Mortality Rate[a] (per 100,000 population) 2016			3.6.1: Death Rate Due to Road Traffic Injuries (per 100,000 population)	
	2000	2016	Total	Female	Male	2000	2016
Developing ADB Member Economies							
Central and West Asia							
Afghanistan	34.4	29.8	4.7	1.5	7.6	14.9	15.1
Armenia	27.8	22.3	6.6	2.8	10.8	19.6	17.1
Azerbaijan	29.3	22.2	2.6	1.1	4.2	8.2	8.7
Georgia	24.7	24.9	8.2	2.7	14.2	10.9	15.3
Kazakhstan	39.1	26.8	22.5	7.6	38.3	14.1	17.6
Kyrgyz Republic	31.4	24.9	8.3	3.5	13.2	12.4	15.4
Pakistan	26.7	24.7	2.9	3.0	2.7	14.3	14.3
Tajikistan	27.3	25.3	2.5	1.3	3.7	19.5	18.1
Turkmenistan	34.0	29.5	6.7	3.5	10.1	16.1	14.5
Uzbekistan	29.3	24.5	7.4	4.8	9.9	9.7	11.5
East Asia							
China, People's Republic of	21.5	17.0	9.7	10.3	9.1	21.5	18.2
Hong Kong, China	...	...	...	...	...	2.4	1.4 (2018)
Korea, Republic of	16.5	7.8	26.9	15.4	38.4	25.6	9.8
Mongolia	38.9	30.2	13.0	3.5	22.6	15.9	16.5
Taipei,China	...	...	16.4 (2018)	...	...	...	...
South Asia							
Bangladesh	21.4	21.6	5.9	7.0	4.7	10.5	15.3
Bhutan	30.8	23.3	11.4	8.5	14.0	12.0	17.4
India	26.6	23.3	16.3	14.7	17.8	14.6	22.6
Maldives	26.8	13.4	2.3	1.3	3.0	1.8	0.9
Nepal	27.3	21.8	8.8	7.9	9.7	15.7	15.9
Sri Lanka	21.5	17.4	14.6	6.4	23.5	15.1	14.9
Southeast Asia							
Brunei Darussalam	20.5	16.6	4.6	2.7	6.4	15.9	9.0
Cambodia	25.5	21.1	5.3	2.9	7.8	17.9	17.8
Indonesia	26.3	26.4	3.4	2.0	4.8	14.5	12.2
Lao People's Democratic Republic	29.2	27.0	8.6	5.7	11.4	13.8	16.6
Malaysia	20.3	17.2	5.5	3.2	7.8	26.8	23.6
Myanmar	25.0	24.2	7.8	9.5	5.9	21.2	19.9
Philippines	26.8	26.8	3.2	2.0	4.3	9.8	12.3
Singapore	16.8	9.3	9.9	6.1	13.8	6.7	2.8
Thailand	19.2	14.5	14.4	5.9	23.4	39.1	32.7
Timor-Leste	26.8	19.9	4.6	2.9	6.2	14.7	12.7
Viet Nam	18.6	17.1	7.3	3.7	10.9	24.0	26.4
The Pacific							
Cook Islands	...	...	...	...	...	5.5	17.3
Fiji	36.4	30.6	5.0	2.4	7.5	9.7	9.6
Kiribati	29.5	28.4	14.4	5.0	24.1	8.3	4.4
Marshall Islands	...	...	...	...	...	15.3	1.9
Micronesia, Federated States of	27.4	26.1	11.1	6.3	15.8	14.9	1.9
Nauru	...	30.0 (2017)	...	...	...	10.0	17.6
Niue	...	18.5	...	...	...	–	–
Palau	...	...	...	...	...	15.6	14.0
Papua New Guinea	31.2	30.0	6.0	3.3	8.6	17.8	14.2
Samoa	29.5	20.6	4.4	1.9	6.7	14.9	11.3
Solomon Islands	31.2	23.8	4.7	2.6	6.8	17.7	17.4
Tonga	26.1	23.3	3.5	2.7	4.3	13.3	16.8
Tuvalu	...	...	...	...	...	10.6	18.0
Vanuatu	27.9	23.3	4.5	2.2	6.6	14.0	15.9
Developed ADB Member Economies							
Australia	13.1	9.1	13.2	7.0	19.5	9.8	5.6
Japan	11.4	8.4	18.5	11.4	26.0	12.5	4.1
New Zealand	15.9	10.1	12.1	6.6	17.9	12.3	7.8

Goal 3. Ensure healthy lives and promote well-being for all at all ages

Table 1.3.3: Selected Indicators for Sustainable Development Goal 3—Mortality Rates, Reproductive Health (*continued*)

ADB Regional Member	Target 3.7: 3.7.1: Proportion of Women of Reproductive Age (Aged 15-49 Years) Who Have Their Need for Family Planning Satisfied with Modern Methods (% of women aged 15-49 years) 2000	2016	3.7.2: Adolescent Birth Rate (women aged 15-19 years per 1,000 women in that age group) 2000	2017	Target 3.8: 3.8.1: Coverage of Essential Health Services[b] (index in a unitless scale of 0 to 100) 2017	Target 3.9: 3.9.1: Mortality Rate Attributed to Household and Ambient Air Pollution (per 100,000 population) 2016	3.9.2: Mortality Rate Attributed to Unsafe Water, Unsafe Sanitation, and Lack of Hygiene (per 100,000 population) 2016
Developing ADB Member Economies							
Central and West Asia							
Afghanistan	...	42.2	193.8	62.0	37.0	95.0	13.9
Armenia	28.3	40.2	31.6	21.2	69.0	81.0	0.2
Azerbaijan	17.8 (2001)	...	29.0	45.0	65.0	55.0	1.1
Georgia	30.8	50.5 (2018)	39.9	32.3 (2018)	66.0	184.0	0.2
Kazakhstan	...	73.2 (2018)	33.0 (2018)	25.6 (2018)	76.0	57.0	0.4
Kyrgyz Republic	...	64.0 (2018)	34.7	33.9	70.0	74.0	0.8
Pakistan	33.3 (2001)	48.6 (2018)	83.0	46.0 (2016)	45.0	113.0	19.6
Tajikistan	...	52.1 (2017)	37.3	54.3 (2016)	68.0	70.0	2.7
Turkmenistan	70.9	75.6	26.1	28.0 (2014)	70.0	51.0	4.0
Uzbekistan	...	...	21.1	18.9	73.0	54.0	0.4
East Asia							
China, People's Republic of	96.6 (2001)	...	6.0	9.2 (2015)	79.0	140.0	0.6
Hong Kong, China	...	...	5.0	2.1 (2018)	...	...	...
Korea, Republic of	...	...	2.5	1.0	86.0	35.0	1.8
Mongolia	79.3 (2003)	63.6 (2018)	27.3	32.6 (2018)	62.0	97.0	1.3
Taipei,China	...	...	...	...	...	...	...
South Asia							
Bangladesh	60.2	72.6 (2014)	134.0	74.0 (2018)	48.0	103.0	11.9
Bhutan	...	84.6 (2010)	61.7	28.4 (2012)	62.0	88.0	3.9
India	61.7 (2004)	72.8	79.1	10.7 (2016)	55.0	141.0	18.6
Maldives	...	29.2 (2017)	28.9	8.9	62.0	14.0	0.3
Nepal	52.8 (2001)	56.0 (2017)	71.0	88.2 (2015)	48.0	133.0	19.8
Sri Lanka	56.1	74.3	30.3	21.0 (2015)	66.0	89.0	1.2
Southeast Asia							
Brunei Darussalam	...	...	31.2	9.8	81.0	9.0	–
Cambodia	33.0	56.5 (2014)	52.0 (2003)	57.4 (2013)	60.0	87.0	6.5
Indonesia	77.1 (2003)	77.0 (2017)	54.0	36.0 (2016)	57.0	81.0	7.1
Lao People's Democratic Republic	40.3	72.3 (2017)	76.0 (2004)	83.4 (2016)	51.0	110.0	11.3
Malaysia	...	...	12.0	9.3	73.0	35.0	0.4
Myanmar	56.0 (2001)	74.9	22.7	28.0 (2015)	61.0	116.0	12.6
Philippines	46.5 (2003)	56.0 (2017)	55.0 (2001)	39.0	61.0	117.0	4.2
Singapore	...	...	8.8	2.5 (2018)	86.0	39.0	0.1
Thailand	94.8 (2006)	89.2	31.1	37.8	80.0	85.0	3.5
Timor-Leste	...	45.9	78.3 (2001)	41.9 (2015)	52.0	77.0	9.9
Viet Nam	66.6 (2002)	69.5 (2014)	24.0	30.1 (2014)	75.0	65.0	1.6
The Pacific							
Cook Islands	...	76.2 (2015)	47.0 (2001)	67.0 (2015)	...	...	– (2012)
Fiji	...	74.5 (2015)	34.8 (2002)	23.1 (2016)	64.0	76.0	2.9
Kiribati	...	35.8 (2009)	42.0	49.0 (2010)	41.0	88.0	16.7
Marshall Islands	80.5 (2007)	...	127.0 (2005)	84.5 (2011)	...	...	7.6 (2012)
Micronesia, Federated States of	66.0 (2002)	...	57.9	...	47.0	93.0	3.6
Nauru	42.5 (2007)	...	71.0	94.0 (2015)	...	...	– (2012)
Niue	...	...	34.9 (2001)	20.0 (2011)	...	...	– (2012)
Palau	...	39.4 (2015)	23.0 (2001)	33.8	...	...	4.8 (2012)
Papua New Guinea	40.6 (2007)	49.2 (2018)	70.0	68.0 (2016)	40.0	90.0	16.3
Samoa	...	39.4 (2014)	33.6 (2001)	39.2 (2011)	58.0	62.0	1.5
Solomon Islands	60.0 (2007)	38.0 (2015)	70.0 (2004)	78.0 (2013)	47.0	67.0	6.2
Tonga	...	47.9 (2012)	18.7	30.0 (2011)	58.0	57.0	1.4
Tuvalu	41.0 (2007)	55.3 (2015)	42.0 (2007)	26.6 (2016)	...	...	(2012)
Vanuatu	...	50.7 (2013)	...	51.2 (2013)	48.0	76.0	10.4
Developed ADB Member Economies							
Australia	...	...	17.8	10.1	87.0	17.0	0.1
Japan	...	...	5.4	3.4	83.0	43.0	0.2
New Zealand	...	...	28.2	13.8 (2018)	87.0	14.0	0.1

... = data not available, – = magnitude equals zero, ADB = Asian Development Bank.

a Data refer to crude suicide rates (per 100,000 population).

b The universal health coverage service coverage index is calculated as the geometric mean of 14 tracer indicators of health service coverage. The index is reported on a unitless scale of 0 to 100, with 100 being the optimal value. The reported values do not directly translate to the percentage of the population covered by universal health coverage services, but they can be viewed as performance scores.

Sources: For Indicators 3.4.1, 3.4.2, 3.6.1, 3.7.1, 3.7.2, 3.8.1, 3.9.1, and 3.9.2: United Nations Statistics Division. Global SDG Indicators Database. https://unstats.un.org/sdgs/indicators/database/ (accessed 14 July 2020). For Indicator 3.4.1 for Nauru and Niue: Pacific Community. Pacific Data Hub: SDG Dashboard. https://pacificdata.org/content/17-goals-transform-pacific (accessed 17 July 2020). For Indicator 3.4.2 for Taipei,China: Government of Taipei,China, Ministry of Health and Welfare. Cause of Death Statistics 2018. https://www.mohw.gov.tw/lp-4650-2.html (accessed 9 July 2020). For Indicator 3.7.1 for Cook Islands, Fiji, Federated States of Micronesia, Palau, and 2015 for Tuvalu: Pacific Community. Pacific Data Hub: SDG Dashboard. https://pacificdata.org/content/17-goals-transform-pacific (accessed 17 July 2020). For Indicator 3.9.2 for Cook Islands, Marshall Islands, Nauru, Niue, Palau, and Tuvalu: Pacific Community. Pacific Data Hub: SDG Dashboard. https://pacificdata.org/content/17-goals-transform-pacific (accessed 17 July 2020).

Click on the indictor name in the table header to access the time series in the Key Indicators Database.

Goal 4. Ensure inclusive and equitable quality education and promote lifelong learning opportunities for all

Table 1.4.1: Selected Indicators for Sustainable Development Goal 4—Early Childhood Education

ADB Regional Member	Target 4.2: By 2030, ensure that all girls and boys have access to quality early childhood development, care, and preprimary education, so that they are ready for primary education											
	4.2.2: Participation Rate in Organized Learning (1 Year before the Official Primary Entry Age)[a] (%)											
	2000						2018					
	Total		Female		Male		Total		Female		Male	
Developing ADB Member Economies												
Central and West Asia												
Afghanistan	...		...		...		...		...		...	
Armenia	...		...		...		47.5		49.5		45.8	
Azerbaijan	15.8		16.1		15.6		69.1		68.6		69.5	
Georgia	49.9	(2004)	54.1	(2004)	46.2	(2004)	...		...		...	
Kazakhstan	...		...		...		90.4	(2019)	92.2	(2019)	88.7	(2019)
Kyrgyz Republic	42.4		43.2		41.6		91.3		91.7		90.8	
Pakistan	...		...		...		93.9		87.3		100.0	
Tajikistan	...		...		...		12.5	(2017)	11.6	(2017)	13.4	(2017)
Turkmenistan	...		...		...		...		...		...	
Uzbekistan	...		...		...		36.7		36.5		37.0	
East Asia												
China, People's Republic of	...		...		...		...		...		...	
Hong Kong, China	...		...		...		96.9		100.0		94.2	
Korea, Republic of	...		...		...		95.9	(2017)	96.0	(2017)	95.7	(2017)
Mongolia	96.5	(2007)	100.0	(2007)	93.1	(2007)	94.1		94.5		93.8	
Taipei,China	...		...		...		...		...		...	
South Asia												
Bangladesh	...		...		...		36.6	(2010)	36.7	(2010)	36.6	(2010)
Bhutan	...		...		...		34.6		35.4		33.9	
India	...		...		...		...		...		...	
Maldives	69.9		70.4		69.5		96.2	(2017)	96.6	(2017)	95.8	(2017)
Nepal	...		...		...		87.0	(2019)	82.9	(2019)	91.0	(2019)
Sri Lanka	...		...		...		...		...		...	
Southeast Asia												
Brunei Darussalam	97.5	(2006)	94.9	(2006)	100.0	(2006)	94.1		94.1		94.1	
Cambodia	26.5	(2006)	27.2	(2006)	25.9	(2006)	43.0	(2012)	43.6	(2012)	42.4	(2012)
Indonesia	...		...		...		95.8		100.0		91.8	
Lao People's Democratic Republic	...		...		...		66.9		67.2		66.7	
Malaysia	78.1		79.3	(2002)	74.6	(2002)	99.3	(2015)	100.0	(2015)	98.6	(2015)
Myanmar	...		...		...		...		...		...	
Philippines	24.0	(2001)	23.8	(2001)	24.1	(2001)	83.0	(2017)	83.6	(2017)	82.4	(2017)
Singapore	...		...		...		...		...		...	
Thailand	98.9	(2006)	100.0	(2006)	97.9	(2006)	95.7	(2015)	91.1	(2015)	100.0	(2015)
Timor-Leste	...		...		...		42.6		42.3		43.0	
Viet Nam	79.3	(2006)	...		...		99.9		99.8		100.0	
The Pacific												
Cook Islands	...		...		...		97.8	(2016)	100.0	(2016)	95.8	(2016)
Fiji	48.6	(2004)	50.3	(2004)	47.1	(2004)	...		...		...	
Kiribati	...		...		...		...		...		...	
Marshall Islands	...		...		...		63.5	(2016)	62.2	(2016)	64.7	(2016)
Micronesia, Federated States of	...		...		...		73.0	(2015)	68.1	(2015)	77.8	(2015)
Nauru	89.0	(2007)	77.8	(2007)	100.0	(2007)	97.8	(2016)	97.0	(2016)	98.5	(2016)
Niue	...		...		...		63.4	(2015)	100.0	(2015)	29.3	(2015)
Palau	...		...		...		90.9	(2014)	81.3	(2014)	100.0	(2014)
Papua New Guinea	...		...		...		71.4	(2016)	71.1	(2016)	71.8	(2016)
Samoa	...		...		...		38.0		41.9		34.3	
Solomon Islands	...		...		...		58.7		60.1		57.4	
Tonga	...		...		...		...		...		...	
Tuvalu	...		...		...		88.0		90.8		85.4	
Vanuatu	...		...		...		...		...		...	
Developed ADB Member Economies												
Australia	52.8	(2001)	53.5	(2001)	52.1	(2001)	86.4	(2017)	86.1	(2017)	86.7	(2017)
Japan	...		...		...		...		...		...	
New Zealand	...		...		...		91.8	(2016)	92.2	(2016)	91.4	(2016)

... = data not available, ADB = Asian Development Bank.

a   The indicator measures the exposure of children to organized learning, but not to the intensity of the learning programs. Participation in both early childhood and primary education are included.

Source: United Nations Statistics Division. Global SDG Indicators Database. https://unstats.un.org/sdgs/indicators/database/ (accessed 15 July 2020).

Goal 4. Ensure inclusive and equitable quality education and promote lifelong learning opportunities for all

Table 1.4.2: Selected Indicators for Sustainable Development Goal 4—Teacher Training and Supply

ADB Regional Member	Target 4.c: By 2030, substantially increase the supply of qualified teachers, including through international cooperation for teacher training in developing countries, especially least developed countries and small island developing states							
	4.c.1.a: Proportion of Teachers in Preprimary Education Who Have Received at least the Minimum Organized Teacher Training (% of total teachers)		4.c.1.b: Proportion of Teachers in Primary Education Who Have Received at least the Minimum Organized Teacher Training (% of total teachers)		4.c.1.c: Proportion of Teachers in Lower Secondary Education Who Have Received at least the Minimum Organized Teacher Training (% of total teachers)		4.c.1.d: Proportion of Teachers in Upper Secondary Education Who Have Received at least the Minimum Organized Teacher Training (% of total teachers)	
	2000	2018	2000	2018	2000	2018	2000	2018
Developing ADB Member Economies								
Central and West Asia								
Afghanistan	...	...	...	...	...	...	...	...
Armenia	97.1 (2002)	82.0 (2017)	66.7 (2004)	...	...	...	...	...
Azerbaijan	79.1	91.3	99.9	99.5	...	99.8	...	71.9
Georgia	99.1	...	94.7	...	76.8	...	93.0	...
Kazakhstan	...	100.0 (2014)	...	100.0 (2019)	...	...	...	...
Kyrgyz Republic	32.1	46.2 (2011)	52.0 (2003)	95.4 (2017)	...	...	...	...
Pakistan	...	...	78.0 (2004)	78.0	...	58.2	...	...
Tajikistan	91.3 (2001)	100.0 (2016)	81.6 (2001)	100.0 (2017)	94.0 (2003)	...	94.3 (2003)	...
Turkmenistan	...	...	...	...	...	...	...	...
Uzbekistan	100.0 (2006)	98.8	100.0 (2006)	99.0	...	99.2	...	90.4
East Asia								
China, People's Republic of	...	...	...	...	...	...	...	...
Hong Kong, China	74.3	96.5	87.5	96.6	...	...	...	...
Korea, Republic of	...	...	...	...	...	...	...	...
Mongolia	100.0	96.9	100.0	93.3	100.0	...	100.0	...
Taipei,China	...	...	...	...	...	...	...	...
South Asia								
Bangladesh	...	...	53.4 (2005)	50.4 (2017)	36.8	67.2 (2016)	22.4	58.5 (2016)
Bhutan	93.8	100.0	94.8	100.0	93.5 (2005)	100.0	72.2 (2008)	100.0
India	...	...	...	69.8 (2017)	...	71.8	...	76.4 (2017)
Maldives	47.2	87.9 (2017)	66.5	90.1 (2017)	76.3	96.8 (2017)	54.3 (2002)	...
Nepal	...	83.4 (2019)	15.4 (2001)	97.3 (2019)	32.6	85.4 (2019)	63.9 (2008)	81.3 (2019)
Sri Lanka	...	51.0	...	82.8	...	85.3	...	78.7
Southeast Asia								
Brunei Darussalam	64.4 (2005)	61.5	84.5 (2005)	86.4	...	91.2	...	88.3
Cambodia	98.1 (2001)	100.0	95.9 (2001)	100.0	99.7 (2001)	100.0	99.1 (2001)	...
Indonesia	...	...	...	...	...	...	...	...
Lao People's Democratic Republic	83.1	90.1	76.7	97.0	98.5	94.8	95.6	98.4
Malaysia	...	96.6	97.9	97.3	...	...	...	...
Myanmar	50.3 (2006)	81.4	62.7	95.3	62.1	89.5	97.1	87.7
Philippines	...	100.0 (2017)	...	100.0 (2017)	...	100.0 (2017)	...	100.0 (2017)
Singapore	...	...	99.2 (2007)	99.0 (2017)	...	...	...	...
Thailand	...	...	...	100.0	...	100.0	...	100.0
Timor-Leste	...	...	...	...	...	...	...	...
Viet Nam	50.5	99.2	80.0	99.9	86.3	99.0	...	...
The Pacific								
Cook Islands	60.9 (2005)	78.1 (2016)	79.2 (2007)	95.3 (2016)	...	...	...	...
Fiji	...	...	97.8 (2008)	100.0 (2012)	...	100.0 (2012)	94.8 (2008)	100.0 (2012)
Kiribati	...	...	93.9 (2005)	72.7 (2016)	83.6 (2005)	86.7 (2014)	43.1 (2005)	...
Marshall Islands	100.0 (2002)	...	...	...	...	...	...	...
Micronesia, Federated States of	...	...	...	...	...	...	...	...
Nauru	77.5 (2006)	100.0 (2016)	74.2 (2007)	100.0 (2016)	...	100.0 (2016)	...	100.0 (2016)
Niue	...	100.0 (2016)	...	92.3 (2016)	...	80.0 (2016)	...	100.0 (2015)
Palau	...	...	...	...	...	...	...	...
Papua New Guinea	...	...	...	...	...	100.0 (2012)	...	100.0 (2012)
Samoa	...	100.0	...	...	...	...	71.9 (2009)	79.5 (2016)
Solomon Islands	...	24.9	...	76.1	...	86.6 (2017)	...	63.0 (2015)
Tonga	...	100.0 (2012)	...	92.5 (2015)	...	...	...	...
Tuvalu	...	91.3	...	80.0	...	67.1	...	62.0
Vanuatu	100.0 (2007)	46.0 (2015)	100.0 (2007)	...	...	21.5 (2015)	...	...
Developed ADB Member Economies								
Australia	...	...	...	...	...	...	...	...
Japan	...	...	...	...	...	...	...	...
New Zealand	...	...	...	...	...	...	...	...

... = data not available, ADB = Asian Development Bank.

Source: United Nations Statistics Division. Global SDG Indicators Database. https://unstats.un.org/sdgs/indicators/database/ (accessed 17 July 2020).

Click on the indictor name in the table header to access the time series in the Key Indicators Database.

Table 1.5.1: Selected Indicators for Sustainable Development Goal 5—Early Marriage and Women in Leadership

ADB Regional Member	Target 5.3: Eliminate all harmful practices such as child, early, and forced marriage, and female genital mutilation				Target 5.5: Ensure women's full and effective participation in, and equal opportunities for leadership at, all levels of decision-making in political, economic, and public life		
	5.3.1: Proportion of Women Aged 20–24 Years Who Were Married or in a Union (%)				5.5.1.a: Proportion of Seats Held by Women in National Parliaments (%)		5.5.2: Proportion of Women in Managerial Positions (%)
	Before Age 15		Before Age 18				
	2000	2017	2000	2017	2000	2019	2018
Developing ADB Member Economies							
Central and West Asia[a]	...	...	...	...	7.0	21.2	...
Afghanistan	...	4.2	...	28.3	27.3 (2006)	27.3	4.1 (2017)
Armenia	...	0.0 (2016)	...	5.3 (2016)	3.1	24.2	28.7 (2017)
Azerbaijan	...	1.9 (2011)	...	11.0 (2011)	10.4	16.8	38.1
Georgia	...	0.3 (2018)	...	13.9 (2018)	7.2	14.8	35.7
Kazakhstan	...	0.2 (2015)	...	7.0 (2015)	10.4	27.1	37.0 (2017)
Kyrgyz Republic	...	0.3 (2018)	...	12.9 (2018)	1.4	19.2	37.8
Pakistan	...	3.6 (2018)	...	18.3 (2018)	21.6 (2003)	20.2	4.9
Tajikistan	...	0.1	...	8.7	2.8	19.1	14.8 (2009)
Turkmenistan	...	0.0 (2016)	...	5.7 (2016)	26.0	25.0	...
Uzbekistan	0.3 (2006)	...	7.2 (2006)	...	6.8	16.0	...
East Asia[a]	...	...	...	...	19.9	24.1	...
China, People's Republic of	...	...	...	...	21.8	24.9	...
Hong Kong, China	...	...	...	...	...	...	...
Korea, Republic of	...	...	...	...	3.7	17.1	14.5
Mongolia	...	0.9 (2018)	...	12.0 (2018)	7.9	17.1	39.0
Taipei,China	...	...	...	...			
South Asia[a]	...	...	...	...	7.2	16.7	...
Bangladesh	...	22.4 (2014)	...	58.6 (2014)	9.1	20.7	10.7 (2017)
Bhutan	...	6.2 (2010)	...	25.8 (2010)	2.0	14.9	18.5 (2015)
India	...	6.6 (2016)	...	27.3 (2016)	9.0	12.6	13.7
Maldives	...	0.0	...	2.2	6.0	4.7	19.6 (2016)
Nepal	...	7.0 (2016)	...	39.5 (2016)	5.9	32.7	13.2 (2017)
Sri Lanka	...	0.9 (2016)	...	9.8 (2016)	4.9	5.3	27.6 (2017)
Southeast Asia[a]	...	...	...	...	12.3	19.6	...
Brunei Darussalam	...	...	...	...	...	9.1	41.3 (2017)
Cambodia	...	1.9 (2014)	...	18.5 (2014)	8.2	20.0	30.9 (2012)
Indonesia	...	2.0	...	16.3	8.0	18.2	27.5 (2017)
Lao People's Democratic Republic	...	7.1	...	32.7	21.2	27.5	31.8 (2010)
Malaysia	...	...	...	...	7.3	14.4	24.7
Myanmar	...	1.9 (2015)	...	16.0 (2015)	...	11.3	32.3
Philippines	...	2.2	...	16.5	12.4	29.5	52.7
Singapore	...	...	...	...	4.3	23.0	36.4
Thailand	...	4.4 (2015)	...	22.5 (2015)	5.6	5.4	33.9
Timor-Leste	...	2.6 (2016)	...	14.9 (2016)	26.1 (2003)	40.0	24.5 (2016)
Viet Nam	...	0.9 (2014)	...	10.6 (2014)	26.0	26.7	27.3
The Pacific[a]	...	...	...	...	3.6	6.1	...
Cook Islands	...	...	...	...	...	...	...
Fiji	...	...	...	...	11.3	19.6	38.9 (2016)
Kiribati	...	2.8 (2009)	...	20.3 (2009)	4.9	6.5	37.2 (2015)
Marshall Islands	5.5 (2007)	...	26.3 (2007)	...	3.0	9.1	...
Micronesia, Federated States of	...	...	...	...	0.0	0.0	20.3 (2014)
Nauru	1.9 (2007)	...	26.8 (2007)	...	0.0	10.5	36.1 (2013)
Niue	...	...	...	...	...	...	...
Palau	...	...	...	...	0.0	12.5	29.9 (2014)
Papua New Guinea	...	8.0 (2018)	...	27.3 (2018)	1.8	0.0	18.1 (2010)
Samoa	...	0.7 (2014)	...	10.8 (2014)	8.2	10.0	43.1 (2017)
Solomon Islands	...	5.6 (2015)	...	21.3 (2015)	2.0	2.0	25.7 (2013)
Tonga	...	0.3 (2012)	...	5.6 (2012)	0.0	7.4	...
Tuvalu	0.0 (2007)	...	9.9 (2007)	...	0.0	6.7	35.9 (2016)
Vanuatu	...	2.5 (2013)	...	21.4 (2013)	0.0	0.0	28.5 (2009)
Developed ADB Member Economies[a]	...	...	...	...	11.9	19.1	...
Australia	...	...	...	...	22.5	30.0	37.8
Japan	...	...	...	...	4.6	10.2	14.9
New Zealand	...	...	...	...	29.2	40.0	...
DEVELOPING ADB MEMBER ECONOMIES[a]	...	...	...	...	13.2	20.3	...
ALL ADB REGIONAL MEMBERS[a]	...	...	...	...	13.1	20.2	...

... = data not available, 0.0 = magnitude is less than half of unit employed, ADB = Asian Development Bank.

a   Aggregates for proportion of seats held by women in national parliaments are estimated as a weighted average based on the number of parliamentary seats in reporting economies.

Sources: United Nations Statistics Division. Global SDG Indicators Database. https://unstats.un.org/sdgs/indicators/database (accessed 9 July 2020). For indicator 5.5.1.a for Afghanistan and Bangladesh: Inter-Parliamentary Union. Women in National Parliaments. http://archive.ipu.org/wmn-e/classif-arc.htm (accessed 31 July 2020).

Click on the indictor name in the table header to access the time series in the Key Indicators Database.

Goal 6. Ensure availability and sustainable management of water and sanitation for all

Table 1.6.1: Selected Indicators for Sustainable Development Goal 6—Clean Water and Sanitation

| ADB Regional Member | Target 6.1: By 2030, achieve universal and equitable access to safe and affordable drinking water for all 6.1.1: Proportion of Population Using Safely Managed Drinking Water Services (%) | | | | | |
| | 2000 | | | 2017 | | |
	Total	Urban	Rural	Total	Urban	Rural
Developing ADB Member Economies						
Central and West Asia						
Afghanistan	...	...	...	...	...	...
Armenia	29.6	...	...	86.5	...	...
Azerbaijan	49.7	...	...	73.6	...	...
Georgia	74.6	...	...	80.0	...	...
Kazakhstan	57.5	...	...	89.5	...	...
Kyrgyz Republic	46.4	80.4	27.8	68.2	93.5	53.9
Pakistan	37.9	50.6	31.6	35.3	40.0	32.6
Tajikistan	35.2	...	...	47.9	...	...
Turkmenistan	65.9	84.4	50.2	93.9	96.9	90.7
Uzbekistan	56.3	84.2	32.5	58.9	86.1	31.1
East Asia						
China, People's Republic of	...	93.3	...	...	92.3	...
Hong Kong, China	79.4	79.4	...	100.0	100.0	...
Korea, Republic of	96.8 (2002)	...	...	98.2	...	...
Mongolia	22.3	...	...	23.7	...	...
Taipei,China	...	...	...	...	...	...
South Asia						
Bangladesh	55.9	44.6	59.4	55.4	44.6	61.5
Bhutan	28.6	48.6	21.7	36.2	48.9	27.6
India	...	...	19.6	...	...	56.0
Maldives	...	...	...	...	...	...
Nepal	23.9	34.9	22.2	27.2	34.1	25.6
Sri Lanka	...	86.1	...	...	90.8	...
Southeast Asia						
Brunei Darussalam	...	...	...	...	...	...
Cambodia	16.9	43.4	10.8	25.8	56.6	16.7
Indonesia	...	...	...	...	...	...
Lao People's Democratic Republic	5.1	21.5	0.5	16.1	26.3	10.8
Malaysia	93.0	...	...	93.3	...	...
Myanmar	...	...	...	...	...	...
Philippines	36.0	53.1	21.4	46.7	61.5	33.7
Singapore	100.0	100.0	...	100.0	100.0	...
Thailand	...	...	...	...	...	...
Timor-Leste	...	...	...	...	...	...
Viet Nam	...	...	...	...	...	...
The Pacific						
Cook Islands	...	...	...	...	...	...
Fiji	...	...	...	...	...	...
Kiribati	...	...	...	...	...	...
Marshall Islands	...	...	...	...	...	...
Micronesia, Federated States of	...	...	...	...	...	...
Nauru	...	...	...	...	...	...
Niue	98.2	...	...	97.2	...	...
Palau	...	...	...	...	...	...
Papua New Guinea	...	...	...	...	...	...
Samoa	57.1	...	...	58.8	...	...
Solomon Islands	...	...	...	...	...	...
Tonga	...	...	...	...	...	...
Tuvalu	...	49.2 (2001)	...	...	49.8	...
Vanuatu	39.6	...	...	44.1	...	...
Developed ADB Member Economies						
Australia	...	98.2	...	...	98.8	...
Japan	97.9	...	...	98.5	...	...
New Zealand	78.1	...	...	100.0	...	...

Goal 6. Ensure availability and sustainable management of water and sanitation for all

Table 1.6.1: Selected Indicators for Sustainable Development Goal 6—Clean Water and Sanitation (*continued*)

ADB Regional Member	Target 6.2: By 2030, achieve access to adequate and equitable sanitation and hygiene for all and end open defecation, paying special attention to the needs of women and girls and those in vulnerable situations 6.2.1a: Proportion of Population Using Safely Managed Sanitation Services (%)					
	2000			2017		
	Total	Urban	Rural	Total	Urban	Rural
Developing ADB Member Economies						
Central and West Asia						
Afghanistan	...	...	...	...	...	...
Armenia	47.4	45.4	...	48.2	45.3	...
Azerbaijan	...	70.2	...	...	92.2	...
Georgia	22.1	5.1	...	27.2	15.9	...
Kazakhstan	...	92.8	...	...	90.5	...
Kyrgyz Republic	...	...	...	...	...	...
Pakistan	...	...	...	...	...	...
Tajikistan	...	...	...	...	...	...
Turkmenistan	...	...	...	...	...	...
Uzbekistan	...	...	...	...	...	...
East Asia						
China, People's Republic of	26.6	29.4	25.0	72.1	83.7	56.1
Hong Kong, China	92.1	92.1	...	91.8	91.8	...
Korea, Republic of	85.9	...	...	99.9	...	...
Mongolia	...	...	...	...	...	...
Taipei,China	...	...	...	...	...	...
South Asia						
Bangladesh	...	...	13.8	...	...	32.3
Bhutan	...	...	...	...	...	...
India	...	...	1.6	...	...	39.0
Maldives	...	...	...	...	...	...
Nepal	...	...	...	...	...	...
Sri Lanka	...	...	...	...	...	...
Southeast Asia						
Brunei Darussalam	...	...	...	...	...	...
Cambodia	...	...	...	...	...	...
Indonesia	...	...	...	...	...	...
Lao People's Democratic Republic	21.8	45.9	15.0	58.1	62.4	55.8
Malaysia	77.8	...	...	88.6	...	...
Myanmar	...	...	...	...	...	...
Philippines	41.5	48.3	35.7	51.6	54.0	49.6
Singapore	100.0	100.0	...	100.0	100.0	...
Thailand	...	...	...	...	...	...
Timor-Leste	...	...	...	...	...	...
Viet Nam	...	...	...	...	...	...
The Pacific						
Cook Islands	...	...	...	...	...	...
Fiji	...	...	...	...	...	...
Kiribati	...	...	...	...	...	...
Marshall Islands	...	...	...	...	...	...
Micronesia, Federated States of	...	...	...	...	...	...
Nauru	...	...	...	...	...	...
Niue	...	...	...	...	...	...
Palau	...	...	...	...	...	...
Papua New Guinea	...	...	...	...	...	...
Samoa	49.4	40.5	52.0	48.5	37.7	50.9
Solomon Islands	...	...	...	...	...	...
Tonga	...	...	...	...	...	...
Tuvalu	4.7 (2001)	5.2 (2001)	4.3 (2001)	6.3	4.2	9.7
Vanuatu	...	...	...	...	...	...
Developed ADB Member Economies						
Australia	64.2	...	...	75.6	...	...
Japan	97.4	...	...	98.8	...	...
New Zealand	78.6	...	...	88.7	...	...

Goal 6: Ensure availability and sustainable management of water and sanitation for all

Table 1.6.1: Selected Indicators for Sustainable Development Goal 6—Clean Water and Sanitation (continued)

ADB Regional Member	Target 6.4: By 2030, substantially increase water-use efficiency across all sectors and ensure sustainable withdrawals and supply of freshwater to address water scarcity and substantially reduce the number of people suffering from water scarcity		Target 6.a: By 2030, expand international cooperation and capacity-building support to developing countries in water- and sanitation-related activities and programmes, including water harvesting, desalination, water efficiency, wastewater treatment, and recycling and reuse technologies	
	6.4.2: Level of Water Stress: Freshwater Withdrawal as a Proportion of Available Freshwater Resources (%)		6.a.1: Amount of Water- and Sanitation-Related Official Development Assistance as Part of a Government-Coordinated Spending Plan ($ million)	
	2000	2017	2000	2018
Developing ADB Member Economies				
Central and West Asia				
Afghanistan	54.8	...	4.5	138.2
Armenia	37.7	57.8	13.5	65.2
Azerbaijan	49.1	56.4	51.8	108.3
Georgia	6.2	5.9	0.8	61.1
Kazakhstan	29.1	31.1	7.6	0.7
Kyrgyz Republic	65.4	50.0 (2014)	14.5	8.4
Pakistan	105.9	122.7	15.4	219.3
Tajikistan	74.9	68.7	16.1	71.8
Turkmenistan	127.9	143.6 (2013)	0.0	0.3 (2011)
Uzbekistan	153.1	168.9	2.3	97.9
East Asia				
China, People's Republic of	40.2	43.2	577.1	74.3
Hong Kong, China	...	...	...	...
Korea, Republic of	80.8	85.2 (2014)	...	...
Mongolia	3.6	3.4	0.3	24.4
Taipei,China	...	...	...	...
South Asia				
Bangladesh	5.7 (2008)	5.7	89.1	279.1
Bhutan	1.4 (2008)	1.4	5.3	19.9
India	62.7	66.5	180.7	594.9
Maldives	17.7	15.7	0.6 (2001)	11.2
Nepal	8.4	8.3 (2015)	61.6	136.2
Sri Lanka	91.2	90.8 (2014)	33.3	179.7
Southeast Asia				
Brunei Darussalam	3.5	...	...	...
Cambodia	1.0 (2006)	1.0 (2015)	24.2	130.3
Indonesia	15.1	29.7	87.5	120.0
Lao People's Democratic Republic	2.3 (2005)	4.8	39.0	70.0
Malaysia	4.8	3.4	534.0	2.4
Myanmar	5.8	...	1.5	114.6
Philippines	24.1 (2006)	28.4	20.9	115.3
Singapore	62.4	83.2	...	...
Thailand	23.0 (2007)	23.0 (2016)	79.0	1.6
Timor-Leste	28.3 (2004)	28.3 (2013)	3.9	2.6
Viet Nam	15.9	18.1 (2014)	174.2	559.7
The Pacific				
Cook Islands	...	...	0.4	6.8
Fiji	0.3	0.3 (2014)	0.4	2.1
Kiribati	...	...	0.6 (2001)	3.9
Marshall Islands	...	...	0.0 (2003)	1.9
Micronesia, Federated States of	...	...	0.0 (2003)	0.2
Nauru	...	...	0.0 (2005)	0.1
Niue	...	...	0.1 (2002)	0.0 (2017)
Palau	...	...	0.0 (2003)	6.9
Papua New Guinea	0.1	0.1 (2015)	12.7	33.9
Samoa	...	...	0.2	19.3
Solomon Islands	...	...	2.2	9.9
Tonga	...	...	10.4	1.1
Tuvalu	...	...	0.5 (2002)	0.1
Vanuatu	...	...	0.5 (2003)	1.5
Developed ADB Member Economies				
Australia	8.7	6.4	...	...
Japan	41.6	37.3	...	...
New Zealand	2.8	8.0	...	...

... = data not available, 0.0 = magnitude is less than half of unit employed, $ = United States dollars, ADB = Asian Development Bank.

Source: United Nations Statistics Division. Global SDG Indicators Database. https://unstats.un.org/sdgs/indicators/database/ (accessed 20 July 2020).

Click on the indictor name in the table header to access the time series in the Key Indicators Database.

Goal 7. Ensure access to affordable, reliable, sustainable and modern energy for all

Table 1.7.1: Selected Indicators for Sustainable Development Goal 7—Affordable and Clean Energy

ADB Regional Member	Target 7.1: By 2030, ensure universal access to affordable, reliable, and modern energy services						Target 7.2: By 2030, increase substantially the share of renewable energy in the global energy mix		Target 7.3: By 2030, double the global rate of improvement in energy efficiency	
	7.1.1: Proportion of Population with Access to Electricity (%)						7.1.2: Proportion of Population with Primary Reliance on Clean Fuels and Technology (%)		7.2.1: Renewable Energy Share in Total Final Energy Consumption (%)		7.3.1: Energy Intensity Measured in Terms of Primary Energy and GDP (MJ/$ 2011 PPP GDP)	
	Total		Urban		Rural							
	2000	2018	2000	2018	2000	2018	2000	2018	2000	2017	2000	2017
Developing ADB Member Economies												
Central and West Asia												
Afghanistan	23.0a	98.7	74.0a	100.0	8.0a	98.3	11.0	37.0	54.2	24.7	1.7	1.9
Armenia	98.9	100.0	99.1	100.0	98.5	100.0	79.0	>95	7.2	12.5	9.4	5.2
Azerbaijan	98.9	100.0	99.7	100.0	98.1	100.0	70.0	>95	2.1	1.9	12.8	3.8
Georgia	99.9b	100.0	100.0b	100.0	99.8b	100.0	49.0	81.0	47.3	28.7	8.4	5.6
Kazakhstan	99.1	100.0	99.6	100.0	98.4	100.0	84.0	>95	2.5	1.6	10.1	8.2
Kyrgyz Republic	99.8	100.0	99.8	100.0	99.7	100.0	53.0	77.0	35.2	24.5	9.6	7.7
Pakistan	70.4	71.1	93.8	100.0	58.9	54.4	24.0	44.0	51.0	41.4	5.5	4.4
Tajikistan	98.5	99.3	99.7	99.2	98.0	99.3	39.0	81.0	62.4	41.7	12.2	5.2
Turkmenistan	99.6	100.0	99.7	100.0	99.5	100.0	>95	>95	0.1	0.1	25.9	12.3
Uzbekistan	99.6	100.0	99.8	100.0	99.4	100.0	84.0	85.0	0.8	2.4	34.1	7.2
East Asia												
China, People's Republic of	96.9	100.0	100.0	100.0	95.2	100.0	43.0	64.0	29.6	12.8	10.2	6.1
Hong Kong, China	100.0	100.0	100.0	100.0	100.0	100.0	...	...	0.6	0.8	2.5	1.4
Korea, Republic of	100.0	100.0	100.0	100.0	100.0	100.0	>95	>95	0.7	2.8	8.1	6.4
Mongolia	67.3	98.1	97.5	99.7	27.1	94.6	23.0	50.0	5.7	3.6	9.0	5.9
Taipei,China	...	...	...	...	...	...	...	...	1.3	2.1c	...	...
South Asia												
Bangladesh	32.0	85.2	81.2	97.1	16.8	78.3	8.0	24.0	59.0	32.0	3.6	2.9
Bhutan	31.2	100.0	96.7	100.0	8.8	100.0	28.0	77.0	91.4	83.4	21.8	9.7
India	59.1	95.2	88.9	99.7	47.7	92.9	23.0	49.0	51.8	32.2	6.5	4.2
Maldives	83.8	100.0	98.7	100.0	78.1	100.0	56.0	>95	2.3	1.2	2.4	3.3
Nepal	27.7	93.9	84.5	95.8	18.9	93.5	7.0	29.0	88.3	76.6	9.3	7.8
Sri Lanka	63.6d	99.6	85.3d	100.0	58.7d	99.5	21.0	31.0	64.2	48.4	3.4	2.0
Southeast Asia												
Brunei Darussalam	100.0	100.0	100.0	100.0	100.0	100.0	>95	>95	–	0.0	3.7	4.9
Cambodia	16.6	91.6	60.6	100.0	6.6	89.0	<5	22.0	81.1	61.5	8.5	5.8
Indonesia	86.3	98.5	95.4	99.9	79.7	96.8	6.0	80.0	45.6	35.0	5.3	3.5
Lao People's Democratic Republic	43.1	97.9	95.9	99.5	28.2	97.1	<5	7.0	81.6	45.9	4.4	5.4
Malaysia	99.3e	100.0	99.9e	100.0	97.9e	100.0	>95	>95	4.5	5.2	5.4	4.2
Myanmar	47.0b	66.3	83.1b	92.2	33.4b	54.8	<5	28.0	80.2	60.6	8.9	3.2
Philippines	74.8	94.9	89.7	97.5	62.0	92.5	38.0	46.0	34.9	23.4	5.1	3.1
Singapore	100.0	100.0	100.0	100.0	100.0	100.0	>95	>95	0.3	0.7	3.7	3.1
Thailand	82.1	100.0	99.9	100.0	74.0	100.0	63.0	79.0	22.0	22.7	5.2	5.1
Timor-Leste	25.6d	85.6	71.7d	100.0	10.6d	79.2	<5	12.0	–	19.0	1.3b	0.9
Viet Nam	87.2	100.0	99.0	100.0	83.4	100.0	13.0	64.0	58.0	32.0	5.9	5.6
The Pacific												
Cook Islandsf	97.5d	100.0	98.5g	100.0	...	...	81.0	77.0	–	1.7	...	...
Fiji	75.8	99.6	91.6	99.9	61.2	99.3	30.0	28.0	52.2	27.0	4.0	4.2
Kiribati	69.7a	100.0	93.6a	93.7	51.2a	100.0	<5	<5	56.5	45.8	5.5	6.3
Marshall Islands	68.6	96.4	89.2	95.7	23.5	98.4	15.0	65.0	19.6	11.8	10.5	11.0
Micronesia, Federated States of	46.0	82.1	70.0	93.5	39.1	78.7	30.0	8.0	2.0	1.6	5.8	6.1
Nauruh	99.8i	99.8	97.6i	100.0	98.1i	99.7j	86.0	90.0	–	0.8	17.1	3.5
Niue	...	100.0	...	100.0	...	...	93.0	84.0	0.6	22.4	...	...
Palau	98.9a	100.0	99.7a	100.0	97.0a	100.0	>95	>95	–	0.1	12.3	11.0
Papua New Guinea	8.7	59.0	62.9	82.1	0.4	55.5	6.0	8.0	66.4	49.7	6.5	5.1
Samoa	87.9	100.0	98.0	100.0	85.0	100.0	21.0	35.0	42.5	26.8	4.2	4.1
Solomon Islandsk	4.7	66.7	58.8	76.7	0.8b	63.5	9.0	9.0	55.2	48.7	8.7	5.5
Tonga	85.5	98.9	96.6	98.9	82.1	98.9	58.0	50.0	2.5	1.5	3.2	3.7
Tuvaluk	94.6b	100.0	95.4b	100.0	94.1l	100.0	31.0	43.0	–	13.5	3.4	3.7
Vanuatu	22.2	61.9	77.9	93.7	6.8	51.1	17.0	8.0	48.7	36.1	4.0	3.7
Developed ADB Member Economies												
Australia	100.0	100.0	100.0	100.0	100.0	100.0	>95	>95	8.4	9.5	6.7	4.8
Japan	100.0	100.0	100.0	100.0	100.0	100.0	>95	>95	3.8	6.9	5.1	3.7
New Zealand	100.0	100.0	100.0	100.0	100.0	100.0	>95	>95	29.0	30.4	6.6	5.0
WORLD	78.3	89.6	95.2	97.3	65.6	82.0	50.0	63.0	17.2	17.3	6.6	5.0

... = data not available, – = magnitude equals zero, 0.0 = magnitude is less than half of unit employed, < = less than, > = greater than, $ = United States dollars, ADB = Asian Development Bank, GDP = gross domestic product, MJ = megajoule, PPP = purchasing power parity.

a   Data are for 2005.
b   Data are for 2002.
c   Data are for 2015.
d   Data are for 2001.
e   Data are for 2009.
f   Initial year data on access to electricity in urban areas are from a different reference year relative to the overall estimate.
g   Data are for 2006.
h   Latest year data on access to electricity in rural areas are from a different reference year relative to the overall estimate.
i   Data are for 2007.
j   Data are for 2017.
k   Initial year data on access to electricity in rural areas are from a different reference year relative to the overall estimate.
l   Data are for 2003.

Sources: For Indicator 7.1.1: World Bank. World Development Indicators. https://data.worldbank.org/indicator (accessed 10 August 2020); and for Nauru (rural): United Nations Statistics Division. Global SDG Indicators Database. http://unstats.un.org/sdgs/indicators/database/ (accessed 14 July 2020). For Indicator 7.1.2, Indicator 7.2.1, and Indicator 7.3.1: United Nations Statistics Division. Global SDG Indicators Database. http://unstats.un.org/sdgs/indicators/database/ (accessed 14 July 2020); and for Taipei,China: World Bank. DataBank: Sustainable Energy for All. http://databank.worldbank.org/data/source/sustainable-energy-for-all# (accessed 28 July 2020).

Click on the indictor name in the table header to access the time series in the Key Indicators Database.

Goal 8. Promote sustained, inclusive and sustainable economic growth, full and productive employment and decent work for all

Table 1.8.1: Selected Indicators for Sustainable Development Goal 8—Decent Work and Economic Growth

ADB Regional Member	Target 8.1: Sustain per capita economic growth in accordance with national circumstances and, in particular, at least 7% gross domestic product per annum in the least developed countries 8.1.1: Annual Growth Rate of Real GDP per Capita at Constant 2015 $ (%)		Target 8.2: Achieve higher levels of economic productivity through diversification, technological upgrading and innovation, including through a focus on high-value added and labor-intensive sectors 8.2.1: Annual Growth Rate of Real GDP per Employed Person at Constant 2010 $ (%)	
	2000	2018	2000	2019
Developing ADB Member Economies				
Central and West Asia				
Afghanistan	-8.3	-4.0	-8.2	-0.4
Armenia	6.6	5.0	6.1	5.3
Azerbaijan	10.2	0.4	10.3	3.0
Georgia	4.0	5.0	3.3	5.8
Kazakhstan	10.6	2.7	8.9	3.4
Kyrgyz Republic	4.2	1.6	2.2	2.9
Pakistan	1.5	3.3	0.1	1.1
Tajikistan	6.6	4.5	5.1	2.7
Turkmenistan	4.3	4.5	1.7	5.0
Uzbekistan	2.5	3.5	-0.3	4.3
East Asia				
China, People's Republic of	7.7	6.1	7.2	6.5
Hong Kong, China	6.3	2.1	4.8	1.3
Korea, Republic of	8.1	2.5	4.4	1.9
Mongolia	0.2	4.8	-1.5	5.3
Taipei,China	...	...	5.6	2.2
South Asia				
Bangladesh	3.9	6.7	2.5	5.9
Bhutan	6.3	4.5	3.2	3.4
India	2.0	5.7	1.6	4.8
Maldives	1.7	2.9	-2.0	2.1
Nepal	4.2	4.9	4.2	3.9
Sri Lanka	5.3	2.7	5.1	2.5
Southeast Asia				
Brunei Darussalam	0.7	-1.0	-1.0	1.0
Cambodia	6.4	5.9	7.4	5.3
Indonesia	3.5	4.0	3.3	3.7
Lao People's Democratic Republic	4.1	4.6	3.5	4.4
Malaysia	6.4	3.3	5.2	2.6
Myanmar	12.4	5.6	12.3	5.4
Philippines	2.2	4.8	1.8	3.3
Singapore	6.9	2.3	5.0	–
Thailand	3.4	3.8	1.3	2.7
Timor-Leste	12.2	0.8	14.5	1.9
Viet Nam	5.6	6.0	4.3	5.8
The Pacific				
Cook Islands	14.6	5.6	...	...
Fiji	-2.3	2.8	-2.0	1.7
Kiribati	10.2	0.8	...	...
Marshall Islands	5.3	1.9	...	...
Micronesia, Federated States of	5.0	0.3	...	...
Nauru	-5.9	-4.9	...	...
Niue	...	...	...	...
Palau	-8.3	1.1	...	...
Papua New Guinea	-4.7	-2.0	-5.5	3.0
Samoa	6.6	0.3	7.7	2.6
Solomon Islands	-16.5	1.2	-17.7	-0.1
Tonga	2.6	-1.6	3.4	1.8
Tuvalu	12.8	5.7	...	...
Vanuatu	3.1	0.7	3.6	1.2
Developed ADB Member Economies				
Australia	0.8	0.7	1.3	0.8
Japan	2.6	1.0	3.1	1.2
New Zealand	1.2	1.9	0.9	1.4

... = data not available, – = magnitude equals zero, $ = United States dollars, ADB = Asian Development Bank, GDP = gross domestic product.

Sources: United Nations Statistics Division. Global SDG Indicators Database. https://unstats.un.org/sdgs/indicators/database/ (accessed 5 August 2020); For Taipei,China: International Labour Organization. ILOSTAT Database. https://ilostat.ilo.org/data/ (accessed 5 August 2020).

Goal 8. Promote sustained, inclusive, and sustainable economic growth; full and productive employment; and decent work for all

Table 1.8.2: Selected Indicators for Sustainable Development Goal 8—Unemployment

ADB Regional Member	Target 8.5: By 2030, achieve full and productive employment and decent work for all women and men, including for young people and persons with disabilities, and equal pay for work of equal value 8.5.2a: Unemployment Rate for Age Group 15+ Years, by Sex (%)					
	2000			**2019**		
	Total	**Male**	**Female**	**Total**	**Male**	**Female**
Developing ADB Member Economies						
Central and West Asia						
Afghanistan	...	...	...	...	...	...
Armenia	9.8 (2007)	9.8 (2007)	9.9 (2007)	19.0 (2018)	20.4 (2018)	17.8 (2018)
Azerbaijan	11.8	12.7	10.9	4.9	5.7	4.0
Georgia	10.8	10.5	11.1	11.6	10.1	12.8
Kazakhstan	12.8	12.1 (2001)	8.9 (2001)	4.8	5.4 (2017)	4.4 (2017)
Kyrgyz Republic	7.5	14.3 (2002)	11.2 (2002)	4.5 (2018)	5.0 (2018)	4.2 (2018)
Pakistan	0.6 (2006)	0.3 (2006)	0.6 (2006)	4.1 (2018)	4.6 (2018)	4.0 (2018)
Tajikistan	...	10.5 (2009)	12.3 (2009)	6.9 (2016)	5.5 (2016)	7.9 (2016)
Turkmenistan	...	...	...	4.0 (2010)	2.3 (2010)	5.3 (2010)
Uzbekistan	5.0 (2007)	5.9 (2009)	4.3 (2009)	9.3 (2018)	5.6 (2017)	6.0 (2017)
East Asia						
China, People's Republic of	...	...	...	...	...	...
Hong Kong, China	...	...	...	...	...	...
Korea, Republic of	4.4	3.6	5.0	3.7	3.6	3.9
Mongolia	6.2 (2002)	6.2 (2002)	6.2 (2002)	10.0	8.9	11.0
Taipei,China	3.0	2.4	3.4	3.7	3.6	3.9
South Asia						
Bangladesh	3.3	3.3	3.2	4.4 (2017)	6.7 (2017)	3.3 (2017)
Bhutan	1.9 (2001)	3.2 (2001)	1.3 (2001)	2.5 (2015)	3.2 (2015)	1.8 (2015)
India	2.7	2.4	2.8	5.3 (2018)	5.3 (2018)	5.3 (2018)
Maldives	11.7 (2009)	13.7 (2009)	10.4 (2009)	6.1 (2016)	5.6 (2016)	6.4 (2016)
Nepal	1.3 (2008)	1.1 (2008)	1.6 (2008)	11.4 (2017)	13.1 (2017)	10.3 (2017)
Sri Lanka	7.7	11.4	5.9	4.3 (2018)	6.9 (2018)	2.9 (2018)
Southeast Asia						
Brunei Darussalam	...	...	...	6.9	8.3	6.0
Cambodia	2.8	3.1	2.4	0.1 (2017)	0.2 (2017)	0.1 (2017)
Indonesia	...	...	...	3.6	3.4	3.8
Lao People's Democratic Republic	...	...	...	0.7 (2010)	0.7 (2010)	0.8 (2010)
Malaysia	3.0	3.1	3.0	3.3	3.6 (2018)	3.1 (2018)
Myanmar	...	...	...	0.5	0.6	0.4
Philippines	3.7 (2001)	4.0 (2001)	3.5 (2001)	2.2	2.5	2.0
Singapore	3.7	3.5	3.9	3.1	4.4 (2017)	4.0 (2017)
Thailand	2.4	2.3	2.4	0.7	0.7	0.7
Timor-Leste	...	...	...	4.7 (2016)	6.3 (2016)	3.3 (2016)
Viet Nam	2.3	2.1	2.4	2.0	2.0	2.1
The Pacific						
Cook Islands	...	...	...	...	...	0.0 (2016)
Fiji	8.2 (2003)	6.0 (2004)	4.1 (2004)	4.3 (2016)	5.5 (2016)	3.7 (2016)
Kiribati	...	...	...	9.3 (2015)	5.6 (2015)	11.9 (2015)
Marshall Islands	25.4 (2005)	...	...	...	...	...
Micronesia, Federated States of	...	...	...	8.9 (2014)	13.9 (2014)	5.4 (2014)
Nauru	...	...	...	13.3 (2013)	18.0 (2013)	10.0 (2013)
Niue	...	...	...	...	...	...
Palau	3.3	3.5	3.1	1.4 (2014)	1.8 (2014)	1.1 (2014)
Papua New Guinea	2.9	...	...	...	...	...
Samoa	...	...	...	14.5 (2017)	21.3 (2017)	10.6 (2017)
Solomon Islands	...	...	2.3 (2009)	0.7 (2013)	0.7 (2013)	0.7 (2013)
Tonga	5.2 (2003)	7.4 (2003)	3.8 (2003)	3.1 (2018)	3.6 (2018)	2.6 (2018)
Tuvalu	...	...	...	8.5 (2016)	16.2 (2016)	4.6 (2016)
Vanuatu	4.6 (2009)	5.2 (2009)	4.1 (2009)	1.8 (2010)	...	...
Developed ADB Member Economies						
Australia	6.3	6.1	6.5	5.2	5.1	5.2
Japan	4.7	4.5	4.9	2.4	2.2	2.5
New Zealand	6.1	6.0	6.3	4.1	4.4	3.8

Click on the indictor name in the table header to access the time series in the Key Indicators Database.

Goal 8. Promote sustained, inclusive, and sustainable economic growth; full and productive employment; and decent work for all

Table 1.8.2: Selected Indicators for Sustainable Development Goal 8—Unemployment *(continued)*

ADB Regional Member	Target 8.5: By 2030, achieve full and productive employment and decent work for all women and men, including for young people and persons with disabilities, and equal pay for work of equal value					
	8.5.2b: Unemployment Rate for Age Group 15–24 Years, by Sex (%)					
	2000			2019		
	Total	Male	Female	Total	Male	Female
Developing ADB Member Economies						
Central and West Asia						
Afghanistan	...	...	...	...	...	...
Armenia	11.7 (2007)	10.1 (2007)	12.5 (2007)	33.6 (2018)	39.0 (2018)	29.1 (2018)
Azerbaijan	22.1	25.4	19.2	12.4	14.2	10.9
Georgia	21.1	20.5	21.6	30.4	32.9	28.9
Kazakhstan	17.3 (2002)	19.3 (2002)	15.7 (2002)	3.8 (2017)	4.0 (2017)	3.6 (2017)
Kyrgyz Republic	20.1 (2002)	21.2 (2002)	19.3 (2002)	9.5 (2018)	13.4 (2018)	7.8 (2018)
Pakistan	0.9 (2006)	0.6 (2006)	1.0 (2006)	7.8 (2018)	6.8 (2018)	8.2 (2018)
Tajikistan	...	...	...	...	...	...
Turkmenistan	...	...	...	...	...	...
Uzbekistan	...	...	...	...	...	...
East Asia						
China, People's Republic of	...	...	...	...	...	...
Hong Kong, China	...	...	...	...	...	...
Korea, Republic of	10.8	9.1	13.5	10.0	9.6	10.4
Mongolia	9.8 (2008)	8.8 (2008)	10.6 (2008)	25.3	25.9	24.9
Taipei,China	...	...	...	...	...	...
South Asia						
Bangladesh	10.7	10.3	11.1	12.8 (2017)	16.8 (2017)	10.8 (2017)
Bhutan	13.0 (2009)	14.7 (2009)	10.7 (2009)	10.7 (2015)	12.7 (2015)	8.2 (2015)
India	8.1	7.0	8.4	22.5 (2018)	24.2 (2018)	22.2 (2018)
Maldives	25.4 (2009)	21.4 (2009)	29.1 (2009)	15.9 (2016)	12.1 (2016)	19.1 (2016)
Nepal	2.2 (2008)	1.6 (2008)	2.9 (2008)	21.4 (2017)	23.9 (2017)	19.7 (2017)
Sri Lanka	23.7	30.8	19.9	21.1 (2018)	29.4 (2018)	16.6 (2018)
Southeast Asia						
Brunei Darussalam	...	...	...	21.4	25.8	19.0
Cambodia	5.3	5.3	5.4	0.4 (2017)	0.4 (2017)	0.0 (2017)
Indonesia	...	...	...	13.5	13.2	13.8
Lao People's Democratic Republic	...	...	...	1.8 (2010)	1.7 (2010)	1.9 (2010)
Malaysia	...	...	...	10.9 (2018)	12.5 (2018)	9.9 (2018)
Myanmar	...	...	...	1.5	1.6	1.4
Philippines	9.7 (2001)	12.8 (2001)	7.9 (2001)	6.8	8.2	5.9
Singapore	7.7 (2001)	10.7 (2001)	5.1 (2001)	11.5	12.5 (2016)	6.2 (2016)
Thailand	6.6	6.0	7.0	4.2	5.3	3.4
Timor-Leste	...	...	...	13.2 (2016)	15.9 (2016)	10.9 (2016)
Viet Nam	4.6 (2004)	4.9 (2004)	4.4 (2004)	6.9	6.9	6.8
The Pacific						
Cook Islands	...	...	...	...	0.0 (2016)	0.0 (2016)
Fiji	9.8 (2005)	16.0 (2005)	7.1 (2005)	15.4 (2016)	22.4 (2016)	11.9 (2016)
Kiribati	...	...	...	17.1 (2015)	7.4 (2015)	22.2 (2015)
Marshall Islands	...	...	...	...	...	...
Micronesia, Federated States of	...	...	...	18.9 (2014)	29.9 (2014)	10.4 (2014)
Nauru	...	...	...	26.6 (2013)	37.5 (2013)	20.9 (2013)
Niue	...	...	...	...	...	...
Palau	9.6	10.6	8.8	5.6 (2014)	0.0 (2014)	0.0 (2014)
Papua New Guinea	5.3	...	...	...	...	...
Samoa	...	...	...	31.9 (2017)	43.4 (2017)	24.6 (2017)
Solomon Islands	...	...	...	1.3 (2013)	1.6 (2013)	1.0 (2013)
Tonga	...	...	...	8.9 (2018)	13.0 (2018)	5.7 (2018)
Tuvalu	...	...	...	20.6 (2016)	45.9 (2016)	9.8 (2016)
Vanuatu	8.9 (2009)	9.2 (2009)	8.6 (2009)	...	...	...
Developed ADB Member Economies						
Australia	12.1	11.2	12.9	11.7	10.6	12.8
Japan	9.1	7.9	10.2	3.8	3.7	3.9
New Zealand	13.5	12.4	14.5	11.2	11.3	11.0

Goal 8. Promote sustained, inclusive, and sustainable economic growth; full and productive employment; and decent work for all

Table 1.8.2: Selected Indicators for Sustainable Development Goal 8—Unemployment (continued)

ADB Regional Member	Target 8.5: By 2030, achieve full and productive employment and decent work for all women and men, including for young people and persons with disabilities, and equal pay for work of equal value					
	8.5.2c: Unemployment Rate for Age Group 25+ Years, by Sex (%)					
	2000			2019		
	Total	Male	Female	Total	Male	Female
Developing ADB Member Economies						
Central and West Asia						
Afghanistan	...	...	...	...	...	...
Armenia	9.6 (2007)	9.7 (2007)	9.5 (2007)	17.3 (2018)	18.1 (2018)	16.6 (2018)
Azerbaijan	9.1	9.6	8.6	3.8	4.6	3.1
Georgia	9.7	9.5	9.8	9.9	8.6	11.1
Kazakhstan	7.9 (2002)	9.9 (2002)	6.0 (2002)	5.0 (2017)	5.6 (2017)	4.5 (2017)
Kyrgyz Republic	10.4 (2002)	12.4 (2002)	8.8 (2002)	3.6 (2018)	3.7 (2018)	3.5 (2018)
Pakistan	0.4 (2006)	0.2 (2006)	0.5 (2006)	2.8 (2018)	3.7 (2018)	2.5 (2018)
Tajikistan	...	...	...	...	...	...
Turkmenistan	...	...	...	...	...	...
Uzbekistan	...	...	...	...	...	...
East Asia						
China, People's Republic of	...	...	...	...	...	...
Hong Kong, China	...	...	...	...	...	...
Korea, Republic of	3.7	2.7	4.3	3.4	3.1	3.6
Mongolia	4.7 (2008)	4.6 (2008)	4.9 (2008)	8.5	7.5	9.4
Taipei,China	...	...	...	...	...	...
South Asia						
Bangladesh	0.9	0.7	1.0	2.6 (2017)	4.4 (2017)	1.8 (2017)
Bhutan	1.5 (2009)	2.3 (2009)	0.9 (2009)	1.3 (2015)	1.6 (2015)	1.1 (2015)
India	1.2	1.1	1.3	2.5 (2018)	2.7 (2018)	2.4 (2018)
Maldives	6.5 (2009)	9.9 (2009)	4.7 (2009)	3.6 (2016)	3.6 (2016)	3.6 (2016)
Nepal	1.0 (2008)	0.9 (2008)	1.1 (2008)	8.8 (2017)	10.2 (2017)	8.0 (2017)
Sri Lanka	3.5	6.2	2.2	2.3 (2018)	4.1 (2018)	1.3 (2018)
Southeast Asia						
Brunei Darussalam	...	...	...	4.8	6.1	4.0
Cambodia	1.6	2.1	1.1	0.0 (2017)	0.0 (2017)	0.0 (2017)
Indonesia	...	...	...	1.8	1.5	2.0
Lao People's Democratic Republic	...	...	...	0.4 (2010)	0.3 (2010)	0.4 (2010)
Malaysia	...	...	...	1.7 (2018)	1.7 (2018)	1.7 (2018)
Myanmar	...	...	...	0.3	0.3	0.2
Philippines	2.0 (2001)	1.7 (2001)	2.2 (2001)	1.4	1.5	1.3
Singapore	3.3 (2001)	3.0 (2001)	3.5 (2001)	3.6 (2016)	3.7 (2016)	3.6 (2016)
Thailand	1.5	1.5	1.4	0.3	0.3	0.4
Timor-Leste	...	...	...	2.5 (2016)	3.8 (2016)	1.5 (2016)
Viet Nam	1.5 (2004)	1.8 (2004)	1.1 (2004)	1.4	1.4	1.4
The Pacific						
Cook Islands	...	...	...	0.0 (2016)	0.0 (2016)	0.0 (2016)
Fiji	2.6 (2005)	2.7 (2005)	2.5 (2005)	2.2 (2016)	2.4 (2016)	2.1 (2016)
Kiribati	...	...	...	7.6 (2015)	5.3 (2015)	9.3 (2015)
Marshall Islands	...	...	...	...	...	...
Micronesia, Federated States of	...	...	...	6.1 (2014)	9.0 (2014)	4.0 (2014)
Nauru	...	...	...	9.1 (2013)	13.1 (2013)	6.1 (2013)
Niue	...	...	...	...	...	...
Palau	2.6	2.8	2.5	1.0 (2014)	1.4 (2014)	0.7 (2014)
Papua New Guinea	2.1	...	...	...	...	...
Samoa	...	...	...	10.0 (2017)	15.1 (2017)	7.3 (2017)
Solomon Islands	...	...	...	0.5 (2013)	0.4 (2013)	0.6 (2013)
Tonga	...	...	...	2.0 (2018)	1.9 (2018)	2.1 (2018)
Tuvalu	...	...	...	5.4 (2016)	9.7 (2016)	3.3 (2016)
Vanuatu	3.1 (2009)	3.7 (2009)	2.7 (2009)	...	...	...
Developed ADB Member Economies						
Australia	4.9	4.7	5.1	3.9	4.0	3.8
Japan	4.2	3.9	4.3	2.2	2.0	2.4
New Zealand	4.6	4.6	4.6	2.8	3.1	2.5

... = data not available, 0.0 = magnitude is less than half of unit employed, ADB = Asian Development Bank.

Sources: International Labour Organisation. ILOSTAT Database. http://www.ilo.org/ilostat (accessed 27 July 2020). For Taipei,China: Government of Taipei,China, Directorate-General of Budget, Accounting and Statistics. National Statistics. https://eng.stat.gov.tw/ (accessed 3 August 2020).

Goal 8. Promote sustained, inclusive, and sustainable economic growth; full and productive employment; and decent work for all

Table 1.8.3: Selected Indicators for Sustainable Development Goal 8—Youth Participation in Education and Work, Child Labor

ADB Regional Member	Target 8.6: By 2020, substantially reduce the proportion of youth not in employment, education, or training		Target 8.7: Take immediate and effective measures to eradicate forced labor, end modern slavery and human trafficking, and secure the prohibition and elimination of the worst forms of child labor, including recruitment and use of child soldiers; and, by 2025, end child labor in all its forms		
	8.6.1: Proportion of Youth (Aged 15–24 Years) not in Education, Employment, or Training (%)		8.7.1: Proportion of Children (Aged 5–17 Years) Engaged in Child Labor, 2015 (%)		
	2000	2018	Total	Female	Male
Developing ADB Member Economies					
Central and West Asia					
Afghanistan	...	42.0 (2017)	16.6 (2013)	12.6 (2013)	20.3 (2013)
Armenia	40.5 (2009)	36.6 (2017)	3.9	2.7	4.9
Azerbaijan	...	...	...	...	...
Georgia	...	26.9	1.5	0.9	2.1
Kazakhstan	18.6 (2001)	9.5 (2016)	...	...	...
Kyrgyz Republic	17.8 (2009)	20.5	20.1 (2018)	15.6 (2018)	24.2 (2018)
Pakistan	36.2 (2006)	31.0	9.0 (2017)	12.4 (2017)	5.1 (2017)
Tajikistan	42.2 (2009)	...	...	...	...
Turkmenistan	...	...	0.3	0.1	0.4
Uzbekistan	...	...	...	...	...
East Asia					
China, People's Republic of	...	...	...	...	...
Hong Kong, China	...	...	...	...	...
Korea, Republic of	...	...	...	...	...
Mongolia	18.5 (2006)	18.9	7.9 (2018)	6.5 (2018)	9.1 (2018)
Taipei,China	...	...	...	...	...
South Asia					
Bangladesh	31.0 (2005)	27.4 (2017)	5.9 (2013)	5.2 (2013)	6.4 (2013)
Bhutan	...	...	1.7 (2010)	1.7 (2010)	1.6 (2010)
India	32.2	30.4	4.3 (2012)	3.1 (2012)	5.3 (2012)
Maldives	...	23.5 (2016)	...	...	...
Nepal	23.1 (2008)	32.1 (2017)	19.0 (2014)	19.3 (2014)	19.2 (2014)
Sri Lanka	...	27.1 (2016)	...	...	...
Southeast Asia					
Brunei Darussalam	...	20.0 (2017)	...	...	...
Cambodia	10.3	12.7 (2012)	11.5 (2012)	12.2 (2012)	10.8 (2012)
Indonesia	29.4	21.7	...	...	...
Lao People's Democratic Republic	...	5.1 (2010)	26.3 (2017)	26.2 (2017)	26.3 (2017)
Malaysia	...	12.5	...	...	...
Myanmar	...	13.6	8.1	7.6	8.7
Philippines	24.7 (2006)	19.9	4.3 (2011)	3.5 (2011)	5.1 (2011)
Singapore	6.8 (2009)	4.1	...	...	...
Thailand	13.7 (2009)	14.8	...	...	...
Timor-Leste	...	21.0 (2016)	...	...	...
Viet Nam	10.6 (2007)	8.3	12.1 (2014)	12.5 (2014)	11.9 (2014)
The Pacific					
Cook Islands	...	...	...	...	...
Fiji	20.6 (2005)	20.1 (2016)	...	...	...
Kiribati	...	46.9 (2015)	...	...	...
Marshall Islands	...	...	...	...	...
Micronesia, Federated States of	...	23.7 (2014)	...	...	...
Nauru	...	36.4 (2013)	...	...	...
Niue	...	...	...	...	...
Palau	27.2	12.9 (2014)	...	...	...
Papua New Guinea	...	27.7 (2010)	...	...	...
Samoa	...	37.9 (2017)	...	...	...
Solomon Islands	...	7.0 (2013)	13.8	13.8	13.8
Tonga	...	...	...	...	...
Tuvalu	...	29.0 (2016)	...	...	...
Vanuatu	26.3 (2009)	...	15.0 (2013)	15.8 (2013)	14.2 (2013)
Developed ADB Member Economies					
Australia	11.4 (2009)	8.9 (2017)	...	...	...
Japan	4.4 (2009)	2.9	...	...	...
New Zealand	10.8 (2004)	11.9	...	...	...

... = data not available, ADB = Asian Development Bank.

Source: United Nations Statistics Division. Global SDG Indicators Database. https://unstats.un.org/sdgs/indicators/database/ (accessed 7 August 2020).

Click on the indictor name in the table header to access the time series in the Key Indicators Database.

Goal 8. Promote sustained, inclusive, and sustainable economic growth; full and productive employment; and decent work for all

Table 1.8.4: Selected Indicators for Sustainable Development Goal 8—Access to Banking, Insurance, and Financial Services; and Trade

ADB Regional Member	Target 8.10: Strengthen the capacity of domestic financial institutions to encourage and expand access to banking, insurance, and financial services for all					8.10.2: Proportion of Adults (15 Years and Older) with an Account at a Bank or Other Financial Institution or with a Mobile-Money Service Provider (%)	
	8.10.1: Number of Commercial Bank Branches and ATMs per 100,000 Adults						
	Commercial Bank Branches		ATMs				
	2004	2018	2004		2018	2011	2017
Developing ADB Member Economies							
Central and West Asia							
Afghanistan	0.4	2.3	0.0		1.6	9.0	14.9
Armenia	10.8	23.6	3.0		64.1	17.5	47.8
Azerbaijan	6.5	10.7 (2015)	17.1 (2006)		32.8	14.9	28.6
Georgia	10.2	31.5	2.1		77.5	33.0	61.2
Kazakhstan	3.7	2.5	10.0		84.3	42.1	58.7
Kyrgyz Republic	5.1	8.1	0.6		37.0	3.8	39.9
Pakistan	7.6	10.3	0.7		10.5	10.3	21.3
Tajikistan	4.9	6.6 (2013)	0.6 (2005)		10.5 (2013)	2.5	47.0
Turkmenistan	...	...	...		...	0.4	40.6
Uzbekistan	39.2	36.4	0.9		28.0	22.5	37.1
East Asia							
China, People's Republic of	...	8.9	9.6 (2006)		97.1	63.8	80.2
Hong Kong, China	23.6	21.2	39.8		51.8	88.7	95.3
Korea, Republic of	16.8	15.4 (2017)	208.2		272.0 (2017)	93.0	94.9
Mongolia	40.0	69.2	9.9 (2008)		106.9	77.7	93.0
Taipei,China	...	...	...		...	...	...
South Asia							
Bangladesh	7.1	8.9	0.1		8.9	31.7	50.0
Bhutan	14.5	18.4 (2017)	0.5		39.4 (2017)	...	...
India	8.9	14.5	2.3 (2005)		21.6	35.2	79.9
Maldives	10.1	13.1	7.2		31.8	...	...
Nepal	2.6	15.5	...		14.3	25.3	45.4
Sri Lanka	8.7	18.6 (2015)	9.3 (2007)		17.2 (2015)	68.5	73.6
Southeast Asia							
Brunei Darussalam	21.0	17.3	35.0		74.5	...	...
Cambodia	2.3 (2006)	7.8	0.0 (2005)		19.4	3.7	21.7
Indonesia	5.2	16.1	8.6		54.4	19.6	48.9
Lao People's Democratic Republic	2.4 (2009)	3.2	2.6 (2008)		25.7	26.8	29.1
Malaysia	14.0	10.2	27.1		46.6	66.2	85.3
Myanmar	1.8	5.1	...		5.6	...	26.0
Philippines	8.2	9.0	10.3		28.9	26.6	34.5
Singapore	11.5	8.1	46.8		64.6	98.2	97.9
Thailand	7.8	11.7	20.9		115.2	72.7	81.6
Timor-Leste	1.1	6.3	2.0 (2008)		11.7	...	...
Viet Nam	3.3 (2008)	3.9	1.4		25.3	21.4	30.8
The Pacific							
Cook Islands	...	...	...		...	...	...
Fiji	9.3	11.9	19.1		54.3	...	...
Kiribati	...	5.7 (2013)	...		14.3 (2013)	...	...
Marshall Islands	11.8	14.1	2.9 (2007)		6.0	...	...
Micronesia, Federated States of	12.3	13.0	3.1		13.0	...	...
Nauru	...	...	...		...	...	...
Niue	...	...	...		...	...	...
Palau	...	...	30.9 (2007)		45.8 (2017)	...	...
Papua New Guinea	1.8	1.5	3.7		8.2	...	...
Samoa	17.7	24.0	12.1		53.7	...	...
Solomon Islands	7.5	4.2 (2017)	1.5		11.9 (2017)	...	...
Tonga	24.2	33.0	22.6		40.5	...	...
Tuvalu	...	...	...		...	...	...
Vanuatu	19.6	20.7	4.9		48.1	...	...
Developed ADB Member Economies							
Australia	30.7	28.2	139.6		146.1	99.1	99.5
Japan	34.6	34.0	124.4		127.4	96.4	98.2
New Zealand	35.0	26.7	59.0		64.6	99.4	99.2

... = data not available, 0.0 = magnitude is less than half of unit employed, ADB = Asian Development Bank.

Sources: United Nations Statistics Division. Global SDG Indicators Database. https://unstats.un.org/sdgs/indicators/database/ (accessed 5 August 2020). For 8.10.2: World Bank. World Development Indicators. https://data.worldbank.org/indicator (accessed 5 August 2020).

Click on the indictor name in the table header to access the time series in the Key Indicators Database.

Goal 9. Build resilient infrastructure, promote inclusive and sustainable industrialization, and foster innovation

Table 1.9.1: Selected Indicators for Sustainable Development Goal 9—Road and Rail Transport, Passenger and Freight Volume

| ADB Regional Member | Target 9.1: Develop quality, reliable, sustainable and resilient infrastructure, including regional and transborder infrastructure, to support economic development and human well-being, with a focus on affordable and equitable access for all | | | |
	9.1.2.a: Passenger Volume, by Road Transport (passenger-km million) 2018	9.1.2.b: Freight Volume, by Road Transport (t-km million) 2018	9.1.2.c: Passenger Volume, by Rail Transport (passenger-km million) 2018	9.1.2.d: Freight Volume, by Rail Transport (t-km million) 2018
Developing ADB Member Economies				
Central and West Asia	**794,358.1**	**627,870.2**	**3,546.7**	**392,598.7**
Afghanistan	29,838.7	8,308.9	2.1	–
Armenia	14,616.6	1,863.2	44.7	385.6
Azerbaijan	63,818.3	11,499.6	1,060.0	11,605.3
Georgia	20,535.6	1,843.2	79.7	2,567.5
Kazakhstan	63,959.8	189,798.9	618.3	275,829.5
Kyrgyz Republic	13,554.1	5,026.1	55.2	164.1
Pakistan	453,782.0	365,188.6	971.7	65,007.5
Tajikistan	14,307.7	2,957.6	0.5	79.0
Turkmenistan	32,099.0	6,316.3	1.1	13,460.2
Uzbekistan	87,846.2	35,068.0	713.2	23,499.9
East Asia[a]	**6,683,971.5**	**7,694,549.5**	**1,478,661.1**	**2,839,677.0**
China, People's Republic of	6,183,373.4	7,488,230.1	1,319,895.2	2,786,167.1
Hong Kong, China	79,123.1	11,536.2	2,533.6	13,067.6
Korea, Republic of	414,046.3	179,592.3	138,305.5	17,775.2
Mongolia	7,428.8	15,190.9	17,926.9	22,667.0
Taipei,China	...	...	...	...
South Asia	**2,609,855.3**	**2,370,534.7**	**980,046.2**	**633,916.9**
Bangladesh	220,182.1	19,007.0	92,733.6	6,857.6
Bhutan	695.5	1,304.8	5,749.3	–
India	2,348,298.9	2,333,311.8	754,212.3	626,592.6
Maldives	352.4	54.3	3,035.1	–
Nepal	17,311.6	6,847.5	3,635.4	–
Sri Lanka	23,014.8	10,009.2	120,680.5	466.7
Southeast Asia	**776,054.0**	**871,077.6**	**1,773,269.8**	**48,425.7**
Brunei Darussalam	53.1	934.9	7,215.4	–
Cambodia	14,491.7	9,782.4	23,295.8	1,452.5
Indonesia	236,758.1	350,247.9	611,785.5	5,896.2
Lao People's Democratic Republic	8,559.6	21,362.4	15,487.4	–
Malaysia	44,426.2	104,133.4	170,097.3	7,239.1
Myanmar	48,134.7	12,757.2	29,067.5	3,991.4
Philippines	158,038.4	53,514.3	286,215.4	–
Singapore	23,023.0	618.1	106,035.4	766.8
Thailand	125,107.6	190,797.6	330,768.7	24,881.0
Timor-Leste	159.6	–	–	–
Viet Nam	117,301.9	126,929.4	193,301.4	4,198.6
The Pacific	**26,563.7**	**4,641.4**	**1,828.8**	**–**
Cook Islands	87.4	–	3.3	–
Fiji	2,680.4	573.3	334.2	–
Kiribati	323.4	–	11.9	–
Marshall Islands	1,205.7	–	21.9	–
Micronesia, Federated States of	529.2	–	37.3	–
Nauru	41.6	–	1.6	–
Niue	4.2	–	0.2	–
Palau	194.0	–	123.1	–
Papua New Guinea	15,884.5	4,067.7	835.0	–
Samoa	1,209.9	–	119.4	–
Solomon Islands	1,920.0	0.4	90.8	–
Tonga	732.9	–	83.8	–
Tuvalu	53.7	–	4.3	–
Vanuatu	1,696.7	–	162.0	–
Developed ADB Member Economies	**1,014,705.0**	**502,606.8**	**449,695.6**	**479,876.9**
Australia	108,455.4	275,076.5	21,328.7	440,500.1
Japan	887,224.7	210,994.4	423,147.9	28,839.1
New Zealand	19,024.9	16,535.9	5,219.0	10,537.7
DEVELOPING ADB MEMBER ECONOMIES[a]	**10,890,802.6**	**11,568,673.4**	**4,237,352.6**	**3,914,618.2**
ALL ADB REGIONAL MEMBERS[a]	**11,905,507.6**	**12,071,280.2**	**4,687,048.2**	**4,394,495.1**
WORLD	**57,305,098.1**	**36,985,778.8**	**9,876,627.3**	**17,275,052.1**

... = data not available, – = magnitude equals zero, ADB = Asian Development Bank, km = kilometer, t = metric ton.

a   For reporting economies only.

Source: United Nations Statistics Division. Global SDG Indicators Database. http://unstats.un.org/sdgs/indicators/database/ (accessed 30 July 2020).

Sustainable Development Goals

Goal 9. Build resilient infrastructure, promote inclusive and sustainable industrialization, and foster innovation

Table 1.9.2: Selected Indicators for Sustainable Development Goal 9—Growth in Manufacturing

ADB Regional Member	Target 9.2: Promote inclusive and sustainable industrialization; and, by 2030, significantly raise industry's share of employment and GDP, in line with national circumstances, and double its share in least developed countries					
	9.2.1: Manufacturing Value Added[a]				9.2.2: Manufacturing Employment as a Proportion of Total Employment (%)	
	As a Proportion of GDP (%)		Per Capita (at constant 2015 $)			
	2000	2019	2000	2019	2000	2018
Developing ADB Member Economies						
Central and West Asia						
Afghanistan	18.5	11.3	47.6	68.8	4.6 (2008)	7.7 (2017)
Armenia	9.8	10.1	124.0	432.2	6.1 (2009)	9.1 (2017)
Azerbaijan	9.0	4.7	134.4	251.1	4.8 (2007)	5.2
Georgia	9.3	10.9	128.2	449.0	5.9	6.2
Kazakhstan	13.0	10.3	567.3	1,159.4	7.7 (2001)	6.8 (2017)
Kyrgyz Republic	24.2	14.2	173.1	173.3	6.7 (2002)	7.6 (2016)
Pakistan	9.9	12.7	101.6	190.4	11.5	16.2
Tajikistan	40.3	16.3	175.1	176.9	4.7 (2004)	5.4
Turkmenistan	33.0	45.0	760.9	3,487.7	...	...
Uzbekistan	29.4	19.7	275.0	495.9	...	12.0
East Asia						
China, People's Republic of	26.1	28.8	562.7	2,863.7	...	...
Hong Kong, China	2.9	0.9	781.0	411.6	...	...
Korea, Republic of	21.6	27.5	3,520.1	8,251.9	20.3	16.8
Mongolia	7.7	8.1	124.4	357.3	5.4 (2003)	8.0
Taipei,China	21.0	31.6	2,936.7	7,662.5	27.7 (2001)	26.7 (2019)
South Asia						
Bangladesh	12.0	19.5	76.8	310.3	7.3	14.4 (2017)
Bhutan	7.3	7.5	84.6	254.4	3.0 (2006)	6.5 (2015)
India	13.5	15.5	102.8	314.9	10.7	12.2
Maldives	2.5	2.2	171.6	223.1	...	11.0 (2016)
Nepal	7.9	5.4	37.4	48.5	...	15.1 (2017)
Sri Lanka	20.8	16.3	398.9	705.4	16.5 (2002)	19.3 (2017)
Southeast Asia						
Brunei Darussalam	17.2	15.9	5,843.6	4,784.9	...	3.8 (2017)
Cambodia	11.2	17.1	54.3	246.8	7.1	16.9 (2016)
Indonesia	23.2	20.8	433.9	807.7	13.0	14.4
Lao People's Democratic Republic	6.7	8.0	61.8	207.4	...	7.9 (2017)
Malaysia	25.6	22.7	1,609.3	2,541.2	22.8	16.9
Myanmar	8.0	23.0	24.2	342.0	...	11.1
Philippines	21.2	20.5	374.2	711.1	8.9 (2006)	8.8
Singapore	21.0	18.3	7,285.6	10,557.5	19.5 (2001)	10.4
Thailand	27.5	26.7	967.5	1,772.4	...	16.5
Timor-Leste	1.8	0.5	20.0	11.7	...	7.2 (2016)
Viet Nam	11.4	16.7	107.3	432.8	9.2	17.9
The Pacific						
Cook Islands	4.0	2.9	498.7	504.8	...	...
Fiji	12.3	9.9	474.9	537.4	13.7 (2005)	5.6 (2016)
Kiribati	4.6	3.7	74.3	58.5	...	14.3 (2015)
Marshall Islands	1.3	0.8	34.9	27.6	0.8 (2009)	0.7 (2010)
Micronesia, Federated States of	...	...	...	...	...	2.4 (2014)
Nauru	...	...	...	...	...	0.5 (2013)
Niue	...	...	...	...	...	...
Palau	1.0	1.0	132.7	155.2	...	0.5 (2014)
Papua New Guinea	2.6	2.3	52.1	60.9	1.1	1.8 (2010)
Samoa	18.0	8.4	549.6	362.8	...	6.8 (2017)
Solomon Islands	6.8	9.4	91.7	170.5	...	5.5 (2013)
Tonga	6.7	5.9	225.5	253.2	24.7 (2003)	...
Tuvalu	0.7	0.7	20.8	26.7	...	3.7 (2016)
Vanuatu	4.5	3.2	122.9	91.6	1.9 (2009)	...
Developed ADB Member Economies						
Australia	9.5	5.2	3,995.8	2,835.5	12.1	8.0
Japan	19.2	21.1	5,896.4	7,644.8	20.5	16.3
New Zealand	16.1	10.7	4,856.6	4,447.3	15.8	9.5

... = data not available, $ = United States dollars, ADB = Asian Development Bank, GDP = gross domestic product.

a   United Nations Statistics Division figures calculated from GDP, manufacturing value added, and population data.

Sources: United Nations Statistics Division. Global SDG Indicators Database. https://unstats.un.org/sdgs/indicators/database/ (accessed 8 July 2020); For Taipei,China: United Nations Industrial Development Organization. Statistics Data Portal. https://stat.unido.org/SDG (accessed 8 July 2020).

Goal 9. Build resilient infrastructure, promote inclusive and sustainable industrialization, and foster innovation

Table 1.9.3: Selected Indicators for Sustainable Development Goal 9—Carbon Dioxide Emissions

ADB Regional Member	Target 9.4: By 2030, upgrade infrastructure and retrofit industries to make them sustainable, with increased resource-use efficiency and greater adoption of clean and environmentally sound technologies and industrial processes, with all countries taking action in accordance with their respective capabilities			
	9.4.1: Carbon Dioxide Emissions[a]			
	Per Unit of GDP (PPP) (kg of CO_2 equivalent per constant 2010 \$)		Per Unit of Manufacturing Value-Added[b] (kg of CO_2 equivalent per constant 2010 \$)	
	2000	2017	2000	2017
Developing ADB Member Economies				
Central and West Asia				
Afghanistan	...	...	...	...
Armenia	0.4	0.2	1.9	0.3
Azerbaijan	0.8	0.2	2.3	0.6
Georgia	0.3	0.2	1.1	0.9
Kazakhstan	0.8	0.6	2.2	2.7
Kyrgyz Republic	0.4	0.4	1.0	0.6
Pakistan	0.2	0.2	1.5	1.4
Tajikistan	0.3	0.2	–	1.0
Turkmenistan	1.6	0.7	0.2	0.1
Uzbekistan	1.9	0.4	2.3	0.6
East Asia				
China, People's Republic of	0.7	0.4	1.2	0.7
Hong Kong, China	0.2	0.1	0.8	2.1
Korea, Republic of	0.4	0.3	0.6	0.2
Mongolia	0.8	0.5	1.7	1.0
Taipei,China	...	...	0.6	0.2
South Asia				
Bangladesh	0.1	0.1	0.4	0.4
Bhutan	...	...	...	...
India	0.3	0.3	1.7	1.5
Maldives	...	...	...	...
Nepal	0.1	0.1	1.3	2.7
Sri Lanka	0.1	0.1	0.1	0.1
Southeast Asia				
Brunei Darussalam	0.2	0.2	0.1	0.2
Cambodia	0.1	0.2	0.1	0.2
Indonesia	0.2	0.2	0.6	0.5
Lao People's Democratic Republic	...	...	...	...
Malaysia	0.3	0.3	0.7	0.4
Myanmar	0.2	0.1	2.1	0.2
Philippines	0.2	0.2	0.4	0.2
Singapore	0.2	0.1	0.1	0.2
Thailand	0.3	0.2	0.5	0.4
Timor-Leste	...	...	...	...
Viet Nam	0.2	0.3	1.7	1.8
The Pacific				
Cook Islands	...	...	...	...
Fiji	...	...	...	...
Kiribati	...	...	...	...
Marshall Islands	...	...	...	...
Micronesia, Federated States of	...	...	...	...
Nauru	...	...	...	...
Niue	...	...	...	...
Palau	...	...	...	...
Papua New Guinea	...	...	...	...
Samoa	...	...	...	...
Solomon Islands	...	...	...	...
Tonga	...	...	...	...
Tuvalu	...	...	...	...
Vanuatu	...	...	...	...
Developed ADB Member Economies				
Australia	0.5	0.3	0.5	0.4
Japan	0.3	0.2	0.3	0.2
New Zealand	0.3	0.2	0.3	0.3

... = data not available, – = magnitude equals zero, \$ = United States dollar, ADB = Asian Development Bank, CO_2 = carbon dioxide, GDP = gross domestic product, kg = kilogram, PPP = purchasing power parity.

a   Refers to carbon dioxide emissions from fuel combustion.

b   For Taipei,China, the unit of measure is kilograms of CO_2 equivalent per constant 2015 United States dollar.

Sources: United Nations Statistics Division. Global SDG Indicators Database. https://unstats.un.org/sdgs/indicators/database/ (accessed 16 July 2020); and United Nations Industrial Development Organization. Statistics Data Portal. https://stat.unido.org/SDG (accessed 16 July 2020).

Click on the indictor name in the table header to access the time series in the Key Indicators Database.

Goal 9. Build resilient infrastructure, promote inclusive and sustainable industrialization, and foster innovation

Table 1.9.4: Selected Indicators for Sustainable Development Goal 9—Research and Development

ADB Regional Member	Target 9.5: Enhance scientific research, upgrade the technological capabilities of industrial sectors in all countries, in particular developing countries, including, by 2030, encouraging innovation and substantially increasing the number of research and development workers per 1 million people and public and private research and development spending							
	9.5.1: Research and Development Expenditure as a Proportion of GDP (%)				9.5.2: Researchers (Full-Time Equivalent) (per million inhabitants)			
	2000		2018		2000		2018	
Developing ADB Member Economies								
Central and West Asia								
Afghanistan	...		...		...		...	
Armenia	0.19		0.19		...		...	
Azerbaijan	0.34		0.18		...		...	
Georgia	0.22		0.30		...		1,464	
Kazakhstan	0.18		0.12		407	(2007)	667	
Kyrgyz Republic	0.16		0.11	(2017)	...		...	
Pakistan	0.13		0.24	(2017)	79	(2005)	336	(2017)
Tajikistan	0.09	(2001)	0.10		...		...	
Turkmenistan	...		...		...		...	
Uzbekistan	0.36		0.13		662		476	
East Asia								
China, People's Republic of	0.89		2.19		539		1,307	
Hong Kong, China	0.46		0.86		1,170		4,026	
Korea, Republic of	2.18		4.81		2,287		7,980	
Mongolia	0.19		0.10		...		...	
Taipei,China	...		...		...		...	
South Asia								
Bangladesh	...		...		...		...	
Bhutan	...		...		...		...	
India	0.76		0.65		110		253	
Maldives	...		...		...		...	
Nepal	0.05	(2008)	0.30	(2010)	61	(2002)	...	
Sri Lanka	0.14		0.11	(2015)	135		106	(2015)
Southeast Asia								
Brunei Darussalam	0.02	(2002)	0.28		285	(2002)	...	
Cambodia	0.05	(2002)	0.12	(2015)	18	(2002)	30	(2015)
Indonesia	0.07		0.23		213		216	
Lao People's Democratic Republic	0.04	(2002)	...		16	(2002)	...	
Malaysia	0.47		1.44	(2016)	277		2,397	(2016)
Myanmar	0.11		0.03	(2017)	12	(2001)	29	(2017)
Philippines	0.14	(2002)	0.16	(2015)	54	(2002)	106	(2015)
Singapore	1.82		1.94	(2017)	4,128		6,803	(2017)
Thailand	0.24		1.00	(2017)	279	(2001)	1,350	(2017)
Timor-Leste	...		...		...		...	
Viet Nam	0.19	(2002)	0.53	(2017)	114	(2002)	708	(2017)
The Pacific								
Cook Islands	...		...		...		...	
Fiji	...		...		...		...	
Kiribati	...		...		...		...	
Marshall Islands	...		...		...		...	
Micronesia, Federated States of	...		...		...		...	
Nauru	...		...		...		...	
Niue	...		...		...		...	
Palau	...		...		...		...	
Papua New Guinea	...		0.03	(2016)	...		35	(2016)
Samoa	...		...		...		...	
Solomon Islands	...		...		...		...	
Tonga	...		...		...		...	
Tuvalu	...		...		...		...	
Vanuatu	...		...		...		...	
Developed ADB Member Economies								
Australia	1.58		1.87	(2017)	3,475		4,532	(2010)
Japan	2.91		3.26		5,078		5,331	
New Zealand	1.10	(2001)	1.37	(2017)	2,643	(2001)	5,530	(2017)

... = data not available, ADB = Asian Development Bank, GDP = gross domestic product.

Source: United Nations Educational, Scientific and Cultural Organization (UNESCO) Institute for Statistics. UIS.Stat Database. http://data.uis.unesco.org/# (accessed 12 August 2020).

Click on the indictor name in the table header to access the time series in the Key Indicators Database.

Goal 9. Build resilient infrastructure, promote inclusive and sustainable industrialization, and foster innovation

Table 1.9.5: Selected Indicators for Sustainable Development Goal 9—Official International Support and Industry Value-Added

ADB Regional Member	Target 9.a: Faciltate sustainable and resilient infrastructure development in developing countries through enhanced financial, technological and technical support to African countries, least developed countries, landlocked developing countries and small island developing States		Target 9.b: Support domestic technology development, research, and innovation in developing countries, including by ensuring a conducive policy environment for, inter alia, industrial diversification and value addition to commodities	
	9.a.1: Total Official International Support to Infrastructure[a] (constant 2018 $ million)		9.b.1: Proportion of Medium- and High-Tech Industry Value-Added in Total Value-Added (%)	
	2000	**2018**	**2000**	**2017**
Developing ADB Member Economies				
Central and West Asia	**1,213.4**	**4,467.2**	...	...
Afghanistan	0.4	469.8	13.6	9.5
Armenia	137.9	242.1	9.5	4.6
Azerbaijan	24.7	794.3	16.5	19.1
Georgia	145.8	480.2	21.4	8.6
Kazakhstan	245.1	299.5	5.2	13.4
Kyrgyz Republic	95.5	122.2	5.9	2.7
Pakistan	496.3	956.6	25.2	24.6
Tajikistan	17.1	220.6	2.7	2.2
Turkmenistan	1.9	4.5	...	...
Uzbekistan	48.8	877.3	...	...
East Asia[b]	**2,478.0**	**2,872.9**	...	...
China, People's Republic of	2,359.0	2,591.2	42.9	41.5
Hong Kong, China	...	...	39.5	37.4
Korea, Republic of	...	...	58.9	63.0
Mongolia	119.0	281.7	2.5	5.4
Taipei,China	...	...	56.2	69.5
South Asia	**4,009.0**	**10,826.0**	...	...
Bangladesh	652.2	2,679.8	21.1	9.8
Bhutan	32.1	45.4	...	...
India	3,115.6	7,150.0	41.3	42.9
Maldives	12.0	87.6	2.6	2.6
Nepal	118.3	334.5	12.1	8.4
Sri Lanka	78.6	528.7	9.4	8.9
Southeast Asia[b]	**3,457.8**	**6,141.2**	...	...
Brunei Darussalam	...	...	3.3	3.3
Cambodia	45.8	272.3	0.3	0.3
Indonesia	113.6	2,592.8	35.7	35.4
Lao People's Democratic Republic	75.9	154.4	10.3	3.8
Malaysia	577.0	5.6	51.2	44.1
Myanmar	0.0	452.5	12.4	7.6
Philippines	799.7	644.3	38.1	43.3
Singapore	...	...	78.5	78.2
Thailand	704.2	535.2	37.9	40.7
Timor-Leste	2.7	56.9	...	...
Viet Nam	1,138.9	1,427.1	23.5	38.7
The Pacific[b]	**259.0**	**738.6**	...	...
Cook Islands	1.0	9.7	...	...
Fiji	0.2	18.9	8.5	7.1
Kiribati	1.5	33.2	...	...
Marshall Islands	3.3	137.5	...	...
Micronesia, Federated States of	5.1	35.1	...	...
Nauru	0.0 (2002)	8.7	...	...
Niue	0.5	5.7	...	...
Palau	0.2	1.6	...	...
Papua New Guinea	219.1	301.3	12.6	12.6
Samoa	3.3	48.2	...	...
Solomon Islands	9.7	62.5	...	...
Tonga	5.0	33.0	1.6	1.6
Tuvalu	0.0 (2002)	3.4	...	...
Vanuatu	10.3	39.8	...	...
Developed ADB Member Economies	...	...	...	...
Australia	...	...	27.2	28.2
Japan	...	...	52.0	56.8
New Zealand	...	...	12.5	18.5
DEVELOPING ADB MEMBER ECONOMIES[b]	**11,417.2**	**25,045.8**		

... = data not available, 0.0 = magnitude is less than half of unit employed, $ = United States dollars, ADB = Asian Development Bank.

a   Gross disbursements of total official development assistance and other official flows from all donors in support of infrastructure.
b   Includes only reporting economies with data corresponding to the year heading.

Sources: United Nations Statistics Division. Global SDG Indicators Database. http://unstats.un.org/sdgs/indicators/database/ (accessed 31 July 2020); and United Nations Industrial Development Organization. Statistics Data Portal. https://stat.unido.org/SDG (accessed 31 July 2020).

Click on the indictor name in the table header to access the time series in the Key Indicators Database.

Goal 9. Build resilient infrastructure, promote inclusive and sustainable industrialization, and foster innovation

Table 1.9.6: Selected Indicators for Sustainable Development Goal 9—Coverage by Mobile Networks

ADB Regional Member	Target 9.c: Significantly increase access to information and communications technology and strive to provide universal and affordable access to the internet in least developed countries by 2020									
	9.c.1.a: Proportion of Population Covered by 2G Mobile Networks (%)				9.c.1.b: Proportion of Population Covered by 3G Mobile Networks (%)				9.c.1.c: Proportion of Population Covered by LTE Mobile Networks (%)	
	2000		2018		2008		2018		2012	2018
Developing ADB Member Economies										
Central and West Asia										
Afghanistan	72.0	(2007)	90.0		...		55.0		– (2014)	7.0
Armenia	38.0	(2001)	100.0		81.1	(2009)	100.0		17.5	99.1
Azerbaijan	93.5		100.0		32.2	(2009)	97.1		6.7	49.0
Georgia	79.0	(2001)	100.0		...		100.0		8.9 (2013)	99.7
Kazakhstan	94.0	(2001)	96.6		...		87.9		2.7	75.3
Kyrgyz Republic	5.2	(2004)	99.2		...		88.0		0.5 (2014)	70.0
Pakistan	27.1	(2001)	88.7		...		88.7		–	68.6
Tajikistan	–	(2001)	90.0	(2017)	...		90.0	(2017)	8.4	80.0 (2017)
Turkmenistan	12.4	(2001)	95.8	(2017)	...		75.8	(2017)	6.0 (2013)	67.0 (2017)
Uzbekistan	75.0	(2002)	98.6		...		75.5		1.0 (2014)	44.0
East Asia										
China, People's Republic of	50.0		99.9		...		99.4		10.0 (2013)	99.4
Hong Kong, China	100.0		100.0		99.0	(2009)	99.0		91.7	99.0
Korea, Republic of	99.0		99.9		99.0		99.9		99.0 (2014)	99.9
Mongolia	58.0		100.0		39.9		95.0		...	45.0
Taipei,China	...		...		...		...		...	...
South Asia										
Bangladesh	40.0	(2001)	99.6		...		95.2		59.0 (2014)	79.0
Bhutan	5.4	(2005)	98.0		15.0	(2010)	90.0		5.0 (2013)	60.0
India	21.1		97.0		–		94.0		2.0 (2014)	94.0
Maldives	40.0		100.0		41.8	(2009)	100.0		11.4 (2013)	100.0
Nepal	10.0	(2006)	92.5	(2017)	20.4	(2009)	54.1	(2017)	– (2014)	15.5 (2017)
Sri Lanka	57.9	(2001)	99.0		...		86.0		5.0	80.0
Southeast Asia										
Brunei Darussalam	...		99.1		...		95.9		5.0 (2013)	94.9
Cambodia	80.0		99.0		43.0	(2009)	85.1		9.0 (2014)	80.3
Indonesia	89.0		98.7		...		97.7		5.0 (2013)	97.6
Lao People's Democratic Republic	55.0	(2005)	94.0		–		78.0		2.0 (2014)	43.0
Malaysia	95.0	(2001)	96.3		74.0	(2009)	96.3		15.0 (2013)	93.0
Myanmar	10.0	(2006)	95.2		...		94.2		– (2014)	75.0
Philippines	70.0		99.0	(2017)	69.0	(2009)	93.0	(2017)	6.0	80.0 (2017)
Singapore	100.0		100.0		99.4		100.0		99.0 (2014)	100.0
Thailand	25.9	(2005)	98.0		...		98.0		– (2014)	98.0
Timor-Leste	38.0	(2003)	96.5		...		96.5		...	40.0
Viet Nam	70.0	(2006)	99.7		...		99.6		– (2014)	93.9
The Pacific										
Cook Islands	...		100.0	(2017)	...		55.0	(2017)	...	55.0 (2017)
Fiji	40.0		98.0		...		94.0		15.0 (2014)	75.0
Kiribati	...		71.0		...		67.0		10.0 (2013)	53.0
Marshall Islands	...		65.0	(2017)	...		...		...	...
Micronesia, Federated States of	–		80.0	(2017)	...		15.0	(2017)	...	– (2017)
Nauru	...		98.0	(2017)	98.0	(2010)	98.0	(2017)	– (2014)	30.0 (2017)
Niue	...		...		...		...		...	...
Palau	30.0	(2005)	98.0	(2015)	...		88.0	(2016)	...	...
Papua New Guinea	...		89.0	(2017)	...		64.4	(2017)	7.0 (2014)	50.0 (2017)
Samoa	...		97.0	(2017)	...		91.0	(2017)	...	49.0 (2017)
Solomon Islands	35.0		95.0		...		45.0		...	20.0
Tonga	70.0	(2001)	98.0		...		96.0		– (2014)	65.0 (2017)
Tuvalu	15.0	(2004)	48.0	(2017)	...		48.0	(2017)	...	– (2017)
Vanuatu	20.0	(2002)	98.0		...		69.0		...	33.0
Developed ADB Member Economies										
Australia	95.6		99.4		98.8		99.4		52.2	99.0
Japan	99.0		99.9		...		99.9		84.0	99.0 (2017)
New Zealand	97.0		98.0		97.0		98.0		50.0 (2014)	97.0

... = data not available, – = magnitude equals zero, ADB = Asian Development Bank, LTE = Long-Term Evolution.

Source: United Nations Statistics Division. Global SDG Indicators Database. http://unstats.un.org/sdgs/indicators/database/ (accessed 6 August 2020).

Click on the indictor name in the table header to access the time series in the Key Indicators Database.

Goal 10. Reduce inequality within and among countries

Table 1.10.1: Selected Indicators for Sustainable Development Goal 10—Household Expenditure or Income Growth

ADB Regional Member	Target 10.1: By 2030, progressively achieve and sustain income growth of the bottom 40% of the population at a rate higher than the national average			
	10.1.1.a: Growth Rates of Household Expenditure or Income per Capita among the Bottom 40% of the Population[a,b] (%)		10.1.1.b: Growth Rates of Household Expenditure or Income per Capita[a,b] (%)	
Developing ADB Member Economies				
Central and West Asia				
Afghanistan	...		...	
Armenia	1.0	(2013–2018)	2.0	(2013–2018)
Azerbaijan	...		...	
Georgia	3.0	(2013–2018)	1.0	(2013–2018)
Kazakhstan	–	(2012–2017)	–1.0	(2012–2017)
Kyrgyz Republic	3.0	(2013–2018)	2.0	(2013–2018)
Pakistan	3.0	(2010–2015)	4.0	(2010–2015)
Tajikistan	...		...	
Turkmenistan	...		...	
Uzbekistan	...		...	
East Asia				
China, People's Republic of	8.0	(2013–2016)	7.0	(2013–2016)
Hong Kong, China	...		...	
Korea, Republic of	...		...	
Mongolia	1.0	(2011–2018)	1.0	(2011–2018)
Taipei,China	...		...	
South Asia				
Bangladesh	1.0	(2010–2016)	2.0	(2010–2016)
Bhutan	2.0	(2012–2017)	2.0	(2012–2017)
India	...		...	
Maldives	...		...	
Nepal	...		...	
Sri Lanka	4.0	(2012–2016)	5.0	(2012–2016)
Southeast Asia				
Brunei Darussalam	...		...	
Cambodia	...		...	
Indonesia	5.0	(2014–2018)	5.0	(2014–2018)
Lao People's Democratic Republic	...		...	
Malaysia	8.0	(2012–2016)	6.0	(2012–2016)
Myanmar	...		...	
Philippines	5.0	(2012–2015)	3.0	(2012–2015)
Singapore	...		...	
Thailand	1.0	(2014–2018)	1.0	(2014–2018)
Timor-Leste	...		...	
Viet Nam	5.0	(2012–2018)	5.0	(2012–2018)
The Pacific				
Cook Islands	...		...	
Fiji	...		...	
Kiribati	...		...	
Marshall Islands	...		...	
Micronesia, Federated States of	...		...	
Nauru	...		...	
Niue	...		...	
Palau	...		...	
Papua New Guinea	...		...	
Samoa	...		...	
Solomon Islands	...		...	
Tonga	...		...	
Tuvalu	...		...	
Vanuatu	...		...	
Developed ADB Member Economies				
Australia	...		...	
Japan	...		...	
New Zealand	...		...	

... = data not available, – = magnitude equals zero, ADB=Asian Development Bank.

a   Based on real mean per capita consumption or income measured at 2011 purchasing power parity using the PovcalNet database (http://iresearch.worldbank.org/PovcalNet). Data reported are based on consumption, except for Malaysia and the Philippines, which are based on income.

b   For the data collection periods in brackets, the initial year refers to the most recently conducted survey prior to the latest survey (only surveys conducted between 3 and 7 years before the latest survey are considered). The final year refers to the latest survey (those available between 2015 and 2018).

Source: United Nations Statistics Division. Global SDG Indicators Database. https://unstats.un.org/sdgs/indicators/database/ (accessed 8 July 2020).

Goal 11. Make cities and human settlements inclusive, safe, resilient, and sustainable

Table 1.11.1: Selected Indicators for Sustainable Development Goal 11—Sustainable Cities and Environment

ADB Regional Member	Target 11.1: By 2030, ensure access for all to adequate, safe, and affordable housing and basic services, and upgrade slums — 11.1.1: Proportion of Urban Population Living in Slums, Informal Settlements, or Inadequate Housing (%)		Target 11.5: ... 11.5.2: Direct Economic Loss Attributed to Disasters[a] ($ million)	Target 11.6: ... 11.6.2: Annual Mean Levels ($\mu g/m^3$) of Fine Particulate Matter (e.g., $PM_{2.5}$ and PM_{10}) in Cities (population weighted) — Total	Urban
	2000	2018	2019	2016	2016
Developing ADB Member Economies					
Central and West Asia					
Afghanistan	...	70.7	558.3	53.2	59.9
Armenia	...	9.3	5.4	30.5	32.9
Azerbaijan	...	...	...	18.2	18.5
Georgia	...	34.1	0.2	21.2	24.0
Kazakhstan	...	...	1.8	11.3	14.5
Kyrgyz Republic	...	9.7	4.8	18.1	17.4
Pakistan	48.7	40.1	18.1 (2018)	55.2	56.2
Tajikistan	...	26.0	12.9 (2018)	40.0	42.8
Turkmenistan	...	...	...	19.0	24.2
Uzbekistan	...	52.2	...	25.3	28.9
East Asia					
China, People's Republic of	37.3	24.6	...	49.2	51.0
Hong Kong, China	...	...	...	...	...
Korea, Republic of	...	...	5.9 (2018)	24.6	24.7
Mongolia	64.9	38.3	45.1	40.4	49.5
Taipei,China	...	...	...	...	...
South Asia					
Bangladesh	77.8	47.2	...	58.3	58.6
Bhutan	...	...	1.9 (2018)	35.3	35.4
India	41.5	35.2	...	65.2	68.0
Maldives	...	30.1	0.3 (2017)	7.6	7.7
Nepal	64.0	49.3	27.7	94.3	99.5
Sri Lanka	...	...	145.7	15.2	15.1
Southeast Asia					
Brunei Darussalam	...	...	...	5.8	5.8
Cambodia	78.9 (2005)	45.1	180.2	24.0	24.9
Indonesia	34.4	30.6	662.8	15.6	16.4
Lao People's Democratic Republic	79.3 (2005)	21.1	11.7 (2012)	24.5	25.5
Malaysia	...	...	21.1	16.0	17.3
Myanmar	45.6 (2005)	56.1	537.4	34.7	34.6
Philippines	47.2	42.9	...	18.4	18.7
Singapore	...	...	...	18.3	18.3
Thailand	26.0 (2005)	23.7	...	26.2	26.6
Timor-Leste	...	33.4	0.7 (2017)	17.9	18.2
Viet Nam	48.8	13.8	981.8 (2010)	29.7	30.1
The Pacific					
Cook Islands	...	...	...	12.0	...
Fiji	...	11.2	21.5 (2018)	10.2	10.5
Kiribati	...	...	...	10.5	10.9
Marshall Islands	...	...	0.4 (2014)	9.4	...
Micronesia, Federated States of	...	...	...	10.2	10.5
Nauru	...	...	...	12.5	12.5
Niue	...	...	...	11.5	...
Palau	...	...	6.1 (2012)	12.2	12.4
Papua New Guinea	...	...	1.7 (2013)	10.9	11.5
Samoa	...	...	27.1 (2009)	10.6	10.9
Solomon Islands	...	...	12.4 (2013)	10.7	11.5
Tonga	...	...	8.4 (2018)	10.1	10.2
Tuvalu	...	...	...	11.4	...
Vanuatu	...	...	0.2 (2014)	10.3	11.0
Developed ADB Member Economies					
Australia	...	...	184.6 (2018)	7.2	7.3
Japan	...	...	400.2 (2018)	11.4	11.8
New Zealand	...	...	120.8 (2018)	5.7	5.8

... = data not available, $ = United States dollars, ADB = Asian Development Bank, m^3 = cubic meter, PM = particulate matter, μg = microgram.

a   The data are submitted to the United Nations' Global SDG Indicators Database by the United Nations Office for Disaster Risk Reduction and have been extracted from two sources: (i) the Sendai Framework Monitoring System as provided by designated national focal points; and (ii) Desinventar disaster loss databases. Some of the data have not undergone an official validation process and may be subject to revision at a later date.

Source: United Nations Statistics Division. Global SDG Indicators Database. https://unstats.un.org/sdgs/indicators/database/ (accessed 8 July 2020).

Click on the indictor name in the table header to access the time series in the Key Indicators Database.

Goal 12. Ensure sustainable consumption and production patterns

Table 1.12.1: Selected Indicators for Sustainable Development Goal 12—Responsible Consumption and Production

ADB Regional Member	Target 12.2: By 2030, achieve the sustainable management and efficient use of natural resources							
	12.2.1: Material Footprint				12.2.2: Domestic Material Consumption			
	Total (t million)		Per Capita (t)		Total (t million)		Per Capita (t)	
	2000	2017	2000	2017	2000	2017	2000	2017
Developing ADB Member Economies								
Central and West Asia	**779.9**	**1,524.7**	...	...	**1,148.2**	**2,089.7**	...	...
Afghanistan	12.2	43.4	0.6	1.2	46.0	67.9	2.3	1.9
Armenia	7.5	23.9	2.4	8.2	13.8	32.5	4.5	11.1
Azerbaijan	20.7	61.5	2.6	6.3	30.2	90.1	3.7	9.2
Georgia	14.6	35.7	3.1	9.1	13.3	26.5	2.8	6.8
Kazakhstan	173.5	330.0	11.5	18.1	249.3	530.4	16.6	29.1
Kyrgyz Republic	30.0	52.3	6.1	8.6	32.0	50.7	6.5	8.4
Pakistan	354.7	628.6	2.6	3.2	514.4	875.8	3.7	4.4
Tajikistan	4.8	33.0	0.8	3.7	10.2	31.2	1.6	3.5
Turkmenistan	45.3	124.0	10.0	21.5	43.4	95.0	9.6	16.5
Uzbekistan	116.6	192.3	4.7	6.0	195.6	289.6	7.9	9.1
East Asia	...	...	...	...	...	...	...	...
China, People's Republic of	9,770.3	29,432.1	7.6	20.9	11,805.8	35,194.1	9.2	25.0
Hong Kong, China	...	...	...	...	...	...	...	...
Korea, Republic of	996.9	1,456.7	21.0	28.6	748.5	808.6	15.8	15.9
Mongolia	9.4	42.6	3.9	13.9	49.0	106.2	20.4	34.5
Taipei,China	...	...	...	...	...	...	...	...
South Asia	**3,239.3**	**6,732.9**	...	...	**4,250.0**	**8,098.0**	...	...
Bangladesh	228.1	388.9	1.7	2.4	255.8	438.3	1.9	2.7
Bhutan	2.9	8.4	5.0	10.4	4.7	8.4	8.3	10.4
India	2,938.7	6,162.0	2.8	4.6	3,868.5	7,417.2	3.7	5.5
Maldives	2.0	6.3	7.3	14.5	1.2	3.0	4.2	6.8
Nepal	30.6	81.6	1.3	2.8	61.7	114.4	2.6	3.9
Sri Lanka	37.0	85.8	2.0	4.1	58.0	116.8	3.1	5.6
Southeast Asia[a]	**2,503.4**	**5,746.3**	...	...	**3,065.8**	**5,840.6**	...	...
Brunei Darussalam	4.4	8.6	13.3	20.0	5.8	9.8	17.4	22.9
Cambodia	20.5	57.9	1.7	3.6	26.9	84.7	2.2	5.3
Indonesia	723.1	1,649.8	3.4	6.2	1,157.3	1,974.2	5.5	7.5
Lao People's Democratic Republic	7.1	51.7	1.3	7.5	13.7	82.2	2.6	12.0
Malaysia	444.5	763.8	19.2	24.2	388.5	609.4	16.8	19.3
Myanmar	24.8	76.4	0.5	1.4	106.9	187.6	2.3	3.5
Philippines	307.3	461.4	3.9	4.4	295.6	416.5	3.8	4.0
Singapore	212.5	434.4	54.3	76.1	260.0	186.3	66.4	32.6
Thailand	482.3	1,033.1	7.7	15.0	477.3	879.1	7.6	12.7
Timor-Leste	...	...	...	...	0.9	10.0	1.1	7.7
Viet Nam	277.0	1,209.2	3.5	12.7	332.8	1,400.7	4.1	14.7
The Pacific[a]	...	...	...	...	**89.9**	**99.9**	...	...
Cook Islands	...	...	...	...	...	...	...	...
Fiji	4.7	6.5	5.8	7.2	8.2	5.9	10.0	6.5
Kiribati	...	...	...	...	0.4	0.7	4.2	6.3
Marshall Islands	...	...	...	...	0.0	0.1	0.4	2.0
Micronesia, Federated States of	...	...	...	...	0.2	0.2	1.4	2.3
Nauru	...	...	...	...	...	...	...	...
Niue	...	...	...	...	...	...	...	...
Palau	...	...	...	...	0.0	0.0	0.2	1.2
Papua New Guinea	11.7	21.3	2.1	2.6	76.9	84.0	13.8	10.2
Samoa	1.0	1.6	5.7	7.9	0.7	1.0	4.0	5.3
Solomon Islands	...	...	...	...	2.2	4.3	5.4	7.1
Tonga	...	...	...	...	0.3	1.8	3.4	16.9
Tuvalu	...	...	...	...	0.0	0.0	0.9	1.1
Vanuatu	0.9	2.1	4.8	7.6	1.0	1.7	5.3	6.1
Developed ADB Member Economies	**4,282.1**	**4,480.9**	...	...	**2,539.6**	**2,182.8**	...	...
Australia	759.6	1,059.9	39.8	43.3	868.4	927.4	45.5	37.9
Japan	3,440.4	3,305.9	27.0	25.9	1,575.4	1,141.6	12.4	9.0
New Zealand	82.1	115.1	21.3	24.5	95.8	113.7	24.8	24.2

... = data not available, 0.0 = magnitude is less than half of unit employed, ADB = Asian Development Bank, t = metric ton.

a   Regional aggregates include reporting economies only.

Sources: For Indicator 12.2.1: United Nations Environment Programme. Environment Live. https://environmentlive.unep.org/ (accessed 20 July 2020). For Indicator 12.2.2: United Nations Statistics Division. Global SDG Indicators Database. https://unstats.un.org/sdgs/indicators/database/ (accessed 8 July 2020).

Click on the indictor name in the table header to access the time series in the Key Indicators Database.

Sustainable Development Goals

Goal 13. Take urgent action to combat climate change and its impacts

Table 1.13.1: Selected Indicators for Sustainable Development Goal 13—Impact of Disasters and Risk Reduction Strategies

ADB Regional Member	Target 13.1: Strengthen resilience and adaptive capacity to climate-related hazards and natural disasters in all countries					13.1.2: Countries that Adopt and Implement National Disaster Risk Reduction Strategies in Line with the Sendai Framework for Disaster Risk Reduction 2015–2030[b,c]
	13.1.1.a: Number of Persons Affected by Disaster[a]		13.1.1.b: Number of Deaths Due to Disaster[a]			
	2005	2019	2005	2019		2019
Developing ADB Member Economies						
Central and West Asia						
Afghanistan	...	332,536	...	368		0.73
Armenia	...	19,447	...	427		0.75
Azerbaijan	...	...	...	...		– (2017)
Georgia	...	91	...	7		0.98 (2018)
Kazakhstan	448	354	6	3		0.83
Kyrgyz Republic	...	1,170	70	19		0.90
Pakistan	5,586,710	11,489 (2018)	45,275	137 (2018)		0.43 (2018)
Tajikistan	...	1,193 (2018)	...	12 (2018)		1.00
Turkmenistan	...	...	...	...		...
Uzbekistan	...	...	...	...		...
East Asia						
China, People's Republic of	...	6,493,721 (2018)	...	589 (2018)		...
Hong Kong, China	...	...	...	...		...
Korea, Republic of	14,246	13,673 (2018)	26	133 (2018)		0.95 (2018)
Mongolia	5,522	9,092	193	203		1.00
Taipei,China	...	...	...	...		...
South Asia						
Bangladesh	...	36,782 (2018)	...	391 (2018)		...
Bhutan	3,801	242 (2018)	568	21		0.50 (2018)
India	...	...	...	...		...
Maldives	1,603	59 (2017)	1	1		– (2017)
Nepal	8,171	183,401	333	489		0.75
Sri Lanka	472,092	81,884	37	106		0.05 (2016)
Southeast Asia						
Brunei Darussalam	...	...	...	...		...
Cambodia	15,307	180,457	29	44		...
Indonesia	569,620	248,087	1,960	517		– (2018)
Lao People's Democratic Republic	731,471	6,229 (2012)	19	19 (2012)		...
Malaysia	10,158	10,529	14	9		0.25
Myanmar	90,925	212,677	8	526		0.70 (2017)
Philippines	112,649	5,562,065 (2018)	98	255 (2018)		0.65
Singapore	...	...	...	...		...
Thailand	...	142,780 (2018)	...	81 (2018)		0.58 (2018)
Timor-Leste	187,482 (2006)	579 (2017)	7 (2006)	2 (2017)		...
Viet Nam	114,264	616,422 (2010)	675	60 (2010)		...
The Pacific						
Cook Islands	1,681	4,443 (2010)	...	3 (2010)		...
Fiji	80 (2006)	77,756	3	2		...
Kiribati	...	...	...	...		0.90
Marshall Islands	96 (2008)	280 (2014)	...	...		...
Micronesia, Federated States of	...	...	...	10 (2015)		...
Nauru	...	...	...	...		...
Niue	...	...	...	...		...
Palau	...	1,528 (2012)	...	...		...
Papua New Guinea	2	358 (2013)	4	30 (2015)		...
Samoa	200 (2008)	...	18	1 (2014)		0.70 (2018)
Solomon Islands	21,343 (2007)	4,800 (2013)	138 (2007)	22 (2014)		...
Tonga	5 (2006)	84,311 (2018)	...	1 (2014)		...
Tuvalu	...	...	...	...		...
Vanuatu	4 (2007)	152 (2014)	2 (2006)	11 (2015)		...
Developed ADB Member Economies						
Australia	...	25,021 (2018)	...	1 (2018)		0.63 (2018)
Japan	...	446,061 (2018)	148	444 (2018)		1.00 (2018)
New Zealand	...	546 (2018)	2 (2006)	1 (2017)		0.88 (2018)

... = data not available, – = magnitude equals zero, ADB = Asian Development Bank.

a The data are submitted to the United Nations' Global SDG Indicators Database by the United Nations Office for Disaster Risk Reduction and have been extracted from two sources: (i) the Sendai Framework Monitoring System as provided by designated national focal points; and (ii) Desinventar disaster loss databases. Some of the data have not undergone an official validation process and may be subject to revision at a later date.

b Economies displaying data have adopted and implemented national disaster risk reduction strategies. The figures refer to the score for adoption and implementation of national disaster risk reduction strategies in line with the Sendai Framework. The scores indicate the degree of alignment of national strategies with the framework, based on self-assessments of the economy using 10 criteria for monitoring the progress of national national disaster risk reduction strategies. The score descriptors are: 1 = comprehensive alignment, 0.75 = substantial alignment, 0.50 = moderate alignment, 0.25 = limited alignment, 0 = no alignment.

c Some of the data have not undergone an official validation process and may be subject to revision at a later date.

Source: United Nations Statistics Division. Global SDG Indicators Database. https://unstats.un.org/sdgs/indicators/database/ (accessed 15 July 2020).

Click on the indictor name in the table header to access the time series in the Key Indicators Database.

Goal 14. Conserve and sustainably use the oceans, seas, and marine resources for sustainable development

Table 1.14.1: Selected Indicators for Sustainable Development Goal 14—Life Below Water

ADB Regional Member	Target 14.5: By 2020, conserve at least 10% of coastal and marine areas, consistent with national and international law and based on the best available scientific information		
	14.5.1.a: Average Proportion of Marine Key Biodiversity Areas Covered by Protected Areas (%)	14.5.1.b: Coverage of Protected Areas in Relation to Marine Areas (Exclusive Economic Zones)[a] (%)	14.5.1.c: Protected Marine Areas (Exclusive Economic Zones)[a] (km²)
	2019	2018	2018
Developing ADB Member Economies			
Central and West Asia			
Afghanistan	...	...	...
Armenia	...		
Azerbaijan	...	0.0	36.5
Georgia	35.6	0.7	152.9
Kazakhstan		2.7	...
Kyrgyz Republic	...	...	
Pakistan	14.6	0.3	570.4
Tajikistan	...	...	...
Turkmenistan	...	2.5	1,955.3
Uzbekistan	...	...	...
East Asia			
China, People's Republic of	8.3	1.5	13,140.2
Hong Kong, China	32.5	...	–
Korea, Republic of	38.5	2.7	8,929.8
Mongolia	...	...	...
Taipei,China	...	...	...
South Asia			
Bangladesh	25.9	5.2	4,432.7
Bhutan	...	...	...
India	18.8	0.1	2,444.0
Maldives	–	0.1	673.0
Nepal	...	...	...
Sri Lanka	50.0	0.1	330.6
Southeast Asia			
Brunei Darussalam	5.4	0.0	4.0
Cambodia	34.2	0.5	260.1
Indonesia	26.1	3.0	180,590.5
Lao People's Democratic Republic	...	...	...
Malaysia	13.7	0.4	1,585.3
Myanmar	20.0	0.5	2,462.9
Philippines	38.0	1.1	21,084.2
Singapore	3.3	0.0	0.1
Thailand	47.5	1.6	4,821.6
Timor-Leste	19.6	2.3	970.0
Viet Nam	23.9	2.5	16,168.3
The Pacific			
Cook Islands	29.3	99.2	1,957,543.5
Fiji	14.6	0.9	11,781.0
Kiribati	32.9	11.8	408,299.6
Marshall Islands	7.8	0.4	7,205.0
Micronesia, Federated States of	1.6	0.0	472.1
Nauru	–	...	...
Niue	...	0.0	4.4
Palau	70.0	99.4	604,201.5
Papua New Guinea	1.6	0.2	4,384.0
Samoa	2.4	0.0	2.3
Solomon Islands	2.4	0.1	1,546.1
Tonga	19.2	0.0	332.5
Tuvalu	...	0.0	212.5
Vanuatu	3.1	0.1	541.4
Developed ADB Member Economies			
Australia	63.2	40.4	3,002,884.8
Japan	64.8	2.3	94,269.6
New Zealand	44.1	29.8	1,222,307.0

... = data not available, – = magnitude equals zero, 0.0 = magnitude is less than half of unit employed, ADB = Asian Development Bank, km2 = square kilometer.

a An Exclusive Economic Zone comprises an area that extends from the coast, or in federal systems from the seaward boundaries of the constituent states (3 to 12 nautical miles, in most cases), to 200 nautical miles (370 kilometres) off the coast.

Sources: United Nations Statistics Division. Global SDG Indicators Database. https://unstats.un.org/sdgs/indicators/database/ (accessed 3 July 2020). For Indicators 14.5.1.b and 14.5.1.c for Kazakhstan: Ministry of National Economy of the Republic of Kazakhstan, Committee on Statistics. Official Statistics. https://stat.gov.kz/official/sustainable_development_goals/goal_14_life_below_water (accessed 24 July 2020).

Click on the indictor name in the table header to access the time series in the Key Indicators Database.

Table 1.15.1: Selected Indicators for Sustainable Development Goal 15—Protection of Ecosystems and Biodiversity

ADB Regional Member	15.1.1: Forest Area as a Proportion of Total Land Area[a] (%) 2000	2019	15.1.2 Terrestrial (%) 2000	2019	Freshwater (%) 2000	2019
Developing ADB Member Economies						
Central and West Asia	**3.9**	**4.0**	…	…	…	…
Afghanistan	1.9	1.9	–	5.7	–	–
Armenia	11.7	11.5	12.5	21.6	25.0	26.8
Azerbaijan	11.9	13.6	22.1	36.6	5.5	14.5
Georgia	39.7	40.6	21.3	40.3	17.6	37.3
Kazakhstan	1.2	1.3	9.2	11.1	8.4	10.1
Kyrgyz Republic	6.2	6.8	25.7	25.7	35.4	35.4
Pakistan	5.9	4.9	34.8	34.8	35.9	35.9
Tajikistan	3.0	3.0	15.8	16.8	27.9	30.5
Turkmenistan	8.8	8.8	14.0	14.0	12.7	12.7
Uzbekistan	7.0	8.6	10.1	10.1	1.1	1.1
East Asia	**18.0**	**21.7**	…	…	2.5	9.4
China, People's Republic of	18.8	23.1	3.2	9.9	2.5	9.4
Hong Kong, China	…	…	48.9	48.9	16.6	16.6
Korea, Republic of	66.5	64.6	24.8	37.5	36.8	36.8
Mongolia	9.2	9.1	33.1	41.7	30.7	38.6
Taipei,China	58.1 (2001)	60.7 (2018)	…	…	…	…
South Asia	**23.9**	**25.3**	…	…	…	…
Bangladesh	14.8	14.5	33.4	43.7	–	–
Bhutan	68.4	71.4	43.3	47.3	23.1	34.3
India	22.7	24.2	17.7	21.0	16.2	18.6
Maldives	2.7	2.7	–	–	…	…
Nepal	40.3	41.6	39.2	50.7	25.0	32.4
Sri Lanka	34.5	33.7	36.8	43.7	34.8	43.9
Southeast Asia	**51.5**	**48.0**	…	…	…	…
Brunei Darussalam	75.3	72.1	41.7	41.7	50.0	50.0
Cambodia	61.1	46.6	35.8	39.5	28.4	33.0
Indonesia	55.9	51.2	8.4	26.1	6.2	41.0
Lao People's Democratic Republic	75.5	72.1	44.0	44.0	29.9	29.9
Malaysia	59.9	58.3	28.5	28.5	50.0	50.0
Myanmar	53.4	44.2	12.4	24.9	14.2	27.1
Philippines	24.5	24.0	28.4	40.1	37.5	49.8
Singapore	24.0	22.2	19.0	21.1	…	…
Thailand	37.2	39.0	67.0	70.7	40.7	40.7
Timor-Leste	63.8	62.0	14.5	39.5	…	…
Viet Nam	38.0	47.0	10.8	39.2	8.5	38.2
The Pacific	**78.4**	**77.9**	…	…	…	…
Cook Islands	64.9	65.0	–	5.7	…	…
Fiji	55.1	62.0	4.4	11.2	–	0.1
Kiribati	1.5	1.5	–	40.0	…	…
Marshall Islands	52.2	52.2	–	10.1	…	…
Micronesia, Federated States of	91.2	92.0	0.0	0.0	…	…
Nauru	–	–	–	–	…	…
Niue	72.4	72.5	–	–	…	…
Palau	86.0	89.8	27.9	44.0	…	…
Papua New Guinea	80.1	79.3	6.8	6.9	…	…
Samoa	60.5	57.3	8.3	13.7	…	…
Solomon Islands	90.7	90.2	3.4	4.4	…	…
Tonga	12.4	12.4	12.5	26.1	…	…
Tuvalu	33.3	33.3	…	…	…	…
Vanuatu	36.3	36.3	2.8	2.8	…	…
Developed ADB Member Economies	**20.0**	**20.3**	…	…	…	…
Australia	17.2	17.4	35.1	55.7	23.3	37.7
Japan	68.2	68.4	54.7	64.8	55.5	62.9
New Zealand	37.4	37.5	42.0	46.4	21.8	29.3
DEVELOPING ADB MEMBER ECONOMIES	**22.8**	**24.0**	…	…	…	…
ALL ADB REGIONAL MEMBERS	**22.1**	**23.1**	…	…	…	…
WORLD	**31.9**	**31.2**	…	…	…	…

Target 15.1: By 2020, ensure the conservation, restoration, and sustainable use of terrestrial and inland freshwater ecosystems and their services, in particular forests, wetlands, mountains, and drylands, in line with obligations under international agreements

15.1.2: Proportion of Important Sites for Terrestrial and Freshwater Biodiversity that are Covered by Protected Areas

Goal 15. Protect, restore, and promote sustainable use of terrestrial ecosystems; sustainably manage forests; combat desertification and halt and reverse land degradation; and halt biodiversity loss

Table 1.15.1: Selected Indicators for Sustainable Development Goal 15—Protection of Ecosystems and Biodiversity (continued)

ADB Regional Member	Target 15.4: By 2030, ensure the conservation of mountain ecosystems, including their biodiversity, in order to enhance their capacity to provide benefits that are essential for sustainable development		Target 15.5: Take urgent and significant action to reduce the degradation of natural habitats, halt the loss of biodiversity and, by 2020, protect and prevent the extinction of threatened species	
	15.4.1: Coverage by Protected Areas of Important Sites for Mountain Biodiversity (%)		15.5.1: Red List Index[b]	
	2000	2019	2000	2019
Developing ADB Member Economies				
Central and West Asia				
Afghanistan	–	7.5	0.84	0.84
Armenia	13.0	22.3	0.85	0.85
Azerbaijan	32.9	55.5	0.91	0.91
Georgia	20.1	40.9	0.89	0.87
Kazakhstan	13.5	16.7	0.88	0.87
Kyrgyz Republic	35.4	35.4	0.99	0.98
Pakistan	35.2	35.2	0.94	0.86
Tajikistan	15.8	16.8	0.99	0.99
Turkmenistan	15.2	15.2	0.98	0.98
Uzbekistan	30.3	30.3	0.98	0.97
East Asia				
China, People's Republic of	3.6	11.6	0.81	0.74
Hong Kong, China	57.0	57.0	0.83	0.83
Korea, Republic of	20.2	20.2	0.76	0.70
Mongolia	38.6	46.7	0.96	0.95
Taipei,China	...	...	...	...
South Asia				
Bangladesh	–	–	0.83	0.75
Bhutan	43.3	47.3	0.80	0.80
India	22.9	29.2	0.75	0.68
Maldives	...	...	0.93	0.85
Nepal	51.2	60.6	0.83	0.83
Sri Lanka	20.5	30.4	0.64	0.57
Southeast Asia				
Brunei Darussalam	69.5	69.5	0.87	0.86
Cambodia	75.7	84.9	0.84	0.79
Indonesia	10.2	27.6	0.83	0.75
Lao People's Democratic Republic	51.9	51.9	0.84	0.83
Malaysia	32.8	32.8	0.84	0.77
Myanmar	17.7	42.4	0.86	0.80
Philippines	27.1	42.2	0.75	0.68
Singapore	...	...	0.91	0.85
Thailand	83.3	88.4	0.84	0.78
Timor-Leste	14.8	46.1	0.92	0.85
Viet Nam	13.0	43.7	0.80	0.73
The Pacific				
Cook Islands	–	–	0.81	0.77
Fiji	3.0	5.7	0.70	0.67
Kiribati	...	...	0.83	0.77
Marshall Islands	...	...	0.90	0.84
Micronesia, Federated States of	–	–	0.77	0.70
Nauru	...	...	0.83	0.77
Niue	...	...	0.77	0.77
Palau	...	...	0.91	0.73
Papua New Guinea	6.7	6.7	0.90	0.84
Samoa	11.1	18.3	0.79	0.77
Solomon Islands	–	0.0	0.83	0.76
Tonga	–	–	0.76	0.72
Tuvalu	...	...	0.90	0.83
Vanuatu	3.8	3.8	0.72	0.66
Developed ADB Member Economies				
Australia	37.8	64.1	0.88	0.82
Japan	63.6	66.9	0.83	0.78
New Zealand	28.4	34.4	0.71	0.62

... = data not available, 0.0 = magnitude is less than half of unit employed, – = magnitude equals zero, ADB = Asian Development Bank.

a   The regional aggregates are calculated by averaging the combined estimates for each economy. The aggregates for East Asia exclude Hong Kong, China.

b   The Red List Index value ranges from 1, which means all species are categorized as "Least Concern" (no species expected to become extinct in the near future), to 0, meaning that all species are categorized as "Extinct". The index therefore indicates how far the set of species has moved overall towards extinction.

Sources: United Nations Statistics Division. Global SDG Indicators Database. https://unstats.un.org/sdgs/indicators/database/ (accessed 8 July 2020). For Indicator 15.1.1 for Taipei,China: Government of Taipei,China, Directorate-General of Budget, Accounting and Statistics. National Statistics. https://eng.stat.gov.tw/ (accessed 8 July 2020).

Click on the indictor name in the table header to access the time series in the Key Indicators Database.

Goal 16. Promote peaceful and inclusive societies for sustainable development; provide access to justice for all; and build effective, accountable, and inclusive institutions at all levels

Table 1.16.1: Selected Indicators for Sustainable Development Goal 16—Peace, Justice, and Strong Institutions

ADB Regional Member	Target 16.1: Significantly reduce all forms of violence and related death rates everywhere		Target 16.3: Promote the rule of law at the national and international levels and ensure equal access to justice for all		Target 16.5: Substantially reduce corruption and bribery in all their forms	Target 16.9: By 2030, provide legal identity for all, including birth registration
	16.1.1: Number of Victims of Intentional Homicide (per 100,000 population)		16.3.2: Unsentenced Detainees as a Proportion of Overall Prison Population (%)		16.5.2: Proportion of Firms Experiencing at least One Bribe Payment Request (%)	16.9.1: Proportion of Children Under 5 Years of Age Whose Births have been Registered with a Civil Authority[a] (%)
	2000	2018	2005	2018	2015	2018
Developing ADB Member Economies						
Central and West Asia						
Afghanistan	3.9 (2009)	6.7	81.0	27.7	46.8 (2014)	42.3 (2015)
Armenia	3.0	1.7	28.2	35.6	8.7 (2013)	98.7 (2016)
Azerbaijan	2.8	2.2	12.0	15.5	16.0 (2013)	93.6 (2006)
Georgia	5.5	2.2	54.2	11.5	1.3 (2019)	99.6 (2015)
Kazakhstan	15.6	5.1 (2017)	15.6	10.9	11.6 (2019)	99.7 (2015)
Kyrgyz Republic	8.7	2.2	16.2	16.4	31.4 (2019)	98.9
Pakistan	6.3	3.9	57.8	66.1	30.8 (2013)	42.2
Tajikistan	4.6	1.6 (2011)	...	...	11.1 (2019)	95.8 (2017)
Turkmenistan	5.9	...	...	...	...	99.6 (2016)
Uzbekistan	4.3	1.1 (2017)	...	...	5.9 (2019)	99.9 (2006)
East Asia						
China, People's Republic of	2.1	0.5	...	...	11.6 (2012)	...
Hong Kong, China	0.7	0.7	11.5	22.2	...	...
Korea, Republic of	0.8	0.6	34.2	35.4	...	...
Mongolia	13.9 (2003)	6.2	21.6	22.9	24.7 (2019)	99.6
Taipei,China	1.4 (2001)	0.8 (2015)	10.9	5.2	...	...
South Asia						
Bangladesh	2.6	2.4	64.0	84.7	47.7 (2013)	56.0 (2019)
Bhutan	3.0	1.2	...	...	0.9	99.9 (2010)
India	4.6	3.1	67.9	67.7	22.7 (2014)	79.7 (2016)
Maldives	2.4 (2001)	0.7 (2013)	...	...	...	98.8 (2017)
Nepal	2.7	2.3 (2016)	...	...	14.4 (2013)	56.2 (2016)
Sri Lanka	6.8 (2003)	2.4	52.4	57.8	10.0 (2011)	97.2 (2007)
Southeast Asia						
Brunei Darussalam	1.2	0.5 (2013)	7.2	7.1	...	...
Cambodia	4.7	1.8 (2011)	32.6	31.7	64.7 (2016)	73.3 (2014)
Indonesia	1.0	0.4 (2017)	46.6	30.7	30.6	71.9
Lao People's Democratic Republic	...	...	...	...	40.3 (2018)	73.0 (2017)
Malaysia	2.4	2.1 (2013)	33.8	33.0	28.2	...
Myanmar	2.2	2.3 (2016)	...	...	29.3 (2016)	81.3 (2016)
Philippines	7.4	6.5	77.0	73.4	17.2	91.8 (2017)
Singapore	1.0	0.2	4.1	11.5	...	99.9
Thailand	8.2	2.6 (2017)	24.6	18.0	9.9 (2016)	99.5 (2016)
Timor-Leste	2.4 (2004)	4.1 (2015)	64.7	23.2	44.2	60.4 (2016)
Viet Nam	1.2 (2001)	1.5 (2011)	...	...	26.1	96.1 (2014)
The Pacific						
Cook Islands	...	3.5 (2012)	3.7	14.6	...	100.0 (2017)
Fiji	3.1 (2003)	2.3 (2014)	8.7	25.9	10.5 (2009)	...
Kiribati	3.6	7.5 (2012)	2.6	5.4	...	93.5 (2009)
Marshall Islands	...	...	...	...	...	83.8 (2017)
Micronesia, Federated States of	...	...	...	...	4.5 (2009)	...
Nauru	...	...	...	...	...	95.9 (2013)
Niue	...	...	...	...	...	...
Palau	...	11.2	...	...	...	...
Papua New Guinea	8.0	9.8 (2010)	31.3	37.8	26.4	13.4
Samoa	8.7 (2009)	3.1 (2013)	8.1	6.5	30.5 (2009)	58.6 (2014)
Solomon Islands	4.4 (2004)	...	35.4	50.4	43.8	88.0 (2015)
Tonga	1.0	1.0 (2012)	2.6	7.4	24.9 (2009)	93.4 (2012)
Tuvalu	0.0 (2002)	18.6 (2012)	...	...	...	49.9 (2007)
Vanuatu	...	...	22.5	22.4	11.9 (2009)	43.4 (2013)
Developed ADB Member Economies						
Australia	1.9	0.9	20.4	31.6	...	100.0 (2015)
Japan	0.5	0.3	15.0	11.3	...	100.0 (2016)
New Zealand	1.3	0.7 (2017)	17.3	18.2	...	100.0 (2016)

... = data not available, – = magnitude equals zero, ADB = Asian Development Bank.

a   Changes in the definition of birth registration were made from the second and third rounds of Multiple Indicator Cluster Surveys (MICS2 and MICS3) to the fourth round (MICS4). In order to allow for comparability with the latter round, data from MICS2 and MICS3 on birth registration were recalculated according to the MICS4 indicator definition. Therefore, the recalculated data presented here may differ from estimates included in MICS2 and MICS3 national reports.

Sources: For 1.16.1: United Nations Office on Drugs and Crime. Statistics Online. https://dataunodc.un.org/ (accessed 23 July 2020) For 16.3.2: United Nations Statistics Division. Global SDG Indicators Database. https://unstats.un.org/sdgs/indicators/database/ (accessed 20 July 2020). For 16.5.2: World Bank. World Development Indicators. https://data.worldbank.org/indicator (accessed 23 July 2020) For 16.9.1: United Nations Children's Fund. UNICEF Data Warehouse. https://data.unicef.org/ (accessed 23 July 2020).

Click on the indictor name in the table header to access the time series in the Key Indicators Database.

Goal 17. Strengthen the means of implementation and revitalize the Global Partnership for Sustainable Development

Table 1.17.1: Selected Indicators for Sustainable Development Goal 17—Financial Sustainability of Developing Countries

ADB Regional Member	Target 17.4: Assist developing countries in attaining long-term debt sustainability through coordinated policies aimed at fostering debt financing, debt relief, and debt restructuring, as appropriate, and address the external debt of highly indebted poor countries to reduce debt distress				Target 17.9: Enhance international support for implementing effective and targeted capacity-building in developing countries to support national plans to implement all the Sustainable Development Goals, including through North-South, South-South, and triangular cooperation	
	17.4.1: Debt Service as a Proportion of Exports of Goods and Services (%)				17.9.1: Dollar Value of Financial and Technical Assistance Committed to Developing Countries[a] (constant 2018 $ million)	
	2000		2018		Average, 2000–2009	Average, 2009–2018
Developing ADB Member Economies						
Central and West Asia[b]	...		...		**1,480.8**	**3,306.5**
Afghanistan	0.4	(2008)	4.0	(2017)	728.7	1,301.5
Armenia	8.2		6.6		67.9	105.0
Azerbaijan	5.5		8.3		34.1	121.6
Georgia	12.2		4.8		86.2	153.4
Kazakhstan	8.8		2.1		54.3	323.2
Kyrgyz Republic	9.8		7.0		52.7	98.3
Pakistan	21.1		16.0		382.3	937.7
Tajikistan	9.1	(2002)	8.7		31.1	45.9
Turkmenistan	...		...		6.2	6.5
Uzbekistan	...		3.0		37.4	213.3
East Asia[b]	...		...		**393.3**	**941.0**
China, People's Republic of	7.1		0.8		351.9	753.4
Hong Kong, China	...		...		...	...
Korea, Republic of	...		...		...	...
Mongolia	6.5		11.6		41.4	187.5
Taipei,China	...		...		...	...
South Asia[b]	...		...		**981.5**	**1,517.6**
Bangladesh	10.3		4.2		239.2	525.6
Bhutan	2.5	(2006)	10.4		16.1	23.8
India	15.4		4.2		523.6	648.6
Maldives	4.0		7.9		3.5	10.5
Nepal	7.4		7.4	(2017)	86.5	188.6
Sri Lanka	10.9		21.7		112.5	120.4
Southeast Asia[b]	...		...		**1,497.7**	**3,121.0**
Brunei Darussalam	...		...		...	...
Cambodia	0.7		1.4		91.4	136.4
Indonesia	11.2		8.5		733.9	1,442.5
Lao People's Democratic Republic	7.9		10.8		50.1	87.5
Malaysia	...		...		17.8	14.2
Myanmar	1.0		4.8		15.5	206.6
Philippines	14.6		4.5		154.0	419.5
Singapore	...		...		...	...
Thailand	5.8		0.5		45.4	70.9
Timor-Leste	–	(2006)	0.3		55.0	47.6
Viet Nam	7.2		1.4		334.5	695.8
The Pacific[b]	...		...		**326.3**	**393.0**
Cook Islands	...		...		2.7	4.1
Fiji	2.3		1.9		17.5	19.7
Kiribati	...		...		8.2	9.6
Marshall Islands	...		...		20.0	7.3
Micronesia, Federated States of	...		...		43.3	16.7
Nauru	...		...		9.9	8.2
Niue	...		...		1.9	6.7
Palau	...		...		1.7	3.3
Papua New Guinea	8.0		1.7		98.5	180.1
Samoa	5.5	(2004)	9.8		15.7	36.8
Solomon Islands	2.8		1.3		85.1	60.2
Tonga	9.8	(2001)	7.2		10.5	16.5
Tuvalu	...		...		3.1	4.7
Vanuatu	1.4		2.0	(2016)	14.9	19.0
Developed ADB Member Economies	...		...		...	...
Australia	...		...		...	...
Japan	...		...		...	...
New Zealand	...		...		...	...
DEVELOPING ADB MEMBER ECONOMIES[b]	...		...		**4,679.6**	**9,279.0**
DEVELOPING ECONOMIES WORLDWIDE[c]	...		...		**20,601.7**	**31,056.0**

... = data not available, $ = United States dollars, ADB = Asian Development Bank.

a   Technical assistance includes assistance through North-South, South-South, and triangular cooperation. The United Nations Statistics Division dataset and metadata refer to this indicator as total official development assistance (gross disbursements) for technical cooperation.

b   For reporting economies only.

c   The figures provided refer to aggregates for all developing economies as reported in the United Nations' Global SDG Indicators Database.

Source: United Nations Statistics Division. Global SDG Indicators Database. http://unstats.un.org/sdgs/indicators/database/ (accessed 17 July 2020).

Goal 17. Strengthen the means of implementation and revitalize the Global Partnership for Sustainable Development

Table 1.17.2: Selected Indicators for Sustainable Development Goal 17—Statistical Capacity Building

ADB Regional Member	Target 17.18: By 2020, enhance capacity-building support to developing countries, including for least developed countries and small island developing states, to increase significantly the availability of high-quality, timely, and reliable data disaggregated by income, gender, age, race, ethnicity, migratory status, disability, geographic location, and other characteristics relevant in national contexts	Target 17.19: By 2030, build on existing initiatives to develop measurements of progress on sustainable development that complement gross domestic product and support statistical capacity-building in developing countries	
	17.18.3: Availability of National Statistical Plan[a]	17.19.1: Value of All Resources Made Available to Strengthen Statistical Capacity in Developing Countries (current $)	17.19.2: Countries that Have Conducted at Least One Population and Housing Census in the Past 10 Years[b]
	2019	2017	2019
Developing ADB Member Economies			
Central and West Asia[c]		**8,082,034.1**	
Afghanistan	B	485,253.9	...
Armenia	A, B, C, D	235,920.0	2011
Azerbaijan	...	22,514.5	2019
Georgia	...	...	2014
Kazakhstan	A, B	174,245.0	...
Kyrgyz Republic	A, B, C, D	3,040,650.7	...
Pakistan	A, B	3,684,806.4	2017
Tajikistan	C, D, E	438,643.6	2010
Turkmenistan	...	...	2012
Uzbekistan	A, B, C, D, E	...	...
East Asia[c]		**149,023.6**	
China, People's Republic of	A, B	91,844.7	2010
Hong Kong, China	A, B	...	2016
Korea, Republic of	B	...	2015
Mongolia	A, B, C, D	57,178.9	2010
Taipei,China	...	...	2010
South Asia[c]		**6,059,569.3**	
Bangladesh	A, B, C, D	652,727.6	2011
Bhutan	A, B, C, D	51,000.0	2017
India	B	2,976,145.4	2011
Maldives	B	86,163.0	2014
Nepal	B, C, D	2,266,612.3	2011
Sri Lanka	C, D	26,921.0	2012
Southeast Asia[c]		**6,526,092.9**	
Brunei Darussalam	A	3,750.0	2011
Cambodia	C, D	475,800.0	2019
Indonesia	...	437,364.9	2010
Lao People's Democratic Republic	B	933,025.0	2015
Malaysia	...	90,287.9	2010
Myanmar	B	2,782,717.1	2014
Philippines	B	267,477.0	2015
Singapore	A, B	...	2010
Thailand	A, B	277,269.4	2010
Timor-Leste	B	1,034,487.8	2015
Viet Nam	B	223,913.8	2019
The Pacific[c]		**2,158,537.2**	
Cook Islands	B	6,261.0	2016
Fiji	...	6,360.6	2017
Kiribati	...	46,471.0	2015
Marshall Islands	...	...	2011
Micronesia, Federated States of	...	6,950.7	2010
Nauru	...	38,983.8	2011
Niue	...	10,092.7	2017
Palau	A	4,851.0	2015
Papua New Guinea	B	921,422.8	2011
Samoa	A, B, C, D	33,010.0	2016
Solomon Islands	B	991,113.2	2019
Tonga	A, B, C, D, E	21,296.7	2016
Tuvalu	B	48,172.3	2012
Vanuatu	...	23,551.4	2016
Developed ADB Member Economies			
Australia	A, B	...	2016
Japan	A, B	...	2015
New Zealand	A, B, E	...	2018

... = data not available, $ = United States dollars, ADB = Asian Development Bank.

a A = a national statistical plan fully funded, B = a national statistical plan under implementation, C = a national statistical plan with funding from government, D = a national statistical plan with funding from donors, E = a national statistical plan with funding from others.

b Refers to the most recent year in which a population and housing census was conducted.

c Aggregates were calculated as the sum of reporting economies with data corresponding to the year heading.

Sources: United Nations Statistics Division. Global SDG Indicators Database. http://unstats.un.org/sdgs/indicators/database/ (accessed 20 July 2020). For Taipei,China: Government of Taipei,China, Directorate-General of Budget, Accounting and Statistics. National Statistics. https://eng.stat.gov.tw/ (accessed 20 July 2020).

Click on the indictor name in the table header to access the time series in the Key Indicators Database.

Regional Trends and Tables

Regional Tables and Trends—Data Stories

Part II of *Key Indicators for Asia and the Pacific 2020* contains 100 regional tables depicting trends in social, economic, and environmental developments in the 49 Asian Development Bank (ADB) member economies located across Asia and the Pacific. These statistical tables are grouped into eight themes, each with a short commentary highlighting important developments regarding select indicators. Each theme concludes with a section on data issues and comparability, detailing issues surrounding the collection and presentation of indicators.

The eight themes are People; Economy and Output; Money, Finance, and Prices; Globalization; Transport and Communications; Energy and Electricity; Environment; and Government and Governance.

Data patterns for the key indicators are summarized and/or visualized through charts and figures. These charts and figures compare indicators across ADB member economies and depict the most recent year for which data were available, which was generally 2019. In some cases, the most recent year for which data were available is compared with either the previous year (e.g., 2018) or an earlier year (e.g., 2000 or 2010). Such comparisons help the reader identify regional, subregional, and economy-level trends.

I. People

People highlights standard demographic indicators such as population size, years of schooling, and the number of physicians and hospital beds per 1,000 people. The tables in this section present data on migration and urbanization; age structure; birth, death, and fertility rates; age dependency ratios; employment; poverty and inequality; health and education resources; and the Human Development Index.

Asia and the Pacific remains home to more than half of all the people on the planet

Asia and the Pacific's total population reached 4,207 million in 2019, up from 3,436 million in 2000 (Table 2.1.1). However, the region's share of the global population decreased slightly from 55.9% in 2000 to 54.5% in 2019 (Figure 2.1.1).

In 2019, the average annual population growth rates of developing ADB member economies in the Pacific (2.7%), Central and West Asia (1.9%), South Asia (1.1%), and Southeast Asia (1.1%) met or exceeded the global average (1.1%). Populations in East Asia expanded an average of 0.3% in 2019, while annual population growth averaged only 0.1% among the three developed ADB member economies in the Asia and Pacific region.

The most populous subregion in 2019 was South Asia (1,562 million). This was followed by East Asia (1,486 million), Southeast Asia (658 million), Central and West Asia (332 million), and the Pacific (12 million). The aggregate population of the region's three developed member economies—Australia, Japan, and New Zealand—was 157 million.

Among the world's 10 most populous countries in 2019, five were located in Asia and the Pacific: the People's Republic of China (PRC) ranked first with 1,400 million, India ranked second with 1,343 million,

Indonesia ranked fourth with 268 million, Pakistan ranked fifth with 211 million, and Bangladesh ranked eighth with 167 million (UN 2019).

The region's economies with the smallest populations in 2019 were all located in the Pacific: Niue (1,900), Tuvalu (10,600), and Nauru (11,600).

Pakistan and Malaysia are leading the way in boosting education for girls

In the 1970s, Asia and the Pacific was home to two-thirds of the world's out-of-school children. Today, about 90% of children, on average, are enrolled in primary school in economies across the region.[1]

From 2000 to 2019 (or from the earliest to the most recent years for which data were available), 19 developing member economies reported an increase in the mean number of years of schooling for both boys and girls, while two developing member economies posted a decrease for both boys and girls, and one economy (Nepal) saw an increase in the mean number of years of schooling for boys but a decrease for girls.

Pakistan and Malaysia reported the largest increases in the mean number of years of schooling

---

[1]   For more information on education issues in Asia and the Pacific, go to https://www.adb.org/sectors/education/issues.

Figure 2.1.1: Distribution of Population by Global Region and by Economy in Asia and the Pacific, 2019 (%)

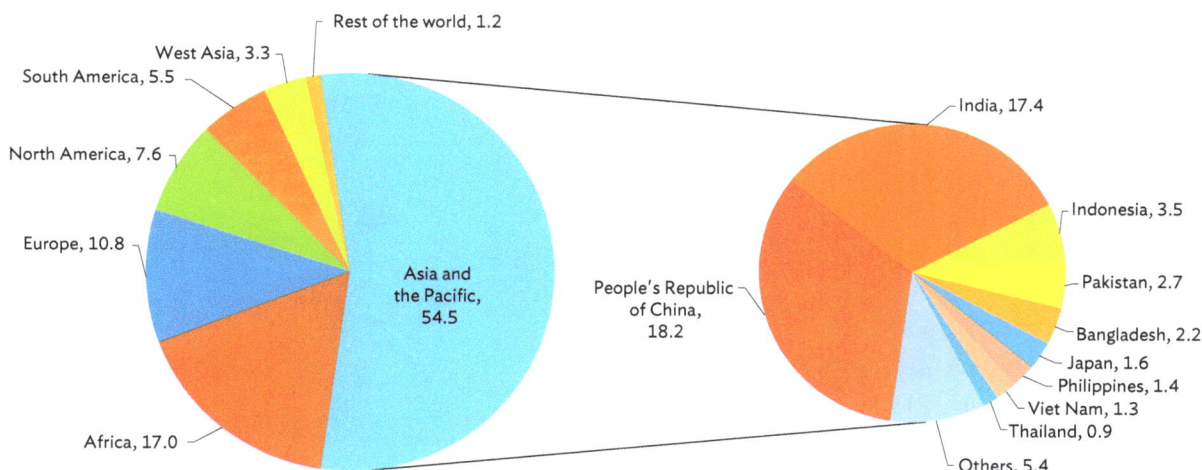

Note: The aggregate for the West Asia region was adjusted to exclude Armenia, Azerbaijan, and Georgia, which are included in the total for Asia and the Pacific.
Source: Table 2.1.1, Key Indicators for Asia and the Pacific 2020.

Click here for figure data

for girls during the review period. Both economies posted increases of 2.3 years, followed by Fiji (1.7 years). For boys, the largest increases in the mean number of years of schooling occurred in Pakistan (2.2 years), Bangladesh (1.7 years), and Fiji (1.5 years).

Using the most recent year for which data were available, the leaders among developing member economies in terms of mean total years of schooling for girls were Georgia (13.2 years), Kazakhstan (12.2 years), and Samoa (12.0 years). The economies with the highest mean total years of schooling for boys were Georgia (13.1 years); the Republic of Korea (12.9 years); and Hong Kong, China (12.7 years).

Emergency preparedness, as measured by the number of physicians and hospital beds per 1,000 people, will help health care systems across Asia and the Pacific respond to the COVID-19 pandemic

Health care systems worldwide are coming under strain due to the coronavirus (COVID-19) pandemic. There are numerous measures of the preparedness of health care systems to effectively cope with diseases such as

Figure 2.1.2: Mean Years of Schooling in Select Economies of Asia and the Pacific, by Sex
(difference between earliest and most recently available annual data)

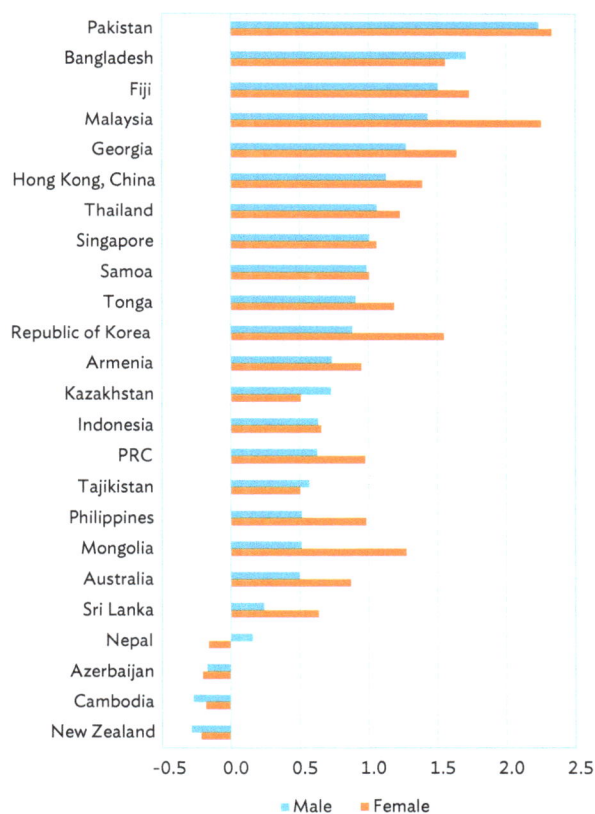

PRC = People's Republic of China.
Note: Earliest year refers to the period 2000 to 2009, while latest year refers to 2010 to 2019, where data are available. Only economies with available data for both earliest and latest years are included.
Source: Table 2.1.12, Key Indicators for Asia and the Pacific 2020.

Click here for figure data

COVID-19, among them the number of physicians and hospital beds per 1,000 people (WHO 2020).

In 2018 (or the most recent year for which data were available), the three leading economies in Asia and the Pacific in terms of physicians per 1,000 people were Georgia (7.1 physicians), Maldives (4.6 physicians), and Armenia (4.4 physicians) as shown in Figure 2.1.3. Those with the fewest number of physicians per 1,000 people were all Pacific economies: Papua New Guinea (0.07 physicians), Vanuatu (0.17 physicians), and the Federated States of Micronesia (FSM) (0.18 physicians) as demonstrated in Table 2.1.14.

In terms of hospital beds per 1,000 people, the region's leading economies in 2018 (or the most recent year for which data were available) were Japan (13.0 beds), the Republic of Korea (12.4 beds), and Mongolia (8.0 beds). Those with the fewest number of hospital beds per 1,000 people include Nepal (0.3 beds), Afghanistan (0.4 beds), and India (0.5 beds).

Data Issues and Comparability

Demographic data are based on vital registration records, censuses, and surveys. Since vital registration records in many developing ADB member economies are incomplete, they cannot be used for statistical purposes. In most economies, population censuses, which are used to provide more accurate estimates of population sizes, are conducted every 10 years. Population numbers in between census years are products of imputation methods that use various population distributional assumptions.

The United Nations (UN) Department of Economics and Social Affairs' Population Division uses future trends on fertility, mortality, and international migration to project population numbers through to 2100. The medium-fertility variant included in the UN's *World Population Prospects 2019* assumes, over the remainder of the century, a decline of fertility in economies where

Figure 2.1.3: Health Care Resources in Select Economies of Asia and the Pacific
(per 1,000 population)

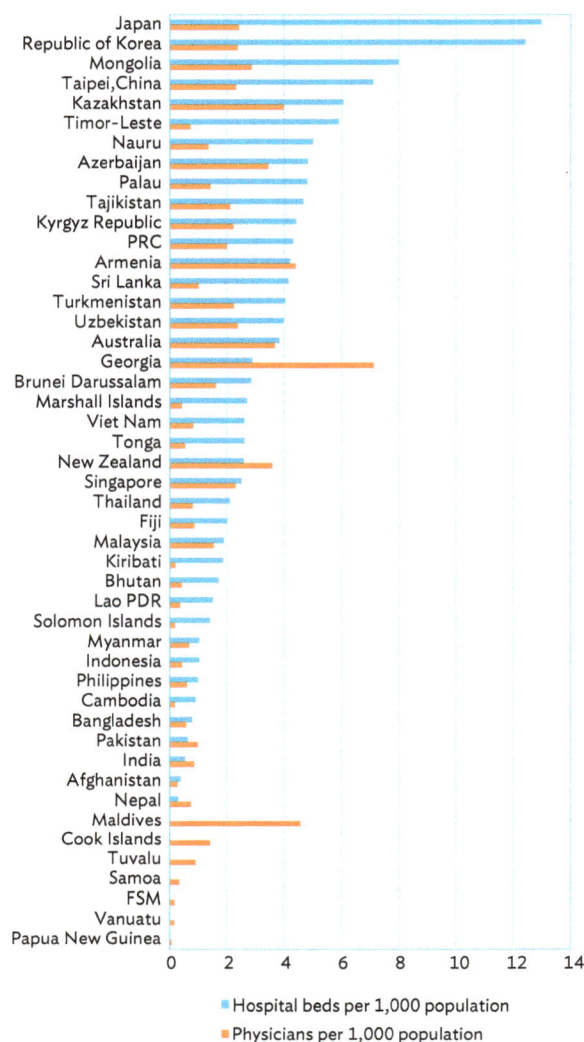

■ Hospital beds per 1,000 population
■ Physicians per 1,000 population

FSM = Federated States of Micronesia, Lao PDR = Lao People's Democratic Republic, PRC = People's Republic of China.

Notes: Data presented refers to the period 2010 to 2019. For the Cook Islands, FSM, Maldives, Papua New Guinea, Samoa, Tuvalu, and Vanuatu, data on the number of hospital beds per 1,000 population is not available for the years 2010 to 2019.

Source: Table 2.1.14 Key Indicators for Asia and the Pacific 2020.

Click here for figure data

large families are still prevalent, a slight increase of fertility in several economies where women have fewer than two live births on average over a lifetime, and continued reductions in mortality at all ages.

Urban population statistics are compiled according to each economy's national definition, as there is no agreed international standard for defining an urban area, which poses constraints in comparability of urban and city indicators across economies. Data from *World Urbanization Prospects* were used when national estimates were not available.

Household surveys, which are the best source of labor force data, are not carried out in all economies on a regular basis. Some economies rely on census data supplemented by enterprise surveys and unemployment registration records, which are often incomplete and may refer only to formal employment.

Furthermore, a breakdown by economic activities also may not be available. An initiative is underway to adopt new standards for work and employment statistics, following the recommendations of the 19th International Conference of Labour Statisticians in 2013. These recommendations were adopted by Timor-Leste in 2010, the Lao People's Democratic Republic (Lao PDR) in 2017, Armenia and Nepal in 2018, and Mongolia in 2019. Hence, data for these years may not be directly comparable with data in other years. For all other economies, the conceptual definitions used are based on the old framework.

Table 2.1.1:   **Midyear Population**

ADB Regional Member	Population (million)				Population Growth Rates[a] (%)			
	2000	**2005**	**2010**	**2019**	**2000**	**2005**	**2010**	**2019**
Developing ADB Member Economies								
Central and West Asia[b]	**230.0**	**251.7**	**276.8**	**332.3***	**2.1**	**1.8**	**2.0**	**1.9***
Afghanistan[c]	19.5	22.1	24.5	30.7	5.0	1.9	2.1	2.2
Armenia	3.2	3.1	3.0	3.0*	-0.3	-0.6	-0.7	-0.2*
Azerbaijan	8.1	8.5	9.1	10.0	1.0	1.2	1.2	0.8
Georgia	4.1	3.9	3.8	3.7	-1.9	-0.6	-0.7	-0.2
Kazakhstan	14.9	15.1	16.3	18.5	-0.3	0.9	1.4	1.4
Kyrgyz Republic[c]	4.9	5.1	5.4	6.4	1.4	1.2	1.3	2.1
Pakistan	140.0	156.0	173.5	211.2	2.4	2.2	2.1	1.9
Tajikistan	6.2	6.8	7.5	9.2*	2.3	1.2	2.5	2.2*
Turkmenistan	4.5	4.8	5.1	5.9	1.1	1.1	1.6	1.6
Uzbekistan	24.7	26.2	28.6	33.6	1.4	1.2	2.9	1.9
East Asia[b]	**1,345.7**	**1,387.8**	**1,423.3**	**1,486.2**	**0.8**	**0.6**	**0.5**	**0.3**
China, People's Republic of[c]	1,267.4	1,307.6	1,340.9	1,400.1	0.8	0.6	0.5	0.3
Hong Kong, China	6.7	6.8	7.0	7.5	0.9	0.4	0.7	0.8
Korea, Republic of	47.0	48.2	49.6	51.7	0.8	0.2	0.5	0.2
Mongolia	2.4	2.5	2.7	3.3	1.3	1.2	1.6	1.8
Taipei,China	22.2	22.7	23.1	23.6	0.8	0.4	0.3	0.1
South Asia[b]	**1,189.6**	**1,290.5**	**1,382.6**	**1,561.9**	**1.8**	**1.6**	**1.4**	**1.1**
Bangladesh	129.3	138.6	148.6	166.5	1.4	1.4	1.4	1.3
Bhutan	0.6	0.6	0.7	0.7	1.3	1.3	1.8	1.0
India[c]	1,019.0	1,106.0	1,186.0	1,342.6	1.8	1.6	1.4	1.1
Maldives	0.3	0.3	0.4	0.5	1.5	3.3	2.3	4.3
Nepal	21.0	25.3	26.3	29.7	3.0	2.3	1.4	2.1
Sri Lanka	19.4	19.6	20.7	21.8	1.3	0.9	1.0	0.6
Southeast Asia[b]	**514.1**	**551.2**	**589.2**	**658.4**	**1.5**	**1.5**	**1.4**	**1.1**
Brunei Darussalam	0.3	0.4	0.4	0.5	2.5	1.8	1.8	3.9
Cambodia	12.5	13.3	14.1	16.0	1.3	1.3	1.3	1.4
Indonesia	205.1	220.9	237.6	268.1	1.4[d]	1.9	1.4	1.2
Lao People's Democratic Republic	5.1	5.6	6.0	6.9	2.0	2.0	1.5	1.4
Malaysia	23.5	26.0	28.6	32.6	2.5	2.1	1.8	0.6
Myanmar[c]	46.1	48.5	50.2	54.3	1.2	0.9	0.7	0.9
Philippines	76.8	84.7	93.1	107.3	2.3	1.9	2.3	1.4
Singapore	4.0	4.3	5.1	5.7	1.7	2.4	1.8	1.2
Thailand	62.2	64.1	65.9	69.3	1.1	0.6	0.6	0.3
Timor-Leste	0.9	1.0	1.1	1.3	1.3	2.4	1.8	2.0
Viet Nam	77.6	82.4	87.1	96.5	1.4	1.2	1.2	1.2
The Pacific[b,e]	**7.2**	**8.2**	**9.3**	**11.8***	**2.7**	**2.6**	**2.7**	**2.7***
Cook Islands	18.0	21.5	23.7	20.2*	9.1	5.9	4.9	8.6*
Fiji	802.0	827.0	850.7	889.3	0.6	0.7	0.6	0.4
Kiribati[c]	84.5	92.5	103.1	116.1*	1.7	1.8	2.2	1.3
Marshall Islands	51.2	51.2	52.9	54.6*	0.8	1.4	1.1	-0.0*
Micronesia, Federated States of[c]	107.0	105.6	102.8	104.5	0.2	-0.3	-0.5	0.2
Nauru	10.1	9.5	9.7	11.6	1.0	-2.2	1.9	1.6
Niue[c]	1.9	1.6 (2006)	1.6 (2011)	1.9*	-3.7[d]	...	...	1.1[f]
Palau	18.9	19.8	18.3	17.5*	0.3	0.8	-1.9	-0.5*
Papua New Guinea	5,190.8	6,051.7	7,055.4	9,300.0	3.3	3.1	3.1	3.1
Samoa	175.2	179.9	186.4	200.9	0.9	0.5	0.8	0.8
Solomon Islands	418.6	470.1	555.5	680.0	2.3	2.3	2.6[g]	1.9
Tonga	99.1	101.2	102.8	99.6	0.4	0.4	0.2	-0.5
Tuvalu	9.5	10.3	11.1	10.6	1.3	3.1	0.5	-0.3
Vanuatu	191.0	214.0	239.7	290.8	2.3	2.3	2.4	2.2
Developed ADB Member Economies[b]	**149.7**	**152.1**	**154.5**	**156.5**	**0.3**	**0.2**	**0.3**	**0.1**
Australia	19.0	20.2	22.0	25.4	1.2	1.2	1.6	1.5
Japan	126.8	127.8	128.1	126.3	0.2	0.0	0.0	-0.2
New Zealand	3.9	4.1	4.4	4.9	0.6	1.1	1.1	1.6
DEVELOPING ADB MEMBER ECONOMIES[b]	**3,286.6**	**3,489.3**	**3,681.3**	**4,050.5***	**1.3**	**1.2**	**1.1**	**0.9***
ALL ADB REGIONAL MEMBERS[b]	**3,436.3**	**3,641.4**	**3,835.7**	**4,207.0***	**1.3**	**1.1**	**1.0**	**0.9***
WORLD	**6,143.5**	**6,541.9**	**6,956.8**	**7,713.5**	**1.3**	**1.2**	**1.2**	**1.1**

... = data not available, * = provisional or preliminary, 0.0 = magnitude is less than half of unit employed, ADB = Asian Development Bank.

a   The annual population growth rate is calculated as the percentage change in population when comparing the reference year with the year prior. For example, the population growth rates under the column heading "2019" refer to population growth from 2018 to 2019.

b   Regional population totals include only reporting economies with data corresponding to the year heading, while regional population growth rates are estimated as a weighted average of the annual population growth rates of the reporting economies. Weights are based on the total population of the region for the years in which the reporting economies have published the annual growth rates.

c   Estimates of population size are as of 1 January for the Kyrgyz Republic; 11 March for Niue; 10 June for Afghanistan; 30 September for the Federated States of Micronesia; 1 October for India and Myanmar; 7 November for Kiribati; and 31 December for the People's Republic of China.

d   Refers to 2001 annual population growth rate.

e   The total population for the Pacific region is expressed in millions, while estimates of population size for ADB developing member economies in the Pacific are expressed in thousands.

f   Refers to the 2017 annual population growth rate.

g   Refers to the 2011 annual population growth rate.

Sources: Economy sources and United Nations. World Population Prospects 2019. https://population.un.org/wpp/Download/Standard/Population/ (accessed 8 June 2020).

Click on the indictor name in the table header to access the time series in the Key Indicators Database.

Table 2.1.2: Migration and Urbanization

ADB Regional Member	Net International Migration Rate[a] (per 1,000 population)				Urban Population[b] (% of total population)			
	2000–2005	2005–2010	2010–2015	2015–2020	2000	2005	2010	2019
Developing ADB Member Economies								
Central and West Asia	...	...	...	...	35.5	36.3	38.8	43.3*
Afghanistan	6.4	-7.6	3.3	-1.7	21.3	21.5	23.2	25.3
Armenia	-10.6	-12.5	-2.1	-1.7	64.8	64.0	63.5	63.9*
Azerbaijan	0.9	1.2	0.2	0.1	51.1	52.5	53.0	52.8
Georgia	-6.9	-5.8	-4.7	-2.5	55.1	56.5	56.5	58.9
Kazakhstan	0.6	-0.4	1.9	-1.0	56.5	57.1	54.5	58.3
Kyrgyz Republic	-6.9	-2.9	-3.3	-0.6	34.7	34.8	34.1	34.0
Pakistan	-0.9	-0.4	-1.1	-1.1	33.0	34.6	36.3	43.2
Tajikistan	-4.5	-4.1	-3.4	-2.2	26.6	26.4	26.4	26.3*
Turkmenistan	-5.4	-2.5	-1.9	-0.9	45.9	47.1	48.5	52.0
Uzbekistan	-1.9	-1.0	-0.4	-0.3	37.2	36.1	51.3	50.6
East Asia	...	...	...	...	38.4	44.9	51.5	61.5
China, People's Republic of	-0.3	-0.3	-0.2	-0.2	36.2	43.0	50.0	60.6
Hong Kong, China	1.9	2.6	2.1	4.0	100.0	100.0	100.0	100.0
Korea, Republic of	0.3	-0.6	1.6	0.2	79.6	81.3	81.9	81.4
Mongolia	-1.2	-0.8	-0.3	-0.3	56.6	61.9	69.2	68.1
Taipei,China[c]	1.8	2.2	1.5	1.3	55.8	57.7	59.3	61.0
South Asia	...	...	...	...	26.8	27.9	29.1	33.9
Bangladesh	-2.2	-4.5	-3.0	-2.3	23.1	24.2	25.9	37.4
Bhutan	2.0	-3.3	0.1	0.4	21.0	30.9	34.8	40.9
India	-0.3	-0.4	-0.4	-0.4	27.7	28.8	29.9	34.0
Maldives	11.6	10.5	28.4	22.8	27.7	33.8	36.4	40.2
Nepal	-6.2	-7.4	-15.1	1.5	14.1	14.6	16.6	21.4
Sri Lanka	-4.7	-5.2	-4.7	-4.6	18.4	18.3	18.2	18.6
Southeast Asia	...	...	...	...	37.9	40.5	44.1	49.4
Brunei Darussalam	0.2	-1.2	-0.4	–	71.2	73.2	75.0	77.9
Cambodia	-0.6	-4.3	-2.0	-1.9	18.6	19.2	20.3	23.8
Indonesia	-1.1	-1.1	-0.4	-0.4	42.0	45.9	49.9	56.0
Lao People's Democratic Republic	-5.3	-3.7	-3.5	-2.1	22.0	27.2	30.1	35.6
Malaysia	5.5	5.7	1.7	1.6	62.0	66.5	71.0	76.2
Myanmar	-5.1	-5.4	-2.0	-3.1	27.0	27.9	28.9	30.0
Philippines	-3.0	-3.4	-1.7	-0.6	46.1	45.7	45.3	47.1
Singapore	4.5	30.7	11.8	4.7	100.0	100.0	100.0	100.0
Thailand	1.2	0.2	0.5	0.3	31.1	32.5	42.0	53.6
Timor-Leste	-5.9	-7.3	-4.9	-4.3	24.3	26.0	27.7	30.9
Viet Nam	-1.6	-1.9	-0.9	-0.8	24.1	27.1	30.4	35.0
The Pacific	...	...	...	...	19.1	19.0	18.8	18.8
Cook Islands	...	...	...	...	65.2	71.0	73.3	75.3
Fiji	-14.4	-5.6	-12.0	-7.0	47.9	49.9	52.2	56.8
Kiribati	-4.4	-0.6	-7.7	-6.9	43.0	43.6	47.4	54.8
Marshall Islands	...	...	...	...	68.6	71.1	73.6	77.4
Micronesia, Federated States of	-23.0	-23.5	-5.7	-5.4	22.3	22.3	22.3	22.8
Nauru	...	...	...	...	100.0	100.0	100.0	100.0
Niue	...	...	...	...	33.1	35.2	38.7	45.5
Palau	...	...	...	...	69.5	77.4	77.0	78.7 (2015)
Papua New Guinea	-2.7	1.1	-0.1	-0.1	13.2	13.1	13.0	13.3
Samoa	-17.7	-16.5	-12.8	-14.3	20.0	22.1	21.0	18.8
Solomon Islands	-3.8	-5.7	-2.8	-2.5	15.8	17.8	20.0	24.2
Tonga	-15.8	-15.2	-25.4	-7.7	23.0	23.2	23.4	22.6
Tuvalu	...	...	...	...	46.0	49.7	54.8	63.2
Vanuatu	-2.6	-2.9	1.4	0.4	21.8	23.2	24.4	25.1
Developed ADB Member Economies	...	...	...	...	79.5	85.7	89.9	90.7
Australia	6.0	11.4	8.6	6.4	84.1 (2001)	84.6	85.7	86.9
Japan	0.3	0.4	0.6	0.6	78.6	86.0	90.8	91.7
New Zealand	6.7	2.9	4.0	3.2	83.5	83.8	83.7	83.7
DEVELOPING ADB MEMBER ECONOMIES	...	...	...	...	33.9	37.2	40.9	47.3*
ALL ADB REGIONAL MEMBERS	...	...	...	...	35.9	39.2	42.8	48.9*
WORLD	...	...	...	...	46.7	49.2	51.6	55.7

... = data not available, – = magnitude equals zero, ADB = Asian Development Bank.

a Refers to annual average migration over the period shown. United Nations population estimates and projections are based on all available sources of data on population size and levels of fertility, mortality, and international migration. Statistics on international migration are sourced from population registers and other administrative sources. These estimates and projections are made for 235 distinct national economies or areas comprising the total population of the world.

b In estimating the aggregates for Asia and the Pacific, imputation was done for economies with missing data by substituting available data from the nearest years. The aggregates were derived using data on total population and percentage of urban population from economy sources and the United Nations publications World Population Prospects 2019 and World Urbanization Prospects: The 2018 Revision.

c For urban population, refers to localities of 100,000 or more inhabitants.

Sources: For net international migration rate: United Nations. World Population Prospects 2019. https://population.un.org/wpp/Download/Standard/Migration/ (accessed 8 June 2020). For urban population: economy sources and United Nations. World Urbanization Prospects: The 2018 Revision. https://population. un.org/wup/Download/ (accessed 1 July 2020).

Table 2.1.3:   Proportion of Total Population by Age Bracket, and Age Dependency Ratio[a]

ADB Regional Member	Population Aged 0–14 Years (% of total population)				Population Aged 15–64 Years (% of total population)			
	2000	2005	2010	2019	2000	2005	2010	2019
Developing ADB Member Economies								
Central and West Asia	**39.9**	**37.7**	**35.9**	**34.2**	**55.6**	**57.7**	**59.7**	**61.2**
Afghanistan	48.9	47.9	48.2	42.5	48.8	49.9	49.5	54.9
Armenia	25.8	21.5	19.5	20.8	64.2	66.6	69.5	67.8
Azerbaijan	31.1	26.2	22.8	23.4	63.0	67.2	71.3	70.1
Georgia	20.8	19.0	18.0	20.0	66.2	66.5	67.8	64.9
Kazakhstan	27.5	24.5	24.1	28.9	65.6	67.8	69.1	63.5
Kyrgyz Republic	34.9	31.0	29.9	32.5	59.6	63.4	65.6	62.9
Pakistan	42.0	40.0	37.7	35.1	54.0	55.9	58.1	60.6
Tajikistan	42.5	38.0	35.7	37.1	53.9	58.2	61.0	59.8
Turkmenistan	36.3	32.6	29.5	30.8	59.5	62.8	66.3	64.6
Uzbekistan	37.3	32.6	29.1	28.8	58.1	62.6	66.4	66.6
East Asia	**24.6**	**20.3**	**18.5**	**17.6**	**68.6**	**72.2**	**73.3**	**70.8**
China, People's Republic of	24.8	20.4	18.7	17.8	68.4	72.2	73.3	70.7
Hong Kong, China	16.9	14.3	11.9	12.3	72.1	73.4	75.1	70.2
Korea, Republic of	20.6	18.8	16.1	12.7	72.2	72.3	73.2	72.2
Mongolia	34.8	28.9	27.0	30.8	61.5	67.3	69.2	65.0
Taipei,China	21.2	19.0	15.9	12.8	70.0	71.3	73.4	72.1
South Asia	**35.0**	**32.9**	**31.0**	**26.7**	**60.7**	**62.4**	**64.0**	**67.0**
Bangladesh	37.0	34.4	32.0	27.2	59.2	61.3	63.2	67.6
Bhutan	39.8	35.1	31.2	25.3	56.3	60.5	63.7	68.6
India	34.7	32.7	30.8	26.6	60.9	62.5	64.1	67.0
Maldives	40.5	31.5	25.3	19.9	55.8	64.1	70.2	76.5
Nepal	41.0	39.3	36.3	29.6	55.3	56.4	58.7	64.7
Sri Lanka	26.8	25.6	25.4	24.0	67.0	67.6	67.2	65.2
Southeast Asia	**31.8**	**29.9**	**27.9**	**25.4**	**63.4**	**64.9**	**66.6**	**67.7**
Brunei Darussalam	30.7	27.8	26.0	22.6	67.0	69.2	70.7	72.2
Cambodia	41.6	37.1	33.3	31.1	55.3	59.5	62.9	64.2
Indonesia	30.7	29.9	28.8	26.2	64.6	65.3	66.2	67.7
Lao People's Democratic Republic	43.4	40.3	36.4	32.3	53.1	56.0	59.9	63.5
Malaysia	33.4	30.5	28.0	23.7	62.7	65.1	67.1	69.4
Myanmar	32.5	31.2	30.0	25.9	63.0	64.2	65.1	68.1
Philippines	38.5	37.1	34.0	30.5	58.3	59.4	61.9	64.2
Singapore	18.7	17.2	14.0	12.3	74.9	75.6	78.7	75.3
Thailand	24.0	21.3	19.2	16.8	69.5	71.0	71.9	70.8
Timor-Leste	44.9	44.7	42.5	37.3	51.7	51.6	53.4	58.4
Viet Nam	31.6	27.1	23.6	23.2	62.0	66.4	69.9	69.2
The Pacific	**39.4**	**38.4**	**37.5**	**35.3**	**57.4**	**58.2**	**59.0**	**60.9**
Cook Islands	34.7	31.4	27.9	25.6	59.1	61.3	63.8	63.8
Fiji	35.0	30.5	29.0	29.3	61.6	65.4	66.2	65.1
Kiribati	40.0	36.9	36.1	35.8	56.7	59.5	60.3	60.1
Marshall Islands	42.3	41.3	41.8	37.7	55.5	56.5	55.9	58.7
Micronesia, Federated States of	40.4	38.9	35.7	31.5	56.0	57.3	61.1	64.4
Nauru	40.1	37.1	35.6	40.0	58.6	61.2	63.1	57.6
Niue	30.0	25.5	24.8	21.0	60.8	64.0	63.0	64.1
Palau	23.9	24.1	20.3	19.9	70.7	70.2	73.2	70.9
Papua New Guinea	39.8	39.2	38.3	35.5	57.2	57.6	58.4	61.0
Samoa	40.8	39.6	38.3	37.9	54.8	55.6	56.7	57.2
Solomon Islands	41.9	41.3	40.8	40.1	55.2	55.7	55.9	56.2
Tonga	38.5	38.2	37.4	35.1	55.9	55.9	56.9	59.0
Tuvalu	37.1	34.3	32.0	31.3	57.0	60.1	62.7	62.1
Vanuatu	41.5	39.7	38.2	38.7	55.2	57.1	57.9	57.7
Developed ADB Member Economies	**15.8**	**14.8**	**14.4**	**13.9**	**68.0**	**66.6**	**64.7**	**60.4**
Australia	20.9	19.8	19.0	19.3	66.8	67.3	67.6	64.8
Japan	14.8	13.8	13.4	12.6	68.2	66.5	64.1	59.4
New Zealand	22.7	21.5	20.5	19.6	65.5	66.4	66.4	64.4
DEVELOPING ADB MEMBER ECONOMIES	**30.6**	**27.8**	**26.1**	**23.8**	**64.0**	**66.3**	**67.6**	**68.0**
ALL ADB REGIONAL MEMBERS	**30.0**	**27.3**	**25.6**	**23.4**	**64.1**	**66.3**	**67.5**	**67.7**
WORLD	**30.1**	**28.1**	**27.0**	**25.6**	**63.0**	**64.6**	**65.5**	**65.3**

continued on next page

Table 2.1.3: Proportion of Total Population by Age Bracket, and Age Dependency Ratio[a] (continued)

ADB Regional Member	Population Aged 65 Years and Older (% of total population)				Age Dependency Ratio for Total Population			
	2000	2005	2010	2019	2000	2005	2010	2019
Developing ADB Member Economies								
Central and West Asia	**4.4**	**4.6**	**4.5**	**4.6**	**79.7**	**73.3**	**67.6**	**63.4**
Afghanistan	2.3	2.2	2.3	2.6	104.9	100.3	102.0	82.1
Armenia	10.0	11.9	11.0	11.5	55.8	50.1	43.8	47.6
Azerbaijan	5.8	6.6	5.9	6.4	58.7	48.8	40.3	42.6
Georgia	12.9	14.5	14.2	15.1	51.0	50.4	47.5	54.1
Kazakhstan	6.8	7.7	6.8	7.7	52.4	47.4	44.6	57.6
Kyrgyz Republic	5.5	5.6	4.5	4.6	67.9	57.7	52.5	59.0
Pakistan	4.0	4.1	4.2	4.3	85.0	78.8	72.2	65.0
Tajikistan	3.6	3.8	3.3	3.1	85.6	71.9	63.9	67.1
Turkmenistan	4.3	4.6	4.1	4.6	68.2	59.2	50.7	54.7
Uzbekistan	4.6	4.8	4.5	4.6	72.1	59.8	50.7	50.1
East Asia	**6.9**	**7.6**	**8.2**	**11.7**	**45.9**	**38.6**	**36.5**	**41.3**
China, People's Republic of	6.8	7.5	8.1	11.5	46.2	38.6	36.5	41.4
Hong Kong, China	11.0	12.2	12.9	17.5	38.7	36.2	33.1	42.5
Korea, Republic of	7.2	8.9	10.7	15.1	38.5	38.3	36.6	38.5
Mongolia	3.7	3.7	3.8	4.2	62.5	48.5	44.6	53.8
Taipei,China	8.7	9.7	10.7	15.1	42.8	40.3	36.2	38.7
South Asia	**4.3**	**4.7**	**5.1**	**6.3**	**64.7**	**60.4**	**56.3**	**49.2**
Bangladesh	3.9	4.3	4.8	5.2	69.0	63.0	58.1	47.9
Bhutan	3.9	4.4	5.1	6.1	77.7	65.3	57.0	45.8
India	4.4	4.7	5.1	6.4	64.2	59.9	56.0	49.2
Maldives	3.8	4.4	4.6	3.6	79.3	56.0	42.5	30.7
Nepal	3.8	4.3	5.0	5.8	80.9	77.2	70.4	54.7
Sri Lanka	6.2	6.8	7.4	10.8	49.2	48.0	48.8	53.4
Southeast Asia	**4.9**	**5.1**	**5.5**	**6.9**	**57.8**	**54.0**	**50.1**	**47.7**
Brunei Darussalam	2.4	3.0	3.4	5.2	49.3	44.5	41.5	38.6
Cambodia	3.1	3.4	3.7	4.7	80.7	67.9	58.9	55.8
Indonesia	4.7	4.8	5.0	6.1	54.8	53.1	51.0	47.6
Lao People's Democratic Republic	3.6	3.7	3.7	4.2	88.4	78.5	67.0	57.4
Malaysia	3.9	4.4	4.9	6.9	59.4	53.5	49.0	44.1
Myanmar	4.5	4.6	4.8	6.0	58.7	55.8	53.5	46.9
Philippines	3.3	3.5	4.1	5.3	71.6	68.2	61.6	55.7
Singapore	6.4	7.2	7.3	12.4	33.5	32.3	27.0	32.8
Thailand	6.5	7.8	8.9	12.4	43.9	40.9	39.0	41.3
Timor-Leste	3.4	3.7	4.0	4.3	93.3	93.7	87.2	71.2
Viet Nam	6.4	6.5	6.5	7.6	61.3	50.7	43.1	44.4
The Pacific	**3.2**	**3.4**	**3.5**	**3.8**	**74.2**	**71.7**	**69.6**	**64.2**
Cook Islands	6.2	7.3	8.2	10.6	69.3	63.1	56.7	56.7
Fiji	3.4	4.1	4.8	5.6	62.5	53.0	51.1	53.7
Kiribati	3.3	3.5	3.6	4.1	76.3	68.0	65.8	66.4
Marshall Islands	2.1	2.2	2.3	3.6	80.0	76.9	78.8	70.5
Micronesia, Federated States of	3.7	3.9	3.2	4.2	78.6	74.7	63.7	55.4
Nauru	1.3	1.7	1.3	2.4	70.7	63.4	58.5	73.6
Niue	9.2	10.5	12.1	14.9	64.6	56.4	58.7	56.0
Palau	5.4	5.7	6.5	9.2	41.4	42.5	36.7	41.0
Papua New Guinea	3.1	3.2	3.3	3.5	74.9	73.5	71.3	63.9
Samoa	4.4	4.8	5.0	4.9	82.3	79.7	76.3	74.8
Solomon Islands	2.9	3.0	3.3	3.6	81.1	79.6	78.9	77.8
Tonga	5.6	5.9	5.7	5.9	78.9	78.9	75.8	69.5
Tuvalu	5.9	5.6	5.3	6.6	75.4	66.5	59.5	61.1
Vanuatu	3.3	3.3	3.9	3.6	81.1	75.3	72.8	73.4
Developed ADB Member Economies	**16.3**	**18.6**	**20.9**	**25.7**	**47.1**	**50.1**	**54.5**	**65.4**
Australia	12.3	12.9	13.4	15.9	49.7	48.6	47.9	54.3
Japan	17.0	19.7	22.5	28.0	46.6	50.3	55.9	68.3
New Zealand	11.8	12.1	13.1	16.0	52.7	50.6	50.5	55.2
DEVELOPING ADB MEMBER ECONOMIES	**5.5**	**5.9**	**6.3**	**8.2**	**56.4**	**50.9**	**47.9**	**47.0**
ALL ADB REGIONAL MEMBERS	**5.9**	**6.4**	**6.9**	**8.9**	**55.9**	**50.8**	**48.1**	**47.6**
WORLD	**6.9**	**7.3**	**7.6**	**9.1**	**58.7**	**54.8**	**52.8**	**53.2**

ADB = Asian Development Bank.

Note: All figures presented in this table are ADB estimates using data from the United Nations' World Population Prospects 2019 and/or official communication from The Pacific Community's Statistics for Development Division.

a United Nations population estimates are based on all available sources of data on population size and levels of fertility, mortality, and international migration for 235 distinct countries or areas comprising the total population of the world.

Sources: United Nations. World Population Prospects 2019. https://population.un.org/wpp/ (accessed 8 June 2020). For the Cook Islands, the Marshall Islands, Nauru, Niue, Palau, and Tuvalu: The Pacific Community, Statistics for Development Division. Official communication, 3 July 2019.

Table 2.1.4:   Labor Force Participation Rates[a]
(%)

ADB Regional Member	2000	2005	2010	2014	2015	2016	2017	2018	2019
Developing ADB Member Economies									
Central and West Asia									
Afghanistan[b]	...	...	49.8 (2011)	...	...	53.9	...	...	...
Armenia[c]	61.4	57.7	61.2	63.1	62.5	61.0	60.9	58.8	58.9*
Azerbaijan	77.6	68.4	64.8	65.1	65.4	66.0	66.2	66.3	66.5
Georgia	65.2	62.7	63.3	65.5	66.8	66.3	65.8	63.9	62.9
Kazakhstan	66.0	69.4	71.2	70.7	69.7	70.0	69.7	70.0	70.1
Kyrgyz Republic	64.4 (2002)	64.8	64.2	62.4	62.4	61.5	60.1	59.8	...
Pakistan	42.8	43.7	45.9	45.5	45.2	...	...	44.3	...
Tajikistan	56.3	55.0	50.3	47.8	47.7	46.7	46.2	45.7	...
Turkmenistan	60.5	62.6	63.3	64.4	64.6	64.7	64.7	64.6	64.5
Uzbekistan	69.7	67.9	70.7	71.3	71.9	72.5	73.5	74.3	...
East Asia									
China, People's Republic of	77.4	73.5	71.3	70.2	69.8	69.4	69.0	68.5	68.0
Hong Kong, China	61.4	60.9	59.6	61.1	61.1	61.1	61.1	61.2	60.6
Korea, Republic of	61.2	62.2	61.1	62.7	62.8	62.9	63.2	63.1	63.3
Mongolia[c]	62.9	63.5	61.6	62.1	61.5	60.5	61.1	61.0	60.5
Taipei,China	57.7	57.8	58.1	58.5	58.7	58.7	58.8	59.0	59.2
South Asia									
Bangladesh	54.9	58.5 (2006)	59.3	...	...	58.5	58.2	...	...
Bhutan[d]	56.5 (2001)	60.4	68.6	62.6	63.1	62.2	63.3	62.6	66.4
India	37.6	39.2	36.4 (2011)	...	...	...	36.9*	37.5*	...
Maldives[e]	47.7	57.7 (2006)	52.1	63.8	...	57.6	...	...	...
Nepal	...	77.2 (2004)	74.3 (2012)	72.2	...	...	...	38.5	...
Sri Lanka	50.3	49.3	48.6	53.2	53.8	53.8	54.1	51.8	52.3
Southeast Asia									
Brunei Darussalam	67.9 (2001)	...	68.9 (2011)	65.6	...	...	62.7	65.4	64.3
Cambodia	65.2	74.6 (2004)	87.0	82.6	82.7	84.0	86.6	...	...
Indonesia	67.8	66.8	67.7	66.6	65.8	66.3	66.7	67.3	67.5
Lao People's Democratic Republic[c]	79.9 (2001)	66.6	79.2	...	...	...	40.8	...	...
Malaysia	65.4	63.3	63.7	67.6	67.9	67.7	68.0	68.3	68.7
Myanmar	...	...	...	67.0	64.7	...	61.2	61.5	...
Philippines[f]	64.9	65.1	64.1	64.6	63.7	63.5	61.2	60.9	61.3
Singapore[g]	63.2	63.0	66.2	67.0	68.3	68.0	67.7	67.7	68.0
Thailand[h]	71.5	72.5	72.3	70.3	69.8	68.8	68.1	68.3	67.5
Timor-Leste[c]	56.0 (2001)	60.2 (2004)	24.0	...	...	46.9	...	...	...
Viet Nam	...	74.7 (2007)	77.4	77.7	77.8	77.3	76.7	76.8	76.2
The Pacific									
Cook Islands	69.0 (2001)	70.2 (2006)	71.0 (2011)	...	...	71.9	...	...	...
Fiji	...	...	...	55.2	...	58.3	57.1	...	...
Kiribati	80.9	63.6	59.3	...	66.0	...	...	...	...
Marshall Islands	51.1	51.1	41.7 (2011)	...	...	...	...	...	...
Micronesia, Federated States of	58.6	...	57.3	...	...	...	...	...	...
Nauru	...	...	64.0 (2011)	...	...	...	...	...	...
Niue	78.7 (2001)	78.0 (2006)	68.9 (2011)	...	...	...	68.6	...	...
Palau	67.5	69.1	68.1 (2012)	...	77.4	...	...	...	...
Papua New Guinea	72.0	61.1	48.3	47.7	47.4	47.3	47.3	47.4	47.2
Samoa[i]	50.6 (2001)	49.8 (2006)	41.3 (2011)	...	...	47.4	43.3	...	...
Solomon Islands	...	...	62.9 (2009)	...	...	...	...	...	...
Tonga	...	94.8 (2003)	...	...	...	63.7	...	46.7	...
Tuvalu	58.2 (2002)	...	59.4 (2012)	...	...	52.3	...	...	...
Vanuatu	68.9	69.6	69.7	69.7	70.0	70.0	69.9	69.9	69.9
Developed ADB Member Economies									
Australia	63.1	64.4	65.4	64.7	65.0	64.9	65.2	65.6	66.0
Japan	62.4	60.4	59.6	59.4	59.6	60.0	60.5	61.5	62.1
New Zealand	65.2	67.7	67.7	68.7	68.7	69.8	70.6	70.6	70.3

... = data not available, * = provisional or preliminary, ADB = Asian Development Bank.

a   Based on varying concepts and definitions of "labor force" across economies.
b   For 2016, data refer to April–September only.
c   Recommendations from the 19th International Conference of Labour Statisticians were adopted by Armenia, for 2018 onward; Mongolia, for 2019; Nepal, for 2018; the Lao People's Democratic Republic, for 2017; and Timor-Leste, for 2010 and 2016. Hence, data for these years may not be directly comparable with data in other years. The conference provides the statistical concept of work for reference purposes; and the operational concepts, definitions, and guidelines for (i) three distinct subsets of work activities, referred to as forms of work (including own-use production work), employment work, and volunteer work; (ii) related classifications of the population according to their labor force status and main work status; and (iii) measures of labor underutilization. The concept of employment has also been refined to refer to work for pay or profit.
d   For 2005 and 2017, data are from censuses of population. For all other years, data are from labor force surveys. Thus, data prior to and after the census years may not be directly comparable with 2005 and 2017 data.
e   Includes local population only.
f   For 2005, annual data on labor force participation rate refer to the average of April, July, and October figures, in view of the adoption of a new definition.
g   Refers to Singapore residents only.
h   Includes seasonally inactive labor force.
i   Figures for different years may not be directly comparable with each other due to changes in methodology and labor concepts adopted.

Sources: Economy sources. For Papua New Guinea, the People's Republic of China, Turkmenistan (for 2005 onward), and Vanuatu: International Labour Organization. ILOSTAT Database. http://www.ilo.org/ilostat/ (accessed 1 July 2020). For the Lao People's Democratic Republic for 2001: International Labour Organization. ILOSTAT Database. http://www.ilo.org/ilostat/ (accessed July 2016). For Timor-Leste for 2001: United Nations Development Programme. East Timor Human Development Report 2002. http://www.tl.undp.org/content/timor_leste/en/home/library/poverty/human-development-report-2002-timor-leste.html (accessed 23 July 2018). For Tuvalu: Secretariat of the Pacific Community. National Minimum Development Indicator Database. http://www.spc.int/nmdi/ (accessed 2 July 2020).

Click on the indictor name in the table header to access the time series in the Key Indicators Database.

Table 2.1.5: **Employment in Agriculture, Industry, and Services**[a]
(% of total employment)

ADB Regional Member	Agriculture			
	2000	2005	2010	2019
Developing ADB Member Economies				
Central and West Asia				
Afghanistan[b]	69.6 (2001)	69.6 (2004)	...	39.5 (2016)
Armenia[c]	44.4	46.2	38.6	22.8
Azerbaijan	39.1	38.7	38.2	36.0
Georgia[d]	52.8 (2001)	50.0	48.0	38.1
Kazakhstan	31.4	31.9	28.3	13.5
Kyrgyz Republic	53.1	38.5	31.2	20.3 (2018)
Pakistan[e]	48.4	43.0	45.0	38.5 (2018)
Tajikistan	65.0	67.5	65.9	60.8 (2018)
Turkmenistan	47.6	...	...	...
Uzbekistan	34.4	29.1	26.8	26.2
East Asia				
China, People's Republic of[f]	50.0	44.8	36.7	25.1
Hong Kong, China[g]	0.3	0.3	–	–
Korea, Republic of[h]	10.7	8.0	6.6	5.1
Mongolia[c]	48.6	39.9	33.5	25.3
Taipei,China	7.8	5.9	5.2	4.9
South Asia				
Bangladesh	50.8	48.1 (2006)	47.5	40.6 (2017)
Bhutan[i]	46.5 (2001)	43.6	59.4	51.1
India	59.9	56.1	53.2 (2009)	...
Maldives[j]	13.7	15.9 (2007)	4.3	9.0 (2016)
Nepal[c]	...	...	64.0 (2011)	21.5 (2018)
Sri Lanka[k]	36.0	32.8	32.5	25.3
Southeast Asia				
Brunei Darussalam	...	...	...	2.0
Cambodia	73.7	60.3	72.3	64.3 (2014)
Indonesia	45.3	44.0	38.3	27.3
Lao People's Democratic Republic[c]	...	76.3	72.2	31.3 (2017)
Malaysia[l]	16.7	14.6	13.6	10.2
Myanmar	...	...	...	48.2 (2018)
Philippines[m]	37.1	35.7	33.2	22.9
Singapore[n]	0.1	0.1	0.2	0.1
Thailand	44.2	38.6	38.2	31.4
Timor-Leste	...	...	26.3	31.6 (2016)
Viet Nam[o]	65.1	55.1	49.5	34.5
The Pacific				
Cook Islands[p]	7.2 (2001)	4.9 (2006)	4.3 (2011)	5.4 (2016)
Fiji[q]	1.5	1.1	1.7	3.2 (2018)
Kiribati[r]	...	2.7	22.1	24.3 (2015)
Marshall Islands	0.9	0.6	1.0	1.2 (2018)
Micronesia, Federated States of	52.2	...	...	...
Nauru	...	...	...	...
Niue	9.0 (2001)	15.9 (2006)	10.4 (2011)	8.7 (2017)
Palau[s]	7.1	7.8	...	6.4 (2015)
Papua New Guinea	...	...	...	...
Samoa[t]	39.9 (2001)	35.4 (2006)	37.0 (2011)	21.9 (2017)
Solomon Islands[u]	...	...	41.5 (2009)	...
Tonga	...	27.9 (2006)	...	20.0 (2018)
Tuvalu	...	...	...	...
Vanuatu	...	...	...	...
Developed ADB Member Economies				
Australia	4.8	3.6	3.2	2.5
Japan	5.1	4.4	4.0	3.3
New Zealand[v]	8.8	6.9	6.7	5.8

continued on next page

Table 2.1.5:   Employment in Agriculture, Industry, and Services[a] *(continued)*
(% of total employment)

ADB Regional Member	Industry			
	2000	2005	2010	2019
Developing ADB Member Economies				
Central and West Asia				
Afghanistan[b]	6.2 (2001)	6.2 (2004)	...	14.8 (2016)
Armenia[c]	20.6	15.9	17.4	22.8
Azerbaijan	12.1	12.4	13.7	14.8
Georgia[d]	5.8 (2001)	7.5	7.2	14.3
Kazakhstan	18.2	17.9	18.7	19.7
Kyrgyz Republic	10.5	17.6	21.1	24.8 (2018)
Pakistan[e]	11.5	20.3	20.9	24.6 (2018)
Tajikistan	9.1	8.7	7.9	8.9 (2018)
Turkmenistan	13.0	...	...	...
Uzbekistan	12.7	13.2	22.7	23.2
East Asia				
China, People's Republic of[f]	22.5	23.8	28.7	27.5
Hong Kong, China[g]	19.6	14.4	11.2	11.4
Korea, Republic of[h]	20.4	26.7	25.0	24.6
Mongolia[c]	14.1	16.8	16.2	21.6
Taipei,China	28.1	36.4	35.9	35.6
South Asia				
Bangladesh	13.1	14.6 (2006)	17.6	20.4 (2017)
Bhutan[i]	5.6 (2001)	17.2	6.6	15.5
India	16.3	18.8	21.5 (2009)	...
Maldives[j]	19.0	27.9 (2007)	9.4	18.4 (2016)
Nepal[c]	...	...	9.5 (2011)	30.8 (2018)
Sri Lanka[k]	23.6	25.4	24.6	27.6
Southeast Asia				
Brunei Darussalam	...	...	...	20.7
Cambodia	7.0	9.7	9.2	9.0 (2014)
Indonesia	17.4	18.8	19.3	23.5
Lao People's Democratic Republic[c]	...	...	8.1	14.1 (2017)
Malaysia[l]	32.5	29.7	27.8	27.9
Myanmar	...	...	...	17.2 (2018)
Philippines[m]	16.2	15.4	15.0	19.1
Singapore[n]	25.7	21.7	21.8	14.8
Thailand	20.2	22.4	20.8	22.8
Timor-Leste	...	...	14.3	17.5 (2016)
Viet Nam[o]	13.1	17.6	21.0	30.1
The Pacific				
Cook Islands[p]	6.0 (2001)	14.2 (2006)	11.7 (2011)	10.3 (2016)
Fiji[q]	30.8	30.8	23.9	23.8 (2018)
Kiribati[r]	...	3.2	16.1	18.2 (2015)
Marshall Islands	15.1	11.9	22.0	15.4 (2018)
Micronesia, Federated States of	...	...	...	...
Nauru	...	...	...	...
Niue	20.4 (2001)	17.1 (2006)	14.2 (2011)	14.2 (2017)
Palau[s]	0.7	2.6	...	11.7 (2015)
Papua New Guinea	...	...	...	...
Samoa[t]	19.7 (2001)	21.8 (2006)	12.2 (2011)	15.4 (2017)
Solomon Islands[u]	...	...	13.0 (2009)	...
Tonga	...	27.8 (2006)	...	29.7 (2018)
Tuvalu	...	...	...	...
Vanuatu	...	...	...	...
Developed ADB Member Economies				
Australia	21.5	21.1	21.0	19.1
Japan	31.2	27.5	25.4	23.7
New Zealand[v]	12.6	22.4	20.6	19.3

continued on next page

Table 2.1.5: Employment in Agriculture, Industry, and Services[a] (continued)
(% of total employment)

ADB Regional Member	Services			
	2000	2005	2010	2019
Developing ADB Member Economies				
Central and West Asia				
Afghanistan[b]	24.2 (2001)	24.2 (2004)	...	45.7 (2016)
Armenia[c]	35.0	37.8	44.0	54.3
Azerbaijan	48.7	48.8	48.1	49.2
Georgia[d]	41.4 (2001)	42.5	44.8	47.6
Kazakhstan	50.5	50.2	53.0	66.8
Kyrgyz Republic	36.5	43.9	47.7	54.9 (2018)
Pakistan[e]	40.0	36.7	34.2	36.9 (2018)
Tajikistan	26.0	23.9	26.3	30.3 (2018)
Turkmenistan	39.4	...	...	...
Uzbekistan	52.8	57.7	50.5	50.7
East Asia				
China, People's Republic of[f]	27.5	31.4	34.6	47.4
Hong Kong, China[g]	79.8	85.1	88.9	88.3
Korea, Republic of[h]	68.9	65.4	68.4	70.3
Mongolia[c]	37.2	43.3	50.2	53.1
Taipei,China	64.1	57.7	58.8	59.6
South Asia				
Bangladesh	36.2	37.6 (2006)	35.3	38.9 (2017)
Bhutan[i]	47.9 (2001)	39.2	33.7	33.4
India	23.7	25.1	25.3 (2009)	...
Maldives[j]	67.3	56.2 (2007)	86.3	72.6 (2016)
Nepal[c]	...	...	25.7 (2011)	47.7 (2018)
Sri Lanka[k]	40.3	41.8	42.9	47.1
Southeast Asia				
Brunei Darussalam	...	...	...	77.4
Cambodia	19.3	30.0	18.6	26.6 (2014)
Indonesia	37.3	37.3	42.3	49.2
Lao People's Democratic Republic[c]	...	...	19.7	54.6 (2017)
Malaysia[l]	50.8	55.6	58.7	61.9
Myanmar	...	...	...	34.6 (2018)
Philippines[m]	46.7	48.1	51.8	58.0
Singapore[n]	74.2	78.2	77.9	84.9
Thailand	35.6	39.0	41.0	45.7
Timor-Leste	...	...	59.4	50.9 (2016)
Viet Nam[o]	21.8	27.3	29.5	35.4
The Pacific				
Cook Islands[p]	86.7 (2001)	80.9 (2006)	84.0 (2011)	85.9 (2016)
Fiji[q]	67.7	68.1	74.4	72.9 (2018)
Kiribati[r]	...	30.7	61.8	57.5 (2015)
Marshall Islands	84.1	87.6	77.1	83.4 (2018)
Micronesia, Federated States of	...	...	...	...
Nauru	...	...	...	...
Niue	70.6 (2001)	66.9 (2006)	75.4 (2011)	77.1 (2017)
Palau[s]	92.2	89.6	...	82.0 (2015)
Papua New Guinea	...	...	...	...
Samoa[t]	40.4 (2001)	42.8 (2006)	50.9 (2011)	62.7 (2017)
Solomon Islands[u]	...	...	44.8 (2009)	...
Tonga	...	44.3 (2006)	...	50.3 (2018)
Tuvalu	...	...	...	...
Vanuatu	...	...	...	...
Developed ADB Member Economies				
Australia	73.7	75.3	75.9	78.4
Japan	63.7	68.1	70.5	73.0
New Zealand[v]	66.3	70.7	72.6	74.9

... = data not available; – = magnitude equals zero, ADB = Asian Development Bank.

a Data are based on varying labor force concepts and definitions adopted by different economies. Some values may not add up to 100% due to limitations on data availability.
b For 2016, data refer to April–September only.
c Recommendations from the 19th International Conference of Labour Statisticians were adopted by Armenia, for 2018 onward; Mongolia, for 2019; Nepal, for 2018; the Lao People's Democratic Republic, for 2017; and Timor-Leste, for 2010 and 2016. Hence, data for these years may not be directly comparable with data in other years. The conference provides the statistical concept of work for reference purposes; and the operational concepts, definitions, and guidelines for (i) three distinct subsets of work activities, referred to as forms of work (including own-use production work), employment work, and volunteer work; (ii) related classifications of the population according to their labor force status and main work status; and (iii) measures of labor underutilization. The concept of employment has also been refined to refer to work for pay or profit.
d Prior to 2017, employment in services includes people who were engaged in construction industries.
e For 2000, employment in services includes people who were engaged in electricity, gas, and water industries.
f Refers to persons engaged in social labor and receiving remuneration or earning business income.
g Employment in services includes people who are engaged in electricity and gas supply; water supply; and sewerage, waste management, and remediation activities.
h For 2000, employment in services includes people who are engaged in electricity, gas, water, and construction industries.
i For 2005 and 2017, data are from censuses of population. For all other years, data are from labor force surveys. Thus, data prior to and after the census years may not be directly comparable with 2005 and 2017 data.
j Figures include local population only. For 2010, employment in services includes people who were engaged in industries other than agriculture, forestry, and fishing; mining and quarrying; or manufacturing.
k Some data may not add up because (i) for 2005 and 2011–2013, data cover all islands; (ii) for 2003, data exclude the Northern Province; (iii) for 2004, data exclude Mullaitivu and Kilinochchi districts; and (iv) for years prior to 2003 and 2006–2010, data exclude northern and eastern provinces.
l For 2005, employment in services includes people who were engaged in water supply; and sewerage, waste management, and remediation activities.
m For 2005, annual data on labor force refer to the average of April, July, and October figures, in view of the adoption of a new definition.
n Refers to Singapore residents only.
o Refers to total number of persons engaged in any activity regardless of age.
p Covers all wage and salary earners from all islands. For 2001, employment in services includes people who were engaged in electricity, gas, water, and construction industries.
q Refers to the number of employed persons excluding those who are engaged in unpaid employment as of end of June.
r Refers to cash work and unpaid village work. For 2005, employment figures by industry include only paid (cash work) workers, and as such, the number of employed for all industries may not add up to the total number of employed, which includes both cash workers and unpaid village workers. For 2010, employment in agriculture includes people who were engaged in mining and quarrying.
s For 2000 and 2005, employment in services includes people who were engaged in electricity, gas, water, and construction industries.
t Figures for 2001, 2006, and 2011 may not be directly comparable to 2017 figures due to differences in the primary data sources.
u For 2009, the figure refers to paid employment.
v For 2000, employment in services includes people who were engaged in industries other than agriculture, forestry, and fishing, or manufacturing.

Source: Asian Development Bank estimates using data from economy sources.

Click on the indictor name in the table header to access the time series in the Key Indicators Database.

Poverty Indicators

Table 2.1.6:   Poverty and Inequality

ADB Regional Member	Proportion of Population Living on Less Than $1.90 a Day (2011 PPP)[a] (%)		Proportion of Population Living on Less Than $3.20 a Day (2011 PPP)[a] (%)		Income Ratio of Highest 20% to Lowest 20%[b]		Gini Coefficient[c]	
	2000	2018	2000	2018	2000	2018	2000	2018
Developing ADB Member Economies								
Central and West Asia								
Afghanistan	...	...	...	...	...	...	...	...
Armenia	19.3 (2001)	2.1	55.6 (2001)	13.0	5.7 (2001)	5.3	0.354 (2001)	0.344
Azerbaijan[d]	2.7 (2001)	...	17.6 (2001)	...	6.0 (2001)	...	0.365 (2001)	...
Georgia	19.4	4.5	44.8	15.7	8.6	6.6	0.405	0.364
Kazakhstan	10.3 (2001)	0.0 (2017)	32.3 (2001)	0.4 (2017)	6.4 (2001)	3.8 (2017)	0.360 (2001)	0.275 (2017)
Kyrgyz Republic	42.1	0.9	77.6	15.5	4.7	3.8	0.310	0.277
Pakistan[e]	28.6 (2001)	3.9 (2015)	72.4 (2001)	34.7 (2015)	4.3 (2001)	4.8 (2015)	0.304 (2001)	0.335 (2015)
Tajikistan	30.8 (2003)	4.8 (2015)	66.8 (2003)	20.3 (2015)	5.2 (2003)	5.6 (2015)	0.327 (2003)	0.340 (2015)
Turkmenistan	...	...	...	...	...	...	...	...
Uzbekistan[f]	62.0	...	86.7	...	6.2	...	0.361	...
East Asia								
China, People's Republic of	31.7 (2002)	0.5 (2016)	57.7 (2002)	5.4 (2016)	8.6 (2002)	7.0 (2016)	0.420 (2002)	0.385 (2016)
Hong Kong, China	...	...	...	...	...	...	...	...
Korea, Republic of	0.2 (2006)	0.2 (2012)	0.5 (2006)	0.5 (2012)	5.4 (2006)	5.3 (2012)	0.317 (2006)	0.316 (2012)
Mongolia	9.7 (2002)	0.5	33.6 (2002)	5.6	5.4 (2002)	5.2	0.329 (2002)	0.327
Taipei,China[g]	0.0 (2002)	0.0	0.0 (2002)	0.0	4.2	3.9	0.294	0.278
South Asia								
Bangladesh	34.8	14.8 (2016)	72.7	52.9 (2016)	5.0	4.8 (2016)	0.334	0.324 (2016)
Bhutan	17.6 (2003)	1.5 (2017)	45.2 (2003)	12.0 (2017)	7.4 (2003)	6.6 (2017)	0.409 (2003)	0.374 (2017)
India[e]	38.2 (2004)	21.2 (2011)	75.2 (2004)	60.4 (2011)	5.7 (2004)	6.0 (2011)	0.368 (2004)	0.378 (2011)
Maldives[e]	10.0 (2002)	0.0 (2016)	39.2 (2002)	0.5 (2016)	7.2 (2002)	4.8 (2016)	0.413 (2002)	0.313 (2016)
Nepal[e]	49.9 (2003)	15.0 (2010)	77.9 (2003)	50.9 (2010)	7.9 (2003)	5.0 (2010)	0.438 (2003)	0.328 (2010)
Sri Lanka	8.3 (2002)	0.8 (2016)	36.0 (2002)	10.1 (2016)	7.1 (2002)	6.8 (2016)	0.410 (2002)	0.398 (2016)
Southeast Asia								
Brunei Darussalam	...	...	...	...	...	...	...	...
Cambodia	...	...	...	...	...	...	...	...
Indonesia	39.3	4.6	79.9	24.2	4.3	6.9	0.302	0.390
Lao People's Democratic Republic[e]	33.8 (2002)	22.7 (2012)	72.1 (2002)	58.7 (2012)	4.8 (2002)	5.9 (2012)	0.326 (2002)	0.364 (2012)
Malaysia	0.4 (2004)	0.0 (2015)	2.6 (2004)	0.2 (2015)	10.9 (2004)	8.2 (2015)	0.461 (2004)	0.410 (2015)
Myanmar	...	2.0 (2017)	...	19.3 (2017)	...	4.5 (2017)	...	0.307 (2017)
Philippines[h]	14.5	7.8 (2015)	43.1	32.7 (2015)	10.5	8.9 (2015)	0.428	0.401 (2015)
Singapore	...	...	...	...	...	...	...	...
Thailand	2.5	0.0	18.6	0.5	8.0	6.1	0.428	0.364
Timor-Leste	46.0 (2001)	30.7 (2014)	75.7 (2001)	73.3 (2014)	6.0 (2001)	4.1 (2014)	0.359 (2001)	0.287 (2014)
Viet Nam	38.0 (2002)	1.9	70.8 (2002)	7.0	6.1 (2002)	6.4	0.370 (2002)	0.357
The Pacific								
Cook Islands	...	...	...	...	...	...	...	...
Fiji[e]	4.9 (2002)	1.4 (2013)	21.9 (2002)	14.1 (2013)	6.8 (2002)	6.0 (2013)	0.381 (2002)	0.367 (2013)
Kiribati	12.9 (2006)	...	34.6 (2006)	...	6.7 (2006)	...	0.370 (2006)	...
Marshall Islands	...	...	...	...	...	...	...	...
Micronesia, Federated States of	8.1 (2005)	15.4 (2013)	24.6 (2005)	38.7 (2013)	8.7 (2005)	8.4 (2013)	0.424 (2005)	0.401 (2013)
Nauru	...	...	...	...	...	...	...	...
Niue	...	...	...	...	...	...	...	...
Palau	...	...	...	...	...	...	...	...
Papua New Guinea[e]	...	38.0 (2009)	...	65.6 (2009)	...	9.3 (2009)	...	0.419 (2009)
Samoa[e]	2.0 (2002)	1.1 (2013)	11.9 (2002)	9.6 (2013)	7.6 (2002)	6.8 (2013)	0.407 (2002)	0.387 (2013)
Solomon Islands	45.6 (2005)	25.1 (2013)	70.6 (2005)	58.8 (2013)	10.4 (2005)	6.4 (2013)	0.461 (2005)	0.371 (2013)
Tonga	2.8 (2001)	1.0 (2015)	8.4 (2001)	7.5 (2015)	7.1 (2001)	6.7 (2015)	0.377 (2001)	0.376 (2015)
Tuvalu	...	3.3 (2010)	...	17.6 (2010)	...	7.0 (2010)	...	0.391 (2010)
Vanuatu	...	13.2 (2010)	...	39.4 (2010)	...	6.7 (2010)	...	0.376 (2010)
Developed ADB Member Economies								
Australia	...	...	...	...	5.5 (2001)	6.3 (2014)	0.335 (2001)	0.344 (2014)
Japan	...	...	...	...	5.4 (2008)	...	0.348 (2008)	0.329 (2013)
New Zealand[i]	...	...	...	...	...	...	...	0.349 (2014)

... = Data not available, 0.0 = magnitude is less than half the unit employed or true zero value, $ = United States dollars, ADB = Asian Development Bank, PPP = purchasing power parity.

a   Poverty estimates are consumption-based, except for Malaysia and the Republic of Korea, whose estimates are income-based.
b   Derived from the income or expenditure shares of the highest 20% and lowest 20% groups by income.
c   Inequality estimates are consumption-based, except for Malaysia; New Zealand; the Republic of Korea; and Taipei,China, whose estimates are income-based.
d   The most recent year data are for 2005: 0.0% for proportion of population below $1.90 a day (2011 PPP); 0.0% for proportion of population below $3.20 a day (2011 PPP); 3.5 for income ratio of highest 20% to lowest 20%; and 0.266 for Gini coefficient.
e   Household income and expenditure surveys for these economies were conducted in overlapping years. The table adopts the approach of the World Bank's World Development Indicators, i.e., using the initial year of the survey as the reference period for the poverty estimates.
f   The most recent year data are for 2003: 62.1% for proportion of population below $1.90 a day (2011 PPP); 86.4% for proportion of population below $3.20 a day (2011 PPP); 5.9 for income ratio of highest 20% to lowest 20%; and 0.353 for Gini coefficient.
g   The Gini coefficient reflected in the table refers to the coefficient using per capita disposable income published by the Government of Taipei,China's Directorate-General of Budget, Accounting and Statistics. The estimates using disposable income of households are 0.326 for 2000 and 0.338 for 2018. Alternative estimates for the Gini coefficient are available in the World Bank's PovcalNet Database.
h   Consumption-based poverty estimates were used. However, income-based estimates are also available for $1.90 poverty line, 13.9% (2000) and 6.1% (2015); for $3.20 poverty line, 38.1% (2000) and 26.0% (2015).
i   The Gini coefficient data are based on disposable income post taxes and transfers. Using the new income definition, the earliest available figure for the Gini coefficient is 0.323 for 2011.

Sources: World Bank. World Development Indicators. http://data.worldbank.org/data-catalog/world-development-indicators (accessed 13 July 2020). For New Zealand's Gini coefficient: Organisation for Economic Co-operation and Development. Income Distribution Database. https://stats.oecd.org/index.aspx?queryid=66670# (accessed 13 July 2020). For Taipei,China's income ratio and Gini coefficient: Government of Taipei,China, Directorate-General of Budget, Accounting and Statistics. https://eng.dgbas. gov.tw/mp.asp?mp=2 (accessed 14 July 2020).

Click on the indictor name in the table header to access the time series in the Key Indicators Database.

Table 2.1.7:   Human Development Index[a]

ADB Regional Member	2000	2005	2010	2014	2015	2016	2017	2018	Rank in 2018[b]
Developing ADB Member Economies									
Central and West Asia	**0.574**	**0.619**	**0.655**	**0.678**	**0.682**	**0.685**	**0.689**	**0.692**	
Afghanistan	0.345	0.410	0.464	0.488	0.490	0.491	0.493	0.496	170
Armenia	0.649	0.694	0.729	0.746	0.748	0.751	0.758	0.760	81
Azerbaijan	0.641	0.681	0.732	0.746	0.749	0.749	0.752	0.754	87
Georgia	0.669	0.705	0.732	0.764	0.771	0.776	0.783	0.786	70
Kazakhstan	0.685	0.747	0.764	0.798	0.806	0.808	0.813	0.817	50
Kyrgyz Republic	0.594	0.616	0.636	0.663	0.666	0.669	0.671	0.674	122
Pakistan	0.449	0.499	0.524	0.546	0.550	0.556	0.558	0.560	152
Tajikistan	0.538	0.590	0.630	0.642	0.642	0.647	0.651	0.656	125
Turkmenistan	...	...	0.673	0.696	0.701	0.706	0.708	0.710	108
Uzbekistan	0.596	0.629	0.665	0.693	0.696	0.701	0.707	0.710	108
East Asia	**0.743**	**0.773**	**0.811**	**0.834**	**0.838**	**0.843**	**0.846**	**0.850**	
China, People's Republic of	0.591	0.643	0.702	0.735	0.742	0.749	0.753	0.758	85
Hong Kong, China	0.827	0.871	0.901	0.924	0.927	0.931	0.937	0.939	4
Korea, Republic of	0.817	0.855	0.882	0.896	0.899	0.901	0.904	0.906	22
Mongolia	0.589	0.649	0.697	0.733	0.736	0.730	0.729	0.735	92
Taipei,China	0.890	0.846	0.873	0.882	0.885	0.903	0.907	0.911	...
South Asia	**0.542**	**0.564**	**0.608**	**0.637**	**0.645**	**0.651**	**0.656**	**0.659**	
Bangladesh	0.470	0.506	0.549	0.572	0.588	0.599	0.609	0.614	135
Bhutan	...	0.512	0.571	0.601	0.606	0.610	0.615	0.617	134
India	0.497	0.539	0.581	0.618	0.627	0.637	0.643	0.647	129
Maldives	0.610	0.632	0.669	0.702	0.709	0.713	0.716	0.719	104
Nepal	0.446	0.474	0.527	0.562	0.568	0.572	0.574	0.579	147
Sri Lanka	0.687	0.721	0.750	0.769	0.772	0.774	0.776	0.780	71
Southeast Asia	**0.602**	**0.635**	**0.677**	**0.698**	**0.704**	**0.708**	**0.711**	**0.714**	
Brunei Darussalam	0.805	0.824	0.832	0.845	0.843	0.844	0.843	0.845	43
Cambodia	0.419	0.490	0.535	0.561	0.566	0.572	0.578	0.581	146
Indonesia	0.604	0.633	0.666	0.691	0.696	0.700	0.704	0.707	111
Lao People's Democratic Republic	0.466	0.505	0.546	0.586	0.594	0.598	0.602	0.604	140
Malaysia	0.724	0.732	0.773	0.792	0.797	0.801	0.802	0.804	61
Myanmar	0.424	0.470	0.523	0.558	0.565	0.571	0.577	0.584	145
Philippines	0.631	0.656	0.672	0.697	0.702	0.704	0.709	0.712	106
Singapore	0.818	0.869	0.909	0.928	0.929	0.933	0.934	0.935	9
Thailand	0.649	0.693	0.721	0.739	0.746	0.753	0.762	0.765	77
Timor-Leste	0.505	0.496	0.620	0.608	0.628	0.628	0.624	0.626	131
Viet Nam	0.578	0.616	0.653	0.675	0.680	0.685	0.690	0.693	118
The Pacific	**0.592**	**0.610**	**0.628**	**0.644**	**0.649**	**0.651**	**0.658**	**0.659**	
Cook Islands	...	...	...	...	...	...	...	...	...
Fiji	0.675	0.687	0.694	0.712	0.718	0.718	0.721	0.724	98
Kiribati	0.564	0.585	0.589	0.613	0.619	0.622	0.623	0.623	132
Marshall Islands	...	...	...	...	...	...	0.696	0.698	117
Micronesia, Federated States of	0.541	0.572	0.595	0.598	0.606	0.608	0.612	0.614	135
Nauru	...	...	...	...	...	...	...	...	...
Niue	...	...	...	...	...	...	...	...	...
Palau	0.736	0.759	0.776	0.809	0.803	0.808	0.811	0.814	55
Papua New Guinea	0.436	0.468	0.510	0.531	0.539	0.541	0.543	0.543	155
Samoa	0.638	0.670	0.690	0.698	0.699	0.704	0.706	0.707	111
Solomon Islands	0.476	0.503	0.524	0.551	0.555	0.553	0.555	0.557	153
Tonga	0.666	0.674	0.692	0.699	0.714	0.715	0.717	0.717	105
Tuvalu	...	...	...	...	...	...	...	...	...
Vanuatu	...	0.569	0.585	0.589	0.592	0.592	0.595	0.597	141
Developed ADB Member Economies	**0.874**	**0.888**	**0.903**	**0.914**	**0.918**	**0.921**	**0.923**	**0.925**	
Australia	0.898	0.902	0.926	0.929	0.933	0.935	0.937	0.938	6
Japan	0.855	0.873	0.885	0.904	0.906	0.910	0.913	0.915	19
New Zealand	0.870	0.889	0.899	0.910	0.914	0.917	0.920	0.921	14
DEVELOPING ADB MEMBER ECONOMIES	**0.604**	**0.632**	**0.667**	**0.689**	**0.694**	**0.698**	**0.701**	**0.704**	
ALL ADB REGIONAL MEMBERS	**0.624**	**0.650**	**0.683**	**0.705**	**0.710**	**0.713**	**0.716**	**0.719**	
WORLD[c]	**0.641**	**0.669**	**0.697**	**0.718**	**0.722**	**0.727**	**0.729**	**0.731**	

... = data not available, ADB = Asian Development Bank.

a   The indexes for each region of Asia and the Pacific are calculated as an arithmetic average of the indexes for their member economies.
b   Rank among the 189 national economies presented in the Human Development Report 2019 of the United Nations Development Programme.
c   Calculated by the Human Development Report Office of the United Nations Development Programme by applying the human development index formula to the weighted group averages of component indicators. Missing values are estimated using cross-country regression models.

Sources: United Nations Development Programme. Human Development Data (1990–2018). http://hdr.undp.org/en/data# (accessed 16 June 2020). For Taipei,China: Government of Taipei,China, Directorate-General of Budget, Accounting and Statistics. https://eng.stat.gov.tw/ct.asp?xItem=25280&ctNode=6032&mp=5 (accessed 16 June 2020).

Table 2.1.8: Life Expectancy at Birth

(years)

ADB Regional Member	Both Sexes		Female		Male	
	2000	2018	2000	2018	2000	2018
Developing ADB Member Economies						
Central and West Asia[a]	**63.3**	**68.1**	**65.2**	**69.7**	**61.6**	**66.5**
Afghanistan	55.8	64.5	57.1	66.0	54.7	63.0
Armenia	71.4	74.9	74.5	78.4	68.1	71.2
Azerbaijan	66.8	72.9	69.9	75.3	63.6	70.3
Georgia	69.9	73.6	73.6	78.0	66.1	69.2
Kazakhstan	65.5	73.2	71.1	77.2	60.2	68.8
Kyrgyz Republic	68.6	71.4	72.4	75.6	64.9	67.4
Pakistan	62.8	67.1	63.7	68.1	62.1	66.2
Tajikistan	62.0	70.9	63.9	73.2	60.2	68.7
Turkmenistan	63.6	68.1	67.7	71.6	59.6	64.6
Uzbekistan	67.2	71.6	70.4	73.7	64.0	69.4
East Asia[a]	**71.7**	**77.0**	**73.8**	**79.4**	**69.8**	**74.8**
China, People's Republic of	71.4	76.7	73.4	79.1	69.6	74.5
Hong Kong, China	80.9	84.9	83.9	87.7	78.0	82.3
Korea, Republic of	75.9	82.6	79.7	85.7	72.3	79.7
Mongolia	62.9	69.7	65.9	74.0	60.1	65.6
Taipei,China	76.5	80.7	79.6	84.0	73.8	77.5
South Asia[a]	**62.9**	**69.8**	**63.8**	**71.2**	**62.1**	**68.6**
Bangladesh	65.4	72.3	66.0	74.3	65.0	70.6
Bhutan	60.9	71.5	61.1	71.8	60.6	71.1
India	62.5	69.4	63.3	70.7	61.7	68.2
Maldives	70.2	78.6	71.4	80.5	69.2	77.2
Nepal	62.3	70.5	63.3	71.9	61.2	69.0
Sri Lanka	71.3	76.8	75.1	80.1	67.9	73.4
Southeast Asia[a]	**67.5**	**72.4**	**70.3**	**75.5**	**64.9**	**69.5**
Brunei Darussalam	72.8	75.7	74.1	77.0	71.7	74.6
Cambodia	58.4	69.6	60.6	71.6	56.2	67.3
Indonesia	65.8	71.5	67.2	73.7	64.3	69.4
Lao People's Democratic Republic	58.8	67.6	60.6	69.4	57.0	65.8
Malaysia	72.6	76.0	74.8	78.2	70.6	74.1
Myanmar	60.1	66.9	63.1	69.9	57.0	63.8
Philippines	68.8	71.1	72.3	75.4	65.5	67.1
Singapore	78.0	83.1	80.0	85.4	76.0	81.0
Thailand	70.6	76.9	74.5	80.7	66.9	73.2
Timor-Leste	59.0	69.3	60.6	71.4	57.5	67.3
Viet Nam	73.0	75.3	77.7	79.4	68.4	71.2
The Pacific[a,b]	**61.1**	**65.6**	**62.6**	**67.0**	**59.7**	**64.2**
Cook Islands	71.9	76.4 (2019)	74.7	79.4 (2019)	69.2	73.6 (2019)
Fiji	65.7	67.3	67.5	69.2	64.0	65.6
Kiribati	63.1	68.1	66.0	72.1	60.4	64.0
Marshall Islands	68.4	73.9 (2019)	70.4	76.2 (2019)	66.6	71.6 (2019)
Micronesia, Federated States of	64.6	67.8	66.2	69.5	63.1	66.1
Nauru	60.9	68.1 (2019)	64.5	71.6 (2019)	57.4	64.0 (2019)
Niue[c]	70.3[d] (2001)	73.6[e] (2016)	73.9[d] (2001)	75.7[e] (2016)	67.2[d] (2001)	71.8[e] (2016)
Palau	68.5	73.9 (2019)	71.7	77.3 (2019)	65.4	70.7 (2019)
Papua New Guinea	59.3	64.3	60.7	65.6	57.9	63.0
Samoa	68.7	73.2	71.4	75.3	66.3	71.2
Solomon Islands	67.4	72.8	68.8	74.7	66.3	71.2
Tonga	69.7	70.8	70.5	72.8	68.7	68.9
Tuvalu	61.6	67.5 (2019)	63.6	69.9 (2019)	59.7	65.3 (2019)
Vanuatu	67.4	70.3	68.7	72.0	66.2	68.8
Developed ADB Member Economies[a]	**80.8**	**83.9**	**84.2**	**86.8**	**77.5**	**81.1**
Australia	79.2	82.7	82.0	84.9	76.6	80.7
Japan	81.1	84.2	84.6	87.3	77.7	81.3
New Zealand	78.6	81.9	81.3	83.6	76.1	80.2
DEVELOPING ADB MEMBER ECONOMIES[a,b]	**67.2**	**72.7**	**69.0**	**74.8**	**65.6**	**70.8**
ALL ADB REGIONAL MEMBERS[a,b]	**67.8**	**73.2**	**69.7**	**75.3**	**66.1**	**71.2**
WORLD[f]	**67.5**	**72.6**	**69.9**	**74.9**	**65.4**	**70.4**

ADB = Asian Development Bank.

a Estimated as weighted averages using total population of appropriate sex(es) from the United Nations' World Population Prospects 2019 as weight. For the Cook Islands, Marshall Islands, Nauru, Niue, Palau, and Tuvalu, sex-disaggregated population figures were derived using total populations from World Population Prospects 2019 and the proportions of total population by sex for Pacific small island states from the World Development Indicators.

b For estimating regional aggregates, imputation was done for economies with missing data by substituting available data from the nearest years.

c Calculated directly from recorded deaths, through 5-year periods.

d Covers 1997–2001.

e Covers 2012–2016.

f Estimated by the World Bank as weighted averages using total population of appropriate sex(es) as weight.

Sources: World Bank. World Development Indicators. https://databank.worldbank.org/source/world-development-indicators (accessed 16 June 2020). For the Cook Islands, the Marshall Islands, Nauru, Palau, and Tuvalu: United States Census Bureau. International Data Base. https://www.census.gov/data-tools/demo/idb/informationGateway.php (accessed 16 June 2020). For Niue: Statistics Niue. Vital Statistics Report 2012–2016. https://niue.prism.spc.int/ (accessed 16 June 2020). For Taipei,China: Government of Taipei,China, Directorate-General of Budget, Accounting and Statistics. https://eng.dgbas.gov.tw/mp.asp?mp=2 (accessed 16 June 2020).

Click on the indictor name in the table header to access the time series in the Key Indicators Database.

Table 2.1.9: Births, Deaths, and Fertility Rates

ADB Regional Member	Crude Birth Rate (per 1,000 people)				Crude Death Rate (per 1,000 people)				Total Fertility Rate (births per woman)			
	2000		2018		2000		2018		2000		2018	
Developing ADB Member Economies												
Central and West Asia[a]	**31.2**		**27.1**		**8.7**		**6.7**		**4.3**		**3.4**	
Afghanistan	48.0		32.5		11.7		6.4		7.5		4.5	
Armenia	12.9		14.0		8.6		9.9		1.6		1.8	
Azerbaijan	14.5		14.0		5.8		5.8		2.0		1.7	
Georgia	12.1		13.5		11.7		12.8		1.6		2.1	
Kazakhstan	14.9		21.8		10.1		7.1		1.8		2.8	
Kyrgyz Republic	19.8		27.1		7.0		5.2		2.4		3.3	
Pakistan	34.7		28.3		8.9		6.9		5.0		3.5	
Tajikistan	30.6		30.8		8.5		4.9		4.0		3.6	
Turkmenistan	23.6		23.8		7.8		7.0		2.8		2.8	
Uzbekistan	21.4		23.3		5.5		4.7		2.6		2.4	
East Asia[a,b]	**14.0**		**10.7**		**6.4**		**7.1**		**1.6**		**1.7**	
China, People's Republic of	14.0		10.9		6.5		7.1		1.6		1.7	
Hong Kong, China	8.1		7.2		5.1		6.4		1.0		1.1	
Korea, Republic of	13.3		6.4		5.2		5.8		1.5		1.0	
Mongolia	19.3		24.1		7.7		6.3		2.1		2.9	
Taipei,China	13.8		7.5	(2019)	5.7		7.5	(2019)	1.7		1.1	(2019)
South Asia[a]	**26.5**		**17.9**		**8.5**		**7.0**		**3.3**		**2.2**	
Bangladesh	27.5		18.2		6.9		5.5		3.2		2.0	
Bhutan	27.1		17.3		8.8		6.2		3.5		2.0	
India	26.4		17.9		8.7		7.2		3.3		2.2	
Maldives	21.4		14.2		4.6		2.8		2.8		1.9	
Nepal	31.5		19.9		8.5		6.4		4.0		1.9	
Sri Lanka	18.5		15.8		6.9		6.7		2.2		2.2	
Southeast Asia[a]	**21.9**		**17.5**		**7.0**		**6.5**		**2.6**		**2.2**	
Brunei Darussalam	22.7		14.9		3.5		4.4		2.3		1.8	
Cambodia	28.1		22.5		9.4		6.0		3.8		2.5	
Indonesia	21.8		18.1		7.5		6.5		2.5		2.3	
Lao People's Democratic Republic	32.0		23.5		9.8		6.4		4.3		2.7	
Malaysia	22.0		16.8		4.5		5.1		2.8		2.0	
Myanmar	24.6		17.6		9.9		8.2		2.9		2.2	
Philippines	29.6		20.5		5.4		5.9		3.8		2.6	
Singapore	13.7		8.8		4.5		5.0		1.6		1.1	
Thailand	14.5		10.3		6.9		7.7		1.7		1.5	
Timor-Leste	39.5		29.4		10.4		6.0		6.1		4.0	
Viet Nam	17.4		16.7		5.7		6.3		2.0		2.0	
The Pacific[a,b]	**32.8**		**26.8**		**8.8**		**7.2**		**4.4**		**3.5**	
Cook Islands	23.1		13.5	(2019)	6.3		8.8	(2019)	3.2		2.1	(2019)
Fiji	24.7		21.3		6.9		8.2		3.1		2.8	
Kiribati	30.6		27.9		7.9		6.3		4.1		3.6	
Marshall Islands	35.0		23.3	(2019)	5.3		4.2	(2019)	4.4		2.9	(2019)
Micronesia, Federated States of	29.9		22.8		7.7		6.6		4.3		3.1	
Nauru	27.9		22.6	(2019)	7.2		6.0	(2019)	3.5		2.7	(2019)
Niue	13.4[c]	(2001)	3.0[c]	(2019)	8.2[c]	(2001)	1.2[d]	(2019)	2.3[c]	(2001)	2.7[e]	(2016)
Palau	14.5		14.0		6.5		7.8		1.8		2.2	(2015)
Papua New Guinea	34.0		27.1		9.5		7.4		4.5		3.6	
Samoa	30.6		24.4		6.3		5.2		4.5		3.9	
Solomon Islands	35.6		32.4		5.6		4.3		4.7		4.4	
Tonga	28.2		24.3		6.9		7.2		4.3		3.6	
Tuvalu	24.6		23.7	(2019)	10.8		8.4	(2019)	3.6		2.9	(2019)
Vanuatu	33.4		29.6		6.1		5.3		4.5		3.8	
Developed ADB Member Economies[a]	**10.0**		**8.4**		**7.6**		**10.1**		**1.4**		**1.5**	
Australia	13.0		12.6		6.7		6.3		1.8		1.7	
Japan	9.4		7.4		7.7		11.0		1.4		1.4	
New Zealand	14.7		12.0		6.9		6.9		2.0		1.7	
DEVELOPING ADB MEMBER ECONOMIES[a,b]	**21.0**		**16.0**		**7.4**		**6.9**		**2.5**		**2.1**	
ALL ADB REGIONAL MEMBERS[a,b]	**20.5**		**15.7**		**7.4**		**7.0**		**2.5**		**2.1**	
WORLD[f]	**21.6**		**18.2**		**8.5**		**7.5**		**2.7**		**2.4**	

ADB = Asian Development Bank.

a   ADB estimates using data on total population from the United Nations. World Population Prospects 2019; data on crude birth rates and crude death rates from the World Bank's World Development Indicators, the United States Census Bureau, and economy sources; and data on the population of women of reproductive age from the World Health Organization, World Population Prospects 2019, and official communication from The Pacific Community, Statistics for Development Division.

b   For estimating aggregates, imputation was done for economies with missing data by substituting available data from the nearest years.

c   Refers to a multiyear average for the intercensal years 1997–2001. Crude birth rate and crude death rate are calculated by dividing the average annual number of births and deaths of the intercensal period 1997–2001 by the midperiod population size of the intercensal period. For total fertility rate, the estimate is based on the average registered number of children born, by age of mother, of the intercensal period 1997–2001, and the estimated midperiod number of women of childbearing age.

d   Refers to July–December 2019.

e   Refers to a multiyear average for the intercensal years 2012–2016. Total fertility rate is estimated based on the average registered number of children born, by age of mother, of the intercensal period 2012–2016, and the estimated midperiod number of women of childbearing age.

f   Estimated by the World Bank as weighted averages of the rates using the value of the denominator or, in some cases, another indicator as a weight. Aggregation is done after imputing values for missing data, which is done according to certain imputation rules by the World Bank, as described in their data compilation methodology.

Sources: Economy sources; Pacific Community, Statistics for Development Division. Official communication, 3 July 2019; United Nations. World Population Prospects 2019. https://population. un.org/wpp/Download/Standard/Population/ (accessed 17 July 2020); World Bank. World Development Indicators. https://data.worldbank.org/indicator (accessed 24 June 2020); and World Health Organization. Maternal, Newborn, Child & Adolescent Health. https://www.who.int/data/maternal-newborn-child-adolescent/indicator-explorer-new/mca/ women-of-reproductive-age-(15-49-years)-population-(thousands)(accessed 17 July 2020). For the Cook Islands, the Marshall Islands, Nauru, and Tuvalu: United States Census Bureau. International Data Base. https://www.census.gov/data-tools/demo/idb/informationGateway.php (accessed 24 June 2020). For Niue: Statistics Niue, Department of Finance and Planning. https://niue.prism.spc.int (accessed 24 June 2020). For Taipei,China: Government of Taipei,China, Directorate-General of Budget, Accounting and Statistics. http://eng.dgbas.gov.tw/mp.asp?mp=2 (accessed 24 June 2020).

Click on the indictor name in the table header to access the time series in the Key Indicators Database.

Social Indicators

Table 2.1.10: Primary Education Completion Rate[a]
(%)

ADB Regional Member	Both Sexes		Female		Male	
	2000	2018	2000	2018	2000	2018
Developing ADB Member Economies						
Central and West Asia						
Afghanistan	...	85.6	...	67.1	...	103.3
Armenia	93.7 (2002)	89.9	94.1 (2002)	89.5	93.3 (2002)	90.2
Azerbaijan	89.5	100.2	85.5	100.6	93.8	99.9
Georgia	118.1	95.5	120.2	96.3	116.2	94.8
Kazakhstan	93.2	106.4 (2019)	93.1	107.0 (2019)	93.3	105.8 (2019)
Kyrgyz Republic	93.6	104.5	93.2	104.4	94.1	104.6
Pakistan	60.2 (2005)	71.1	50.1 (2005)	64.2	69.7 (2005)	77.4
Tajikistan[b]	92.6	94.9 (2017)	97.4 (2009)	94.7 (2017)	100.5 (2009)	95.1 (2017)
Turkmenistan	...	...	...	...	...	...
Uzbekistan[b]	95.8	103.0	100.6 (2001)	102.5	100.8 (2001)	103.6
East Asia						
China, People's Republic of	91.6 (2006)	...	91.4 (2006)	...	91.8 (2006)	...
Hong Kong, China	...	104.5	...	105.7	...	103.4
Korea, Republic of	103.2	91.4 (2017)	105.0	91.1 (2017)	101.7	91.6 (2017)
Mongolia	86.9	101.8	89.3	101.9	84.6	101.7
Taipei,China	...	...	...	...	...	...
South Asia						
Bangladesh	66.3 (2005)	67.8 (2010)	68.9 (2005)	71.8 (2010)	63.9 (2005)	64.1 (2010)
Bhutan	51.1	100.0 (2017)	47.5	104.4 (2017)	54.5	95.7 (2017)
India	71.5	91.6	64.0	93.1	78.3	90.2
Maldives	134.5 (2005)	97.4 (2017)	133.2 (2005)	92.3 (2017)	135.8 (2005)	102.4 (2017)
Nepal	66.7	120.4 (2019)	56.8	123.2 (2019)	76.4	117.7 (2019)
Sri Lanka	107.3 (2001)	102.6	106.6 (2001)	101.5	108.0 (2001)	103.6
Southeast Asia						
Brunei Darussalam	114.8	108.0	109.9	108.4	119.5	107.6
Cambodia	51.3 (2001)	88.0	46.0 (2001)	90.3	56.3 (2001)	85.8
Indonesia	93.8 (2001)	102.3	94.2 (2001)	101.6	93.4 (2001)	103.0
Lao People's Democratic Republic	67.4	97.9	61.4	97.1	73.2	98.6
Malaysia	100.7	99.5 (2017)	100.8	101.1 (2017)	100.6	98.0 (2017)
Myanmar	76.5	95.4	74.1	94.8	78.8	96.0
Philippines	100.4 (2001)	108.7 (2017)	105.5 (2001)	109.6 (2017)	95.6 (2001)	107.8 (2017)
Singapore	...	99.3 (2017)	...	99.3 (2017)	...	99.3 (2017)
Thailand	84.9	93.4	84.3	94.1	85.5	92.7
Timor-Leste	89.1 (2008)	103.8	88.0 (2008)	106.3	90.1 (2008)	101.4
Viet Nam	99.8	110.0	98.0	111.5	101.5	108.6
The Pacific						
Cook Islands	88.3 (2007)	107.0 (2016)	...	103.5 (2016)	...	110.3 (2016)
Fiji	95.0	107.0 (2016)	93.9	106.3 (2016)	96.0	107.7 (2016)
Kiribati	99.0	100.9 (2016)	95.1	103.2 (2016)	102.6	98.6 (2016)
Marshall Islands	108.8 (2002)	70.9 (2016)	112.3 (2002)	72.8 (2016)	105.4 (2002)	69.0 (2016)
Micronesia, Federated States of	...	...	...	...	...	...
Nauru	101.3 (2001)	131.0 (2016)	97.3 (2001)	133.3 (2016)	105.4 (2001)	128.7 (2016)
Niue	102.4 (2001)	111.5 (2016)	95.0 (2001)	92.3 (2016)	109.5 (2001)	130.8 (2016)
Palau	95.2	100.4 (2014)	83.3	94.7 (2014)	107.3	105.8 (2014)
Papua New Guinea	50.0	77.1 (2016)	45.8	71.5 (2016)	54.0	82.4 (2016)
Samoa	94.0	104.8	95.5	103.8	92.7	105.7
Solomon Islands	...	86.8	...	89.7	...	84.0
Tonga	105.5 (2001)	116.1 (2013)	104.0 (2001)	110.1 (2013)	106.9 (2001)	121.6 (2013)
Tuvalu	108.6 (2001)	78.7	110.3 (2001)	69.4	107.0 (2001)	87.5
Vanuatu	92.1	91.7 (2013)	94.4	94.9 (2013)	89.9	88.7 (2013)
Developed ADB Member Economies						
Australia	...	...	...	...	...	...
Japan	...	...	...	...	...	...
New Zealand	...	...	...	...	...	...
WORLD[c]	81.8	89.6	78.6	89.3	84.8	89.9

... = data not available, ADB = Asian Development Bank.

a Represented by the total number of new entrants in the last grade of primary education, regardless of age, expressed as a percentage of the population at the theoretical age to enter the last grade of primary education.

b For the initial year, sex-disaggregated data were available for a different reference year relative to the overall estimate.

c Estimated by the United Nations Educational, Scientific and Cultural Organization's Institute of Statistics as a weighted average using the population at the theoretical age to enter the last grade of primary education as weight.

Source: United Nations Educational, Scientific and Cultural Organization (UNESCO) Institute for Statistics. UIS.Stat Database. UIS.Stat. http://data.uis.unesco.org/ (accessed 26 June 2020).

Table 2.1.11:   Adult (15 Years and Older) Literacy Rate
(%)

ADB Regional Member	Both Sexes		Female		Male	
	2000	2018	2000	2018	2000	2018
Developing ADB Member Economies						
Central and West Asia						
Afghanistan	...	43.0	...	29.8	...	55.5
Armenia	99.4 (2001)	99.7 (2017)	99.2 (2001)	99.7 (2017)	99.7 (2001)	99.8 (2017)
Azerbaijan	99.6 (2007)	99.8 (2017)	99.4 (2007)	99.7 (2017)	99.8 (2007)	99.9 (2017)
Georgia	99.7 (2002)	99.4 (2017)	99.6 (2002)	99.3 (2017)	99.8 (2002)	99.4 (2017)
Kazakhstan	99.7 (2009)	99.8	99.7 (2009)	99.7	99.8 (2009)	99.8
Kyrgyz Republic	99.2 (2009)	99.6	99.0 (2009)	99.5	99.5 (2009)	99.7
Pakistan	49.9 (2005)	59.1 (2017)	35.4 (2005)	46.5 (2017)	64.1 (2005)	71.1 (2017)
Tajikistan	99.5	99.8 (2014)	99.2	99.7 (2014)	99.7	99.8 (2014)
Turkmenistan	...	99.7 (2014)	...	99.6 (2014)	...	99.8 (2014)
Uzbekistan	98.6	100.0	98.1	100.0	99.2	100.0
East Asia						
China, People's Republic of	90.9	96.8	86.5	95.2	95.1	98.5
Hong Kong, China	...	...	...	...	...	...
Korea, Republic of	...	...	...	...	...	...
Mongolia	97.8	98.4	97.5	98.6	98.0	98.2
Taipei,China	...	...	...	...	...	...
South Asia						
Bangladesh	47.5 (2001)	73.9	40.8 (2001)	71.2	53.9 (2001)	76.7
Bhutan	52.8 (2005)	66.6 (2017)	38.7 (2005)	57.1 (2017)	65.0 (2005)	75.0 (2017)
India	61.0 (2001)	74.4	47.8 (2001)	65.8	73.4 (2001)	82.4
Maldives	98.4 (2006)	97.7 (2016)	98.4 (2006)	98.1 (2016)	98.4 (2006)	97.3 (2016)
Nepal	48.6 (2001)	67.9	34.9 (2001)	59.7	62.7 (2001)	78.6
Sri Lanka	90.7 (2001)	91.7	89.1 (2001)	90.8	92.3 (2001)	92.8
Southeast Asia						
Brunei Darussalam	92.7 (2001)	97.2	90.2 (2001)	96.3	95.2 (2001)	98.1
Cambodia	73.6 (2004)	80.5 (2015)	64.1 (2004)	75.0 (2015)	84.7 (2004)	86.5 (2015)
Indonesia	90.4 (2004)	95.7	86.8 (2004)	94.0	94.0 (2004)	97.3
Lao People's Democratic Republic	69.6	84.7 (2015)	58.5	79.4 (2015)	81.4	90.0 (2015)
Malaysia	88.7	94.9	85.4	93.5	92.0	96.1
Myanmar	89.9	75.6 (2016)	86.4	71.8 (2016)	93.9	80.0 (2016)
Philippines	92.6	98.2 (2015)	92.7	98.2 (2015)	92.5	98.1 (2015)
Singapore	92.5	97.3	88.6	95.9	96.6	98.9
Thailand	92.6	93.8	90.5	92.4	94.9	95.2
Timor-Leste	37.6 (2001)	68.1	30.0 (2001)	64.2	45.3 (2001)	71.9
Viet Nam	90.2	95.0	86.6	93.6	93.9	96.5
The Pacific						
Cook Islands	...	...	...	...	...	...
Fiji	...	99.1 (2017)	...	99.1 (2017)	...	99.1 (2017)
Kiribati	...	...	...	...	...	...
Marshall Islands	...	98.3 (2011)	...	98.2 (2011)	...	98.3 (2011)
Micronesia, Federated States of	...	...	...	...	...	...
Nauru	...	...	...	...	...	...
Niue	...	...	...	...	...	...
Palau	...	96.6 (2015)	...	96.3 (2015)	...	96.8 (2015)
Papua New Guinea	57.3	61.6 (2010)	50.9	57.9 (2010)	63.4	65.3 (2010)
Samoa	...	99.1	...	99.2	...	99.0
Solomon Islands	76.6 (2009)	...	69.0 (2009)	...	83.7 (2009)	...
Tonga	99.0 (2006)	99.4	99.1 (2006)	99.5	99.0 (2006)	99.4
Tuvalu	...	...	...	...	...	...
Vanuatu	78.4 (2004)	87.5	76.2 (2004)	86.7	80.5 (2004)	88.3
Developed ADB Member Economies						
Australia	...	...	...	...	...	...
Japan	...	...	...	...	...	...
New Zealand	...	...	...	...	...	...
WORLD	**80.8**	**86.3**	**75.4**	**82.8**	**86.2**	**89.8**

... = data not available, ADB = Asian Development Bank.

Source: United Nations Educational, Scientific and Cultural Organization (UNESCO) Institute for Statistics. UIS.Stat Database. http://data.uis.unesco.org/ (accessed 26 June 2020).

Click on the indictor name in the table header to access the time series in the Key Indicators Database.

Table 2.1.12: Years of Schooling
(years)

ADB Regional Member	Expected[a]					
	Both Sexes		Female		Male	
	2000	2018	2000	2018	2000	2018
Developing ADB Member Economies						
Central and West Asia						
Afghanistan	6.4 (2003)	10.2	4.4 (2003)	7.7	8.3 (2003)	12.5
Armenia	11.2	13.1	11.7	13.6	10.7	12.6
Azerbaijan	…	13.3	…	13.4	…	13.2
Georgia	13.2	15.3	13.5	15.5	13.0	15.0
Kazakhstan	12.4	15.6 (2019)	12.7	16.0 (2019)	12.1	15.3 (2019)
Kyrgyz Republic	11.8	13.0	12.0	13.2	11.7	12.7
Pakistan[c]	5.3 (2003)	8.3	5.5 (2006)	7.6	7.0 (2006)	8.9
Tajikistan	9.7	11.4 (2013)	8.8	10.7 (2013)	10.6	12.1 (2013)
Turkmenistan	…	10.8 (2014)	…	10.5 (2014)	…	11.1 (2014)
Uzbekistan	10.8	12.1 (2017)	10.7	11.9 (2017)	11.0	12.2 (2017)
East Asia						
China, People's Republic of[c]	9.9 (2001)	12.4 (2010)	11.3 (2006)	12.4 (2010)	11.5 (2006)	12.4 (2010)
Hong Kong, China	…	16.9	…	17.1	…	16.8
Korea, Republic of	15.6	16.5 (2017)	14.7	15.9 (2017)	16.5	17.0 (2017)
Mongolia	9.4	14.6 (2010)	10.3	15.3 (2010)	8.5	13.9 (2010)
Taipei,China	…	16.5 (2019)	…	16.7 (2019)	…	16.4 (2019)
South Asia						
Bangladesh	8.7 (2005)	12.0	8.8 (2005)	12.4	8.6 (2005)	11.7
Bhutan	9.4 (2005)	13.1	9.1 (2005)	13.5	9.6 (2005)	12.8
India	8.3	12.2 (2017)	7.3	12.6 (2017)	9.2	11.7 (2017)
Maldives	11.8	…	11.9	…	11.8	…
Nepal	9.0	12.8 (2017)	7.5	13.0 (2017)	10.4	12.6 (2017)
Sri Lanka	…	14.1	…	14.5	…	13.8
Southeast Asia						
Brunei Darussalam	13.2	14.3	13.2	14.8	13.1	13.9
Cambodia	7.6	…	6.8	…	8.4	…
Indonesia	10.6	13.6	10.4	13.7	10.8	13.5
Lao People's Democratic Republic	8.0	10.6	7.0	10.4	9.0	10.9
Malaysia	11.9	13.7 (2017)	12.2	14.0 (2017)	11.7	13.3 (2017)
Myanmar	7.7 (2001)	10.7	…	10.9	…	10.5
Philippines	11.4 (2001)	13.1 (2017)	11.6 (2001)	13.5 (2017)	11.2 (2001)	12.8 (2017)
Singapore	…	16.4 (2017)	…	16.7 (2017)	…	16.3 (2017)
Thailand	11.5 (2001)	15.4 (2016)	11.6 (2001)	15.8 (2016)	11.5 (2001)	15.1 (2016)
Timor-Leste[c]	10.0 (2002)	12.4 (2010)	12.0 (2009)	12.0 (2010)	13.2 (2009)	12.9 (2010)
Viet Nam	…	…	…	…	…	…
The Pacific						
Cook Islands	10.1	14.8 (2012)	10.3	14.2 (2012)	9.9	15.5 (2012)
Fiji	13.4 (2003)	…	13.7 (2003)	…	13.2 (2003)	…
Kiribati	10.4	…	10.8	…	10.0	…
Marshall Islands	12.2 (2002)	…	12.2 (2002)	…	12.2 (2002)	…
Micronesia, Federated States of	…	…	…	…	…	…
Nauru	9.5	…	10.3	…	8.8	…
Niue[c]	11.7	…	11.5 (2001)	…	11.9 (2001)	…
Palau	14.1	16.6 (2013)	14.8	17.2 (2013)	13.4	16.1 (2013)
Papua New Guinea	…	…	…	…	…	…
Samoa	12.0	…	12.4	…	11.7	…
Solomon Islands	6.6	…	6.2	…	7.0	…
Tonga[c]	13.2	…	13.9 (2002)	…	13.4 (2002)	…
Tuvalu	10.9 (2001)	…	11.0 (2001)	…	10.8 (2001)	…
Vanuatu	10.1	…	10.1	…	10.1	…
Developed ADB Member Economies						
Australia	…	22.0 (2017)	…	22.4 (2017)	…	21.5 (2017)
Japan	…	…	…	…	…	…
New Zealand	…	18.8 (2017)	…	19.7 (2017)	…	17.9 (2017)
WORLD[h]	**9.8**	**12.4**	**9.4**	**12.4**	**10.2**	**12.3**

continued on next page

Table 2.1.12: Years of Schooling (continued)
(years)

ADB Regional Member	Mean[b]					
	Both Sexes		Female		Male	
	2000	2018	2000	2018	2000	2018
Developing ADB Member Economies						
Central and West Asia						
Afghanistan	...	...	...	...	...	...
Armenia	10.5 (2001)	11.3 (2017)	10.3 (2001)	11.3 (2017)	10.6 (2001)	11.3 (2017)
Azerbaijan	10.8 (2007)	10.6 (2017)	10.5 (2007)	10.2 (2017)	11.1 (2007)	10.9 (2017)
Georgia	11.7 (2002)	13.1 (2017)	11.5 (2002)	13.2 (2017)	11.8 (2002)	13.1 (2017)
Kazakhstan	11.6 (2007)	12.2	11.7 (2007)	12.2	11.5 (2007)	12.2
Kyrgyz Republic	11.0 (2009)	...	11.1 (2009)	...	10.9 (2009)	...
Pakistan[c]	2.7 (2005)	5.0 (2017)	1.5 (2005)	3.8 (2017)	4.0 (2005)	6.3 (2017)
Tajikistan	10.8	11.4 (2017)	10.3	10.8 (2017)	11.4	11.9 (2017)
Turkmenistan	...	...	...	...	...	...
Uzbekistan	...	11.8	...	11.6	...	12.0
East Asia						
China, People's Republic of[c]	5.9	6.7 (2010)	5.3	6.2 (2010)	6.6	7.2 (2010)
Hong Kong, China	11.0 (2006)	12.3 (2017)	10.5 (2006)	11.9 (2017)	11.6 (2006)	12.7 (2017)
Korea, Republic of	10.9	12.1 (2015)	9.9	11.4 (2015)	12.0	12.9 (2015)
Mongolia	9.2	10.1 (2010)	9.1	10.4 (2010)	9.3	9.8 (2010)
Taipei,China	...	...	...	...	...	...
South Asia						
Bangladesh	4.8 (2001)	6.4	4.3 (2001)	5.8	5.3 (2001)	7.0
Bhutan	...	4.1 (2017)	...	3.3 (2017)	...	4.8 (2017)
India	...	5.3 (2011)	...	4.1 (2011)	...	6.5 (2011)
Maldives	3.8[d] (2006)	...	3.5[d] (2006)	...	4.0[d] (2006)	...
Nepal	3.6[e] (2001)	3.5 (2011)	2.5[e] (2001)	2.3 (2011)	4.8[e] (2001)	4.9 (2011)
Sri Lanka	10.2 (2001)	10.6	10.0 (2001)	10.6	10.4 (2001)	10.6
Southeast Asia						
Brunei Darussalam	...	11.6 (2011)	...	11.4 (2011)	...	11.8 (2011)
Cambodia	4.0 (2007)	3.7 (2015)	3.0 (2007)	2.8 (2015)	5.0 (2007)	4.8 (2015)
Indonesia	7.6 (2006)	8.2	7.1 (2006)	7.8	7.9 (2006)	8.6
Lao People's Democratic Republic	...	...	...	...	...	...
Malaysia	8.5	10.4 (2016)	8.0	10.3 (2016)	9.0	10.5 (2016)
Myanmar	...	...	...	...	...	...
Philippines	7.7	8.5 (2017)	7.7	8.7 (2017)	7.7	8.2 (2017)
Singapore	10.6 (2005)	11.6	10.1 (2005)	11.2	11.1 (2005)	12.1
Thailand	7.3 (2004)	8.5	7.0 (2004)	8.3	7.6 (2004)	8.7
Timor-Leste[c]	...	...	...	...	...	...
Viet Nam	7.6 (2009)	...	7.1 (2009)	...	8.2 (2009)	...
The Pacific						
Cook Islands	9.9 (2006)	...	9.8 (2006)	...	10.0 (2006)	...
Fiji	9.3 (2007)	10.9 (2017)	9.3 (2007)	11.0 (2017)	9.3 (2007)	10.8 (2017)
Kiribati	...	...	...	...	...	...
Marshall Islands	...	10.9 (2011)	...	10.7 (2011)	...	11.1 (2011)
Micronesia, Federated States of	...	...	...	...	...	...
Nauru	...	...	...	...	...	...
Niue[c]	...	...	...	...	...	...
Palau	...	12.9 (2013)	...	12.9 (2013)	...	12.8 (2013)
Papua New Guinea	...	...	...	...	...	...
Samoa	10.8 (2001)	11.8 (2011)	11.0 (2001)	12.0 (2011)	10.7 (2001)	11.7 (2011)
Solomon Islands	...	...	...	...	...	...
Tonga[c]	9.9 (2006)	10.9 (2011)	9.7 (2006)	10.9 (2011)	10.0 (2006)	11.0 (2011)
Tuvalu	...	...	...	...	...	...
Vanuatu	...	...	...	...	...	...
Developed ADB Member Economies						
Australia	11.8[f] (2004)	12.5[g]	11.7[f] (2004)	12.6[g]	11.9[f] (2004)	12.4[g]
Japan	...	12.3[d] (2010)	...	12.0[d] (2010)	...	12.7[d] (2010)
New Zealand	13.4[d] (2001)	13.1 (2016)	13.3[d] (2001)	13.1 (2016)	13.5[d] (2001)	13.2 (2016)

... = data not available, ADB = Asian Development Bank.

a   Refers to the expected number of years of schooling from primary to tertiary level of education.
b   Refers to the mean of years of schooling among the population aged 25 years or older.
c   For the initial year data on the expected years of schooling, sex-disaggregated data are available for a different reference year relative to the overall estimate.
d   Based on data for which the proportion of the population with unknown educational attainment exceeds 5%.
e   Estimated by the United Nations Educational, Scientific and Cultural Organization's Institute for Statistics.
f   Data for the population aged 25 to 64 years.
g   Data for the population aged 25 to 74 years.
h   Estimated by the United Nations Educational, Scientific and Cultural Organization's Institute of Statistics as the sum of the age-specific enrolment rates for primary to tertiary level of education. The part of the enrolment that is not distributed by age is divided by the school-age population for the level of education, then multiplied by the duration of that level of education. The result is then added to the sum of the age-specific enrolment rates.

Sources: United Nations Educational, Scientific and Cultural Organization (UNESCO) Institute for Statistics. UIS.Stat Database. http://data.uis.unesco.org/ (accessed 26 June 2020). For Taipei,China, expected years of schooling: Government of Taipei,China, Ministry of Education. https://english.moe.gov.tw/cp-87-14508-95005-1.html (accessed 15 June 2020).

Click on the indictor name in the table header to access the time series in the Key Indicators Database.

Table 2.1.13:   Education Resources

ADB Regional Member	Primary Pupil–Teacher Ratio		Secondary Pupil–Teacher Ratio	
	2000	2018	2000	2018
Developing ADB Member Economies				
Central and West Asia				
Afghanistan	42.3 (2006)	48.8	31.6 (2007)	33.5
Armenia	20.3 (2001)	15.4	...	8.0
Azerbaijan	18.7	15.4	...	7.6
Georgia	16.8	9.0	7.5	7.6
Kazakhstan	18.7 (2001)	17.2 (2019)	...	7.7 (2019)
Kyrgyz Republic	24.1	25.0	13.3	10.6
Pakistan	33.0	44.1	24.2 (2003)	20.4
Tajikistan	21.8	22.3 (2017)	16.4	15.4 (2011)
Turkmenistan	...	...		...
Uzbekistan	21.4	21.5	11.5	10.3 (2017)
East Asia				
China, People's Republic of	22.2 (2001)	16.4	17.1	13.3
Hong Kong, China	21.5	13.3	18.8 (2001)	11.2
Korea, Republic of	32.1	16.3 (2017)	21.0	13.3 (2017)
Mongolia	32.6	30.4	19.9	14.5 (2010)
Taipei,China	19.0	12.1 (2019)	17.6	12.2 a (2019)
South Asia				
Bangladesh	47.0 (2005)	30.1	38.4	35.1
Bhutan	41.1	34.7	28.1 (2005)	10.8
India	40.0	32.7 (2017)	33.6	28.5
Maldives	22.7	10.2 (2017)	15.3	...
Nepal	38.0	19.7 (2019)	30.2	28.3 (2019)
Sri Lanka	26.3 (2001)	21.7	...	17.5
Southeast Asia				
Brunei Darussalam	13.7	9.9	10.9	8.3
Cambodia	50.1	41.7	18.5	...
Indonesia	22.1	17.0	14.6	15.2
Lao People's Democratic Republic	30.1	22.3	21.3	18.2
Malaysia	19.6	11.7 (2017)	18.4	11.4
Myanmar	32.8	24.4	31.9	27.2
Philippines	35.3	29.1 (2017)	36.4 (2001)	23.9 (2017)
Singapore	21.1 (2007)	14.7 (2017)	17.8 (2007)	11.5 (2017)
Thailand	20.8	16.6	24.0 (2001)	25.9
Timor-Leste	61.9 (2001)	26.9	28.0 (2001)	26.5
Viet Nam	29.5	20.3	...	...
The Pacific				
Cook Islands	17.8	17.4 (2016)	13.9	15.7 (2016)
Fiji	28.1	28.0 (2012)	20.2	19.3 (2012)
Kiribati	31.7	25.5 (2017)	21.0 (2001)	...
Marshall Islands	16.9 (2002)	...	16.7 (2002)	...
Micronesia, Federated States of	...	19.7 (2015)	...	...
Nauru	21.5	40.2 (2016)	17.4	24.8 (2016)
Niue	14.7	15.5 (2016)	7.8	7.9 (2015)
Palau	15.7	...	15.1	...
Papua New Guinea	35.4	35.5 (2016)	...	34.3 (2016)
Samoa	24.0	30.2 (2010)	21.2	21.5 (2010)
Solomon Islands	...	25.4	10.1	25.9 (2012)
Tonga	22.1	21.6 (2015)	14.6	14.5 (2015)
Tuvalu	19.7	15.6	...	8.6
Vanuatu	22.5	26.6 (2015)	24.7	20.6 (2015)
Developed ADB Member Economies				
Australia	...	...	...	...
Japan	...	15.7 (2017)	...	11.1 (2017)
New Zealand	18.4	14.9 (2017)	15.5	13.6 (2017)

... = data not available, ADB = Asian Development Bank.

a   Includes pupils and teachers in vocational secondary schools.

Sources: United Nations Educational, Scientific and Cultural Organization (UNESCO) Institute for Statistics. UIS.Stat Database. http://data.uis.unesco.org/ (accessed 9 June 2020). For Taipei,China: Government of Taipei,China, Directorate-General of Budget, Accounting and Statistics. Social Indicators. http://eng.dgbas.gov.tw/mp.asp?mp=2 (accessed 9 June 2020).

Table 2.1.14: Health Care Resources
(per 1,000 population)

ADB Regional Member	Physicians[a]		Hospital Beds[a]	
	2000	2018	2000	2018
Developing ADB Member Economies				
Central and West Asia				
Afghanistan	0.19 (2001)	0.28 (2016)	0.3	0.4 (2017)
Armenia	2.70	4.40 (2017)	6.4	4.2[b] (2015)
Azerbaijan	3.57	3.45 (2014)	8.7	4.8 (2014)
Georgia	3.84	7.12	4.8	2.9 (2014)
Kazakhstan	3.28	3.98 (2014)	7.2	6.1 (2014)
Kyrgyz Republic	2.80	2.21 (2014)	7.0	4.4 (2014)
Pakistan	0.65	0.98	0.7	0.6 (2017)
Tajikistan	2.17	2.10 (2014)	6.5	4.7 (2014)
Turkmenistan	2.75	2.22 (2014)	5.4	4.0 (2014)
Uzbekistan	2.96	2.37 (2014)	5.3	4.0 (2014)
East Asia				
China, People's Republic of	1.24	1.98 (2017)	1.7	4.3 (2017)
Hong Kong, China	...	...	...	...
Korea, Republic of	1.30[b]	2.36 (2017)	4.7	12.4
Mongolia	2.76 (2002)	2.86 (2016)	7.5[b] (2002)	8.0 (2017)
Taipei,China	1.54 (2001)	2.30	5.7 (2001)	7.1
South Asia				
Bangladesh	0.25 (2001)	0.58	0.3[b] (2001)	0.8 (2016)
Bhutan	0.18 (2004)	0.42	1.6[b] (2001)	1.7[b] (2012)
India	0.53	0.86	0.7	0.5 (2017)
Maldives	0.78[b]	4.56	1.7[b]	...
Nepal	0.05[b] (2001)	0.75	0.2[b] (2001)	0.3[b] (2012)
Sri Lanka	0.42	1.00	2.9[b]	4.2 (2017)
Southeast Asia				
Brunei Darussalam	1.01	1.61 (2017)	2.5	2.9 (2017)
Cambodia	0.17	0.19 (2014)	0.6[b] (2001)	0.9 (2016)
Indonesia	0.16[b]	0.43	0.6[b] (2002)	1.0 (2017)
Lao People's Democratic Republic	0.29	0.37 (2017)	0.9[b] (2002)	1.5[b] (2012)
Malaysia	0.70	1.54 (2015)	1.8[b] (2001)	1.9 (2017)
Myanmar	0.30[b]	0.68	0.7[b]	1.0 (2017)
Philippines	1.22	0.60 (2017)	1.0[b] (2001)	1.0 (2014)
Singapore	1.41 (2001)	2.29 (2016)	2.9[b] (2001)	2.5 (2017)
Thailand	0.37[b]	0.81	2.2[b]	2.1[b] (2010)
Timor-Leste	0.08[b] (2004)	0.72	5.9[b] (2009)	5.9[b] (2010)
Viet Nam	0.52 (2001)	0.83 (2016)	2.3	2.6[b] (2014)
The Pacific				
Cook Islands	0.78 (2001)	1.41 (2014)	...	...
Fiji	0.47 (2003)	0.86 (2015)	2.1[b] (2004)	2.0 (2016)
Kiribati	0.25 (2008)	0.20 (2013)	1.5[b] (2004)	1.9 (2016)
Marshall Islands	0.47[b]	0.42 (2012)	2.7[b] (2009)	2.7[b] (2010)
Micronesia, Federated States of	0.60[b]	0.18[b] (2010)	2.8[b]	...
Nauru	1.01 (2004)	1.35 (2015)	3.5[b] (2004)	5.0[b] (2010)
Niue	2.35 (2003)	...	...	...
Palau	1.58[b]	1.42 (2014)	5.9[b] (2006)	4.8[b] (2010)
Papua New Guinea	0.05	0.07	...	...
Samoa	0.28 (2003)	0.34 (2016)	3.3[b]	...
Solomon Islands	0.13 (2003)	0.19 (2016)	2.2[b] (2003)	1.4[b] (2012)
Tonga	0.50[b]	0.54 (2013)	3.2[b] (2001)	2.6[b] (2010)
Tuvalu	0.63 (2002)	0.91 (2014)	5.6[b] (2001)	...
Vanuatu	0.15 (2004)	0.17 (2016)	3.1[b] (2001)	...
Developed ADB Member Economies				
Australia	2.50[b]	3.68 (2017)	4.0	3.8 (2016)
Japan	2.01	2.41 (2016)	14.7	13.0
New Zealand	2.31 (2001)	3.59	6.2 (2002)	2.6 (2019)
WORLD	**1.24**[b]	**1.57**[b] (2017)	**2.9**[b] (2002)	**2.7**[b] (2011)

... = data not available, ADB = Asian Development Bank.

a Main source of data is the World Health Organization Global Health Observatory.
b Data sourced from the World Bank's World Development Indicators database.

Sources: World Bank. World Development Indicators. https://data.worldbank.org/indicator/SH.MED.PHYS.ZS and https://data.worldbank.org/indicator/SH.MED.BEDS.ZS (both accessed 8 July 2020); and World Health Organization. Global Health Observatory. http://apps.who.int/gho/data/node.main.HWFGRP_0020?lang=en (accessed 29 June 2020) and http://apps.who.int/gho/data/view.main.HS07v (accessed 8 July 2020). For Taipei,China: Government of Taipei,China, Directorate-General of Budget, Accounting and Statistics. Statistical Yearbook 2018. https://eng.dgbas.gov.tw/lp.asp?ctNode=2351&CtUnit=1072&BaseDSD=36&MP=2 (accessed 29 June 2020).

Click on the indictor name in the table header to access the time series in the Key Indicators Database.

Social Indicators

Table 2.1.15: Adults Aged 15 Years and Older Living with HIV[a]
('000)

ADB Regional Member	All Adults		Women	
	2000	2018	2000	2018
Developing ADB Member Economies				
Central and West Asia[b]	**20.7**	**269.3**	**6.3**	**85.1**
Afghanistan	1.5	6.9	0.4	2.0
Armenia	0.9	3.5	0.3	1.2
Azerbaijan	...	...	...	...
Georgia	1.0	9.3	0.3	3.0
Kazakhstan	1.1	25.3	0.4	9.2
Kyrgyz Republic	0.7	8.2	0.2	2.7
Pakistan	0.4	157.5	0.1	47.7
Tajikistan	1.4	12.4	0.3	3.5
Turkmenistan	...	...	...	...
Uzbekistan	13.7	46.2	4.2	15.7
East Asia				
China, People's Republic of	...	...	...	...
Hong Kong, China	...	...	...	...
Korea, Republic of	...	...	...	...
Mongolia	0.0	0.6	0.0	0.1
Taipei,China	...	...	...	...
South Asia				
Bangladesh	0.9	13.5	0.2	4.8
Bhutan	0.5	1.3	0.1	0.4
India	...	...	...	...
Maldives	...	...	...	...
Nepal	15.4	28.7	2.4	11.6
Sri Lanka	2.1	3.4	0.5	1.0
Southeast Asia[b]	**1,211.7**	**1,802.6**	**379.9**	**655.9**
Brunei Darussalam	...	...	...	...
Cambodia	78.3	69.9	33.2	37.0
Indonesia	79.7	622.1	14.9	222.5
Lao People's Democratic Republic	2.1	11.3	0.8	5.0
Malaysia	54.9	86.6	11.2	14.6
Myanmar	147.4	227.3	34.2	86.9
Philippines	1.0	76.7	0.2	4.6
Singapore	2.9	7.9	0.3	0.8
Thailand	724.4	476.4	261.5	209.9
Timor-Leste	...	...	...	...
Viet Nam	120.8	224.3	23.6	74.5
The Pacific				
Cook Islands	...	...	...	...
Fiji	...	...	...	...
Kiribati	...	...	...	...
Marshall Islands	...	...	...	...
Micronesia, Federated States of	...	...	...	...
Nauru	...	...	...	...
Niue	...	...	...	...
Palau	...	...	...	...
Papua New Guinea	18.8	42.5	10.3	24.5
Samoa	...	...	...	...
Solomon Islands	...	...	...	...
Tonga	...	...	...	...
Tuvalu	...	...	...	...
Vanuatu	...	...	...	...
Developed ADB Member Economies[b]	**20.4**	**60.8**	**2.5**	**6.8**
Australia	13.0	27.6	1.3	3.3
Japan	6.1	29.7	0.9	2.8
New Zealand	1.3	3.6	0.3	0.6

... = data not available, 0.0 = magnitude is less than half of unit employed, ADB = Asian Development Bank.

a The modeled HIV estimates are calculated by the Joint United Nations Programme on HIV/AIDS (UNAIDS) using the software Spectrum developed by Avenir Health (www.avenirhealth.org), and the Estimates and Projections Package developed by the East-West Center (www.eastwestcenter.org). The UNAIDS Reference Group on Estimates, Modelling and Projections (www.epidem.org) provides technical guidance on the development of the HIV component of the software.
b The aggregates shown for the two regions of Asia and the Pacific and for the developed ADB member economies are approximations of the actual total and, due to rounding, may not equal the sum of the figures for the individual economies.

Source: Joint United Nations Programme on HIV/AIDS (UNAIDS). AIDSInfo. https://onlinedb.unaids.org/epi/libraries/aspx/Home.aspx (accessed 1 July 2020).

Click on the indictor name in the table header to access the time series in the Key Indicators Database.

II.   Economy and Output

Economy and Output presents figures comparing the relative size of economies, both within Asia and the Pacific and across the world, using data on gross domestic product (GDP) expressed in current United States (US) dollars. The economic growth rates and gross fixed capital formation levels of ADB member economies in the region are also discussed under this theme. Statistical tables generated from the national accounts include GDP, value added, consumption expenditure, exports and imports, and gross domestic saving. Other tables present production indicators and trends in external trade and domestic consumption.

Asia and the Pacific now makes the highest regional contribution to global GDP

The Asia and Pacific region's share of global GDP in current US dollars has increased steadily from 26.3% in 2000, to 29.0% in 2010, and 34.9% in 2019 (Figure 2.2.1). Meanwhile, its ranking among all regions for share of global output has improved from third in 2000, to second in 2010, and to first in 2019. During the review period, the region's share of global GDP increased 8.6 percentage points, while the shares of North America and Europe declined 6.9 percentage points and 4.1 percentage points, respectively.

In 2019, the region with the second-largest share of global GDP was North America at 28.1%, followed by Europe at 25.3%. The remaining regions and their respective shares of global GDP in 2019 are as follows: South America (4.4%), West Asia (3.2%), Africa (2.8%), and the rest of the world (1.3%). These percentages compare with the following global GDP shares in 2000: South America (4.0%), West Asia (2.0%), Africa (1.9%), and the rest of the world (1.4%).

Figure 2.2.1 Global Distribution of Gross Domestic Product at Current US Dollar (%)

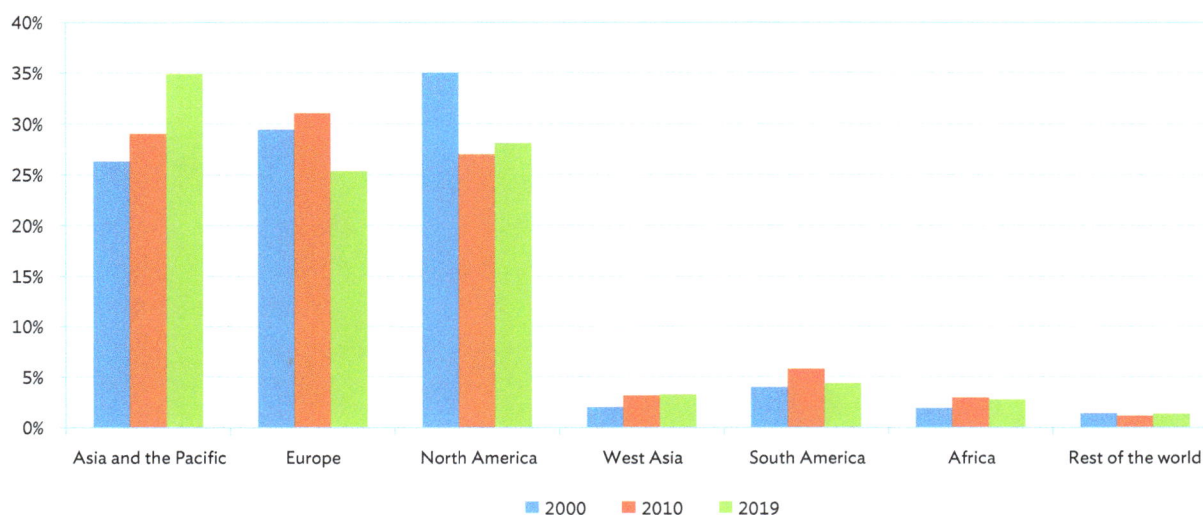

Note: Asia and the Pacific region refers to all ADB regional member economies.
Sources: Table 2.2.1, Key Indicators for Asia and the Pacific 2020; and World Bank. World Development Indicators. https://data.worldbank.org/ (accessed 3 July 2020).

Click here for figure data

More than half the reporting economies in Asia and Pacific posted GDP growth of 4.0% or higher in 2019

A majority of ADB member economies with available data (19 of 35) experienced GDP growth of 4.0% or higher in 2019, led by Bangladesh (8.2%); Armenia (7.6%); and Nepal and Viet Nam (7.0% each) as shown in Figure 2.2.2. Bangladesh's economy expanded on increased manufacturing to meet rising export demand for garments and growth in services (e.g., wholesale and retail trade, transport, education, and health and social services). Growth in Armenia was driven by gains in services, industry, and private consumption. In Viet Nam, a combination of robust domestic demand, growth in manufacturing, and rising foreign direct investment contributed to another year of solid economic growth (ADB 2020).

Economies with the slowest (or negative) growth rates included Hong Kong, China (–1.2%); Palau (0.3%); and Japan, Singapore, and Tonga (0.7% each). In Hong Kong, China, domestic political tensions were exacerbated by weakening global trade growth, leading to an economic contraction for the first time in a decade. In Palau, economic growth weakened on falling visitor arrivals. In Japan, the growth rate represented an acceleration from only 0.3% in 2018. However, global trade tensions as well as a sales tax hike and a destructive typhoon (both coming in the fourth quarter of 2019), kept Japan's economy from expanding further (ADB 2020).

More than 60% of reporting economies had a higher gross capital formation as a percentage of GDP in 2019 than in 2000

Capital formation comprises fixed investment in buildings, civil engineering, machinery, and equipment. While developed economies tend to have a larger and more modern stock of capital assets, rapidly developing economies often attempt to

Figure 2.2.2: Growth Rates of Real Gross Domestic Product, 2019 (%)

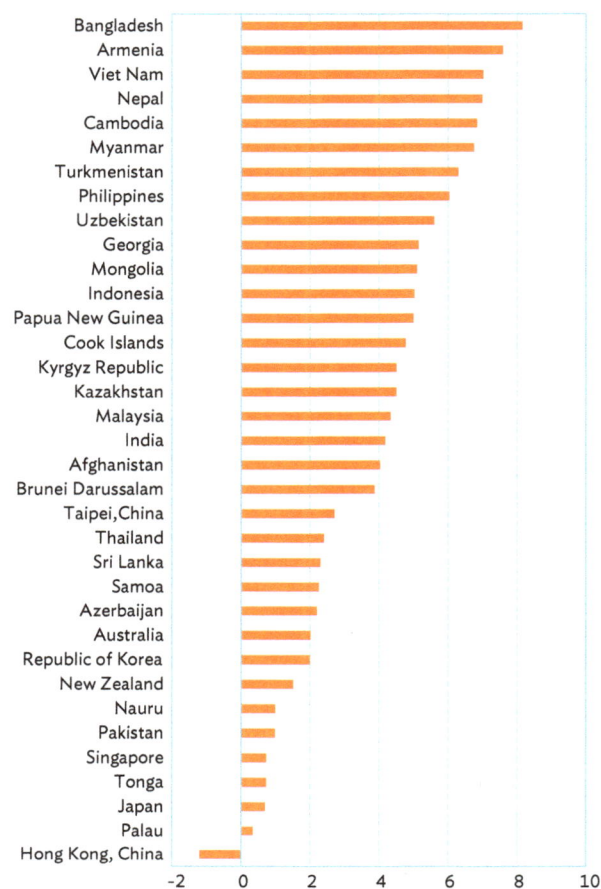

Note: Only economies with data for 2019 are included in the chart.
Source: Table 2.2.11, Key Indicators for Asia and the Pacific 2020.

Click here for figure data

narrow this gap with increased investments and the incorporation of new technology.

Figure 2.2.3 shows gross capital formation as a percentage of GDP for 28 regional economies with available data for 2000 and 2019. Of these 28 economies, 17 experienced an increase in gross capital formation as a percentage of GDP from 2000 to 2019.

The largest average annual gains in gross capital formation from 2000 to 2019 were observed in Nepal (1.7 percentage points), Brunei Darussalam (1.3 percentage points), and Uzbekistan (1.1 percentage points). The largest average annual declines occurred in the newly industrialized economies of Hong Kong, China and Singapore (0.5 percentage points each), and Malaysia (0.3 percentage points).

In 2019 (or the most recent year for which data were available), gross capital formation as a percentage of GDP ranged from a low of 15.6% in Pakistan to a high of 56.6% in Nepal, where major infrastructure investments are ongoing under a program of national pride projects (Poudel 2019). The next highest levels of gross capital formation as a percentage of GDP in 2019 were observed in the PRC (43.3%), Uzbekistan (39.8%), and Brunei Darussalam (38.7%).

Data Issues and Comparability

Indicators in this theme were derived from national accounts statistics compiled in accordance with the UN System of National Accounts. As national statistical offices gradually adopt the latest 2008 System of National Accounts framework with regard to data compilation and methodologies, these indicators will become more consistent across economies. Currently, economies in the region have varying reference periods (e.g., calendar year versus fiscal year) and price valuation methods. Due to a lack of reliable data and limited technical and financial resources dedicated for national accounts compilation, some economies with small statistical offices are not able to provide timely estimates, while some are dependent upon the estimates of external institutions.

Figure 2.2.3. Share of Gross Capital Formation to Gross Domestic Product
(%)

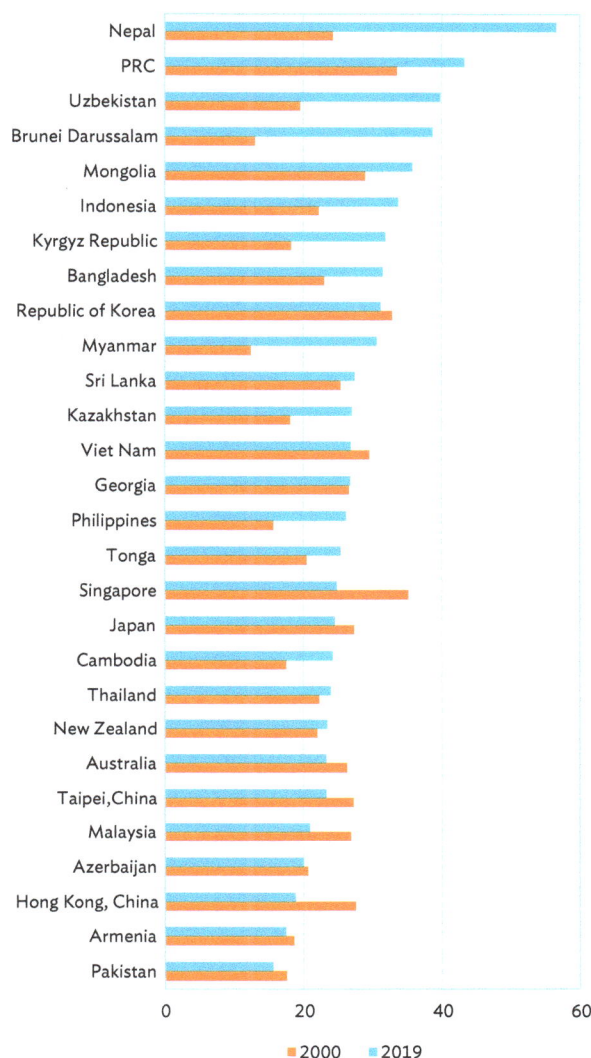

- ■ 2000 ■ 2019

PRC = People's Republic of China.
Note: This chart includes economies with available data between 2000 and 2019.
Source: Table 2.2.8, Key Indicators for Asia and the Pacific 2020.

Click here for figure data

National Accounts

Table 2.2.1:   Gross Domestic Product at Purchasing Power Parity[a]
(current international dollars, million)

ADB Regional Member	2000	2005	2010	2014	2015	2016	2017	2018	2019
Developing ADB Member Economies									
Central and West Asia[b]	**653,160**	**1,019,836**	**1,479,140**	**1,881,316**	**1,898,465**	**1,951,080**	**2,051,068**	**2,202,623**	**2,300,140**
Afghanistan	22,037 (2002)	27,913	51,342	71,677	74,020	70,168	73,631	76,662	81,770
Armenia	8,160	16,264	21,598	29,231	29,167	31,429	35,677	38,417	42,058
Azerbaijan	27,708	57,490	135,151	166,329	144,146	140,230	139,153	144,574	150,358
Georgia	12,657	20,172	28,643	43,054	45,036	47,930	50,663	54,383	58,174
Kazakhstan	115,107	211,070	313,789	427,478	407,416	423,833	448,473	477,876	508,088
Kyrgyz Republic	9,129	12,309	16,810	24,987	25,107	28,459	31,280	33,222	35,324
Pakistan	379,138	546,046	698,014	827,826	872,097	898,016	950,382	1,029,590	1,057,890
Tajikistan	6,518	11,573	17,527	27,631	26,634	26,986	28,887	31,103	32,808
Turkmenistan	11,238	27,716	49,909	73,681	76,309	78,516	81,788	88,908	...
Uzbekistan	61,468	89,283	146,357	189,421	198,534	205,512	211,135	227,888	244,761
East Asia	**5,235,492**	**8,730,000**	**15,207,193**	**20,408,530**	**21,276,211**	**22,304,058**	**23,613,760**	**25,611,969**	**27,450,891**
China, People's Republic of	3,687,573	6,588,683	12,378,799	17,121,277	17,796,747	18,712,097	19,887,033	21,730,685	23,460,170
Hong Kong, China	188,308	259,288	345,487	396,044	411,294	419,811	442,388	465,790	467,868
Korea, Republic of	872,060	1,213,618	1,572,870	1,792,600	1,933,849	2,026,536	2,105,893	2,174,501	2,224,986
Mongolia	8,941	13,704	20,621	32,507	32,285	32,833	35,222	38,666	41,346
Taipei,China	478,612	654,707	889,416	1,066,102	1,102,036	1,112,781	1,143,224	1,202,327	1,256,521
South Asia[b]	**2,462,040**	**3,740,541**	**5,815,813**	**7,618,310**	**8,043,414**	**8,688,636**	**9,318,055**	**10,126,022**	**10,814,995**
Bangladesh	150,089	211,662	359,947	520,423	555,570	608,047	664,404	733,561	807,200
Bhutan	1,594	2,631	4,588	6,232	6,915	7,704	8,307	8,761	...
India	2,214,209	3,389,017	5,229,334	6,781,022	7,159,798	7,735,002	8,280,935	8,995,057	9,590,504
Maldives	2,303	2,857	4,649	6,957	7,628	8,279	8,930	9,770	...
Nepal	26,423	37,524	51,265	69,781	71,141	70,414	85,625	93,519	101,801
Sri Lanka	67,421	96,848	166,030	233,895	242,361	259,190	269,854	285,354	296,959
Southeast Asia[b]	**2,454,854**	**3,539,549**	**5,058,508**	**6,451,162**	**6,618,131**	**6,936,388**	**7,361,216**	**7,923,668**	**8,423,924**
Brunei Darussalam	22,135	27,462	31,199	33,344	25,949	23,633	25,891	26,515	28,022
Cambodia	13,072	22,874	34,739	48,654	52,598	57,942	62,891	69,183	75,355
Indonesia	1,003,410	1,415,353	2,056,981	2,622,252	2,647,707	2,744,897	2,894,126	3,115,566	3,329,169
Lao People's Democratic Republic	9,237	14,678	22,601	39,000	41,583	46,850	50,445	54,882	...
Malaysia	299,511	422,719	578,512	734,948	750,777	783,874	828,897	888,687	943,336
Myanmar	43,013	88,204	164,098	221,974	227,959	213,835	225,517	243,729	261,324
Philippines	268,256	377,278	528,684	699,662	733,864	798,601	854,095	929,690	1,003,038
Singapore	176,555	250,474	382,249	461,772	481,405	501,213	532,833	564,158	578,204
Thailand	459,736	670,930	886,663	1,059,446	1,087,225	1,146,218	1,205,675	1,285,351	1,338,781
Timor-Leste	1,122	1,379	2,148	3,195	3,489	3,830	3,936	3,997	...
Viet Nam	158,806	248,198	370,634	526,915	565,575	615,496	676,910	741,909	807,816
The Pacific[b]	**14,972**	**19,220**	**32,636**	**44,895**	**49,295**	**51,477**	**54,419**	**56,827**	**...**
Cook Islands	...	...	...	...	...	...	...	...	...
Fiji	4,717	5,923	6,805	9,831	10,782	11,020	11,784	12,487	...
Kiribati	134	161	177	210	234	249	256	268	...
Marshall Islands	126	158	183	197	202	207	220	233	...
Micronesia, Federated States of	267	309	336	345	365	373	390	400	...
Nauru	...	43	62	146	158	143	138	149	152
Niue	...	...	...	...	...	...	...	...	...
Palau	189	247	241	286	316	320	320	333	...
Papua New Guinea	7,759	9,669	21,314	29,904	33,090	34,816	36,733	38,313	40,087
Samoa	541	807	1,019	1,109	1,190	1,243	1,267	1,301	1,344
Solomon Islands	392	944	1,282	1,482	1,526	1,576	1,685	...	...
Tonga	364	445	505	557	592	646	690	719	...
Tuvalu	23	26	30	36	40	45	48	...	...
Vanuatu	418	487	682	791	801	838	891	...	...
Developed ADB Member Economies[b]	**3,991,391**	**4,816,244**	**5,482,679**	**6,255,219**	**6,410,608**	**6,409,178**	**6,582,404**	**6,714,446**	**7,018,679**
Australia	504,077	664,362	865,883	1,100,545	1,102,113	1,145,438	1,203,164	1,275,027	1,352,432
Japan	3,404,300	4,045,734	4,480,784	4,986,566	5,136,019	5,076,057	5,180,326	5,230,147	5,456,974
New Zealand	83,014	106,148	136,011	168,108	172,477	187,684	198,913	209,273	...
DEVELOPING ADB MEMBER ECONOMIES[b]	**10,820,518**	**17,049,146**	**27,593,291**	**36,404,214**	**37,885,516**	**39,931,639**	**42,398,518**	**45,921,108**	**49,048,597**
ALL ADB REGIONAL MEMBERS[b]	**14,811,909**	**21,865,390**	**33,075,969**	**42,659,433**	**44,296,124**	**46,340,817**	**48,980,922**	**52,635,554**	**56,067,276**

... = data not available, ADB = Asian Development Bank.

a Gross domestic product figures in local currency units are obtained from economy sources and converted into a common currency using the purchasing power parity (PPP) from the World Bank's World Development Indicators. Prior to 2011, the PPP figures are extrapolated from the revised 2011 International Comparison Program (ICP). For 2012–2016, PPP estimates are interpolated from the two ICP reference years 2011 and 2017. For 2017 onward, the PPP figures are extrapolated from the 2017 ICP PPPs or imputed based on a regression model. Moreover, for 2005, 2011, and 2017, PPP figures are based on results from the ICP benchmark rounds. For Taipei,China, the PPP figures for 2000–2010 and 2018–2019 are Asian Development Bank estimates using data from economy sources and the World Bank, while the PPP conversion factor used for 2011–2017 was from the World Bank's ICP 2017 database.
b For estimating aggregates, imputation was done for economies with missing data by substituting available data from the nearest years.

Source: Asian Development Bank estimates.

Click on the indictor name in the table header to access the time series in the Key Indicators Database.

Table 2.2.2: Gross Domestic Product[a]
(current $ million)

ADB Regional Member	2000	2005	2010	2014	2015	2016	2017	2018	2019
Developing ADB Member Economies									
Central and West Asia[b]	**132,839**	**244,384**	**492,971**	**733,020**	**683,267**	**628,155**	**669,100**	**665,839**	**651,604**
Afghanistan	4,285 (2002)	6,622	16,079	21,329	20,609	18,037	18,622	17,988	17,876
Armenia	1,912	4,900	9,260	11,610	10,553	10,546	11,527	12,458	13,673
Azerbaijan	5,273	13,245	52,906	75,240	53,076	37,867	40,867	47,112	48,048
Georgia	3,058	6,411	12,243	17,627	14,954	15,142	16,243	17,600	17,743
Kazakhstan	18,292	57,124	148,047	221,416	184,388	137,278	166,806	179,340	180,162
Kyrgyz Republic	1,370	2,460	4,794	7,468	6,678	6,813	7,703	8,271	8,455
Pakistan	79,097	119,739	174,508	248,949	267,035	277,521	302,710	284,151	253,086
Tajikistan	861	2,312	5,642	9,237	8,271	6,992	7,536	7,765	8,117
Turkmenistan	4,932	17,174	22,582	43,486	35,855	36,180	37,926	40,761	46,525
Uzbekistan	13,759	14,396	46,909	76,659	81,847	81,779	59,160	50,393	57,921
East Asia	**2,291,092**	**3,779,148**	**7,911,445**	**12,798,997**	**13,383,157**	**13,608,657**	**14,877,859**	**16,598,558**	**16,975,986**
China, People's Republic of	1,211,331	2,285,961	6,087,192	10,475,625	11,061,573	11,233,315	12,310,490	13,894,907	14,342,934
Hong Kong, China	171,669	181,569	228,639	291,460	309,386	320,840	341,242	361,697	365,711
Korea, Republic of	576,179	934,901	1,144,067	1,484,318	1,465,773	1,500,112	1,623,901	1,720,579	1,642,384
Mongolia	1,137	2,523	7,189	12,227	11,750	11,187	11,426	13,109	13,853
Taipei,China	330,776	374,192	444,357	535,368	534,676	543,204	590,800	608,267	611,105
South Asia[b]	**544,720**	**915,864**	**1,861,270**	**2,321,100**	**2,448,743**	**2,621,345**	**2,991,436**	**3,167,781**	**3,311,898**
Bangladesh	45,468	57,627	114,508	173,062	194,466	220,837	245,633	269,628	301,051
Bhutan	424	797	1,548	1,907	2,004	2,159	2,450	2,447	...
India	476,168	823,612	1,669,620	2,042,939	2,146,759	2,290,587	2,625,598	2,774,000	2,888,349
Maldives	624	1,163	2,588	3,697	4,109	4,379	4,736	5,327	...
Nepal	5,338	8,259	16,281	20,138	20,801	20,982	25,590	27,953	30,715
Sri Lanka	16,717	24,406	56,726	79,356	80,604	82,401	87,428	88,426	84,009
Southeast Asia[b]	**616,700**	**942,573**	**1,997,444**	**2,549,598**	**2,480,736**	**2,598,193**	**2,798,758**	**2,995,340**	**3,167,930**
Brunei Darussalam	6,001	9,531	13,707	17,098	12,930	11,400	12,128	13,567	13,469
Cambodia	3,667	6,293	11,242	16,703	18,050	20,017	22,177	24,572	27,089
Indonesia	165,021	285,869	755,094	890,815	860,854	931,877	1,015,619	1,042,240	1,119,191
Lao People's Democratic Republic	1,638	2,717	6,747	13,279	14,426	15,913	17,065	18,142	...
Malaysia	93,790	143,534	255,018	338,066	301,355	301,255	318,955	358,579	364,702
Myanmar	...	...	...	66,300	62,543	60,100	60,793	64,896	69,329
Philippines	83,670	107,420	208,369	297,484	306,446	318,627	328,481	346,842	376,796
Singapore	96,077	127,808	239,808	314,864	307,997	318,641	341,856	373,206	372,073
Thailand	126,392	189,318	341,105	407,339	401,296	413,430	456,295	506,514	543,650
Timor-Leste	367	462	882	1,447	1,597	1,656	1,610	1,569	...
Viet Nam	31,173	57,633	115,932	186,205	193,241	205,276	223,780	245,214	261,921
The Pacific[b]	**6,866**	**10,431**	**21,198**	**32,856**	**31,065**	**30,599**	**33,327**	**34,910**	**...**
Cook Islands	92	183	241	319	302	310	346	362	379
Fiji	1,678	2,980	3,140	4,857	4,682	4,930	5,353	5,537	...
Kiribati	68	112	156	180	171	178	187	197	...
Marshall Islands	115	142	162	185	185	201	213	221	...
Micronesia, Federated States of	233	250	297	319	316	332	367	402	...
Nauru	...	31	51	115	90	102	111	120	115
Niue	8	14	18	27	24	25	26	30	31
Palau	146	185	184	244	279	297	288	285	280
Papua New Guinea	3,499	4,866	14,251	23,211	21,723	20,759	22,743	24,035	24,960
Samoa	231	434	692	781	787	822	824	834	845
Solomon Islands	286	556	903	1,336	1,307	1,379	1,484	...	...
Tonga	191	261	371	432	403	421	461	480	508
Tuvalu	14	22	31	37	35	40	44	...	...
Vanuatu	273	395	701	815	760	804	880	...	...
Developed ADB Member Economies[b]	**5,325,283**	**5,574,516**	**7,040,314**	**6,492,279**	**5,787,447**	**6,345,297**	**6,423,969**	**6,546,905**	**6,643,350**
Australia	383,319	704,383	1,193,597	1,440,944	1,220,504	1,234,535	1,351,689	1,382,145	1,353,658
Japan	4,887,520	4,755,410	5,700,098	4,850,414	4,389,476	4,922,538	4,866,864	4,954,807	5,079,739
New Zealand	54,444	114,722	146,619	200,922	177,468	188,224	205,416	209,953	...
DEVELOPING ADB MEMBER ECONOMIES[b]	**3,592,217**	**5,892,399**	**12,284,328**	**18,435,571**	**19,026,968**	**19,486,948**	**21,370,480**	**23,462,428**	**24,143,301**
ALL ADB REGIONAL MEMBERS[b]	**8,917,500**	**11,466,915**	**19,324,642**	**24,927,850**	**24,814,415**	**25,832,245**	**27,794,449**	**30,009,333**	**30,786,652**

... = data not available, $ = United States dollars, ADB = Asian Development Bank.

a Gross domestic product figures in local currency units are obtained from economy sources and converted to United States dollars using the official exchange rates from the International Monetary Fund. The exchange rates used are expressed as the average rate for a period of time (average of period), calculated as annual averages based on the monthly averages (local currency units relative to the United States dollar). For Myanmar, the 2000–2012 figures for GDP in US dollars were converted from the domestic currency using the World Bank's alternative conversion factor to calculate the aggregate for Southeast Asia.

b For estimating aggregates, imputation was done for economies with missing data by substituting available data from the nearest years.

Source: Asian Development Bank estimates.

Click on the indictor name in the table header to access the time series in the Key Indicators Database.

National Accounts

Table 2.2.3:   Gross Domestic Product per Capita at Purchasing Power Parity[a]
(current international dollars)

ADB Regional Member	2000	2005	2010	2014	2015	2016	2017	2018	2019
Developing ADB Member Economies									
Central and West Asia[b]	**2,831**	**4,052**	**5,344**	**6,305**	**6,246**	**6,236**	**6,336**	**6,754**	**6,925**
Afghanistan	1,086 (2002)	1,263	2,097	2,699	2,731	2,537	2,609	2,549	2,661
Armenia	2,533	5,169	7,093	9,699	9,707	10,503	11,974	12,939	14,197
Azerbaijan	3,432	6,763	14,927	17,444	14,938	14,371	14,121	14,545	14,999
Georgia	3,104	5,169	7,564	11,576	12,089	12,858	13,590	14,593	15,638
Kazakhstan	7,734	13,935	19,225	24,726	23,224	23,819	24,863	26,147	27,421
Kyrgyz Republic	1,873	2,396	3,103	4,326	4,259	4,728	5,094	5,310	5,529
Pakistan	2,709	3,499	4,023	4,403	4,549	4,518	4,574	4,972	5,010
Tajikistan	1,052	1,707	2,331	3,347	3,151	3,121	3,269	3,451	3,561
Turkmenistan	2,488	5,829	9,811	13,479	13,712	13,866	14,205	15,196	...
Uzbekistan	2,494	3,412	5,124	6,159	6,343	6,453	6,519	6,915	7,289
East Asia	**3,891**	**6,291**	**10,684**	**14,054**	**14,579**	**15,195**	**16,004**	**17,291**	**18,471**
China, People's Republic of	2,909	5,039	9,232	12,517	12,947	13,533	14,306	15,573	16,757
Hong Kong, China	28,253	38,057	49,185	54,782	56,409	57,221	59,849	62,514	62,321
Korea, Republic of	18,551	25,187	31,740	35,324	37,907	39,567	41,001	42,136	43,029
Mongolia	3,725	5,482	7,637	10,836	10,762	10,591	11,362	12,083	12,529
Taipei,China	21,574	28,804	38,435	45,553	46,969	47,320	48,533	50,989	53,251
South Asia[b]	**2,070**	**2,898**	**4,206**	**5,166**	**5,386**	**5,750**	**6,099**	**6,555**	**6,925**
Bangladesh	1,161	1,527	2,422	3,319	3,496	3,781	4,084	4,457	4,848
Bhutan	2,677	4,144	6,594	8,363	9,135	10,024	11,425	11,930	...
India	2,173	3,064	4,409	5,347	5,575	5,953	6,303	6,772	7,143
Maldives	8,527	8,439	11,813	15,901	16,786	17,525	18,165	19,081	...
Nepal	1,256	1,483	1,953	2,530	2,545	2,485	2,982	3,213	3,427
Sri Lanka	3,483	4,930	8,039	11,261	11,560	12,224	12,584	13,168	13,620
Southeast Asia[b]	**4,775**	**6,422**	**8,585**	**10,374**	**10,512**	**10,887**	**11,415**	**12,149**	**12,797**
Brunei Darussalam	68,150	76,601	80,659	81,806	62,922	56,638	60,282	59,935	60,984
Cambodia	1,049	1,717	2,459	3,269	3,485	3,786	4,053	4,396	4,722
Indonesia	4,892	6,406	8,656	10,399	10,364	10,610	11,051	11,756	12,418
Lao People's Democratic Republic	1,815	2,611	3,741	6,094	6,405	7,113	7,550	8,096	...
Malaysia	12,751	16,230	20,236	23,933	24,074	24,780	25,885	27,444	28,953
Myanmar	933	1,819	3,272	4,270	4,346	4,041	4,224	4,525	4,809
Philippines	3,494	4,455	5,677	7,005	7,226	7,735	8,142	8,721	9,348
Singapore	43,833	58,717	75,295	84,424	86,975	89,386	94,940	100,051	101,376
Thailand	7,387	10,475	13,450	15,680	15,993	16,796	17,503	18,599	19,314
Timor-Leste	1,268	1,386	1,965	2,721	2,917	3,141	3,166	3,153	...
Viet Nam	2,046	3,012	4,257	5,777	6,132	6,600	7,179	7,778	8,373
The Pacific[b]	**2,092**	**2,363**	**3,514**	**4,352**	**4,654**	**4,734**	**4,871**	**4,963**	**...**
Cook Islands	...	...	...	...	...	...	...	...	...
Fiji	5,882	7,162	7,999	11,356	12,401	12,620	13,317	14,091	...
Kiribati	1,587	1,741	1,714	1,930	2,125	2,229	2,261	2,337	...
Marshall Islands	2,453	3,094	3,465	3,659	3,743	3,820	4,035	4,264	...
Micronesia, Federated States of	2,499	2,927	3,268	3,336	3,521	3,585	3,745	3,835	...
Nauru	...	4,599	6,361	13,687	14,539	13,002	12,291	13,139	13,152
Niue	...	...	...	...	...	...	...	...	...
Palau	9,994	12,482	13,181	16,485	17,881	17,897	17,850	18,967	...
Papua New Guinea	1,495	1,598	3,021	3,749	4,023	4,105	4,200	4,248	4,310
Samoa	3,086	4,488	5,465	5,756	6,126	6,345	6,410	6,532	6,690
Solomon Islands	935	2,009	2,308	2,424	2,440	2,465	2,579	...	...
Tonga	3,668	4,395	4,911	5,453	5,819	6,387	6,859	7,185	...
Tuvalu	2,407	2,480	2,726	3,349	3,706	4,242	4,507	...	...
Vanuatu	2,188	2,275	2,846	3,012	2,981	3,074	3,197	...	...
Developed ADB Member Economies[b]	**26,657**	**31,668**	**35,498**	**40,290**	**41,214**	**41,120**	**42,153**	**42,944**	**44,856**
Australia	26,490	32,927	39,302	46,880	46,276	47,350	48,905	51,036	53,318
Japan	26,839	31,663	34,987	39,179	40,396	39,971	40,859	41,336	43,218
New Zealand	21,519	25,677	31,262	37,320	37,613	40,120	41,741	43,232	...
DEVELOPING ADB MEMBER ECONOMIES[b]	**3,292**	**4,886**	**7,496**	**9,437**	**9,722**	**10,136**	**10,645**	**11,435**	**12,110**
ALL ADB REGIONAL MEMBERS[b]	**4,310**	**6,005**	**8,623**	**10,631**	**10,931**	**11,315**	**11,833**	**12,616**	**13,328**

... = data not available, ADB = Asian Development Bank.

a   Calculated as gross domestic product (GDP) at purchasing power parity (PPP), divided by the midyear population. GDP figures in local currency units are obtained from economy sources and converted into a common currency using the purchasing power parity (PPP) from the World Bank's World Development Indicators. Prior to 2011, the PPP figures are extrapolated from the revised 2011 International Comparison Program (ICP). For 2012–2016, PPP estimates are interpolated from the two ICP reference years 2011 and 2017. For 2017 onward, the PPP figures are extrapolated from the 2017 ICP PPPs or imputed based on a regression model. Moreover, for 2005, 2011, and 2017, PPP figures are based on results from the ICP benchmark rounds. For Taipei,China, the PPP figures for 2000–2010 and 2018–2019 are Asian Development Bank estimates using data from economy sources and the World Bank, while the PPP conversion factor used for 2011–2017 was from the World Bank's ICP 2017 database.

b   For estimating aggregates, imputation was done for economies with missing data by substituting available data from the nearest years.

Source: Asian Development Bank estimates.

Click on the indictor name in the table header to access the time series in the Key Indicators Database.

Table 2.2.4: Gross National Income per Capita, Atlas Method[a]
(current $)

ADB Regional Member	2000	2005	2010	2014	2015	2016	2017	2018	2019
Developing ADB Member Economies									
Central and West Asia[b]	561	920	1,609	2,321	2,262	2,081	2,025	2,061	2,055
Afghanistan	...	...	510	630	600	570	560	550	540
Armenia	660	1,540	3,470	4,140	4,010	3,760	3,950	4,230	4,680
Azerbaijan	610	1,270	5,370	7,690	6,570	4,760	4,090	4,060	4,480
Georgia	790	1,520	3,210	4,740	4,410	4,080	4,040	4,460	4,740
Kazakhstan	1,270	2,930	7,440	12,080	11,380	8,770	8,040	8,070	8,810
Kyrgyz Republic	280	450	850	1,250	1,180	1,110	1,110	1,220	1,240
Pakistan	490	770	1,030	1,320	1,360	1,420	1,500	1,590	1,530
Tajikistan	170	380	920	1,350	1,250	1,100	1,010	1,000	1,030
Turkmenistan	600	1,590	4,070	7,200	7,030	6,820	6,380	6,740	...
Uzbekistan	630	530	1,370	2,470	2,600	2,660	2,350	2,020	1,800
East Asia	1,646	2,736	5,357	8,650	9,078	9,413	9,917	10,876	11,685
China, People's Republic of	940	1,760	4,340	7,510	7,940	8,270	8,740	9,620	10,410
Hong Kong, China	26,930	28,890	33,620	40,240	41,180	42,970	46,390	50,060	50,840
Korea, Republic of	11,030	18,520	22,290	28,160	28,720	29,330	30,300	32,610	33,720
Mongolia	470	900	2,000	4,210	3,820	3,500	3,230	3,630	3,780
Taipei,China	14,738	17,582	19,899	23,533	23,316	23,440	24,473	26,217	27,357
South Asia[b]	444	690	1,182	1,530	1,580	1,664	1,808	1,992	2,121
Bangladesh	440	550	800	1,110	1,220	1,370	1,520	1,750	1,940
Bhutan	730	1,200	2,040	2,460	2,520	2,650	2,800	2,970	...
India	440	710	1,220	1,560	1,600	1,680	1,830	2,010	2,130
Maldives	2,070	3,460	5,960	7,320	7,650	8,070	8,570	9,140	9,650
Nepal	230	310	540	770	780	770	860	970	1,090
Sri Lanka	870	1,210	2,410	3,640	3,760	3,810	3,870	4,040	4,020
Southeast Asia[b]	1,074	1,641	2,999	4,112	4,003	3,993	4,091	4,422	4,676
Brunei Darussalam	14,680	23,090	33,300	43,090	38,850	33,170	29,800	29,390	32,230
Cambodia	300	460	750	1,020	1,060	1,140	1,230	1,380	1,480
Indonesia	580	1,220	2,530	3,620	3,430	3,400	3,530	3,850	4,050
Lao People's Democratic Republic	280	460	1,000	1,820	1,970	2,120	2,240	2,450	2,570
Malaysia	3,460	5,270	8,260	11,140	10,680	10,150	9,940	10,590	11,200
Myanmar	170 (2002)	270	850	1,230	1,260	1,280	1,290	1,370	1,390
Philippines	1,150	1,380	2,370	3,330	3,380	3,450	3,530	3,710	3,850
Singapore	23,680	28,820	44,930	56,380	53,160	53,020	54,320	57,900	59,590
Thailand	1,980	2,790	4,580	5,760	5,710	5,700	5,960	6,600	7,260
Timor-Leste	750 (2002)	930	2,850	2,690	2,200	1,750	1,790	1,810	1,890
Viet Nam	410	630	1,250	1,880	1,970	2,080	2,120	2,360	2,540
The Pacific[b]	908	1,133	2,012	3,198	3,156	2,995	2,904	2,947	3,120
Cook Islands	6,129	8,475	9,349	17,088	17,157	16,573	17,360	19,429	19,289
Fiji	2,240	3,590	3,650	5,020	5,200	5,360	5,480	5,860	5,860
Kiribati	1,330	1,700	2,050	3,220	3,470	2,920	3,020	3,080	3,350
Marshall Islands	2,960	3,460	3,600	4,070	4,310	4,280	4,460	4,860	...
Micronesia, Federated States of	2,210	2,560	2,900	3,150	3,490	3,410	3,450	3,400	...
Nauru	...	...	8,750 (2012)	12,950	11,390	10,220	10,160	12,040	14,230
Niue	...	8,728 (2006)	10,896 (2011)	...	...	...	14,546	...	...
Palau	9,180 (2002)	10,570	11,430	14,020	16,180	16,870	16,400	17,280	...
Papua New Guinea	570	650	1,740	2,990	2,910	2,700	2,570	2,570	2,780
Samoa	1,520 (2002)	2,320	3,230	3,820	3,960	4,110	4,060	4,020	4,180
Solomon Islands	1,010	890	900	1,840	1,870	1,830	1,870	2,020	2,050
Tonga	2,050	2,450	3,570	4,570	4,520	4,300	4,250	4,300	...
Tuvalu	2,710 (2001)	3,630	4,400	4,670	5,440	5,070	4,810	5,430	5,620
Vanuatu	1,430	1,780	2,690	3,120	2,910	2,850	2,880	3,110	3,170
Developed ADB Member Economies	33,726	38,778	43,504	47,086	42,204	40,429	40,547	43,084	43,860
Australia	21,120	30,310	46,630	65,150	60,500	54,140	51,600	53,250	54,910
Japan	36,230	40,560	43,440	43,950	38,840	37,860	38,490	41,150	41,690
New Zealand	14,080	25,440	29,690	41,630	40,560	39,390	38,170	41,100	42,670
DEVELOPING ADB MEMBER ECONOMIES[b]	1,039	1,662	3,091	4,660	4,804	4,932	5,173	5,638	6,008
ALL ADB REGIONAL MEMBERS[b]	2,453	3,201	4,692	6,285	6,226	6,272	6,499	7,031	7,405
WORLD	5,491	7,361	9,420	11,005	10,673	10,412	10,477	11,160	11,570

... = data not available, $ = United States dollars, ADB = Asian Development Bank.

a Refers to a conversion factor that averages the exchange rate for a given year and the 2 preceding years, adjusted for differences in rates of inflation between the member economy and the G5 economies.
b Aggregates are weighted averages estimated using midyear population. Imputation was done for economies with missing data by substituting available data from the nearest 2 years.

Sources: World Bank. World Development Indicators. https://data.worldbank.org (accessed 6 July 2020). For the Cook Islands; Niue; and Taipei,China: Asian Development Bank estimates using the Atlas method based on economy sources.

National Accounts

Table 2.2.5: Gross Domestic Product per Capita[a]
(current $)

ADB Regional Member	2000	2005	2010	2014	2015	2016	2017	2018	2019
Developing ADB Member Economies									
Central and West Asia[b]	**576**	**971**	**1,781**	**2,457**	**2,248**	**2,008**	**2,067**	**2,042**	**1,961**
Afghanistan	211 (2002)	300	657	803	760	652	660	598	582
Armenia	593	1,557	3,041	3,852	3,512	3,524	3,869	4,196	4,615
Azerbaijan	653	1,558	5,843	7,891	5,501	3,881	4,147	4,740	4,793
Georgia	750	1,643	3,233	4,739	4,014	4,062	4,357	4,723	4,769
Kazakhstan	1,229	3,771	9,070	12,807	10,511	7,715	9,248	9,813	9,723
Kyrgyz Republic	281	479	885	1,293	1,133	1,132	1,255	1,322	1,323
Pakistan	565	767	1,006	1,324	1,393	1,396	1,457	1,372	1,198
Tajikistan	139	341	750	1,119	979	809	853	862	881
Turkmenistan	1,092	3,612	4,439	7,955	6,443	6,390	6,587	6,967	7,830
Uzbekistan	558	550	1,642	2,492	2,615	2,568	1,827	1,529	1,725
East Asia	**1,703**	**2,723**	**5,558**	**8,814**	**9,170**	**9,271**	**10,083**	**11,206**	**11,423**
China, People's Republic of	956	1,748	4,540	7,659	8,047	8,124	8,856	9,958	10,245
Hong Kong, China	25,757	26,650	32,550	40,315	42,432	43,731	46,166	48,543	48,713
Korea, Republic of	12,257	19,403	23,087	29,250	28,732	29,289	31,617	33,340	31,762
Mongolia	474	1,009	2,663	4,076	3,917	3,609	3,686	4,096	4,198
Taipei,China	14,910	16,463	19,202	22,875	22,788	23,099	25,081	25,796	25,899
South Asia[b]	**458**	**710**	**1,346**	**1,574**	**1,640**	**1,735**	**1,958**	**2,051**	**2,121**
Bangladesh	352	416	771	1,104	1,224	1,373	1,510	1,638	1,808
Bhutan	713	1,255	2,225	2,559	2,647	2,809	3,370	3,332	...
India	467	745	1,408	1,611	1,671	1,763	1,998	2,089	2,151
Maldives	2,311	3,436	6,576	8,450	9,043	9,269	9,634	10,404	...
Nepal	254	326	620	730	744	741	891	961	1,034
Sri Lanka	863	1,242	2,747	3,821	3,845	3,886	4,077	4,081	3,853
Southeast Asia[b]	**1,199**	**1,710**	**3,390**	**4,100**	**3,940**	**4,078**	**4,340**	**4,593**	**4,812**
Brunei Darussalam	18,477	26,587	35,437	41,947	31,354	27,322	28,238	30,667	29,313
Cambodia	294	472	796	1,122	1,196	1,308	1,429	1,561	1,698
Indonesia	804	1,294	3,177	3,533	3,370	3,602	3,878	3,933	4,175
Lao People's Democratic Republic	322	483	1,117	2,075	2,222	2,416	2,554	2,676	...
Malaysia	3,993	5,511	8,920	11,009	9,663	9,523	9,960	11,073	11,194
Myanmar	...	...	...	1,275	1,192	1,136	1,139	1,205	1,276
Philippines	1,090	1,268	2,237	2,978	3,017	3,086	3,131	3,254	3,512
Singapore	23,853	29,961	47,237	57,565	55,645	56,826	60,912	66,187	65,235
Thailand	2,031	2,956	5,174	6,029	5,903	6,058	6,624	7,329	7,843
Timor-Leste	415	465	806	1,232	1,335	1,358	1,295	1,237	...
Viet Nam	402	700	1,332	2,042	2,095	2,201	2,373	2,571	2,715
The Pacific[b]	**957**	**1,279**	**2,276**	**3,179**	**2,927**	**2,809**	**2,977**	**3,044**	**...**
Cook Islands	5,091	8,491	10,160	17,362	16,422	17,773	17,725	19,477	18,741
Fiji	2,093	3,604	3,691	5,610	5,385	5,646	6,050	6,248	...
Kiribati	799	1,212	1,515	1,654	1,554	1,598	1,656	1,717	...
Marshall Islands	2,252	2,772	3,065	3,433	3,419	3,700	3,913	4,053	...
Micronesia, Federated States of	2,180	2,371	2,887	3,083	3,051	3,197	3,522	3,854	...
Nauru	...	3,291	5,275	10,778	8,329	9,280	9,951	10,515	9,944
Niue	4,107	8,197 (2006)	13,021 (2011)	...	...	...	15,197	...	16,772
Palau	7,728	9,315	10,045	14,041	15,786	16,598	16,064	16,263	16,062
Papua New Guinea	674	804	2,020	2,910	2,641	2,447	2,600	2,665	2,684
Samoa	1,319	2,413	3,713	4,053	4,051	4,193	4,172	4,184	4,205
Solomon Islands	682	1,182	1,625	2,184	2,089	2,156	2,271	...	...
Tonga	1,926	2,581	3,612	4,224	3,966	4,162	4,585	4,795	5,107
Tuvalu	1,450	2,108	2,816	3,429	3,275	3,705	4,125	...	...
Vanuatu	1,431	1,846	2,923	3,104	2,828	2,952	3,157	...	...
Developed ADB Member Economies	**35,566**	**36,654**	**45,582**	**41,817**	**37,208**	**40,710**	**41,139**	**41,873**	**42,457**
Australia	20,144	34,911	54,176	61,380	51,247	51,033	54,942	55,324	53,366
Japan	38,532	37,218	44,508	38,109	34,524	38,762	38,386	39,159	40,231
New Zealand	14,113	27,752	33,700	44,605	38,701	40,235	43,106	43,372	...
DEVELOPING ADB MEMBER ECONOMIES[b]	**1,093**	**1,689**	**3,337**	**4,779**	**4,883**	**4,946**	**5,365**	**5,842**	**5,961**
ALL ADB REGIONAL MEMBERS[b]	**2,595**	**3,149**	**5,038**	**6,212**	**6,123**	**6,307**	**6,715**	**7,193**	**7,318**
WORLD	**5,498**	**7,297**	**9,551**	**10,952**	**10,247**	**10,282**	**10,817**	**11,382**	**11,436**

... = data not available, $ = United States dollars, ADB = Asian Development Bank.

a   Calculated as gross domestic product (GDP) at current United States (US) dollar value, divided by the midyear population. GDP figures in local currency units are obtained from economy sources and are converted to US dollars using the official exchange rates from the International Monetary Fund. The exchange rates used are expressed as the average rate for a period of time (average of period), calculated as annual averages based on the monthly averages (local currency units relative to the US dollar). For Myanmar, the 2000–2012 figures for GDP in US dollars were converted from the domestic currency using the World Bank's alternative conversion factor to calculate the aggregate for Southeast Asia.

b   For estimating aggregates, imputation was done for economies with missing data by substituting available data from the nearest years.

Sources: Economy sources. For "World": World Bank. World Development Indicators. https://data.worldbank.org/ (accessed 12 August 2020).

Click on the indictor name in the table header to access the time series in the Key Indicators Database.

Table 2.2.6:   Agriculture, Industry, and Services Value-Added
(% of GDP)[a]

ADB Regional Member	Agriculture				Industry				Services			
	2000	2005	2010	2019	2000	2005	2010	2019	2000	2005	2010	2019
Developing ADB Member Economies												
Central and West Asia												
Afghanistan	43.7 (2002)	35.2	28.8	26.9	21.7 (2002)	26.0	21.3	12.8	34.6 (2002)	38.8	49.8	60.4
Armenia	25.1	20.6	18.8	13.2	38.3	44.7	36.3	26.8	36.5	34.6	45.0	59.9
Azerbaijan	17.1	9.8	5.9	6.3	45.3	63.3	64.1	53.3	37.5	26.9	30.0	40.4
Georgia	21.9	16.7	9.6	7.2	22.4	26.8	19.1	23.0	55.7	56.5	71.4	69.8
Kazakhstan	8.6	6.6	4.7	4.8	40.1	39.2	41.9	35.6	51.3	54.2	53.4	59.7
Kyrgyz Republic	36.6	31.3	18.8	13.4	31.3	22.0	28.2	30.7	32.1	46.7	53.1	55.9
Pakistan	27.4	24.4	24.3	23.4	18.8	21.1	20.6	19.5	53.8	54.5	55.1	57.1
Tajikistan	27.3	23.8	21.8	22.1	38.4	30.7	27.9	29.3	34.3	45.6	50.3	48.6
Turkmenistan	22.9	18.8	11.5	…	41.8	37.6	60.0	…	35.2	43.6	28.5	…
Uzbekistan	34.4	29.5	32.9	28.1	23.1	29.1	25.9	36.4	42.5	41.4	41.1	35.5
East Asia												
China, People's Republic of	14.9	12.0	9.6	7.4	45.7	47.2	46.7	39.2	39.4	40.9	43.7	53.4
Hong Kong, China	0.1	0.1	0.1	0.1 (2018)	12.6	8.7	7.0	6.8 (2018)	87.3	91.3	93.0	93.1 (2018)
Korea, Republic of	4.3	2.9	2.4	1.9	38.5	37.7	37.5	36.1	57.2	59.4	60.1	62.1
Mongolia	27.4	19.8	11.6	10.9	26.0	34.9	36.1	42.0	46.6	45.3	52.4	47.1
Taipei,China	2.0	1.6	1.6	1.8	30.9	31.8	33.4	35.8	67.1	66.6	65.0	62.4
South Asia												
Bangladesh	25.5	20.1	17.8	13.3	25.3	27.2	26.1	31.2	49.2	52.6	56.0	55.5
Bhutan	24.3	20.2	14.8	15.9 (2018)	36.4	36.9	43.8	38.3 (2018)	39.3	42.9	41.4	45.8 (2018)
India	23.6	19.2	18.4	17.8	29.9	32.2	33.1	27.5	46.8	48.5	48.5	54.8
Maldives	6.9 (2001)	8.7	6.1	6.5 (2018)	13.2 (2001)	13.2	10.2	15.0 (2018)	79.9 (2001)	78.1	83.8	78.6 (2018)
Nepal	39.6	35.2	35.4	27.5	21.5	17.1	15.1	15.1	38.9	47.7	49.5	57.4
Sri Lanka	17.6	11.8	9.5	8.0	29.9	30.2	29.7	29.4	52.5	58.0	60.9	62.6
Southeast Asia												
Brunei Darussalam	1.0	0.9	0.7	1.0	63.7	71.6	67.4	61.5	35.3	27.5	31.9	37.5
Cambodia	37.8	32.4	36.0	22.1	23.0	26.4	23.3	36.5	39.1	41.2	40.7	41.4
Indonesia	15.6	13.1	14.3	13.3	45.9	46.5	43.9	40.6	38.5	40.3	41.8	46.1
Lao People's Democratic Republic	48.5	36.7	30.6	17.7 (2018)	19.1	23.5	29.8	35.5 (2018)	32.4	39.8	39.6	46.8 (2018)
Malaysia	8.3	8.4	10.2	7.4	46.8	46.9	40.9	37.8	44.9	44.7	48.9	54.8
Myanmar	57.2	46.7	36.9	21.4	9.7	17.5	26.5	38.0	33.1	35.8	36.7	40.7
Philippines	13.9	13.5	13.7	8.8	35.0	33.8	32.3	30.2	51.1	52.7	53.9	61.0
Singapore	0.1	0.1	0.0	0.0	34.8	32.9	28.2	25.8	65.1	67.1	71.8	74.2
Thailand[b]	8.5	9.2	10.5	8.0	33.7	35.5	37.1	30.9	57.8	55.3	52.4	61.1
Timor-Leste	29.8	29.7	24.7	17.2 (2018)	16.8	5.4	8.7	16.2 (2018)	53.4	64.8	66.6	66.6 (2018)
Viet Nam	24.5	19.3	21.0	15.5	36.7	38.1	36.7	38.3	38.7	42.6	42.2	46.2
The Pacific												
Cook Islands	10.3	6.9	3.4	2.7	8.3	9.6	7.9	8.9	81.4	83.5	88.7	88.4
Fiji	16.5	14.1	11.0	13.4 (2018)	21.6	19.2	20.9	19.4 (2018)	61.9	66.8	68.1	67.2 (2018)
Kiribati	20.0	21.8	24.2	27.4 (2018)	12.2	9.3	11.9	12.0 (2018)	67.8	68.9	63.9	60.6 (2018)
Marshall Islands	8.9	7.8	11.2	15.9 (2018)	14.0	9.9	14.5	13.4 (2018)	80.2	85.2	76.8	74.3 (2018)
Micronesia, Federated States of	25.3	24.2	26.7	23.9 (2018)	8.6	5.7	7.8	5.2 (2018)	66.1	70.1	65.5	70.9 (2018)
Nauru	…	5.2	6.3	…	…	9.1	32.7	…	…	85.7	61.0	…
Niue	22.2	23.3	23.0	19.1 (2018)	3.9	4.5	4.0	3.7 (2018)	73.9	72.2	73.0	77.2 (2018)
Palau	4.3	4.2	4.2	3.4	16.1	15.2	11.0	10.4	79.7	80.6	84.8	86.2
Papua New Guinea	35.2	34.0	20.2	17.9	40.7	44.3	34.2	39.2	24.1	21.7	45.5	42.9
Samoa	16.7	12.3	9.1	10.1	26.8	30.6	18.1	15.7	56.6	57.2	72.8	74.2
Solomon Islands	…	36.7	34.8	33.2 (2017)	…	10.1	13.8	17.4 (2017)	…	53.2	51.4	49.3 (2017)
Tonga	22.4	20.7	18.7	23.4	20.7	19.4	20.5	18.0	56.9	59.9	60.9	58.6
Tuvalu	20.4	22.2	27.3	20.0 (2017)	7.4	8.3	5.7	17.8 (2017)	72.2	69.4	67.0	62.2 (2017)
Vanuatu	25.4	24.1	21.9	23.1 (2017)	12.2	8.5	13.0	11.0 (2017)	62.3	67.4	65.0	65.9 (2017)
Developed ADB Member Economies												
Australia	3.4	3.1	2.4	2.2	26.8	26.8	27.0	27.0	69.9	70.1	70.6	70.8
Japan	1.5	1.1	1.1	1.2 (2018)	32.7	30.1	28.5	29.2 (2018)	65.8	68.8	70.4	69.6 (2018)
New Zealand	8.3	4.9	7.1	6.4 (2017)	25.3	25.8	23.0	22.3 (2017)	66.4	69.3	69.9	71.3 (2017)

… = data not available, 0.0 = magnitude is less than half of the unit employed, ADB = Asian Development Bank, GDP = gross domestic product.

a   Calculated as a share of GDP at current prices.
b   For Thailand, value-added for construction is included under services.

Sources: Economy sources.

Click on the indictor name in the table header to access the time series in the Key Indicators Database.

National Accounts

Table 2.2.7:   Household and Government Consumption Expenditure
(% of GDP)[a]

ADB Regional Member	Household Consumption				Government Consumption			
	2000	2005	2010	2019	2000	2005	2010	2019
Developing ADB Member Economies								
Central and West Asia[a]	**71.7**	**66.0**	**59.8**	**63.9**	**10.4**	**10.1**	**11.1**	**11.5**
Afghanistan	111.2 (2002)	115.7	97.4	93.6	7.7 (2002)	10.0	14.0	24.1
Armenia[b]	97.1	75.5	82.0	84.5	11.8	10.6	13.1	12.5
Azerbaijan	63.0	41.6	38.9	56.4	15.2	10.4	10.9	10.8
Georgia	80.5	64.6	79.5	67.1	8.5	17.3	15.3	12.8
Kazakhstan[b]	61.9	49.9	45.4	52.4	12.1	11.2	10.8	9.3
Kyrgyz Republic[b]	65.7	84.5	84.6	82.0	20.0	17.5	18.1	16.8
Pakistan[b]	75.5	78.4	79.7	82.9	8.1	7.5	10.3	11.7
Tajikistan[b]	87.7	81.1	84.7	76.4 (2018)	11.6	14.6	11.3	11.2 (2018)
Turkmenistan[b]	37.1	46.6	5.0	...	14.5	13.2	9.3	...
Uzbekistan[b]	61.9	46.7	57.0	54.4	18.7	17.6	13.3	16.4
East Asia	**50.4**	**44.9**	**38.3**	**40.8**	**14.6**	**14.1**	**14.4**	**16.5**
China, People's Republic of	46.7	39.6	34.3	38.9	16.8	14.8	14.6	16.7
Hong Kong, China[b]	58.6	57.5	61.4	68.7	9.4	9.2	8.9	10.8
Korea, Republic of	53.3	51.0	49.1	46.8	10.9	12.9	14.2	17.3
Mongolia[b]	75.1	55.2	55.2	55.2	15.3	12.1	12.7	12.1
Taipei,China[b]	55.2	56.3	53.2	52.2	15.7	15.4	15.1	14.0
South Asia[a]	**65.2**	**58.9**	**56.5**	**61.3**	**11.4**	**10.1**	**10.6**	**11.4**
Bangladesh	77.5	74.4	74.1	68.7	4.6	5.5	5.1	6.3
Bhutan[b]	48.3	52.0	45.3	60.5 (2018)	21.9	21.8	20.5	17.1 (2018)
India[b]	63.7	57.4	54.7	60.3	11.9	10.4	11.0	12.0
Maldives	...	...	...	...	...	...	...	...
Nepal[b]	75.9	79.5	78.6	69.5	8.9	8.9	10.0	11.6
Sri Lanka	70.9	69.0	68.5	69.3	13.7	13.1	8.5	9.4
Southeast Asia[a]	**54.6**	**56.1**	**52.0**	**54.6**	**10.1**	**10.0**	**10.8**	**10.8**
Brunei Darussalam[b]	24.8	22.5	14.7	20.5	25.8	18.4	22.2	25.0
Cambodia[b]	88.8	84.3	81.3	69.4	5.2	4.1	6.3	4.8
Indonesia[b]	61.7	64.4	56.2	57.9	6.5	8.1	9.0	8.8
Lao People's Democratic Republic	...	...	...	...	...	...	...	...
Malaysia[b]	43.8	44.2	48.1	59.8	10.2	11.5	12.6	11.7
Myanmar[c]	87.7	86.9	67.3	70.4				
Philippines[b]	71.7	74.0	70.2	73.2	11.1	8.9	9.7	12.5
Singapore	41.9	39.8	36.3	36.0	10.5	9.9	9.7	10.3
Thailand	53.1	54.9	51.2	49.1	13.6	13.7	15.8	16.1
Timor-Leste	84.7	88.6	68.7	65.3 (2018)	133.3	52.6	103.2	55.7 (2018)
Viet Nam	66.5	65.5	66.6	68.2	6.4	5.5	6.0	6.5
The Pacific	**...**	**...**	**...**	**...**	**...**	**...**	**...**	**...**
Cook Islands	...	...	...	...	...	...	...	...
Fiji[d]	57.2	73.3	70.3	60.9 (2018)	17.3	15.9	15.0	19.9 (2018)
Kiribati	...	...	...	...	...	...	...	...
Marshall Islands	...	78.0	72.2	66.8 (2018)	...	58.9	53.8	52.8 (2018)
Micronesia, Federated States of	...	...	...	...	...	...	...	...
Nauru	...	...	...	...	...	...	...	...
Niue	...	...	...	...	...	...	...	...
Palau	...	63.7	67.8	64.5	...	31.3	37.4	33.4
Papua New Guinea[b]	44.6	48.0	...	...	16.6	16.1	...	...
Samoa	...	...	...	...	...	...	...	...
Solomon Islands	...	59.3	61.6	56.2 (2017)	...	34.9	31.4	29.3 (2017)
Tonga	87.3	95.0	89.1	89.4	18.1	15.9	18.7	20.3
Tuvalu	...	...	...	...	...	...	...	...
Vanuatu	62.4	65.8	60.6	60.5 (2017)	15.4	13.2	17.5	17.4 (2017)
Developed ADB Member Economies[a]	**53.7**	**54.9**	**56.5**	**54.2**	**16.9**	**18.0**	**19.2**	**19.8**
Australia	58.1	57.6	56.2	55.6	17.8	17.6	18.0	18.9
Japan[b]	54.4	55.6	57.8	55.2	16.9	18.1	19.5	20.0
New Zealand	57.9	58.1	57.9	57.2	17.1	17.9	19.7	19.0
DEVELOPING ADB MEMBER ECONOMIES[a]	**54.2**	**49.8**	**44.2**	**46.1**	**13.2**	**12.7**	**13.1**	**15.0**
ALL ADB REGIONAL MEMBERS[a]	**53.9**	**52.3**	**48.7**	**47.9**	**15.4**	**15.3**	**15.4**	**16.0**
WORLD	**58.5**	**57.5**	**57.3**	**57.6 (2018)**	**16.1**	**16.5**	**17.7**	**17.1 (2018)**

... = data not available, ADB = Asian Development Bank, GDP = gross domestic product.

a   Calculated as a share of GDP at current prices. For estimating aggregates, GDP figures in domestic currencies were converted to United States dollars using official exchange rates, and imputation was done for economies with missing data by substituting available data from the nearest years.
b   Data for household consumption includes nonprofit institutions serving households.
c   Data refers to total final consumption expenditure.
d   Prior to 2005, data for household consumption includes nonprofit institutions serving households.

Sources: Economy sources. For "World": World Bank. World Development Indicators. https://data.worldbank.org/ (accessed 6 August 2020).

Click on the indictor name in the table header to access the time series in the Key Indicators Database.

Table 2.2.8:   Gross Capital Formation and Changes in Inventories
(% of GDP)[a]

ADB Regional Member	Gross Capital Formation				Changes in Inventories			
	2000	2005	2010	2019	2000	2005	2010	2019
Developing ADB Member Economies								
Central and West Asia[a]	**18.6**	**23.7**	**22.3**	**23.9**	...	...	...	...
Afghanistan[b,c]	11.3 (2002)	21.8	17.5	12.3	...	...	5.3	...
Armenia	18.6	30.5	32.9	17.4	0.2	0.7	-0.6	1.7
Azerbaijan	20.7	41.5	18.1	20.1	-2.5	0.2	-0.1	-0.3
Georgia	26.6	33.5	20.5	26.8	1.1	5.4	1.6	3.1
Kazakhstan	18.1	31.0	25.4	27.0	0.8	3.0	1.0	3.8
Kyrgyz Republic[d]	18.3	16.2	28.1	31.9	1.7	0.2	-0.7	1.0
Pakistan	17.6	17.7	15.8	15.6	1.6	1.6	1.6	1.6
Tajikistan	9.4	11.6	23.8	37.3 (2018)	2.0	0.5	-0.6	1.9 (2018)
Turkmenistan	35.4	22.9	51.9	...	...	...	...	...
Uzbekistan	19.6	26.5	26.5	39.8	-4.4	4.5	2.4	-0.2
East Asia[a]	**32.0**	**35.9**	**42.7**	**40.8**	...	...	...	...
China, People's Republic of	33.6	40.3	46.6	43.3	1.0	0.9	2.6	0.7
Hong Kong, China	27.6	21.1	23.9	18.9	1.1	-0.3	2.1	-0.2
Korea, Republic of	32.9	32.5	32.6	31.2	1.1	2.0	2.3	1.4
Mongolia	29.0	37.5	42.1	35.8	3.8	9.6	7.6	4.4
Taipei,China	27.2	24.6	25.1	23.3	0.9	0.3	1.4	-0.1
South Asia[a]	**26.0**	**35.3**	**38.7**	**31.1**	...	...	...	...
Bangladesh[b,e]	23.0	24.5	26.2	31.6	...	...	...	...
Bhutan	48.7	52.3	63.2	47.5 (2018)	-1.8	0.5	0.5	0.3 (2018)
India[f]	26.2	36.4	39.8	32.2 (2018)	-1.1	3.5	4.4	1.7
Maldives	...	...	...	...	...	...	...	...
Nepal[g]	24.3	26.5	38.3	56.6	5.0	6.5	16.1	22.9
Sri Lanka	25.4	26.1	30.4	27.4	0.6	2.8	5.9	-0.1
Southeast Asia[a]	**24.2**	**24.7**	**28.2**	**27.8**	...	...	...	...
Brunei Darussalam	13.1	11.4	23.7	38.7	0.1	0.0	0.2	0.2
Cambodia	17.5	20.2	17.4	24.2	-0.8	1.3	1.2	0.9
Indonesia	22.2	25.1	32.9	33.8	2.4	1.4	1.9	1.4
Lao People's Democratic Republic	...	...	...	...	...	...	...	...
Malaysia[h]	26.9	22.4	23.4	20.9	1.6	0.1	1.0	-2.0
Myanmar	12.4	13.2	23.2	30.6	0.7	0.5	0.3	0.7
Philippines	15.7	18.6	20.4	26.2	-3.7	0.3	0.0	-1.0
Singapore	35.2	21.5	27.7	24.9	2.8	-1.7	2.1	1.7
Thailand	22.3	30.4	25.4	23.9	0.7	2.7	1.4	1.3
Timor-Leste	33.5	15.8	42.7	34.0 (2018)	-4.5	0.1	0.0	1.5 (2018)
Viet Nam	29.6	33.8	35.7	26.8	2.0	2.5	3.0	2.6
The Pacific	...	...	...	...	...	...	...	...
Cook Islands	...	...	...	...	...	...	...	...
Fiji	17.3	21.0	18.7	17.8 (2018)	1.9	1.4	2.9	0.0 (2018)
Kiribati	...	...	...	...	...	...	...	...
Marshall Islands	...	18.5	39.4	21.9 (2018)	...	-0.1	-2.1	1.5 (2018)
Micronesia, Federated States of	...	...	...	...	...	...	...	...
Nauru	...	...	...	...	...	...	...	...
Niue	...	...	...	...	...	...	...	...
Palau	...	42.9	24.5	30.4	...	0.4	0.7	–
Papua New Guinea	21.9	17.5	...	...	1.5	1.0	...	...
Samoa	...	...	...	...	...	...	...	...
Solomon Islands	...	...	...	...	...	...	-1.4 (2012)	1.3 (2017)
Tonga	20.5	22.5	29.6	25.4	0.5	0.3	0.5	1.0
Tuvalu	...	...	...	...	...	...	...	...
Vanuatu	22.9	24.1	34.7	27.9 (2017)	0.5	0.7	0.8	0.7 (2017)
Developed ADB Member Economies[a]	**27.2**	**25.1**	**22.2**	**24.3**	...	...	...	...
Australia	26.3	27.6	26.9	23.3	0.3	0.5	-0.2	-0.1
Japan	27.3	24.7	21.3	24.6	-0.1	0.1	-0.0	0.2
New Zealand	22.0	25.4	20.1	23.5	1.2	0.7	0.4	-0.1
DEVELOPING ADB MEMBER ECONOMIES[a]	**29.3**	**33.5**	**38.9**	**37.3**	...	...	...	...
ALL ADB REGIONAL MEMBERS[a]	**28.0**	**29.4**	**32.8**	**34.5**	...	...	...	...
WORLD	**24.4**	**24.9**	**24.2**	**24.4 (2018)**	...	...	...	...

... = data not available, -0.0 or 0.0 = magnitude is less than half of unit employed, – = magnitude equals zero, ADB = Asian Development Bank, GDP = gross domestic product.

a   Calculated as a share of GDP at current prices. For estimating aggregates, GDP figures in domestic currencies were converted to United States dollars using official exchange rates, and imputation was done for economies with missing data by substituting available data from the nearest years.
b   Refers to gross fixed capital formation.
c   Changes in inventories include statistical discrepancy.
d   Refers to gross fixed capital formation and acquisitions less disposals of valuables.
e   Includes data on changes in inventories.
f   Refers to gross capital formation, which refers to the sum of gross fixed capital formation, valuables, increases in stocks, and errors and omissions.
g   Changes in inventories were derived residually; hence, statistical discrepancies or errors are included in this entry.
h   Changes in inventories includes valuables and statistical discrepancy.

Sources: Economy sources. For "World": World Bank. World Development Indicators. https://data.worldbank.org/ (accessed 24 July 2020).

National Accounts

Table 2.2.9:   Exports and Imports of Goods and Services
(% of GDP)[a]

ADB Regional Member	Exports of goods and services				Imports of goods and services			
	2000	2005	2010	2019	2000	2005	2010	2019
Developing ADB Member Economies								
Central and West Asia[b]	**25.8**	**32.7**	**32.4**	**28.2**	**26.7**	**32.5**	**27.0**	**30.1**
Afghanistan	29.7 (2002)	26.0	9.8	12.7	59.8 (2002)	73.6	43.9	46.0
Armenia	23.4	28.8	20.8	38.5	50.5	43.2	45.3	52.9
Azerbaijan	40.2	62.9	54.3	49.2	38.4	52.9	20.7	36.9
Georgia	23.0	33.7	33.0	54.0	39.7	51.6	49.9	62.9
Kazakhstan	56.6	53.2	44.2	36.5	49.1	44.6	29.9	27.9
Kyrgyz Republic	41.8	38.3	51.6	37.4	47.6	56.8	81.7	65.7
Pakistan	12.1	14.3	13.5	10.1	13.2	17.8	19.4	20.3
Tajikistan	92.4	54.3	26.8	14.4 (2018)	100.2	72.8	59.0	41.5 (2018)
Turkmenistan	97.2	65.0	76.3	...	82.4	47.8	44.5	...
Uzbekistan	26.5	37.9	27.9	31.2	26.7	28.7	19.7	41.8
East Asia[b]	**36.7**	**44.2**	**38.2**	**...**	**34.4**	**39.4**	**34.4**	**...**
China, People's Republic of	20.9	33.8	27.2	19.1 (2018)	18.5	28.4	23.5	18.3 (2018)
Hong Kong, China[c]	126.0	177.5	205.3	177.5	121.6	165.2	199.4	175.8
Korea, Republic of	33.9	35.3	47.1	39.8	32.2	33.0	44.3	36.9
Mongolia	54.0	58.8	46.7	61.1	67.9	63.6	56.7	64.2
Taipei,China	52.7	65.2	79.6	64.1	50.9	61.5	73.0	53.6
South Asia[b]	**14.0**	**19.7**	**21.8**	**18.2**	**15.6**	**23.0**	**26.7**	**21.6**
Bangladesh	14.0	16.6	16.0	15.3	19.2	23.0	21.8	21.4
Bhutan	29.4	38.0	43.5	30.8 (2018)	48.3	64.1	72.4	55.9 (2018)
India	13.0	19.6	22.4	18.4	13.9	22.4	26.9	21.1
Maldives	...	...	...	...	...	...	...	...
Nepal	23.3	14.6	9.6	8.7	32.4	29.5	36.4	46.3
Sri Lanka	38.2	32.3	19.6	23.1	48.4	41.3	26.8	29.2
Southeast Asia[b]	**82.2**	**81.9**	**64.4**	**58.6**	**72.5**	**73.4**	**57.8**	**54.2**
Brunei Darussalam	67.4	70.2	67.4	57.9	35.8	27.3	28.0	50.6
Cambodia	49.8	64.1	54.1	61.1	61.8	72.7	59.5	62.5
Indonesia	41.0	34.1	24.3	18.4	30.5	29.9	22.4	18.9
Lao People's Democratic Republic	...	...	...	...	...	...	...	...
Malaysia	119.8	112.9	86.9	65.3	100.6	91.0	71.0	57.8
Myanmar	0.5	0.2	19.6	30.4	0.6	0.1	15.1	30.3
Philippines	43.3	41.2	32.9	28.3	41.8	42.6	33.2	40.3
Singapore	188.4	225.2	198.0	173.5	176.0	195.3	171.7	145.6
Thailand	64.8	68.4	66.5	59.7	56.5	69.5	60.8	50.6
Timor-Leste	10.6	7.1	8.6	2.7 (2018)	164.9	67.5	125.8	60.3 (2018)
Viet Nam	55.0	63.7	72.0	106.8	57.5	67.0	80.2	103.6
The Pacific	**...**	**...**	**...**	**...**	**...**	**...**	**...**	**...**
Cook Islands	...	...	...	...	...	...	...	...
Fiji	65.4	54.1	57.4	48.3 (2018)	70.5	63.7	63.8	56.0 (2018)
Kiribati	...	...	...	...	...	...	...	...
Marshall Islands	...	33.5	36.9	38.0 (2018)	...	90.4	103.9	81.6 (2018)
Micronesia, Federated States of	...	...	...	...	...	...	...	...
Nauru	...	...	...	...	...	...	...	...
Niue	...	...	...	...	...	...	...	...
Palau	...	46.9	49.7	41.9	...	78.5	77.0	78.8
Papua New Guinea	66.2	74.5	...	...	49.2	56.1	...	...
Samoa	...	...	...	...	...	...	...	...
Solomon Islands	...	27.2	35.0	38.3 (2017)	...	39.1	60.7	43.1 (2017)
Tonga	15.2	17.8	12.5	22.0	46.3	58.4	58.3	65.2
Tuvalu	...	...	...	...	...	...	...	...
Vanuatu	34.7	45.4	46.6	47.7 (2017)	43.7	54.8	52.7	57.9 (2017)
Developed ADB Member Economies[b]	**11.5**	**14.8**	**16.2**	**19.2**	**10.3**	**13.9**	**15.1**	**18.5**
Australia	19.4	18.3	19.8	24.1	21.6	21.0	20.8	21.6
Japan	10.6	14.0	15.0	17.5	9.2	12.5	13.6	17.3
New Zealand	35.7	28.3	30.3	27.6	32.8	29.7	28.0	27.3
DEVELOPING ADB MEMBER ECONOMIES[b]	**40.6**	**46.0**	**39.7**	**...**	**37.8**	**42.0**	**36.7**	**...**
ALL ADB REGIONAL MEMBERS[b]	**23.2**	**30.8**	**31.1**	**...**	**21.4**	**28.4**	**28.9**	**...**

.... = data not available, ADB = Asian Development Bank, GDP = gross domestic product.

a   Calculated as a share of GDP at current prices.
b   For estimating aggregates, imputation was done for economies with missing data by substituting available data from the nearest years.
c   The statistics for trade in goods and services are compiled based on the change of ownership principle in recording goods sent abroad for processing and merchanting under the standards stipulated in the System of National Accounts 2008.

Sources: Economy sources.

Click on the indictor name in the table header to access the time series in the Key Indicators Database.

Table 2.2.10: Gross Domestic Saving
(% of GDP)[a]

ADB Regional Member	2000	2005	2010	2014	2015	2016	2017	2018	2019
Developing ADB Member Economies									
Central and West Asia[b]	**17.6**	**23.6**	**28.6**	**26.9**	**23.6**	**21.4**	**22.1**	**23.4**	**...**
Afghanistan	-18.8 (2002)	-25.8	-11.4	7.9	5.0	-2.6	6.4	-8.5	-20.9
Armenia	-8.9	14.0	4.9	2.4	8.8	9.2	7.7	6.7	3.1
Azerbaijan	20.4	47.5	49.8	43.7	30.9	28.5	31.1	35.4	32.5
Georgia	9.9	15.7	3.5	8.5	9.3	14.9	16.3	17.5	17.9
Kazakhstan	26.0	38.9	43.8	40.8	34.6	33.8	36.9	39.6	...
Kyrgyz Republic	14.3	-2.1	-2.7	-13.5	-8.3	-0.2	0.8	0.3	...
Pakistan	16.5	14.2	10.0	8.2	9.3	8.7	6.8	6.2	5.4
Tajikistan	0.6	4.3	4.0	-12.7	17.2	8.5	8.2	12.4	...
Turkmenistan	48.4	40.2	85.6	81.6 (2013)	...	...	...	...	...
Uzbekistan	19.4	35.7	29.6	26.0	24.3	22.1	26.9	30.0	29.2
East Asia[b]	**34.3**	**40.8**	**46.4**	**45.2**	**44.4**	**43.1**	**43.0**	**42.8**	**...**
China, People's Republic of	35.9	45.8	50.2	47.9	46.5	44.9	44.8	44.6	...
Hong Kong, China	32.0	33.3	29.8	24.0	23.9	23.8	23.1	21.8	20.6
Korea, Republic of	34.6	34.8	35.4	34.8	36.4	36.8	37.0	35.9	34.2
Mongolia	9.6	32.7	32.1	30.4	27.4	30.5	33.7	34.0	32.4
Taipei,China	29.1	28.5	31.5	33.1	34.4	34.1	34.7	34.0	33.2
South Asia	**...**	**...**	**...**	**...**	**...**	**...**	**...**	**...**	**...**
Bangladesh	17.9	20.0	20.8	22.1	22.2	25.0	25.3	22.8	25.0
Bhutan	27.3	23.8	31.8	29.7	22.1	30.8	29.3	26.6	...
India	...	...	...	...	...	...	...	...	...
Maldives	...	...	...	...	...	...	...	...	...
Nepal	15.2	11.6	11.5	11.9	9.2	4.1	13.4	16.6	19.0
Sri Lanka	15.4	17.9	23.1	24.2	23.6	20.6	24.4	23.0	21.3
Southeast Asia[b]	**36.7**	**34.9**	**37.0**	**35.3**	**35.1**	**35.3**	**35.1**	**...**	**...**
Brunei Darussalam	49.4	59.1	63.1	63.1	55.2	52.6	53.0	56.3	54.5
Cambodia	8.1	14.0	14.5	18.9	19.6	20.4	23.2	26.0	27.2
Indonesia	31.8	27.5	34.8	33.4	32.8	32.7	33.6	...	...
Lao People's Democratic Republic	...	...	...	...	...	...	...	...	...
Malaysia	46.1	44.3	39.3	34.3	33.0	32.6	32.4	30.6	28.5
Myanmar	12.3	13.1	32.7	22.9	23.4	22.6	22.3	24.2	28.3
Philippines	...	...	...	...	...	...	...	...	...
Singapore	47.5	51.4	54.0	52.9	52.7	53.0	52.8	53.9	52.7
Thailand	31.7	30.3	32.0	31.8	34.9	36.6	32.6	30.8	30.9
Timor-Leste	-117.7	-44.6	-74.6	-30.5	-17.0	-14.0	-17.7	-23.5	...
Viet Nam	27.1	29.0	27.4	27.9	25.7	24.9	27.7	26.0	26.5
The Pacific	**...**	**...**	**...**	**...**	**...**	**...**	**...**	**...**	**...**
Cook Islands	...	...	...	...	...	...	...	...	...
Fiji	25.6	7.1	12.7	22.1	22.6	19.4	20.7	19.2	...
Kiribati	...	...	...	...	...	...	...	...	...
Marshall Islands	...	-37.1	-30.9	-28.2	-30.7	-28.0	-29.5	-29.9	...
Micronesia, Federated States of	...	...	...	...	...	...	...	...	...
Nauru	...	...	...	...	...	...	...	...	...
Niue	...	...	...	...	...	...	...	...	...
Palau[c]	...	3.1	-7.5	-2.8	4.9	4.6	0.9	-1.8	-0.9
Papua New Guinea	38.8	35.9	...	...	...	...	...	...	...
Samoa	...	...	...	...	...	...	...	...	...
Solomon Islands	...	...	...	...	...	...	...	...	...
Tonga	-10.2	-19.2	-15.1	-19.1	-22.3	-17.1	-16.4	-20.3	-15.8
Tuvalu	...	...	...	...	...	...	...	...	...
Vanuatu	21.2	13.9	27.0	24.0	...	...	...	...	...
Developed ADB Member Economies[b]	**28.6**	**26.5**	**23.4**	**22.6**	**23.9**	**24.1**	**24.8**	**24.7**	**...**
Australia	24.1	24.8	25.8	26.3	24.7	23.1	24.7	24.9	25.5
Japan	29.0	26.8	22.9	21.4	23.6	24.4	24.8	24.7	...
New Zealand	25.0	24.0	22.4	23.7	24.2	24.1	25.0	24.8	...

.... = data not available, ADB = Asian Development Bank, GDP = gross domestic product.

a Calculated as a share of GDP at current prices.

b For estimating aggregates, the figures for gross domestic saving and GDP were converted from domestic currencies to United States dollars using official exchange rates and imputation was done for economies with missing data by substituting available data from the nearest years.

c Estimated as the difference between GDP by industrial origin at producer's prices and final consumption expenditure.

Sources: Economy sources.

Click on the indictor name in the table header to access the time series in the Key Indicators Database.

Table 2.2.11:   Growth Rates of Real Gross Domestic Product
(%)

ADB Regional Member	2000	2005	2010	2014	2015	2016	2017	2018	2019
Developing ADB Member Economies									
Central and West Asia									
Afghanistan	...	9.9	3.2	3.1	-1.8	3.5	2.7	1.6	4.0
Armenia	5.9	13.9	2.2	3.6	3.2	0.2	7.5	5.2	7.6
Azerbaijan	11.1	26.4	5.0	2.8	1.1	-3.1	0.2	1.5	2.2
Georgia	1.8	9.6	6.2	4.4	3.0	2.9	4.8	4.8	5.1
Kazakhstan	9.8	9.7	7.3	4.2	1.2	1.1	4.1	4.1	4.5
Kyrgyz Republic	5.4	-0.2	-0.5	4.0	3.9	4.3	4.7	3.8	4.5
Pakistan	3.6 (2001)	6.5	1.6	4.7	4.7	5.5	5.6	5.8	1.0
Tajikistan	8.3	6.7	6.5	6.7	6.0	6.9	7.1	7.6	...
Turkmenistan	5.5	13.0	9.2	10.3	6.5	6.2	6.5	6.2	6.3
Uzbekistan	4.0	7.0	7.3	7.2	7.4	6.1	4.5	5.4	5.6
East Asia									
China, People's Republic of	8.5	11.4	10.6	7.3	6.9	6.7	6.8	6.6	...
Hong Kong, China	7.7	7.4	6.8	2.8	2.4	2.2	3.8	2.8	-1.2
Korea, Republic of	4.9 (2001)	4.3	6.8	3.2	2.8	2.9	3.2	2.7	2.0
Mongolia	1.1	7.3	17.3 (2011)	7.9	2.4	1.2	5.3	7.2	5.1
Taipei,China	6.3	5.4	10.3	4.7	1.5	2.2	3.3	2.7	2.7
South Asia									
Bangladesh	6.0	6.0	5.6	6.1	6.6	7.1	7.3	7.9	8.2
Bhutan	7.0	7.3	11.9	5.8	6.6	8.1	4.7	3.0	...
India	3.8	7.9	8.5	7.4	8.0	8.3	7.0	6.1	4.2
Maldives	3.8	-13.1	7.3	7.3	2.9	6.3	6.8	6.9	...
Nepal	6.0	3.5	4.8	6.0	3.3	0.6	8.2	6.7	7.0
Sri Lanka	6.0	6.2	8.0	5.0	5.0	4.5	3.6	3.3	2.3
Southeast Asia									
Brunei Darussalam	2.8	0.4	3.7 (2011)	-2.5	-0.4	-2.5	1.3	0.1	3.9
Cambodia	10.7	13.3	6.0	7.1	7.0	7.0	7.0	7.5	6.8
Indonesia	4.9	5.7	6.2	5.0	4.9	5.0	5.1	5.2	5.0
Lao People's Democratic Republic	6.3	6.8	8.1	7.6	7.3	7.0	6.9	6.3	...
Malaysia	8.9	5.3	7.4	6.0	5.1	4.4	5.7	4.7	4.3
Myanmar	13.7	13.6	9.6	8.0	7.0	5.9	5.8	6.4	6.8
Philippines	4.4	4.9	7.3	6.3	6.3	7.1	6.9	6.3	6.0
Singapore	8.8	7.4	14.5	3.9	3.0	3.2	4.3	3.4	0.7
Thailand	4.5	4.2	7.5	1.0	3.1	3.4	4.1	4.2	2.4
Timor-Leste	16.3 (2001)	3.0	9.5	4.5	3.1	3.6	-3.8	-0.7	...
Viet Nam	6.8	7.5	6.4	6.0	6.7	6.2	6.8	7.1	7.0
The Pacific									
Cook Islands	3.7 (2001)	-1.1	-4.9	5.4	5.7	4.9	9.5	5.7	4.8
Fiji	-1.7	-1.3	3.0	5.6	4.7	2.5	5.4	3.5	...
Kiribati	5.3	-0.0 (2006)	-0.9	-0.7	10.4	5.1	0.9	2.3	...
Marshall Islands	1.4	2.3	7.6	-0.9	1.6	1.3	4.1	3.6	...
Micronesia, Federated States of	4.8	2.0	2.3	-2.3	4.6	0.9	2.7	0.2	...
Nauru	...	-0.6	13.6	36.5	2.8	3.0	-5.5	5.7	1.0
Niue	...	8.9	0.6	4.1	4.0	3.5	2.4	6.5	...
Palau	5.7 (2001)	3.9	-0.5	5.4	8.6	-0.4	-2.4	5.1	0.3
Papua New Guinea	-2.5	3.9	10.1	13.5	9.5	4.1	3.5	-0.8	5.0
Samoa	8.6	4.7	2.4	2.6	6.7	3.7	-0.6	0.7	2.3
Solomon Islands	-14.2	7.4	9.7	1.0	1.4	5.9	5.3	...	...
Tonga	3.8	-0.4	0.8	2.0	1.2	6.6	3.3	0.3	0.7
Tuvalu	1.5 (2001)	-4.1	-3.3	1.2	9.2	5.9	5.9	...	...
Vanuatu	5.9	5.3	1.6	2.3	0.2	3.5	4.4	...	...
Developed ADB Member Economies									
Australia	3.9	3.2	2.1	2.5	2.2	2.8	2.4	2.9	2.0
Japan	2.8	1.7	4.2	0.4	1.2	0.5	2.2	0.3	0.7
New Zealand	2.9	3.3	1.6	3.6	3.6	3.7	3.2	3.1	1.5

... = data not available, -0.0 = magnitude is less than half of unit employed, ADB = Asian Development Bank.

Sources: Economy sources.

Table 2.2.12: Growth Rates of Real Gross Domestic Product per Capita
(%)

ADB Regional Member	2000	2005	2010	2014	2015	2016	2017	2018	2019
Developing ADB Member Economies									
Central and West Asia									
Afghanistan	...	7.8	1.2	1.0	-3.8	1.5	0.6	-4.7	1.8
Armenia	6.2	14.5	2.9	3.9	3.6	0.6	8.0	5.6	7.8
Azerbaijan	10.0	24.9	3.8	1.5	-0.1	-4.2	-0.8	0.6	1.3
Georgia	3.8	10.3	7.0	4.4	2.9	2.8	4.8	4.9	5.3
Kazakhstan	10.2	8.7	5.7	2.7	-0.3	-0.3	2.7	2.8	3.1
Kyrgyz Republic	4.0	-1.4	-1.8	2.0	1.8	2.2	2.7	1.8	2.3
Pakistan	1.5 (2001)	4.2	-0.5	2.6	2.7	3.4	3.1	3.8	-0.9
Tajikistan	5.8	5.5	3.9	4.3	3.5	4.5	4.8	5.3	...
Turkmenistan	4.3	11.8	7.5	8.3	4.6	4.4	4.7	4.5	4.7
Uzbekistan	2.6	5.7	4.3	5.4	5.5	4.3	2.8	3.6	3.6
East Asia									
China, People's Republic of	7.7	10.7	10.1	6.7	6.4	6.1	6.2	6.2	...
Hong Kong, China	6.8	6.9	6.0	2.1	1.5	1.6	3.0	2.0	-2.0
Korea, Republic of	4.1 (2001)	4.1	6.3	2.6	2.3	2.5	2.9	2.2	1.8
Mongolia	-0.2	6.0	15.2 (2011)	5.6	0.3	-0.8	3.4	5.2	3.2
Taipei,China	5.5	5.0	10.0	4.5	1.3	1.9	3.1	2.6	2.6
South Asia									
Bangladesh	4.5	4.5	4.2	4.6	5.1	5.6	5.9	6.4	6.7
Bhutan	5.6	5.9	9.9	4.1	5.0	6.5	3.3	2.0	...
India	2.0	6.3	7.0	6.1	6.7	7.0	5.9	5.0	3.1
Maldives	2.3	-15.9	4.9	5.2	-0.9	2.3	2.6	2.6	...
Nepal	2.9	1.2	3.4	4.5	1.9	-0.8	6.8	5.3	4.8
Sri Lanka	4.6	5.3	7.0	4.0	4.0	3.3	2.4	2.2	1.7
Southeast Asia									
Brunei Darussalam	0.3	-1.3	2.0 (2011)	-3.5	-1.6	-3.6	-1.6	-2.9	0.0
Cambodia	9.2	11.7	4.6	5.7	5.6	5.5	5.5	6.0	5.4
Indonesia	2.2 (2001)	3.7	4.8	3.6	3.5	3.7	3.8	3.9	3.8
Lao People's Democratic Republic	4.2	4.7	6.6	6.1	5.7	5.5	5.3	4.8	...
Malaysia	6.2	3.2	5.5	4.3	3.5	3.0	4.5	3.6	3.7
Myanmar	12.4	12.6	8.9	6.9	6.1	4.9	4.8	5.5	5.8
Philippines	2.0	3.0	4.9	4.6	4.6	5.5	5.2	4.7	4.6
Singapore	7.0	4.8	12.5	2.6	1.8	1.9	4.2	2.9	-0.5
Thailand	3.3	3.6	6.9	0.4	2.5	3.0	3.1	3.9	2.1
Timor-Leste	14.2 (2001)	0.6	7.5	2.6	1.2	1.6	-5.7	-2.6	...
Viet Nam	5.4	6.3	5.1	4.8	5.5	5.0	5.6	5.8	5.8
The Pacific									
Cook Islands	3.5 (2001)	-6.7	-9.3	6.5	5.7	...	...	10.8	-3.5
Fiji	-2.3	-2.0	2.3	5.2	4.2	2.1	4.8	2.9	...
Kiribati	3.5	-2.2 (2006)	-3.0	-2.0	8.9	3.8	-0.4	1.0	...
Marshall Islands	0.6	0.9	6.3	-1.3	1.2	0.9	3.7	3.2	...
Micronesia, Federated States of	4.6	2.3	2.8	-2.5	4.4	0.7	2.5	0.0	...
Nauru	...	1.6	11.4	34.2	1.1	1.3	-7.0	4.0	-0.6
Niue	...	...	...	...	...	...	1.3	...	...
Palau	4.1 (2001)	3.1	1.4	5.7	6.7	-1.6	-2.6	7.3	0.8
Papua New Guinea	-5.5	0.8	6.8	10.1	6.2	0.9	0.4	-3.8	1.8
Samoa	7.6	4.2	1.6	1.8	5.9	2.8	-1.5	-0.2	1.4
Solomon Islands	-16.2	4.9	4.7 (2011)	-1.3	-0.9	3.6	3.1	...	...
Tonga	3.3	-0.8	0.6	2.6	1.7	7.1	3.9	0.8	1.3
Tuvalu	1.1 (2001)	-7.0	-3.8	1.4	9.5	6.2	6.2	...	...
Vanuatu	3.5	2.9	-0.8	0.0	-2.1	2.0	2.1	...	...
Developed ADB Member Economies									
Australia	2.8	2.0	0.5	1.0	0.7	1.2	0.7	1.4	0.5
Japan	2.6	1.7	4.2	0.5	1.3	0.6	2.4	0.5	0.9
New Zealand	2.3	2.2	0.4	2.2	1.8	1.6	1.3	1.5	-0.1

... = data not available, 0.0 = magnitude is less than half of unit employed, ADB = Asian Development Bank.

Source: Asian Development Bank estimates using economy sources.

Table 2.2.13:   Growth Rates of Agriculture Real Value-Added
(%)

ADB Regional Member	2000	2005	2010	2014	2015	2016	2017	2018	2019
Developing ADB Member Economies									
Central and West Asia									
Afghanistan	...	12.2	-18.0	3.7	-16.9	12.4	9.3	-5.9	20.8
Armenia	-1.0	11.2	-16.0	6.1	13.2	-5.0	-5.1	-6.9	-2.6
Azerbaijan	12.1	6.7	-4.7	-2.6	6.6	2.6	4.2	4.6	7.3
Georgia	-12.0	11.7	-4.2	-0.9	-0.1	-2.8	-7.7	13.8	-1.1
Kazakhstan	-3.2	7.1	-12.9	1.3	3.5	5.4	3.2	3.8	0.9
Kyrgyz Republic	2.6	-4.2	-2.6	-0.5	6.2	2.9	2.2	2.6	2.6
Pakistan	-0.7 (2001)	7.0	0.2	2.5	2.1	0.2	2.2	4.0	0.6
Tajikistan	8.0 (2001)	2.8	6.8	9.2	3.4	5.2	7.6	7.0	...
Turkmenistan	-2.6	14.1	17.7	1.7	...	...	...	...	...
Uzbekistan	3.2	5.9	6.1	6.0	6.1	6.2	1.2	0.3	2.5
East Asia									
China, People's Republic of	2.3	5.2	4.3	4.2	4.0	3.5	4.1	3.6	...
Hong Kong, China[a]	0.3 (2001)	-0.2	3.9	-6.0	-6.8	-2.0	-5.2	-1.8	-0.4
Korea, Republic of	0.4 (2001)	0.6	-3.6	5.1	-0.2	-5.6	2.3	1.5	2.4
Mongolia	-16.3	11.3	-0.3 (2011)	13.7	10.7	6.2	1.8	4.5	8.4
Taipei,China	2.1	-4.2	2.1	2.0	-7.7	-9.7	8.3	4.5	-1.6
South Asia									
Bangladesh	7.4	2.2	6.2	4.4	3.3	2.8	3.0	4.2	3.9
Bhutan	5.5	1.0	0.8	2.1	4.7	4.2	2.9	4.4	...
India	-0.0	4.8	8.8	-0.2	0.6	6.8	5.9	2.4	4.0
Maldives	-0.8	11.4	-3.5	-0.3	-0.4	1.5	8.3	4.8	...
Nepal	4.9	3.5	2.0	4.5	1.1	0.2	5.2	2.8	5.1
Sri Lanka	2.3	1.8	7.0	4.6	4.7	-3.7	-0.4	6.5	0.6
Southeast Asia									
Brunei Darussalam	6.6	1.3	-2.6 (2011)	4.7	6.4	-3.6	-1.6	-1.6	-1.4
Cambodia	2.5	15.7	4.0	0.3	0.2	1.3	1.7	1.2	-0.7
Indonesia	1.9	2.7	3.0	4.2	3.8	3.4	3.9	3.9	3.6
Lao People's Democratic Republic	4.2	0.7	3.2	4.1	3.6	2.8	2.9	1.3	...
Malaysia	6.1	2.6	2.4	2.0	1.4	-3.7	5.7	0.1	1.8
Myanmar	11.0	12.1	4.7	2.8	3.4	-0.5	-1.5	0.1	1.6
Philippines	3.4	3.5	1.3	1.9	0.7	-1.0	4.2	1.1	1.2
Singapore[a]	-6.0	6.8	2.7	3.3	-0.5	1.7	-0.9	-0.1	5.1
Thailand	6.8	-0.1	-0.5	-0.3	-6.5	-1.2	4.7	5.5	0.1
Timor-Leste	-1.0 (2001)	2.2	4.4	-3.5	-4.7	-0.9	-3.3	4.4	...
Viet Nam	4.6	4.2	0.5	3.4	2.4	1.4	2.9	3.8	2.0
The Pacific									
Cook Islands	-18.0 (2001)	-3.5	0.4	-1.4	-2.2	-3.1	3.2	-2.5	-3.0
Fiji	-1.2	0.9	-2.6	1.9	14.9	-10.9	10.8	4.2	...
Kiribati	-7.2	10.4 (2006)	-3.9	5.9	1.3	10.7	9.0	0.3	...
Marshall Islands	3.0	-0.3	11.1	-6.0	6.1	-1.6	1.8	4.2	...
Micronesia, Federated States of	7.0	4.2	-3.1	5.6	9.5	-4.8	-0.9	0.1	...
Nauru	...	0.3	3.7	9.5	5.2	10.6	43.4	-8.7	24.9
Niue	...	8.6	-0.4	0.2	2.0	1.2	3.5	1.7	...
Palau	-0.6 (2001)	6.9	-5.2	-7.9	-5.2	7.7	10.8	-5.2	-5.6
Papua New Guinea	2.1	5.6	2.8	3.4	-2.6	2.7	2.4	2.9	2.5
Samoa	8.1	2.4	-9.0	0.7	1.9	7.1	7.1	-12.4	2.4
Solomon Islands	-17.1	-0.4	13.0	6.7	1.8	5.7	3.6	...	...
Tonga	4.0	-5.0	4.7	2.5	-1.7	-1.3	-2.5	0.4	3.6
Tuvalu	-2.2 (2001)	-1.1	12.8	-0.5	-1.8	2.9	0.8	...	...
Vanuatu	4.3	2.3	4.8	4.2	-15.8	5.1	0.4	...	...
Developed ADB Member Economies									
Australia	6.7	4.3	-0.7	1.1	1.4	-7.4	9.4	-2.6	-9.8
Japan	7.3	-0.0	-5.8	-3.1	-4.5	-7.3	0.9	1.5	...
New Zealand	3.6	5.2	-7.9	5.1	2.2	0.5	-6.1	8.9	1.6

... = data not available, -0.0 = magnitude is less than half of unit employed, ADB = Asian Development Bank.

a Refers to other goods industries comprising agriculture, forestry, and fishing; and mining and quarrying.

Sources: Economy sources.

Click on the indictor name in the table header to access the time series in the Key Indicators Database.

Table 2.2.14:   Growth Rates of Industry Real Value-Added
(%)

ADB Regional Member	2000	2005	2010	2014	2015	2016	2017	2018	2019
Developing ADB Member Economies									
Central and West Asia									
Afghanistan	...	13.0	6.3	2.4	4.5	-1.8	8.1	19.4	-4.4
Armenia	12.8	14.8	5.7	-2.3	2.8	-0.3	9.0	3.7	7.1
Azerbaijan	5.7	43.6	3.7	0.4	-1.9	-5.7	-3.1	-0.7	0.6
Georgia[a]	4.9	9.6	8.2	7.4	2.6	6.7	4.4	-0.5	3.0
Kazakhstan	15.3	10.7	9.5	1.5	-0.4	1.1	7.7	4.4	5.2
Kyrgyz Republic	8.8	-9.8	2.5	5.7	2.9	7.1	8.6	5.9	8.1
Pakistan	5.8 (2001)	6.5	3.4	4.5	5.2	5.7	4.6	4.6	-2.3
Tajikistan	15.6 (2001)	7.7	5.6	14.9	16.3	22.2	7.3	14.4	...
Turkmenistan	1.0	10.6	6.0	11.6	...	...	...	...	...
Uzbekistan	1.8	5.3	5.5	7.4	8.3	5.9	5.4	11.5	8.9
East Asia									
China, People's Republic of	9.5	12.1	12.7	7.3	6.2	6.2	5.8	5.8	...
Hong Kong, China[a,b]	-3.8 (2001)	-1.4	7.7	7.4	2.4	3.0	-0.7	2.5	-3.9
Korea, Republic of[a]	3.5 (2001)	4.4	9.6	2.9	2.4	3.1	4.2	2.2	1.3
Mongolia	1.5	4.2	8.8 (2011)	12.7	9.9	-0.4	0.7	7.9	2.9
Taipei,China[a]	6.8	7.9	21.5	9.3	0.9	3.7	4.8	3.2	0.6
South Asia									
Bangladesh	6.2	8.3	7.0	8.2	9.7	11.1	10.2	12.1	12.7
Bhutan	7.3	3.8	12.5	3.7	8.2	6.9	2.5	-4.8	...
India	5.8	9.6	7.9	7.0	9.6	7.7	6.3	4.9	0.9
Maldives	-3.8	14.3	7.3	16.2	18.1	8.9	10.7	10.5	...
Nepal	8.6	3.0	4.0	7.1	1.4	-6.4	12.4	9.6	7.7
Sri Lanka	9.0	8.0	8.4	4.7	2.2	5.7	4.7	1.2	2.7
Southeast Asia									
Brunei Darussalam	3.0	-1.8	3.2 (2011)	-4.4	-0.0	-2.9	1.5	-0.4	4.2
Cambodia	31.2	12.7	13.6	10.1	11.7	10.9	9.8	11.6	10.7
Indonesia	5.9	4.7	4.9	4.2	3.0	3.8	4.1	4.3	3.8
Lao People's Democratic Republic	9.3	10.6	17.5	7.3	7.0	12.0	11.6	7.8	...
Malaysia	13.6	3.6	8.4	5.9	5.2	4.3	4.7	3.2	2.4
Myanmar	21.3	19.9	18.6	12.1	8.3	8.9	8.7	8.3	8.4
Philippines	6.6	5.1	9.8	7.5	6.5	8.2	7.0	7.3	4.7
Singapore[a,b]	11.1	7.9	24.0	3.7	-2.7	2.6	6.8	4.8	-0.7
Thailand[a,c]	4.0	4.9	10.6	0.1	1.9	2.2	2.1	2.7	-0.0
Timor-Leste	-3.4 (2001)	-7.6	7.9	-10.9	22.2	7.6	-26.5	5.3	...
Viet Nam	10.1	8.4	-9.9	6.4	9.6	7.6	8.0	8.9	8.9
The Pacific									
Cook Islands	7.5 (2001)	-6.3	-8.9	-1.8	25.4	-13.5	19.1	7.0	10.5
Fiji	-5.5	-6.7	6.5	1.2	20.8	7.2	4.2	4.4	...
Kiribati	-6.4	15.0 (2006)	9.5	-2.6	23.6	-2.4	-15.1	8.0	...
Marshall Islands	-2.2	-17.4	20.1	-0.1	-12.9	-5.6	2.7	13.0	...
Micronesia, Federated States of	6.6	-2.4	18.0	-28.6	-6.2	6.4	2.9	-7.3	...
Nauru	...	16.1	39.4	-3.6	-17.1	77.3	-26.8	-37.9	-21.0
Niue	...	81.4	14.4	6.1	0.9	2.3	-4.7	90.4	...
Palau	29.2 (2001)	6.2	4.2	3.4	38.1	0.2	-6.1	2.3	6.0
Papua New Guinea	-0.8	4.1	12.0	39.1	35.3	8.1	4.7	-7.0	8.2
Samoa	14.4	4.7	7.7	1.6	8.7	-2.6	-9.7	-5.3	12.0
Solomon Islands	-29.7	-3.5	13.2	-13.1	-4.1	4.3	10.5	...	...
Tonga	-6.5	-5.0	4.1	8.0	-0.6	12.7	9.7	-14.4	4.6
Tuvalu	5.0 (2001)	-18.2	-41.6	-5.8	36.7	20.2	21.1	...	...
Vanuatu	46.4	5.3	12.6	3.2	35.3	4.3	7.1	...	...
Developed ADB Member Economies									
Australia[a]	...	...	...	...	...	...	...	...	...
Japan[a]	...	...	...	...	...	...	...	...	...
New Zealand[a]	...	...	...	...	...	...	...	...	...

... = data not available, -0.0 = magnitude is less than half of unit employed, ADB = Asian Development Bank.

a   National accounts are compiled using chain volume measures.
b   Industry refers to manufacturing, construction, and utilities comprising of electricity, gas, steam, and air-conditioning supply; water supply; sewerage, waste management, and remediation activities.
c   Industry refers to mining and quarrying; manufacturing; electricity, gas, steam, and air-conditioning supply; water supply; sewerage, waste management, and remediation activities.

Sources: Economy sources.

Click on the indictor name in the table header to access the time series in the Key Indicators Database.

Table 2.2.15: Growth Rates of Services Real Value-Added
(%)

ADB Regional Member	2000	2005	2010	2014	2015	2016	2017	2018	2019
Developing ADB Member Economies									
Central and West Asia									
Afghanistan	...	5.4	18.1	4.0	1.4	2.3	-1.8	2.1	-1.0
Armenia	3.1	14.7	4.7	6.7	1.0	3.4	10.4	9.2	10.4
Azerbaijan	9.6	9.6	8.8	7.6	4.4	-0.8	3.2	3.8	3.7
Georgia[a]	5.5	6.5	8.2	3.6	3.8	2.8	6.4	5.8	6.5
Kazakhstan	8.4	10.4	6.0	5.7	3.1	0.9	2.5	3.9	4.5
Kyrgyz Republic	5.8	8.4	-1.3	4.5	3.5	3.2	3.3	2.9	2.9
Pakistan	5.1 (2001)	8.1	3.2	4.5	4.4	5.7	6.5	6.3	3.8
Tajikistan	3.9 (2001)	7.7	7.1	1.7	1.9	-1.5	6.2	2.6	...
Turkmenistan	18.0	27.1	13.8	-13.2	...	...	...	...	...
Uzbekistan	5.4	7.6	10.6	8.3	8.3	6.3	6.4	5.5	5.1
East Asia									
China, People's Republic of	9.8	12.3	9.6	7.9	8.3	7.7	8.0	7.6	...
Hong Kong, China[a,b]	1.8 (2001)	7.8	6.9	2.5	1.7	2.3	3.5	3.1	-0.3
Korea, Republic of[a]	5.6 (2001)	4.1	4.6	2.7	2.7	3.1	2.7	3.4	2.7
Mongolia	10.5	9.7	17.8 (2011)	7.8	0.6	1.1	7.7	4.7	5.8
Taipei,China[a]	6.4	4.1	6.4	3.2	1.2	1.3	2.9	2.9	2.8
South Asia									
Bangladesh	5.5	6.4	5.5	5.6	5.8	6.3	6.7	6.4	6.8
Bhutan	8.7	13.7	15.2	8.9	5.6	10.3	7.1	10.0	...
India	5.2	9.1	7.8	9.8	9.4	8.5	6.9	7.7	5.5
Maldives	5.1	-17.7	7.3	7.0	2.4	6.7	6.0	6.5	...
Nepal	5.9	3.3	5.8	6.2	4.6	2.4	8.1	7.2	7.3
Sri Lanka	6.1	6.4	8.0	4.8	6.0	4.8	3.6	4.6	2.3
Southeast Asia									
Brunei Darussalam	2.5	4.1	4.9 (2011)	0.6	-1.1	-1.7	1.1	0.8	3.4
Cambodia	8.9	13.1	3.3	8.7	7.1	6.8	7.0	6.7	6.2
Indonesia	5.2	7.9	8.4	6.0	5.5	5.7	5.7	5.8	6.4
Lao People's Democratic Republic	6.9	10.8	7.6	8.1	8.0	4.7	4.4	6.9	...
Malaysia	6.0	7.3	7.4	6.8	5.3	5.7	6.4	6.9	6.1
Myanmar	13.4	13.1	9.5	9.1	8.7	8.1	8.1	8.7	8.3
Philippines	3.3	5.3	7.6	6.7	7.4	8.2	7.4	6.7	7.5
Singapore[a,c]	7.5	6.9	10.9	4.3	4.2	2.7	3.5	3.4	1.5
Thailand[a,d]	4.4	4.5	6.9	1.8	5.6	4.8	5.1	4.8	4.0
Timor-Leste	42.4 (2001)	4.4	10.5	7.8	4.6	5.7	3.2	-2.6	...
Viet Nam	5.3	8.6	-7.7	6.2	6.3	7.0	7.4	7.0	7.3
The Pacific									
Cook Islands	6.5 (2001)	-0.3	-5.8	3.3	2.4	12.3	6.6	5.1	6.4
Fiji	0.8	-17.0	2.9	7.4	15.5	0.2	3.8	1.2	...
Kiribati	1.7	0.9 (2006)	-0.1	-0.3	7.2	6.6	3.5	0.7	...
Marshall Islands	4.8	3.0	3.2	-0.1	3.7	2.2	5.0	2.6	...
Micronesia, Federated States of	3.3	0.7	2.4	-1.3	3.0	2.8	2.9	0.9	...
Nauru	...	-2.1	4.2	41.9	11.6	-7.0	3.1	13.4	-3.3
Niue	...	0.8	0.4	5.2	4.6	4.2	2.4	4.7	...
Palau	2.4 (2001)	2.8	-0.6	5.5	8.9	-0.7	-3.0	8.9	0.8
Papua New Guinea	-12.7	3.6	12.4	0.9	-2.3	2.3	1.4	3.9	2.8
Samoa	6.2	5.2	3.0	3.2	6.9	4.8	0.4	3.9	0.3
Solomon Islands	-5.7	15.1	5.1	2.2	2.8	6.7	4.9	...	...
Tonga	5.7	1.3	0.7	-1.0	1.4	5.5	1.8	3.3	0.8
Tuvalu	-0.5 (2001)	-4.9	2.3	2.4	7.1	2.0	3.2	...	...
Vanuatu	2.2	6.6	3.0	2.4	2.0	2.9	2.9	...	...
Developed ADB Member Economies									
Australia[a]	...	...	...	...	...	...	...	...	...
Japan[a]	...	...	...	...	...	...	...	...	...
New Zealand[a]	...	...	...	...	...	...	...	...	...

... = data not available, ADB = Asian Development Bank.

a National accounts are compiled using chain volume measures.
b Refers to import, export, wholesale, and retail trades; accommodation and food services; transportation, storage, postal, and courier services; information and communications; financing and insurance; real estate, professional, and business services; public administration, social services, and personal services; and ownership of premises.
c Refers to services-producing industries, including ownership of dwellings.
d Includes construction.

Sources: Economy sources.

Table 2.2.16: Growth Rates of Real Household Final Consumption
(%)

ADB Regional Member	2000	2005	2010	2014	2015	2016	2017	2018	2019
Developing ADB Member Economies									
Central and West Asia									
Afghanistan	...	...	...	...	...	...	...	...	...
Armenia[a]	8.3	8.8	3.9	1.0	-7.7	-1.0	12.7	7.4	10.3
Azerbaijan[a]	10.0	13.2	10.8	8.1	10.3	1.7	0.8	4.6	...
Georgia[a]	...	...	9.0 (2011)	5.7	3.8	-5.7	7.4	5.8	...
Kazakhstan[a]	1.2	10.7	11.5	1.1	1.8	1.2	1.5	6.1	5.8
Kyrgyz Republic[a]	-5.0	8.3	2.7	3.0	-0.9	-0.6	6.3	5.0	1.6
Pakistan[a]	3.5 (2001)	10.8	2.2	5.6	2.9	7.6	8.5	6.2	2.9
Tajikistan[a]	8.6 (2001)	20.6	10.5	1.8	-15.1	13.2	4.6	4.0	...
Turkmenistan[a]	-48.3	-15.2	-61.4	...	...	...	...	...	...
Uzbekistan[a]	...	...	51.7	10.7	11.9	9.4	3.9	5.9	6.7
East Asia									
China, People's Republic of	...	...	...	...	...	...	...	...	...
Hong Kong, China[a]	4.5	3.5	6.1	3.3	4.8	2.0	5.5	5.3	-1.1
Korea, Republic of	5.8 (2001)	4.7	4.6	2.0	2.2	2.3	2.8	2.7	1.9
Mongolia[a]	...	12.4 (2006)	15.8 (2011)	6.3	8.1	-2.6	5.4	12.4	10.9
Taipei,China	5.1	3.3	3.7	3.4	3.1	2.7	2.7	1.7	2.4
South Asia									
Bangladesh	4.1	3.9	4.6	4.0	5.8	3.0	7.4	11.0	3.9
Bhutan[a]	-5.3	22.4	5.7	-3.9	13.8	-4.9	5.1	14.9	...
India[a]	3.4	7.5	6.7	6.4	7.9	8.1	7.0	7.2	5.3
Maldives	...	...	...	...	...	...	...	...	...
Nepal[a]	3.5 (2002)	4.7	6.2	4.2	2.9	-0.7	2.6	3.3	5.5
Sri Lanka	4.0	1.7	9.9 (2011)	3.7	7.5	7.4	3.6	3.7	2.9
Southeast Asia									
Brunei Darussalam[a]	-7.0	-0.6	5.4 (2011)	-3.7	5.2	-1.3	4.7	2.2	5.9
Cambodia[a]	4.9	12.2	8.8	4.5	6.0	6.8	4.6	4.6	5.6
Indonesia[a]	1.6	4.0	4.7	5.3	4.8	5.0	4.9	5.1	5.0
Lao People's Democratic Republic	...	...	...	...	...	...	...	...	...
Malaysia[a]	13.0	9.1	6.9	7.0	6.0	5.9	6.9	8.0	7.6
Myanmar[b]	4.3	14.6	2.6	11.1	4.7	2.2	4.1	4.5	1.5
Philippines[a]	5.2	4.4	3.6	5.8	6.4	7.1	6.0	5.8	5.9
Singapore	13.6	4.1	4.4	3.6	5.2	3.2	3.0	4.2	3.7
Thailand[a]	7.0	4.2	5.5	0.5	2.6	2.9	3.1	4.6	4.5
Timor-Leste	12.9 (2001)	-1.2	5.2	6.2	2.0	3.4	7.0	2.2	...
Viet Nam	3.1	5.8	8.2	6.1	9.3	7.3	7.3	7.3	7.4
The Pacific									
Cook Islands	...	...	...	...	...	...	...	...	...
Fiji	...	...	...	...	...	...	...	...	...
Kiribati	...	...	...	...	...	...	...	...	...
Marshall Islands	...	0.0	-0.4	-4.5	-1.2	3.1	10.5	-0.8	...
Micronesia, Federated States of	...	...	...	...	...	...	...	...	...
Nauru	...	...	...	...	...	...	...	...	...
Niue	...	...	...	...	...	...	...	...	...
Palau	...	0.6 (2006)	-3.1	1.9	4.2	6.0	-0.5	5.2	-2.9
Papua New Guinea[a]	-28.5	9.8	...	...	...	...	...	...	...
Samoa	...	...	...	...	...	...	...	...	...
Solomon Islands	...	9.3	8.7	3.1	2.5	3.5	0.0	...	...
Tonga	3.4	1.4	2.3	1.6	8.2	6.5	1.0	4.2	0.5
Tuvalu	...	...	...	...	...	...	...	...	...
Vanuatu	...	2.4	2.6	3.9	1.3	8.9	-1.9	...	...
Developed ADB Member Economies									
Australia	4.3	4.5	3.3	2.4	2.3	2.7	2.3	2.9	2.0
Japan	1.8	1.2	2.3	-0.8	-0.4	-0.4	1.3	0.1	0.1
New Zealand	1.4	4.6	2.3	3.0	3.9	6.2	4.4	3.1	2.2

... = data not available, 0.0 = magnitude is less than half of unit employed, ADB = Asian Development Bank.

a   Includes expenditure of nonprofit institutions serving households.
b   Data refers to total final consumption expenditure.

Sources: Economy sources.

Table 2.2.17: Growth Rates of Real Government Consumption Expenditure
(%)

ADB Regional Member	2000	2005	2010	2014	2015	2016	2017	2018	2019
Developing ADB Member Economies									
Central and West Asia									
Afghanistan	...	...	...	...	...	...	...	...	...
Armenia	2.8	19.0	3.9	-1.2	4.7	-2.4	-2.1	-3.0	12.5
Azerbaijan	2.3	3.4	3.4	3.7	1.5	6.8	1.1	-3.9	...
Georgia	...	...	-3.3 (2011)	9.0	4.4	10.9	1.1	1.6	...
Kazakhstan	15.0	10.8	2.7	9.8	2.4	2.3	2.1	-14.1	15.5
Kyrgyz Republic	5.9	-2.7	-1.1	-0.5	0.9	1.5	1.3	1.3	0.5
Pakistan	-6.7 (2001)	3.4	-0.6	1.5	8.1	8.2	5.3	8.6	0.8
Tajikistan	10.8 (2001)	0.4	0.9	4.1	3.3	1.7	5.7	4.5	...
Turkmenistan	28.0	17.9	3.7	...	...	...	...	...	...
Uzbekistan	...	...	7.0	8.4	6.7	2.7	1.5	4.8	6.1
East Asia									
China, People's Republic of	...	...	...	...	...	...	...	...	...
Hong Kong, China	2.4	-2.6	3.4	3.1	3.4	3.4	2.8	4.2	5.1
Korea, Republic of	6.5 (2001)	5.3	5.6	4.3	3.8	4.4	3.9	5.6	6.5
Mongolia	...	5.5 (2006)	15.3 (2011)	12.2	-4.7	10.6	-1.8	0.5	13.6
Taipei,China	0.6	0.5	1.2	3.8	-0.1	3.7	-0.4	4.0	0.1
South Asia									
Bangladesh	0.9	7.7	6.8	7.9	8.8	8.4	7.8	15.4	9.0
Bhutan	–	2.8	7.5	2.4	10.8	4.2	4.4	3.1	...
India	1.4	8.8	5.2	7.6	7.5	6.1	11.8	10.1	11.8
Maldives	...	...	...	...	...	...	...	...	...
Nepal	7.8 (2002)	1.2	1.3	10.0	7.4	-0.4	10.5	13.5	7.8
Sri Lanka	5.3	12.0	-2.1 (2011)	6.0	10.2	2.3	-6.0	-5.1	9.6
Southeast Asia									
Brunei Darussalam	7.7	-1.0	5.3 (2011)	1.9	-3.6	-6.5	7.4	1.6	1.8
Cambodia	12.4	2.9	12.5	2.4	4.4	5.7	6.5	6.5	5.8
Indonesia	-0.9	6.6	0.3	1.2	5.3	-0.1	2.1	4.8	3.2
Lao People's Democratic Republic	...	...	...	...	...	...	...	...	...
Malaysia	1.6	6.5	3.4	4.4	4.5	1.1	5.5	3.3	2.0
Myanmar	...	...	...	...	...	...	...	...	...
Philippines	-1.0	3.0	4.2	3.6	7.9	9.4	6.5	13.4	9.6
Singapore	18.3	4.0	10.2	0.6	8.9	3.8	3.1	2.9	2.8
Thailand	2.8	8.0	8.9	2.8	2.5	2.2	0.1	2.6	1.4
Timor-Leste	33.8 (2001)	-28.1	2.1	11.8	3.6	-1.2	-5.8	-1.0	...
Viet Nam	5.0	8.2	12.3	7.0	7.0	7.5	7.4	6.3	5.8
The Pacific									
Cook Islands	...	...	...	...	...	...	...	...	...
Fiji	...	...	...	...	...	...	...	...	...
Kiribati	...	...	...	...	...	...	...	...	...
Marshall Islands	...	1.8	-0.7	-5.8	4.8	9.9	0.4	5.6	...
Micronesia, Federated States of	...	...	...	...	...	...	...	...	...
Nauru	...	...	...	...	...	...	...	...	...
Niue	...	...	...	...	...	...	...	...	...
Palau	...	5.9 (2006)	-1.5	1.4	1.3	4.1	-0.9	4.4	0.3
Papua New Guinea	3.7	1.1	...	...	...	...	...	...	...
Samoa	...	...	...	...	...	...	...	...	...
Solomon Islands	...	80.5	10.0	3.1	4.9	4.2	4.8	...	...
Tonga	1.9	-1.1	-8.3	-0.3	3.1	-1.4	2.4	1.1	9.7
Tuvalu	...	...	...	...	...	...	...	...	...
Vanuatu	...	-0.1	4.3	-3.7	16.9	-1.4	19.5	...	...
Developed ADB Member Economies									
Australia	3.1	3.2	1.7	1.5	2.4	4.3	5.0	3.7	4.5
Japan	3.9	0.8	1.9	0.5	1.5	1.4	0.2	0.9	1.9
New Zealand	1.3	7.2	-0.4	3.4	2.3	2.3	3.0	3.9	4.4

... = data not available, – = magnitude equals zero, ADB = Asian Development Bank.

Sources: Economy sources.

Click on the indictor name in the table header to access the time series in the Key Indicators Database.

Table 2.2.18: Growth Rates of Real Gross Capital Formation
(%)

ADB Regional Member	2000	2005	2010	2014	2015	2016	2017	2018	2019
Developing ADB Member Economies									
Central and West Asia									
Afghanistan	...	...	...	...	...	...	...	...	...
Armenia	5.2	26.9	0.5	-3.0	-1.2	-8.7	15.4	28.4	-13.8
Azerbaijan	2.6	5.8	2.0	-1.7	-8.2	-19.0	1.2	-4.3	...
Georgia	...	...	14.3 (2011)	31.0	7.5	13.3	-2.3	6.5	...
Kazakhstan	10.7	35.0	2.0	8.6	5.5	2.5	3.1	2.9	9.0
Kyrgyz Republic	22.1	13.7	-5.2	15.7	-2.3	8.1	6.9	16.0	-5.2
Pakistan	2.5 (2001)	13.2	-6.5	2.8	14.6	7.3	9.8	10.7	-11.5
Tajikistan	39.2 (2001)	2.6	7.5	17.6	25.2	-6.6	-12.0	25.5	...
Turkmenistan	-6.0	12.4	21.5	...	...	...	...	...	...
Uzbekistan	...	...	18.9	12.5	7.9	8.4	21.5	30.6	17.9
East Asia									
China, People's Republic of	...	...	...	...	...	...	...	...	...
Hong Kong, China	16.1	0.0	11.3	1.6	-8.1	4.0	5.4	1.9	-14.9
Korea, Republic of	1.7 (2001)	2.2	17.1	3.6	6.5	6.3	10.9	-1.8	-2.5
Mongolia	...	15.0 (2006)	62.8 (2011)	-30.1	-26.5	2.1	34.6	18.6	17.9
Taipei,China	6.6	1.2	35.6	6.2	2.6	1.7	-0.8	6.7	5.4
South Asia									
Bangladesh	7.3	10.7	8.6	9.9	7.1	8.9	10.1	10.5	8.4
Bhutan	26.5	-12.2	46.1	26.8	16.5	12.0	-2.2	-5.5	...
India	-5.5	19.3	20.1	6.1	7.0	9.8	15.3	0.2	...
Maldives	...	...	...	...	...	...	...	...	...
Nepal	-14.0 (2002)	9.5	34.4	22.8	9.4	10.7	37.8	19.9	9.7
Sri Lanka	8.7	9.4	20.2 (2011)	11.5	3.8	5.0	6.7	4.3	-9.5
Southeast Asia									
Brunei Darussalam	6.7 (2001)	0.5	37.0 (2011)	-31.2	6.6	-11.1	8.0	28.1	-4.4
Cambodia	12.7	30.7	-7.9	8.8	9.9	10.0	6.0	6.0	6.5
Indonesia	12.9	12.4	8.8	5.7	3.0	5.0	5.7	8.5	2.4
Lao People's Democratic Republic	...	...	...	...	...	...	...	...	...
Malaysia	29.2	-2.5	25.3	2.5	6.7	4.4	6.2	-3.2	-3.8
Myanmar	11.3	29.8	34.6	7.5	16.1	4.3	8.1	-1.5	1.6
Philippines	1.1	-4.3	30.5	8.3	13.4	20.8	10.9	11.3	2.5
Singapore	29.9	0.6	22.5	0.2	-9.8	10.5	9.6	-1.4	-2.5
Thailand	8.0	21.7	32.0	-12.3	2.1	-3.8	11.0	16.2	...
Timor-Leste	10.5 (2001)	-7.9	2.8	7.3	-5.0	15.7	-16.0	-2.2	...
Viet Nam	10.1	11.2	10.4	8.9	9.0	9.7	9.8	8.2	7.9
The Pacific									
Cook Islands	...	...	...	...	...	...	...	...	...
Fiji	...	...	...	...	...	...	...	...	...
Kiribati	...	...	...	...	...	...	...	...	...
Marshall Islands	...	10.0	18.8	-13.1	-12.2	20.8	30.6	3.3	...
Micronesia, Federated States of	...	...	...	...	...	...	...	...	...
Nauru	...	...	...	...	...	...	...	...	...
Niue	...	...	...	...	...	...	...	...	...
Palau	...	-11.0 (2006)	3.3	37.1	0.3	9.8	12.0	-10.0	8.5
Papua New Guinea	36.8	-9.8	...	...	...	...	...	...	...
Samoa	...	...	...	...	...	...	...	...	...
Solomon Islands	...	71.0	85.2	-6.7	19.9	4.9	13.4	...	...
Tonga	-9.4	1.7	4.7	6.5	11.1	9.6	18.9	-23.2	7.9
Tuvalu	...	...	...	...	...	...	...	...	...
Vanuatu	...	7.7	-5.2	9.0	33.2	-21.5	15.9	...	...
Developed ADB Member Economies									
Australia	...	...	...	...	...	...	...	...	...
Japan	2.9	2.3	2.9	3.4	2.9	-0.9	3.5	0.5	1.5
New Zealand	-3.9	4.1	7.4	8.3	2.3	3.3	8.0	2.2	-0.9

... = data not available, 0.0 = magnitude is less than half of unit employed, ADB = Asian Development Bank.

Sources: Economy sources.

Click on the indictor name in the table header to access the time series in the Key Inaicators Database.

National Accounts

Table 2.2.19:   Growth Rates of Real Exports of Goods and Services
(%)

ADB Regional Member	2000	2005	2010	2014	2015	2016	2017	2018	2019
Developing ADB Member Economies									
Central and West Asia									
Afghanistan	...	...	...	...	...	...	...	...	...
Armenia	19.0	15.9	26.5	6.4	4.9	19.1	18.7	2.9	13.2
Azerbaijan	15.4	52.8	9.1	-1.9	-0.2	-2.0	-2.2	0.5	...
Georgia	...	...	16.6 (2011)	0.2	4.2	8.7	11.7	10.1	...
Kazakhstan	27.9	0.4	3.1	-2.5	-4.1	-4.5	8.0	9.6	2.2
Kyrgyz Republic	10.5	-11.0	-11.7	-6.2	-5.6	-3.8	6.1	-2.7	19.8
Pakistan	12.2 (2001)	11.7	15.7	-1.5	-6.3	-1.6	-0.6	12.7	14.5
Tajikistan	-20.8 (2001)	2.9	23.0	–	–	15.1	6.8	-5.2	...
Turkmenistan	82.7	19.2	11.7	...	...	...	...	...	...
Uzbekistan	...	...	2.1	-7.5	2.3	11.1	1.3	9.3	23.9
East Asia									
China, People's Republic of	...	...	...	...	...	...	...	...	...
Hong Kong, China[a]	16.9	12.2	17.6	1.0	-1.4	0.7	5.8	3.7	-5.6
Korea, Republic of	-1.8 (2001)	7.9	13.0	2.1	0.2	2.4	2.5	3.5	1.7
Mongolia	...	6.1 (2006)	18.2 (2011)	53.2	0.1	13.8	14.8	24.0	9.9
Taipei,China	17.4	8.4	27.6	6.0	0.4	-0.9	4.5	0.7	1.2
South Asia									
Bangladesh	14.4	15.6	0.9	3.2	-2.8	2.2	-2.3	8.1	8.5
Bhutan	3.3	34.3	7.5	-5.3	-3.2	-5.3	6.5	4.6	...
India	18.2	26.1	19.5	1.8	-5.6	5.0	4.6	12.3	-3.6
Maldives	...	...	...	...	...	...	...	...	...
Nepal	-23.2 (2002)	-3.0	-10.4	18.8	6.8	-13.7	11.3	6.2	4.7
Sri Lanka	17.1	6.6	10.2 (2011)	4.3	4.7	-0.7	7.6	0.5	7.1
Southeast Asia									
Brunei Darussalam	11.9	-1.3	-3.0 (2011)	-0.1	-9.9	-1.9	-5.3	5.7	14.9
Cambodia	30.3	16.4	20.6	11.3	7.2	8.6	5.3	5.3	7.8
Indonesia	26.5	16.6	15.3	1.1	-2.1	-1.7	8.9	6.5	-0.9
Lao People's Democratic Republic	...	...	...	...	...	...	...	...	...
Malaysia	16.1	8.3	11.1	5.0	0.3	1.3	8.7	2.2	-1.1
Myanmar	79.3	3.6	10.9	18.7	15.1	-0.4	13.5	12.0	11.3
Philippines	13.7	12.5	20.3	12.1	10.0	9.2	17.4	11.8	2.4
Singapore	14.3	12.8	17.8	3.6	5.0	-0.0	6.2	8.1	-1.6
Thailand	15.8	7.8	14.2	0.3	1.3	2.7	5.2	3.3	-2.6
Timor-Leste	23.2 (2001)	-10.6	28.0	-22.5	-28.3	8.5	-39.1	8.4	...
Viet Nam	11.0 (2002)	7.8	14.6	11.6	12.6	13.9	16.7	14.3	6.7
The Pacific									
Cook Islands	...	...	...	...	...	...	...	...	...
Fiji	...	...	...	...	...	...	...	...	...
Kiribati	...	...	...	...	...	...	...	...	...
Marshall Islands	...	-11.6	44.3	10.9	-2.9	-11.3	-2.3	8.6	...
Micronesia, Federated States of	...	...	...	...	...	...	...	...	...
Nauru	...	...	...	...	...	...	...	...	...
Niue	...	...	...	...	...	...	...	...	...
Palau	...	0.3 (2006)	5.7	9.7	12.7	-3.9	-9.3	-5.4	-13.1
Papua New Guinea	7.1	6.8	...	...	...	...	...	...	...
Samoa	...	...	...	...	...	...	...	...	...
Solomon Islands	...	9.3	32.7	-11.3	-6.5	10.7	5.2	...	...
Tonga	-5.4	-5.4	-9.4	1.9	7.9	27.2	-5.8	1.3	-3.3
Tuvalu	...	...	...	...	...	...	...	...	...
Vanuatu	...	7.1	0.4	-0.7	4.9	19.5	-1.1	...	...
Developed ADB Member Economies									
Australia	9.9	3.5	4.7	6.0	6.8	6.8	5.5	4.1	3.9
Japan	12.7	7.2	24.9	9.3	2.9	1.7	6.8	3.4	-1.8
New Zealand	6.1	-0.4	2.8	4.7	6.2	1.6	3.6	2.8	-0.4

... = data not available, -0.0 = magnitude is less than half of unit employed, – = magnitude equals zero, ADB = Asian Development Bank.

a   The statistics for trade in goods and services are compiled based on the change of ownership principle in recording goods sent abroad for processing and merchanting under the standards stipulated in the System of National Accounts 2008.

Sources: Economy sources.

Table 2.2.20:   Growth Rates of Real Imports of Goods and Services
(%)

ADB Regional Member	2000	2005	2010	2014	2015	2016	2017	2018	2019
Developing ADB Member Economies									
Central and West Asia									
Afghanistan	...	...	...	...	...	...	...	...	...
Armenia	7.2	14.3	12.8	-1.0	-15.1	7.6	24.6	12.9	7.8
Azerbaijan	17.3	19.8	12.4	-2.1	8.4	-3.2	-0.8	-0.3	...
Georgia	...	...	15.6 (2011)	14.5	7.2	2.4	8.1	10.3	...
Kazakhstan	28.0	12.1	2.9	-4.0	-0.1	-2.0	1.0	6.6	11.6
Kyrgyz Republic	0.4	6.5	-6.9	1.6	-13.2	-1.1	7.4	7.4	2.9
Pakistan	2.2 (2001)	39.5	4.3	0.3	-1.6	16.0	21.2	17.6	4.3
Tajikistan	-14.5 (2001)	16.5	8.0	1.0	–	-7.5	-6.5	9.3	...
Turkmenistan	4.1	-9.3	7.3	...	...	...	...	...	...
Uzbekistan	...	...	-6.6	0.3	-11.2	-2.2	15.5	39.4	...
East Asia									
China, People's Republic of	...	...	...	...	...	...	...	...	...
Hong Kong, China[a]	17.1	9.3	18.2	1.0	-1.8	0.9	6.6	4.5	-6.8
Korea, Republic of	-3.5 (2001)	7.8	17.5	1.3	2.1	5.2	8.9	0.8	-0.4
Mongolia	...	6.7 (2006)	49.5 (2011)	6.8	-11.4	12.7	24.8	30.9	19.1
Taipei,China	14.7	3.6	30.1	5.6	1.3	-1.0	1.6	1.4	0.8
South Asia									
Bangladesh	10.2	19.1	0.7	1.2	3.2	-7.1	2.9	27.0	8.4
Bhutan	4.2	13.0	28.7	-0.0	17.2	-9.3	-1.0	8.2	...
India	4.6	32.3	15.8	0.9	-5.9	4.4	17.4	8.6	-6.8
Maldives	...	...	...	...	...	...	...	...	...
Nepal	-15.1 (2002)	6.9	28.3	21.0	9.6	2.8	27.2	16.5	7.8
Sri Lanka	14.8	2.7	23.6 (2011)	9.6	10.6	7.9	7.1	1.8	-5.8
Southeast Asia									
Brunei Darussalam	-6.2	10.2	33.7 (2011)	-22.9	-8.9	-10.8	1.3	28.1	13.8
Cambodia	23.7	17.3	16.8	10.1	6.5	8.6	4.1	4.1	6.0
Indonesia	25.9	17.8	17.3	2.1	-6.2	-2.4	8.1	11.9	-7.7
Lao People's Democratic Republic	...	...	...	...	...	...	...	...	...
Malaysia	24.4	8.9	15.6	4.0	0.8	1.4	10.2	1.3	-2.3
Myanmar	-8.0	2.2	51.9	22.3	21.6	-11.4	10.0	-2.2	-7.7
Philippines	11.8	3.7	20.7	9.9	15.0	18.8	15.1	14.6	1.8
Singapore	20.0	11.6	16.3	2.8	3.4	0.2	7.5	7.3	-1.7
Thailand	26.0	16.2	23.0	-5.3	0.0	-1.0	6.2	8.3	-4.4
Timor-Leste	27.4 (2001)	-33.2	-1.9	11.6	-7.6	8.2	-8.7	2.3	...
Viet Nam	15.8 (2002)	5.9	13.7	12.8	18.1	15.3	17.5	12.8	8.3
The Pacific									
Cook Islands	...	...	...	...	...	...	...	...	...
Fiji	...	...	...	...	...	...	...	...	...
Kiribati	...	...	...	...	...	...	...	...	...
Marshall Islands	...	2.5	9.5	-6.4	-0.9	0.5	10.9	3.1	...
Micronesia, Federated States of	...	...	...	...	...	...	...	...	...
Nauru	...	...	...	...	...	...	...	...	...
Niue	...	...	...	...	...	...	...	...	...
Palau	...	2.1 (2006)	0.9	11.6	2.5	8.3	-1.5	-3.6	0.6
Papua New Guinea	-4.7	4.7	...	...	...	...	...	...	...
Samoa	...	...	...	...	...	...	...	...	...
Solomon Islands	...	14.3	52.2	-2.1	0.8	4.1	-2.9	...	...
Tonga	-0.7	2.1	3.0	-8.4	22.6	16.9	3.5	-1.4	4.8
Tuvalu	...	...	...	...	...	...	...	...	...
Vanuatu	...	2.9	-2.2	0.2	26.2	2.3	3.3	...	...
Developed ADB Member Economies									
Australia	12.0	12.5	7.1	-2.3	1.0	-0.1	4.7	7.2	0.2
Japan	9.3	6.1	11.2	8.3	0.8	-1.6	3.4	3.4	-0.8
New Zealand	-1.1	4.9	11.5	7.4	2.3	5.2	7.2	3.9	0.7

... = data not available, -0.0 = magnitude is less than half of unit employed, – = magnitude equals zero, ADB = Asian Development Bank.

a   The statistics for trade in goods and services are compiled based on the change of ownership principle in recording goods sent abroad for processing and merchanting under the standards stipulated in the System of National Accounts 2008.

Sources: Economy sources.

Production

Table 2.2.21:   Growth Rates of Agriculture Production Index
(%)

ADB Regional Member	2000	2005	2010	2014	2015	2016	2017	2018	2019
Developing ADB Member Economies									
Central and West Asia									
Afghanistan	-15.9	10.7	-0.8	3.6	-3.7	5.3	...	...	...
Armenia	4.7	36.9	-18.3	0.3	6.1	-10.0	...	...	...
Azerbaijan	10.1	15.8	-0.7	-3.4	6.4	1.9	...	...	...
Georgia	-13.7	17.1	-6.2	-15.7	2.1	-5.2	...	...	...
Kazakhstan	-4.4	7.1	-10.4	1.0	3.4	5.4	3.0	3.5	0.9
Kyrgyz Republic	2.6	-4.2	-2.6	-0.5	6.2	3.1	2.4	2.7	2.6
Pakistan	1.3	-2.6	-1.9	7.4	-4.8	2.6	11.5	5.8	-13.4
Tajikistan	12.6	-6.8	1.1	-1.8	6.0	-2.7	...	...	...
Turkmenistan	7.4	3.4	2.8	-4.0	-5.2	3.2	...	...	...
Uzbekistan	3.1	5.0	4.5	-2.1	6.1	6.1	1.2	0.3	2.5
East Asia									
China, People's Republic of	5.1	3.8	2.4	1.4	2.9	2.2	...	...	...
Hong Kong, China	2.4	13.5	0.0	-5.9	0.0	0.0	6.3	5.9	0.0
Korea, Republic of	0.8	0.6	-5.9	2.5	-1.7	-1.4	...	...	...
Mongolia	-1.8	-7.1	-20.2	8.6	-1.9	5.6	...	...	...
Taipei,China	2.2	-5.8	2.1	1.0	-3.4	-3.7	5.7	2.6	-4.7
South Asia									
Bangladesh	6.1	13.0	5.9	4.3	0.7	2.3	...	...	...
Bhutan	-10.2	23.5	4.5	2.1	0.1	3.4	...	...	...
India	-1.1	5.7	8.6	2.7	-1.2	2.3	...	...	...
Maldives	5.9	-20.0	-3.9	3.9	2.4	0.2	...	...	...
Nepal	5.1	2.0	1.0	4.3	-0.2	1.4	...	...	...
Sri Lanka	2.3	8.7	10.5	-9.5	4.5	0.6	...	...	...
Southeast Asia									
Brunei Darussalam	13.0	-26.6	4.9	-0.2	2.1	-0.3	...	...	...
Cambodia	1.8	26.7	8.7	0.3	1.4	5.0	...	...	...
Indonesia	3.3	2.7	2.6	2.0	2.2	0.5	...	...	...
Lao People's Democratic Republic	14.3	4.0	6.9	17.1	11.0	4.0	...	...	...
Malaysia	3.5	4.6	0.5	-0.8	0.9	0.6	...	...	...
Myanmar[a]	10.3	7.2	1.9	1.3	2.3	-0.8	0.1	-3.9	-3.3
Philippines	2.7	2.2	-0.8	-3.3	-1.3	-2.2	...	...	...
Singapore	-59.2	-22.8	0.5	-0.3	-2.0	4.9	...	...	...
Thailand	8.8	-1.9	0.9	0.3	-3.5	-0.4	6.0	8.5	-0.7
Timor-Leste	6.0	6.0	-0.7	-0.4	0.2	-1.3	...	...	...
Viet Nam	3.2	3.7	2.7	2.2	2.4	-1.5	...	...	...
The Pacific									
Cook Islands	-3.3	3.3	-2.5	-0.5	-0.2	-1.8	...	...	...
Fiji	-0.1	1.6	-6.9	2.2	-3.3	-2.1	...	...	...
Kiribati	-5.5	1.1	-48.4	0.7	0.1	-0.2	...	...	...
Marshall Islands	-74.9	15.2	-5.0	0.0	-4.3	-5.6	...	...	...
Micronesia, Federated States of	-0.0	-3.5	-0.4	12.2	13.1	-20.8	...	...	...
Nauru	0.8	1.2	1.0	0.9	1.0	0.7	...	...	...
Niue	-4.3	-0.3	0.6	0.5	0.9	0.5	...	...	...
Palau	...	...	...	...	...	...	...	...	...
Papua New Guinea	3.2	1.8	-1.4	1.2	0.8	1.1	...	...	...
Samoa	3.1	2.1	0.0	1.1	4.1	-1.1	...	...	...
Solomon Islands	2.9	12.2	2.9	1.7	-0.8	-3.1	...	...	...
Tonga	-3.3	-0.2	-1.4	0.8	3.6	-1.5	...	...	...
Tuvalu	6.1	1.4	-1.3	-0.4	0.9	1.0	...	...	...
Vanuatu	-4.6	1.9	24.0	-8.8	0.2	1.0	...	...	...
Developed ADB Member Economies									
Australia	-1.4	-0.4	-2.0	-0.3	0.5	-3.5	...	...	...
Japan	-0.5	1.0	-2.4	-0.2	-1.1	-3.8	...	...	...
New Zealand	6.9	-2.1	1.2	5.8	1.9	-0.8	...	...	...

... = data not available, -0.0 or 0.0 = magnitude is less than half of unit employed, ADB = Asian Development Bank.

a   For 2010–2015, fiscal year is April–March. For 2016 onward, fiscal year is October–September.

Sources: Food and Agriculture Organization of the United Nations. FAOSTAT Database. http://www.fao.org/faostat/en/#home (accessed 7 July 2020). For Kazakhstan; the Kyrgyz Republic; Pakistan (2001-2019); Uzbekistan (2015–2019); Hong Kong, China; Taipei,China; Myanmar (2011–2019); and Thailand (2006–2019): Economy sources.

Click on the indictor name in the table header to access the time series in the Key Indicators Database.

Table 2.2.22:   Growth Rates of Manufacturing Production Index
(%)

ADB Regional Member	2000	2005	2010	2014	2015	2016	2017	2018	2019
Developing ADB Member Economies									
Central and West Asia									
Afghanistan	...	...	...	...	...	...	...	...	...
Armenia	...	...	...	...	...	...	...	...	...
Azerbaijan	...	...	...	...	...	...	...	...	...
Georgia	34.6 (2002)	40.6	18.5	3.2	-12.6	3.7	1.5	4.8	1.4
Kazakhstan	22.8	6.4	13.9	1.1	0.2	0.6	5.6	4.5	4.4
Kyrgyz Republic	3.4	-15.6	10.1	-3.0	-7.8	5.4	7.6	5.0	8.3
Pakistan	1.0 (2001)	18.2	0.5	5.4	3.4	3.1	5.8	5.2	-2.3
Tajikistan	12.0	10.5	-6.2 (2009)	...	...	...	...	...	...
Turkmenistan	13.4	...	...	...	...	...	...	...	...
Uzbekistan	0.8	6.4	8.9	8.0	5.9	6.7	4.2	7.9	9.4
East Asia									
China, People's Republic of	...	18.2 (2006)	16.6	9.4	7.0	6.8	7.2	6.5	6.0
Hong Kong, China	-0.5	2.5	3.5	-0.4	-1.6	-0.4	0.4	1.3	0.4
Korea, Republic of	10.4	3.3	7.9	2.9	-0.3	2.3	2.3	1.3	0.1
Mongolia	...	...	...	...	...	...	...	...	...
Taipei,China	7.8	3.2	29.7	6.8	-1.2	1.9	5.3	3.9	-0.4
South Asia									
Bangladesh	4.9	8.5	6.3	9.2	10.7	13.5	11.2	15.0	14.7
Bhutan	...	...	...	...	...	...	...	...	...
India	5.3	10.3	9.0	3.8	3.0	4.1	4.6	3.9	-1.3
Maldives	...	...	...	...	...	...	...	...	...
Nepal	-9.1	2.6	-2.7	7.0	0.3	-9.8	17.1	10.0	...
Sri Lanka	...	...	...	...	...	...	...	...	...
Southeast Asia									
Brunei Darussalam	...	...	...	...	...	...	...	...	...
Cambodia	48.8	...	...	...	...	...	...	...	...
Indonesia	3.6	1.3	4.4	4.8	4.8	4.0	4.7	4.0	4.1
Lao People's Democratic Republic	...	...	...	...	...	...	...	...	...
Malaysia	24.9	5.1	11.1	6.0	4.8	4.3	6.1	4.8	3.6
Myanmar[a]	...	...	10.1 (2011)	9.4	10.2	9.1	9.8	9.7	7.3
Philippines	-8.1	1.1	23.2	7.3	0.5	13.1	11.3	7.1	-8.5
Singapore	15.3	9.5	29.7	2.7	-5.1	3.7	10.4	7.0	-1.5
Thailand	6.9	5.0	14.2	-4.0	0.1	1.4	1.8	3.7	-3.6
Timor-Leste	...	...	...	...	...	...	...	...	...
Viet Nam	...	...	...	1.0	1.6	0.8	2.9	-2.0	-1.6
The Pacific									
Cook Islands	...	...	...	...	...	...	...	...	...
Fiji	-5.6	2.3 (2006)	7.6	-2.8	8.9	2.1	1.5	3.6	-2.8
Kiribati	...	...	...	...	...	...	...	...	...
Marshall Islands	...	...	...	...	...	...	...	...	...
Micronesia, Federated States of	...	...	...	...	...	...	...	...	...
Nauru	...	...	...	...	...	...	...	...	...
Niue	...	...	...	...	...	...	...	...	...
Palau	...	...	...	...	...	...	...	...	...
Papua New Guinea	...	...	...	...	...	...	...	...	...
Samoa[b]	2.8	–	15.2	3.2 (2013)	...	...	...	...	...
Solomon Islands	...	...	...	...	...	...	...	...	...
Tonga	...	...	...	...	...	...	...	...	...
Tuvalu	...	...	...	...	...	...	...	...	...
Vanuatu	...	...	...	...	...	...	...	...	...
Developed ADB Member Economies									
Australia	1.4	-0.9	0.4	-1.1	-1.7	-2.4	-0.6	2.0	-1.5
Japan	5.7	1.4	15.6	1.9	-1.1	–	3.1	1.1	-3.0
New Zealand	4.3	0.6	4.6	2.3	1.8	3.0	2.6	1.4	1.1

... = data not available, – = magnitude equals zero, ADB = Asian Development Bank.

a For 2010–2015, fiscal year is April–March. For 2016 onward, fiscal year is October-September.
b Refers to volume indices of industrial production.

Sources: Economy sources.

Click on the indictor name in the table header to access the time series in the Key Inaicators Database.

III.   Money, Finance, and Prices

Money, Finance, and Prices summarizes the latest statistics on consumer price inflation and nonperforming loans. Other monetary and financial statistics include producer price inflation, interest rates, bank lending, official exchange rates, and stock market capitalization and growth rates.

Consumer price inflation slowed in 60% of reporting economies from 2018 to 2019

From 2018 to 2019, consumer price inflation decelerated in 26 economies of Asia and the Pacific, while accelerating in 17 economies (Figure 2.3.1). Brunei Darussalam and Kiribati recorded deflation in 2019 (–0.4% and –1.8%, respectively) after recording subdued inflation in 2018 (1.0% and 0.6%, respectively). In Maldives, inflation returned in 2019 (0.2%), reversing the deflation posted in 2018 (–0.1%).

Subdued inflation allowed central banks in many developing member economies to cut official interest rates to support growth in 2019. In addition to further cutting rates amid the global recession caused by the COVID-19 pandemic, policymakers will continue to employ other instruments to extend credit to affected small businesses and households, and to lower their financial costs (ADB 2020).

Comparing 2019 to 2018, inflation rose the most in Nauru (3.4 percentage points) on higher alcohol and tobacco tariffs and due to disruptions to shipping, and in Pakistan (3.4 percentage points) on a sharp depreciation in the country's currency (ADB 2020). The next largest increases were observed in Tajikistan (2.6 percentage points), Georgia (2.2 percentage points), and Myanmar (2.1 percentage points).

The largest declines in inflation occurred in Niue (–8.2 percentage points), led by a slowdown in price increases for alcoholic beverages and transportation,

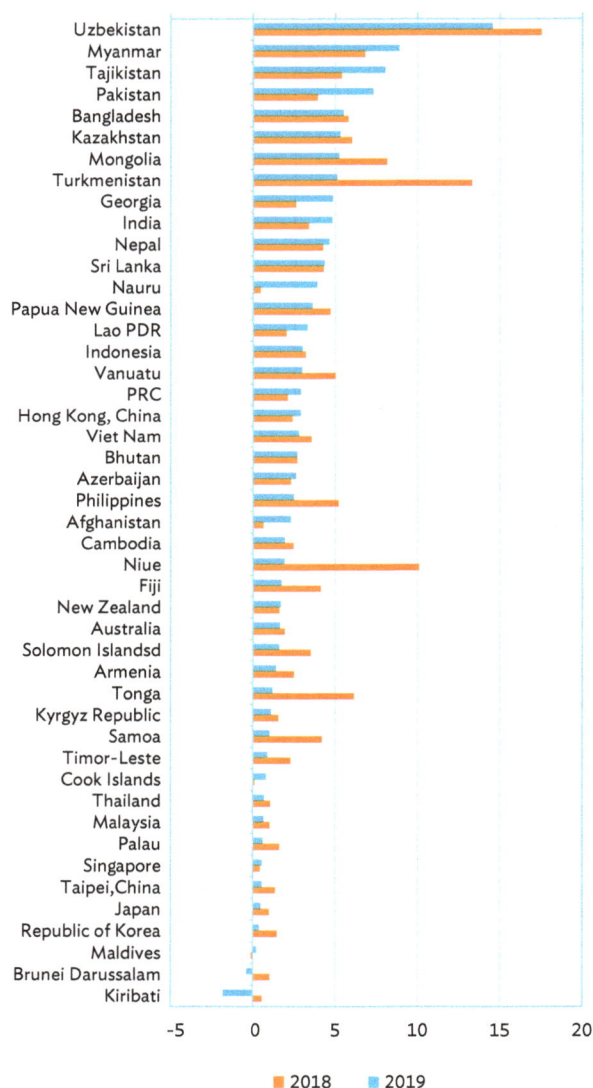

Figure 2.3.1: Inflation Rates in Select Economies of Asia and the Pacific
(% annual change)

■ 2018   ■ 2019

Lao PDR = Lao People's Democratic Republic, PRC = People's Republic of China.
Note: This chart includes economies with available data for both 2018 and 2019.
Source: Table 2.3.1, Key Indicators for Asia and the Pacific 2020.

Click here for figure data

and in Turkmenistan (–8.2 percentage points). The next largest decreases in inflation were observed in Tonga (–4.9 percentage points), Samoa (–3.2 percentage points), and Uzbekistan (–3.0 percentage points).

Banks in two-thirds of reporting economies have strengthened their balance sheets since 2010

The 2008–2009 global financial crisis led to a sharp increase in the value of nonperforming bank loans (NPLs) within economies of Asia and the Pacific. The crisis also saw a hike in the percentage of NPLs as a share of total gross loans. From 2010 to 2018, these indicators recovered in the majority of the region's economies. However, NPLs are expected to rise again in developing Asia as the global economy contracts as a result of the COVID-19 pandemic. A sharp increase in NPLs could compromise the eventual economic recovery for many developing ADB member economies (Park and Shin 2020).

From 2010 to 2018 (or from the earliest to latest years for which data were available), the percentage of NPLs as a share of total gross loans fell in 22 of the 31 economies with available data. These economies were led by Afghanistan (–41.0 percentage points), Kazakhstan (–13.5 percentage points), and Maldives (–11.5 percentage points) as illustrated in Figure 2.3.2.

Of the nine economies in which the percentage of NPLs as a share of total gross loans rose from 2010 to 2018, the largest increases were observed in Vanuatu (10.3 percentage points), India (6.8 percentage points), and Bangladesh (4.0 percentage points).

Data Issues and Comparability

Not all reporting economies meet the standards and classifications of the International Monetary Fund (IMF) on the compilation of monetary and financial

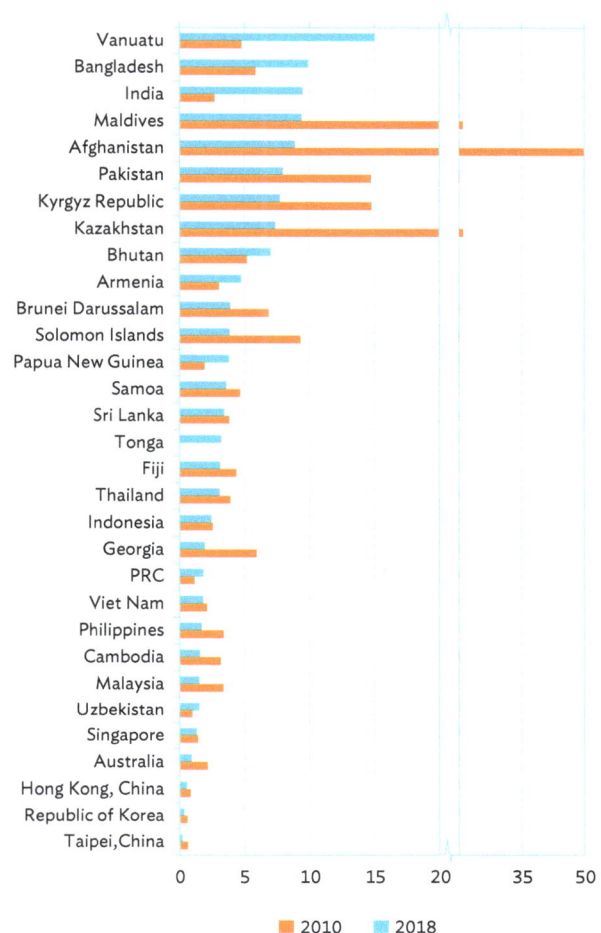

Figure 2.3.2: Nonperforming Bank Loans in Select Economies of Asia and the Pacific
(% of total gross loans)

■ 2010   ■ 2018

PRC = People's Republic of China
Note: This chart includes economies with available data for both 2010 and 2018. For 2010, data included are for 2010 to 2012. For 2018, data included are for 2016 to 2019.
Source: Table 2.3.9, Key Indicators for Asia and the Pacific 2020.

Click here for figure data

statistics available on the fund's Dissemination Standards Bulletin Board.[2]

Consumer price index coverage differs across economies. Most economies try to follow the Classification of Individual Consumption by Purpose guidelines, but the implementation varies across economies. In some instances, the basket of goods and services in the index is outdated or represents

[2]   For more information on the IMF's standards and classifications on the compilation of monetary and financial statistics, go to http://dsbb.imf.org/Pages/SDDS/StatMethod.aspx.

only urban areas (or the capital city). Other price measurements, such as the wholesale price index and the producer price index, are not available in Pacific economies.

Broad money supply in most economies relates to M2, which includes cash, checking deposits, savings deposits, money market securities, mutual funds, and other time deposits. However, 12 of the 44 economies with available data reported M3, thereby posing limits to comparability as M3 also includes less liquid financial assets. Not all economies publish the same types of aggregates, and even when aggregates have the same name (i.e., M1, M2, M3, etc.), their asset composition often differs significantly. For example, the definition of M2 in one economy may include time deposits with maturities of 1 year or less, whereas another economy's M2 definition may include time deposits with maturities of 2 years or less.

Finally, some economies use the central bank policy rate, while others use commercial bank rates in measuring banks' average deposit and lending rates.

Table 2.3.1: **Growth Rates of Consumer Price Index[a]**
(%)

ADB Regional Member	2000	2005	2010	2014	2015	2016	2017	2018	2019
Developing ADB Member Economies									
Central and West Asia									
Afghanistan	...	11.4	4.9	4.7	-0.7	4.4	5.0	0.6	2.3
Armenia	-0.8	0.6	8.2	3.0	3.7	-1.4	1.0	2.5	1.4
Azerbaijan	1.8	9.6	5.7	1.4	4.0	12.4	12.9	2.3	2.6
Georgia	4.0	8.2	7.1	3.1	4.0	2.1	6.0	2.6	4.9
Kazakhstan	13.2	7.6	7.1	6.7	6.6	14.6	7.4	6.0	5.3
Kyrgyz Republic	18.7	4.3	8.0	7.5	6.5	0.4	3.2	1.5	1.1
Pakistan	3.6	9.3	10.1	8.6	4.5	2.9	4.2	3.9	7.3
Tajikistan	60.6	7.1	9.8	7.4	5.1	6.1	6.7	5.4	8.0
Turkmenistan	8.0	10.7	4.4	6.0	7.4	3.6	8.0	13.3	5.1
Uzbekistan[b]	24.9	6.4	7.6	6.4	5.5	9.5	13.9	17.5	14.5
East Asia									
China, People's Republic of	0.4	1.8	3.3	2.0	1.4	2.0	1.6	2.1	2.9
Hong Kong, China	-3.7	0.8	2.3	4.4	3.0	2.4	1.5	2.4	2.9
Korea, Republic of	2.3	2.8	2.9	1.3	0.7	1.0	1.9	1.5	0.4
Mongolia	8.1	9.5	12.9	11.0	1.9	1.3	6.4	8.1	5.2
Taipei,China	1.3	2.3	1.0	1.2	-0.3	1.4	0.6	1.4	0.6
South Asia									
Bangladesh	2.8	6.5	6.8	7.3	6.4	5.9	5.4	5.8	5.5
Bhutan	4.0	5.3	7.0	8.3	4.6	3.2	5.0	2.7	2.7
India	3.7	4.2	10.4	5.8	4.9	4.6	3.7	3.4	4.8
Maldives	-1.2	1.3	6.1	2.1	1.0	0.5	2.8	-0.1	0.2
Nepal	3.4	4.6	9.6	9.1	7.2	9.9	4.5	4.2	4.6
Sri Lanka[c]	6.2	11.0	6.2	5.1	2.2	4.0	6.5	4.3	4.4
Southeast Asia									
Brunei Darussalam	1.2	1.1	0.4	-0.2	-0.5	-0.3	-1.3	1.0	-0.4
Cambodia[c]	-0.8	5.8	4.0	3.9	1.2	3.0	2.9	2.5	1.9
Indonesia[d]	3.8	10.5	5.1	6.4	6.4	3.5	3.8	3.2	3.0
Lao People's Democratic Republic	23.2	7.2	6.0	4.1	1.3	1.6	0.8	2.0	3.3
Malaysia	1.5	2.9	1.7	3.2	2.1	2.1	3.7	1.0	0.6
Myanmar	-0.2	9.4	7.7	5.0	9.5	6.9	4.6	6.8	8.9
Philippines	6.7	6.5	3.8	3.6	0.7	1.3	2.9	5.2	2.5
Singapore	1.3	0.5	2.8	1.0	-0.5	-0.5	0.6	0.4	0.6
Thailand	1.6	4.4	3.3	1.9	-0.9	0.2	0.7	1.1	0.7
Timor-Leste	...	1.6	5.2	0.8	0.6	-1.5	0.5	2.3	0.9
Viet Nam	-0.3 (2001)	8.3	9.2	4.8	0.6	1.9	3.5	3.5	2.8
The Pacific									
Cook Islands	3.2	2.5	-0.3	2.1	1.9	-0.3	-0.1	0.1	0.8
Fiji	1.1	2.5 (2006)	3.7	0.6	1.4	3.9	3.3	4.1	1.7
Kiribati[c]	0.4	-0.3	-3.0	2.1	0.6	1.9	0.4	0.6	-1.8
Marshall Islands[c]	0.9	3.5	1.8	1.1	-2.2	-1.5	0.1	0.8	...
Micronesia, Federated States of	1.8	4.1	3.6	0.7	0.0	-1.0	0.2	1.5	...
Nauru	2.3	9.8	-3.1	0.3	9.8	8.2	5.1	0.5	3.9
Niue	...	0.8	5.3	0.4	1.8	1.3	5.0	10.1	1.9
Palau	-1.8 (2001)	3.9	1.4	4.2	0.9	-1.0	0.7	1.6	0.6
Papua New Guinea	15.6	1.8	4.4 (2011)	5.2	6.0	6.7	5.4	4.7	3.6
Samoa	0.9	1.9	0.8	-0.4	0.7	1.3	1.8	4.2	1.0
Solomon Islands[c]	7.1	7.2	0.9	5.3	-0.6	0.5	0.5	3.5	1.6
Tonga	6.3	8.7	3.5	2.5	-1.1	2.6	7.5	6.1	1.2
Tuvalu	3.9	3.2	-1.9	1.1	3.2	3.5	4.1	2.2	...
Vanuatu	1.9	1.2	3.1	0.8	2.5	0.8	3.3	5.0	3.0
Developed ADB Member Economies									
Australia	2.4	2.4	2.3	2.7	1.7	1.4	1.7	1.9	1.6
Japan	-0.7	-0.3	-0.7	2.8	0.8	-0.1	0.5	1.0	0.5
New Zealand	2.6	3.0	2.3	1.2	0.3	0.6	1.9	1.6	1.7

... = data not available, 0.0 = magnitude is less than half of unit employed, ADB = Asian Development Bank.

a Data refer to the whole economy, unless otherwise indicated.
b Prior to 2016, values were calculated based on variable weights. From 2016 onward, values were calculated based on fixed weights.
c Data refer to capital city.
d Consumer price index data for Indonesia for 2000–2002 refer to the consumer price indexes for 43 cities; for 2003–2007, 45 cities; for 2008–2013, 66 cities; and for 2014–2019, 82 cities.

Sources: Economy sources.

Table 2.3.2:   Growth Rates of Food and Nonalcoholic Beverages Consumer Price Index[a]
(%)

ADB Regional Member	2000	2005	2010	2014	2015	2016	2017	2018	2019
Developing ADB Member Economies									
Central and West Asia									
Afghanistan	...	10.8	3.5	7.7	-0.8	5.7	6.9	-1.1	3.8
Armenia	-5.9	0.8	9.4	1.7	3.1	-3.3	4.1	2.3	1.9
Azerbaijan	...	12.4 (2006)	7.5	0.7	4.8	13.7	17.2	2.0	3.3
Georgia	...	8.9	11.7	5.1	4.2	1.6	6.8	2.2	8.1
Kazakhstan	16.4	8.8	5.9	5.8	5.7	12.9	8.5	4.7	8.1
Kyrgyz Republic[b]	18.5	7.0	6.5	8.2	3.7	-6.5	2.5	-2.2	1.3
Pakistan[c]	2.5 (2002)	12.5	12.6	8.6	2.6	1.0	3.3	2.8	4.2
Tajikistan	...	...	...	10.0	3.8	6.5	7.8	4.9	11.4
Turkmenistan	...	...	...	...	...	...	...	...	...
Uzbekistan	30.0	4.3	4.9	3.7	2.7	7.9	18.1	20.1	17.0
East Asia									
China, People's Republic of[d]	-2.6	2.9	7.2	3.1	2.3	4.6	-1.4	1.8	9.2
Hong Kong, China	...	2.4 (2006)	3.5	3.6	3.3	3.6	1.1	4.3	9.9
Korea, Republic of	0.8	3.1	6.4	0.3	1.6	2.3	3.4	2.8	0.0
Mongolia	8.8 (2001)	15.6	18.6	6.6	-4.8	1.7	7.3	9.1	8.3
Taipei,China	0.2	10.3	1.1	4.0	3.9	7.9	-1.8	0.6	2.2
South Asia									
Bangladesh[e]	...	...	7.7 (2012)	8.6	6.7	4.9	6.0	7.1	5.5
Bhutan	...	5.3	9.4	10.2	3.3	4.0	7.5	5.0	3.6
India	...	...	...	6.1	4.7	4.4	1.9	0.4	6.6
Maldives[f]	-4.8	7.8	7.5	0.7	0.5	0.6	5.6	-1.1	-0.8
Nepal[g]	0.5	4.0	15.5	11.6	9.6	10.9	1.9	2.7	3.1
Sri Lanka[h]	4.5	11.4	6.9	4.3	5.5	6.1	9.3	3.4	0.8
Southeast Asia									
Brunei Darussalam	...	...	-0.0 (2011)	-0.2	1.0	-0.5	0.3	1.9	-0.7
Cambodia[h]	...	...	4.3	4.9	4.0	5.6	3.4	2.5	2.1
Indonesia[i]	-4.8	10.0	9.4	...	7.2	7.2	2.1	4.2	3.7
Lao People's Democratic Republic	...	...	5.6 (2012)	6.9	4.5	4.3	-0.1	1.2	4.7
Malaysia	2.1	3.7	2.5	3.3	3.6	3.8	3.9	1.7	1.6
Myanmar	...	18.7 (2007)	7.4	6.9	13.1	9.2	4.4	6.6	9.0
Philippines	3.0	6.4	4.0	5.9	1.8	1.6	3.0	6.8	2.1
Singapore	0.5	2.0	2.3	3.0	1.2	2.3	1.3	1.3	1.1
Thailand	-1.1	4.8	5.4	3.9	1.1	1.6	–	0.4	2.3
Timor-Leste	...	–	6.4	0.7	0.3	-2.1	0.9	1.7	0.9
Viet Nam	-1.3 (2001)	11.2	10.7	4.0	1.5	2.6	-1.1	3.2	4.1
The Pacific									
Cook Islands[h,j]	3.4	1.1	2.9	3.3	-0.1	1.3	0.3	0.4	2.9
Fiji	-3.2	1.8 (2006)	4.1	1.9	4.7	6.0	-2.1	3.4	4.9
Kiribati[k]	...	6.1 (2007)	-4.6	0.6	-0.6	1.7	1.8	-1.1	-1.9
Marshall Islands[h,l]	-0.8	0.3	-1.5	2.0	2.3	-1.4	-0.5	1.3	...
Micronesia, Federated States of	1.1	3.4	2.2	0.8	0.8	-1.2	-1.6	-1.5	...
Nauru	...	...	-0.4	...	...	...	...	...	...
Niue[m]	...	1.1	8.2	–	2.7	-0.2	3.4	0.6	5.1
Palau	-2.4 (2001)	-1.5	1.8	1.5	1.7	-3.0	1.6	3.3	1.0
Papua New Guinea	13.6	3.5	-1.0 (2011)	4.8	4.9	5.1	2.8	0.8	3.0
Samoa	...	0.2	-6.6	-3.4	3.3	5.9	1.4	5.6	1.0
Solomon Islands[h,n]	...	...	-2.9	3.2	-3.0	0.5	-0.9	1.9	-0.4
Tonga	0.4	6.0	3.0	3.8	1.8	1.3	8.5	6.7	1.8
Tuvalu	1.1	5.5	-5.9	0.6	4.0	3.4	4.5	3.3	...
Vanuatu	1.1	-0.4	4.5	1.7	3.6	2.3	6.8	3.5	6.0
Developed ADB Member Economies									
Australia[o]	2.1	1.6	1.6	1.3	2.1	0.1	1.8	-0.0	2.0
Japan	-2.4	-1.3	-0.3	4.3	3.6	2.1	0.7	1.6	0.2
New Zealand	1.5	1.2	1.0	0.3	–	-0.6	2.1	-0.2	1.1

... = data not available, – = magnitude equals zero, -0.0 or 0.0 = magnitude is less than half of unit employed, ADB = Asian Development Bank.

a Data refer to the whole economy, unless otherwise indicated.
b For 2000–2002, refers to food and drinks, which includes alcoholic beverages.
c For 2002–2008, growth rates were calculated using price indexes for food, nonalcoholic beverages, alcoholic beverages, tobacco, and narcotics. For 2009 onward, growth rates were calculated using price indexes for food and nonalcoholic beverages only.
d For 2016 onward, excludes nonalcoholic beverages.
e Refers to food, nonalcoholic and alcoholic beverages, and tobacco.
f Refers to food (including fish) and nonalcoholic beverages. Prior to 2004, also includes tobacco and narcotics.
g Includes alcoholic beverages, tobacco, and narcotics; and restaurants and hotels.
h Refers to capital city.
i Consumer price index (CPI) data for Indonesia for 2000–2002 refer to CPI for 43 cities; for 2003–2007, 45 cities; for 2008–2013, 66 cities; and for 2014–2019, 82 cities. Refers to Indonesia's CPI group "Foodstuff" consisting of cereals, cassava, and their products; meat and their products; fresh fish; preserved fish; eggs, milk, and their products; vegetables; beans and nuts; fruits; spices; fats and oils; and other food items. The group does not include nonalcoholic and alcoholic beverages.
j Refers to fruits and vegetables; meat, poultry, and fish; cereal products; soft drink and sweets; farm products; fats and oils; other food; and prepared food.
k For 2006 onward, refers to the Tarawa Retail Price Index, which is based on data for South Tarawa to represent all of Kiribati. Data refer to the weighted averages of food and nonalcoholic drinks price indexes.
l Refers to food.
m For 2003–2011, data refer to food.
n For 2008–2017, excludes nonalcoholic beverages.
o Includes restaurants and hotels.

Sources: Economy sources.

Click on the indictor name in the table header to access the time series in the Key Indicators Database.

Table 2.3.3:   Growth Rates of Wholesale and/or Producer Price Indexes
  (%)

ADB Regional Member	2000	2005	2010	2014	2015	2016	2017	2018	2019
Developing ADB Member Economies									
Central and West Asia									
Afghanistan	...	...	...	...	...	...	...	...	...
Armenia	0.8	7.7	22.6	8.5	-0.8	1.5	3.9	1.6	0.5
Azerbaijan	3.3 (2001)	17.3	30.5	-5.1	-30.6	27.5	36.8	26.0	3.2
Georgia	5.8	7.5	11.3	2.9	7.5	-0.1	11.0	6.1	7.2
Kazakhstan	38.0	23.7	25.2	9.5	-20.5	16.8	15.3	19.0	5.1
Kyrgyz Republic	29.6	2.8	22.8	1.5	8.8	6.4	1.7	1.5	4.3
Pakistan	1.8	6.8	13.8	8.2	-0.3	-1.1	4.0	3.5	12.0
Tajikistan	39.2	10.4	27.2	4.7	3.0	14.7	1.6	1.8	1.1
Turkmenistan	...	...	...	...	...	...	...	...	...
Uzbekistan	60.9	25.6	15.6	13.6	13.5	14.8	17.5	31.8	43.2
East Asia									
China, People's Republic of	2.8	4.9	5.5	-1.9	-5.2	-1.4	6.3	3.5	-0.3
Hong Kong, China	0.2	0.8	6.0	-1.7	-2.7	1.3	3.8	2.0	1.0
Korea, Republic of	2.1	2.1	3.8	-0.5	-4.0	-1.8	3.5	1.9	0.0
Mongolia	...	...	...	...	...	11.3	17.5	-8.1	23.9
Taipei,China	1.8	0.6	5.5	-0.6	-8.9	-3.0	0.9	3.6	-2.3
South Asia									
Bangladesh[a]	-0.4	3.4	...	...	...	...	...	...	...
Bhutan	...	...	5.8 (2012)	3.0	0.6	1.2	5.8	4.7	-3.7
India	7.2	4.5	9.6	1.3	-3.7	1.7	2.9	4.3	1.8
Maldives	-2.4 (2002)	4.6	3.9	2.1	-2.4	...	...	...	...
Nepal	1.3 (2001)	7.4	12.2	8.3	6.1	6.3	2.7	1.7	6.2
Sri Lanka	1.7	11.5	2.6	3.2	1.0	4.2	7.4	3.4	...
Southeast Asia									
Brunei Darussalam	...	...	...	...	...	...	...	...	...
Cambodia									
Indonesia[b]	12.5	15.3	4.9	5.4	4.4	7.9	4.6	5.5	0.9
Lao People's Democratic Republic	...	...	...	...	...	...	...	...	...
Malaysia	-1.8 (2001)	3.8 (2006)	12.3 (2011)	1.5	-7.4	-1.1	6.7	-1.1	-1.4
Myanmar	...								
Philippines	5.8	11.3	5.9	3.5	1.6	0.9	1.9	1.9	1.6
Singapore	10.1	9.6	4.7	-3.3	-15.3	-6.9	7.0	6.4	-3.3
Thailand	3.9	9.1	9.4	0.1	-4.1	-1.2	0.7	0.4	-1.0
Timor-Leste	...	...	...	...	...	...	...	...	...
Viet Nam	-0.2	4.4	12.6	3.3	-0.6	-0.6	2.8	3.1	1.3
The Pacific									
Cook Islands	...	...	...	...	...	...	...	...	...
Fiji	...	...	...	...	...	...	...	...	...
Kiribati	...	...	...	...	...	...	...	...	...
Marshall Islands	...	...	...	...	...	...	...	...	...
Micronesia, Federated States of	...	...	...	...	...	...	...	...	...
Nauru	...	...	...	...	...	...	...	...	...
Niue	...	...	...	...	...	...	...	...	...
Palau	...	...	...	...	...	...	...	...	...
Papua New Guinea	...	...	...	...	...	...	...	...	...
Samoa	...	...	...	...	...	...	...	...	...
Solomon Islands	...	...	...	...	...	...	...	...	...
Tonga	...	...	...	...	...	...	...	...	...
Tuvalu	...	...	...	...	...	...	...	...	...
Vanuatu	...	...	...	...	...	...	...	...	...
Developed ADB Member Economies									
Australia	2.6	3.6	-0.1	2.1	1.0	1.5	1.0	1.6	2.0
Japan	0.0	1.6	-0.1	1.1	-3.0	-3.5	2.3	2.6	-0.2
New Zealand	5.2	3.4	2.3	1.1	-1.3	0.8	4.8	3.4	2.1

... = data not available, 0.0 = magnitude is less than half of unit employed, ADB = Asian Development Bank.

a   For agricultural and industrial products only.
b   For 2013, change of the wholesale price index was estimated by rebasing January–October 2013 and 2012 data to 2005.

Sources: Economy sources.

Click on the indictor name in the table header to access the time series in the Key Indicators Database.

Table 2.3.4:   Growth Rates of Gross Domestic Product Deflator
(%)

ADB Regional Member	2000	2005	2010	2014	2015	2016	2017	2018	2019
Developing ADB Member Economies									
Central and West Asia									
Afghanistan	...	11.6	14.3	-1.0	5.1	5.2	0.8	0.8	3.0
Armenia	-1.4	3.2	7.8	2.3	1.2	0.3	2.1	2.8	1.6
Azerbaijan	12.5	16.1	13.6	-1.3	-8.9	14.7	16.2	12.2	-0.2
Georgia	4.7	7.9	8.5	4.2	5.8	2.6	8.5	4.4	6.6
Kazakhstan	17.4	17.9	19.6	5.8	1.9	13.6	8.4	9.2	6.7
Kyrgyz Republic	27.2	7.1	10.0	8.4	3.4	6.1	6.3	3.4	-0.8
Pakistan	5.3 (2001)	7.8	10.9	7.4	4.1	0.4	4.0	2.5	8.6
Tajikistan	22.7	9.5	12.4	5.5	...	...	...	2.5	...
Turkmenistan	21.3	7.0	2.3	0.6	-4.9	-5.0	-1.6	1.2	7.4
Uzbekistan	47.1	21.4	18.9	14.3	10.4	8.7	19.4	27.5	19.2
East Asia									
China, People's Republic of	2.1	3.9	6.9	1.1	0.1	1.9	4.4	3.7	...
Hong Kong, China	-3.4	-0.2	0.3	2.9	3.6	1.6	2.9	3.7	2.4
Korea, Republic of	3.5 (2001)	1.0	2.7	0.9	3.2	2.0	2.2	0.5	-0.9
Mongolia	12.0	20.1	15.1 (2011)	7.4	1.7	2.2	10.6	8.3	8.3
Taipei,China	-0.9	-1.5	-1.3	1.7	3.4	0.8	-0.8	-0.7	0.3
South Asia									
Bangladesh	1.9	5.1	7.1	5.7	5.9	6.7	6.3	5.6	4.5
Bhutan	3.7	5.9	6.0	6.9	3.6	4.4	5.1	1.8	...
India	3.6	5.6	10.5	3.3	2.3	3.2	3.8	4.6	2.9
Maldives	36.7 (2001)	9.2	2.9	4.6	7.9	0.2	1.4	5.3	...
Nepal	4.6	5.8	14.4	9.0	5.1	5.0	9.1	5.9	4.1
Sri Lanka	6.7	10.4	7.3	2.9	0.6	4.8	7.3	4.3	2.2
Southeast Asia									
Brunei Darussalam	29.0	18.8	5.3	-1.8	-17.6	-9.2	5.0	9.2	-3.3
Cambodia	-4.9	6.1	3.1	2.6	1.7	3.4	3.3	3.1	3.4
Indonesia	9.6	14.3	8.2	5.4	4.0	2.4	4.2	3.8	1.6
Lao People's Democratic Republic	21.8	7.8	3.1	5.7	2.3	3.0	1.8	2.0	...
Malaysia	-1.6 (2001)	4.0 (2006)	5.4 (2011)	2.5	-0.4	1.7	3.8	0.7	0.1
Myanmar	2.5	19.2	7.0	4.2	4.1	...	5.4	5.4	6.3
Philippines	5.8	5.9	4.4	3.1	-0.7	1.3	2.3	3.7	0.8
Singapore	4.1	1.9	1.2	-0.3	3.1	0.7	2.8	3.1	0.1
Thailand	1.3	5.1	4.1	1.4	0.7	2.7	2.0	1.5	0.7
Timor-Leste	11.8 (2001)	1.8	10.8	-0.7	7.0	0.2	1.0	-1.9	...
Viet Nam	3.4	9.0	12.1	3.7	-0.2	1.1	4.1	3.4	1.8
The Pacific									
Cook Islands	2.2	-2.6	1.9	3.6	6.4	-2.1	-0.2	4.2	2.5
Fiji	-2.4	3.1 (2006)	2.5	...	2.4	2.5	1.6	0.9	...
Kiribati	3.2	-0.3 (2006)	1.2	4.7	3.5	0.2	1.0	5.3	...
Marshall Islands	-0.5	3.7	-0.7	-0.7	-1.6	7.2	2.0	0.3	...
Micronesia, Federated States of	1.1	2.1	3.6	3.0	-5.3	4.0	7.5	9.4	...
Nauru	...	-6.8	-18.1	-11.8	-8.3	...	11.8	4.2	2.3
Niue	...	0.5	7.6	1.6	-0.3	0.5	1.9	11.2	...
Palau	1.5 (2001)	7.6	0.5	3.2	5.3	6.9	-0.7	-5.6	-2.0
Papua New Guinea	13.1	7.9	9.9	5.4	-3.9	3.9	7.7	10.1	1.7
Samoa	1.1	5.1	-0.0	0.5	3.7	0.9	0.6	1.7	1.5
Solomon Islands	6.9	10.7	1.7	3.9	3.6	0.0	1.4	...	...
Tonga	2.6	8.0	7.8	0.0	5.3	3.1	5.6	5.1	7.7
Tuvalu	6.1 (2001)	0.7	2.5	4.9	4.6	7.7	1.7	...	...
Vanuatu	2.4	0.4	2.6	2.0	4.5	1.8	4.2	...	...
Developed ADB Member Economies									
Australia	2.6	3.8	1.2	1.5	-0.5	-0.5	3.7	1.9	3.2
Japan	-1.4	-1.0	-1.9	1.7	2.1	0.3	-0.2	-0.1	0.6
New Zealand	3.5	2.1	3.7	0.5	0.7	2.4	2.8	1.1	3.0

... = data not available; -0.0 or 0.0 = magnitude is less than half of unit employed, ADB = Asian Development Bank.

Sources: Economy sources.

Table 2.3.5: **Growth Rates of Money Supply**[a]
(%)

ADB Regional Member	2000	2005	2010	2014	2015	2016	2017	2018	2019
Developing ADB Member Economies									
Central and West Asia									
Afghanistan	...	38.3 (2006)	39.3	6.0	3.7	9.7	4.1	2.6	5.7
Armenia	38.6	27.8	11.8	8.3	10.8	17.5	18.5	7.4	11.2
Azerbaijan[b]	21.8	22.3	24.3	11.8	-1.3	-1.9	9.0	5.7	20.0
Georgia[b]	39.2	27.9	30.1	13.8	19.3	20.2	14.8	14.7	16.7
Kazakhstan[b]	45.0	25.2	13.3	10.4	33.8	15.6	-1.7	7.0	2.4
Kyrgyz Republic	12.1	9.9	21.1	3.0	14.9	14.6	17.9	5.5	12.8
Pakistan	9.4	19.8	13.0	12.6	12.8	14.5	13.9	9.5	10.8
Tajikistan	43.3	62.9	17.6	3.5	12.2	56.7	36.6	10.0	23.1
Turkmenistan[b]	94.6	5.6	74.2	10.0	18.0	9.4	11.4	8.4	8.6
Uzbekistan	37.1	54.4	52.4	14.9	25.2	23.5	40.2	14.4	7.7
East Asia									
China, People's Republic of	12.3	16.5	19.7	11.0	13.3	11.3	9.0	8.1	8.7
Hong Kong, China	7.8	5.1	8.1	9.5	5.5	7.7	10.0	4.3	2.8
Korea, Republic of	5.2	7.0	6.0	8.1	8.2	7.1	5.1	6.7	7.9
Mongolia	17.6	34.6	62.5	12.5	-5.5	21.0	30.5	22.8	7.0
Taipei,China	6.5	6.6	5.5	6.1	5.8	3.6	3.6	2.7	4.5
South Asia									
Bangladesh	18.6	16.7	22.4	16.1	12.4	16.3	10.9	9.2	9.9
Bhutan	16.1	13.2	16.5	26.0	3.8	23.0	17.4	6.5	13.1
India[b]	16.8	21.1	16.1	10.9	10.1	10.1	9.2	10.5	8.9
Maldives	4.2	10.6	14.6	14.9	12.1	-0.2	5.2	3.4	9.6
Nepal	21.8	8.3	14.1	19.1	19.9	19.5	15.5	19.4	15.8
Sri Lanka	13.0	19.6	18.0	13.1	17.2	18.9	17.5	13.5	7.6
Southeast Asia									
Brunei Darussalam	1.9 (2002)	-4.5	4.8	3.2	-1.8	1.5	-0.4	2.8	4.3
Cambodia	26.9	15.8	21.3	31.5	17.0	21.0	23.1	26.6	18.2
Indonesia	15.6	16.3	15.4	11.9	9.0	10.0	8.3	6.3	6.5
Lao People's Democratic Republic	45.9	8.2	39.5	25.2	14.7	10.9	12.2	8.4	18.9
Malaysia[b]	5.1	8.3	6.8	7.3	3.0	3.2	4.9	9.1	3.5
Myanmar	42.2	27.3	42.5	21.0	30.7	17.4	20.5	14.6	15.5
Philippines[b]	4.6	16.8	10.0	11.2	9.4	12.8	11.9	9.5	11.3
Singapore	-2.0	6.2	8.6	3.3	1.5	8.0	3.2	3.9	5.0
Thailand	4.0	6.1	10.9	4.7	4.4	4.2	5.0	4.7	3.6
Timor-Leste	155.5 (2001)	17.6	18.2	19.9	7.1	14.2	12.1	3.1	-7.1
Viet Nam	56.2	29.7	33.3	17.7	16.2	18.4	15.0	12.4	14.8
The Pacific									
Cook Islands	12.2 (2001)	-0.9	0.1	-1.0	9.5	0.1	6.4	9.9	7.9
Fiji[b]	-2.1	15.2	3.5	10.4	13.9	4.8	8.3	2.8	2.7
Kiribati	...	...	...	...	...	...	...	...	...
Marshall Islands	16.6	-0.8	9.4	31.0	28.6	19.9	23.9	-3.3	...
Micronesia, Federated States of	...	...	...	...	...	...	...	...	...
Nauru	...	...	...	...	...	...	...	...	...
Niue	...	...	...	...	...	...	...	...	...
Palau	...	...	-12.4	22.6	30.0	17.3	0.5	0.6	-2.7
Papua New Guinea[b]	5.4	29.5	11.4	3.4	8.0	10.9	-0.7	-4.0	4.4
Samoa	16.4	15.6	6.4	9.6	6.0	9.2	15.2	8.8	4.6
Solomon Islands[b]	0.4	46.1	13.3	5.1	15.5	13.4	3.5	6.8	-3.1
Tonga	8.3	12.1	5.1	7.3	9.3	16.7	13.7	7.6	4.4
Tuvalu	...	...	...	...	...	...	...	...	...
Vanuatu	5.5	11.6	-6.0	8.5	11.4	10.7	9.3	13.1	...
Developed ADB Member Economies									
Australia[b]	7.3	8.9	4.5	6.9	6.7	5.8	7.8	1.9	4.0
Japan[c]	1.9	0.4	1.9	2.8	2.5	3.2	2.9	2.2	2.1
New Zealand[d]	6.6	7.8	3.2	6.3	8.1	7.7	7.3	6.4	4.7

... = data not available, ADB = Asian Development Bank.

a Data are based on money supply M2 (M2), unless otherwise stated.
b Refers to money supply M3 (M3).
c Refers to M3, except for 2000–2002 (M2).
d Refers to M3, except for 2016–2019 (M2).

Sources: Economy sources.

Money and Finance

Table 2.3.6: Money Supply[a]
(% of GDP)

ADB Regional Member	2000	2005	2010	2014	2015	2016	2017	2018	2019
Developing ADB Member Economies									
Central and West Asia									
Afghanistan	11.0 (2002)	17.9	30.3	29.6	29.7	37.2	37.4	37.5	37.0
Armenia	14.7	16.3	26.3	34.7	36.8	43.0	46.4	46.2	47.1
Azerbaijan[b]	10.8	14.7	24.8	36.5	39.1	34.6	32.4	30.0	35.3
Georgia[b]	10.1	16.9	28.4	36.0	39.3	44.8	45.2	47.4	49.3
Kazakhstan[b]	15.3	27.2	38.9	32.3	41.9	42.2	35.8	33.7	31.1
Kyrgyz Republic	11.3	21.1	31.4	31.1	33.3	34.4	36.5	35.8	39.0
Pakistan	33.0	41.6	37.8	38.9	40.2	43.5	45.1	45.5	46.0
Tajikistan	5.8	11.2	12.0	12.8	12.8	18.7	21.7	21.6	24.5
Turkmenistan[b]	19.4	10.5	17.3	41.4	48.2	55.9	62.5	64.8	66.4
Uzbekistan	12.2	14.4	18.9	19.1	20.1	21.5	24.2	20.5	17.6
East Asia									
China, People's Republic of	134.2	158.0	176.1	190.9	202.1	207.7	203.1	198.7	200.5
Hong Kong, China	272.9	310.1	401.7	487.2	484.4	502.2	517.2	506.1	514.6
Korea, Republic of	108.6	106.7	125.5	132.9	135.5	138.3	137.8	142.6	152.2
Mongolia	21.1	37.5	48.0	47.8	43.4	50.8	56.9	60.5	56.5
Taipei,China	183.0	202.8	220.2	231.9	233.9	235.3	237.8	239.4	242.8
South Asia									
Bangladesh	31.5	40.9	45.5	52.1	52.0	52.9	51.4	49.3	48.0
Bhutan	52.6	59.4	72.2	63.0	59.2	64.6	68.9	70.0	79.2
India[b]	61.4	74.9	85.2	84.6	84.4	83.1	81.7	81.3	82.2
Maldives	41.1	45.2	47.9	47.8	48.3	45.2	43.9	40.4	40.8
Nepal	49.0	51.0	60.3	79.7	88.2	99.6	96.9	102.1	103.4
Sri Lanka	31.4	33.6	28.3	33.4	37.1	40.2	42.5	44.7	46.0
Southeast Asia									
Brunei Darussalam	77.8 (2001)	57.8	67.3	67.5	80.8	92.6	86.7	81.6	84.7
Cambodia	13.0	19.3	41.6	67.4	72.4	79.2	88.2	100.7	107.7
Indonesia	53.8	43.4	36.0	39.5	39.5	40.4	39.9	38.8	38.8
Lao People's Democratic Republic	17.4	18.7	38.0	49.0	51.2	51.5	53.1	53.1	...
Malaysia[b]	128.6	123.8	132.2	140.8	136.3	132.5	126.6	130.9	129.8
Myanmar	32.7	21.6	23.6	39.5	46.4	53.4	57.7	58.9	60.0
Philippines[b]	38.6	40.1	47.7	58.3	60.5	62.8	64.2	63.7	66.4
Singapore	103.2	103.3	123.3	128.4	122.9	127.7	122.9	119.7	124.6
Thailand	122.4	104.1	109.0	127.0	127.7	125.4	124.1	123.2	123.2
Timor-Leste	5.4	16.5	33.5	41.4	40.2	44.3	51.1	54.1	...
Viet Nam	50.5	75.6	129.3	131.5	143.6	158.3	163.7	166.2	175.1
The Pacific									
Cook Islands	50.1	56.4	83.1	60.9	59.3	57.7	56.2	57.3	56.3
Fiji[b]	42.4	58.9	67.6	68.9	73.3	73.0	73.8	72.7	72.2
Kiribati	...	...	...	...	...	...	...	...	...
Marshall Islands	53.3	52.3	63.0	64.4	82.9	91.4	106.7	99.3	...
Micronesia, Federated States of	...	...	...	...	...	...	...	...	...
Nauru	...	...	...	...	...	...	...	...	...
Niue	...	...	...	...	...	...	...	...	...
Palau	...	...	50.8	66.0	75.0	82.7	85.7	86.9	86.0
Papua New Guinea[b]	31.2	33.6	34.0	32.8	33.6	34.5	30.7	27.0	26.4
Samoa	33.5	35.7	44.2	45.0	43.1	45.0	49.9	52.6	52.5
Solomon Islands[b]	14.7	22.5	28.5	36.7	40.4	43.3	41.9	41.6	38.9
Tonga	28.9	39.4	41.2	46.3	47.5	50.5	52.6	53.6	51.6
Tuvalu	...	...	...	...	...	...	...	...	...
Vanuatu	89.7	98.6	83.3	73.7	78.5	82.5	82.9	...	...
Developed ADB Member Economies									
Australia[b]	65.4	73.5	94.4	104.2	109.4	113.2	114.9	111.6	110.2
Japan[c]	123.4	198.7	218.8	237.4	235.5	241.0	243.4	248.1	250.3
New Zealand[d]	86.3	98.7	110.5	116.9	122.0	102.5	102.6	104.6	104.8

... = data not available, ADB = Asian Development Bank, GDP = gross domestic product.

a Refers to money supply M2 (M2), unless otherwise stated.
b Refers to money supply M3 (M3).
c Refers to M3, except for 2000–2002 (M2).
d Refers to M3, except for 2016–2019 (M2).

Sources: Economy sources.

Table 2.3.7: **Interest Rates on Savings and Time Deposits**
(% per annum, period averages)

ADB Regional Member	Savings Deposits				Time Deposits[a]			
	2000	2005	2010	2019	2000	2005	2010	2019
Developing ADB Member Economies								
Central and West Asia								
Afghanistan	...	4.3 (2006)	5.4	1.5	...	4.7 (2006)	8.2	3.4
Armenia	...	...	...	...	20.7	6.7	10.7	9.3
Azerbaijan	...	...	...	...	10.4	9.4	11.0	9.4
Georgia[b]	11.0	6.8	8.7	4.7	9.8	10.2	11.6	5.7
Kazakhstan	...	...	...	...	7.5	10.3	9.8	9.1
Kyrgyz Republic[c]	...	...	...	...	28.1	9.8	11.5	9.5
Pakistan	5.8	1.2	5.0	8.7	7.4	4.2	7.2	8.6
Tajikistan	5.3 (2002)	3.6	3.8	0.6	14.8 (2002)	20.2	17.8	11.6
Turkmenistan	...	...	...	...	22.8	...	...	...
Uzbekistan[d]	...	...	...	18.3	...	...	...	18.6
East Asia								
China, People's Republic of	1.0	0.7	0.4	0.4	2.3	2.3	2.3	1.5
Hong Kong, China	4.5	1.0	0.0	0.1	5.4	1.7	0.2	0.3
Korea, Republic of[e]	7.1	3.6	3.2	1.7	7.9	3.7	3.9	1.9
Mongolia[f]	13.8	12.6	10.7	10.5	...	...	...	...
Taipei,China	3.5	0.6	0.2	0.2	5.0	1.8	1.0	1.1
South Asia								
Bangladesh[g]	5.8	4.2	4.9	3.3	9.0	8.3	9.0	8.2
Bhutan[h]	6.0	4.5	4.8	5.4	9.5	6.5	6.8	7.8
India	4.0	3.5	3.5	4.0 (2016)	7.1	5.3	7.5	5.5 (2016)
Maldives[i]	5.5	2.3	2.3	1.5	6.5	4.5	3.8	4.7
Nepal	5.3	3.4	7.0	5.0	6.9	3.6	8.1	9.8
Sri Lanka	8.4	5.0	5.0	4.0	15.0	9.0	8.5	9.8
Southeast Asia								
Brunei Darussalam	...	1.0	0.5	0.3	...	1.6	0.7	0.8
Cambodia	6.1	2.1	1.2	0.6	7.2	6.8	6.6	6.3
Indonesia	8.9	4.3	3.9	1.1	12.2	11.0	7.9	6.8
Lao People's Democratic Republic	...	...	...	...	...	...	...	...
Malaysia	2.7	1.4	0.9	1.0	4.2	3.7	2.8	3.2
Myanmar	...	...	...	...	...	...	...	...
Philippines[j]	7.4	3.8	1.6	1.2	10.5	6.0	2.1	4.6
Singapore	1.3	0.2	0.1	0.2	2.5	0.8	0.5	0.6
Thailand[k]	2.5	1.9	0.5	0.5	3.5	3.0	1.6	1.3
Timor-Leste	0.2 (2002)	0.8	0.8	0.5	– (2002)	1.3	1.3	0.7
Viet Nam[l]	0.2	3.0	3.0	0.5 (2018)	6.2	8.4	11.5	7.1 (2018)
The Pacific								
Cook Islands	...	...	...	...	...	...	...	...
Fiji	...	...	...	...	...	...	...	...
Kiribati	...	...	...	...	...	...	...	...
Marshall Islands	2.5	1.2	0.5	0.2 (2018)	6.8	3.5	3.5	1.1 (2018)
Micronesia, Federated States of	...	...	...	...	...	...	...	...
Nauru	...	...	...	...	...	...	...	...
Niue	...	...	...	...	...	...	...	...
Palau	...	...	0.9	0.1	...	...	0.8	0.4
Papua New Guinea	3.9	1.8	1.0	1.0	9.4	1.3	4.8	1.3
Samoa[m]	3.0	2.8	1.0	1.0	7.4	6.4	2.9	2.9
Solomon Islands	...	...	...	...	...	...	...	...
Tonga	3.2	3.4	1.5	2.5	5.1	5.9	3.0	4.8
Tuvalu	...	...	...	...	...	...	...	...
Vanuatu	...	...	...	...	...	...	...	...
Developed ADB Member Economies								
Australia[n]	...	5.4	4.5	0.6	5.9	4.6	6.0	1.8
Japan[o]	0.1	0.0	0.0	0.0	0.2	0.0	0.1	0.0
New Zealand[p]	...	...	...	...	6.5	6.9	4.7	2.6

... = data not available, – = magnitude equals zero, 0.0 = magnitude is less than half of unit employed, ADB = Asian Development Bank.

a   Refers to interest rate on time deposits of 12 months, unless otherwise indicated.
b   Refers to interest rate on time deposits of over 12 months.
c   Rates for time deposits refer to interest rates of commercial banks in national currency for 6–12 months.
d   Refers to weighted average interest rate on all time household savings deposits and time deposits from 181 to 365 days.
e   Refers to weighted averages of interest rates on newly extended time and savings deposits of commercial and specialized banks.
f   Refers to interest rate from deposit accounts in domestic currency.
g   Refers to savings bank accounts with checking facilities.
h   For savings deposits, actual range of rates for 2000–2001 is 5.0%–7.0%; for 2012, 4.5%–5.0%; for 2013, 5.0%–5.5%; for 2014–2016, 5.0%–7.0%; for 2017, 5.0%–6.0%; and for 2019, 5.0%–5.75%. For time deposits, rate refers to fixed deposits of 1 year to less than 3 years for 2000–2001, and actual range of rates is 9.0%–10.0%. For 2010–2016, rate refers to fixed deposits of 1 year to less than 2 years and actual range of rates for 2010 is 4.5%–6.5%; for 2011, 6.0%–7.0%; for 2012, 7.0%–7.3%; for 2013–2014, 7.0%–7.5%; for 2015–2017, 6.5%–7.5%; and for 2018–2019, 6.0%–9.5%.
i   Refers to interest rate on time deposits of 2–3 years.
j   Rates for time deposits refer to rates charged on interest-bearing deposits with maturities of over 1 year.
k   For 2001, actual range of rates on time deposits is 2.75%–3.00%.
l   For 2000–2010, time deposits refer to maximum interest per annum for state enterprise deposits.
m   For savings deposits actual range of rates for 2007 is 2.50%–3.00%; for 2008, 2.50%–3.00%; and for 2009, 1.00%–2.50%. For time deposits actual range of rates for 2007 is 7.00%–7.50%; for 2008, 4.75%–5.50%; and for 2009, 2.25%–3.50%.
n   Refers to interest rates of online savings deposits.
o   Refers to savings deposits of at least ¥0.3 million, calculated as the arithmetic average of weekly figures. Refers to time deposits from 12 months to less than 2 years, calculated as the arithmetic average of the monthly figures.
p   Refers to interest rate on time deposits of 6 months.

Sources: Economy sources. For the People's Republic of China: CEIC Database. https://www.ceicdata.com/en (accessed 6 July 2020).

Click on the indictor name in the table header to access the time series in the Key Indicators Database.

Table 2.3.8:   Yield on Short-Term Treasury Bills and Lending Interest Rates
(% per annum, period averages)

ADB Regional Member	Yield on Short-Term Treasury Bills[a]				Lending Interest Rates			
	2000	2005	2010	2019	2000	2005	2010	2019
Developing ADB Member Economies								
Central and West Asia								
Afghanistan	...	...	...	6.0	...	18.0 (2006)	15.6	14.8 (2017)
Armenia[b]	20.6 (2001)	4.1	10.6	6.0	31.6	18.0	19.2	12.1
Azerbaijan	16.7	7.5	1.8	14.3 (2017)	19.7	17.0	20.7	17.3
Georgia	29.9 (2001)	12.6	9.6	7.2	...	17.6	15.8	10.8
Kazakhstan	...	...	...	...	...	...	...	...
Kyrgyz Republic	61.9	8.4	10.4	5.1	56.5	21.5	23.7	19.0
Pakistan[c]	8.4	7.2	12.5	13.3	...	9.1	14.0	12.2
Tajikistan[d]	4.5 (2002)	...	6.7	1.0 (2017)	1.6	23.3	23.4	27.2 (2018)
Turkmenistan	...	...	...	...	...	...	...	...
Uzbekistan	...	...	...	13.2	...	...	...	23.6
East Asia								
China, People's Republic of[e]	2.6	1.9	2.6	...	5.9	5.6	5.8	4.4
Hong Kong, China[f]	5.9	2.7	0.2	1.3 (2018)	9.3	6.2	5.0	5.0 (2018)
Korea, Republic of[g]	7.1	3.6	2.7	1.7	8.5	5.6	5.5	3.4
Mongolia[h]	...	13.7	12.9 (2012)	13.9 (2017)	37.0	30.6	20.1	16.9
Taipei,China[i]	...	1.3	0.3	0.3 (2018)	7.7	3.8	2.7	2.6
South Asia								
Bangladesh[d]	...	7.5 (2006)	4.5	5.7	12.8	10.6	12.2	9.6
Bhutan[d]	7.3	3.5	2.0	4.3	16.0	14.5	13.9	14.0
India[d,j]	9.0	5.7	6.2	6.6 (2018)	12.3	10.8	8.3	9.5
Maldives[k]	...	5.0 (2006)	4.9	3.5	13.0	13.0	10.4	11.5
Nepal[d]	5.3	3.0	6.9	3.3	...	...	...	...
Sri Lanka[l]	13.7 (2001)	9.0	8.6	9.1	14.3 (2001)	10.8	10.2	11.2
Southeast Asia								
Brunei Darussalam	...	...	...	...	5.5	5.5	5.5	5.5
Cambodia	...	...	...	...	...	...	...	...
Indonesia	...	...	...	...	18.5	14.1	13.3	10.4
Lao People's Democratic Republic[m]	29.9	18.6	8.0	...	32.0	26.8	22.6	...
Malaysia	2.9	2.5	2.6	...	7.7	6.0	5.0	4.9
Myanmar	...	...	...	...	15.3	15.0	17.0	15.8
Philippines[d]	9.9	6.1	3.5	4.3	10.9	10.2	7.7	7.1
Singapore	2.2	2.1	0.3	...	5.8	5.3	5.4	5.3
Thailand[d]	2.3 (2001)	2.7	1.4	1.6	7.8	4.7	4.3	4.1
Timor-Leste	...	...	...	...	17.4 (2002)	16.7	11.0	15.4
Viet Nam[n]	5.4	6.1	11.1	...	10.6	11.0	13.1	7.7
The Pacific								
Cook Islands	...	...	...	...	...	...	...	...
Fiji[d]	3.5	1.9	3.4	1.4 (2018)	8.4	6.8	7.5	5.7 (2018)
Kiribati	...	...	...	...	...	...	...	...
Marshall Islands	...	...	...	...	...	...	...	...
Micronesia, Federated States of	...	...	...	...	15.3	16.4	15.1	15.7 (2018)
Nauru	...	...	...	...	...	...	...	...
Niue	...	...	...	...	...	...	...	...
Palau	...	...	...	...	...	...	...	...
Papua New Guinea[o]	17.0	3.8	4.6	6.1	17.5	11.5	10.4	8.7
Samoa	...	...	...	...	11.6 (2001)	11.4	10.7	8.9
Solomon Islands[d]	7.0	4.5	3.7	0.5 (2018)	10.3	9.3	14.4	10.7 (2018)
Tonga	...	...	...	...	11.3	11.4	11.5	8.1
Tuvalu	...	...	...	...	...	...	...	...
Vanuatu	...	...	...	...	9.9	7.5	5.5	2.0
Developed ADB Member Economies								
Australia[p]	6.0	...	4.4	...	7.7	7.3	7.3	5.1
Japan	0.2	0.0	0.1	-0.2 (2017)	2.1	1.7	1.6	1.0 (2017)
New Zealand	6.4	6.5	2.8	1.3	7.8	7.8	6.3	– (2018)

... = data not available, 0.0 = magnitude is less than half of unit employed, ADB = Asian Development Bank.

a   Refers to 3-month Treasury bills, unless otherwise indicated.
b   Refers to average yield on 9-month to 12-month Treasury bills since March 2001.
c   Refers to weighted average yield on 6-month Treasury securities.
d   Refers to 91-day Treasury bills.
e   Refers to 3-month Treasury bonds trading rate.
f   Refers to annualized yields on 91-day Exchange Fund bills.
g   Refers to 91-day certificates of deposit.
h   Refers to weighted average rate on Treasury bills of all maturities. From December 2012 onward, refers to yield on 12-week Treasury bills.
i   Refers to prime lending rates.
j   Figures are for fiscal year ending March.
k   Refers to rate on 28-day Treasury bills.
l   Refers to weighted average rate on the last monthly issuance of 364-day Treasury bills since December 2001.
m   Refers to weighted average auction rate for 12-month Treasury bills.
n   Refers to average monthly yield on 360-day Treasury bills sold at auction.
o   Refers to rate on 182-day Treasury bills.
p   Refers to estimated closing yield in the secondary market on 13-week Treasury notes.

Sources: International Monetary Fund. International Financial Statistics. http://data.imf.org/ (accessed 3 July 2020); and Organisation for Economic Co-operation and Development. Main Economic Indicators. http://dx.doi.org/10.1787/data-00043-en (accessed 6 July 2020). For Bangladesh; Bhutan; India; and Taipei,China: Economy sources.

Click on the indictor name in the table header to access the time series in the Key Indicators Database.

Table 2.3.9:   Domestic Credit Provided by Banking Sector and Bank Nonperforming Loans

ADB Regional Member	Domestic Credit Provided by Banking Sector[a] (% of GDP)				Bank Nonperforming Loans[b] (% of total gross loans)	
	2000	2005	2010	2018	2010	2018
Developing ADB Member Economies						
Central and West Asia						
Afghanistan	...	...	...	...	49.9	8.9
Armenia	...	...	27.8	65.2 (2019)	3.0	4.8
Azerbaijan	...	...	...	14.7 (2019)	...	...
Georgia	...	...	33.8	69.8 (2019)	5.9	1.9 (2019)
Kazakhstan	...	...	...	35.3 (2019)	20.9	7.4
Kyrgyz Republic	...	...	...	...	14.8	7.7 (2019)
Pakistan	...	...	...	...	14.7	8.0
Tajikistan	...	...	7.6	15.8 (2019)	7.4	...
Turkmenistan	...	...	...	...	...	...
Uzbekistan	...	...	...	...	1.0	1.5 (2019)
East Asia						
China, People's Republic of	...	...	...	...	1.1	1.8
Hong Kong, China	...	...	...	...	0.8	0.6 (2019)
Korea, Republic of	...	...	...	...	0.6	0.4 (2017)
Mongolia	...	...	...	...	...	...
Taipei,China	1.8	1.9	0.9	...	0.6	0.2 (2019)
South Asia						
Bangladesh	...	...	...	...	5.8 (2011)	9.9
Bhutan	...	...	...	...	5.2	7.0
India	...	...	...	...	2.7 (2011)	9.5
Maldives	...	47.0	76.9	63.6 (2019)	20.9 (2012)	9.4 (2019)
Nepal	...	...	...	...	...	1.6
Sri Lanka	...	...	...	...	3.8 (2011)	3.4
Southeast Asia						
Brunei Darussalam	...	16.5 (2006)	22.7	29.5 (2019)	6.9	3.9 (2019)
Cambodia	...	...	...	...	3.1	1.6 (2019)
Indonesia	...	...	34.2	46.5 (2019)	2.5	2.4 (2019)
Lao People's Democratic Republic	...	...	...	...	...	...
Malaysia	...	...	...	...	3.4	1.5 (2019)
Myanmar	...	...	...	...	...	...
Philippines	...	...	...	82.9	3.4	1.7
Singapore	...	...	...	...	1.4	1.3 (2019)
Thailand	...	123.6 (2007)	133.4	169.0 (2019)	3.9	3.1
Timor-Leste	...	...	...	...	...	...
Viet Nam	...	...	...	...	2.1	1.8
The Pacific						
Cook Islands	...	...	...	...	...	...
Fiji	71.6 (2001)	111.5	131.7	125.7	4.4	3.1
Kiribati	...	...	...	...	...	...
Marshall Islands	...	...	...	...	...	...
Micronesia, Federated States of	...	...	...	...	...	...
Nauru	...	...	...	...	...	...
Niue	...	...	...	...	...	...
Palau	...	...	...	...	...	...
Papua New Guinea	...	...	23.7	37.0 (2019)	1.9	3.8 (2019)
Samoa	...	61.2 (2007)	61.5	82.7 (2019)	4.7	3.6
Solomon Islands	26.5	29.4	26.8	28.2	9.3	3.8 (2016)
Tonga	...	...	...	...	–	3.2 (2019)
Tuvalu	...	...	...	...	...	...
Vanuatu	...	...	...	...	4.8	15.0 (2017)
Developed ADB Member Economies						
Australia	...	...	...	...	2.1	0.9
Japan	295.0	296.1	314.0	361.3 (2019)	...	...
New Zealand	...	...	...	172.8 (2019)	...	...

... = data not available, ADB = Asian Development Bank, GDP = gross domestic product.

a   Domestic credit provided by the financial sector includes all credit to various sectors on a gross basis, with the exception of credit to the central government, which is net. The financial sector includes monetary authorities and deposit money banks, as well as other financial corporations where data were available (including corporations that do not accept transferable deposits, but do incur such liabilities as time and savings deposits). Examples of other financial corporations are finance and leasing companies, money lenders, insurance corporations, pension funds, and foreign exchange companies.

b   Bank nonperforming loans to total gross loans are the value of nonperforming loans divided by the total value of the loan portfolio (including nonperforming loans before the deduction of specific loan-loss provisions). The loan amount recorded as nonperforming should be the gross value of the loan as recorded on the balance sheet, not just the amount that is overdue.

Sources: World Bank. World Development Indicators. http://databank.worldbank.org/data/home.aspx (accessed 6 July 2020). For Taipei,China: Central bank of Taipei,China. http://www.cbc.gov.tw (accessed 6 July 2020).

Click on the indictor name in the table header to access the time series in the Key Indicators Database.

Money and Finance

Table 2.3.10:   Growth Rates of Stock Market Price Index[a]

(%)

ADB Regional Member	2000	2005	2010	2014	2015	2016	2017	2018	2019
Developing ADB Member Economies									
Central and West Asia									
Afghanistan	...	...	...	...	...	...	...	...	...
Armenia	...	...	...	...	...	...	...	...	...
Azerbaijan	...	...	...	...	...	...	...	...	...
Georgia	...	...	...	...	...	...	...	...	...
Kazakhstan	...	...	...	...	...	...	...	...	...
Kyrgyz Republic	...	...	...	...	...	...	...	...	...
Pakistan[b]	7.0	53.7	28.2	27.2	2.1	45.7	...	...	...
Tajikistan	...	...	...	...	...	...	...	...	...
Turkmenistan	...	...	...	...	...	...	...	...	...
Uzbekistan	...	...	...	...	...	...	-0.5	0.7	-42.7
East Asia									
China, People's Republic of	37.3	-22.1	3.4	1.5	66.0	-19.0	6.7	...	...
Hong Kong, China	26.5	11.1	19.3	2.7	4.8	-12.0	22.3	10.2	...
Korea, Republic of	-8.7	28.5	23.6	1.1	1.4	-1.2	16.5	0.5	-9.4
Mongolia	81.3 (2001)	18.7	88.7	4.2	-14.6	-14.0	33.5	30.5	-0.8
Taipei,China	5.7	1.0	23.1	11.1	-0.4	-2.2	16.5	4.0	1.6
South Asia									
Bangladesh[b]	31.8	-14.9	82.8	14.0	-4.8	8.8	24.0	-13.8	-17.3
Bhutan	...	...	...	...	...	...	...	...	...
India	11.2	32.6	29.8	25.2	10.9	-3.6	8.6	...	...
Maldives	...	51.8	-20.4	-4.8	8.9	4.8	7.4	6.8	5.2
Nepal	...	...	...	...	...	...	...	...	...
Sri Lanka[b]	...	27.6	96.0	23.4	-5.5	-9.7	...	...	...
Southeast Asia									
Brunei Darussalam	...	...	...	...	...	...	...	...	...
Cambodia	...	...	...	...	...	...	...	...	...
Indonesia[b]	-38.5	16.2	46.1	22.3	-12.1	15.3	20.0	-2.5	1.7
Lao People's Democratic Republic	...	...	...	...	...	...	...	...	...
Malaysia	21.4	6.4	27.1	5.5	-6.1	-3.8	5.0	2.2	-8.4
Myanmar	...	...	...	...	...	...	...	...	...
Philippines	-6.3	17.5	43.1	1.8	5.5	0.9	8.0	0.1	...
Singapore	8.6	16.7	30.3	1.2	-2.5	-11.6	10.3	...	...
Thailand	-18.7	4.2	45.6	-0.2	0.2	-2.1	12.7	6.6	-4.7
Timor-Leste	...	...	...	...	...	...	...	...	...
Viet Nam[b]	50.0 (2001)	8.3	12.2	8.1	6.1	14.8	...	...	...
The Pacific									
Cook Islands	...	...	...	...	...	...	...	...	...
Fiji	8.7 (2001)	13.5	-11.1	0.5	20.8	27.6	22.4	...	...
Kiribati	...	...	...	...	...	...	...	...	...
Marshall Islands	...	...	...	...	...	...	...	...	...
Micronesia, Federated States of	...	...	...	...	...	...	...	...	...
Nauru	...	...	...	...	...	...	...	...	...
Niue	...	...	...	...	...	...	...	...	...
Palau	...	...	...	...	...	...	...	...	...
Papua New Guinea	34.8 (2002)	52.5	26.2	-12.3	-6.3	...	...	7.5	-2.9
Samoa	...	...	...	...	...	...	...	...	...
Solomon Islands	...	...	...	...	...	...	...	...	...
Tonga	...	...	...	...	...	...	...	...	...
Tuvalu	...	...	...	...	...	...	...	...	...
Vanuatu	...	...	...	...	...	...	...	...	...
Developed ADB Member Economies									
Australia[b]	1.7	17.6	-2.6	1.1	-2.1	7.0	7.0	-6.9	...
Japan	11.6	13.5	2.0	12.6	22.7	-12.6	...	...	...
New Zealand	2.3	19.4	9.7	14.1	12.7	17.4	11.1	14.8	18.0

... = data not available, ADB = Asian Development Bank.

a   Growth rates are calculated from stock market price index at period average, unless otherwise indicated.
b   Refers to growth rates of stock market price index at end of period.

Sources: International Monetary Fund. International Financial Statistics. http://data.imf.org/IFS (accessed 29 June 2020). For Taipei,China: Stock exchange corporation in Taipei,China. Indices Monthly Statistics. http://www.twse.com.tw/en/statistics/ (accessed 29 June 2020).

Click on the indictor name in the table header to access the time series in the Key Indicators Database.

Table 2.3.11: Stock Market Capitalization

ADB Regional Member	Stock Market Capitalization ($ million)				Stock Market Capitalization (% of GDP)			
	2000	2005	2010	2019	2000	2005	2010	2019
Developing ADB Member Economies								
Central and West Asia								
Afghanistan	...	...	...	...	...	...	...	...
Armenia	...	...	...	...	...	...	...	...
Azerbaijan	...	...	...	...	...	...	...	...
Georgia	...	...	...	...	...	...	...	...
Kazakhstan	802	10,529	26,673	40,640	4.4	18.4	18.0	22.6
Kyrgyz Republic	...	...	...	...	...	...	...	...
Pakistan	6,625	45,317	38,007	...	8.1	37.7	21.5	...
Tajikistan	...	...	...	...	...	...	...	...
Turkmenistan	...	...	...	...	...	...	...	...
Uzbekistan	...	...	...	...	...	...	...	...
East Asia								
China, People's Republic of	...	401,852	4,027,840	8,515,504	...	17.6	66.2	59.4
Hong Kong, China	623,398	1,054,999	2,711,316	4,899,235	363.1	581.0	1,185.9	1,338.5
Korea, Republic of	171,262	718,011	1,091,911	1,413,717 (2018)	29.7	76.8	95.4	82.2 (2018)
Mongolia	...	...	...	...	...	...	...	...
Taipei,China	262,335	486,021	752,526	1,177,470	79.3	129.9	169.4	192.7
South Asia								
Bangladesh	2,192	3,300	41,617	77,391 (2018)	4.1	4.8	36.1	28.2 (2018)
Bhutan	53	101	219	515 (2018)	12.4	12.7	14.1	21.1 (2018)
India	...	553,074	1,631,830	2,179,781	...	67.4	97.4	75.8
Maldives	...	...	...	...	...	...	...	...
Nepal	...	...	...	...	...	...	...	...
Sri Lanka	1,074	5,720	19,924	15,721	6.6	23.4	35.1	18.7
Southeast Asia								
Brunei Darussalam	...	...	...	...	...	...	...	...
Cambodia	...	...	...	...	...	...	...	...
Indonesia	26,813	81,428	360,388	523,322	16.2	28.5	47.7	46.8
Lao People's Democratic Republic	...	...	...	...	...	...	...	...
Malaysia	113,156	180,518	408,689	403,957	120.6	125.8	160.3	110.8
Myanmar	...	...	...	...	...	...	...	...
Philippines	25,981	39,799	157,321	275,302	31.1	37.0	75.5	73.1
Singapore	152,826	257,340	647,226	697,271	159.1	201.3	269.9	187.4
Thailand	29,217	123,885	277,732	569,228	23.1	65.4	81.4	104.7
Timor-Leste	...	...	...	...	...	...	...	...
Viet Nam	...	...	36,855	149,817	...	...	31.8	57.2
The Pacific								
Cook Islands	...	...	...	...	...	...	...	...
Fiji	...	...	...	...	...	...	...	...
Kiribati	...	...	...	...	...	...	...	...
Marshall Islands	...	...	...	...	...	...	...	...
Micronesia, Federated States of	...	...	...	...	...	...	...	...
Nauru	...	...	...	...	...	...	...	...
Niue	...	...	...	...	...	...	...	...
Palau	...	...	...	...	...	...	...	...
Papua New Guinea	...	6,138	11,027	...	...	126.2	77.4	...
Samoa	...	...	...	...	...	...	...	...
Solomon Islands	...	...	...	...	...	...	...	...
Tonga	...	...	...	...	...	...	...	...
Tuvalu	...	...	...	...	...	...	...	...
Vanuatu	...	...	...	...	...	...	...	...
Developed ADB Member Economies								
Australia	372,794	804,015	1,454,491	1,487,599	89.8	116.0	126.9	106.8
Japan	3,157,222	4,572,901	3,827,774	6,191,073	64.6	96.2	67.2	121.8
New Zealand	18,613	40,592	43,516	107,880	35.4	35.4	29.7	52.1

... = data not available, $ = United States dollars, ADB = Asian Development Bank, GDP = gross domestic product.

Sources: World Bank. World Development Indicators. https://databank.worldbank.org/source/world-development-indicators (accessed 30 June 2020). For Bhutan and Taipei,China: Asian Development Bank estimates using data from economy sources.

Click on the indictor name in the table header to access the time series in the Key Indicators Database.

Table 2.3.12:   Official Exchange Rates
(local currency units per $, period averages)

ADB Regional Member	2000	2005	2010	2013	2014	2015	2016	2017	2018	2019
Developing ADB Member Economies										
Central and West Asia										
Afghanistan	47.4	49.5	46.5	57.3	61.1	67.9	68.0	72.1	77.7	77.7
Armenia	539.5	457.7	373.7	415.9	477.9	480.5	482.7	483.0	480.4	480.4
Azerbaijan	0.9	0.9	0.8	0.8	1.0	1.6	1.7	1.7	1.7	1.7
Georgia	2.0	1.8	1.8	1.8	2.3	2.4	2.5	2.5	2.8	2.8
Kazakhstan	142.1	132.9	147.4	179.2	221.7	342.2	326.0	344.7	382.7	382.7
Kyrgyz Republic	47.7	41.0	46.0	53.7	64.5	69.9	68.9	68.8	69.8	69.8
Pakistan	53.6	59.5	85.2	101.1	102.8	104.8	105.5	121.8	150.0	150.0
Tajikistan	2.1	3.1	4.4	4.9	6.2	7.8	8.5	9.2	9.5	9.5
Turkmenistan	1.0	1.0	2.9	2.9	3.5	3.5	3.5	3.5	3.5	3.5
Uzbekistan[a]	236.6	1,106.1	1,578.4	2,310.9	2,568.0	2,965.3	5,113.9	8,069.6	8,836.8	8,836.8
East Asia										
China, People's Republic of	8.3	8.2	6.8	6.1	6.2	6.6	6.8	6.6	6.9	6.9
Hong Kong, China	7.8	7.8	7.8	7.8	7.8	7.8	7.8	7.8	7.8	7.8
Korea, Republic of	1,131.0	1,024.1	1,156.1	1,053.0	1,131.2	1,160.4	1,130.4	1,100.5	1,165.4	1,165.4
Mongolia	1,076.7	1,205.2	1,357.1	1,817.9	1,970.3	2,140.3	2,439.8	2,472.5	2,663.5	2,663.5
Taipei,China	31.2	32.2	31.6	30.4	31.9	32.3	30.4	30.2	30.9	30.9
South Asia										
Bangladesh	52.1	64.3	69.6	77.6	77.9	78.5	80.4	83.5	84.5	84.5
Bhutan	44.9	44.1	45.7	61.0	64.2	67.2	65.1	68.4	70.4	70.4
India	44.9	44.1	45.7	61.0	64.2	67.2	65.1	68.4	70.4	70.4
Maldives	11.8	12.8	12.8	15.4	15.4	15.4	15.4	15.4	15.4	15.4
Nepal	71.1	71.4	73.3	97.6	102.4	107.4	104.5	108.9	112.6	112.6
Sri Lanka	77.0	100.5	113.1	130.6	135.9	145.6	152.4	162.5	178.7	178.7
Southeast Asia										
Brunei Darussalam	1.7	1.7	1.4	1.3	1.4	1.4	1.4	1.3	1.4	1.4
Cambodia	3,840.8	4,092.5	4,184.9	4,037.5	4,067.8	4,058.7	4,050.6	4,051.2	4,061.1	4,061.1
Indonesia	8,421.8	9,704.7	9,090.4	11,865.2	13,389.4	13,308.3	13,380.8	14,236.9	14,147.7	14,147.7
Lao People's Democratic Republic	7,887.6	10,655.2	8,254.2	8,042.4	8,127.6	8,124.4	8,244.8	8,401.3	8,679.4	8,679.4
Malaysia	3.8	3.8	3.2	3.3	3.9	4.1	4.3	4.0	4.1	4.1
Myanmar[b]	6.5	5.8	5.6	984.3	1,162.6	1,234.9	1,360.4	1,429.8	1,518.3	1,518.3
Philippines	44.2	55.1	45.1	44.4	45.5	47.5	50.4	52.7	51.8	51.8
Singapore	1.7	1.7	1.4	1.3	1.4	1.4	1.4	1.3	1.4	1.4
Thailand	40.1	40.2	31.7	32.5	34.2	35.3	33.9	32.3	31.0	31.0
Timor-Leste[c]	1.0	1.0	1.0	1.0	1.0	1.0	1.0	1.0	1.0	1.0
Viet Nam	14,167.8	15,858.9	18,612.9	21,148.0	21,697.6	21,935.0	22,370.1	22,602.1	23,050.2	23,050.2
The Pacific										
Cook Islands	2.2	1.4	1.4	1.2	1.4	1.4	1.4	1.4	1.5	1.5
Fiji	2.1	1.7	1.9	1.9	2.1	2.1	2.1	2.1	2.2	2.2
Kiribati	1.7	1.3	1.1	1.1	1.3	1.3	1.3	1.3	1.4	1.4
Marshall Islands[c]	1.0	1.0	1.0	1.0	1.0	1.0	1.0	1.0	1.0	1.0
Micronesia, Federated States of[c]	1.0	1.0	1.0	1.0	1.0	1.0	1.0	1.0	1.0	1.0
Nauru	1.7	1.3	1.1	1.1	1.3	1.3	1.3	1.3	1.4	1.4
Niue	2.2	1.4	1.4	1.2	1.4	1.4	1.4	1.4	1.5	1.5
Palau[c]	1.0	1.0	1.0	1.0	1.0	1.0	1.0	1.0	1.0	1.0
Papua New Guinea	2.8	3.1	2.7	2.5	2.8	3.1	3.2	3.3	3.4	3.4
Samoa	3.3	2.7	2.5	2.3	2.6	2.6	2.6	2.6	2.6	2.6
Solomon Islands	5.1	7.5	8.1	7.4	7.9	7.9	7.9	8.0	8.2	8.2
Tonga	1.8	1.9	1.9	1.8	2.1	2.2	2.2	2.2	2.3	2.3
Tuvalu	1.7	1.3	1.1	1.1	1.3	1.3	1.3	1.3	1.4	1.4
Vanuatu	137.6	109.2	96.9	97.1	109.0	108.5	107.8	110.2	114.3	114.3
Developed ADB Member Economies										
Australia	1.7	1.3	1.1	1.1	1.3	1.3	1.3	1.3	1.4	1.4
Japan	107.8	110.2	87.8	105.9	121.0	108.8	112.2	110.4	109.0	109.0
New Zealand	2.2	1.4	1.4	1.2	1.4	1.4	1.4	1.4	1.5	1.5

$ = United States (US) dollars, ADB = Asian Development Bank.

a   Data show weighted averages of the official, bank, and parallel market rates.
b   From 1 April 2012, the Central Bank of Myanmar adopted the managed float exchange rate regime for kyat vis-à-vis the US dollar.
c   Unit of currency is the US dollar.

Sources: International Monetary Fund. International Financial Statistics. http://data.imf.org/ (accessed 22 June 2020). For Turkmenistan for 2000–2009: United Nations Statistics Division. National Accounts Database. https://unstats.un.org/unsd/snaama/resCountry.asp (accessed 19 May 2020); and for 2010–2019: Interstate Statistical Committee of the Commonwealth of Independent States. http://www.cisstat.org/eng/index.htm (accessed 26 May 2020). For Uzbekistan for 2000–2012: United Nations Statistics Division. National Accounts Database. http://unstats.un.org/unsd/snaama/resCountry.asp (accessed 1 June 2020); and for 2013–2019: Central Bank of the Republic of Uzbekistan. Statistics Database. http://cbu.uz/en/statistics/ (accessed 1 June 2020). For Taipei,China: Central bank of Taipei,China. http://www.cbc.gov.tw (accessed 20 April 2020).

Table 2.3.13: **Purchasing Power Parity Conversion Factor**[a,b]
(local currency units per $, period averages)

ADB Regional Member	2000	2005	2010	2011	2015	2016	2017	2018	2019
Developing ADB Member Economies									
Central and West Asia									
Afghanistan	9.2 (2002)	11.7	14.5	16.6	17.0	17.4	17.2	16.9	17.0
Armenia	126.4	137.9	160.2	163.7	172.9	161.2	156.0	156.6	156.2
Azerbaijan	0.2	0.2	0.3	0.4	0.4	0.4	0.5	0.6	0.5
Georgia	0.5	0.6	0.8	0.8	0.8	0.7	0.8	0.8	0.9
Kazakhstan	22.6	36.0	69.5	82.1	100.3	110.8	121.3	129.4	135.7
Kyrgyz Republic	7.2	8.2	13.1	15.7	17.1	16.7	17.0	17.1	16.7
Pakistan	11.2	13.1	21.3	25.0	31.5	32.4	33.6	33.6	35.9
Tajikistan	0.3	0.6	1.4	1.6	1.9	2.0	2.2	2.3	2.4
Turkmenistan	0.5	0.6	1.3	1.4	1.6	1.6	1.6	1.6	...
Uzbekistan	53.0	178.3	505.9	602.0	1,058.7	1,180.0	1,432.9	1,784.4	2,091.2
East Asia									
China, People's Republic of	2.7	2.8	3.3	3.5	3.9	4.0	4.2	4.2	4.2
Hong Kong, China	7.1	5.4	5.1	5.2	5.8	5.9	6.0	6.1	6.1
Korea, Republic of	747.2	788.9	840.9	854.6	857.4	859.0	871.7	870.8	860.2
Mongolia	136.9	221.9	473.1	533.5	717.1	729.2	791.4	838.2	892.4
Taipei,China	21.6	18.4	15.8	15.2	15.5	15.8	15.7	15.3	15.0
South Asia									
Bangladesh	15.8	17.5	22.2	23.4	27.3	28.5	29.7	30.7	31.5
Bhutan	12.0	13.4	15.4	16.4	18.6	18.8	19.2	19.1	...
India	9.7	10.7	14.6	15.5	19.2	19.9	20.6	21.1	21.2
Maldives	3.2	5.2	7.1	7.9	8.3	8.1	8.2	8.4	8.4
Nepal	14.4	15.7	23.3	25.3	29.9	32.0	31.2	32.6	34.0
Sri Lanka	19.1	25.3	38.6	39.3	45.2	46.3	49.4	50.3	50.6
Southeast Asia									
Brunei Darussalam	0.5	0.6	0.6	0.7	0.7	0.7	0.6	0.7	0.7
Cambodia	1,077.3	1,125.9	1,354.3	1,371.2	1,395.9	1,402.1	1,428.4	1,438.8	1,459.9
Indonesia	1,385.0	1,960.1	3,337.0	3,512.8	4,353.3	4,518.1	4,695.7	4,762.6	4,756.1
Lao People's Democratic Republic	1,398.4	1,972.2	2,464.3	2,666.5	2,819.7	2,759.4	2,789.1	2,777.1	2,795.7
Malaysia	1.2	1.3	1.4	1.5	1.6	1.6	1.7	1.6	1.6
Myanmar	59.3	139.3	242.4	261.8	319.0	347.1	366.7	380.7	402.8
Philippines	13.8	15.7	17.8	18.1	19.0	18.9	19.4	19.6	19.5
Singapore	0.9	0.8	0.9	0.8	0.9	0.9	0.9	0.9	0.9
Thailand	11.0	11.3	12.2	12.4	12.6	12.7	12.8	12.7	12.6
Timor-Leste	0.3	0.3	0.4	0.5	0.5	0.4	0.4	0.4	0.4
Viet Nam	2,781.0	3,682.5	5,822.0	6,915.3	7,413.5	7,315.6	7,395.3	7,470.4	7,473.7
The Pacific									
Cook Islands	...	...	...	...	...	...	...	...	...
Fiji	0.8	0.9	0.9	0.9	0.9	0.9	0.9	0.9	0.9
Kiribati	0.9	0.9	1.0	1.0	1.0	1.0	1.0	1.0	1.0
Marshall Islands	0.9	0.9	0.9	0.9	0.9	1.0	1.0	1.0	...
Micronesia, Federated States of	0.9	0.8	0.9	0.9	0.9	0.9	0.9	1.0	...
Nauru	...	0.9	0.9	1.0	0.8	1.0	1.1	1.1	1.1
Niue	...	...	...	...	...	...	...	...	...
Palau	0.8	0.7	0.8	0.7	0.9	0.9	0.9	0.9	...
Papua New Guinea	1.3	1.6	1.8	1.9	1.8	1.9	2.0	2.1	2.1
Samoa	1.4	1.5	1.7	1.7	1.7	1.7	1.7	1.7	1.7
Solomon Islands	3.7	4.4	5.7	6.4	6.8	7.0	6.9	7.0	7.1
Tonga	0.9	1.1	1.4	1.5	1.4	1.4	1.5	1.5	...
Tuvalu	1.0	1.1	1.1	1.1	1.2	1.2	1.2	1.2	1.3
Vanuatu	90.1	88.6	99.5	100.5	103.4	104.2	106.5	106.5	106.7
Developed ADB Member Economies									
Australia	1.3	1.4	1.5	1.5	1.5	1.4	1.5	1.5	1.4
Japan	154.7	129.6	111.7	107.5	103.4	105.5	105.4	104.6	101.5
New Zealand	1.4	1.5	1.5	1.5	1.5	1.4	1.5	1.4	1.5

... = data not available, $ = United States dollars, ADB = Asian Development Bank.

a Prior to 2011, purchasing power parity (PPP) figures are extrapolated from the revised 2011 International Comparison Program (ICP) PPP estimates. For 2012–2016, figures are interpolated from the two ICP reference years 2011 and 2017. For 2017 onward, figures are extrapolated from the 2017 ICP PPPs or imputed based on a regression model.
b For 2005, 2011, and 2017, PPP figures are based on results from the ICP benchmark rounds.

Sources: World Bank. World Development Indicators. http://databank.worldbank.org/data/home.aspx (accessed 8 July 2020). For Taipei,China: for 2000–2010 and 2018–2019, Asian Development Bank estimates using data from economy sources; for 2011–2017, World Bank. DataBank: ICP 2017. https://databank.worldbank.org/source/icp-2017 (accessed 28 July 2020).

Exchange Rates

Table 2.3.14:   Price Level Indexes
(PPPs to official exchange rates, period averages, United States = 100)

ADB Regional Member	2000	2005	2010	2011	2015	2016	2017	2018	2019
Developing ADB Member Economies									
Central and West Asia									
Afghanistan	20.5 (2002)	23.7	31.8	34.8	27.7	25.7	25.3	23.4	21.9
Armenia	23.4	30.1	42.9	43.9	36.2	33.6	32.3	32.4	32.5
Azerbaijan	19.0	23.0	39.1	48.6	36.8	27.0	29.4	32.6	32.0
Georgia	24.2	31.8	42.7	48.1	33.2	31.6	32.1	32.4	30.5
Kazakhstan	15.9	27.1	47.2	56.0	45.3	32.4	37.2	37.5	35.5
Kyrgyz Republic	15.0	20.0	28.5	34.1	26.6	23.9	24.6	24.9	23.9
Pakistan	21.6	22.0	25.4	29.2	31.0	31.0	32.0	30.6	26.3
Tajikistan	13.2	20.0	32.2	33.9	31.1	25.9	26.1	25.0	24.7
Turkmenistan	25.4	29.2	45.2	50.0	47.0	46.1	46.4	45.8	...
Uzbekistan	22.4	16.0	31.9	35.1	41.2	39.8	28.0	22.1	23.7
East Asia									
China, People's Republic of	32.8	34.7	49.2	54.5	62.2	60.0	61.9	63.9	61.1
Hong Kong, China	91.2	70.0	66.2	67.2	75.2	76.4	77.1	77.7	78.2
Korea, Republic of	66.1	77.0	72.7	77.1	75.8	74.0	77.1	79.1	73.8
Mongolia	12.7	18.4	34.9	42.2	36.4	34.1	32.4	33.9	33.5
Taipei,China	69.1	57.2	50.0	51.4	48.5	48.8	51.7	50.6	48.6
South Asia									
Bangladesh	31.4	28.5	32.0	32.9	35.1	36.4	37.6	37.4	37.5
Bhutan	26.6	30.3	33.7	35.1	29.0	28.0	29.5	27.9	...
India	21.2	24.2	32.0	32.4	29.4	29.7	32.0	30.2	29.9
Maldives	27.1	40.7	55.7	53.8	53.9	52.9	53.0	54.5	54.8
Nepal	20.8	21.7	31.2	34.9	30.1	30.1	29.4	31.2	30.1
Sri Lanka	24.8	25.2	34.2	35.5	33.3	31.8	32.4	31.0	28.3
Southeast Asia									
Brunei Darussalam	27.1	34.7	43.9	56.1	49.8	48.2	46.8	51.2	48.1
Cambodia	28.0	27.5	32.4	33.8	34.3	34.5	35.3	35.5	35.9
Indonesia	16.4	20.2	36.7	40.1	32.5	33.9	35.1	33.5	33.6
Lao People's Democratic Republic	17.8	18.5	29.8	33.2	34.6	33.7	33.4	32.7	31.1
Malaysia	31.3	34.0	44.1	47.9	40.1	38.4	38.5	40.3	38.7
Myanmar	20.7	13.6	30.2	33.9	29.2	28.2	27.2	27.5	26.3
Philippines	31.2	28.5	39.4	41.8	41.8	39.9	38.5	37.3	37.6
Singapore	54.4	51.0	62.7	67.3	64.0	63.6	64.2	66.2	64.3
Thailand	27.5	28.2	38.5	40.6	36.9	36.1	37.8	39.4	40.6
Timor-Leste	32.7	33.5	41.0	45.5	45.8	43.2	40.9	39.2	39.8
Viet Nam	19.6	23.2	31.3	33.7	34.2	33.4	33.1	33.1	32.4
The Pacific									
Cook Islands	...	...	...	...	...	...	...	...	...
Fiji	35.6	50.3	46.2	52.9	43.4	44.7	45.4	44.3	43.1
Kiribati	50.3	69.6	88.4	99.2	73.1	71.7	73.2	73.4	69.9
Marshall Islands	91.8	89.6	88.5	93.9	91.3	96.9	97.0	95.0	...
Micronesia, Federated States of	87.2	81.0	88.4	87.9	86.6	89.2	94.0	100.5	...
Nauru	...	...	79.6	98.5	63.4	69.9	79.7	83.0	77.8
Niue	...	...	...	...	...	...	...	...	...
Palau	77.3	74.6	76.2	74.9	88.3	92.7	90.0	85.7	...
Papua New Guinea	45.4	50.3	66.9	78.4	65.6	59.6	61.9	62.7	62.3
Samoa	44.2	53.8	66.5	69.6	69.9	64.8	65.6	64.6	63.6
Solomon Islands	72.9	58.8	70.4	83.4	85.6	87.4	88.1	88.3	86.3
Tonga	56.3	58.9	72.7	79.3	73.9	65.1	66.7	68.0	...
Tuvalu	60.2	85.0	103.3	114.5	88.4	87.3	91.5	91.5	90.9
Vanuatu	65.4	81.1	102.7	112.3	94.9	96.0	98.8	96.6	93.4
Developed ADB Member Economies									
Australia	82.4	104.4	132.4	149.0	122.6	105.5	110.6	112.5	103.0
Japan	143.6	117.5	127.2	134.6	85.5	97.0	93.9	94.7	93.1
New Zealand	63.4	108.1	107.8	117.4	102.9	100.3	103.3	100.3	95.7

... = data not available, ADB = Asian Development Bank, PPP = purchasing power parity.

Sources: World Bank. World Development Indicators. http://databank.worldbank.org/data/home.aspx (accessed 19 August 2020). For Taipei,China: Asian Development Bank estimates using data from economy sources and World Bank. DataBank: ICP 2017. https://databank.worldbank.org/source/icp-2017 (accessed 28 July 2020).

Click on the indictor name in the table header to access the time series in the Key Indicators Database.

IV. Globalization

Globalization focuses on trends in remittances, foreign direct investment (FDI), and merchandise exports. The statistical tables cover balance of payments, external trade, international reserves, capital flows, external indebtedness, and tourism.

Five economies of Asia and the Pacific ranked in the world's top 10 recipients of FDI in 2019

While the region's largest recipient of FDI, the PRC, recorded declining investment inflows in 2019 (compared with 2018), developing Asia remained the largest recipient of global FDI flows in 2019, accounting for 33.5% of the world total.

Five of the region's economies ranked among the world's top 10 recipients of FDI in 2019: The PRC ranked second with $155.8 billion; Singapore ranked third with $105.5 billion; Hong Kong, China ranked sixth with $53.2 billion; India ranked eighth with $50.6 billion; and Australia ranked tenth with $38.6 billion (Figure 2.4.1). The next largest FDI recipients in Asia and the Pacific for 2019 included Japan ($37.2 billion), Indonesia ($24.6 billion), and the Republic of Korea ($10.6 billion) as shown in Figure 2.4.2.

FDI flows to developing Asia are projected to fall between 30% and 45% in 2020 due to measures to mitigate the COVID-19 pandemic. Following the initial economic shock caused by border closures and lockdowns, investment flows in Asia and the Pacific have recovered somewhat. However, the region's high level of FDI related to global value chains leaves developing Asia exposed to negative trends in developed economies (UN 2020).

Figure 2.4.1: Top 10 Economies in Terms of Net Inflows of Foreign Direct Investments, 2019
($ billion)

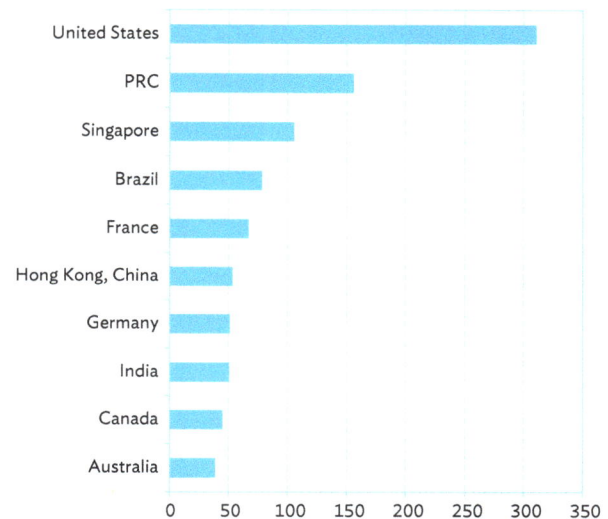

PRC = People's Republic of China.
Source: World Bank. World Development Indicators. http://data.worldbank.org/indicator/BX.KLT.DINV.CD.WD?locations=MH (accessed 22 July 2020).

Click here for figure data

East Asia was the powerhouse for merchandise exports from Asia and the Pacific in 2019

After falling to $5.8 trillion in 2016, merchandise exports from Asia and the Pacific rose to $6.4 trillion in 2017 and $7.0 trillion in 2018, before falling slightly to $6.8 trillion in 2019.

Figure 2.4.2: Top 10 Economies in Asia and the Pacific in Terms of Net Inflows of Foreign Direct Investments, 2019
($ billion)

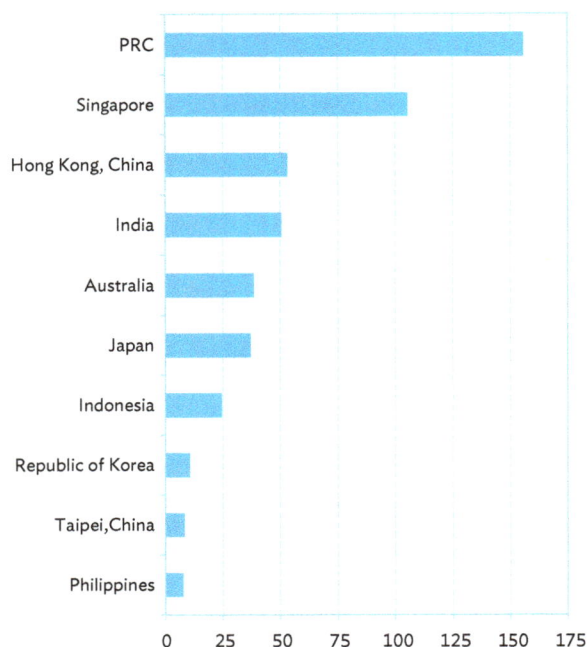

PRC = People's Republic of China.
Source: Table 2.4.6, Key Indicators for Asia and the Pacific 2020.

Click here for figure data

The region's merchandise exports experienced significant growth from 2000 to 2019 (Figure 2.4.3). By subregion, the following average annual growth rates were achieved: South Asia (29.2%), Central and West Asia (21.7%), East Asia (21.1%), the Pacific (18.3%), and Southeast Asia (12.3%), while the three developed ADB member economies averaged 4.3% annual growth. In value terms, merchandise exports from East Asia ($3.9 trillion) exceeded that of all other subregions and the developed economies combined in 2019: Southeast Asia ($1.4 trillion), developed member economies ($1.0 trillion), South Asia ($0.37 trillion), Central and West Asia ($0.14 trillion), and the Pacific ($0.01 trillion).

As a percentage of global merchandise exports, Asia and the Pacific's share increased from 28.4% in 2000 to 36.5% in 2019 (Table 2.4.8).

Figure 2.4.3: Total Merchandise Exports by Subregion within Asia and the Pacific

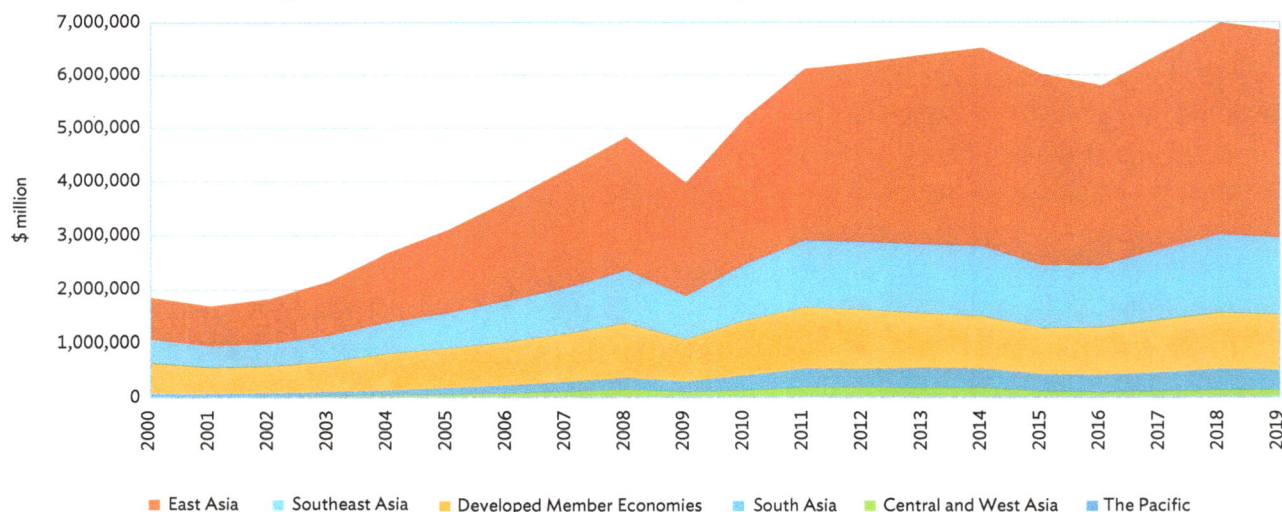

$ = United States dollars.
Source: Table 2.4.8, Key Indicators for Asia and the Pacific 2020.

Click here for figure data

Aggregate remittances to economies in Asia and the Pacific rose for the third consecutive year in 2019, but they are expected to decline in 2020

Remittances provide many families in developing economies with the money needed for food, health care, and other basic needs. ADB estimates that Asia and the Pacific economies face total remittance losses in 2020 ranging from $31.4 billion to $54.3 billion due to the international travel restrictions and economic slowdowns caused by the COVID-19 pandemic (Takenaka et al. 2020).

Aggregate remittances to economies in Asia and the Pacific increased for the third consecutive year in 2019, reaching $317.5 billion (Table 2.4.4). The region's top five recipients of remittances in 2019 were India ($83.1 billion), the PRC ($68.4 billion), the Philippines ($35.2 billion), Pakistan ($22.5 billion), and Bangladesh ($18.3 billion).

As a share of GDP, remittances accounted for at least 10.0% of GDP in 9 of the 44 economies with available data for 2019 (Figure 2.4.4). These were led by Tonga (36.1%), the Kyrgyz Republic (28.5%), and Tajikistan (28.3%). From 2000 (or the earliest year for which data were available) to 2019 (or the latest year for which data were available), remittances as a share of GDP increased in 29 of 44 regional economies. The largest increases were observed in the Kyrgyz Republic (27.9 percentage points), Nepal (24.4 percentage points), and Tajikistan (21.9 percentage points).

Data Issues and Comparability

Most of the data on international transactions presented in this section were taken from balance-of-payments statistics as reported by individual economies. IMF guidelines are followed by most governments in compiling these statistics. However, authorities have difficulty accurately recording

Figure 2.4.4: Total Remittances, Inflows
(% of GDP)

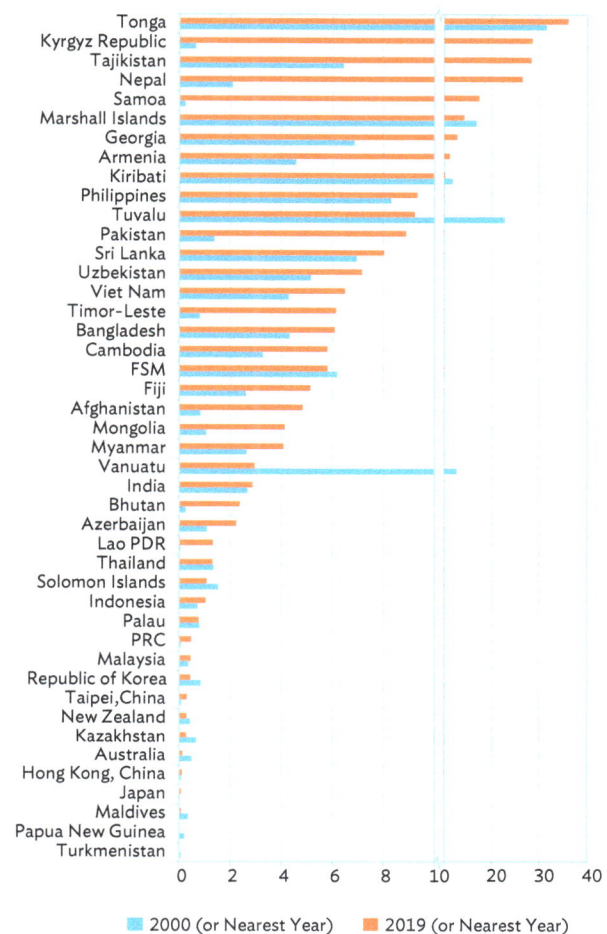

■ 2000 (or Nearest Year)   ■ 2019 (or Nearest Year)

FSM = Federated States of Micronesia, Lao PDR = Lao People's Democratic Republic, PRC = People's Republic of China.
Note: For 2000, includes economies with data from 2000 to 2010; for 2019, from 2017 to 2019.
Source: Table 2.4.5, Key Indicators for Asia and the Pacific 2020.

Click here for figure data

nonofficial transactions such as migrant workers' remittances and private capital flows, which is one of the reasons that the IMF's Balance of Payments Manual (BPM) was updated to the sixth edition (BPM6) in 2009. All economies in the region have adopted BPM6 in recent years except two economies, which still rely on BPM5. However, there is not a single framework for an extended time series available for all economies. Several economies are reporting a mix of BPM5 and BPM6, and two economies are reporting a mix of BPM4 and BPM6. This therefore affects the comparability of data across economies.

The World Trade Organization and other international agencies closely monitor international trade statistics. Common definitions are used by all economies, with the larger economies throughout Asia and the Pacific using standard forms and procedures for data processing.

Data on official development assistance, other official flows, and private direct investment and other private capital are compiled by the Organisation for Economic Co-operation and Development's Development Assistance Committee. These data are standardized on a calendar-year basis for all donors, but may have discrepancies for some economies owing to the fiscal-year data available in budget documents. Commitments from donors do not necessarily translate to actual disbursements to recipient economies of official development assistance.

Table 2.4.1: **Trade in Goods Balance**
(% of GDP)

ADB Regional Member	2000	2005	2010	2014	2015	2016	2017	2018	2019
Developing ADB Member Economies									
Central and West Asia									
Afghanistan[a]	-28.4 (2002)	-65.5		-26.9	-28.7	-32.4	-27.7	-31.9	-31.9	-29.6
Armenia	-24.4	-13.0	-22.3	-17.7	-11.2	-9.0	-11.9	-14.4	-15.0
Azerbaijan	6.1	24.9	37.3	25.2	11.0	11.1	15.0	21.0	17.8
Georgia	-17.5	-19.0	-21.5	-24.3	-26.4	-25.6	-23.5	-23.4	-21.1
Kazakhstan	12.2	18.1	19.3	16.5	6.3	6.7	10.0	14.3	10.7
Kyrgyz Republic[a]	0.3	-17.0		-25.2	-38.1	-34.3	-31.1	-30.9	-36.7	-30.4
Pakistan[a]	-1.8		-3.7	-6.5	-6.8	-6.4	-6.9	-8.5	-9.8	-9.9
Tajikistan[a]	-9.5		-34.1	-43.9	-33.2	-27.7	-27.0	-20.1	-24.3	-23.7
Turkmenistan	...	11.6	9.9	9.5	-5.3	-15.6	-6.3	10.2	4.9
Uzbekistan[b]	3.6	10.1	6.4		-3.9	-2.6	-2.9	-3.7	-13.6	-12.6
East Asia									
China, People's Republic of	2.5	5.4	3.9	4.2	5.2	4.4	3.9	2.8	3.0
Hong Kong, China	11.9	17.1	1.4	-11.1	-7.4	-5.2	-6.7	-8.9	-4.3
Korea, Republic of	2.7	3.5	4.2	5.8	8.2	7.8	7.0	6.4	4.7
Mongolia	-6.4	-3.9	-2.4	1.5	4.8	12.0	13.0	5.2	8.4
Taipei,China	5.8	6.6	8.3	11.3	13.7	13.1	13.8	11.0	9.5
South Asia									
Bangladesh	-4.0	-5.5	-4.5	-3.9	-3.6	-2.9	-3.8	-6.6	-5.1
Bhutan[a]	-15.6	-35.5		-20.5	-22.6	-22.3	-27.6	-21.6	-17.5	-17.9
India[a]	-2.7	-6.3		-7.6	-7.1	-6.2	-4.9	-6.0	-6.6	-5.5
Maldives[a]	-37.4	-42.4	-40.9		-45.0	-40.4	-42.1	-40.4	-45.6	-41.5
Nepal[c]	-14.4	-14.6	-25.5	-30.4	-31.3	-30.3	-33.5	-37.5	-37.1
Sri Lanka[a]	-10.8	-10.3	-8.5		-10.4	-10.4	-10.8	-11.0	-11.7	-9.5
Southeast Asia									
Brunei Darussalam[a]	45.4 (2001)	50.7		45.3	43.5	22.4	18.9	19.8	17.4	16.4
Cambodia[a]	-14.7	-16.1		-23.9	-23.1	-21.9	-19.2	-19.3	-23.8	-26.8
Indonesia	15.2	6.2	4.1	0.8	1.6	1.6	1.9	-0.0	0.3
Lao People's Democratic Republic[a]	-12.5	-12.1	-4.7		-12.8	-14.0	-7.1	-4.7	-4.8	...
Malaysia[a]	22.2		23.9	15.1	10.2	9.3	8.2	8.5	8.2	8.3
Myanmar[a]	-0.1	0.1	0.1		-2.8	-6.1	-5.9	-9.5	-6.3	...
Philippines[a]	-7.1		-11.3	-8.1	-5.8	-7.6	-11.2	-12.2	-14.7	-12.3
Singapore	16.4	37.3	26.4	27.5	30.1	28.5	28.5	27.9	26.3
Thailand	4.3	1.8	7.8	4.2	6.5	8.7	7.1	4.4	4.9
Timor-Leste[a]	...	-22.9 (2006)	-31.8		-41.7	-39.8	-33.0	-38.2	-37.5	...
Viet Nam[a]	1.2	-4.2	-4.4		6.5	3.8	5.4	4.8	6.7	8.2
The Pacific									
Cook Islands	...	...	-25.2	-36.4	-43.3	-44.9	-46.3	-43.6	...
Fiji[a]	-14.0		-23.0	-23.5	-21.2	-19.5	-20.2	-20.4	-24.4	...
Kiribati[a]	-52.2	-62.8		-40.9	-52.2	-52.4	-53.5	-52.4	-46.7	...
Marshall Islands	-52.2	-36.4	-49.4	-30.2	-28.6	-24.6	-25.6	-28.6	...
Micronesia, Federated States of	-38.1	-42.8	-43.2	-36.8	-40.4	-33.2	-32.8	-32.0	...
Nauru	...	...	33.6 (2012)	-27.1	-47.9	-21.1	-30.8	-40.8	-47.0
Niue	...	-33.4 (2007)	-60.3	-42.1	-40.2	-35.7	-43.6	-41.4	...
Palau	-79.0	-49.6	-45.7	-62.3	-49.1	-45.3	-48.5	-48.4	-51.7
Papua New Guinea[d]	31.4		36.8	15.5	22.6	27.0	28.3	29.8	29.1	30.9
Samoa[a]	-107.5		-28.4	-35.0	-40.4	-35.0	-35.3	-36.3	-37.5	-39.6
Solomon Islands[a]	-3.8	-3.1		-15.1	-0.4	-1.3	1.0	0.5	0.2	-2.5
Tonga[b]	-44.3	-66.3	-53.0		-57.0	-70.4	-71.9	-74.5	-80.5	-83.5
Tuvalu[b]	-64.9	-40.1 (2006)	-54.3		-47.0	-121.0	-61.0	-61.0	...	...
Vanuatu[a]	-18.2	-23.3	-27.1		-25.3	-35.6	-33.6	-29.1	...	...
Developed ADB Member Economies									
Australia	-1.9	-2.6	-0.7	0.6	-0.8	-1.7	0.8	0.7	2.7
Japan	2.4	2.2	1.9	-2.0	-0.2	1.0	0.9	0.2	0.1
New Zealand	1.6	-3.0	1.4	-0.2	-1.0	-1.1	-1.0	-1.5	...

... = data not available, | = marks break in series due to change in compilation methodology, -0.0 = magnitude is less than half of unit employed, ADB = Asian Development Bank, GDP = gross domestic product.

a Change in compilation methodology from the International Monetary Fund's Balance of Payments Manual (fifth edition) [BPM5] to the International Monetary Fund's Balance of Payments and International Investment Position Manual (sixth edition) [BPM6].
b Change in compilation methodology from BPM4 to BPM6.
c Based on BPM5.
d Change in compilation methodology from BPM4 to BPM5.

Sources: Economy sources.

Click on the indictor name in the table header to access the time series in the Key Indicators Database.

Balance of Payments

Table 2.4.2: **Trade in Services Balance**
(% of GDP)

ADB Regional Member	2000	2005	2010	2014	2015	2016	2017	2018	2019
Developing ADB Member Economies									
Central and West Asia									
Afghanistan[a]	-3.6 (2002)	-8.2 |	6.0	-0.7	-1.8	-3.3	-4.7	-3.6	-3.2
Armenia	-3.4	-3.0	-2.8	-1.0	-0.9	-0.7	-0.3	-1.3	0.6
Azerbaijan	-4.3	-14.9	-3.3	-8.1	-8.0	-8.3	-8.3	-4.4	-5.4
Georgia	2.4	1.6	4.5	7.4	9.4	10.4	12.5	12.7	12.2
Kazakhstan	-5.3	-9.5	-4.9	-3.1	-2.6	-2.7	-2.1	-2.6	-2.0
Kyrgyz Republic[a]	-12.2	-4.9 |	-4.2	-4.4	-3.1	-3.0	-1.2	-1.6	2.1
Pakistan[a]	-3.5 |	-2.8	-1.0	-1.1	-1.1	-1.3	-1.5	-2.0	-1.8
Tajikistan[a]	-1.7 |	-4.6	-0.5	-3.1	-2.5	-2.0	-1.6	-2.8	-3.0
Turkmenistan	...	...	...	...	...	...	...	...	...
Uzbekistan[b]	-0.5	-1.1	-1.2 |	-0.7	-0.9	-1.9	-3.1	-4.8	-3.9
East Asia									
China, People's Republic of	-0.1	0.0	-0.2	-2.0	-2.0	-2.1	-2.1	-2.1	-1.8
Hong Kong, China	-7.5	-4.9	4.4	11.3	9.8	7.5	7.7	8.7	6.1
Korea, Republic of	-0.1	-1.0	-1.2	-0.2	-1.0	-1.2	-2.3	-1.7	-1.4
Mongolia	-7.5	0.5	-4.2	-10.5	-6.1	-12.0	-10.6	-15.1	-14.4
Taipei,China	-3.8	-3.8	-2.5	-2.1	-2.0	-1.9	-1.5	-1.1	-0.8
South Asia									
Bangladesh	-1.4	-1.5	-1.1	-2.4	-1.6	-1.2	-1.3	-1.6	-1.2
Bhutan[a]	-1.8	-4.9 |	-4.6	-3.4	-3.5	-2.8	-2.2	-1.6	...
India[a]	0.4	2.8 |	2.6	3.7	3.2	3.0	3.0	3.0	2.9
Maldives[a]	33.4	6.8	34.8 |	59.6	49.4	40.8	36.4	35.8	...
Nepal[c]	7.2	-0.4	-1.3	1.1	1.3	0.4	0.1	0.1	-0.5
Sri Lanka[a]	0.2	1.4	1.2 |	2.4	2.9	3.5	3.8	4.3	3.4
Southeast Asia									
Brunei Darussalam[a]	11.0 (2001)	0.6 |	-5.9	-9.5	-7.8	-9.8	-5.7	-7.4	-8.8
Cambodia[a]	-0.6	2.9 |	9.0	10.3	9.5	8.0	8.4	9.8	10.6
Indonesia	-11.1	-3.2	-1.3	-1.1	-1.0	-0.8	-0.7	-0.6	-0.7
Lao People's Democratic Republic[a]	5.1	2.5	2.4 |	-2.9	-1.6	-1.2	-2.0	-1.3	...
Malaysia[a]	-11.1 |	-2.0	0.8	-1.0	-1.8	-1.5	-1.7	-1.2	-0.7
Myanmar[d]	-0.0	-0.1	-0.0 |	1.4	2.2	2.1	1.5	1.8	...
Philippines[a]	-2.2 |	2.0	2.8	1.5	1.8	2.2	2.6	3.3	3.5
Singapore	-4.1	-7.4	-0.1	-4.1	-2.8	-2.2	-3.1	0.6	1.5
Thailand	3.7	-3.6	-2.1	1.6	3.9	4.9	5.3	4.4	4.3
Timor-Leste[a]	...	-63.4 (2006)	-107.7 |	-41.0	-36.5	-34.3	-21.3	-22.3	...
Viet Nam[a]	-1.8	-0.5	-2.1 |	-2.1	-2.5	-2.1	-1.8	-1.6	-0.9
The Pacific									
Cook Islands	...	...	41.4	52.1	62.5	70.8	73.4	71.7	...
Fiji[a]	7.1 |	9.4	14.7	14.8	16.0	16.3	15.5	16.7	...
Kiribati[a]	-27.4	-30.3 |	-25.4	-37.1	-39.4	-36.8	-35.7	-30.1	...
Marshall Islands	-19.9	-20.6	-19.9	-18.0	-18.0	-16.6	-19.0	-17.2	...
Micronesia, Federated States of	-16.5	-16.3	-15.2	-5.4	-10.8	-12.1	-8.3	2.1	...
Nauru	...	...	-13.5 (2012)	-23.5	-15.9	-21.5	-15.6	-12.5	-12.5
Niue	...	-17.5 (2007)	-40.5	8.4	13.0	13.6	16.5	21.1	...
Palau	13.5	16.4	19.1	32.1	32.5	25.9	21.4	19.2	16.1
Papua New Guinea[d]	-21.2 |	-17.8	-17.2	-9.0	-5.4	-4.6	-5.7	-5.1	-4.9
Samoa[a]	44.1 |	15.6	10.4	15.8	15.8	15.1	18.6	20.5	20.1
Solomon Islands[a]	-8.2	1.2 |	-10.6	-8.3	-5.8	-6.6	-6.0	...	...
Tonga[b]	1.7	-7.4	-2.1 |	-0.7	1.2	4.1	5.8	6.7	6.3
Tuvalu[b]	-51.2	5.6 (2006)	-4.1 |	-74.0	-95.0	-74.0	-80.0	...	...
Vanuatu[a]	17.1	14.9	17.6 |	23.1	13.7	22.4	22.1	...	...
Developed ADB Member Economies									
Australia	-0.2	-0.2	-0.3	-1.1	-0.7	-0.6	-0.2	-0.3	-0.2
Japan	-1.0	-0.8	-0.5	-0.6	-0.4	-0.2	-0.1	-0.2	0.0
New Zealand	1.4	1.5	0.9	1.0	2.0	2.0	2.1	1.5	...

... = data not available, | = marks break in series due to change in compilation methodology, -0.0 or 0.0 = magnitude is less than half of unit employed, ADB = Asian Development Bank, GDP = gross domestic product.

a Change in compilation methodology from the International Monetary Fund's Balance of Payments Manual (fifth edition) [BPM5] to the International Monetary Fund's Balance of Payments and International Investment Position Manual (sixth edition) [BPM6].
b Change in compilation methodology from BPM4 to BPM6.
c Based on BPM5.
d Change in compilation methodology from BPM4 to BPM5.

Sources: Economy sources.

Click on the indictor name in the table header to access the time series in the Key Indicators Database.

Table 2.4.3:   **Current Account Balance**
(% of GDP)

ADB Regional Member	2000	2005	2010	2014	2015	2016	2017	2018	2019
Developing ADB Member Economies									
Central and West Asia									
Afghanistan[a]	-3.5 (2002)	-2.7 |	-4.6	-15.2	-20.3	-12.4	-17.7	-21.7	-21.2
Armenia	-15.8	-2.5	-13.6	-7.8	-2.7	-2.1	-3.0	-9.4	-8.2
Azerbaijan	-3.2	1.3	28.4	13.9	-0.4	-3.6	4.1	12.9	9.1
Georgia	-5.8	-10.9	-9.8	-10.1	-11.8	-12.5	-8.0	-6.8	-5.1
Kazakhstan	2.0	-1.8	0.9	2.8	-3.3	-5.9	-3.1	-0.1	-3.6
Kyrgyz Republic[a]	-5.5	-1.4 |	-6.5	-17.1	-16.4	-11.5	-6.3	-12.1	-9.9
Pakistan[a]	-0.3 |	-1.3	-2.2	-1.3	-1.0	-1.8	-4.0	-6.1	-4.8
Tajikistan[a]	-7.2 |	-12.8	-10.3	-3.4	-5.8	-4.2	2.1	-4.9	-2.3
Turkmenistan	8.2	5.1	-12.9	-6.1	-15.6	-20.2	-10.4	5.5	5.1
Uzbekistan[b]	1.6	13.5	5.1 |	3.3	1.3	0.4	2.5	-7.1	-5.6
East Asia									
China, People's Republic of	1.7	5.8	3.9	2.3	2.7	1.8	1.6	0.2	1.0
Hong Kong, China	4.4	11.9	7.0	1.4	3.3	4.0	4.6	3.7	6.2
Korea, Republic of	1.8	1.3	2.4	5.6	7.2	6.5	4.6	4.5	3.7
Mongolia	-6.1	3.5	-12.3	-15.8	-8.1	-6.3	-10.1	-16.8	-15.6
Taipei,China	2.5	4.0	8.3	11.3	13.6	13.1	14.1	11.6	10.5
South Asia									
Bangladesh	-0.9	-1.0	3.7	0.8	1.8	1.9	-0.5	-3.5	-1.7
Bhutan[a]	-9.4	-33.5 |	-24.3	-28.2	-28.6	-32.2	-25.1	-19.5	-23.7
India[a]	-0.6	-1.2 |	-2.9	-1.3	-1.1	-0.6	-1.8	-2.1	-0.9
Maldives[a]	-8.2	-23.5	-13.8 |	-3.2	-7.4	-23.7	-21.7	-28.3	-26.0
Nepal[c]	-2.2	2.0	-2.3	4.6	5.1	6.2	-0.4	-8.2	-7.7
Sri Lanka[a]	-6.4	-2.7	-1.9 |	-2.5	-2.3	-2.1	-2.6	-3.2	-2.2
Southeast Asia									
Brunei Darussalam[a]	51.5 (2001)	47.3 |	36.5	30.7	16.6	12.9	16.4	6.9	6.6
Cambodia[a]	-2.7	-3.6 |	-8.7	-8.6	-8.9	-8.7	-8.1	-12.2	-15.5
Indonesia	4.8	0.1	0.7	-3.1	-2.0	-1.8	-1.6	-2.9	-2.7
Lao People's Democratic Republic[a]	-0.3	-7.1	0.4 |	-14.5	-15.7	-8.7	-7.4	-7.9	...
Malaysia[a]	9.0 |	14.4	10.1	4.4	3.0	2.4	2.8	2.1	3.3
Myanmar[a]	-0.1	0.0	0.0 |	-3.6	-4.9	-3.0	-7.9	-3.6	...
Philippines[a]	-2.7 |	1.9	3.4	3.6	2.4	-0.4	-0.7	-2.5	-0.1
Singapore	11.1	23.3	22.9	18.0	18.7	17.6	16.3	17.2	17.0
Thailand	7.4	-4.0	3.4	2.9	6.9	10.5	9.6	5.6	7.0
Timor-Leste[a]	...	119.8 (2006)	180.2 |	75.6	12.8	-32.9	-17.6	-12.2	...
Viet Nam[a]	4.2	-1.0	-3.7 |	4.6	-1.1	0.3	-0.7	2.4	5.0
The Pacific									
Cook Islands	...	...	15.5	18.2	29.4	36.4	35.9	32.6	...
Fiji[a]	-1.6 |	-11.0	-7.1	-6.1	-3.5	-3.6	-6.7	-8.5	...
Kiribati[a]	-3.2	-32.4 |	0.1	31.3	32.8	10.5	37.6	39.2	...
Marshall Islands	-10.8	7.8	-14.8	3.4	17.2	16.1	7.5	6.5	...
Micronesia, Federated States of	-14.7	-10.1	-17.5	6.1	4.5	7.2	10.3	21.0	...
Nauru	...	...	38.1 (2012)	-13.5	-18.5	2.0	12.7	-4.6	5.0
Niue	...	-8.0 (2007)	-53.9	8.2	11.1	17.6	14.9	15.7	...
Palau	-49.3	-23.1	-8.9	-17.8	-8.7	-13.5	-18.8	-15.9	-26.7
Papua New Guinea[d]	10.1 |	13.3	-4.4	12.4	20.2	24.0	23.1	23.0	22.3
Samoa[a]	-2.9	-6.0	-8.4	-5.9	-1.6	-5.0	-1.3	2.9	1.9
Solomon Islands[a]	-6.0	-1.1 |	-16.0	-3.7	-2.7	-3.9	-4.1	-3.3	-8.9
Tonga[b]	-8.4	-4.3	-8.7 |	-9.2	-9.0	5.0	7.0	4.4	-0.5
Tuvalu[b]	54.5	-1.3 (2006)	-3.8 |	3.0	-53.0	23.0	6.0	...	...
Vanuatu[a]	-5.0	-3.5	-5.8 |	6.2	-1.6	0.8	-6.4	...	...
Developed ADB Member Economies									
Australia	-5.1	-6.6	-5.0	-3.2	-3.7	-4.7	-2.2	-2.8	-0.7
Japan	2.7	3.6	3.9	0.8	3.1	4.0	4.2	3.5	3.6
New Zealand	-2.3	-7.8	-2.8	-3.4	-2.4	-2.5	-2.8	-3.6	...

... = data not available, | = marks break in series due to change in compilation methodology, 0.0 = magnitude is less than half of unit employed, ADB = Asian Development Bank, GDP = gross domestic product.

a Change in compilation methodology from the International Monetary Fund's Balance of Payments Manual (fifth edition) [BPM5] to the International Monetary Fund's Balance of Payments and International Investment Position Manual (sixth edition) [BPM6].
b Change in compilation methodology from BPM4 to BPM6.
c Based on BPM5.
d Change in compilation methodology from BPM4 to BPM5.

Sources: Economy sources.

Click on the indictor name in the table header to access the time series in the Key Indicators Database.

Balance of Payments

Table 2.4.4:   Total Remittances, Inflows[a]
($ million)

ADB Regional Member	2000	2005	2010	2014	2015	2016	2017	2018	2019
Developing ADB Member Economies									
Central and West Asia[b]	**1,565**	**7,106**	**20,737**	**35,120**	**31,193**	**30,699**	**34,018**	**35,926**	**37,603**
Afghanistan	...	...	378	253	349	628	1,084	804	868
Armenia	87	915	1,669	2,079	1,491	1,382	1,539	1,488	1,528
Azerbaijan	57	623	1,410	1,846	1,270	643	1,133	1,226	1,077
Georgia	210	446	1,184	1,986	1,459	1,521	1,794	2,034	2,258
Kazakhstan	122	62	226	401	294	384	560	618	506
Kyrgyz Republic	9	313	1,266	2,243	1,688	1,995	2,486	2,689	2,410
Pakistan	1,080	4,280	9,690	17,244	19,306	19,808	19,807	21,193	22,507
Tajikistan	79 (2002)	467	2,021	3,384	2,259	1,867	2,237	2,183	2,298
Turkmenistan	...	14 (2006)	35	30	16	9	4	2	1
Uzbekistan	...	898 (2006)	2,858	5,653	3,062	2,462	3,374	3,689	4,150
East Asia	**6,042**	**29,601**	**59,419**	**70,393**	**71,964**	**69,180**	**72,295**	**76,904**	**78,641**
China, People's Republic of	758	23,626	52,460	62,332	63,938	61,000	63,876	67,414	68,398
Hong Kong, China	136	297	340	372	387	399	437	425	447
Korea, Republic of	4,862	5,178	5,854	6,574	6,464	6,524	6,526	7,125	7,374
Mongolia	12	177	266	255	261	260	273	441	575
Taipei,China	274	323	500	860	915	997	1,183	1,500	1,846
South Asia[b]	**16,092**	**29,957**	**71,929**	**98,319**	**97,958**	**90,231**	**96,635**	**109,752**	**116,406**
Bangladesh	1,969	4,642	10,850	14,988	15,296	13,574	13,502	15,562	18,348
Bhutan	...	2 (2006)	8	14	20	34	43	58	47
India	12,845	22,125	53,480	70,389	68,910	62,744	68,967	78,790	83,131
Maldives	2	2	3	3	4	4	4	4	4
Nepal	112	1,212	3,464	5,889	6,730	6,612	6,928	8,294	8,128
Sri Lanka	1,163	1,976	4,123	7,036	7,000	7,262	7,190	7,043	6,747
Southeast Asia[b]	**11,752**	**24,900**	**43,120**	**60,544**	**63,438**	**65,738**	**69,371**	**74,782**	**77,366**
Brunei Darussalam	...	...	...	...	...	...	...	...	...
Cambodia	121	164	557	1,103	1,185	1,200	1,295	1,433	1,575
Indonesia	1,190	5,420	6,916	8,551	9,659	8,907	8,990	11,215	11,667
Lao People's Democratic Republic	1	1	42	188	189	189	243	239	285
Malaysia	342	1,117	1,103	1,580	1,644	1,604	1,649	1,686	1,659
Myanmar	102	129	115	1,864	2,005	2,346	2,578	2,840	2,840
Philippines	6,957	13,733	21,557	28,691	29,799	31,142	32,810	33,809	35,167
Singapore	...	...	...	...	...	...	...	...	...
Thailand	1,700	1,187	4,433	6,524	5,895	6,270	6,720	7,463	7,075
Timor-Leste	...	4 (2006)	137	44	62	80	87	96	98
Viet Nam	1,340	3,150	8,260	12,000	13,000	14,000	15,000	16,000	17,000
The Pacific[b]	**...**	**403**	**479**	**642**	**729**	**703**	**693**	**755**	**756**
Cook Islands	...	...	...	...	...	...	...	...	...
Fiji	44	203	176	221	251	269	274	285	288
Kiribati	...	13 (2006)	16	16	14	16	18	20	20
Marshall Islands	...	24	22	26	27	28	30	31	31
Micronesia, Federated States of	...	...	18	23	23	23	23	23	23
Nauru	...	...	...	...	...	...	...	...	...
Niue	...	...	...	...	...	...	...	...	...
Palau	...	1	2	2	2	2	2	2	2
Papua New Guinea	7	7	4	10	4	3	4	4	3
Samoa	...	82	139	139	130	130	136	147	147
Solomon Islands	4	7	14	16	19	20	16	19	19
Tonga	53 (2001)	69	74	119	150	126	159	183	183
Tuvalu	...	5	4	4	4	4	4	4	4
Vanuatu	35	5	12	64	104	81	26	35	35
Developed ADB Member Economies	**3,514**	**2,197**	**3,919**	**6,488**	**5,920**	**6,307**	**7,058**	**6,846**	**6,693**
Australia	1,904	940	1,864	2,292	2,175	2,057	2,002	1,861	1,727
Japan	1,374	905	1,684	3,734	3,325	3,830	4,443	4,366	4,380
New Zealand	236	352	371	462	421	420	613	619	585
DEVELOPING ADB MEMBER ECONOMIES[b]	**35,541**	**91,968**	**195,685**	**265,019**	**265,283**	**256,551**	**273,012**	**298,118**	**310,772**
ALL ADB REGIONAL MEMBERS[b]	**39,055**	**94,165**	**199,604**	**271,507**	**271,203**	**262,858**	**280,071**	**304,964**	**317,465**
WORLD[b]	**126,750**	**288,121**	**474,839**	**611,596**	**602,849**	**597,332**	**643,270**	**694,479**	**714,249**

... = data not available, $ = United States dollars, ADB = Asian Development Bank.

a For 2000, figures are based on the International Monetary Fund's Balance of Payments Manual (fifth edition). For 2005 onward, figures are based on the International Monetary Fund's Balance of Payments and International Investment Position Manual (sixth edition).
b Includes only reporting economies with data corresponding to the year heading.

Source: World Bank. Migration and Remittances Data. http://www.worldbank.org/en/topic/migrationremittancesdiasporaissues/brief/migration-remittances-data (accessed 30 June 2020). For Taipei,China: Central bank of Taipei,China. https://www.cbc.gov.tw/ct.asp?xItem=1061&ctNode=535&mp=2 (accessed 30 June 2020).

Table 2.4.5: Total Remittances, Inflows
(% of GDP)

ADB Regional Member	2000	2005	2010	2014	2015	2016	2017	2018	2019
Developing ADB Member Economies									
Central and West Asia[a]	**1.4**	**3.4**	**4.2**	**4.8**	**4.6**	**4.9**	**5.1**	**5.4**	**5.8**
Afghanistan	...	...	2.4	1.2	1.7	3.5	5.8	4.5	4.9
Armenia	4.6	18.7	18.0	17.9	14.1	13.1	13.3	11.9	11.2
Azerbaijan	1.1	4.7	2.7	2.5	2.4	1.7	2.8	2.6	2.2
Georgia	6.9	7.0	9.7	11.3	9.8	10.0	11.0	11.6	12.7
Kazakhstan	0.7	0.1	0.2	0.2	0.2	0.3	0.3	0.3	0.3
Kyrgyz Republic	0.6	12.7	26.4	30.0	25.3	29.3	32.3	32.5	28.5
Pakistan	1.4	3.6	5.6	6.9	7.2	7.1	6.5	7.5	8.9
Tajikistan	6.4 (2002)	20.2	35.8	36.6	27.3	26.7	29.7	28.1	28.3
Turkmenistan	...	0.1 (2006)	0.2	0.1	0.0	0.0	0.0	0.0	0.0
Uzbekistan	...	5.2 (2006)	6.1	7.4	3.7	3.0	5.7	7.3	7.2
East Asia	**0.3**	**0.8**	**0.8**	**0.5**	**0.5**	**0.5**	**0.5**	**0.5**	**0.5**
China, People's Republic of	0.1	1.0	0.9	0.6	0.6	0.5	0.5	0.5	0.5
Hong Kong, China	0.1	0.2	0.1	0.1	0.1	0.1	0.1	0.1	0.1
Korea, Republic of	0.8	0.6	0.5	0.4	0.4	0.4	0.4	0.4	0.4
Mongolia	1.1	7.0	3.7	2.1	2.2	2.3	2.4	3.4	4.2
Taipei,China	0.1	0.1	0.1	0.2	0.2	0.2	0.2	0.2	0.3
South Asia[a]	**3.0**	**3.3**	**3.9**	**4.2**	**4.0**	**3.4**	**3.2**	**3.5**	**3.5**
Bangladesh	4.3	8.1	9.5	8.7	7.9	6.1	5.5	5.8	6.1
Bhutan	...	0.3 (2006)	0.5	0.7	1.0	1.6	1.8	2.4	...
India	2.7	2.7	3.2	3.4	3.2	2.7	2.6	2.8	2.9
Maldives	0.4	0.2	0.1	0.1	0.1	0.1	0.1	0.1	...
Nepal	2.1	14.7	21.3	29.2	32.4	31.5	27.1	29.7	26.5
Sri Lanka	7.0	8.1	7.3	8.9	8.7	8.8	8.2	8.0	8.0
Southeast Asia[a]	**2.3**	**3.1**	**2.5**	**2.7**	**2.9**	**2.9**	**2.8**	**2.9**	**2.8**
Brunei Darussalam	...	...	...	...	...	...	...	...	...
Cambodia	3.3	2.6	5.0	6.6	6.6	6.0	5.8	5.8	5.8
Indonesia	0.7	1.9	0.9	1.0	1.1	1.0	0.9	1.1	1.0
Lao People's Democratic Republic	0.0	0.0	0.6	1.4	1.3	1.2	1.4	1.3	...
Malaysia	0.4	0.8	0.4	0.5	0.5	0.5	0.5	0.5	0.5
Myanmar	...	...	...	2.8	3.2	3.9	4.2	4.4	4.1
Philippines	8.3	12.8	10.3	9.6	9.7	9.8	10.0	9.7	9.3
Singapore	...	...	...	...	...	...	...	...	...
Thailand	1.3	0.6	1.3	1.6	1.5	1.5	1.5	1.5	1.3
Timor-Leste	...	0.8 (2006)	15.6	3.0	3.9	4.8	5.4	6.1	...
Viet Nam	4.3	5.5	7.1	6.4	6.7	6.8	6.7	6.5	6.5
The Pacific[a]	**...**	**4.1**	**2.3**	**2.0**	**2.4**	**2.3**	**2.1**	**2.4**	**...**
Cook Islands	...	...	...	...	...	...	...	...	...
Fiji	2.6	6.8	5.6	4.5	5.4	5.5	5.1	5.1	...
Kiribati	...	11.8 (2006)	10.0	9.1	8.2	9.1	9.6	10.2	...
Marshall Islands	...	16.7	13.7	14.1	14.8	14.1	14.3	14.2	...
Micronesia, Federated States of	...	...	6.1	7.3	7.4	7.0	6.4	5.8	...
Nauru	...	...	...	...	...	...	...	...	...
Niue	...	...	...	...	...	...	...	...	...
Palau	...	0.8	0.9	0.9	0.8	0.8	0.8	0.8	0.8
Papua New Guinea	0.2	0.1	0.0	0.0	0.0	0.0	0.0	0.0	0.0
Samoa	...	18.8	20.0	17.7	16.6	15.8	16.4	17.7	17.4
Solomon Islands	1.5	1.3	1.6	1.2	1.4	1.5	1.1	...	...
Tonga	31.5 (2001)	26.4	19.9	27.6	37.2	30.0	34.4	38.2	36.1
Tuvalu	...	22.7	12.5	11.0	11.6	10.3	9.2	...	...
Vanuatu	12.7	1.3	1.7	7.9	13.7	10.0	3.0	...	...
Developed ADB Member Economies[a]	**0.1**	**0.0**	**0.1**	**0.1**	**0.1**	**0.1**	**0.1**	**0.1**	**0.1**
Australia	0.5	0.1	0.2	0.2	0.2	0.2	0.1	0.1	0.1
Japan	0.0	0.0	0.0	0.1	0.1	0.1	0.1	0.1	0.1
New Zealand	0.4	0.3	0.3	0.2	0.2	0.2	0.3	0.3	...
DEVELOPING ADB MEMBER ECONOMIES[a]	**1.0**	**1.6**	**1.6**	**1.5**	**1.4**	**1.3**	**1.3**	**1.3**	**1.3**
ALL ADB REGIONAL MEMBERS[a]	**0.4**	**0.8**	**1.0**	**1.1**	**1.1**	**1.0**	**1.0**	**1.0**	**1.1**

... = data not available, 0.0 = magnitude is less than half of unit employed, ADB = Asian Development Bank, GDP = gross domestic product.

a Aggregate percentages calculated using only reporting economies with data available for both remittances and GDP in the years specified in the column headings.

Sources: Economy sources; and World Bank. Migration and Remittances Data. http://www.worldbank.org/en/topic/migrationremittancesdiasporaissues/brief/migration-remittances-data (accessed 30 June 2020). For Taipei,China: Central bank of Taipei,China. https://www.cbc.gov.tw/ct.asp?xItem=1061&ctNode=535&mp=2 (accessed 30 June 2020).

Table 2.4.6:   Foreign Direct Investment, Net Inflows
($ million)

ADB Regional Member	2000	2005	2010	2014	2015	2016	2017	2018	2019
Developing ADB Member Economies									
Central and West Asia[a]	**2,271**	**10,946**	**20,308**	**21,220**	**20,069**	**31,147**	**16,243**	**7,921**	**11,356**
Afghanistan	0	271	191	43	169	94	52	119	23
Armenia	104	292	529	407	184	334	251	254	254
Azerbaijan	130	4,476	3,353	4,430	4,048	4,500	2,867	1,403	1,504
Georgia	131	453	921	1,837	1,735	1,656	1,902	1,219	1,269
Kazakhstan	1,371	2,546	7,456	7,308	6,578	17,221	4,713	214	3,588
Kyrgyz Republic	-2	43	473	343	1,144	619	-107	144	...
Pakistan	308	2,201	2,022	1,887	1,673	2,576	2,496	1,737	2,218
Tajikistan	24	54	94	327	454	242	186	221	213
Turkmenistan	131	418	3,632	3,830	3,043	2,243	2,086	1,985	...
Uzbekistan	75	192	1,636	809	1,041	1,663	1,797	625	2,286
East Asia	**129,082**	**160,528**	**340,093**	**410,384**	**430,126**	**325,218**	**314,499**	**353,533**	**230,241**
China, People's Republic of	42,095	104,109	243,703	268,097	242,489	174,750	166,084	235,365	155,815
Hong Kong, China	70,496	40,963	82,709	129,847	181,047	133,259	125,717	97,036	53,171
Korea, Republic of	11,509	13,643	9,497	9,274	4,104	12,104	17,913	12,183	10,566
Mongolia	54	188	1,691	338	94	-4,156	1,494	1,952	2,443
Taipei,China	4,928	1,625	2,492	2,828	2,391	9,261	3,291	6,998	8,245
South Asia[a]	**4,059**	**8,417**	**29,486**	**38,397**	**47,877**	**48,263**	**43,787**	**47,278**	**...**
Bangladesh	280	813	1,232	2,539	2,831	2,333	1,810	2,940	1,597
Bhutan	2 (2002)	6	75	24	6	12	-17	3	13
India	3,584	7,269	27,397	34,577	44,009	44,459	39,966	42,117	50,605
Maldives	22	53	216	333	298	457	458	539	...
Nepal	-0	2	88	30	52	106	196	68	...
Sri Lanka	173	272	478	894	680	897	1,373	1,611	...
Southeast Asia[a]	**21,860**	**44,229**	**108,413**	**129,852**	**132,976**	**118,967**	**169,189**	**163,557**	**...**
Brunei Darussalam	550	175	481	568	171	-151	468	516	373
Cambodia	118	379	1,404	1,853	1,823	2,476	2,788	3,213	3,706
Indonesia	-4,550	8,336	15,292	25,121	19,779	4,542	20,510	18,910	24,582
Lao People's Democratic Republic	34	28	279	868	1,078	935	1,693	1,320	...
Malaysia	3,788	3,925	10,886	10,619	9,857	13,470	9,368	8,570	...
Myanmar	255	235	901	2,175	4,084	3,278	4,002	1,291	...
Philippines	1,487	1,664	1,070	5,740	5,639	8,280	10,256	9,949	7,647
Singapore	15,515	19,316	55,322	68,698	69,775	70,721	97,766	91,036	105,466
Thailand	3,366	8,216	14,747	4,975	8,928	2,810	8,229	13,205	6,316
Timor-Leste	1 (2002)	1	30	34	43	5	7	48	75
Viet Nam	1,298	1,954	8,000	9,200	11,800	12,600	14,100	15,500	...
The Pacific[a]	**133**	**247**	**433**	**550**	**545**	**535**	**668**	**1,728**	**...**
Cook Islands	...	...	...	...	...	...	...	...	...
Fiji	1	173	178	378	205	392	388	469	323
Kiribati	1	3	-7	3	-1	2	1	-1	...
Marshall Islands	1	3	-9	9	-5	-3	6	10	...
Micronesia, Federated States of	-0 (2001)	0	0	20	1	...	...	...	...
Nauru	1	1	0	0	0	0	0	0	...
Niue	...	...	...	...	...	...	...	...	...
Palau	3	4	3	40	35	35	27	22	...
Papua New Guinea	96	40	36	29	214	19	161	1,135	...
Samoa	-1	4	-1	23	27	3	9	17	...
Solomon Islands	2	1	166	21	32	37	43	25	30
Tonga	9	6	5	13	6	6	-6	15	1
Tuvalu	-0 (2001)	-0	0	0	0	0	0	0	...
Vanuatu	20	13	63	13	31	44	38	38	...
Developed ADB Member Economies	**24,073**	**-17,727**	**42,938**	**86,197**	**52,072**	**85,810**	**68,437**	**88,908**	**79,732**
Australia	14,893	-25,093	35,211	63,195	46,893	42,981	47,541	62,173	38,606
Japan	10,688	5,460	7,441	19,752	5,252	40,954	18,802	24,606	37,177
New Zealand	-1,508	1,907	286	3,249	-73	1,875	2,094	2,129	3,949
DEVELOPING ADB MEMBER ECONOMIES[a]	**157,406**	**224,367**	**498,733**	**600,403**	**631,593**	**524,129**	**544,386**	**574,017**	**442,330**
ALL ADB REGIONAL MEMBERS[a]	**181,479**	**206,640**	**541,671**	**686,599**	**683,665**	**609,939**	**612,823**	**662,925**	**522,061**
WORLD[a]	**1,569,119**	**1,563,482**	**1,916,740**	**1,942,619**	**2,675,558**	**2,672,992**	**2,065,300**	**1,350,143**	**1,321,823**

... = data not available, -0 or 0 = magnitude is less than half of unit employed, $ = United States dollars, ADB = Asian Development Bank.

a   Includes only reporting economies with data corresponding to the year heading.

Sources: World Bank. World Development Indicators. http://data.worldbank.org/indicator/BX.KLT.DINV.CD.WD?locations=MH (accessed 22 July 2020). For Taipei,China: Central bank of Taipei,China. https://www.cbc.gov.tw/ct.asp?xItem=1061&ctNode=535&mp=2 (accessed 22 July 2020).

Table 2.4.7: Foreign Direct Investment, Net Inflows
(% of GDP)

ADB Regional Member	2000	2005	2010	2014	2015	2016	2017	2018	2019
Developing ADB Member Economies									
Central and West Asia[a]	**1.8**	**4.5**	**4.1**	**2.9**	**2.9**	**5.0**	**2.4**	**1.2**	**1.9**
Afghanistan	1.2 (2002)	4.1	1.2	0.2	0.8	0.5	0.3	0.7	0.1
Armenia	5.5	6.0	5.7	3.5	1.7	3.2	2.2	2.0	1.9
Azerbaijan	2.5	33.8	6.3	5.9	7.6	11.9	7.0	3.0	3.1
Georgia	4.3	7.1	7.5	10.4	11.6	10.9	11.7	6.9	7.2
Kazakhstan	7.5	4.5	5.0	3.3	3.6	12.5	2.8	0.1	2.0
Kyrgyz Republic	-0.2	1.7	9.9	4.6	17.1	9.1	-1.4	1.7	...
Pakistan	0.4	1.8	1.2	0.8	0.6	0.9	0.8	0.6	0.9
Tajikistan	2.7	2.4	1.7	3.5	5.5	3.5	2.5	2.8	2.6
Turkmenistan	2.7	2.4	16.1	8.8	8.5	6.2	5.5	4.9	...
Uzbekistan	0.5	1.3	3.5	1.1	1.3	2.0	3.0	1.2	3.9
East Asia	**5.6**	**4.2**	**4.3**	**3.2**	**3.2**	**2.4**	**2.1**	**2.1**	**1.4**
China, People's Republic of	3.5	4.6	4.0	2.6	2.2	1.6	1.3	1.7	1.1
Hong Kong, China	41.1	22.6	36.2	44.6	58.5	41.5	36.8	26.8	14.5
Korea, Republic of	2.0	1.5	0.8	0.6	0.3	0.8	1.1	0.7	0.6
Mongolia	4.7	7.4	23.5	2.8	0.8	-37.2	13.1	14.9	17.6
Taipei,China	1.5	0.4	0.6	0.5	0.4	1.7	0.6	1.2	1.3
South Asia[a]	**0.7**	**0.9**	**1.6**	**1.7**	**2.0**	**1.8**	**1.5**	**1.5**	**...**
Bangladesh	0.6	1.4	1.1	1.5	1.5	1.1	0.7	1.1	0.5
Bhutan	0.5 (2002)	0.8	4.9	1.2	0.3	0.6	-0.7	0.1	...
India	0.8	0.9	1.6	1.7	2.1	1.9	1.5	1.5	1.8
Maldives	3.6	4.6	8.4	9.0	7.3	10.4	9.7	10.1	...
Nepal	-0.0	0.0	0.5	0.2	0.2	0.5	0.8	0.2	...
Sri Lanka	1.0	1.1	0.8	1.1	0.8	1.1	1.6	1.8	...
Southeast Asia[a]	**3.6**	**4.8**	**5.6**	**5.1**	**5.4**	**4.6**	**6.0**	**5.5**	**...**
Brunei Darussalam	9.2	1.8	3.5	3.3	1.3	-1.3	3.9	3.8	2.8
Cambodia	3.2	6.0	12.5	11.1	10.1	12.4	12.6	13.1	13.7
Indonesia	-2.8	2.9	2.0	2.8	2.3	0.5	2.0	1.8	2.2
Lao People's Democratic Republic	2.1	1.0	4.1	6.5	7.5	5.9	9.9	7.3	...
Malaysia	4.0	2.7	4.3	3.1	3.3	4.5	2.9	2.4	...
Myanmar	...	...	...	3.3	6.5	5.5	6.6	2.0	...
Philippines	1.8	1.5	0.5	1.9	1.8	2.6	3.1	2.9	2.0
Singapore	16.1	15.1	23.1	21.8	22.7	22.2	28.6	24.4	28.3
Thailand	2.7	4.3	4.3	1.2	2.2	0.7	1.8	2.6	1.2
Timor-Leste	0.2 (2002)	0.2	3.4	2.3	2.7	0.3	0.4	3.1	...
Viet Nam	4.2	3.4	6.9	4.9	6.1	6.1	6.3	6.3	...
The Pacific[a]	**2.0**	**2.4**	**2.1**	**1.7**	**1.8**	**1.8**	**2.1**	**5.5**	**...**
Cook Islands	...	...	...	...	...	...	...	...	...
Fiji	0.0	5.8	5.7	7.8	4.4	7.9	7.2	8.5	...
Kiribati	1.1	2.3	-4.2	1.5	-0.5	1.0	0.4	-0.6	...
Marshall Islands	0.6	2.3	-5.8	4.9	-2.9	-1.5	2.7	4.4	...
Micronesia, Federated States of	-0.1 (2001)	0.0	0.0	6.3	0.3	...	...	...	...
Nauru	...	3.2	0.0	0.0	0.0	0.0	0.0	0.0	...
Niue	...	...	...	...	...	...	...	...	...
Palau	2.2	2.2	1.5	16.4	12.4	11.9	9.6	7.5	...
Papua New Guinea	2.8	0.8	0.2	0.1	1.0	0.1	0.7	4.7	...
Samoa	-0.5	0.9	-0.2	2.9	3.4	0.3	1.1	2.0	...
Solomon Islands	0.7	0.1	18.4	1.6	2.5	2.7	2.9	...	...
Tonga	4.8	2.3	1.3	3.1	1.6	1.4	-1.2	3.1	0.3
Tuvalu	-0.1 (2001)	-0.1	1.4	0.8	0.9	0.8	0.7	...	...
Vanuatu	7.4	3.4	9.0	1.6	4.1	5.5	4.3	...	...
Developed ADB Member Economies[a]	**0.5**	**-0.3**	**0.6**	**1.3**	**0.9**	**1.4**	**1.1**	**1.4**	**1.2**
Australia	3.9	-3.6	2.9	4.4	3.8	3.5	3.5	4.5	2.9
Japan	0.2	0.1	0.1	0.4	0.1	0.8	0.4	0.5	0.7
New Zealand	-2.8	1.7	0.2	1.6	-0.0	1.0	1.0	1.0	...
DEVELOPING ADB MEMBER ECONOMIES[a]	**4.4**	**3.8**	**4.1**	**3.3**	**3.3**	**2.7**	**2.5**	**2.4**	**1.9**
ALL ADB REGIONAL MEMBERS[a]	**2.0**	**1.8**	**2.8**	**2.8**	**2.8**	**2.4**	**2.2**	**2.2**	**1.7**

... = data not available, -0.0 or 0.0 = magnitude is less than half of the unit employed, ADB = Asian Development Bank, GDP = gross domestic product.

a Aggregate percentages calculated using only reporting economies with data available for both foreign direct investment and GDP in the years specified in the column headings.

Sources: World Bank. World Development Indicators. http://data.worldbank.org/indicator/BX.KLT.DINV.CD.WD?locations=MH (accessed 15 July 2020). For Taipei,China: Central bank of Taipei,China. https://www.cbc.gov.tw/ct.asp?xItem=1061&ctNode=535&mp=2 (accessed 15 July 2020).

Table 2.4.8:   Merchandise Exports
($ million)

ADB Regional Member	2000	2005	2010	2014	2015	2016	2017	2018	2019
Developing ADB Member Economies									
Central and West Asia	**26,716**	**64,110**	**134,768**	**174,603**	**116,373**	**97,395**	**113,221**	**135,984**	**136,794**
Afghanistan	137	384	388	571	571	596	723	875	864
Armenia	300	974	1,041	1,547	1,485	1,792	2,238	2,412	2,640
Azerbaijan	1,745	7,649	26,476	28,260	15,586	13,211	15,152	20,794	19,868
Georgia	324	865	1,677	2,861	2,204	2,113	2,736	3,356	3,764
Kazakhstan	8,812	27,849	60,271	79,460	45,956	36,737	48,503	61,111	57,723
Kyrgyz Republic	505	674	1,756	1,884	1,483	1,573	1,764	1,837	1,966
Pakistan	8,335	14,453	19,261	25,715	23,526	20,859	20,566	21,296	21,222
Tajikistan	784	909	1,195	977	891	899	1,198	1,073	1,174
Turkmenistan	2,508	4,944	9,679	19,782	12,164	7,520	7,788	9,239	9,670
Uzbekistan	3,265	5,409	13,023	13,546	12,508	12,095	12,554	13,991	17,902
East Asia	**775,319**	**1,536,558**	**2,713,946**	**3,712,596**	**3,552,566**	**3,338,638**	**3,656,155**	**3,962,925**	**3,887,188**
China, People's Republic of	249,203	761,953	1,577,754	2,342,293	2,273,468	2,097,631	2,263,345	2,486,682	2,499,029
Hong Kong, China	201,855	289,325	390,134	473,654	465,092	462,269	497,340	530,472	509,026
Korea, Republic of	172,268	284,419	466,384	572,665	526,757	495,426	573,694	604,860	542,233
Mongolia	536	1,064	2,909	5,774	4,669	4,916	6,201	7,012	7,620
Taipei,China	151,458	199,798	276,765	318,211	282,580	278,395	315,574	333,900	329,280
South Asia	**56,445**	**119,305**	**276,096**	**353,306**	**310,212**	**320,174**	**346,730**	**386,588**	**369,647**
Bangladesh	4,780	8,259	16,099	29,807	30,588	33,352	33,462	35,691	39,731
Bhutan	103	214	535	539	561	488	566	604	751
India	45,297	103,496	249,951	310,742	267,550	275,233	300,440	337,439	316,182
Maldives	109	162	62	144	144	139	199	206	178
Nepal	701	823	830	943	833	653	699	747	862
Sri Lanka	5,456	6,351	8,618	11,130	10,536	10,309	11,364	11,901	11,943
Southeast Asia	**426,344**	**654,632**	**1,048,353**	**1,297,828**	**1,172,202**	**1,151,010**	**1,311,959**	**1,446,426**	**1,420,308**
Brunei Darussalam	3,906	6,247	8,887	10,606	6,338	4,915	5,585	6,577	7,248
Cambodia	1,397	2,908	3,903	8,170	9,336	10,273	11,224	12,963	14,987
Indonesia	62,124	85,660	157,779	176,293	150,393	144,490	168,828	180,013	167,497
Lao People's Democratic Republic	330	553	1,746	3,276	3,653	4,245	4,873	5,295	5,764
Malaysia	98,229	141,595	198,325	233,868	199,041	189,708	217,403	248,712	238,113
Myanmar	1,756	3,836	8,872	11,452	11,432	11,837	13,878	16,704	18,110
Philippines	38,078	41,255	51,498	62,102	58,827	57,406	68,713	69,307	70,927
Singapore	137,954	230,523	352,553	415,191	357,729	337,962	372,938	411,958	390,360
Thailand	68,083	109,564	192,511	226,615	213,397	213,431	233,376	251,155	242,958
Timor-Leste	4 (2001)	43	42	39	38	162	24	46	154
Viet Nam	14,483	32,447	72,237	150,217	162,017	176,581	215,119	243,697	264,189
The Pacific[a]	**2,817**	**4,262**	**7,003**	**10,716**	**9,261**	**8,872**	**11,251**	**11,635**	**12,668**
Cook Islands	9	5	5	18	14	14	20	17	17
Fiji	543	705	837	1,220	982	922	985	1,016	1,032
Kiribati	4	4	4	10	9	10	15	8	12
Marshall Islands	25	34	34 (2009)	...	...	...	...	...	...
Micronesia, Federated States of	17	13	30	32	40	49	46	47	...
Nauru	4 (2002)	0	32	22	14	36	19	12	4
Niue	0	1 (2006)	1	1	1	1	2	2	...
Palau	12	14	16	19	18	...	...	...	...
Papua New Guinea	2,089	3,311	5,737	8,794	7,638	7,248	9,526	9,827	10,923
Samoa	14	12	23	27	34	36	37	42	51
Solomon Islands	65	105	227	455	421	432	468	536	460
Tonga	9	10	8	19	18	21	19	13	20
Tuvalu	0	0	1	0	0	0	0	...	...
Vanuatu	26	46	48	63	39	50	61	63	48
Developed ADB Member Economies	**556,592**	**723,605**	**1,011,217**	**971,165**	**846,359**	**869,646**	**967,003**	**1,034,971**	**1,016,198**
Australia	63,980	106,211	212,027	239,708	187,525	192,140	230,950	257,480	271,003
Japan	479,320	595,696	767,826	689,916	624,681	643,753	697,951	737,877	705,733
New Zealand	13,292	21,698	31,365	41,541	34,152	33,753	38,102	39,613	39,463
DEVELOPING ADB MEMBER ECONOMIES[a]	**1,287,641**	**2,378,867**	**4,180,164**	**5,549,049**	**5,160,614**	**4,916,088**	**5,439,316**	**5,943,558**	**5,826,604**
ALL ADB REGIONAL MEMBERS[a]	**1,844,233**	**3,102,472**	**5,191,381**	**6,520,214**	**6,006,973**	**5,785,733**	**6,406,319**	**6,978,529**	**6,842,803**
WORLD[b]	**6,483,466**	**10,506,556**	**15,169,220**	**18,765,054**	**16,345,970**	**15,809,520**	**17,486,341**	**19,271,006**	**18,724,006**

... = data not available, 0 = magnitude is less than half of unit employed, $ = United States dollars, ADB = Asian Development Bank.

a   For estimating aggregates, imputation was done for economies with missing data by substituting available data from the nearest years.
b   The world aggregate includes estimates derived from reports of partner economies for nonreporting and slow-reporting economies.

Sources: Economy sources; and International Monetary Fund. International Financial Statistics. http://data.imf.org/ (accessed 3 July 2020). For Nauru: for 2002–2015, data are from the media release on International Merchandise Trade Statistics (IMTS Release No. 01/2016) of the Nauru Bureau of Statistics, published on 3 November 2016; for 2016–2019, data are from the IMF 2019 Article IV Staff Country Reports for the Republic of Nauru. For "World": International Monetary Fund. Direction of Trade Statistics. http://data.imf.org/?sk=9D6028D4-F14A-464C-A2F2-59B2CD424B85 (accessed 30 June 2020).

Table 2.4.9:   Growth Rates of Merchandise Exports[a]
(%)

ADB Regional Member	2000	2005	2010	2014	2015	2016	2017	2018	2019
Developing ADB Member Economies									
Central and West Asia	**27.6**	**32.7**	**25.3**	**-3.6**	**-33.3**	**-16.3**	**16.3**	**20.1**	**0.6**
Afghanistan	-17.4	25.9	-3.7	10.9	–	4.5	21.2	21.1	-1.3
Armenia	29.7	34.7	46.6	4.6	-4.0	20.6	24.9	7.8	9.4
Azerbaijan	87.7	111.6	25.5	-10.9	-44.8	-15.2	14.7	37.2	-4.5
Georgia	36.1	33.8	48.0	-1.7	-23.0	-4.1	29.5	22.7	12.2
Kazakhstan	50.1	38.6	39.5	-6.2	-42.2	-20.1	32.0	26.0	-5.5
Kyrgyz Republic	11.1	-6.5	5.0	-6.1	-21.3	6.1	12.1	4.1	7.0
Pakistan	4.8	14.9	12.0	10.0	-8.5	-11.3	-1.4	3.6	-0.3
Tajikistan	13.9	-0.7	18.3	-15.9	-8.9	0.9	33.3	-10.4	9.5
Turkmenistan	115.5	28.3	3.8	4.9	-38.5	-38.2	3.6	18.6	4.7
Uzbekistan	0.9	11.5	10.6	-5.4	-7.7	-3.3	3.8	11.4	28.0
East Asia	**21.8**	**19.0**	**29.8**	**4.8**	**-4.3**	**-6.0**	**9.5**	**8.4**	**-1.9**
China, People's Republic of	27.8	28.4	31.3	6.0	-2.9	-7.7	7.9	9.9	0.5
Hong Kong, China	16.1	11.6	22.5	3.2	-1.8	-0.6	7.6	6.7	-4.0
Korea, Republic of	19.9	12.0	28.3	2.3	-8.0	-5.9	15.8	5.4	-10.4
Mongolia	18.0	22.4	54.3	35.3	-19.1	5.3	26.1	13.1	8.7
Taipei,China	22.6	8.6	35.1	2.8	-11.2	-1.5	13.4	5.8	-1.4
South Asia	**21.0**	**22.9**	**38.9**	**-3.1**	**-12.2**	**3.2**	**8.3**	**11.5**	**-4.4**
Bangladesh	12.5	11.3	3.7	7.9	2.6	9.0	0.3	6.7	11.3
Bhutan	-11.3	35.8	6.5	5.5	4.1	-13.0	16.0	6.6	24.3
India	22.2	25.0	43.1	-4.4	-13.9	2.9	9.2	12.3	-6.3
Maldives	18.8	-10.5	-63.6	-13.0	-0.6	-3.2	43.0	3.6	-13.6
Nepal	34.0	12.4	-4.9	14.1	-11.6	-21.6	7.0	6.9	15.5
Sri Lanka	18.5	10.1	21.7	6.9	-5.3	-2.2	10.2	4.7	0.4
Southeast Asia	**19.0**	**15.0**	**29.7**	**1.4**	**-9.7**	**-1.8**	**14.0**	**10.2**	**-1.8**
Brunei Darussalam	53.1	23.3	23.9	-7.3	-40.2	-22.4	13.6	17.8	10.2
Cambodia	23.6	12.3	24.4	16.0	14.3	10.0	9.3	15.5	15.6
Indonesia	27.7	19.7	35.4	-3.4	-14.7	-3.9	16.8	6.6	-7.0
Lao People's Democratic Republic	9.6	52.2	65.9	44.7	11.5	16.2	14.8	8.7	8.9
Malaysia	16.1	11.8	26.5	2.3	-14.9	-4.7	14.6	14.4	-4.3
Myanmar	53.1	61.8	32.4	1.9	-0.2	3.5	17.2	20.4	8.4
Philippines	8.7	4.0	34.0	9.5	-5.3	-2.4	19.7	0.9	2.3
Singapore	20.3	15.7	30.5	-1.1	-13.8	-5.5	10.3	10.5	-5.2
Thailand	16.2	15.3	27.2	-0.4	-5.8	0.0	9.3	7.6	-3.3
Timor-Leste	1,850.9 (2002)	-58.9	20.7	-26.7	-1.7	321.2	-85.1	91.5	232.0
Viet Nam	25.5	22.5	26.5	13.8	7.9	9.0	21.8	13.3	8.4
The Pacific[b]	**1.1**	**20.7**	**30.2**	**37.7**	**-13.6**	**-4.2**	**26.8**	**3.4**	**8.9**
Cook Islands	154.4	-26.9	88.0	65.8	-20.3	-2.9	48.9	-14.3	0.1
Fiji	-12.1	1.4	25.1	6.0	-19.5	-6.1	6.8	3.1	1.6
Kiribati	-59.1	58.2	-38.0	51.9	-11.0	16.3	45.2	-46.3	49.3
Marshall Islands	48.7	14.0	5.6 (2009)	...	...	...	...	...	...
Micronesia, Federated States of	688.9	-7.3	63.5	-7.8	23.0	23.3	-5.6	1.7	...
Nauru	...	-69.8	249.5	-53.4	-39.4	...	-45.4	-38.7	-64.9
Niue	-49.9 (2001)	65.6 (2004)	1.0	1.4	-20.2	8.8	23.0	12.8	...
Palau	65.9	116.9	15.9	-8.7	-5.3	...	...	...	...
Papua New Guinea	7.3	26.8	30.9	47.8	-13.2	-5.1	31.4	3.2	11.2
Samoa	-24.9	0.6	114.2	14.7	23.8	6.3	3.1	13.5	19.6
Solomon Islands	-48.1	22.3	37.4	1.7	-7.6	2.7	8.3	14.5	-14.2
Tonga	-27.1	-35.2	7.1	34.2	-6.5	21.1	-12.1	-31.2	56.1
Tuvalu	-91.7	-54.0	76.5	464.8	-12.0	7.2	-8.1	...	...
Vanuatu	9.6	-6.5	-14.8	62.6	-38.0	28.8	22.1	2.9	-24.3
Developed ADB Member Economies	**14.5**	**7.6**	**33.6**	**-3.6**	**-12.9**	**2.8**	**11.2**	**7.0**	**-1.8**
Australia	14.1	22.6	38.3	-5.2	-21.8	2.5	20.2	11.5	5.3
Japan	14.8	5.4	32.6	-3.5	-9.5	3.1	8.4	5.7	-4.4
New Zealand	6.5	6.6	26.6	5.4	-17.8	-1.2	12.9	4.0	-0.4
DEVELOPING ADB MEMBER ECONOMIES[b]	**20.9**	**18.4**	**30.2**	**3.3**	**-7.0**	**-4.7**	**10.6**	**9.3**	**-2.0**
ALL ADB REGIONAL MEMBERS[b]	**18.9**	**15.7**	**30.8**	**2.2**	**-7.9**	**-3.7**	**10.7**	**8.9**	**-1.9**
WORLD[c]	**14.5**	**13.7**	**22.3**	**0.5**	**-12.9**	**-3.3**	**10.6**	**10.2**	**-2.8**

... = data not available, – = magnitude equals zero, 0.0 = magnitude is less than half of unit employed, ADB = Asian Development Bank.

a   Growth rates are based on the value of exports in United States dollars.
b   For estimating aggregates, imputation was done for economies with missing data by substituting available data from the nearest years.
c   The world aggregate includes estimates derived from reports of partner economies for nonreporting and slow-reporting economies.

Sources: Economy sources; and International Monetary Fund. International Financial Statistics. http://data.imf.org/ (accessed 3 July 2020).

Table 2.4.10:   Merchandise Imports
($ million)

ADB Regional Member	2000	2005	2010	2014	2015	2016	2017	2018	2019
Developing ADB Member Economies									
Central and West Asia	**24,868**	**58,649**	**109,439**	**157,857**	**138,055**	**128,493**	**141,955**	**154,294**	**160,876**
Afghanistan	1,176	2,470	5,154	7,729	7,723	6,534	7,065	7,407	6,777
Armenia	885	1,802	3,749	4,424	3,239	3,273	4,097	4,976	5,514
Azerbaijan	1,172	4,350	6,746	9,332	9,774	9,004	9,037	10,952	11,335
Georgia	710	2,488	5,236	8,602	7,300	7,294	7,943	9,136	9,098
Kazakhstan	5,040	17,353	31,127	41,296	30,568	25,377	29,600	33,659	38,357
Kyrgyz Republic	554	1,189	3,223	5,735	4,154	4,000	4,495	5,292	4,904
Pakistan	9,967	20,630	34,169	45,820	45,394	44,665	52,742	55,189	49,869
Tajikistan	675	1,330	2,657	4,297	3,436	3,031	2,775	3,151	3,349
Turkmenistan	1,742	2,947	8,204	16,638	14,051	13,177	10,189	5,094	7,397
Uzbekistan	2,947	4,091	9,176	13,984	12,417	12,138	14,012	19,439	24,276
East Asia	**739,620**	**1,407,125**	**2,512,913**	**3,314,086**	**2,876,632**	**2,742,411**	**3,143,063**	**3,563,903**	**3,435,801**
China, People's Republic of	225,094	659,953	1,396,244	1,959,235	1,679,565	1,587,926	1,843,793	2,135,734	2,077,097
Hong Kong, China	212,800	299,520	433,102	544,106	522,001	516,395	559,074	602,335	563,487
Korea, Republic of	160,481	261,238	425,212	525,515	436,499	406,193	478,478	535,202	503,343
Mongolia	615	1,177	3,200	5,237	3,798	3,358	4,337	5,875	6,128
Taipei,China	140,630	185,237	255,155	279,994	234,770	228,539	257,380	284,757	285,746
South Asia	**67,978**	**173,194**	**409,681**	**514,757**	**455,084**	**452,970**	**537,469**	**617,000**	**561,342**
Bangladesh	7,300	11,329	21,245	36,608	37,528	39,795	42,779	53,571	55,142
Bhutan[a]	193	466	810	936	977	1,046	1,044	1,001	755
India	51,372	149,753	368,166	448,486	388,189	383,609	460,836	525,618	469,747
Maldives	389	683	909	1,988	1,890	2,121	2,355	3,179	3,156
Nepal	1,526	2,094	5,110	7,323	7,565	7,204	9,474	11,430	12,597
Sri Lanka	7,198	8,869	13,441	19,417	18,935	19,195	20,982	22,200	19,945
Southeast Asia	**363,000**	**571,362**	**934,616**	**1,224,566**	**1,089,776**	**1,071,162**	**1,233,058**	**1,405,578**	**1,368,556**
Brunei Darussalam	1,107	1,448	2,536	3,596	3,235	2,671	3,083	4,168	5,100
Cambodia[a]	1,936	3,918	6,588	12,022	13,285	14,119	15,502	18,806	22,242
Indonesia	33,515	57,701	135,663	178,179	142,695	135,653	156,986	188,711	170,727
Lao People's Democratic Republic[a]	535	882	2,060	4,976	5,675	5,372	5,667	6,164	6,252
Malaysia	81,963	114,302	164,177	208,667	175,593	168,459	194,497	218,036	204,966
Myanmar	2,407	1,934	4,866	16,220	16,913	15,706	19,253	19,355	18,607
Philippines	34,491	47,418	54,933	65,398	71,067	84,108	96,093	112,841	111,593
Singapore	134,675	200,861	312,668	377,714	307,967	291,922	327,389	370,833	358,985
Thailand	56,481	106,027	165,988	209,392	187,079	177,662	200,820	228,857	216,416
Timor-Leste	253(2001)	109	298	554	491	512	554	565	597
Viet Nam	15,637	36,761	84,839	147,849	165,776	174,978	213,215	237,242	253,071
The Pacific[b]	**2,657**	**4,339**	**7,091**	**9,430**	**7,323**	**6,740**	**7,962**	**8,403**	**9,028**
Cook Islands	51	81	91	121	110	106	135	134	134
Fiji	856	1,610	1,806	2,656	2,268	2,301	2,402	2,729	2,782
Kiribati	39	76	73	107	103	111	108	103	112
Marshall Islands	116	132	158(2009)	...	...	...	...	...	...
Micronesia, Federated States of	107	128	168	161	160	186	183	198	...
Nauru	18(2002)	9	13	114	93	57	54	61	58
Niue	2	4(2006)	9	15	13	13	15	18	...
Palau	127	108	103	149	156	...	...	...	...
Papua New Guinea	999	1,519	3,522	4,548	2,866	2,240	3,280	3,316	3,885
Samoa	91	187	280	341	298	312	321	333	357
Solomon Islands	92	185	405	505	485	465	516	593	560
Tonga	70	121	158	219	209	229	238	228	267
Tuvalu	5	13	22	22	37	23	27	...	...
Vanuatu	84	165	284	314	367	382	370	350	315
Developed ADB Member Economies	**461,654**	**661,780**	**915,836**	**1,081,267**	**885,006**	**832,052**	**933,113**	**1,020,015**	**977,248**
Australia	67,806	118,836	193,071	227,859	200,643	189,074	220,954	227,172	213,810
Japan	379,884	516,697	692,242	810,886	647,744	607,043	672,032	748,967	721,032
New Zealand	13,963	26,248	30,523	42,523	36,619	35,935	40,128	43,876	42,405
DEVELOPING ADB MEMBER ECONOMIES[b]	**1,198,123**	**2,214,669**	**3,973,740**	**5,220,695**	**4,566,870**	**4,401,776**	**5,063,507**	**5,749,177**	**5,535,602**
ALL ADB REGIONAL MEMBERS[b]	**1,659,777**	**2,876,449**	**4,889,577**	**6,301,962**	**5,451,876**	**5,233,828**	**5,996,620**	**6,769,192**	**6,512,850**
WORLD[c]	**6,607,666**	**10,692,867**	**15,456,765**	**18,918,188**	**16,563,307**	**16,131,693**	**17,721,718**	**19,537,386**	**18,974,119**

... = data not available, $ = United States dollars, ADB = Asian Development Bank.

a   Compilation methodology shifted from cost, insurance, and freight to free on board from 2004 onward for Bhutan; from 2005 onward for Cambodia; and from 2017 onward for the Lao People's Democratic Republic.
b   For estimating aggregates, imputation was done for economies with missing data by substituting available data from the nearest years.
c   The world aggregate includes estimates derived from reports of partner economies for nonreporting and slow-reporting economies.

Sources: Economy sources; and International Monetary Fund. International Financial Statistics. http://data.imf.org/ (accessed 3 July 2020). For Nauru: for 2002–2015, data are from the media release on International Merchandise Trade Statistics (IMTS Release No. 01/2016) of the Nauru Bureau of Statistics, published on 3 November 2016; for 2016–2019, data are from the IMF 2019 Article IV Staff Country Reports for the Republic of Nauru. For "World": International Monetary Fund. Direction of Trade Statistics. http://data.imf.org/?sk=9D6028D4-F14A-464C-A2F2-59B2CD424B85 (accessed 30 June 2020).

Table 2.4.11: Growth Rates of Merchandise Imports[a]
(%)

ADB Regional Member	2000	2005	2010	2014	2015	2016	2017	2018	2019
Developing ADB Member Economies									
Central and West Asia	**11.1**	**27.0**	**5.8**	**-3.3**	**-12.5**	**-6.9**	**10.5**	**8.7**	**4.3**
Afghanistan	16.2	13.5	54.5	-11.4	-0.1	-15.4	8.1	4.8	-8.5
Armenia	9.1	33.4	12.9	0.9	-26.8	1.1	25.2	21.4	10.8
Azerbaijan	13.1	23.7	3.6	-9.6	4.7	-7.9	0.4	21.2	3.5
Georgia	2.9	34.9	17.0	7.2	-15.1	-0.1	8.9	15.0	-0.4
Kazakhstan	37.9	35.8	9.6	-15.4	-26.0	-17.0	16.6	13.7	14.0
Kyrgyz Republic	-7.7	25.5	6.0	-4.2	-27.6	-3.7	12.4	17.7	-7.3
Pakistan	5.7	33.7	2.5	7.1	-0.9	-1.6	18.1	4.6	-9.6
Tajikistan	1.8	11.7	3.4	4.3	-20.1	-11.8	-8.4	13.6	6.3
Turkmenistan	26.8	-6.4	-8.8	3.4	-15.5	-6.2	-22.7	-50.0	45.2
Uzbekistan	-5.2	7.2	-2.8	0.3	-11.2	-2.2	15.4	38.7	24.9
East Asia	**28.2**	**14.4**	**35.5**	**1.3**	**-13.2**	**-4.7**	**14.6**	**13.4**	**-3.6**
China, People's Republic of	35.8	17.6	38.8	0.5	-14.3	-5.5	16.1	15.8	-2.7
Hong Kong, China	18.5	10.5	24.7	3.9	-4.1	-1.1	8.3	7.7	-6.4
Korea, Republic of	34.0	16.4	31.6	1.9	-16.9	-6.9	17.8	11.9	-6.0
Mongolia	19.8	15.5	49.7	-17.6	-27.5	-11.6	29.2	35.5	4.3
Taipei,China	26.3	7.8	44.4	1.4	-16.2	-2.7	12.6	10.6	0.3
South Asia	**4.7**	**32.2**	**29.1**	**-1.8**	**-11.6**	**-0.5**	**18.7**	**14.8**	**-9.0**
Bangladesh	3.3	16.3	5.1	6.5	2.5	6.0	7.5	25.2	2.9
Bhutan	2.9	77.2	40.7	8.3	4.4	7.0	-0.1	-4.1	-24.6
India	2.8	35.4	30.7	-3.2	-13.4	-1.2	20.1	14.1	-10.6
Maldives	-3.4	21.3	-5.6	15.0	-4.9	12.2	11.1	35.0	-0.7
Nepal	19.0	13.2	39.3	22.4	3.3	-4.8	31.5	20.7	10.2
Sri Lanka	20.5	10.7	31.8	7.9	-2.5	1.4	9.3	5.8	-10.2
Southeast Asia[b]	**20.5**	**15.7**	**31.1**	**-0.6**	**-11.0**	**-1.7**	**15.1**	**14.0**	**-2.6**
Brunei Darussalam	-16.7	1.5	5.6	-0.5	-10.0	-17.4	15.4	35.2	22.4
Cambodia	21.6	19.8	35.0	12.6	10.5	6.3	9.8	21.3	18.3
Indonesia	39.6	24.0	40.1	-4.5	-19.9	-4.9	15.7	20.2	-9.5
Lao People's Democratic Republic	-3.4	23.8	41.0	63.1	14.1	-5.3	5.5	8.8	1.4
Malaysia	25.3	8.7	33.1	1.4	-15.9	-4.1	15.5	12.1	-6.0
Myanmar	3.3	-11.6	11.0	34.7	4.3	-7.1	22.6	0.5	-3.9
Philippines	5.9	7.7	27.5	4.8	8.7	18.3	14.2	17.4	-1.1
Singapore	21.3	15.4	26.9	-2.7	-18.5	-5.2	12.1	13.3	-3.2
Thailand	12.0	25.8	38.2	-7.8	-10.7	-5.0	13.0	14.0	-5.4
Timor-Leste	24.8 (2002)	-25.3	1.0	4.7	-11.3	4.2	8.2	2.1	5.6
Viet Nam	33.2	15.0	21.3	12.0	12.1	5.6	21.9	11.3	6.7
The Pacific[b]	**-3.5**	**10.3**	**19.5**	**-16.3**	**-22.3**	**-8.0**	**18.1**	**5.5**	**7.4**
Cook Islands	21.9	7.0	11.2	4.1	-9.3	-3.0	26.9	-0.6	0.2
Fiji	-8.3	11.5	17.0	-5.9	-14.6	1.5	4.4	13.6	2.0
Kiribati	-4.2	28.7	5.4	0.0	-3.7	7.6	-3.0	-4.8	8.7
Marshall Islands	16.7	15.3	15.0 (2009)	...	...	...	...	...	...
Micronesia, Federated States of	766.0	-3.2	-1.8	-14.3	-0.3	16.0	-1.4	7.9	...
Nauru	...	-27.0	-47.3	-25.3	-18.0	...	-5.9	13.2	-4.1
Niue	0.9 (2001)	269.9 (2004)	28.5	1.4	-15.4	5.2	13.1	17.8	...
Palau	-5.7	0.7	9.3	3.1	4.4	...	...	...	...
Papua New Guinea	-7.0	4.5	23.0	-26.6	-37.0	-21.9	46.5	1.1	17.2
Samoa	-21.7	20.7	36.6	4.8	-12.7	4.8	2.7	3.8	7.2
Solomon Islands	-16.1	52.4	51.2	-1.0	-4.1	-4.1	11.1	14.8	-5.4
Tonga	-3.8	15.3	10.3	10.4	-4.4	9.5	3.7	-4.0	17.2
Tuvalu	-38.0	13.3	59.2	7.0	66.4	-36.2	13.1	...	...
Vanuatu	-6.8	22.4	-2.5	-0.0	17.0	4.0	-3.1	-5.3	-10.2
Developed ADB Member Economies	**18.5**	**13.7**	**25.1**	**-2.1**	**-18.2**	**-6.0**	**12.1**	**9.3**	**-4.2**
Australia	3.5	14.4	23.4	-2.1	-11.9	-5.8	16.9	2.8	-5.9
Japan	22.7	13.6	25.8	-2.6	-20.1	-6.3	10.7	11.4	-3.7
New Zealand	-2.7	13.4	21.5	7.2	-13.9	-1.9	11.7	9.3	-3.4
DEVELOPING ADB MEMBER ECONOMIES[b]	**23.8**	**16.3**	**32.7**	**0.3**	**-12.5**	**-3.6**	**15.0**	**13.5**	**-3.7**
ALL ADB REGIONAL MEMBERS[b]	**22.3**	**15.7**	**31.2**	**-0.1**	**-13.5**	**-4.0**	**14.6**	**12.9**	**-3.8**
WORLD[c]	**13.6**	**13.1**	**21.4**	**0.5**	**-12.4**	**-2.6**	**9.9**	**10.2**	**-2.9**

... = data not available, -0.0 or 0.0 = magnitude is less than half of unit employed, ADB = Asian Development Bank.

a Growth rates are based on the value of imports in United States dollars.
b For estimating aggregates, imputation was done for economies with missing data by substituting available data from the nearest years.
c The world aggregate includes estimates derived from reports of partner countries for nonreporting and slow-reporting countries.

Sources: Economy sources; and International Monetary Fund. International Financial Statistics. http://data.imf.org/ (accessed 3 July 2020).

Table 2.4.12:   Trade in Goods[a]
(% of GDP)

ADB Regional Member	2000	2005	2010	2014	2015	2016	2017	2018	2019
Developing ADB Member Economies									
Central and West Asia[b]	**38.8**	**50.2**	**49.5**	**45.4**	**37.2**	**36.0**	**38.1**	**43.6**	**45.7**
Afghanistan	59.6 (2002)	43.1	34.5	38.9	40.2	39.5	41.8	46.0	42.7
Armenia	62.0	56.6	51.7	51.4	44.8	48.0	55.0	59.3	59.6
Azerbaijan	55.3	90.6	62.8	50.0	47.8	58.7	59.2	67.4	64.9
Georgia	33.8	52.3	56.5	65.0	63.6	62.1	65.7	71.0	72.5
Kazakhstan	75.7	79.1	61.7	54.5	41.5	45.2	46.8	52.8	53.3
Kyrgyz Republic	77.3	75.7	103.8	102.0	84.4	81.8	81.3	86.2	81.2
Pakistan	23.1	29.3	30.6	28.7	25.8	23.6	24.2	26.9	28.1
Tajikistan	169.6	96.8	68.3	57.1	52.3	56.2	52.7	54.4	55.7
Turkmenistan	86.2	45.9	79.2	83.8	73.1	57.2	47.4	35.2	36.7
Uzbekistan	45.1	66.0	47.3	35.9	30.5	29.6	44.9	66.3	72.8
East Asia	**66.1**	**77.9**	**66.1**	**54.9**	**48.0**	**44.7**	**45.7**	**45.3**	**43.1**
China, People's Republic of	39.2	62.2	48.9	41.1	35.7	32.8	33.4	33.3	31.9
Hong Kong, China	241.5	324.3	360.1	349.2	319.0	305.0	309.6	313.2	293.0
Korea, Republic of	57.8	58.4	77.9	74.0	65.7	60.1	64.8	66.3	63.7
Mongolia	101.2	88.8	85.0	90.1	72.1	74.0	92.2	98.3	99.2
Taipei,China	88.3	102.9	119.7	111.7	96.8	93.3	97.0	101.7	100.6
South Asia[b]	**22.8**	**31.9**	**36.8**	**37.4**	**31.3**	**29.5**	**29.6**	**31.7**	**28.1**
Bangladesh	26.6	34.0	32.6	38.4	35.0	33.1	31.0	33.1	31.5
Bhutan[c]	69.7	85.4	86.9	77.3	76.8	71.0	65.7	65.6	...
India	20.3	30.7	37.0	37.2	30.5	28.8	29.0	31.1	27.2
Maldives	79.7	72.6	37.5	57.7	49.5	51.6	53.9	63.6	...
Nepal	41.7	35.3	36.5	41.0	40.4	37.4	39.8	43.6	43.8
Sri Lanka	75.7	62.4	38.9	38.5	36.6	35.8	37.0	38.6	38.0
Southeast Asia[b]	**128.0**	**130.1**	**99.3**	**98.9**	**91.2**	**85.5**	**90.9**	**95.2**	**88.0**
Brunei Darussalam	83.5	80.7	83.3	83.1	74.0	66.5	71.5	79.2	91.7
Cambodia[c]	90.9	108.5	93.3	120.9	125.3	121.9	120.5	129.3	137.4
Indonesia	58.0	50.1	38.9	39.8	34.0	30.1	32.1	35.4	30.2
Lao People's Democratic Republic[c]	52.9	52.8	56.4	62.1	64.7	60.4	61.8	63.2	...
Malaysia	192.1	178.3	142.1	130.9	124.3	118.9	129.1	130.2	121.5
Myanmar	...	...	...	41.7	45.3	45.8	54.5	55.6	53.0
Philippines	86.7	82.5	51.1	42.9	42.4	44.4	50.2	52.5	48.4
Singapore[d]	283.8	337.5	277.4	251.8	216.1	197.7	204.9	209.7	201.4
Thailand	98.6	113.9	105.1	107.0	99.8	94.6	95.2	94.8	84.5
Timor-Leste	53.9 (2001)	33.0	38.5	41.0	33.2	40.7	35.9	39.0	...
Viet Nam	96.6	120.1	135.5	160.1	169.6	171.3	191.4	196.1	197.5
The Pacific[b]	**79.7**	**82.5**	**66.5**	**61.3**	**53.4**	**51.0**	**57.6**	**57.4**	**...**
Cook Islands	65.3	47.3	39.8	43.4	40.9	38.7	44.9	41.9	40.1
Fiji	83.3	77.7	84.2	79.8	69.4	65.4	63.3	67.6	...
Kiribati	63.6	72.0	49.3	65.3	65.6	68.2	65.7	56.3	...
Marshall Islands	122.2	116.8	126.9 (2009)	...	...	...	...	...	...
Micronesia, Federated States of	53.0	56.5	66.6	60.5	63.1	70.6	62.6	60.9	...
Nauru	...	30.4	86.3	118.5	118.4	90.5	65.6	60.8	54.3
Niue	28.9	35.8 (2006)	56.5	60.8	58.7	59.7	63.9	65.0	...
Palau	95.0	66.1	64.6	69.0	62.3	...	...	...	...
Papua New Guinea	88.3	99.3	65.0	57.5	48.4	45.7	56.3	54.7	59.3
Samoa	45.1	45.9	43.7	47.2	42.2	42.4	43.4	45.0	48.3
Solomon Islands	55.1	52.2	70.0	71.9	69.3	65.0	66.3	...	...
Tonga	41.5	50.1	44.9	55.1	56.3	59.5	55.6	50.2	56.5
Tuvalu	37.3	59.8	72.7	60.8	105.7	60.0	61.0	...	...
Vanuatu	40.5	53.5	47.4	46.2	53.4	53.7	49.0	...	...
Developed ADB Member Economies[b]	**19.1**	**24.9**	**27.4**	**31.6**	**29.9**	**26.8**	**29.6**	**31.4**	**30.0**
Australia	34.4	31.9	33.9	32.4	31.8	30.9	33.4	35.1	35.8
Japan	17.6	23.4	25.6	30.9	29.0	25.4	28.1	30.0	28.1
New Zealand	50.1	41.8	42.2	41.8	39.9	37.0	38.1	39.8	...
DEVELOPING ADB MEMBER ECONOMIES[b]	**69.2**	**78.0**	**66.4**	**58.4**	**51.1**	**47.8**	**49.1**	**49.8**	**47.1**
ALL ADB REGIONAL MEMBERS[b]	**39.3**	**52.1**	**52.2**	**51.4**	**46.2**	**42.7**	**44.6**	**45.8**	**43.4**

... = data not available, ADB = Asian Development Bank, GDP = gross domestic product.

a The sum of merchandise exports and imports in United States dollars.
b For estimating aggregates, imputation was done for economies with missing data by substituting available data from the nearest years.
c The compilation methodology shifted from cost, insurance, and freight to free on board from 2004 onward for Bhutan; from 2005 onward for Cambodia; and from 2017 onward for the Lao People's Democratic Republic.
d Prior to 2003, data excludes Indonesia.

Sources: Economy sources; and International Monetary Fund. International Financial Statistics. http://data.imf.org/ (accessed 3 July 2020).

Click on the indictor name in the table header to access the time series in the Key Indicators Database.

Table 2.4.13: Direction of Trade: Merchandise Exports
(% of total merchandise exports)

To From ADB Regional Member	Asia and the Pacific		Europe		North and Central America		Middle East		South America		Africa		Rest of the World	
	2000	2019	2000	2019	2000	2019	2000	2019	2000	2019	2000	2019	2000	2019
Developing ADB Member Economies														
Central and West Asia[a]	**21.7**	**32.4**	**46.9**	**51.3**	**13.7**	**4.5**	**7.6**	**4.7**	**0.4**	**0.3**	**1.2**	**1.2**	**8.5**	**5.7**
Afghanistan	73.4	86.7	19.1	5.1	0.2	0.5	7.1	7.5	0.0	0.0	0.0	0.0	0.2	0.1
Armenia	8.0	11.1	56.0	69.0	12.9	4.4	12.5	14.9	0.0	0.0	0.0	0.0	10.7	0.6
Azerbaijan	7.3	16.8	82.4	74.6	0.5	0.8	8.6	7.6	0.4	0.0	0.6	0.0	0.1	0.2
Georgia	15.9	37.5	75.5	50.4	2.7	3.7	4.0	5.0	0.1	0.7	1.4	0.3	0.5	2.4
Kazakhstan	11.1	28.6	48.9	63.1	14.8	2.1	2.5	2.3	0.1	0.1	0.1	0.4	22.6	3.4
Kyrgyz Republic	19.9	25.3	58.9	65.2	0.6	0.3	1.6	2.0	0.0	0.0	1.5	0.1	17.6	7.1
Pakistan	24.7	27.6	29.7	36.8	28.1	18.8	12.4	10.1	1.2	1.1	3.6	5.6	0.2	0.1
Tajikistan	4.1	30.9	80.0	46.3	0.1	0.0	1.7	5.6	0.7	0.0	0.8	6.2	12.5	11.0
Turkmenistan	5.8	86.0	81.2	9.9	1.1	0.2	10.2	0.3	0.0	0.2	0.2	0.0	1.5	3.3
Uzbekistan	60.5	38.1	30.4	24.7	0.0	0.1	8.9	2.6	0.1	0.0	0.0	0.0	0.0	34.5
East Asia[a]	**52.1**	**54.7**	**16.9**	**17.2**	**25.4**	**18.3**	**2.6**	**4.0**	**1.5**	**2.6**	**1.2**	**2.9**	**0.4**	**0.3**
China, People's Republic of	51.8	46.1	18.3	20.6	23.5	20.9	2.9	4.9	1.4	3.4	1.7	3.9	0.4	0.3
Hong Kong, China	53.9	75.9	16.7	11.0	26.1	8.8	1.4	2.6	1.1	0.8	0.7	0.8	0.1	0.0
Korea, Republic of	49.0	63.0	16.2	12.7	26.4	17.7	4.3	3.0	2.2	1.7	1.5	1.4	0.3	0.5
Mongolia	57.7	93.7	17.6	5.7	24.6	0.4	0.1	0.2	0.0	0.0	0.0	0.0	0.0	0.0
Taipei,China	53.6	71.7	15.7	9.0	26.1	15.9	1.7	1.6	1.1	0.7	0.9	0.6	0.8	0.5
South Asia[a]	**23.4**	**29.4**	**29.9**	**23.9**	**26.8**	**19.1**	**10.6**	**15.6**	**1.1**	**2.4**	**3.5**	**7.3**	**4.7**	**2.4**
Bangladesh	6.9	11.8	41.5	51.7	33.8	16.1	2.4	1.8	0.2	1.0	0.6	0.5	14.6	17.1
Bhutan	82.6	98.1	5.2	1.8	3.4	0.1	0.0	0.0	0.6	0.0	8.0	0.0	0.2	0.0
India	26.2	31.3	28.5	20.6	23.8	19.1	12.2	17.3	1.3	2.6	4.3	8.2	3.7	0.8
Maldives	36.9	51.7	18.6	38.6	44.4	9.2	0.0	0.4	0.0	0.0	0.0	0.1	0.0	0.0
Nepal	46.1	75.5	24.1	12.1	28.0	9.3	0.1	1.2	0.0	0.0	0.0	0.1	1.6	1.8
Sri Lanka	14.8	21.9	29.9	34.5	43.5	30.0	7.7	8.9	0.6	1.9	0.7	1.4	2.7	1.4
Southeast Asia[a]	**59.8**	**68.1**	**15.6**	**12.6**	**20.7**	**14.1**	**2.1**	**2.6**	**0.5**	**0.9**	**1.0**	**1.5**	**0.2**	**0.1**
Brunei Darussalam	87.7	98.8	0.5	0.3	11.8	0.5	0.1	0.3	0.0	0.0	0.0	0.0	0.0	0.0
Cambodia	28.2	37.2	17.3	29.5	54.4	31.3	0.0	0.6	0.0	0.6	0.0	0.5	0.0	0.3
Indonesia	64.1	71.0	15.1	10.4	15.1	11.9	3.4	3.4	0.9	1.1	1.4	2.2	0.1	0.0
Lao People's Democratic Republic	58.1	88.2	38.0	7.0	3.4	4.1	0.1	0.3	0.0	0.1	0.2	0.3	0.0	0.0
Malaysia	60.0	72.9	14.5	11.1	22.3	11.1	2.0	2.4	0.6	0.6	0.6	1.7	0.0	0.0
Myanmar	77.6	73.4	6.2	22.1	15.0	0.9	0.6	1.3	0.2	0.2	0.4	2.0	0.0	0.1
Philippines	48.8	67.1	18.3	12.6	31.7	18.2	0.5	1.2	0.2	0.6	0.1	0.3	0.4	0.0
Singapore	62.8	75.1	14.6	10.2	19.2	10.8	1.7	2.1	0.4	0.5	1.1	1.3	0.2	0.0
Thailand	53.0	64.9	17.5	12.6	23.3	14.9	3.1	3.4	0.6	1.6	1.7	2.3	0.7	0.3
Timor-Leste[b]	75.5	85.8	17.1	5.0	6.7	8.3	0.0	0.1	0.0	0.0	0.6	0.8	0.0	0.0
Viet Nam	65.9	49.7	23.1	19.9	6.1	24.7	2.9	3.4	0.3	1.4	0.8	0.9	0.9	0.0
The Pacific[a]	**70.6**	**81.0**	**16.4**	**12.7**	**12.2**	**4.1**	**0.1**	**0.7**	**0.0**	**0.8**	**0.7**	**0.4**	**0.0**	**0.1**
Cook Islands	87.1	76.4	0.0	0.0	7.8	0.1	0.0	0.0	0.0	0.0	0.0	0.0	5.1	23.5
Fiji	56.0	69.3	20.2	7.3	23.7	23.1	0.0	0.2	0.1	0.0	0.0	0.1	0.0	0.0
Kiribati	87.2	99.5	0.6	0.0	0.1	0.5	0.0	0.0	12.1	0.0	0.0	0.0	0.0	0.0
Marshall Islands	0.0	37.7	42.6	49.5	57.4	1.3	0.0	8.4	0.0	0.8	0.0	2.2	0.0	0.0
Micronesia, Federated States of	42.1	98.2	0.3	0.1	57.4	1.6	0.0	0.1	0.0	0.1	0.0	0.0	0.2	0.0
Nauru	84.1	55.2	1.3	0.5	7.5	10.5	0.0	0.7	0.1	0.0	7.0	33.0	0.0	0.1
Niue	...	...	...	...	...	...	...	...	...	...	...	...	...	...
Palau	64.6	80.5	6.8	0.6	12.2	15.8	0.0	1.4	1.2	1.0	14.8	0.6	0.4	0.2
Papua New Guinea	72.0	87.1	19.9	10.3	6.9	1.4	0.2	0.0	0.0	1.0	1.1	0.0	0.0	0.1
Samoa	71.1	78.8	1.6	1.3	27.0	10.5	0.2	6.9	0.0	0.0	0.1	1.9	0.0	0.5
Solomon Islands	97.6	82.1	1.0	16.3	0.1	1.0	0.0	0.0	0.0	0.0	1.3	0.5	0.0	0.0
Tonga	99.0	81.8	0.1	0.2	0.9	17.9	0.0	0.0	0.0	0.0	0.0	0.0	0.0	0.0
Tuvalu	4.8	3.7	79.3	8.8	0.6	6.9	0.0	0.9	8.5	70.6	5.7	7.6	1.1	1.5
Vanuatu	28.0	74.8	69.2	6.0	2.6	12.7	0.0	0.1	0.1	4.7	0.0	1.7	0.1	0.0
Developed ADB Member Economies[a]	**46.4**	**64.0**	**17.3**	**12.0**	**31.3**	**18.3**	**2.6**	**3.0**	**1.2**	**1.1**	**1.0**	**1.0**	**0.3**	**0.6**
Australia	66.4	82.5	12.4	7.9	11.6	4.5	5.1	2.2	0.8	0.5	1.9	0.7	1.7	1.8
Japan	43.4	56.5	17.9	13.8	34.3	23.9	2.3	3.2	1.2	1.3	0.9	1.1	0.1	0.0
New Zealand	59.0	70.1	15.6	9.0	18.0	11.8	2.8	4.0	1.5	0.7	0.9	1.9	2.2	2.4
DEVELOPING ADB MEMBER ECONOMIES[a]	**52.8**	**55.7**	**17.7**	**17.3**	**23.6**	**17.0**	**2.9**	**4.4**	**1.1**	**2.1**	**1.3**	**2.8**	**0.7**	**0.5**
ALL ADB REGIONAL MEMBERS[a]	**50.8**	**57.0**	**17.6**	**16.6**	**25.9**	**17.2**	**2.8**	**4.2**	**1.1**	**2.0**	**1.2**	**2.5**	**0.6**	**0.5**
WORLD[a]	**24.6**	**33.1**	**42.1**	**38.2**	**25.2**	**18.3**	**3.0**	**4.2**	**2.2**	**2.4**	**1.8**	**2.6**	**1.1**	**1.2**

... = data not available, 0.0 = magnitude is less than half of unit employed, ADB = Asian Development Bank.

a Aggregates include estimates derived from reports of partner economies for nonreporting and slow-reporting economies.
b For 2000, data refer to 2004.

Sources: International Monetary Fund. Direction of Trade Statistics. http://data.imf.org/?sk=9D6028D4-F14A-464C-A2F2-59B2CD424B85 (accessed 17 July 2020).
For the Cook Islands and Taipei,China: Economy sources.

Click on the indictor name in the table header to access the time series in the Key Indicators Database.

External Trade

Table 2.4.14:   Direction of Trade: Merchandise Imports
(% of total merchandise imports)

From To ADB Regional Member	Asia and the Pacific		Europe		North and Central America		Middle East		South America		Africa		Rest of the World	
	2000	2019	2000	2019	2000	2019	2000	2019	2000	2019	2000	2019	2000	2019
Developing ADB Member Economies														
Central and West Asia[a]	**27.1**	**39.7**	**44.1**	**39.4**	**5.8**	**5.0**	**18.3**	**11.1**	**1.2**	**1.2**	**1.3**	**1.9**	**2.2**	**1.6**
Afghanistan	47.1	64.9	3.7	5.4	1.8	1.0	36.1	20.5	0.4	0.1	0.3	0.9	10.6	7.2
Armenia	4.3	25.5	60.4	57.3	14.6	6.1	15.4	7.3	0.0	1.9	0.0	0.9	5.4	1.0
Azerbaijan	14.4	23.2	65.1	61.1	10.5	9.4	7.3	4.3	0.5	1.4	2.1	0.2	0.2	0.5
Georgia	16.9	26.5	66.7	60.1	10.2	4.7	4.2	4.6	0.9	3.7	0.1	0.3	1.1	0.2
Kazakhstan	10.3	32.5	78.5	59.3	6.3	4.2	1.1	0.8	1.0	0.8	0.5	0.4	2.2	2.0
Kyrgyz Republic	26.3	51.1	45.5	41.0	11.7	2.1	2.9	0.9	0.1	0.2	0.0	0.3	13.5	4.5
Pakistan	31.2	45.5	19.8	12.6	7.0	6.6	38.3	27.4	1.0	1.3	2.7	5.3	0.1	1.2
Tajikistan	29.1	25.7	40.6	59.0	0.1	0.9	1.6	5.4	0.0	1.0	1.1	0.0	27.4	7.9
Turkmenistan	15.5	25.6	58.9	71.3	3.5	1.1	13.5	0.0	0.1	0.3	0.0	0.0	8.4	1.7
Uzbekistan	43.4	52.6	47.3	42.0	1.5	2.9	5.0	1.6	2.6	0.7	0.1	0.1	0.0	0.1
East Asia[a]	**62.5**	**55.6**	**13.6**	**15.9**	**13.8**	**9.1**	**6.0**	**7.6**	**1.3**	**4.9**	**1.7**	**2.9**	**1.1**	**4.0**
China, People's Republic of	58.2	48.0	17.5	18.3	11.8	8.2	4.5	7.8	2.1	7.1	2.4	4.3	3.4	6.5
Hong Kong, China	80.5	82.8	10.3	9.1	7.6	5.5	0.8	1.4	0.5	0.8	0.3	0.5	0.0	0.0
Korea, Republic of	48.1	51.6	12.5	15.2	20.0	14.9	15.9	13.9	1.6	2.6	1.8	1.4	0.2	0.5
Mongolia	47.1	54.8	47.8	38.6	4.8	5.7	0.2	0.1	0.0	0.7	0.0	0.2	0.0	0.0
Taipei,China	58.9	63.2	13.6	12.8	19.3	13.5	4.8	8.4	1.0	1.5	2.3	0.6	0.0	0.0
South Asia[a]	**34.5**	**44.8**	**24.8**	**15.3**	**6.3**	**8.6**	**8.7**	**20.5**	**1.3**	**3.1**	**4.7**	**7.0**	**19.7**	**0.8**
Bangladesh	59.9	61.8	12.4	10.2	3.7	4.9	5.2	8.6	1.4	3.9	0.9	3.3	16.6	7.4
Bhutan	92.7	95.1	7.0	3.2	0.2	0.3	0.0	0.6	0.1	0.0	0.0	0.0	0.0	0.7
India	23.6	40.2	28.9	16.4	7.2	9.4	9.4	23.0	1.4	3.2	6.1	7.8	23.5	0.0
Maldives	76.4	62.0	10.6	12.9	3.7	3.3	8.8	20.4	0.1	0.6	0.4	0.7	0.0	0.0
Nepal	71.6	87.0	12.8	3.7	2.0	4.0	5.8	2.0	0.8	1.4	0.1	0.2	7.0	1.7
Sri Lanka	70.4	73.1	14.2	11.8	4.6	4.4	9.4	7.3	0.5	0.3	0.5	3.1	0.2	0.1
Southeast Asia[a]	**62.8**	**70.0**	**13.0**	**11.9**	**14.9**	**9.0**	**7.0**	**5.8**	**0.6**	**1.5**	**0.7**	**1.4**	**1.1**	**0.3**
Brunei Darussalam	74.7	61.3	12.9	13.5	11.6	6.7	0.3	7.0	0.1	0.3	0.0	9.5	0.4	1.7
Cambodia	88.5	92.3	8.3	5.0	2.8	2.0	0.1	0.2	0.1	0.4	0.0	0.1	0.2	0.0
Indonesia	60.4	72.1	14.1	10.6	12.3	7.8	8.4	2.0	1.5	2.2	2.3	5.2	0.9	0.0
Lao People's Democratic Republic	92.2	96.9	7.0	2.8	0.7	0.3	0.0	0.0	0.0	0.0	0.0	0.0	0.0	0.0
Malaysia	65.2	71.6	12.6	11.1	17.3	8.8	2.0	5.1	0.6	2.0	0.4	1.4	1.9	0.0
Myanmar	88.4	89.8	9.2	4.9	2.4	0.4	0.0	2.1	0.0	0.6	0.0	2.2	0.0	0.0
Philippines	58.4	78.1	10.1	9.8	19.4	7.3	10.5	3.3	0.7	1.3	0.2	0.1	0.7	0.0
Singapore	60.7	58.7	14.2	16.8	15.8	13.6	8.2	9.3	0.3	0.6	0.4	0.9	0.4	0.0
Thailand	60.2	67.3	12.6	11.9	12.6	8.2	10.2	8.3	1.1	1.5	1.3	1.2	2.0	1.7
Timor-Leste[b]	94.0	94.3	5.3	2.8	0.6	1.2	0.0	0.3	0.1	1.2	0.0	0.2	0.0	0.0
Viet Nam	82.8	80.1	11.8	8.0	2.6	6.0	1.2	2.7	0.4	2.7	0.3	0.4	0.8	0.0
The Pacific[a]	**84.3**	**87.7**	**6.4**	**8.5**	**6.2**	**2.6**	**0.0**	**0.5**	**0.2**	**0.1**	**1.2**	**0.2**	**1.7**	**0.4**
Cook Islands	87.0	86.9	0.0	0.0	8.6	5.2	0.0	0.0	0.0	0.0	0.0	0.0	4.5	7.9
Fiji	84.6	80.2	3.8	15.7	5.5	2.5	0.1	0.8	0.3	0.1	0.2	0.3	5.5	0.4
Kiribati	85.4	93.8	2.4	2.6	12.0	3.2	0.0	0.0	0.0	0.1	0.1	0.2	0.0	0.0
Marshall Islands	0.1	88.4	99.8	9.7	0.1	0.9	0.0	0.7	0.0	0.0	0.0	0.3	0.0	0.0
Micronesia, Federated States of	98.0	58.1	1.7	0.5	0.0	27.3	0.0	0.0	0.0	0.1	0.0	0.3	0.2	13.7
Nauru	32.3	95.3	7.9	2.1	10.6	2.4	0.0	0.0	0.0	0.1	49.2	0.1	0.0	0.0
Niue	...	...	...	...	...	...	...	...	...	...	...	...	...	...
Palau	40.8	67.2	0.6	1.0	58.5	31.3	0.0	0.0	0.0	0.3	0.0	0.0	0.0	0.0
Papua New Guinea	94.1	93.6	3.2	3.8	2.3	2.2	0.0	0.2	0.2	0.1	0.1	0.2	0.0	0.0
Samoa	80.6	85.5	0.8	2.8	18.3	10.9	0.0	0.0	0.2	0.4	0.0	0.1	0.0	0.4
Solomon Islands	90.6	91.5	3.0	4.2	6.1	4.3	0.0	0.0	0.1	0.0	0.2	0.0	0.0	0.0
Tonga	88.7	83.1	0.6	4.4	10.3	11.6	0.0	0.1	0.2	0.7	0.1	0.1	0.0	0.0
Tuvalu	65.6	93.7	32.8	0.8	0.2	3.8	0.0	0.3	1.0	0.0	0.0	1.3	0.4	0.0
Vanuatu	91.0	92.1	7.5	5.1	0.7	2.0	0.0	0.2	0.2	0.3	0.4	0.3	0.1	0.1
Developed ADB Member Economies[a]	**47.0**	**57.5**	**16.5**	**16.7**	**22.1**	**13.4**	**11.2**	**8.6**	**1.8**	**2.2**	**1.2**	**1.1**	**0.2**	**0.4**
Australia	49.5	60.6	23.5	20.0	22.1	13.8	2.8	1.8	0.8	0.8	0.9	1.1	0.4	1.8
Japan	46.4	56.5	15.1	15.5	22.2	13.4	13.0	10.9	2.0	2.7	1.3	1.1	0.1	0.0
New Zealand	53.1	59.3	18.8	21.2	19.6	12.1	5.6	5.4	1.1	1.2	1.2	0.6	0.5	0.3
DEVELOPING ADB MEMBER ECONOMIES[a]	**60.3**	**57.6**	**14.7**	**15.5**	**13.5**	**8.9**	**6.7**	**8.6**	**1.1**	**3.8**	**1.5**	**2.9**	**2.2**	**2.7**
ALL ADB REGIONAL MEMBERS[a]	**56.6**	**57.6**	**15.2**	**15.7**	**15.9**	**9.6**	**7.9**	**8.6**	**1.3**	**3.5**	**1.4**	**2.7**	**1.6**	**2.3**
WORLD[a]	**29.1**	**35.8**	**40.6**	**38.5**	**19.9**	**13.9**	**4.2**	**4.9**	**2.6**	**2.9**	**2.2**	**2.5**	**1.3**	**1.4**

... = data not available, 0.0 = magnitude is less than half of unit employed, ADB = Asian Development Bank.

a Aggregates include estimates derived from reports of partner economies for nonreporting and slow-reporting economies.
b For 2000, data refer to 2004.

Sources: International Monetary Fund. Direction of Trade Statistics. http://data.imf.org/?sk=9D6028D4-F14A-464C-A2F2-59B2CD424B85 (accessed 17 July 2020).
For the Cook Islands and Taipei,China: Economy sources.

Table 2.4.15: International Reserves and Ratio to Imports

ADB Regional Member	International Reserves[a] ($ million)				Ratio to Imports[b] (months)			
	2000	2005	2010	2019	2000	2005	2010	2019
Developing ADB Member Economies								
Central and West Asia	**9,909**	**27,063**	**77,894**	**100,349**	**4.4**	**6.0**	**9.6**	**8.0**
Afghanistan	...	...	5,147	8,467	...	...	12.9	16.5
Armenia	314	669	1,866	2,850	4.8	4.8	6.9	6.9
Azerbaijan	680	1,178	6,409	7,043	5.3	3.2	11.5	7.5
Georgia	116	479	2,264	3,506	1.4	2.2	5.4	4.8
Kazakhstan	2,096	7,070	28,275	28,958	3.6	4.7	10.3	9.0
Kyrgyz Republic	262	612	1,720	2,425	6.2	6.6	6.9	6.3
Pakistan	2,056	10,948	17,210	16,463	2.6	6.9	6.6	3.8
Tajikistan	94	189	403	1,466	1.2	2.0	1.7	6.0
Turkmenistan	...	...	...	...	...	...	...	...
Uzbekistan	1,273	2,900	14,600	29,172	6.3	10.5	22.0	16.5
East Asia	**484,185**	**1,418,542**	**3,825,703**	**4,560,345**	**9.0**	**13.7**	**20.0**	**16.6**
China, People's Republic of	168,855	825,588	2,875,894	3,222,900	10.8	17.5	27.8	19.6
Hong Kong, China	107,560	124,278	268,743	441,349	7.9	6.1	8.4	9.4
Korea, Republic of	96,198	210,391	291,571	408,500	7.5	10.0	8.4	10.1
Mongolia	202	333	2,288	4,356	4.0	3.4	8.9	8.7
Taipei,China	111,370	257,952	387,207	483,240	9.7	17.0	18.5	21.2
South Asia	**44,209**	**143,747**	**320,425**	**510,953**	**7.1**	**9.5**	**9.0**	**10.8**
Bangladesh	1,516	2,825	11,178	32,692	2.4	2.9	6.3	7.1
Bhutan	318	467	1,002	1,238	20.6	12.2	15.1	15.4
India	40,155	136,026	297,746	460,209	8.3	10.4	9.3	11.6
Maldives	123	189	364	762	4.3	3.5	3.5	3.3
Nepal	952	1,504	2,939	8,407	7.3	8.9	7.2	8.2
Sri Lanka	1,147	2,735	7,196	7,645	1.9	3.7	6.4	4.6
Southeast Asia	**190,733**	**303,674**	**688,196**	**933,800**	**6.0**	**6.6**	**9.3**	**8.7**
Brunei Darussalam	408	492	1,563	4,273	4.2 (2001)	4.2	7.3	10.3
Cambodia	611	1,159	3,802	18,762	3.8	3.5	6.9	10.1
Indonesia	29,268	34,731	96,211	129,183	8.7	6.5	9.7	9.4
Lao People's Democratic Republic	140	257	817	1,068	3.1	3.5	4.8	2.0
Malaysia	28,624	70,152	106,525	103,613	4.4	7.8	8.6	7.4
Myanmar	234	782	5,729	5,822	1.3	5.3	16.0	4.5 (2018)
Philippines	15,063	18,494	62,373	87,840	4.2	5.9	14.0	10.6
Singapore	80,170	116,172	225,715	279,451	6.9	7.2	8.7	9.8
Thailand	32,661	52,065	172,129	224,322	6.3	5.9	12.4	12.4
Timor-Leste	43 (2002)	153	406	656	...	8.9 (2006)	15.9	13.3
Viet Nam	3,510	9,216	12,926	78,810	3.0	3.2	2.0	3.9
The Pacific	**981**	**1,408**	**4,611**	**...**	**4.3**	**4.3**	**8.3**	**...**
Cook Islands	...	...	...	...	...	...	...	...
Fiji	412	321	721	1,043	6.4	2.8	5.6	5.2
Kiribati	0	0	8	7	0.0	0.0	1.3	0.7 (2018)
Marshall Islands	0	0	5	5 (2017)	0.0	0.0	0.5	0.5 (2017)
Micronesia, Federated States of	113	50	56	204 (2018)	12.4	4.8	4.2	13.9 (2018)
Nauru	...	...	...	1 (2018)	...	...	...	0.2 (2018)
Niue	...	...	...	...	...	...	...	...
Palau	0	0	5	4 (2018)	0.0	0.0	0.6	0.3 (2018)
Papua New Guinea	296	749	3,092	2,309	3.5	5.9	10.5	7.5
Samoa	64	77	189	185	2.4	5.0	8.1	6.2
Solomon Islands	32	95	266	571	4.2	9.4	8.9	13.7
Tonga	25	47	105	229	2.9	2.8	6.0	6.2
Tuvalu	0	0	3	2 (2017)	0.0	0.0	1.8	1.1 (2017)
Vanuatu	39	67	161	512	6.1	6.2	8.1	16.7 (2018)
Developed ADB Member Economies	**384,408**	**899,045**	**1,163,670**	**1,398,998**	**11.2**	**17.8**	**16.4**	**17.5**
Australia	18,817	43,257	42,268	58,742	3.5	4.5	2.6	3.2
Japan	361,639	846,896	1,104,680	1,322,443	12.9	21.9	21.2	22.9
New Zealand	3,952	8,893	16,723	17,814	3.7	4.2	6.5	4.9 (2018)
DEVELOPING ADB MEMBER ECONOMIES	**730,018**	**1,894,434**	**4,916,830**	**6,110,522**	**7.7**	**11.2**	**15.9**	**13.8**
ALL ADB REGIONAL MEMBERS	**1,114,426**	**2,793,480**	**6,080,501**	**7,509,520**	**8.6**	**12.7**	**16.0**	**14.4**

... = data not available, 0 or 0.0 = magnitude is less than half of the unit employed, $ = United States dollars, ADB = Asian Development Bank.

a Data refer to international reserves with gold at national valuation, unless otherwise specified, as of the end of the year. For Afghanistan (prior to 2008), Bhutan, Kiribati, Nauru, Palau, Samoa, Solomon Islands (prior to 2012), Tonga, Turkmenistan, and Vanuatu, data refer to international reserves without gold. For estimating aggregates, imputation was done for economies with missing data using available data from the nearest years.

b Merchandise imports from the balance of payments were used in the calculation. Aggregate ratios calculated using only reporting economies with data available for both reserves and imports in the years specified in the column headings.

Sources: For international reserves: International Monetary Fund. International Financial Statistics. http://data.imf.org/ (accessed 11 July 2020); for Taipei,China: economy source. For the reserves-to-imports ratio: Asian Development Bank estimates using data from economy sources and International Monetary Fund. International Financial Statistics. http://data.imf.org/ (accessed 11 July 2020).

Table 2.4.16:   **Net Official Development Assistance from All Sources to Developing Economies**[a]
($ million)

ADB Regional Member	2000	2005	2010	2013	2014	2015	2016	2017	2018
Developing ADB Member Economies									
Central and West Asia[b]	**1,925**	**5,856**	**11,448**	**9,555**	**11,042**	**10,667**	**9,384**	**8,524**	**7,454**
Afghanistan	136	2,815	6,235	5,153	4,943	4,274	4,069	3,812	3,792
Armenia	216	173	320	280	267	347	326	257	141
Azerbaijan	141	210	156	-71	217	70	79	124	87
Georgia	172	293	589	646	564	449	463	447	590
Kazakhstan	185	225	212	91	93	82	63	59	80
Kyrgyz Republic	193	238	372	539	627	775	519	465	416
Pakistan	550	1,477	2,933	2,194	3,616	3,764	2,961	2,364	1,367
Tajikistan	112	226	388	391	356	432	360	328	403
Turkmenistan	36	29	44	36	34	23	32	28	20
Uzbekistan	185	169	198	295	325	451	511	639	558
East Asia[b]	**1,935**	**1,994**	**959**	**-226**	**-630**	**-70**	**-466**	**-225**	**-373**
China, People's Republic of	1,749	1,798	672	-657	-947	-306	-791	-990	-706
Hong Kong, China	...	...	...	...	...	...	...	...	...
Korea, Republic of	...	...	...	...	...	...	...	...	...
Mongolia	186	195	287	431	317	236	326	765	333
Taipei,China	...	...	...	...	...	...	...	...	...
South Asia[b]	**2,959**	**4,726**	**5,670**	**6,525**	**6,943**	**7,558**	**6,724**	**8,724**	**6,926**
Bangladesh	976	1,252	1,327	2,634	2,423	2,593	2,533	3,782	3,044
Bhutan	47	79	97	137	131	97	52	119	106
India	1,383	1,876	2,831	2,456	2,992	3,174	2,679	3,198	2,462
Maldives	18	72	88	22	23	24	23	43	119
Nepal	311	407	767	873	884	1,224	1,065	1,269	1,452
Sri Lanka	222	1,040	559	403	492	445	373	313	-256
Southeast Asia[b]	**5,349**	**5,659**	**6,365**	**9,689**	**7,797**	**6,243**	**6,145**	**6,176**	**5,930**
Brunei Darussalam	...	...	...	...	...	...	...	...	...
Cambodia	346	453	681	808	803	679	728	856	773
Indonesia	1,645	2,489	1,324	69	-382	-28	-108	280	962
Lao People's Democratic Republic	234	241	389	423	474	471	399	480	568
Malaysia	49	29	-6	-113	20	-1	-52	-29	-35
Myanmar	106	145	355	3,936	1,384	1,169	1,537	1,542	1,690
Philippines	553	588	582	192	677	515	284	160	547
Singapore	...	...	...	...	...	...	...	...	...
Thailand	701	-165	-20	29	355	59	228	250	-420
Timor-Leste	231	185	290	259	250	212	224	232	207
Viet Nam	1,485	1,693	2,770	4,086	4,216	3,167	2,906	2,404	1,638
The Pacific[b]	**670**	**906**	**1,435**	**1,752**	**1,527**	**1,576**	**1,345**	**1,571**	**1,857**
Cook Islands	4	7	14	16	28	26	17	19	34
Fiji	29	66	76	91	94	102	117	146	116
Kiribati	17	27	24	65	81	65	61	77	75
Marshall Islands	47	56	25	94	56	57	13	73	54
Micronesia, Federated States of	97	105	64	143	117	81	51	98	99
Nauru	4	9	28	29	23	31	23	26	32
Niue	3	21	15	18	14	20	14	15	19
Palau	39	24	29	35	23	14	18	22	85
Papua New Guinea	275	268	514	657	582	591	532	533	790
Samoa	29	43	124	113	94	94	89	131	121
Solomon Islands	68	197	333	290	201	190	176	187	196
Tonga	16	33	66	81	80	68	83	87	88
Tuvalu	4	9	14	28	34	50	24	27	20
Vanuatu	35	40	109	91	100	187	129	132	130
DEVELOPING ADB MEMBER ECONOMIES[b]	**12,837**	**19,139**	**25,876**	**27,294**	**26,678**	**25,974**	**23,133**	**24,770**	**21,793**
DEVELOPING ECONOMIES WORLDWIDE[c]	**48,993**	**107,452**	**129,264**	**151,138**	**161,730**	**146,741**	**158,808**	**165,026**	**166,299**

... = data not available, $ = United States dollars, ADB = Asian Development Bank.

a   Net official development assistance refers to concessional flows to developing economies and multilateral institutions provided by official agencies, including state and local governments, or by their executing agencies, administered with the objective of promoting the economic development and welfare of developing economies, and containing a grant element of at least 25%. Net flow takes into account principal repayments for loans, offsetting entries for forgiven debt, and recoveries made on grants.
b   For reporting economies only.
c   Includes data for all developing economies as reported in the Organisation for Economic Co-operation and Development's OECD.Stat database.

Source: Organisation for Economic Co-operation and Development. OECD.Stat Database. http://stats.oecd.org (accessed 14 August 2020).

Table 2.4.17: Net Other Official Flows from All Sources to Developing Economies[a]
($ million)

ADB Regional Member	2000	2005	2010	2013	2014	2015	2016	2017	2018
Developing ADB Member Economies									
Central and West Asia[b]	**158.5**	**-41.0**	**4,070.1**	**2,840.5**	**3,063.7**	**5,251.1**	**5,540.1**	**2,663.7**	**1,782.9**
Afghanistan	...	56.9	71.2	60.5	-24.2	127.4	97.2	56.1	0.2
Armenia	16.9	7.8	288.3	112.1	103.6	111.1	197.2	157.6	156.7
Azerbaijan	314.3	226.5	179.9	391.0	630.1	801.8	1,114.7	1,738.5	490.7
Georgia	62.7	86.3	250.2	-0.7	2.9	342.4	486.6	262.1	219.0
Kazakhstan	-41.7	-502.3	2,247.2	1,548.0	549.5	1,256.7	441.4	-853.7	-673.2
Kyrgyz Republic	-4.0	56.3	18.3	69.7	16.5	0.4	-43.2	-6.0	51.2
Pakistan	-592.9	127.4	345.3	-236.7	-97.1	-343.9	1,102.3	378.2	-137.0
Tajikistan	0.7	22.8	6.4	6.6	-5.5	68.1	13.6	15.6	48.2
Turkmenistan	130.3	-74.1	647.4	135.4	1,143.9	2,356.6	926.1	532.3	127.6
Uzbekistan	272.1	-48.7	16.0	754.6	743.9	530.5	1,204.2	383.0	1,499.5
East Asia[b]	**-1,790.9**	**408.6**	**3,355.5**	**997.1**	**852.8**	**1,429.0**	**896.3**	**1,016.7**	**816.4**
China, People's Republic of	-1,782.4	423.1	3,196.3	742.1	343.0	1,215.8	139.9	1,227.3	650.9
Hong Kong, China	...	...	...	...	...	...	...	...	...
Korea, Republic of	...	...	...	...	...	...	...	...	...
Mongolia	-8.5	-14.6	159.3	255.0	509.8	213.3	756.4	-210.6	165.6
Taipei,China	...	...	...	...	...	...	...	...	...
South Asia[b]	**-231.9**	**2,589.2**	**6,175.1**	**3,659.0**	**4,615.0**	**2,531.9**	**3,653.6**	**3,636.7**	**2,832.9**
Bangladesh	-30.5	186.8	35.1	187.7	247.0	417.9	1,421.5	2,337.4	938.4
Bhutan	-1.1	4.8	24.0	-5.0	-6.0	-2.8	8.0	3.1	-5.2
India	-196.4	2,322.3	5,967.5	3,010.8	4,029.7	1,811.5	1,935.6	1,190.1	1,650.3
Maldives	-4.8	44.0	-33.9	13.3	-3.7	-8.1	-24.7	-23.8	18.0
Nepal	23.7	-8.3	-6.9	16.2	-2.4	-7.4	0.7	-2.3	-0.2
Sri Lanka	-22.7	39.8	189.3	436.0	350.5	320.8	312.6	132.3	231.7
Southeast Asia[b]	**-1,110.2**	**1,043.0**	**3,916.6**	**6,358.4**	**2,846.1**	**8,205.9**	**3,110.3**	**60.5**	**4,784.1**
Brunei Darussalam	...	...	...	...	...	...	...	...	...
Cambodia	-0.4	7.6	-5.0	89.3	96.3	84.6	-12.3	84.1	-23.1
Indonesia	100.1	1,443.8	1,783.7	120.8	-1,715.7	3,775.4	3,708.7	2,963.1	3,784.7
Lao People's Democratic Republic	-8.8	59.4	-120.5	4.6	194.8	73.1	38.6	74.7	34.1
Malaysia	519.9	-1,369.3	159.2	-126.4	1,339.4	-231.8	-1,494.5	-739.8	-963.0
Myanmar	20.1	-31.5	30.9	227.2	107.6	427.5	100.6	96.4	18.5
Philippines	499.6	-945.9	-680.3	-1,245.5	1,029.6	1,148.5	203.1	-32.2	956.6
Singapore	...	...	...	...	...	...	...	...	...
Thailand	-2,112.2	1,629.6	-71.5	2,454.4	-349.0	138.7	-39.3	-1,051.6	-613.9
Timor-Leste	417.8	1.1	4.6	5.7	9.9	7.8	24.8	11.8	26.5
Viet Nam	-546.4	248.4	2,815.4	4,828.3	2,133.3	2,782.1	580.6	-1,345.9	1,563.6
The Pacific[b]	**59.0**	**-20.2**	**4,982.0**	**1,132.3**	**-2,765.2**	**18.1**	**-144.7**	**-164.0**	**-2.6**
Cook Islands	-0.2	-0.3	9.7	4.9	-1.3	-0.6	-1.2	1.8	0.6
Fiji	-11.8	1.2	14.2	73.6	66.1	-11.4	40.6	48.3	27.1
Kiribati	0.1 (2002)	0.2	0.5	0.6	0.2	0.2	0.3	0.1	0.3
Marshall Islands	-0.2	-0.1	-0.6	-21.1	146.2	7.6	36.7	17.1	58.7
Micronesia, Federated States of	-0.1	0.3	0.8	-1.0	1.1	0.2	2.3	1.5	0.2
Nauru	-5.6	0.2	0.3	-0.1	...	...	62.5	19.4	0.4
Niue	7.5	...	...	...	...	...	–	...	...
Palau	-1.5	-2.1	6.4 (2011)	6.4	-11.1	0.3	6.6	9.9	8.7
Papua New Guinea	85.4	-9.1	4,892.3	1,025.2	-2,991.6	19.4	-320.7	-267.2	-120.7
Samoa	0.4	-0.1	4.1	4.2	-0.9	-1.3	5.6	1.3	-0.2
Solomon Islands	1.2	-11.7	59.2	37.4	25.0	0.7	19.1	0.5	11.0
Tonga	0.0	0.4	0.3	0.3	0.0	2.1	2.5	1.2	2.3
Tuvalu	...	0.5 (2006)	-0.1	0.2	0.2	0.2	0.2	0.1	0.2
Vanuatu	-16.2	0.8	1.3	1.7	0.8	0.7	0.9	2.1	8.9
DEVELOPING ADB MEMBER ECONOMIES[b]	**-2,915.5**	**3,979.7**	**22,499.2**	**14,987.2**	**8,612.3**	**17,436.0**	**13,055.7**	**7,213.5**	**10,213.8**
DEVELOPING ECONOMIES WORLDWIDE[c]	**9,856.9**	**9,605.9**	**70,855.8**	**38,808.2**	**22,461.4**	**50,604.3**	**29,284.9**	**21,460.1**	**30,665.2**

... = data not available, 0.0 = magnitude is less than half of unit employed, $ = United States dollars, ADB = Asian Development Bank.

a Net other official flows refer to official sector transactions with economies on the Development Assistance Committee List of Official Development Assistance Recipients (http://www.oecd.org/dac/financing-sustainable-development/development-finance-standards/daclist.htm) that do not meet the conditions for eligibility as official development assistance, either because they are not primarily aimed at development or because they have a grant element of less than 25%. Also includes net export credits. Net flow takes into account principal repayments for loans, offsetting entries for forgiven debt, and recoveries made on grants.

b For reporting economies only.

c Includes data for all developing economies as reported in the Organisation for Economic Co-operation and Development's OECD.Stat database.

Source: Organisation for Economic Co-operation and Development. OECD.Stat Database. http://stats.oecd.org (accessed 14 August 2020).

Table 2.4.18:   Net Private Flows from All Sources to Developing Economies[a]
($ million)

ADB Regional Member	2000	2005	2010	2013	2014	2015	2016	2017	2018
Developing ADB Member Economies									
Central and West Asia[b]	**1,023**	**4,081**	**-822**	**3,981**	**827**	**5,055**	**1,243**	**-1,189**	**-6,731**
Afghanistan	21	-14	-21	26	32	-5	-5	3	1
Armenia	-21	35	-69	208	-0	57	179	88	88
Azerbaijan	219	1,082	798	869	-129	436	404	145	218
Georgia	23	-32	22	52	-59	1,249	190	359	337
Kazakhstan	603	2,252	-1,511	2,947	1,251	3,090	-86	-3,002	-7,651
Kyrgyz Republic	12	7	23	18	10	6	-23	15	11
Pakistan	60	833	-75	-172	155	131	192	703	-97
Tajikistan	-8	-1	18	47	4	-8	-2	-42	43
Turkmenistan	124	1	-46	103	42	-11	285	107	-21
Uzbekistan	-10	-84	39	-117	-478	110	108	436	339
East Asia[b]	**926**	**21,123**	**46,322**	**54,436**	**61,744**	**17,370**	**42,706**	**38,821**	**27,606**
China, People's Republic of	923	21,125	46,301	53,925	61,702	17,154	42,121	38,753	27,415
Hong Kong, China	...	...	...	...	...	...	...	...	...
Korea, Republic of	...	...	...	...	...	...	...	...	...
Mongolia	3	-2	22	511	42	216	586	68	191
Taipei,China	...	...	...	...	...	...	...	...	...
South Asia[b]	**1,274**	**4,776**	**20,237**	**6,571**	**11,446**	**7,900**	**14,938**	**19,621**	**14,471**
Bangladesh	93	186	-3	-105	249	100	-380	225	79
Bhutan	-8	1	18	-163	9	16	-0	-1	-7
India	1,099	4,548	19,976	6,292	10,655	7,288	14,813	18,950	13,477
Maldives	-4	8	38	-16	100	112	17	-1	158
Nepal	-4	-2	-11	115	7	-3	6	53	25
Sri Lanka	98	35	218	447	427	387	482	394	739
Southeast Asia[b]	**286**	**20,767**	**21,463**	**31,547**	**38,906**	**16,972**	**23,388**	**25,424**	**21,382**
Brunei Darussalam	...	...	...	...	...	...	...	...	...
Cambodia	9	9	256	310	399	380	403	412	456
Indonesia	606	4,012	3,348	7,291	13,343	9,678	10,235	11,225	6,559
Lao People's Democratic Republic	14	0	172	59	50	-19	44	72	27
Malaysia	-872	2,064	6,573	9,719	6,165	3,689	2,134	2,962	117
Myanmar	-70	17	260	534	566	865	356	452	415
Philippines	330	3,496	2,424	2,510	4,839	1,908	2,738	4,251	3,077
Singapore	...	...	...	...	...	...	...	...	...
Thailand	32	10,944	6,394	6,096	10,076	-2,337	2,760	1,497	6,714
Timor-Leste	54 (2001)	0	-3	25	2	17	-41	15	1
Viet Nam	237	224	2,038	5,002	3,467	2,790	4,758	4,537	4,018
The Pacific[b]	**106**	**3,025**	**978**	**-59**	**153**	**179**	**925**	**1,211**	**-2,061**
Cook Islands	-31	-29	-0	3	-2	-2	-1	0	-18
Fiji	6	51	-3	2	49	53	-15	45	40
Kiribati	0	1	-0	0	3	3	-9	-1	9
Marshall Islands	108	2,737	974	-1,048	-365	2,245	9	572	-513
Micronesia, Federated States of	-0 (2001)	0	3	93	320	798	714	453	-1,641
Nauru	4	2	-0 (2011)	...	...	...	-0	0	-0
Niue	12	-1	-0 (2012)	...	0	0	0	0	0
Palau	18	1	3	2	6	7	9	10	9
Papua New Guinea	-27	238	-40	879	65	-2,931	211	134	8
Samoa	1	30	17	-36	37	3	8	6	54
Solomon Islands	-15	-17	3	4	23	11	-1	-8	-0
Tonga	-7	2	-10	1	1	-1	-0	0	0
Tuvalu	-4	-1	1 (2011)	-2	-1	0	0	0	...
Vanuatu	41	11	31	43	15	-5	1	-1	-10
DEVELOPING ADB MEMBER ECONOMIES[b]	**3,615**	**53,771**	**88,177**	**96,474**	**113,076**	**47,476**	**83,201**	**83,887**	**54,667**
DEVELOPING ECONOMIES WORLDWIDE[c]	**75,170**	**173,009**	**324,145**	**251,386**	**414,308**	**116,530**	**128,651**	**233,815**	**90,853**

... = data not available, -0 or 0 = magnitude is less than half of unit employed, $ = United States dollars, ADB = Asian Development Bank.

a   Net private flows refer to the sum of direct investments and portfolio investments.
b   For reporting economies only.
c   Includes data for all developing economies as reported in the Organisation for Economic Co-operation and Development's OECD.Stat database.

Source: Organisation for Economic Co-operation and Development. OECD.Stat Database. http://stats.oecd.org (accessed 14 August 2020).

Table 2.4.19: Aggregate Net Resource Flows from All Sources to Developing Economies[a]
($ million)

ADB Regional Member	2000	2005	2010	2013	2014	2015	2016	2017	2018
Developing ADB Member Economies									
Central and West Asia[b]	**3,106**	**9,895**	**14,696**	**16,376**	**14,933**	**20,973**	**16,168**	**9,998**	**2,506**
Afghanistan	157	2,858	6,285	5,239	4,951	4,396	4,162	3,871	3,794
Armenia	211	216	539	600	371	515	703	502	386
Azerbaijan	673	1,519	1,135	1,189	718	1,308	1,598	2,007	796
Georgia	258	347	861	698	508	2,040	1,139	1,068	1,145
Kazakhstan	746	1,975	948	4,586	1,893	4,429	419	-3,797	-8,245
Kyrgyz Republic	201	302	413	627	653	781	453	474	478
Pakistan	17	2,437	3,203	1,786	3,673	3,551	4,255	3,446	1,133
Tajikistan	105	248	413	444	355	492	371	302	494
Turkmenistan	290	-44	645	274	1,220	2,369	1,244	667	127
Uzbekistan	447	37	253	933	590	1,092	1,823	1,458	2,397
East Asia[b]	**1,069**	**23,525**	**50,636**	**55,207**	**61,967**	**18,729**	**43,137**	**39,612**	**28,050**
China, People's Republic of	889	23,346	50,169	54,011	61,098	18,063	41,469	38,990	27,360
Hong Kong, China	...	...	...	...	...	...	...	...	...
Korea, Republic of	...	...	...	...	...	...	...	...	...
Mongolia	180	179	468	1,196	869	665	1,668	622	690
Taipei,China	...	...	...	...	...	...	...	...	...
South Asia[b]	**4,001**	**12,091**	**32,082**	**16,754**	**23,004**	**17,990**	**25,315**	**31,982**	**24,229**
Bangladesh	1,039	1,625	1,360	2,717	2,918	3,111	3,574	6,344	4,061
Bhutan	38	85	140	-32	133	110	60	121	93
India	2,286	8,746	28,774	11,760	17,676	12,274	19,428	23,339	17,589
Maldives	10	124	93	19	119	128	15	18	295
Nepal	331	397	749	1,005	888	1,215	1,071	1,320	1,477
Sri Lanka	298	1,115	966	1,286	1,269	1,153	1,168	839	715
Southeast Asia[b]	**4,525**	**27,468**	**31,744**	**47,594**	**49,549**	**31,420**	**32,644**	**31,660**	**32,096**
Brunei Darussalam	...	...	...	...	...	...	...	...	...
Cambodia	354	470	932	1,207	1,298	1,144	1,120	1,353	1,205
Indonesia	2,352	7,945	6,456	7,481	11,245	13,425	13,835	14,468	11,306
Lao People's Democratic Republic	239	301	441	487	719	526	482	627	629
Malaysia	-304	724	6,726	9,480	7,524	3,457	588	2,193	-882
Myanmar	56	131	646	4,697	2,058	2,460	1,993	2,090	2,123
Philippines	1,383	3,138	2,326	1,457	6,546	3,571	3,225	4,379	4,580
Singapore	...	...	...	...	...	...	...	...	...
Thailand	-1,380	12,409	6,302	8,579	10,081	-2,139	2,949	696	5,681
Timor-Leste	649	186	292	290	262	238	207	259	235
Viet Nam	1,176	2,166	7,623	13,916	9,816	8,739	8,244	5,595	7,219
The Pacific[b]	**835**	**3,911**	**7,395**	**2,825**	**-1,086**	**1,773**	**2,126**	**2,618**	**-207**
Cook Islands	-27	-23	23	23	25	23	15	20	17
Fiji	24	118	87	166	210	144	143	239	184
Kiribati	17	28	24	66	84	68	52	77	84
Marshall Islands	156	2,793	998	-975	-163	2,309	58	662	-400
Micronesia, Federated States of	97	105	68	236	438	879	767	552	-1,542
Nauru	2	12	28	29	23	31	85	45	32
Niue	23	20	15	18	14	20	14	15	19
Palau	55	22	32	44	18	21	33	42	102
Papua New Guinea	333	498	5,366	2,562	-2,344	-2,320	422	400	677
Samoa	30	73	145	81	130	95	103	139	175
Solomon Islands	55	169	395	331	249	202	194	179	206
Tonga	10	35	57	83	82	70	85	88	90
Tuvalu	-0	8	14	26	34	50	25	27	20
Vanuatu	60	52	142	136	117	182	131	134	129
DEVELOPING ADB MEMBER ECONOMIES[b]	**13,536**	**76,890**	**136,553**	**138,756**	**148,366**	**90,885**	**119,389**	**115,871**	**86,674**
DEVELOPING ECONOMIES WORLDWIDE[c]	**134,020**	**290,067**	**524,265**	**441,332**	**598,499**	**313,876**	**316,744**	**420,301**	**287,817**

... = data not available, $ = United States dollars, ADB = Asian Development Bank.

a Aggregate net resource flows refer to the sum of net official development assistance, net other official flows, and net private flows.
b For reporting economies only.
c Includes data for all developing economies as reported in the Organisation for Economic Co-operation and Development's OECD.Stat database.

Source: Organisation for Economic Co-operation and Development. OECD.Stat Database. http://stats.oecd.org (accessed 14 August 2020).

Table 2.4.20:   Total External Debt of Developing Economies[a]
($ million)

ADB Regional Member	Total External Debt				External Debt, Public and Publicly Guaranteed			
	2000	2005	2010	2018	2000	2005	2010	2018
Developing ADB Member Economies								
Central and West Asia[b]	**60,998**	**93,506**	**222,929**	**327,466**	**41,583**	**43,302**	**67,086**	**132,724**
Afghanistan	0	979 (2006)	2,436	2,605	0	920 (2006)	1,976	1,949
Armenia	1,018	1,970	6,307	11,019	684	924	2,560	5,371
Azerbaijan	1,585	2,247	7,258	16,212	794	1,491	3,819	13,957
Georgia	1,826	2,151	8,790	17,118	1,274	1,531	3,274	6,280
Kazakhstan	12,890	43,862	119,151	156,921	3,623	2,177	3,845	24,181
Kyrgyz Republic	1,938	2,257	4,118	8,120	1,220	1,665	2,446	3,685
Pakistan	33,026	34,118	62,975	90,957	27,196	30,189	43,577	64,493
Tajikistan	1,141	1,117	3,561	5,977	755	821	1,806	2,857
Turkmenistan	2,627	1,153	531	907	2,271	878	362	469
Uzbekistan	4,948	4,632	7,802	17,630	3,766	3,626	3,423	9,481
East Asia[b]	**525,059**	**1,003,874**	**2,077,093**	**4,318,832**	**147,681**	**125,558**	**224,629**	**...**
China, People's Republic of	145,874	283,501	734,639	1,962,304	94,697	84,404	94,176	243,455
Hong Kong, China	208,260	470,288	879,034	1,673,614 (2019)	...	...	...	...
Korea, Republic of	135,208	161,956	355,911	466,979 (2019)	52,128	39,665	120,636	...
Mongolia	960	1,396	5,928	29,377	833	1,267	1,782	7,856
Taipei,China	34,757	86,732	101,581	184,659 (2019)	23	222	8,035	629 (2019)
South Asia[b]	**129,277**	**155,211**	**344,632**	**636,500**	**107,345**	**85,873**	**143,502**	**260,917**
Bangladesh	15,603	18,506	26,881	52,124	14,992	17,441	21,453	36,664
Bhutan	212	657	935	2,549	202	636	919	2,482
India	101,131	121,195	290,428	521,391	81,196	54,726	100,563	180,508
Maldives	203	362	917	2,332	185	300	628	2,003
Nepal	2,878	3,191	3,789	5,478	2,826	3,112	3,509	4,941
Sri Lanka	9,250	11,300	21,684	52,626	7,945	9,658	16,430	34,319
Southeast Asia[b]	**568,374**	**656,353**	**...**	**...**	**174,236**	**187,673**	**273,649**	**370,235**
Brunei Darussalam	...	...	...	...	...	...	...	...
Cambodia	1,946	2,769	3,825	13,347	1,853	2,666	2,874	6,808
Indonesia	144,049	142,132	198,278	379,664	70,043	77,717	102,748	215,147
Lao People's Democratic Republic	2,531	3,279	6,554	15,588	2,474	2,354	3,751	9,161
Malaysia	41,946	64,911	133,800	200,364 (2016)	19,125	34,387	61,858	65,721 (2016)
Myanmar	6,477	7,171	10,157	14,936	5,895	6,323	8,602	13,701
Philippines	58,456	58,693	65,358	78,824	33,744	35,364	45,094	36,346
Singapore	220,298	300,359	...	...	...	...	...	...
Thailand	79,830	58,467	106,358	169,241	29,462	12,602	15,929	35,606
Timor-Leste	0	0	0	158	0	0	0	145
Viet Nam	12,841	18,572	44,936	108,096	11,640	16,260	32,794	53,321
The Pacific[b]	**3,227**	**2,920**	**7,795**	**20,330**	**...**	**...**	**...**	**...**
Cook Islands	59	68	99	71 (2019)	...	...	...	...
Fiji	122	230	535	852	101	112	353	714
Kiribati	8	11	14	47 (2019)	...	...	...	...
Marshall Islands	105	92	105	78	...	...	...	...
Micronesia, Federated States of	63	62	86	76	...	...	...	...
Nauru	...	...	...	...	...	...	...	...
Niue	...	...	...	...	...	...	...	...
Palau	58	60	66	87 (2019)	...	...	...	...
Papua New Guinea	2,325	1,871	5,987	17,718	1,454	1,264	1,042	3,408
Samoa	139	169	325	427	138	167	299	403
Solomon Islands	156	167	231	389	121	144	125	96
Tonga	74	89	154	189	65	80	144	180
Tuvalu	4	10 (2006)	15	16 (2017)	...	...	...	...
Vanuatu	112	100	178	402	73	72	103	314
DEVELOPING ADB MEMBER ECONOMIES[b]	**1,286,935**	**1,911,863**	**3,221,714**	**6,082,982**	**472,798**	**444,244**	**710,932**	**1,020,469**
DEVELOPING ECONOMIES WORLDWIDE[b,c]	**2,690,727**	**3,552,004**	**5,884,897**	**10,138,706**	**1,323,120**	**1,327,726**	**1,802,802**	**2,936,572**

... = data not available, 0 = magnitude is less than half of unit employed, $ = United States dollars, ADB = Asian Development Bank.

a   Refers to the sum of public and publicly guaranteed long-term debt, private nonguaranteed long-term debt, use of International Monetary Fund credit, and estimated short-term debt.
b   Aggregates include only reporting economies with data corresponding to the year heading.
c   Refers to all low- and middle-income countries as classified by the World Bank. For developing ADB member economies not covered by the World Bank, data are from economy sources.

Sources: World Bank. International Debt Statistics. https://data.worldbank.org/products/ids (accessed 15 August 2020); and Asian Development Bank estimates using economy sources.

Click on the indictor name in the table header to access the time series in the Key Indicators Database.

Table 2.4.21: Total External Debt of Developing ADB Member Economies
(% of GNI)

ADB Regional Member	Total External Debt				External Debt, Public and Publicly Guaranteed			
	2000	2005	2010	2018	2000	2005	2010	2018
Developing ADB Member Economies								
Central and West Asia								
Afghanistan	...	13.8 (2006)	15.3	13.4	...	13.0 (2006)	12.4	10.0
Armenia	51.8	38.6	64.9	87.5	34.8	18.1	26.3	42.6
Azerbaijan	31.8	19.4	14.6	36.4	15.9	12.9	7.7	31.4
Georgia	57.5	33.2	77.9	110.6	40.1	23.7	29.0	40.6
Kazakhstan	75.7	84.7	92.6	105.7	21.3	4.2	3.0	16.3
Kyrgyz Republic	150.5	95.1	91.7	103.0	94.8	70.2	54.5	46.7
Pakistan	45.2	30.5	34.2	27.6	37.2	27.0	23.7	19.6
Tajikistan	138.4	50.0	51.1	67.7	91.6	36.8	25.9	32.3
Turkmenistan	96.3	15.3	2.6	2.3	83.3	11.6	1.7	1.2
Uzbekistan	36.5	32.4	19.3	33.9	27.8	25.4	8.4	18.2
East Asia								
China, People's Republic of	12.2	12.5	12.1	14.5	7.9	3.7	1.6	1.8
Hong Kong, China[a]	121.3	259.0	384.5	457.6 (2019)	...	...	...	...
Korea, Republic of	23.6	17.4	31.1	28.2 (2019)	9.1	4.3	10.5	...
Mongolia	84.8	56.5	89.7	253.9	73.6	51.2	27.0	67.9
Taipei,China	10.4	22.6	22.2	29.5 (2019)	0.0	0.1	1.8	0.1 (2019)
South Asia								
Bangladesh	28.3	25.5	21.6	18.2	27.2	24.1	17.2	12.8
Bhutan	48.2	81.3	62.4	109.2	46.1	78.7	61.4	106.3
India	21.8	14.9	17.5	19.3	17.5	6.7	6.1	6.7
Maldives	34.2	32.0	40.3	48.0	31.1	26.5	27.6	41.2
Nepal	52.2	39.1	23.5	18.9	51.2	38.2	21.8	17.0
Sri Lanka	57.8	46.9	38.6	60.8	49.6	40.1	29.3	39.7
Southeast Asia								
Brunei Darussalam	...	...	...	...	...	...	...	...
Cambodia	55.1	46.1	35.7	58.2	52.4	44.4	26.8	29.7
Indonesia	93.5	52.3	27.0	37.6	45.5	28.6	14.0	21.3
Lao People's Democratic Republic	152.4	122.8	98.2	90.2	149.0	88.2	56.2	53.0
Malaysia	48.7	47.3	54.2	69.6 (2016)	22.2	25.1	25.1	22.8 (2016)
Myanmar	72.8	59.9	20.5	21.5	66.2	52.8	17.4	19.8
Philippines	61.6	48.0	27.2	19.9	35.5	28.9	18.7	9.2
Singapore	16.0	...	...	...	...	...	...	...
Thailand	64.4	32.3	32.5	35.1	23.8	7.0	4.9	7.4
Timor-Leste	0.0	0.0	0.0	6.7	0.0	0.0	0.0	6.1
Viet Nam	38.7	32.8	40.3	46.7	35.1	28.7	29.4	23.0
The Pacific								
Cook Islands[a]	64.3	37.4	41.0	12.3 (2019)	...	...	...	...
Fiji	7.1	7.5	17.6	16.7	5.9	3.7	11.6	14.0
Kiribati[a]	1.5	11.2	8.5	23.0 (2019)	...	...	...	...
Marshall Islands[a]	93.8	65.8	62.7	32.8	...	...	...	...
Micronesia, Federated States of[a]	27.1	24.7	28.9	21.8	...	...	...	...
Nauru	...	...	...	...	...	...	...	...
Niue	...	...	...	...	...	...	...	...
Palau[a]	40.0	32.3	36.2	31.1 (2019)	...	...	...	...
Papua New Guinea	70.4	41.3	45.7	78.4	44.0	27.9	8.0	15.1
Samoa	51.7	39.5	52.2	51.3	51.2	39.1	48.0	48.4
Solomon Islands	35.9	40.3	46.5	29.1	27.7	34.7	25.2	7.2
Tonga	36.7	34.0	40.3	41.3	32.2	30.3	37.6	39.3
Tuvalu[a]	28.9	45.7 (2006)	49.1	37.0 (2017)	...	...	...	...
Vanuatu	43.3	27.2	26.3	45.9	28.2	19.5	15.2	35.8

... = data not available, 0.0 = magnitude is less than half of unit employed, ADB = Asian Development Bank, GNI = gross national income.

a   For total external debt as a percentage of GNI, gross domestic product is used in lieu of GNI.

Sources: World Bank. International Debt Statistics. https://data.worldbank.org/products/ids (accessed 15 August 2020); and Asian Development Bank estimates using economy sources.

External Indebtedness

Table 2.4.22:   **Total External Debt of Developing ADB Member Economies**
(% of exports of goods, services, and primary income)

ADB Regional Member	2000	2005	2010	2013	2014	2015	2016	2017	2018
Developing ADB Member Economies									
Central and West Asia									
Afghanistan	...	...	90.2	162.9	119.9	155.1	201.5	209.8	...
Armenia	182.6	101.3	193.5	196.7	188.8	222.0	229.0	193.8	196.4
Azerbaijan	72.9	26.9	25.1	28.6	35.4	63.2	79.8	73.2	59.8
Georgia	183.7	89.1	191.5	161.9	169.3	206.8	223.1	183.3	168.2
Kazakhstan	123.0	139.8	174.7	160.3	178.6	288.0	373.6	282.5	225.7
Kyrgyz Republic	328.5	234.4	181.2	176.8	220.1	308.2	326.6	313.5	307.3
Pakistan	326.5	172.6	219.1	191.7	200.1	228.0	266.0	290.6	295.3
Tajikistan	163.0 (2002)	126.6	158.4	130.3	160.8	200.6	229.6	225.7	224.6
Turkmenistan	...	...	...	...	...	...	...	...	...
Uzbekistan	...	...	...	...	...	...	123.8	112.4	101.8
East Asia									
China, People's Republic of	72.0	34.9	42.1	58.0	65.5	51.3	58.4	62.9	68.0
Hong Kong, China[a]	76.8	121.2	149.2	152.0	166.2	168.8	177.6	190.5	190.6
Korea, Republic of[a]	64.7	46.6	62.6	56.4	56.3	59.5	60.4	58.9	57.7
Mongolia	153.3	93.6	173.2	423.4	345.4	422.4	453.7	418.4	370.1
Taipei,China[a]	19.3	35.9	30.0	38.2	39.3	38.8	45.3	43.1	44.0
South Asia									
Bangladesh	214.0	173.5	123.5	100.2	99.6	103.4	102.8	120.1	117.7
Bhutan	...	188.8 (2006)	154.0	233.9	271.3	268.8	343.4	349.4	313.1
India	161.9	75.6	81.1	89.1	91.8	108.0	102.2	100.7	93.1
Maldives	43.4	73.1	45.6	35.3	33.2	32.0	37.8	43.8	63.0
Nepal	212.5	224.2	212.7	159.5	142.2	154.8	167.2	165.7	...
Sri Lanka	141.7	141.9	189.8	258.5	250.2	257.3	265.4	263.3	256.4
Southeast Asia									
Brunei Darussalam	...	...	...	...	...	...	...	...	...
Cambodia	102.8	67.6	62.7	68.8	66.0	67.8	67.3	69.1	70.3
Indonesia	197.1	146.5	117.6	127.0	145.6	176.7	185.6	177.0	174.2
Lao People's Democratic Republic	493.1	430.1	284.0	259.1	231.6	251.7	259.8	253.6	245.4
Malaysia	36.7	38.9	57.2	72.8	74.0	86.0	94.5	...	...
Myanmar	302.0	186.8	129.4	111.1	102.8	97.8	101.0	101.2	87.3
Philippines	189.8	152.4	106.7	86.9	91.8	93.6	87.3	76.5	77.9
Singapore	104.5	87.6	...	...	...	...	...	...	...
Thailand	92.8	44.4	45.7	51.8	50.4	47.0	47.7	49.3	49.0
Timor-Leste	...	...	0.0	2.6	4.6	8.3	12.3	14.2	15.7
Viet Nam	73.5	50.2	56.1	45.8	44.9	44.8	45.2	45.6	41.6
The Pacific									
Cook Islands[a]	...	...	61.3	32.6	29.7	23.8	20.0	17.9	16.8
Fiji	11.9	13.6	28.3	30.9	32.0	33.7	35.6	34.5	31.3
Kiribati[a]	16.3	17.6	14.9	9.8	7.4	15.8	23.5	21.0	22.1
Marshall Islands[a]	135.0	93.2	94.1	60.2	60.9	57.2	55.5	47.7	42.7
Micronesia, Federated States of[a]	100.3	98.2	91.3	64.3	58.1	51.3	49.5	43.1	34.2
Nauru	...	...	...	...	...	...	...	...	...
Niue	...	...	...	...	...	...	...	...	...
Palau[a]	83.1	64.3	62.8	43.1	43.0	35.1	43.1	48.7	55.8
Papua New Guinea	98.2	51.3	98.2	337.3	227.4	237.4	231.0	167.6	166.5
Samoa	...	114.8	161.1	179.4	184.4	182.6	162.7	154.5	137.2
Solomon Islands	121.3	108.1	68.9	33.7	30.6	35.9	44.2	57.7	53.8
Tonga	246.2 (2001)	167.6	283.9	171.4	201.4	145.9	145.7	141.1	122.5
Tuvalu[a]	85.9	54.9 (2006)	64.1	59.5	78.8	55.2	43.2	44.6	...
Vanuatu	63.9	49.0	48.9	37.3	46.9	71.7	69.9	...	...

... = data not available, 0.0 = magnitude is less than half of unit employed, ADB = Asian Development Bank.

a   External debt as a percentage of exports of goods, services, and primary income was derived using balance-of-payments data.

Sources: World Bank. International Debt Statistics. https://data.worldbank.org/products/ids (accessed 15 August 2020); and Asian Development Bank estimates using economy sources.

Click on the indictor name in the table header to access the time series in the Key Indicators Database.

Table 2.4.23: Total Debt Service Paid by Developing ADB Member Economies

ADB Regional Member	Debt Service Payment ($ million)				Debt Service Payment (% of exports of goods, services, and primary income)			
	2000	2005	2010	2018	2000	2005	2010	2018
Developing ADB Member Economies								
Central and West Asia[a]	**8,199**	**17,525**	**48,012**	**49,203**	...	...	...	...
Afghanistan	0	11 (2006)	10	61	...	...	0.4	4.9 (2017)
Armenia	48	142	969	1,679	8.7	7.3	29.7	29.9
Azerbaijan	138	242	415	2,857	6.4	2.9	1.4	10.5
Georgia	126	195	803	2,410	12.7	8.1	17.5	23.7
Kazakhstan	3,392	13,158	39,475	33,602	32.4	41.9	57.9	48.3
Kyrgyz Republic	178	143	557	826	30.2	14.8	24.5	31.3
Pakistan	2,871	2,466	4,314	6,125	28.4	12.5	15.0	19.9
Tajikistan	66	73	695	586	12.6 (2002)	8.2	30.9	22.0
Turkmenistan	472	310	155	54	...	...	...	...
Uzbekistan	907	795	618	1,003	...	...	...	5.8
East Asia[a]	**49,602**	**45,751**	**58,712**	**...**	...	...	...	...
China, People's Republic of	26,610	27,476	52,000	235,548	13.1	3.4	3.0	8.2
Hong Kong, China	...	...	...	...	...	...	...	...
Korea, Republic of[b,c]	22,905	7,224	2,843	...	10.9	...	...	...
Mongolia	41	45	239	8,068	6.6	3.0	7.0	101.6
Taipei,China[b,c]	45	11,006	3,630	18,078 (2019)	0.0	4.6	1.1	4.3 (2019)
South Asia[a]	**12,362**	**25,335**	**27,306**	**74,522**	...	...	...	...
Bangladesh	773	812	1,129	2,806	10.6	7.6	5.2	6.3
Bhutan	7	7	87	87	...	2.8 (2006)	14.4	10.7
India	10,668	23,922	24,413	63,649	17.1	14.9	6.8	11.4
Maldives	20	31	81	342	4.2	6.3	4.0	9.2
Nepal	103	120	188	243	7.6	8.5	10.6	8.5 (2017)
Sri Lanka	791	441	1,408	7,394	12.1	5.5	12.3	36.0
Southeast Asia[a]	**45,589**	**58,368**	**62,054**	**111,245**	...	...	...	...
Brunei Darussalam	...	...	...	...	...	...	...	...
Cambodia	13	30	65	1,279	0.7	0.7	1.1	6.7
Indonesia	16,697	20,283	31,569	56,689	22.8	20.9	18.7	26.0
Lao People's Democratic Republic	41	136	302	926	8.0	17.8	13.1	14.6
Malaysia	6,441	9,381	5,575	10,385 (2016)	5.6	5.6	2.4	4.9 (2016)
Myanmar	21	25	244	843	1.0	0.6	3.1	4.9
Philippines	7,066	9,528	11,461	8,766	22.9	24.7	18.7	8.7
Singapore	...	...	...	...	...	...	...	...
Thailand	14,013	18,044	10,965	18,532	16.3	13.7	4.7	5.4
Timor-Leste	0	0	0	3	...	...	0.0	0.3
Viet Nam	1,306	948	1,880	18,432	7.5	2.6	2.3	7.1
The Pacific[a]	**401**	**362**	**896**	**2,955**	...	...	...	...
Cook Islands[b,c]	4	4	3	4 (2019)	...	...	2.0	1.4
Fiji	24	14	25	53	2.4	0.8	1.3	2.0
Kiribati[c]	1	1	1	2 (2019)	1.7	1.9	0.9	0.5
Marshall Islands[c]	22	4	9	7	28.5	4.5	7.7	3.9
Micronesia, Federated States of[c]	23	2	5	6	36.1	3.9	5.2	2.9
Nauru	...	...	...	...	...	...	...	...
Niue	...	...	...	...	...	...	...	...
Palau	...	...	...	...	...	...	...	...
Papua New Guinea	305	308	812	2,780	12.9	8.4	13.3	26.1
Samoa	6	6	11	30	...	3.9	5.3	9.8
Solomon Islands	9	14	21	40	7.1	9.1	6.2	5.6
Tonga	5	5	5	11	9.8 (2001)	9.8	9.3	7.2
Tuvalu	...	...	...	...	...	...	...	...
Vanuatu	3	3	6	19	1.6	1.6	1.6	2.1 (2016)
DEVELOPING ADB MEMBER ECONOMIES[a]	**116,154**	**147,340**	**196,980**	**18,084 (2019)**	...	...	...	...

... = data not available, 0 or 0.0 = magnitude is less than half of unit employed, $ = United States dollars; ADB = Asian Development Bank.

a For reporting economies only.
b Refers to principal repayments on long-term debt plus interest on short-term and long-term debt.
c Debt service payment as a percentage of exports of goods, services, and primary income was derived using balance-of-payments data.

Sources: World Bank. International Debt Statistics. https://data.worldbank.org/products/ids (accessed 15 August 2020); and Asian Development Bank estimates using economy sources.

Tourism

Table 2.4.24:   International Tourist Arrivals[a]
('000)

ADB Regional Member	2000	2005	2010	2015	2016	2017	2018	2019*
Developing ADB Member Economies								
Central and West Asia[b]	**2,559**	**5,526**	**9,288**	**12,458**	**12,825**	**15,707**	**22,557**	**...**
Afghanistan	...	...	...	...	...	...	...	...
Armenia	45	319	684	1,192	1,260	1,495	1,652	1,894
Azerbaijan	576 (2002)	693	1,280	1,922	2,044	2,454	2,605	...
Georgia	...	...	1,067	3,012	3,297	4,069	4,757	5,080
Kazakhstan	1,471	3,143	2,991	4,560 (2014)	...	...	...	...
Kyrgyz Republic	173	319	1,224	4,000	3,853	4,568	6,947	...
Pakistan	557	798	907	...	...	...	...	...
Tajikistan	8	...	160	414	344	431	1,250	...
Turkmenistan	3	12	...	...	...	...	...	...
Uzbekistan	302	242	975	1,918	2,027	2,690	5,346	6,749
East Asia	**48,143**	**71,322**	**90,570**	**107,630**	**114,159**	**113,170**	**119,106**	**119,396**
China, People's Republic of	31,229	46,809	55,664	56,886	59,270	60,740	62,900	65,700
Hong Kong, China	8,814	14,773	20,085	26,686	26,553	27,885	29,263	23,752
Korea, Republic of	5,322	6,023	8,798	13,232	17,242	13,336	15,347	17,503
Mongolia	154	339	456	386	404	469	529	577
Taipei,China	2,624	3,378	5,567	10,440	10,690	10,740	11,067	11,864
South Asia[b]	**4,187**	**5,460**	**8,169**	**17,653**	**19,700**	**20,244**	**22,692**	**23,040**
Bangladesh	199	208	303	643	830	...	...	...
Bhutan	8	14	41	155	210	255	274	316
India	2,649	3,919	5,776	13,284	14,570	15,543	17,427	17,910
Maldives	467	395	792	1,234	1,286	1,390	1,484	1,703
Nepal	464	375	603	539	753	940	1,173	1,197
Sri Lanka	400	549	654	1,798	2,051	2,116	2,334	1,914
Southeast Asia[b]	**36,132**	**49,059**	**70,471**	**104,242**	**110,771**	**120,569**	**128,620**	**114,298**
Brunei Darussalam	...	126	214	218	219	259	278	323
Cambodia	466	1,422	2,508	4,775	5,012	5,602	6,201	6,611
Indonesia[c]	5,064	5,002	7,003	9,963	11,072	12,948	13,396	...
Lao People's Democratic Republic	191	672	1,670	3,543	3,315	3,257	3,770	...
Malaysia	10,222	16,431	24,577	25,721	26,757	25,948	25,832	26,101
Myanmar	416	660	792	4,681	2,907	3,443	3,551	...
Philippines	1,992	2,623	3,520	5,361	5,967	6,621	7,168	8,261
Singapore	6,062	7,079	9,161	12,051	12,913	13,903	14,673	15,115
Thailand	9,579	11,567	15,936	29,923	32,530	35,592	38,178	39,797
Timor-Leste	...	14 (2006)	40	62	66	74	75	81
Viet Nam	2,140	3,477	5,050	7,944	10,013	12,922	15,498	18,009
The Pacific[b]	**703**	**1,035**	**1,310**	**1,570**	**1,619**	**1,664**	**1,683**	**...**
Cook Islands	73	88	104	125	146	161	169	172
Fiji	294	545	632	755	792	843	870	894
Kiribati	5	4	5	4	6	6	7	...
Marshall Islands	5	9	5	6	5	6	7	...
Micronesia, Federated States of	21	19	45	31	30	27	19	...
Nauru	...	...	...	...	...	...	...	...
Niue	2	3	6	8	9	10	...	...
Palau	58	81	85	162	138	123	106	94
Papua New Guinea	58	69	140	183	179	143	140	160
Samoa	88	102	122	128	134	146	164	172
Solomon Islands	5	9	21	22	23	26	28	...
Tonga	35	42	47	54	59	62	54	...
Tuvalu	1	1	2	2	3	2	3	...
Vanuatu	58	62	97	90	95	109	116	121
Developed ADB Member Economies[b]	**11,475**	**14,593**	**16,931**	**30,315**	**35,803**	**41,229**	**44,124**	**41,648**
Australia	4,931	5,499	5,790	7,449	8,269	8,815	9,246	9,466
Japan	4,757	6,728	8,611	19,737	24,040	28,691	31,192	32,182
New Zealand	1,787	2,366	2,530	3,129	3,494	3,723	3,686	...
DEVELOPING ADB MEMBER ECONOMIES[b]	**91,723**	**132,401**	**179,808**	**243,553**	**259,074**	**271,354**	**294,658**	**272,070**
ALL ADB REGIONAL MEMBERS[b]	**103,198**	**146,994**	**196,739**	**273,868**	**294,877**	**312,583**	**338,782**	**313,718**
WORLD[d]	**676,655**	**808,570**	**955,675**	**1,197,427**	**1,240,866**	**1,332,972**	**1,408,776**	**1,459,724**

... = data not available, | = marks break in the series, * = provisional or preliminary, ADB = Asian Development Bank.

a For Australia; Japan; the Kyrgyz Republic; the Republic of Korea; New Zealand; Taipei,China; Tajikistan; Uzbekistan; and Viet Nam, data refer to international visitor arrivals at frontiers (including tourists and same-day visitors). For the rest of the economies, data refer to international tourist arrivals at frontiers (overnight visitors only, i.e., excluding same-day visitors).

b Includes only reporting economies with data corresponding to the year heading.

c Prior to 2015, data refer to international tourist arrivals at frontiers (overnight visitors only, i.e., excluding same-day visitors). For 2015 onward, data refer to international visitor arrivals at frontiers (including tourists and same-day visitors).

d Aggregations were done by the United Nations World Tourism Organization with approximations based on trends in the economies with data available.

Sources: United Nations World Tourism Organization. UNWTO eLibrary. https://www.e-unwto.org/action/showLogin?uri=%2F& (accessed 17 July 2020); World Tourism Barometer, Statistical Annex. July 2020. Volume 18.

Click on the indictor name in the table header to access the time series in the Key Indicators Database.

Table 2.4.25: International Tourism Receipts
($ million)

ADB Regional Member	2000	2005	2010	2015	2016	2017	2018	2019*
Developing ADB Member Economies								
Central and West Asia[a]	677	1,528	3,631	7,568	8,916	10,451	11,351	9,965
Afghanistan	...	...	75	79	49	2	28	72
Armenia	38	223	646	936	968	1,120	1,208	1,528
Azerbaijan	63	78	657	2,309	2,714	3,012	2,634	...
Georgia	97	241	659	1,868	2,111	2,704	3,222	3,269
Kazakhstan	356	701	1,005	1,632	1,858	2,135	2,255	2,463
Kyrgyz Republic	15	73	160	426	432	429	460	644
Pakistan	81	182	305	317	322	352	391	494
Tajikistan	2 (2002)	2	3	1	4	8	9	14
Turkmenistan	...	...	...	...	...	...	...	...
Uzbekistan	27	28	121	...	458	689	1,144	1,481
East Asia	32,707	50,427	86,731	110,195	106,407	97,977	109,968	101,389
China, People's Republic of	16,231	29,296	45,814	44,969	44,432	38,559	40,386	35,832
Hong Kong, China	5,868	10,179	21,689	35,795	31,398	33,339	36,866	29,043
Korea, Republic of	6,834	5,798	10,263	14,798	16,886	13,368	18,567	21,628
Mongolia	36	177	244	246	316	396	445	513
Taipei,China	3,738	4,977	8,721	14,387	13,375	12,315	13,704	14,373
South Asia[a]	4,237	8,954	17,244	27,290	29,203	35,117	37,074	37,815
Bangladesh	50	75	81	150	214	341	353	388
Bhutan	...	23 (2006)	40	94	92	103	103	...
India	3,460	7,493	14,490	21,013	22,427	27,365	28,568	29,962
Maldives	321	826	1,713	2,569	2,506	2,744	3,028	3,157
Nepal	158	131	344	483	446	639	641	701
Sri Lanka	248	429	576	2,981	3,518	3,925	4,381	3,607
Southeast Asia[a]	25,347	34,977	68,484	105,091	112,991	126,145	138,158	146,483
Brunei Darussalam	155 (2001)	191	254 (2009)	147	144	177	190	217
Cambodia	304	840	1,519	3,137	3,212	3,636	4,352	4,769
Indonesia	4,975	4,522	6,958	10,761	11,206	13,139	16,426	16,912
Lao People's Democratic Republic	114	139	382	724	716	648	734	...
Malaysia	5,011	8,846	18,152	17,666	18,085	18,357	19,622	19,823
Myanmar	162	67	72	2,120	2,197	1,969	1,652	2,483
Philippines	2,156	2,287	2,645	5,272	5,143	6,988	8,240	9,806
Singapore	5,142	6,209	14,178	16,617	18,944	19,892	20,418	20,052
Thailand	7,483	9,576	20,104	41,246	44,786	52,376	56,366	60,521
Timor-Leste	...	20 (2006)	24	51	58	73	78	70
Viet Nam	...	2,300	4,450	7,350	8,500	8,890	10,080	11,830
The Pacific[a]	...	819	1,256	819	1,677	1,780	...	...
Cook Islands	36	91	111	116	137	153	...	...
Fiji	189	485	635	816	878	940	972	963
Kiribati	...	2 (2006)	4	2	3	4	3	...
Marshall Islands	...	3	4	1	5	7	9	...
Micronesia, Federated States of	...	...	24	25	...	...	...	...
Nauru	...	...	1	2	3	4	...	...
Niue	...	...	...	...	7	8	...	...
Palau	45	60	73	149	141	116	...	...
Papua New Guinea	7	4	2	2	1	2	3	...
Samoa	41	73	123	142	148	166	191	199
Solomon Islands	4	2	44	51	59	67	81	70
Tonga	7	15	16	43	51	48	48	57
Tuvalu	...	1	2	2 (2013)	...	...	...	...
Vanuatu	56	85	217	228	243	265	295	...
Developed ADB Member Economies[a]	15,020	35,666	48,219	68,701	77,544	86,390	98,006	91,763
Australia	9,375	16,750	28,472	34,269	37,019	41,732	45,035	45,709
Japan	3,373	12,430	13,224	24,968	30,752	34,054	42,096	46,054
New Zealand	2,272	6,486	6,523	9,464	9,773	10,604	10,875	...
DEVELOPING ADB MEMBER ECONOMIES[a]	63,353	96,704	177,599	251,721	259,193	271,470	298,153	296,941
ALL ADB REGIONAL MEMBERS[a]	78,373	132,370	225,818	320,422	336,737	357,860	396,159	388,704
WORLD[b]	475,510	703,779	979,163	1,221,823	1,246,391	1,347,047	1,456,664	1,478,311

... = data not available, * = provisional or preliminary, $ = United States dollars, ADB = Asian Development Bank.

a Includes only reporting economies with data corresponding to the year heading.
b Aggregations were done by the United Nations World Tourism Organization with approximations for nonreporting economies based on the previous year's values and the trend in neighboring economies.

Sources: United Nations World Tourism Organization. UNWTO eLibrary. https://www.e-unwto.org/action/showLogin?uri=%2F& (accessed 17 July 2020); World Tourism Barometer, Statistical Annex. July 2020. Volume 18.

V.   Transport and Communications

Transport and Communications features a discussion on air carrier departures and passenger traffic in Asia and the Pacific. Other data topics include container port traffic; road and rail networks; motor vehicle ownership, injuries, and fatalities; internet usage and penetration rates; mobile telephone subscriptions; and fixed telephone subscriptions.

The Asia and Pacific region has become the global leader in air carrier departures and passengers carried

In 2018, Asia and the Pacific was the busiest region in the world in terms of air carrier departures and passengers carried, accounting for 33.7% and 38.6%, respectively, of the global totals. By comparison, North America accounted for 30.0% and 22.6% of air carrier departures and passengers carried, respectively, and Europe 23.6% and 26.0% (ICAO 2018). Amid the COVID-19 pandemic, the International Civil Aviation Organization is forecasting that international seat capacity could drop by up to 75% for 2020 (ICAO 2019).

From 2000 to 2018, air carrier departures increased in 30 of 39 economies with available data (Table 2.5.6). The economies of Asia and the Pacific with the most air carrier departures in 2018 were the PRC (4.69 million); India (1.20 million); Japan (0.99 million); Indonesia (0.96 million); and Australia (0.67 million). For historical comparison, the most air carrier departures in 2000 were in Japan (0.65 million); Taipei,China (0.59 million); the PRC (0.57 million); Australia (0.38 million); and New Zealand (0.24 million).

The economies with the highest average annual growth rates in air carrier departures from 2000 to 2018 were Bangladesh (83.7%), Kazakhstan (52.0%), and Viet Nam (48.8%). The most notable average annual declines in air carrier departures were observed in Fiji (–3.2%), Samoa (–2.1%), and Uzbekistan (–1.6%).

By subregion, average annual growth in air carrier departures from 2000 to 2018 was most pronounced in South Asia (29.3%), Southeast Asia (20.0%), and East Asia (17.2%) as demonstrated in Figure 2.5.1. Much lower average annual growth rates were observed in Central and West Asia (3.4%) and the developed ADB member economies (2.6%).

Figure 2.5.1: Air Carrier Departures by Subregion within Asia and the Pacific
('000)

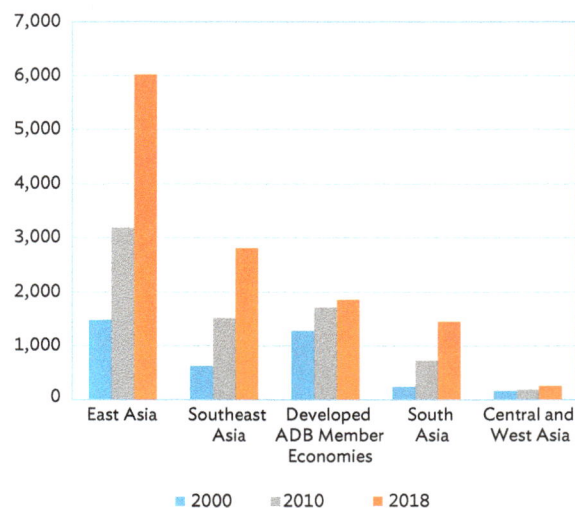

ADB = Asian Development Bank
Note: The Pacific is not included due to multiple missing data.
Source: Table 2.5.6, Key Indicators for Asia and the Pacific 2020.

Click here for figure data

Data Issues and Comparability

Issues with data organization, collection, compilation, and dissemination affect the availability, quality, and timeliness of road statistics. Some regions, especially the Pacific, have incomplete or no data. The most recent road data are usually 2–3 years old at the time of review.

Most data on telephone and internet subscriptions came from questionnaires sent by the International Telecommunication Union to participating economies. Other information and reports were sourced from national ministries in charge of telecommunications and from staff estimates.

Table 2.5.1:   Road Indicators—Network[a]
(km)

ADB Regional Member	Primary	Class I	Class II	Class III	Below III	Other	Year[b]
Developing ADB Member Economies							
Central and West Asia							
Afghanistan	–	10	2,549	–	1,461	–	2015
Armenia	–	147	721	58	40	–	2013
Azerbaijan	–	544	905	–	–	–	2017
Georgia	–	90	1,058	–	–	–	2017
Kazakhstan	–	557	5,407	6,389	475	–	2010
Kyrgyz Republic	–	–	303	1,324	136	–	2013
Pakistan	357	1,116	275	2,442	1,138	–	2015
Tajikistan	–	20	978	–	914	–	2015
Turkmenistan	–	60	–	2,120	24	–	2008
Uzbekistan	–	1,195	1,101	670	–	–	2008
East Asia							
China, People's Republic of	8,437	230	1,855	321	5	...	2015
Hong Kong, China	...	...	...	...	...	...	
Korea, Republic of	457	423	40	–	–	–	2017
Mongolia	–	8	2,593	233	1,480	–	2017
Taipei,China	...	...	...	...	...	...	
South Asia							
Bangladesh	–	321	1,680	44	5	–	2017
Bhutan	–	7	116	–	47	–	2017
India	90	7,067	1,071	3,556	117	–	2015
Maldives	...	...		...	...	...	
Nepal	–	–	218	1,082	13	–	2013
Sri Lanka	–	60	545	45	–	–	2017
Southeast Asia							
Brunei Darussalam	...	...		...	...	...	
Cambodia			633	1,321	–	–	2017
Indonesia	409	603	3,045	–	–	34	2010
Lao People's Democratic Republic	–	–	244	2,307	306	–	2010
Malaysia	795	61	817	–	–	–	2010
Myanmar	–	320	575	1,702	1,928	–	2015
Philippines	–	665	2,048	687	–	–	2017
Singapore	13	6	–	–	–	–	2015
Thailand	572	4,075	848	27	–	–	2017
Timor-Leste	...	...	...	...	...	...	
Viet Nam	–	1,202	1,915	–	–	–	2017
The Pacific							
Cook Islands	...	...	...	...	...	...	
Fiji	...	...	...	...	...	...	
Kiribati	...	...	...	...	...	...	
Marshall Islands	...	...	...	...	...	...	
Micronesia, Federated States of	...	...	...	...	...	...	
Nauru	...	...	...	...	...	...	
Niue	...	...	...	...	...	...	
Palau	...	...	...	...	...	...	
Papua New Guinea	...	...	...	...	...	...	
Samoa	...	...	...	...	...	...	
Solomon Islands	...	...	...	...	...	...	
Tonga	...	...	...	...	...	...	
Tuvalu	...	...	...	...	...	...	
Vanuatu	...	...	...	...	...	...	
Developed ADB Member Economies							
Australia	...	...	...	...	...	...	
Japan	1,138	–	–	–	–	–	2015
New Zealand	...	...	...	...	...	...	

... = data not available, – = magnitude equals zero, ADB = Asian Development Bank, km = kilometer.

a   The road network refers to the Asian Highway that consists of highway routes of international importance within Asia, including highway routes substantially crossing more than one subregion; highway routes within subregions that connect neighboring subregions; and highway routes located within member states that provide access to (a) capital cities; (b) main industrial and agricultural centers; (c) major air, sea, and river ports; (d) major container terminals and depots; and (e) major tourist attractions. "Primary" class in the classification refers to access-controlled motorways. Access-controlled motorways are used exclusively by automobiles. Motorcycles, bicycles, and pedestrians will not be allowed to enter the motorway to ensure traffic safety and the high running speed of automobiles.
Class I refers to asphalt, cement, or concrete roads with four or more lanes.
Class II refers to double bituminous-treated roads with two lanes.
Class III is regarded as the minimum desirable standard usually described as a two-lane (narrow) road.
Roads classified below Class III are road sections below the minimum desirable standard.
b   The year data were received by the Secretariat of the United Nations Economic and Social Commission for Asia and the Pacific.

Source: United Nations Economic and Social Commission for Asia and the Pacific. ESCAP Online Statistical Database. http://data.unescap.org/escap_stat/(accessed 24 July 2019).

Click on the indictor name in the table header to access the time series in the Key Indicators Database.

Table 2.5.2: Road Indicators—Vehicles

ADB Regional Member	Number of Registered Vehicles, 2016						
	Total	(per 1,000 people)[b]	By type[a]				
			Four-Wheeled Vehicles	Two- and Three-Wheeled Vehicles	Heavy Trucks	Buses	Others
Developing ADB Member Economies							
Central and West Asia							
Afghanistan	655,357 (2013)	25.2	407,608	68,090	81,416	20,589	77,654
Armenia	300,091 (2010)	98.6	247,723	28	40,924	11,396	20
Azerbaijan	1,330,551	136.4	1,136,983	3,290	141,525	30,958	17,795
Georgia	1,126,470	302.2	919,199	63,083	93,497	50,691	–
Kazakhstan	4,383,120	246.3	3,835,609	9,692	439,167	98,652	–
Kyrgyz Republic	993,000 (2015)	168.4	...	...	...	...	...
Pakistan	18,352,500	92.3	2,835,400	13,538,200	259,900	229,200	1,489,800
Tajikistan	439,972	50.9	380,496	4,546	39,261	15,669	–
Turkmenistan	...	...	...	...	...	...	...
Uzbekistan	...	...	...	...	...	...	...
East Asia							
China, People's Republic of[c]	294,694,457	213.1	...	...	...	...	...
Hong Kong, China	...	...	...	...	...	...	...
Korea, Republic of	25,680,967	501.4	17,338,160	2,180,688	3,492,173	892,539	1,777,407
Mongolia	841,537	271.5	547,299	42,751	175,648	6,823	69,016
Taipei,China[d]	21,871,240 (2018)	927.5	6,845,711	13,835,520	1,090,789	33,877	65,343
South Asia							
Bangladesh	2,879,708	17.9	613,149	1,980,246	158,379	64,608	63,326
Bhutan[e]	86,981 (2017)	119.6	56,232	9,786	12,891	681	7,391
India	210,023,289 (2015)	163.7	38,523,053	154,297,746	4,461,059	1,970,786	10,770,645
Maldives	92,983	196.8	14,314	75,053	3,438	178	–
Nepal	2,339,169 (2015)	83.7	187,014	1,547,312	56,250	52,388	496,205
Sri Lanka	6,795,469	320.5	717,674	4,815,617	762,912	104,104	395,162
Southeast Asia							
Brunei Darussalam	349,279 (2010)	903.0	...	...	...	...	...
Cambodia	3,751,715	245.1	97,239	2,714,193	57,321	5,972	876,990
Indonesia	128,398,594	496.3	...	...	...	...	...
Lao People's Democratic Republic	1,850,020	280.9	370,043	1,422,869	52,443	4,665	–
Malaysia	27,613,120	872.9	13,123,638	12,677,041	1,191,310	59,977	561,154
Myanmar[e]	6,381,136 (2017)	119.5	516,707	5,391,505	59,680	28,383	384,861
Philippines	9,251,565	89.6	3,434,329	5,329,770	407,357	29,794	50,315
Singapore	933,534	166.5	727,533	142,439	45,224	18,338	0
Thailand	37,338,139	547.1	15,003,774	20,497,296	1,055,717	157,799	623,553
Timor-Leste	146,596	120.2	24,438	108,409	1,120	207	12,422
Viet Nam	50,666,855	543.3	3,033,527	47,131,928	...	...	501,400
The Pacific							
Cook Islands	12,453 (2014)	676.8	5,085	6,846	491	31	–
Fiji	110,763	126.8	...	...	...	...	...
Kiribati[e]	3,706 (2017)	32.8	2,547	757	4	398	–
Marshall Islands	2,116 (2013)	39.5	1,917	52	26	63	58
Micronesia, Federated States of	5,673	54.6	5,436	25	55	62	95
Nauru	...	...	...	...	...	...	...
Niue	...	...	...	...	...	...	...
Palau	7,102 (2013)	408.2	...	...	...	...	...
Papua New Guinea	100,993	11.9	66,017	1,289	22,072	11,615	–
Samoa	25,235	128.8	23,557	95	1,184	326	73
Solomon Islands	...	...	...	...	...	...	...
Tonga	8,154 (2012)	78.9	6,039	184	1,882	49	–
Tuvalu	...	...	...	...	...	...	...
Vanuatu	...	...	...	...	...	...	...
Developed ADB Member Economies							
Australia	18,326,236	757.6	16,946,125	828,965	430,997	96,582	23,567
Japan	81,602,046	642.6	...	...	...	...	...
New Zealand	3,656,300	781.6	...	...	...	...	...

... = data not available, – = magnitude equals zero, ADB = Asian Development Bank.

a Figures by type refer to the year indicated in brackets in the "Total" column, unless otherwise specified.
b Calculated by dividing the total number of registered vehicles by the midyear population in thousands.
c The "per 1,000 people" calculation used end-of-year population data instead of midyear data.
d "Heavy Trucks" includes a combination of heavy and light trucks.
e For 2017, data covers only 1 January to April 30.

Sources: World Health Organization. 2018. Global Status Report on Road Safety 2018. Geneva. For the number of registered vehicles per 1,000 people: Asian Development Bank estimates. For Armenia and Brunei Darussalam: World Health Organization. 2013. Global Status Report on Road Safety 2013. Geneva. For Taipei,China: National Development Council. Statistical Data Book. https://www.ndc.gov.tw/en/News.aspx?n=607ED34345641980&sms=B8A915763E3684AC (accessed 3 July 2020).

Click on the indictor name in the table header to access the time series in the Key Indicators Database.

Table 2.5.3:   Road Indicators—Safety

ADB Regional Member	Estimated Road Traffic Deaths, 2016		Road User Deaths, 2016 (%)				
	Total	Death Rate (per 100,000 population)	Four-Wheeled Vehicles	Two- and Three-Wheeled Vehicles	Cyclists	Pedestrians	Others
Developing ADB Member Economies							
Central and West Asia	**44,846**	**14.3**					
Afghanistan	5,230	15.0	...	...	...	...	...
Armenia	499	17.0	59.6	1.5	0.4	34.8	3.7
Azerbaijan	845	9.0	51.8	0.9	0.9	42.0	4.3
Georgia	599	15.0	44.9	0.5	0.7	26.5	27.4
Kazakhstan	3,158	18.0	59.8	4.3	1.7	30.9	3.3
Kyrgyz Republic	916	15.0	27.6	2.1	0.2	40.0	30.0
Pakistan	27,582	14.0	...	...	...	...	...
Tajikistan	1,577	18.0	57.4	...	2.3	40.3	–
Turkmenistan	823	15.0	...	...	...	...	...
Uzbekistan	3,617	12.0	...	...	...	...	...
East Asia[a]	**261,669**	**17.9**					
China, People's Republic of	256,180	18.2	...	...	...	...	...
Hong Kong, China	...	...	...	...	...	39.9	...
Korea, Republic of	4,990	9.8	...	20.5	5.9	28.7	33.7
Mongolia	499	16.5	39.3	18.6	1.2	...	12.2
Taipei,China	...	...					
South Asia	**331,906**	**21.6**					
Bangladesh	24,954	15.3	...	...	...	...	...
Bhutan	139	17.4	...	...	...	10.4	...
India	299,091	22.6	17.9	39.6	1.7	25.0	30.4
Maldives	4	0.9	–	75.0	–	...	–
Nepal	4,622	15.9	...	...	...	29.2	...
Sri Lanka	3,096	14.9	6.2	50.8	8.1	...	5.7
Southeast Asia[a]	**114,030**	**17.8**					
Brunei Darussalam	...	...					
Cambodia	2,803	17.8	6.2	73.5	2.3	9.6	8.4
Indonesia	31,726	12.2	4.9	73.6	3.2	15.5	2.7
Lao People's Democratic Republic	1,120	16.6	...	...	...	...	...
Malaysia	7,374	23.6	...	...	...	...	...
Myanmar	10,540	19.9	10.8	64.8	3.1	14.2	7.1
Philippines	12,690	12.3	0.3	4.7	0.1	1.0	93.9
Singapore	155	2.8	7.8	44.0	14.2	33.3	0.7
Thailand	22,491	32.7	12.3	74.4	3.5	7.6	2.3
Timor-Leste	161	12.7	...	...	...	...	...
Viet Nam	24,970	26.4	...	...	...	...	...
The Pacific[a]	**1,428**	**13.7**					
Cook Islands	3	17.3	20.0	80.0	–	–	–
Fiji	86	9.6	63.3	...	...	36.7	–
Kiribati	5	4.4	40.0	20.0	–	40.0	–
Marshall Islands	...	...	...	...	...	...	...
Micronesia, Federated States of	2	1.9	50.0	–	–	50.0	–
Nauru	...	...	...	...	...	...	...
Niue	...	...	...	...	...	...	...
Palau	...	...	...	...	...	...	–
Papua New Guinea	1,145	14.2	52.5	...	...	47.5	–
Samoa	22	11.3	41.2	–	5.9	47.1	5.9
Solomon Islands	104	17.4	...	...	...	...	...
Tonga	18	16.8	66.7	–	–	27.8	5.6
Tuvalu	...	...	...	...	...	...	...
Vanuatu	43	15.9	...	...	...	...	...
Developed ADB Member Economies	**6,939**	**4.4**					
Australia	1,351	5.6	60.9	19.3	2.2	14.0	3.5
Japan	5,224	4.1	32.4	17.2	15.1	35.0	1.0
New Zealand	364	7.8	68.5	15.9	1.5	7.6	6.4
DEVELOPING ADB MEMBER ECONOMIES[a]	**753,879**	**19.0**					
ALL ADB REGIONAL MEMBERS[a]	**760,818**	**18.4**					

... = data not available, – = magnitude equals zero; ADB = Asian Development Bank.

a Regional aggregates include reporting economies only.

Source: World Health Organization. 2018. Global Status Report on Road Safety 2018. Geneva.

Click on the indictor name in the table header to access the time series in the Key Indicators Database.

Table 2.5.4: Rail Indicators

ADB Regional Member	Rail Lines, Total Route (km)				Rail Network, Length per Land Area (km per km² '000)			
	2000	2005	2010	2018	2000	2005	2010	2018
Developing ADB Member Economies								
Central and West Asia								
Afghanistan	...	...	...	...	...	...	...	...
Armenia	843.0	845.0 (2006)	826.1	843.0 (2019)	29.6	29.7 (2006)	29.0	24.1 (2017)
Azerbaijan	2,116.0	2,122.0	2,079.1	2,133.1	25.6	25.7	25.2	25.8
Georgia	1,562.0	1,336.0	1,566.4	1,285.0 (2017)	22.5	19.2	22.5	18.5 (2017)
Kazakhstan	13,545.0	14,204.0	14,184.1	16,060.8	5.0	5.3	5.3	5.9
Kyrgyz Republic	417.0	417.0	417.2	424.0 (2017)	2.2	2.2	2.2	2.2 (2017)
Pakistan	7,791.0	7,791.0	7,791.0	7,791.0	10.1	10.1	10.1	10.1
Tajikistan	533.0	617.0	620.7	620.0 (2017)	3.8	4.4	4.4	4.5 (2017)
Turkmenistan	2,521.0	2,529.0	3,115.0	7,680.0 (2017)	5.4	5.4	6.6	16.3 (2017)
Uzbekistan	3,645.0	4,014.0	4,227.2	4,642.0 (2017)	8.6	9.4	9.9	10.9 (2017)
East Asia								
China, People's Republic of	58,656.0	62,200.0	66,239.0	67,515.0	6.2	6.6	7.1	7.2
Hong Kong, China	...	113.0	...	...	...	107.6	...	...
Korea, Republic of	3,123.0	3,392.0	3,618.3	4,191.7 (2017)	32.4	35.0	37.2	43.0 (2017)
Mongolia	1,810.0	1,810.0	1,814.0	1,810.0 (2017)	1.2	1.2	1.2	1.2 (2017)
Taipei,China	1,190.0	1,336.0	1,743.0	1,836.0	33.2	37.2	48.6	51.2
South Asia								
Bangladesh	2,745.0	2,855.0	2,835.0	2,877.0 (2016)	21.1	21.9	21.8	22.1 (2016)
Bhutan	...	...	...	...	...	...	...	...
India	62,759.0	63,485.0	63,974.0	68,443.0	21.1	21.4	21.5	23.0
Maldives	...	...	...	...	...	...	...	...
Nepal	...	...	...	...	...	...	...	...
Sri Lanka	...	1,463.0 (2007)	1,148.3 (2011)	1,561.7 (2016)	...	23.3 (2007)	18.3 (2011)	24.9 (2016)
Southeast Asia								
Brunei Darussalam	...	...	...	...	...	...	...	...
Cambodia	601.0	650.0 (2004)	...	...	3.4	3.7 (2004)	...	...
Indonesia	...	3,370.0 (2006)	4,684.0	...	...	1.9 (2006)	2.6	...
Lao People's Democratic Republic	...	...	...	...	...	...	...	...
Malaysia	1,636.0	1,667.0	2,209.7	...	5.0	5.1	6.7	...
Myanmar	...	...	...	...	...	...	...	...
Philippines	...	...	479.0 (2008)	509.0 (2016)	...	...	1.6 (2008)	1.7 (2016)
Singapore	...	...	...	...	...	...	...	...
Thailand	4,044.0	4,429.0 (2007)	4,458.0	...	7.9	8.7 (2007)	8.7	...
Timor-Leste	...	...	...	...	...	...	...	...
Viet Nam	3,142.0	3,147.0	2,576.6	2,382.0	10.1	10.1	8.3	7.7
The Pacific								
Cook Islands	...	...	...	...	...	...	...	...
Fiji	...	...	...	...	...	...	...	...
Kiribati	...	...	...	...	...	...	...	...
Marshall Islands	...	...	...	...	...	...	...	...
Micronesia, Federated States of	...	...	...	...	...	...	...	...
Nauru	...	...	...	...	...	...	...	...
Niue	...	...	...	...	...	...	...	...
Palau	...	...	...	...	...	...	...	...
Papua New Guinea	...	...	...	...	...	...	...	...
Samoa	...	...	...	...	...	...	...	...
Solomon Islands	...	...	...	...	...	...	...	...
Tonga	...	...	...	...	...	...	...	...
Tuvalu	...	...	...	...	...	...	...	...
Vanuatu	...	...	...	...	...	...	...	...
Developed ADB Member Economies								
Australia	9,499.0	9,528.0	8,615.4	...	1.2	1.2	1.1	...
Japan	29,799.0	20,052.3	20,140.3	16,851.7	81.8	55.0	55.2	46.2
New Zealand	...	...	...	...	...	...	...	...

... = data not available, ADB = Asian Development Bank, km = kilometer, km² = square kilometer.

Sources: World Bank. World Development Indicators. http://data.worldbank.org/indicator (accessed 3 July 2020); and Asian Development Bank estimates. For Taipei,China: National Development Council. Statistical Data Book. https://www.ndc.gov.tw/en/News.aspx?n=607ED34345641980&sms=B8A915763 E3684AC (accessed 3 July 2020).

Click on the indictor name in the table header to access the time series in the Key Indicators Database.

Table 2.5.5:   Railways—Passengers Carried and Goods Transported

ADB Regional Member	Passengers Carried (passenger-km million)				Goods Transported (t-km million)			
	2000	2005	2010	2017	2000	2005	2010	2017
Developing ADB Member Economies								
Central and West Asia								
Afghanistan	...	...	...	...	...	...	...	...
Armenia	47	27	50	25	354	654	346	689
Azerbaijan	493	878	917	468 (2018)	5,770	11,059 (2006)	8,250	4,633
Georgia	453	720	654	597	3,912	6,127	6,228	2,963
Kazakhstan	10,215	12,129	15,448	19,241	124,983	171,855	213,174	206,258
Kyrgyz Republic	44	60 (2006)	99	43	337	752 (2006)	738	935
Pakistan	18,495	24,238	20,619 (2011)	24,903 (2018)	3,612	5,014	1,757 (2011)	8,080 (2018)
Tajikistan	73	52 (2006)	33	28	1,326	1,220 (2006)	808	165
Turkmenistan	943	1,435 (2006)	1,811	2,340	7,588	10,441 (2006)	11,765	13,327
Uzbekistan	2,163	2,012	2,905	4,294	15,441	18,007	22,282	22,940
East Asia								
China, People's Republic of	441,468	583,320	791,158	681,203 (2018)	1,333,606	1,953,336	2,451,185	2,238,435 (2018)
Hong Kong, China	...	...	...	...	...	...	...	...
Korea, Republic of	28,097	31,004	33,012	23,002 (2018)	10,621	10,108	9,452	7,878 (2018)
Mongolia	1,070	1,289 (2006)	2,440	973	4,293	9,219 (2006)	20,574	13,493
Taipei,China	12,269 (2001)	19,066 (2008)	20,931	29,624 (2018)	1,010 (2001)	933 (2008)	873	544 (2018)
South Asia								
Bangladesh	3,941	4,164	7,304	10,040 (2016)	777	817	710	1,053 (2016)
Bhutan	...	...	...	...	...	...	...	...
India	430,666	575,702	903,465	1,149,835	305,201	407,398	600,548	620,175
Maldives	...	...	...	...	...	...	...	...
Nepal	...	...	...	...	...	...	...	...
Sri Lanka	3,208	4,358	4,574 (2011)	7,407 (2015)	127 (2003)	135	154 (2011)	127 (2015)
Southeast Asia								
Brunei Darussalam	...	...	...	...	92	...	...	...
Cambodia	45	45	...	...	4,997	4,390 (2006)	7,166	...
Indonesia	19,228	14,345	20,340	25,654	...	...	...	...
Lao People's Democratic Republic	...	...	...	...	...	...	...	...
Malaysia	1,220	2,152	2,415	2,029	916	1,177	1,483	1,234
Myanmar	4,451	4,163 (2004)	...	...	1,222	885 (2004)	...	...
Philippines	123	83 (2004)	...	384 (2016)	1 (2003)	1 (2004)	...	...
Singapore	...	...	...	...	...	...	...	...
Thailand	9,935	9,195	8,187	...	2,247	4,037	2,701	...
Timor-Leste	...	...	...	...	...	...	...	...
Viet Nam	3,200	4,558	4,378	3,542 (2018)	1,921	2,928	3,901	3,989 (2018)
The Pacific								
Cook Islands	...	...	...	...	...	...	...	...
Fiji	...	...	...	...	...	...	...	...
Kiribati	...	...	...	...	...	...	...	...
Marshall Islands	...	...	...	...	...	...	...	...
Micronesia, Federated States of	...	...	...	...	...	...	...	...
Nauru	...	...	...	...	...	...	...	...
Niue	...	...	...	...	...	...	...	...
Palau	...	...	...	...	...	...	...	...
Papua New Guinea	...	...	...	...	...	...	...	...
Samoa	...	...	...	...	...	...	...	...
Solomon Islands	...	...	...	...	...	...	...	...
Tonga	...	...	...	...	...	...	...	...
Tuvalu	...	...	...	...	...	...	...	...
Vanuatu	...	...	...	...	...	...	...	...
Developed ADB Member Economies								
Australia	1,265	1,290	1,500	...	33,592	46,164	64,172	...
Japan	240,657	245,957	244,591	1,410 (2018)	21,800	22,632	20,255	21,265 (2016)
New Zealand	...	...	...	...	4,078	...	...	...

... = data not available, ADB = Asian Development Bank, km = kilometer, t = metric ton.

Sources: World Bank. World Development Indicators. http://data.worldbank.org/indicator (accessed 30 June 2020). For Taipei,China: Government of Taipei,China, Directorate-General of Budget, Accounting and Statistics. Statistical Yearbook. https://eng.dgbas.gov.tw/ct.asp?xItem=41882&ctNode=2351&mp=2 (accessed 30 June 2020).

Click on the indictor name in the table header to access the time series in the Key Indicators Database.

Table 2.5.6: Air Transport

ADB Regional Member	Carrier Departures Worldwide (takeoffs)				Freight (t-km million)				Passengers Carried ('000)			
	2000	2005	2010	2018	2000	2005	2008	2018	2000	2005	2010	2018
Developing ADB Member Economies												
Central and West Asia[a]	151,667	159,458	180,767	243,394	515.1	640.9	660.2	450.9	10,303	14,461	16,759	25,258
Afghanistan	3,409	...	21,677	24,433	7.8	...	108.0	29.6	150	...	1,999	1,723
Armenia	4,406	5,939	8,761	...	8.8	7.0	6.0	...	298	556	705	...
Azerbaijan	8,012	12,470	9,885	19,960	47.2	11.9	7.8	44.1	546	1,134	797	2,280
Georgia	1,906	4,673	2,803	7,108	2.0	2.8	0.9	0.8	118	249	164	516
Kazakhstan	8,041	17,302	33,483	83,287	11.8	15.8	42.4	50.2	461	1,160	3,098	7,144
Kyrgyz Republic	6,051	5,228	7,371	16,344	3.7	2.0	1.3	0.0(2017)	241	226	376	709
Pakistan	63,956	48,905	64,932	48,542	340.3	407.9	333.0	217.5	5,294	5,364	6,588	6,881
Tajikistan	3,953	6,987	5,710	4,021	2.0	3.7	1.0	2.3	168	479	617	492
Turkmenistan	21,858	14,094	3,221	18,184	11.9	10.1	6.2	16.9	1,284	1,654	301	2,457
Uzbekistan	30,075	22,183	22,924	21,514	79.6	71.6	153.7	89.4	1,745	1,639	2,114	3,057
East Asia[a]	1,471,773	2,178,229	3,183,408	6,018,498	16,672.7	22,783.7	40,516.3	49,872.8	159,262	235,402	373,111	816,274
China, People's Republic of	572,921	1,349,269	2,377,789	4,692,008	3,900.1	7,579.4	17,193.9	25,256.2	61,892	136,722	266,293	611,440
Hong Kong, China	79,182	122,705	158,255	245,146	5,111.5	7,763.9	10,373.4	12,676.7	14,378	20,230	28,348	47,102
Korea, Republic of	226,910	221,424	280,427	526,374	7,651.3	7,432.6	12,942.7	11,929.6	34,331	33,888	36,988	88,158
Mongolia	6,200	5,332	6,528	7,777	8.4	6.1	3.9	7.8	254	295	391	670
Taipei,China[b]	586,560	479,499	360,409	547,193	1.3	1.8	2.3	2.5	48,407	44,268	41,091	68,904
South Asia[a]	229,183	370,837	717,432	1,439,804	1,027.4	1,275.1	2,141.3	3,217.1	21,379	32,943	70,386	180,622
Bangladesh	6,313	7,399	19,300	101,383	193.9	183.5	164.4	63.8	1,331	1,634	1,819	5,984
Bhutan	1,138	2,467	3,053	5,187	0.0	0.3	0.4	0.7	34	49	182	276
India	198,426	330,484	623,197	1,200,111	547.7	774.0	1,631.0	2,704.0	17,299	27,879	64,374	164,036
Maldives[c]	5,970	4,520	4,971	26,789	13.2	0.0	0.0	7.7	315	82	85	1,147
Nepal	12,130	6,255	45,990	71,908	17.0	6.9	6.5	4.7	643	480	918	3,297
Sri Lanka	5,206	19,712	20,921	34,425	255.7	310.4	339.0	436.2	1,756	2,818	3,008	5,882
Southeast Asia[a]	608,596	862,178	1,519,936	2,797,219	10,544.2	13,284.5	14,328.2	11,851.1	70,845	100,305	187,126	389,525
Brunei Darussalam	12,739	11,808	12,333	11,310	140.2	134.1	148.5	129.4	864	978	1,263	1,234
Cambodia[d]	4,648	3,207	5,105	14,387	4.1	1.2	0.0	0.7	125	169	278	1,411
Indonesia	159,027	320,724	520,932	959,307	408.5	439.8	665.7	1,131.9	9,916	26,836	59,384	115,154
Lao People's Democratic Republic	6,411	9,002	11,374	10,173	1.7	2.5	0.1	1.5	211	293	444	1,252
Malaysia	169,263	176,152	302,185	476,733	1,863.8	2,577.6	2,564.7	1,404.4	16,561	20,369	34,239	60,482
Myanmar	10,329	26,460	20,485	64,398	0.8	2.7	2.1	4.7	438	1,504	924	3,408
Philippines	44,547	58,944	205,318	292,450	289.9	322.7	460.2	835.9	5,756	8,057	22,575	43,080
Singapore	71,042	77,119	131,722	208,787	6,004.9	7,571.3	7,121.4	5,194.9	16,704	17,744	24,860	40,402
Thailand	101,591	124,347	201,306	475,886	1,712.9	2,002.4	2,938.7	2,666.3	17,392	18,903	28,781	76,053
Timor-Leste	...	...	...	...	...	...	...	...	...	...	...	...
Viet Nam	28,999	54,415	109,176	283,787	117.3	230.2	426.9	481.4	2,878	5,454	14,378	47,050
The Pacific												
Cook Islands	...	...	...	...	...	...	...	...	...	...	...	...
Fiji	57,776	41,886	26,127	24,134	90.8	92.1	77.1	106.8	586	871	1,259	1,670
Kiribati	...	...	...	5,005	...	...	...	...	...	...	...	67
Marshall Islands[c]	2,324	3,083	3,480	2,244	0.2	0.3	0.3	0.1	16	26	28	24
Micronesia, Federated States of	...	...	...	...	...	...	...	...	...	...	...	...
Nauru	...	...	342	842	...	...	6.3	7.9	...	...	30	45
Niue	...	...	...	...	...	...	...	...	...	...	...	...
Palau	...	...	...	...	...	...	...	...	...	...	...	...
Papua New Guinea	27,512	19,606	32,741	41,545	22.3	21.1	28.5	30.9	1,100	819	1,405	965
Samoa[c]	10,877	11,439	12,492	6,848	2.2	1.8	1.6	0.0(2016)	164	267	271	138
Solomon Islands	11,481	12,318	7,388	14,365	1.0	0.8	2.5	3.8	75	91	143	428
Tonga[e]	3,814	5,255	...	...	0.0	0.0	...	...	52	75	...	...
Tuvalu	...	...	...	...	...	...	...	...	...	...	...	...
Vanuatu	1,402	1,580	17,212	11,723	1.8	1.8	0.2	1.7	102	112	248	375
Developed ADB Member Economies[a]	1,267,647	1,203,836	1,715,265	1,852,829	11,219.9	11,775.3	11,105.8	12,797.6	152,482	158,888	183,553	219,304
Australia	382,514	342,509	572,906	665,384	1,730.7	2,444.6	2,938.3	2,027.6	32,578	44,657	60,641	75,668
Japan	645,087	651,858	934,487	999,594	8,672.0	8,549.2	7,698.8	9,420.7	109,123	102,279	109,617	126,388
New Zealand	240,046	209,469	207,872	187,851	817.1	781.5	468.6	1,349.3	10,781	11,952	13,295	17,249
DEVELOPING ADB MEMBER ECONOMIES[a]	2,583,408	3,672,872	5,711,585	10,610,876	28,880.7	38,105.0	57,762.7	65,543.1	264,161	385,649	650,908	1,415,466
ALL ADB REGIONAL MEMBERS[a]	3,851,055	4,876,708	7,426,850	12,463,705	40,100.6	49,880.3	68,868.5	78,340.7	416,643	544,538	834,461	1,634,771
WORLD	22,008,658	24,215,712	29,637,930	36,999,575	118,257.2	141,483.6	182,025.6	220,707.2	1,674,065	1,969,591	2,628,261	4,232,645

... = data not available, 0.0 = magnitude is less than half of unit employed, ADB = Asian Development Bank, km = kilometer, t = metric ton.

a For estimating regional aggregates, imputation was done for economies with missing data by substituting available data from the closest years.

b Carried departures worldwide are based on the number of aircraft movements, both domestic and international. Freight is based on millions of tons per kilometer.

c For all indicators, data for 2010 refer to 2009.

d For the freight indicator, data for 2000 refer to 2002.

e For all indicators, data for 2005 refer to 2004.

Sources: World Bank. World Development Indicators. http://databank.worldbank.org/data/reports.aspx?source=world-development-indicators (accessed 3 July 2020). For Taipei,China: National Development Council. Statistical Data Book 2019. https://www.ndc.gov.tw/en/News_Content.aspx?n=607ED34345641980&sms=B8A915763E3684AC&s=EDDF6690A4EE6CCB (accessed 3 July 2020).

Click on the indictor name in the table header to access the time series in the Key Indicators Database.

Transport

Table 2.5.7:   Container Port Traffic
(teu '000)

ADB Regional Member	2000	2005	2006	2007	2008	2009	2010	2013	2014	2015	2016	2017	2018
Developing ADB Member Economies													
Central and West Asia													
Afghanistan	...	...	...	...	...	...	...	...	...	...	...	...	...
Armenia	...	...	...	...	...	...	...	...	...	...	...	...	...
Azerbaijan	...	...	...	...	...	...	...	...	...	...	...	...	...
Georgia	...	...	...	185	254	182	210	226	256	222	222	285	285
Kazakhstan	...	...	...	...	...	...	...	...	...	...	...	...	...
Kyrgyz Republic	...	...	...	...	...	...	...	...	...	...	...	...	...
Pakistana	879	1,686	1,777	1,936	1,938	2,058	2,149	2,262	2,535	2,756	2,756	3,275	3,275
Tajikistan	...	...	...	...	...	...	...	...	...	...	...	...	...
Turkmenistan	...	...	...	...	...	...	...	...	...	...	...	...	...
Uzbekistan	...	...	...	...	...	...	...	...	...	...	...	...	...
East Asia													
China, People's Republic of	41,000	67,245	84,811	103,823	115,942	108,800	142,970	175,936	186,679	195,277	199,552	216,684	225,829
Hong Kong, China	...	22,602	23,539	23,998	24,494	21,040	23,600	22,290	22,300	20,114	19,580	20,760	19,641
Korea, Republic of	9,030	15,113	15,514	17,086	17,418	15,700	19,456	23,711	24,819	25,354	26,153	27,416	28,945
Mongolia	...	...	...	...	...	...	...	...	...	...	...	...	...
Taipei,China	...	12,791	13,102	13,720	12,971	11,352	13,592	14,353	15,270	14,634	14,885	14,911	15,322
South Asia													
Bangladesh	456	809	902	978	1,091	1,182	1,350	1,489	1,643	2,045	2,377	2,587	2,827
Bhutan	...	...	...	...	...	...	...	...	...	...	...	...	...
India	2,451	4,982	6,141	7,398	7,672	8,014	8,923	10,626	11,323	11,882	12,086	15,426	16,383
Maldives	...	...	...	48	54	56	50	80	84	84	82	87	89
Nepal	...	...	...	...	...	...	...	...	...	...	...	...	...
Sri Lanka	1,733	2,455	3,079	3,687	3,687	3,464	4,100	4,310	4,908	5,185	5,550	6,200	7,000
Southeast Asia													
Brunei Darussalam	...	...	...	...	90	86	93	122	128	128	125	133	139
Cambodia	...	...	...	253	259	208	224	230	342	392	400	645	742
Indonesia	3,798	5,503	4,316	6,583	7,405	7,255	9,692	11,862	11,620	11,979	12,479	12,710	12,853
Lao People's Democratic Republic	...	...	...	...	...	...	...	...	...	...	...	...	...
Malaysia	4,642	12,198	13,419	14,829	16,094	15,923	18,142	21,377	22,645	24,260	24,570	23,784	24,956
Myanmar	...	...	...	170	180	164	335	567	717	827	1,026	1,120	1,288
Philippines	3,032	3,634	3,676	4,351	4,471	4,307	5,087	5,826	6,176	7,210	7,621	8,090	8,638
Singapore	17,100	23,192	24,792	28,768	30,891	26,593	29,147	33,388	34,688	31,710	32,668	33,667	36,600
Thailand	3,179	5,115	5,574	6,339	6,726	5,898	7,553	8,891	9,420	9,522	9,940	10,732	11,185
Timor-Leste	...	...	...	...	...	...	...	...	...	...	...	...	...
Viet Nam	1,190	2,537	3,000	4,009	4,394	4,937	5,968	8,967	10,189	11,479	11,853	15,326	16,374
The Pacific													
Cook Islands	...	...	...	...	...	...	...	...	...	...	...	...	...
Fiji	...	...	...	...	...	...	87	88	260	89	89	89	93
Kiribati	...	...	...	...	...	...	...	...	...	...	...	...	...
Marshall Islands	...	...	...	...	...	...	...	...	...	...	...	...	...
Micronesia, Federated States of	...	...	...	...	...	...	...	...	...	...	...	...	...
Nauru	...	...	...	...	...	...	...	...	...	...	...	...	...
Niue	...	...	...	...	...	...	...	...	...	...	...	...	...
Palau	...	...	...	...	...	...	...	...	...	...	...	...	...
Papua New Guinea	...	...	...	282	255	262	283	279	279	279	279	335	341
Samoa	...	...	...	...	...	...	22	24	27	28	28	29	30
Solomon Islands	...	...	...	...	...	...	...	...	...	...	...	...	...
Tonga	...	...	...	...	...	...	...	...	...	...	...	...	...
Tuvalu	...	...	...	...	...	...	...	...	...	...	...	...	...
Vanuatu	...	...	...	...	...	...	...	...	...	...	...	...	...
Developed ADB Member Economies													
Australia	3,543	5,191	5,742	6,290	6,102	6,200	6,412	7,180	7,405	7,634	7,690	8,010	8,747
Japan	13,100	17,055	18,470	19,165	18,944	16,286	19,548	21,050	21,139	20,577	20,785	22,055	22,434
New Zealand	1,067	1,603	1,807	2,312	2,318	2,325	2,526	2,891	3,003	3,173	3,165	3,189	3,329

... = data not available, – = magnitude equals zero, ADB = Asian Development Bank, teu = twenty-foot equivalent unit.

a   For 2000, the figure refers to 2001.

Sources: World Bank. World Development Indicators. http://data.worldbank.org/indicator (accessed 7 July 2020). For Taipei,China for 2005–2007: United Nations Conference on Trade and Development (UNCTAD). 2008 and 2010. Review of Maritime Transport. New York, New York: United Nations Publications; for 2008–2009: UNCTAD. UNCTADstat. http://unctadstat.unctad.org/EN/ (accessed 15 August 2016); and for 2010–2018: UNCTAD. UNCTADstat. http://unctadstat.unctad.org/EN/ (accessed 7 July 2020).

Table 2.5.8: Access to Fixed Telephone, Mobile Phones, and Internet
('000)

ADB Regional Member	Telephone Subscribers		Mobile Phone Subscribers		Fixed Broadband Subscribers	
	2000	2018	2000	2018	2000	2018
Developing ADB Member Economies						
Central and West Asia[a]	**9,374.1**	**13,993.4**	**1,232.2**	**272,649.2**	**20.1**	**11,859.4**
Afghanistan	29.0	127.8	25.0 (2002)	21,976.4	0.2 (2004)	16.0
Armenia	533.4	477.9	17.5	3,579.3	0.0 (2001)	347.4
Azerbaijan	801.2	1,681.4	420.4	10,339.7	1.0 (2002)	1,890.9
Georgia	508.8	604.3	194.7	5,459.2	0.4 (2001)	840.6
Kazakhstan	1,834.2	3,350.9	197.3	26,065.6	1.0 (2003)	2,462.9
Kyrgyz Republic	376.1	331.1	9.0	8,735.2	0.0 (2002)	355.6
Pakistan	3,053.5	2,798.6	306.5	153,986.6	14.6 (2005)	1,811.4
Tajikistan	218.5	479.0 (2017)	1.2	9,904.0 (2017)	0.0 (2003)	6.0 (2017)
Turkmenistan	364.4	682.0 (2017)	7.5	9,377.0 (2017)	0.1 (2008)	5.0 (2017)
Uzbekistan	1,655.0	3,460.3	53.1	23,226.2	2.8 (2003)	4,123.5
East Asia[a]	**187,377.5**	**235,732.1**	**135,552.2**	**1,769,122.3**	**4,566.2**	**437,413.7**
China, People's Republic of	144,829.0	192,085.0	85,260.0	1,649,301.7	22.7	407,382.0
Hong Kong, China	3,925.8	4,196.1	5,447.3	19,901.9	444.5	2,714.7
Korea, Republic of	25,863.0	25,906.8	26,816.4	66,355.8	3,870.0	21,285.9
Mongolia	117.5	369.9	154.6	4,222.0	0.0 (2001)	306.2
Taipei,China	12,642.2	13,174.3	17,873.8	29,340.9	229.0	5,725.0
South Asia[a]	**34,000.3**	**26,631.9**	**4,304.2**	**1,408,816.4**	**97.3**	**30,807.5**
Bangladesh	491.3	1,449.6	279.0	161,771.6	43.7 (2007)	10,237.0
Bhutan	14.1	22.0	0.0	703.6	2.1 (2008)	10.8
India	32,436.1	21,868.2	3,577.1	1,176,021.9	50.0 (2001)	18,170.0
Maldives	24.4	18.8	7.6	857.9	0.2 (2002)	53.5
Nepal	266.9	799.4	10.2	39,178.5	1.0 (2006)	792.0
Sri Lanka	767.4	2,473.9	430.2	30,283.0	0.3 (2001)	1,544.3
Southeast Asia[a]	**24,857.4**	**30,271.7**	**22,109.1**	**857,004.0**	**91.9**	**39,674.5**
Brunei Darussalam	80.5	82.6	95.0	565.9	1.9 (2001)	49.5
Cambodia	30.9	88.2	130.5	19,417.1	0.1 (2002)	166.2
Indonesia	6,662.6	8,303.5	3,669.3	319,434.6	4.0	8,874.1
Lao People's Democratic Republic	40.9	1,482.3	12.7	3,662.3	0.0 (2003)	45.4
Malaysia	4,628.0	6,433.3	5,121.7	42,413.4	4.0 (2001)	2,696.0
Myanmar	271.4	520.9	13.4	61,144.0	0.2 (2005)	129.1
Philippines	3,061.4	4,132.5	6,454.4	134,592.6	10.0 (2001)	3,919.7
Singapore	1,946.0	2,001.0	2,747.4	8,568.4	69.0	1,610.5
Thailand	5,591.1	2,929.0	3,056.0	125,098.0	1.6 (2001)	9,189.0
Timor-Leste	2.0 (2003)	2.2	20.1 (2003)	1,468.5	0.0 (2003)	0.6
Viet Nam	2,542.7	4,296.3	788.6	140,639.1	1.1 (2002)	12,994.5
The Pacific[a]	**211.2**	**288.8**	**72.6**	**6,157.9**	**12.9**	**49.7**
Cook Islands	...	...	...	...	...	...
Fiji	86.4	76.5	55.1	1,033.9 (2017)	7.0 (2005)	13.0
Kiribati	3.4	0.0	0.3	58.8	0.3 (2005)	0.9
Marshall Islands	4.0	2.4 (2014)	0.4	16.0 (2017)	...	1.0 (2017)
Micronesia, Federated States of	9.6	6.9 (2017)	0.0	23.1 (2017)	0.0 (2003)	3.8 (2017)
Nauru	1.8	0.0 (2014)	1.2	10.0 (2017)	...	1.0 (2010)
Niue	1.1	1.0 (2015)	0.4	...	...	...
Palau	6.9 (2002)	7.2 (2015)	2.5 (2002)	23.7 (2015)	0.1 (2004)	1.2 (2015)
Papua New Guinea	64.8	158.0 (2017)	8.6	4,018.0 (2017)	3.0 (2008)	18.0 (2017)
Samoa	8.5	8.5 (2017)	2.5	124.2 (2017)	0.0 (2004)	1.7 (2017)
Solomon Islands	7.7	7.4	1.2	482.0	0.2 (2004)	1.5
Tonga	9.7	14.7	0.2	107.9	0.0 (2002)	2.5
Tuvalu	0.7	2.0 (2017)	0.0	8.0 (2017)	0.1 (2004)	0.5 (2017)
Vanuatu	6.6	4.2	0.4	251.4	0.0 (2003)	4.7
Developed ADB Member Economies[a]	**73,838.1**	**73,375.7**	**76,888.4**	**214,551.8**	**982.1**	**50,783.3**
Australia	10,050.0	8,090.0	8,562.0	28,279.0	122.8 (2001)	7,640.0
Japan	61,957.1	63,525.7	66,784.4	179,872.8	854.7	41,496.3
New Zealand	1,831.0	1,760.0	1,542.0	6,400.0	4.7	1,647.0
DEVELOPING ADB MEMBER ECONOMIES[a]	**255,820.5**	**306,917.8**	**163,270.2**	**4,313,749.7**	**4,788.4**	**519,804.8**
ALL ADB REGIONAL MEMBERS[a]	**329,658.6**	**380,293.5**	**240,158.6**	**4,528,301.5**	**5,770.5**	**570,588.1**

... = data not available, – = magnitude equals zero, 0.0 = magnitude is less than half of unit employed, ADB = Asian Development Bank.

a   Regional aggregates include reporting economies only. Imputation was done for economies with missing data by substituting available data from the closest years.

Source: International Telecommunication Union. World Telecommunication/ICT Indicators Database. https://www.itu.int/en/ITU-D/Statistics/Pages/publications/wtid.aspx (accessed 9 July 2020).

Table 2.5.9: Access to Fixed Telephone, Mobile Phones, and Internet
(per 100 people)

ADB Regional Member	Fixed Telephone				Mobile Cellular				Fixed Broadband				Internet Users[a]			
	2000	2005	2010	2018	2000	2005	2010	2018	2000	2005	2010	2018	2000	2005	2010	2018
Developing ADB Member Economies																
Central and West Asia[b]	**4.0**	**5.6**	**5.8**	**4.0**	**0.5**	**9.5**	**63.0**	**78.3**	**...**	**0.0**	**0.9**	**3.7**				
Afghanistan[c,d]	0.1	0.2	0.1	0.3	0.1	4.7	35.0	59.1	...	0.0	0.0	0.0	0.0	1.2	4.0	13.5
Armenia[e]	17.4	19.9	20.6	16.2	0.6	10.7	134.3	121.3	0.0	0.1	3.3	11.8	1.3	5.3	25.0	64.7
Azerbaijan	9.9	12.8	16.7	16.9	5.2	26.3	100.7	103.9	0.0	0.0	5.3	19.0	0.1	8.0	46.0	79.8
Georgia	11.7	13.5	27.1	15.1	4.5	27.9	97.1	136.4	0.0	0.1	4.5	21.0	0.5	6.1	26.9	62.7
Kazakhstan	12.3	17.6	25.0	18.3	1.3	35.0	119.4	142.3	...	0.0	5.4	13.4	0.7	3.0	31.6	78.9
Kyrgyz Republic[e]	7.6	8.7	9.0	5.3	0.2	10.7	97.3	138.6	0.0	0.0	0.4	5.6	1.0	10.5	16.3	38.0
Pakistan[f]	2.1	3.3	3.4	1.3	0.2	8.0	55.3	72.6	...	0.0	0.4	0.9	1.3	6.3	8.0	15.5
Tajikistan[g]	3.5	4.1	4.9	5.4	0.0	3.9	78.9	111.5	...	0.1	0.1	0.1	0.0	0.3	11.6	22.0
Turkmenistan[g]	8.1	8.4	10.2	11.8	0.2	2.2	62.9	162.9	...	...	0.0	0.1	0.1	1.0	3.0	21.3
Uzbekistan	6.7	6.8	6.6	10.7	0.2	2.7	73.5	71.5	...	0.0	0.4	12.7	0.5	3.3	15.9	55.2
East Asia[b]	**13.7**	**27.8**	**23.7**	**15.6**	**9.9**	**32.8**	**65.7**	**116.9**	**0.3**	**3.9**	**10.4**	**28.9**				
China, People's Republic of[e]	11.2	26.3	21.5	13.5	6.6	29.6	62.8	115.5	0.0	2.8	9.2	28.5	1.8	8.5	34.3	54.3
Hong Kong, China	59.4	56.0	62.6	56.9	82.5	126.2	198.0	270.0	6.7	24.5	31.1	36.8	27.8	56.9	72.0	90.5
Korea, Republic of	54.6	49.1	57.6	50.6	56.6	78.7	102.5	129.7	8.2	25.0	34.7	41.6	44.7	73.5	83.7	96.0
Mongolia[h]	4.9	6.2	7.1	11.7	6.4	22.1	92.3	133.2	0.0	0.1	2.8	9.7	1.3	9.0	10.2	47.2
Taipei,China	57.6	63.8	70.9	55.5	81.4	97.6	120.1	123.7	1.0	19.1	22.9	24.1	28.1	58.0	71.5	86.2
South Asia[b]	**3.1**	**4.4**	**3.2**	**1.9**	**0.4**	**7.7**	**59.3**	**90.0**	**...**	**...**	**0.8**	**2.0**				
Bangladesh[e]	0.4	0.8	0.9	0.9	0.2	6.5	46.0	100.2	...	0.0	0.3	6.3	0.1	0.2	3.7	15.0
Bhutan[e]	2.4	5.1	3.8	2.9	0.0	5.5	57.5	93.3	...	...	1.3	1.4	0.4	3.8	13.6	48.1
India[e]	3.1	4.4	2.8	1.6	0.3	7.9	60.9	86.9	0.0	0.1	0.9	1.3	0.5	2.4	7.5	34.5
Maldives[e]	8.7	10.1	7.8	3.6	2.7	63.7	135.2	166.4	0.1	1.0	4.3	10.4	2.2	6.9	26.5	63.2
Nepal[e]	1.1	1.9	3.1	2.8	0.0	0.9	34.0	139.4	...	0.0	0.2	2.8	0.2	0.8	7.9	34.0
Sri Lanka[e]	4.1	6.4	17.7	11.7	2.3	17.2	85.7	142.7	0.0	0.1	1.1	7.3	0.6	1.8	12.0	34.1
Southeast Asia[b]	**4.7**	**6.5**	**12.2**	**4.6**	**4.2**	**26.3**	**89.2**	**130.8**	**...**	**0.4**	**2.5**	**6.1**				
Brunei Darussalam[e]	24.2	23.0	20.6	19.3	28.5	63.8	112.0	131.9	0.6	2.2	5.6	11.5	9.0	36.5	53.0	94.9
Cambodia	0.3	0.2	2.5	0.5	1.1	8.0	56.9	119.5	0.0	0.0	0.2	1.0	0.0	0.3	1.3	40.0
Indonesia	3.1	6.0	16.9	3.1	1.7	20.7	87.4	119.3	0.0	0.0	0.9	3.3	0.9	3.6	10.9	39.9
Lao People's Democratic Republic[e]	0.8	1.6	1.6	21.0	0.2	11.4	64.1	51.9	...	0.0	0.1	0.6	0.1	0.9	7.0	25.5
Malaysia	20.0	17.0	16.3	20.4	22.1	76.1	120.0	134.5	0.0	1.9	7.4	8.6	21.4	48.6	56.3	81.2
Myanmar[f]	0.6	1.0	1.0	1.0	0.0	0.3	1.2	113.8	...	0.0	0.0	0.2	0.0	0.1	0.3	30.7
Philippines[e]	3.9	3.9	3.5	3.9	8.3	40.3	88.5	126.2	0.0	0.1	1.9	3.7	2.0	5.4	25.0	60.1
Singapore	48.3	43.2	38.9	34.8	68.2	102.8	143.9	148.8	1.7	15.4	26.1	28.0	36.0	61.0	71.0	88.2
Thailand	8.9	10.8	10.2	4.2	4.9	46.6	106.7	180.2	0.0	0.8	4.8	13.2	3.7	15.0	22.4	56.8
Timor-Leste[i]	...	0.2	0.3	0.2	...	3.3	43.3	115.8	...	0.0	0.0	0.0	0.0	0.1	3.0	27.5
Viet Nam[j]	3.2	10.1	16.3	4.5	1.0	11.4	126.8	147.2	0.0	0.3	4.2	13.6	0.3	12.7	30.7	70.3
The Pacific[b]	**2.6**	**3.0**	**3.5**	**2.6**	**0.9**	**4.4**	**32.7**	**56.1**	**...**	**...**	**0.4**	**0.4**				
Cook Islands	...	...	...	...	...	...	...	...	...	...	...	...	...	...	...	...
Fiji[k]	10.7	13.7	15.1	8.7	6.8	25.0	81.2	117.8	...	0.9	2.7	1.5	1.5	8.5	20.0	50.0
Kiribati[e]	4.0	4.5	8.2	0.0	0.4	0.7	10.3	50.8	...	0.3	0.8	0.8	1.8	4.0	9.1	14.6
Marshall Islands[l]	7.9	10.1	...	4.1	0.9	1.2	...	27.6	...	...	...	1.7	1.5	3.9	7.0	38.7
Micronesia, Federated States of[g]	9.0	11.7	8.2	6.2	0.0	13.3	26.7	20.7	...	0.0	1.0	3.4	3.7	11.9	20.0	35.3
Nauru[m]	17.4	18.3	0.0	0.0	11.6	...	62.0	94.6	...	...	9.5	...	3.0	...	54.0	57.0
Niue[n]	55.3	62.4	61.8	61.8	21.6	37.9	...	...	...	...	...	...	26.5	51.7	77.0	...
Palau[o]	35.3	40.3	38.9	40.8	12.5	30.6	80.8	134.4	...	0.5	1.3	...	20.2	27.0	...	...
Papua New Guinea[g]	1.1	1.0	1.7	1.9	0.1	1.2	26.1	47.6	...	0.1	0.2	0.8	1.7	1.3	11.2
Samoa[g]	4.9	10.8	4.3	4.3	1.4	13.4	48.4	63.6	...	0.0	0.1	0.9	0.6	3.4	7.0	33.6
Solomon Islands[e]	1.9	1.6	1.6	1.1	0.3	1.3	21.9	73.8	...	0.1	0.5	0.2	0.5	0.8	5.0	11.9
Tonga[e]	9.9	13.6	29.8	14.2	0.2	29.6	52.2	104.6	0.0	0.6	1.1	2.4	2.4	4.9	16.0	41.2
Tuvalu[p]	7.0	8.9	11.4	17.6	0.0	13.0	15.2	70.4	...	1.5	2.3	4.0	5.2	10.0	25.0	49.3
Vanuatu[e]	3.6	3.3	3.0	1.4	0.2	6.1	71.9	85.9	...	0.0	0.2	1.6	2.1	5.1	8.0	25.7
Developed ADB Member Economies[b]	**49.1**	**45.8**	**50.4**	**46.8**	**51.1**	**77.6**	**97.1**	**136.8**	**0.7**	**16.8**	**26.2**	**32.4**				
Australia[e]	52.9	50.2	48.0	32.5	45.1	91.3	101.6	113.6	0.6	10.0	24.9	30.7	46.8	63.0	76.0	86.5
Japan	48.6	45.2	51.0	49.9	52.4	75.2	95.9	141.4	0.7	18.2	26.5	32.6	30.0	66.9	78.2	91.3
New Zealand[e]	47.4	41.8	43.0	37.1	40.0	85.4	107.8	134.9	0.1	7.8	25.0	34.7	47.4	62.7	80.5	90.8
DEVELOPING ADB MEMBER ECONOMIES[b]	**7.9**	**14.7**	**13.1**	**7.8**	**4.9**	**20.7**	**66.7**	**105.7**	**...**	**1.7**	**4.8**	**12.8**				
ALL ADB REGIONAL MEMBERS[b]	**9.7**	**16.1**	**14.6**	**9.3**	**6.8**	**23.0**	**67.9**	**106.9**	**...**	**2.4**	**5.7**	**13.5**				

... = data not available, – = magnitude equals zero, 0.0 = magnitude is less than half of unit employed, ADB = Asian Development Bank.

a   The reference population differs across countries. For example, some countries refer to population of people aged 6 years and older, some refer to 7 years and older, and others refer to ages from 16 to 74 years.
b   Regional aggregates are derived from table 2.5.8 regional aggregate levels and population data from the United Nations' World Population Prospects 2019.
c   For fixed telephone, data for 2005 refers to 2003. For internet users, data for 2000 refers to 2001 and data for 2018 refers to 2017.
d   For mobile cellular, 2002 refers to the first non-zero available data.
e   For internet users, data for 2018 refers to 2017.
f   For internet users, data for 2000 refers to 2001. Data for 2018 refers to 2017.
g   For fixed telephone, data for 2018 refers to 2017. For mobile cellular, data for 2018 refers to 2017. For fixed broadband, data for 2018 refers to 2017. For internet users, data for 2018 refers to 2017.
h   For internet users, data for 2005 refers to 2007.
i   For internet users, data for 2000 refers to 2002 and data for 2018 refers to 2017.
j   For fixed telephone, data for 2005 refers to 2006.
k   All aggregates for the Pacific region for 2018 refer to 2017.
l   For mobile cellular, data for 2018 refers to 2017. For internet users, data for 2018 refers to 2017.
m   For fixed telephone, data for 2005 refers to 2004 and data for 2018 refers to 2014. For mobile cellular, fixed broadband, and internet users, data for 2018 refers to 2017.
n   For fixed telephone, data for 2018 refers to 2014. For mobile cellular, data for 2018 refers to 2017. For internet users, data for 2000 refers to 2001, data for 2010 refers to 2011, and data for 2018 refers to 2017.
o   For fixed telephone, data for 2018 refers to 2015.
p   For fixed telephone, data for 2000 refers to 2002 and data for 2018 refers to 2015. For mobile cellular, data for 2018 refers to 2015. For internet users, data for 2000 refers to 2002 and data for 2005 refers to 2004.
q   For fixed telephone, mobile cellular, and fixed broadband, data for 2018 refers to 2017. For internet users, data for 2005 refers to 2007 and data for 2018 refers to 2017.

Sources: International Telecommunication Union. World Telecommunication/ICT Indicators Database. https://www.itu.int/en/ITU-D/Statistics/Pages/publications/wtid.aspx (accessed 9 July 2020); and United Nations. World Population Prospects 2019. https://population.un.org/wpp/Download/Standard/Population/ (accessed 15 July 2020).

Click on the indictor name in the table header to access the time series in the Key Indicators Database.

VI. Energy and Electricity

Energy and Electricity discusses trends in energy productivity, total production and sources, and energy imports. The statistical tables cover key issues such as energy demand, supplies and uses of primary energy, and electricity consumption and generation.

Energy efficiency is an increasing priority in the most populous economies of Asia and the Pacific

From 2000 to 2017, the five most populous economies in Asia and the Pacific all increased their energy efficiency, as measured by the amount of GDP per unit use of energy (i.e., one petajoule) as shown in Figure 2.6.1.[3] Bangladesh led these economies with an increase in

GDP per unit of energy use of $97.2 million in constant 2017 US dollars at purchasing power parity (constant 2017 $ at PPP), followed by India at $80.2 million.

By comparison, energy efficiency gains from 2000 to 2017 averaged $71.0 million (constant 2017 $ at PPP) among developed member economies, $55.1 million among developing member economies, and $40.4 million for the world average.

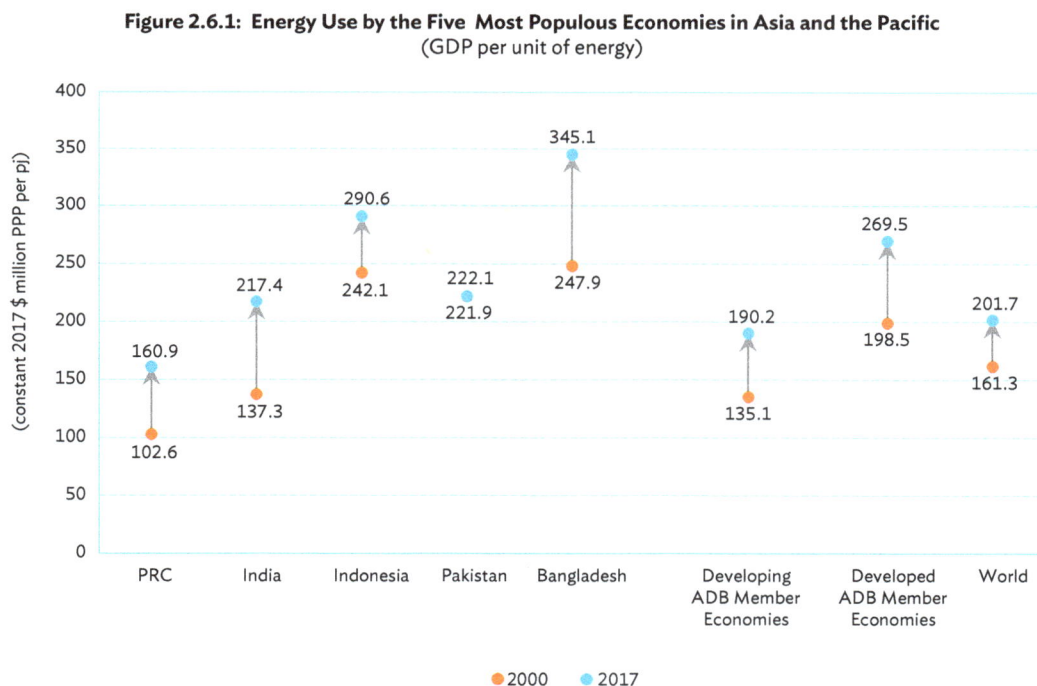

Figure 2.6.1: Energy Use by the Five Most Populous Economies in Asia and the Pacific
(GDP per unit of energy)

$ = United States dollars, ADB = Asian Development Bank, GDP = gross domestic product, PJ = petajoule, PPP = purchasing power parity, PRC = People's Republic of China.
Source: Table 2.6.3, Key Indicators for Asia and the Pacific 2020.

Click here for figure data

[3]   Energy use refers to the consumption of both renewable and nonrenewable energy sources.

In absolute terms, the most energy efficient among the five most populous economies in 2017 were Bangladesh with GDP per unit use of energy at $345.1 million (constant 2017 $ at PPP) and Indonesia at $290.6 million. Among developed member economies, the average for GDP per unit of energy use in 2017 was $269.5 million. For developing member economies, the average was $190.2 million. The global average was $201.7 million.

The region's largest energy producers continue to expand their share of production

Asia and the Pacific's energy production as a share of the global total rose from 24.7% in 2000 to 34.1% in 2017 (Figure 2.6.2, Table 2.6.4,). The increase was mainly driven by expanded energy production in the PRC, which saw its global share rise from 9.9% in 2000 to 17.1% in 2017. The PRC accounted for more than half (50.1%) of all energy production in Asia and the Pacific in 2017, up from 40.2% in 2000.

The region's next four largest energy producers also increased their respective share of global energy production from 2000 to 2017: India (from 3.8% to 4.0%), Indonesia (from 2.0% to 3.3%), Australia (2.4% and 2.9%), and Kazakhstan (0.8% to 1.3%).

More than two-thirds of regional economies were net energy importers in 2017

In 2017, only 14 of 47 reporting economies from Asia and the Pacific were net energy exporters, with the remaining 33 dependent on energy imports (Table 2.6.4). From 2000 (or the earliest year for which data were available) to 2017, the Lao PDR, Mongolia, and Timor-Leste each switched from being a net energy importer to a net energy exporter. As a percentage of domestic energy use, Timor-Leste's energy exports were 592.9% in 2017, Mongolia's were 232.3%, and the Lao PDR's were 16.6%. Viet Nam, which had been a net energy exporter in 2000, with energy exports equivalent to 37.4% of domestic energy use, was importing 5.7% of its domestic energy needs by 2017.

Figure 2.6.2: Energy production by global region and by economy in Asia and the Pacific, 2017
(petajoules, %)

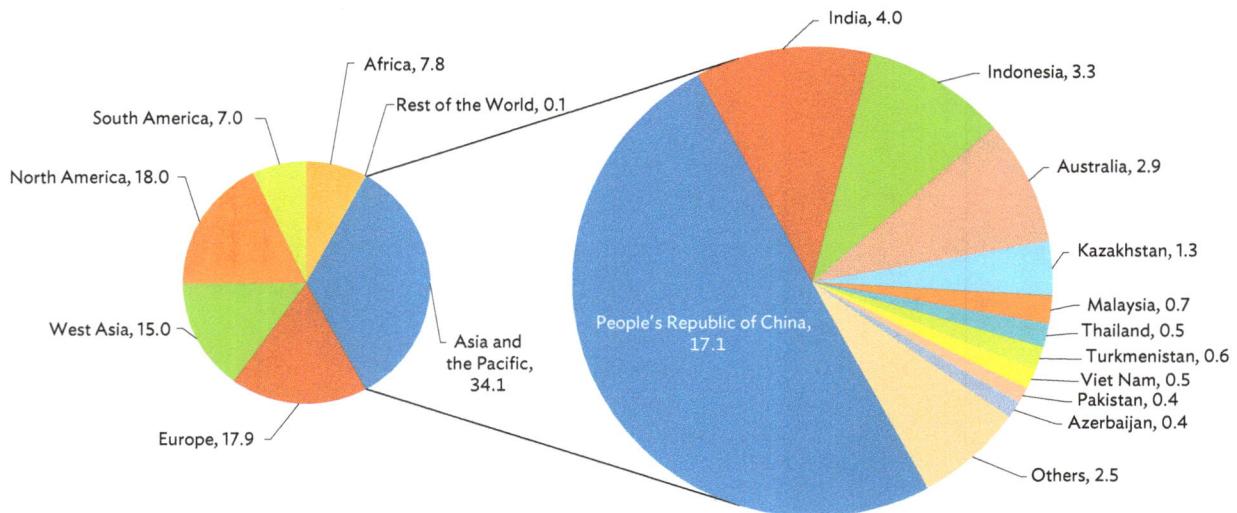

Africa, 7.8
South America, 7.0
Rest of the World, 0.1
North America, 18.0
West Asia, 15.0
Europe, 17.9
Asia and the Pacific, 34.1
India, 4.0
Indonesia, 3.3
Australia, 2.9
Kazakhstan, 1.3
Malaysia, 0.7
Thailand, 0.5
Turkmenistan, 0.6
Viet Nam, 0.5
Pakistan, 0.4
Azerbaijan, 0.4
Others, 2.5
People's Republic of China, 17.1

Source: Table 2.6.4, Key Indicators for Asia and the Pacific 2020.

Click here for figure data

Considering all reporting economies in 2017, Timor-Leste (figures as stated above), Brunei Darussalam, and Azerbaijan—all of which are rich in oil and gas deposits—led the region in energy exports as a share of domestic energy use (Figure 2.6.3). Energy exports from Brunei Darussalam in 2017 were equivalent to 327.2% of domestic energy use. For Azerbaijan, energy exports were equivalent to 283.6%.

In 2017, the economies of Asia and the Pacific that relied on imports to meet 90.0% or more of domestic energy demand included the Marshall Islands (100.0%), Palau (100.0%), Nauru (99.3%), Maldives (99.0%), the Cook Islands (98.7%), the Federal States of Micronesia (98.6%), Tonga (98.4%), Singapore (97.6%), Tuvalu (91.5%), and Japan (90.5%) (Table 2.6.4).

Data Issues and Comparability

Energy data are compiled by the United Nations Statistics Division (UNSD) using standard procedures that follow the definitions of the United Nations International Recommendations for Energy Statistics.[4] The UNSD Annual Questionnaire on Energy Statistics to the UN member economies is the primary source of information for the UNSD energy database. Additional sources of information include national, regional, and international statistical publications. These include, but are not limited to, publications from the International Energy Agency, the Statistical Office of the European Communities (Eurostat), the International Atomic Energy Agency, the Organization of the Petroleum Exporting Countries, and the Organización Latinoamericana de Energía. The UNSD sometimes prepares estimates where official data are incomplete or inconsistent. For the indicator on GDP per unit use of energy, the energy statistics adopt the territory principle, while national accounts are being compiled on the residency principle, which could be a potential source of inconsistency, although in practice differences are not huge (UN 2016).

Data for the household electrification indicator are lacking. Data are posted over a varied range of years (i.e., different starting and ending years) depending on data availability. These data may therefore not be comparable, limiting possibilities for analysis.

Figure 2.6.3: Net Energy Imports as Share of Energy Use in Select Economies of Asia and the Pacific (%)

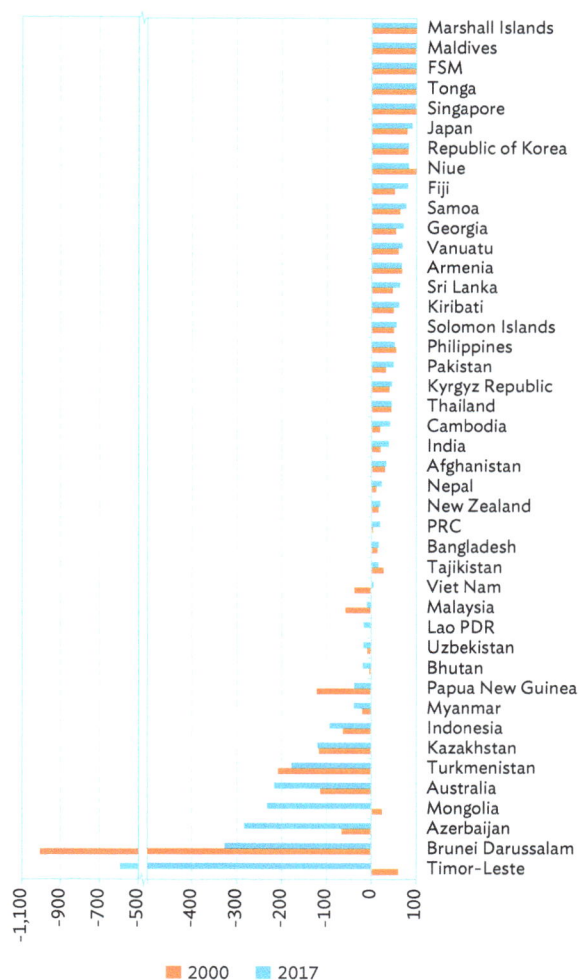

FSM = Federated States of Micronesia, Lao PDR = Lao People's Democratic Republic, PRC = People's Republic of China.
Note: The chart includes economies with available data for 2000 (or the earliest year) and 2017. For Timor-Leste, the earliest year for which data are vailable is 2002.
Source: Table 2.6.4, Key Indicators for Asia and the Pacific 2020.

Click here for figure data

---

4   The full definitions can be found at https://unstats.un.org/UNSD/energy/ires/.

Table 2.6.1:   Electricity Production and Sources

ADB Regional Member	Total Electricity Production (billion kWh)		Sources of Electricity (% of total)							
			Combustible Fuels[a]		Hydropower		Solar		Others[b]	
	2000	2017	2000	2017	2000	2017	2000	2017	2000	2017
Developing ADB Member Economies										
Central and West Asia[c]	**237.1**	**388.6**	**69.7**	**71.8**	**29.3**	**25.0**	**–**	**0.2**	**1.0**	**2.9**
Afghanistan	0.7	1.0 (2018)	25.0	15.3 (2018)	75.0	84.7 (2018)	–	–	–	–
Armenia	6.0	7.8	45.2	37.0	21.2	29.2	–	0.0	33.7	33.8
Azerbaijan	18.7	24.3	91.8	92.6	8.2	7.2	–	0.2	–	0.1
Georgia	7.4	12.1 (2018)	21.1	17.4 (2018)	78.9	81.9 (2018)	–	–	–	0.7 (2018)
Kazakhstan	51.6	103.1	85.4	88.7	14.6	10.9	–	0.1	–	0.3
Kyrgyz Republic	16.0	15.5	14.4	8.5	85.6	91.5	–	–	–	–
Pakistan	65.8	135.0 (2018)	70.1	70.1 (2018)	29.3	20.5 (2018)	–	0.5 (2018)	0.6	8.9 (2018)
Tajikistan	14.2	19.7 (2018)	2.3	6.8 (2018)	97.7	93.2 (2018)	–	–	–	–
Turkmenistan	9.8	22.5	100.0	100.0	–	–	–	–	–	–
Uzbekistan	46.9	61.0	87.5	86.2	12.5	13.8	–	0.0	–	–
East Asia[c]	**1,864.8**	**7,375.3**	**78.9**	**71.9**	**13.6**	**16.8**	**0.0**	**1.5**	**7.5**	**9.8**
China, People's Republic of	1,355.6	6,495.1	82.4	71.8	16.4	18.3	–	1.5	1.2	8.4
Hong Kong, China	31.3	36.6 (2018)	100.0	100.0 (2018)	–	–	–	–	–	–
Korea, Republic of	290.1	566.9	60.5	70.6	1.9	1.2	0.0	1.2	37.6	26.9
Mongolia	2.9	6.5 (2018)	100.0	100.0 (2018)	–	–	–	–	–	–
Taipei,China	184.8	274.1 (2019)	...	...	...	...	...	...	...	...
South Asia[c]	**587.2**	**1,591.5**	**82.9**	**81.7**	**14.0**	**9.0**	**0.0**	**1.6**	**3.1**	**7.7**
Bangladesh	15.8	73.2	94.0	98.3	6.0	1.4	–	0.2	–	0.0
Bhutan	1.8	7.7	0.0 (2001)	0.0	100.0	100.0	–	–	–	0.0
India	560.8	1,490.3	83.4	81.7	13.3	8.5	–	1.7	3.3	8.2
Maldives	0.1	0.7	100.0	97.6	–	–	–	2.1	–	0.3
Nepal	1.7	4.6	1.6	–	98.4	99.8	–	0.0	–	0.1
Sri Lanka	7.0	15.0	54.0	69.2	46.0	26.9	0.0	1.4	0.0	2.4
Southeast Asia[c]	**380.3**	**1,044.0**	**81.7**	**79.0**	**14.5**	**17.9**	**–**	**0.6**	**3.8**	**2.5**
Brunei Darussalam	2.5	4.3 (2018)	100.0	100.0 (2018)	–	–	–	0.0 (2018)	–	–
Cambodia	0.3	7.0	85.9	60.9	14.1	39.1	–	0.1	–	–
Indonesia	99.5	283.6	83.5	88.8	13.8	6.6	–	0.0	2.7	4.7
Lao People's Democratic Republic	4.0	31.6	9.1	37.0	90.9	62.9	–	0.0	–	–
Malaysia	69.2	164.5	89.3	83.6	10.7	16.2	–	0.2	–	–
Myanmar	5.1	19.5	63.0	43.9	37.0	56.1	–	–	–	–
Philippines	45.3	95.7	57.1	76.8	17.2	10.1	–	1.3	25.6	11.9
Singapore	31.7	53.1 (2018)	100.0	99.7 (2018)	–	–	–	0.3 (2018)	–	–
Thailand	96.0	186.5	93.7	91.9	6.3	5.1	–	2.4	0.0	0.6
Timor-Leste	0.1 (2002)	0.4	100.0 (2002)	100.0	–	–	–	–	–	–
Viet Nam	26.6	198.5	45.2	55.1	54.8	44.8	–	–	–	0.1
The Pacific[c]	**3.7**	**6.3**	**57.0**	**70.1**	**38.0**	**22.4**	**0.0**	**0.7**	**5.1**	**6.8**
Cook Islands	0.0	0.0	100.0	90.2	–	–	–	9.8	–	–
Fiji	0.7	1.0 (2018)	39.8	44.9 (2018)	60.2	54.9 (2018)	–	–	–	0.2 (2018)
Kiribati	0.0	0.0	100.0	84.0	–	–	–	16.0	–	–
Marshall Islands	0.1	0.1	100.0	97.8	–	–	–	2.2	–	–
Micronesia, Federated States of	0.1	0.1	96.0	97.2	3.9	0.2	0.1	2.6	–	–
Nauru	0.0	0.0	100.0	96.6	–	–	–	3.4	–	–
Niue	0.0	0.0	100.0	97.9	–	–	–	2.1	–	–
Palau	0.1	0.1	100.0	99.8	–	–	–	0.2	–	–
Papua New Guinea	2.4	4.5	52.9	71.3	39.2	19.4	–	0.0	7.8	9.3
Samoa	0.1	0.1	50.4	66.2	49.6	22.3	–	10.8	–	0.7
Solomon Islands	0.1	0.1 (2018)	100.0	98.7 (2018)	–	0.4 (2018)	–	0.8 (2018)	–	–
Tonga	0.0	0.1	100.0	93.3	–	–	–	6.7	–	0.0
Tuvalu	0.0	0.0	100.0	59.3	–	–	–	38.4	–	2.3
Vanuatu	0.0	0.1	100.0	79.5	–	9.6	–	3.4	–	7.5
Developed ADB Member Economies	**1,317.3**	**1,370.6**	**63.0**	**79.6**	**10.5**	**9.6**	**0.0**	**4.6**	**26.5**	**6.2**
Australia	210.2	258.0	92.0	85.7	8.0	6.3	0.0	3.1	0.0	4.9
Japan	1,067.8	1,068.3	58.5	80.6	9.1	8.4	0.0	5.2	32.4	5.8
New Zealand	39.2	44.2	29.8	20.0	62.3	57.0	–	0.2	7.9	22.8
DEVELOPING ADB MEMBER ECONOMIES[c]	**3,073.1**	**10,405.6**	**79.3**	**74.1**	**15.1**	**16.0**	**0.0**	**1.3**	**5.6**	**8.5**
ALL ADB REGIONAL MEMBERS[c]	**4,390.4**	**11,776.2**	**74.2**	**74.8**	**13.6**	**15.3**	**0.0**	**1.7**	**12.1**	**8.2**

... = data not available, 0.0 = magnitude is less than half of unit employed, ADB = Asian Development Bank, kWh = kilowatt-hour.

a Electricity from combustible fuels refers to the production of electricity from the combustion of fuels that are capable of igniting or burning, which would include coal, natural gas, oil, and other combustible fuels.
b Includes chemical heat, geothermal, nuclear, tide, other marine electricity, wind, wave, and other sources of energy.
c Includes only reporting economies with data corresponding to the year heading.

Sources: United Nations Statistics Division. Energy Statistics Database. http://data.un.org/Data.aspx?d=EDATA&f=cmID%3aEL (accessed 14 July 2020). For Taipei,China: Government of Taipei,China; Directorate-General of Budget, Accounting and Statistics; Official communication, 20 April 2020.

Table 2.6.2: Electric Power Consumption and Electrification

ADB Regional Member	Electric Power Consumption (per capita kWh)		Household Electrification Rate (% of households)	
	2000	2017	2000	2016
Developing ADB Member Economies				
Central and West Asia[a]	**785.5**	**946.7**		
Afghanistan	29.7	127.5 (2018)	25.0 (2005)	71.5 (2015)
Armenia	1,169.9	1,912.5	98.9	100.0
Azerbaijan	1,913.7	2,028.3	99.5 (2006)	…
Georgia	1,541.8	3,010.6	…	…
Kazakhstan	2,773.0	4,409.2	…	…
Kyrgyz Republic	1,891.2	1,805.4	100.0 (2002)	99.8 (2012)
Pakistan	320.3	496.8	89.2 (2006)	92.7 (2018)
Tajikistan	2,145.8	1,526.2 (2018)	99.0 (2002)	99.2 (2017)
Turkmenistan	1,525.6	2,559.2	99.6	…
Uzbekistan	1,669.3	1,908.5 (2018)	99.7 (2002)	…
East Asia[a]	**1,297.7**	**4,424.0**		
China, People's Republic of	992.7	4,077.4	…	…
Hong Kong, China	5,446.2	5,946.2 (2018)	…	…
Korea, Republic of	5,597.4	10,482.2	…	…
Mongolia	970.2	2,034.5 (2018)	67.3	…
Taipei,China	8,332.0	11,614.6 (2019)	…	…
South Asia	**273.9**	**786.1**		
Bangladesh	97.7	376.9	32.0	62.4 (2014)
Bhutan	675.1	2,931.7	41.1 (2003)	…
India	299.6	848.1	67.9 (2006)	88.2
Maldives	486.8	1,202.7	83.8	99.8 (2017)
Nepal	54.3	206.7	24.6 (2001)	90.5
Sri Lanka	289.9	629.0	…	…
Southeast Asia[a]	**617.1**	**1,404.9**		
Brunei Darussalam	7,560.8	8,585.8 (2018)	…	…
Cambodia	29.2	423.1	16.6	56.1 (2014)
Indonesia	374.4	924.4	90.7 (2003)	96.0 (2012)
Lao People's Democratic Republic	120.2	714.3	46.3 (2002)	…
Malaysia	2,636.7	4,710.5	…	…
Myanmar	70.0	313.5	47.0 (2002)	55.6
Philippines	468.7	739.7	76.6 (2003)	92.7 (2017)
Singapore	7,232.6	8,946.9 (2018)	…	…
Thailand	1,396.8	2,677.6	…	…
Timor-Leste	51.8 (2002)	275.2	27.0 (2002)	…
Viet Nam	284.0	2,017.0 (2018)	89.1 (2002)	…
The Pacific[a]	**437.9**	**510.1**		
Cook Islands	1,393.9	2,368.9 (2018)	97.0 (2006)	99.5
Fiji	749.2	1,026.6 (2018)	84.0 (2009)	…
Kiribati	169.4	214.6	…	92.6 (2015)
Marshall Islands	1,517.2	1,336.6	…	90.0 (2011)
Micronesia, Federated States of	737.4	420.4	…	72.8 (2013)
Nauru	2,902.2	2,485.2	100.0 (2002)	100.0 (2013)
Niue	1,577.3	1,898.3	…	98.7
Palau	4,480.5	4,161.1	99.0 (2005)	98.3 (2015)
Papua New Guinea	389.7	473.8	…	19.5 (2010)
Samoa	515.9	680.8	98.0 (2006)	96.4
Solomon Islands	138.9	137.7 (2018)	14.0 (2005)	19.5 (2015)
Tonga	369.5	539.2	89.0 (2006)	97.0
Tuvalu	308.7	756.4	94.0 (2005)	97.3
Vanuatu	224.1	223.8 (2018)	…	57.8
Developed ADB Member Economies	**8,007.2**	**7,987.3**		
Australia	9,390.3	9,326.2	…	…
Japan	7,768.3	7,716.6	…	…
New Zealand	8,994.2	8,274.9	…	…
DEVELOPING ADB MEMBER ECONOMIES[a]	**775.8**	**2,233.3**		
ALL ADB REGIONAL MEMBERS[a]	**1,086.8**	**2,449.0**		

… = data not available, ADB = Asian Development Bank, kWh = kilowatt-hour.

a   Includes only reporting economies with data corresponding to the year heading.

Sources: For electric power consumption: United Nations. Energy Statistics Database. http://data.un.org/Explorer.aspx?d=EDATA (accessed 7 August 2020); and World Bank. World Development Indicators. https://data.worldbank.org/indicator/SP.POP.TOTL (accessed 7 August 2020); for Taipei,China: Asian Development Bank estimates using economy source. For household electrification rate: International Development Association. Results Measurement System Online. http://data.worldbank.org/data-catalog/IDA-results-measurement (accessed 17 July 2019); United States Agency for International Development, Demographic and Health Surveys Program. DHS Program STAT compiler. http://www.statcompiler.com/ (accessed 7 August 2020); and Secretariat of the Pacific Community, Statistics for Development Division. National Minimum Development Indicator Database. http://www.spc.int/nmdi/MdiHome.aspx (accessed 7 August 2020).

Click on the indictor name in the table header to access the time series in the Key Indicators Database.

Table 2.6.3:　Use of Energy

ADB Regional Member	Energy Use (PJ)				GDP per Unit Use of Energy (constant 2017 $ million PPP per PJ)			
	2000	2005	2010	2017	2000	2005	2010	2017
Developing ADB Member Economies								
Central and West Asia[a]	**7,338.6**	**8,955.8**	**10,141.2**	**12,067.4**	**108.4**	**127.0**	**148.9**	**170.4**
Afghanistan	25.3	36.1	136.2	122.9	904.6 (2002)	978.1	448.7	650.4
Armenia	84.4	104.9	119.4	136.8	147.2	210.8	223.8	260.8
Azerbaijan	485.5	572.9	485.9	601.7	67.4	105.8	266.7	231.3
Georgia	120.3	134.6	139.8	204.3	166.7	212.1	263.8	248.0
Kazakhstan	1,551.0	2,352.0	3,363.4	3,335.4	98.6	106.5	100.7	134.5
Kyrgyz Republic	100.7	113.9	115.5	161.6	149.8	159.4	195.3	193.6
Pakistan	2,082.2	2,642.4	2,880.3	4,279.9	221.9	224.9	243.4	222.1
Tajikistan	141.0	148.4	143.4	186.5	55.2	83.2	118.6	147.1
Turkmenistan	624.6	804.9	951.4	1,158.2	33.4	33.3	46.1	70.6
Uzbekistan	2,123.5	2,045.7	1,806.0	1,880.1	32.3	43.6	73.6	112.3
East Asia[a]	**51,028.2**	**78,338.2**	**112,824.1**	**136,399.9**	**111.5**	**110.4**	**123.8**	**164.7**
China, People's Republic of	42,460.5	68,832.9	101,618.2	123,597.5	102.6	101.0	117.0	160.9
Hong Kong, China	569.5	579.5	544.0	587.0	425.0	513.7	663.2	753.6
Korea, Republic of	7,911.5	8,822.2	10,497.6	11,820.8	136.6	156.6	162.5	178.2
Mongolia	86.6	103.6	164.4	394.6	125.4	143.4	123.8	89.3
Taipei,China	...	...	...	...	...	...	...	...
South Asia	**21,502.0**	**24,664.8**	**31,562.3**	**41,129.1**	**145.5**	**171.5**	**187.0**	**226.6**
Bangladesh	997.8	1,191.0	1,493.3	1,925.3	247.9	266.1	285.0	345.1
Bhutan	44.2	48.2	56.8	67.0	54.3	73.5	98.9	124.1
India	19,808.1	22,705.6	29,193.2	38,083.2	137.3	163.7	178.7	217.4
Maldives	6.5	8.7	13.4	21.5	575.0	462.1	444.9	415.2
Nepal	349.0	387.8	445.6	570.9	124.2	132.1	142.8	150.0
Sri Lanka	296.4	323.5	360.1	461.2	376.9	419.5	513.5	585.1
Southeast Asia[a]	**14,387.8**	**18,934.2**	**22,410.1**	**27,275.9**	**216.0**	**211.7**	**232.5**	**270.9**
Brunei Darussalam	73.4	76.4	135.7	152.6	313.3	333.5	194.1	169.7
Cambodia	142.1	143.6	223.3	338.9	127.5	196.0	174.1	185.6
Indonesia	4,969.5	7,087.4	8,331.1	9,958.8	242.1	213.9	240.5	290.6
Lao People's Democratic Republic	57.6	68.5	100.2	237.1	264.3	301.1	302.4	212.9
Malaysia	1,959.1	2,745.4	2,965.0	3,482.2	188.5	169.5	195.4	238.0
Myanmar	537.6	618.1	661.8	854.1	95.1	151.4	239.3	296.2
Philippines	1,551.2	1,469.4	1,631.1	2,320.8	223.9	296.9	341.0	368.0
Singapore	760.6	898.8	1,079.0	1,166.4	296.6	318.0	367.7	456.8
Thailand	3,074.7	4,066.9	4,944.8	5,777.2	201.0	198.1	195.9	208.7
Timor-Leste	3.8 (2002)	3.8	4.4	7.9	590.2 (2002)	592.0	723.2	500.5
Viet Nam	1,261.8	1,755.7	2,333.6	2,980.0	187.1	187.7	191.9	227.1
The Pacific[a]	**143.4**	**174.2**	**187.8**	**230.6**	**200.2**	**183.0**	**207.0**	**236.0**
Cook Islands	0.7	0.8	0.7	1.0	...	...	...	...
Fiji	21.6	23.8	21.5	34.4	358.5	366.6	421.1	342.2
Kiribati	0.9	1.3	1.3	1.5	200.1	153.5	148.6	175.9
Marshall Islands	2.0	2.0	2.0	2.0	86.9	97.8	103.0	109.8
Micronesia, Federated States of	1.9	1.8	1.5	2.2	191.8	216.9	244.3	180.5
Nauru	1.2	0.8	0.6	0.6	...	65.3	114.9	222.0
Niue	0.1	0.1	0.1	0.1	...	...	...	...
Palau	2.9	3.1	2.9	3.2	89.8	98.1	93.7	98.4
Papua New Guinea	98.8	126.2	140.9	168.1	170.3	148.4	177.2	218.5
Samoa	3.2	3.5	3.9	4.9	262.4	307.2	288.2	260.2
Solomon Islands	6.5	7.3	7.9	7.4	127.0	119.1	136.9	200.9
Tonga	1.5	1.7	1.7	2.1	339.2	330.5	342.4	300.0
Tuvalu	0.1	0.1	0.1	0.1	327.2	258.0	281.7	299.1
Vanuatu	2.1	1.7	2.7	2.9	276.6	352.3	284.1	302.8
Developed ADB Member Economies	**27,048.2**	**27,469.7**	**27,277.1**	**24,423.8**	**198.5**	**211.0**	**218.6**	**269.5**
Australia	4,567.3	4,790.0	5,440.7	5,352.7	162.1	181.2	183.7	224.8
Japan	21,731.5	21,931.6	20,997.4	18,115.7	207.3	217.8	228.6	286.0
New Zealand	749.5	748.2	838.9	955.4	166.2	202.6	192.2	208.2
DEVELOPING ADB MEMBER ECONOMIES[a]	**94,398.0**	**131,065.2**	**177,123.6**	**217,101.0**	**135.1**	**137.8**	**150.4**	**190.2**
ALL ADB REGIONAL MEMBERS[a]	**121,446.2**	**158,534.9**	**204,400.7**	**241,524.8**	**149.2**	**150.5**	**159.5**	**198.2**
WORLD[a]	**400,572.2**	**459,255.2**	**512,382.3**	**558,732.1**	**161.3**	**161.0**	**170.7**	**201.7**

... = data not available, – = magnitude equals zero, $ = United States dollars, ADB = Asian Development Bank, GDP = gross domestic product, PJ = petajoule, PPP = purchasing power parity.

a　Aggregates include only reporting economies with data corresponding to the year heading.

Sources:　For Energy Use: United Nations. Energy Statistics Database. https://data.un.org/SdmxBrowser/start (accessed 09 July 2020). For GDP per Unit Use of Energy: Asian Development Bank estimates.

Table 2.6.4: Energy Production and Imports

ADB Regional Member	Energy Production (PJ)				Energy Imports, Net (% of energy use)			
	2000	2005	2010	2017	2000	2005	2010	2017
Developing ADB Member Economies								
Central and West Asia	**10,070.1**	**13,622.8**	**16,177.8**	**17,700.1**	**-37.2**	**-52.1**	**-59.5**	**-46.7**
Afghanistan	17.7	22.7	41.4	82.3	30.3	37.1	69.6	33.0
Armenia	26.7	36.1	52.1	45.2	68.4	65.6	56.3	66.9
Azerbaijan	803.2	1,155.4	2,758.9	2,308.1	-65.4	-101.7	-467.8	-283.6
Georgia	55.3	52.9	57.5	58.3	54.1	60.7	58.8	71.4
Kazakhstan	3,366.8	5,131.1	6,769.9	7,359.3	-117.1	-118.2	-101.3	-120.6
Kyrgyz Republic	60.4	60.6	53.1	87.7	40.0	46.8	54.1	45.7
Pakistan	1,402.8	2,019.7	2,039.6	2,174.7	32.6	23.6	29.2	49.2
Tajikistan	102.8	114.9	114.7	156.7	27.1	22.5	20.0	16.0
Turkmenistan	1,927.9	2,583.6	1,981.9	3,222.5	-208.6	-221.0	-108.3	-178.2
Uzbekistan	2,306.6	2,445.7	2,308.7	2,205.2	-8.6	-19.6	-27.8	-17.3
East Asia[a]	**42,276.8**	**65,750.5**	**91,160.0**	**102,557.1**	**16.2**	**15.4**	**18.8**	**24.5**
China, People's Republic of	40,783.1	63,831.3	88,642.0	99,218.1	4.0	7.3	12.8	19.7
Hong Kong, China	...	...	...	...	...	...	...	...
Korea, Republic of	1,427.6	1,781.3	1,863.1	2,027.9	82.0	79.8	82.3	82.8
Mongolia	66.1	137.9	654.8	1,311.0	23.7	-33.1	-298.4	-232.3
Taipei,China	...	...	...	...	...	...	...	...
South Asia	**17,132.9**	**19,804.5**	**24,833.8**	**25,700.3**	**20.3**	**19.7**	**21.3**	**37.5**
Bangladesh	857.3	1,027.5	1,304.1	1,605.1	14.1	13.7	12.7	16.6
Bhutan	46.4	53.3	72.9	79.5	-4.8	-10.5	-28.4	-18.7
India	15,762.6	18,211.7	22,888.0	23,410.1	20.4	19.8	21.6	38.5
Maldives	0.1	0.1	0.2	0.2	98.1	98.5	98.9	99.0
Nepal	310.2	348.5	384.4	438.5	11.1	10.1	13.7	23.2
Sri Lanka	156.3	163.4	184.3	166.9	47.3	49.5	48.8	63.8
Southeast Asia[a]	**16,974.2**	**22,790.1**	**29,140.3**	**32,471.0**	**-18.0**	**-20.4**	**-30.0**	**-19.0**
Brunei Darussalam	813.0	848.4	775.2	651.9	-1,007.7	-1,010.3	-471.3	-327.2
Cambodia	114.0	104.5	151.7	197.9	19.8	27.2	32.1	41.6
Indonesia	8,128.5	11,350.8	16,863.4	19,187.4	-63.6	-60.2	-102.4	-92.7
Lao People's Democratic Republic	57.5	64.1	97.7	276.5	0.3	6.4	2.6	-16.6
Malaysia	3,081.9	3,769.6	3,450.0	3,829.6	-57.3	-37.3	-16.4	-10.0
Myanmar	647.7	926.1	968.5	1,185.8	-20.5	-49.8	-46.3	-38.8
Philippines	694.7	762.4	923.7	1,097.9	55.2	48.1	43.4	52.7
Singapore	4.2	8.3	24.9	27.6	99.4	99.1	97.7	97.6
Thailand	1,699.6	2,143.8	2,951.7	3,150.3	44.7	47.3	40.3	45.5
Timor-Leste	1.5 (2002)	200.6	186.3	54.5	60.0 (2002)	-5,149.9	-4,105.9	-592.9
Viet Nam	1,733.1	2,611.7	2,747.2	2,811.6	-37.4	-48.8	-17.7	5.7
The Pacific[a]	**236.0**	**188.9**	**106.4**	**244.9**	**-72.8**	**-12.9**	**41.6**	**-7.1**
Cook Islands	...	...	0.0 (2011)	0.0	...	...	99.6 (2011)	98.7
Fiji	10.4	8.8	5.2	6.6	51.8	62.9	75.9	80.7
Kiribati	0.5	0.5	0.5	0.6	49.6	64.1	62.4	61.6
Marshall Islands	0.0	0.0	0.0	0.0	100.0	100.0	100.0	100.0
Micronesia, Federated States of	0.0	0.0	0.0	0.0	98.3	98.8	98.4	98.6
Nauru	...	0.0 (2006)	0.0	0.0	...	99.9 (2006)	99.9	99.3
Niue	0.0	0.0	0.0	0.0	99.4	99.3	80.3	82.7
Palau	...	...	...	0.0	...	...	...	100.0
Papua New Guinea	219.8	174.3	95.4	232.3	-122.5	-38.1	32.3	-38.2
Samoa	1.2	1.2	1.2	1.1	63.4	65.3	68.5	77.5
Solomon Islands	3.3	3.3	3.2	3.3	49.8	55.3	59.8	55.9
Tonga	0.0	0.0	0.0	0.0	98.6	98.8	98.8	98.4
Tuvalu	...	...	...	0.0	...	...	...	91.5
Vanuatu	0.8	0.8	0.9	0.9	60.0	51.0	67.2	69.0
Developed ADB Member Economies	**14,812.9**	**16,377.2**	**18,649.2**	**19,448.3**	**45.2**	**40.4**	**31.6**	**20.4**
Australia	9,778.7	11,490.5	13,646.0	16,963.0	-114.1	-139.9	-150.8	-216.9
Japan	4,402.0	4,312.9	4,227.9	1,727.2	79.7	80.3	79.9	90.5
New Zealand	632.2	573.8	775.3	758.2	15.6	23.3	7.6	20.6
DEVELOPING ADB MEMBER ECONOMIES[a]	**86,690.1**	**122,156.8**	**161,418.3**	**178,673.4**	**7.6**	**6.4**	**8.6**	**17.5**
ALL ADB REGIONAL MEMBERS[a]	**101,503.0**	**138,534.1**	**180,067.5**	**198,121.7**	**16.0**	**12.3**	**11.7**	**17.8**
WORLD[a]	**411,029.6**	**475,724.4**	**528,908.7**	**581,312.2**	**-2.8**	**-3.7**	**-3.3**	**-4.2**

... = data not available, – = magnitude equals zero, ADB = Asian Development Bank, PJ = petajoule.

a   The aggregates for energy production include only economies with available data. The aggregates for net energy imports include only economies with available data for both energy use and energy production. Net energy imports are calculated as the difference between total energy use and total energy production divided by total energy use.

Sources: For Energy Production: United Nations. Energy Statistics Database. https://data.un.org/SdmxBrowser/start (accessed 09 July 2020). For Net Energy Imports: Asian Development Bank estimates.

Table 2.6.5:   Retail Prices of Fuel Energy
($/L)

ADB Regional Member	Gasoline (Premium)				Diesel			
	2000	2005	2010	2019	2000	2005	2010	2019
Developing ADB Member Economies								
Central and West Asia								
Afghanistan	...	...	...	...	...	...	...	...
Armenia	0.51	0.73	1.01	0.87	0.34	0.60	0.92	0.92
Azerbaijan	...	...	...	...	...	...	...	...
Georgia	0.52	0.46 (2003)	1.03	0.89	0.38	0.70	1.00	0.92
Kazakhstan	0.35	0.47	0.58	0.38	0.30	0.39	0.53	0.50
Kyrgyz Republic	...	...	...	...	...	...	...	...
Pakistan	0.48	0.82	0.80	0.71	0.22	0.54	0.83	0.81
Tajikistan	...	...	...	...	...	...	...	...
Turkmenistan	...	...	...	...	...	...	...	...
Uzbekistan	0.44	0.33 (2004)	...	...	...	...	...	...
East Asia								
China, People's Republic of	...	...	...	...	...	...	...	...
Hong Kong, China	1.32	1.60	1.75	2.00	0.80	1.00	1.25	1.82
Korea, Republic of	1.10	1.40	1.48	1.26	0.54	1.05	1.30	1.15
Mongolia	0.33	0.56	1.01	0.64	0.38	0.81 (2006)	0.96	0.88
Taipei,China	0.57	0.73	0.94	0.87	0.44	0.60	0.82	0.81
South Asia								
Bangladesh	...	...	...	...	...	...	...	...
Bhutan	...	...	...	...	...	...	...	...
India	0.58	0.86	1.05	...	0.32	0.64	0.83	...
Maldives	...	...	...	...	...	...	...	...
Nepal	0.58	0.87	1.22	0.98	0.33	0.58	0.95	0.86
Sri Lanka	0.65	0.80	1.02	0.77	0.32	0.50	0.65	0.58
Southeast Asia								
Brunei Darussalam	...	...	...	...	...	...	...	...
Cambodia	...	...	...	...	...	...	...	...
Indonesia	0.14	0.30	0.50	0.65 (2018)	0.07	0.27	0.50	0.55 (2018)
Lao People's Democratic Republic	...	...	...	...	...	...	...	...
Malaysia	0.29	0.40	0.67	0.52	0.18	0.29	0.57	0.53
Myanmar	...	...	1.69 (2012)	0.59	...	...	1.54 (2012)	0.65
Philippines	0.37	0.57	0.96	1.02	0.28	0.51	0.76	0.81
Singapore	0.82	0.92	1.35	1.83	0.33	0.56	0.89	1.23
Thailand	0.39	0.59	1.02	0.89	0.32	0.50	0.91	0.85
Timor-Leste	...	...	...	...	...	...	...	...
Viet Nam	...	...	0.99 (2011)	0.85 (2015)	...	...	0.93 (2011)	0.68 (2015)
The Pacific								
Cook Islands	...	...	...	...	...	...	...	...
Fiji	...	...	...	...	...	...	...	...
Kiribati	...	...	...	...	...	...	...	...
Marshall Islands	...	...	...	...	...	...	...	...
Micronesia, Federated States of	...	...	...	...	...	...	...	...
Nauru	...	...	...	...	...	...	...	...
Niue	...	...	...	...	...	...	...	...
Palau	...	...	...	...	...	...	...	...
Papua New Guinea	...	...	...	...	...	...	...	...
Samoa	...	...	...	...	...	...	...	...
Solomon Islands	...	0.86 (2007)	1.14	1.05	...	0.86 (2007)	1.15	1.11
Tonga	...	...	...	...	...	...	...	...
Tuvalu	...	...	...	...	...	...	...	...
Vanuatu	0.78	1.23	1.50	...	...	...	...	...
Developed ADB Member Economies								
Australia	0.49	0.82	1.09	0.90	...	0.87	1.09	0.94
Japan	1.05	1.23	1.64	1.44	0.76	0.91	1.28	1.16
New Zealand	0.51	0.97	1.34	1.49	0.33	0.64	0.85	0.96

... = data not available, $ = United States dollars, ADB = Asian Development Bank, L = liter.

Sources: Economy sources.

Click on the indictor name in the table header to access the time series in the Key Indicators Database.

VII.   Environment

Environment includes the key issues of deforestation and greenhouse gas emissions. Indicators related to land use, forest resources, air and water pollution, and freshwater resources per capita are presented in the tables.

The amount of forested land increased in slightly more than half of Asia and Pacific economies in 2017

Forests cover about 30% of the earth's surface and are home to about 80% of the world's terrestrial biology. An estimated 1.6 billion people use forests for part of their livelihoods, and many millions more depend on forest resources for clean air and fresh water (UN-REDD 2020). Forests also play a crucial role in the fight against climate change by absorbing and storing more carbon dioxide (CO_2) than is currently in the atmosphere.[5]

In 2017, the total amount of forested land increased in 16 economies of Asia and the Pacific, while decreasing in 15 economies (Figure 2.7.1). The region's leaders in terms of reforestation in 2017 were Taipei,China (4.5%); the Philippines (3.1%); Azerbaijan (2.4%); and the Lao PDR (1.0%). The highest levels of deforestation occurred in Pakistan (2.8%), Myanmar (1.8%), Timor-Leste (1.6%), and Cambodia (1.3%).

On an aggregate basis, the amount of forested land in Asia and the Pacific reporting economies increased 0.2% in 2017 (Table 2.7.2).

Figure 2.7.1: Deforestation Rates in Select Economies of Asia and the Pacific, 2017
(%)

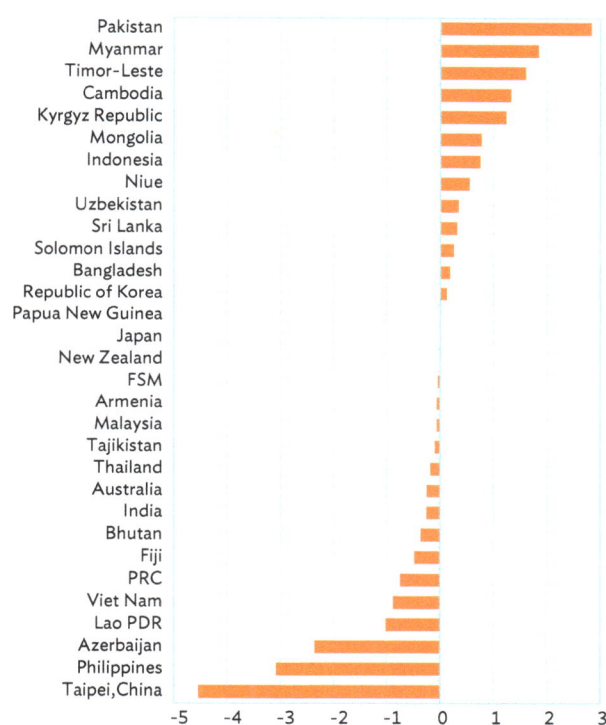

FSM = Federated States of Micronesia, Lao PDR = Lao People's Democratic Republic, PRC = People's Republic of China.

Notes: A negative deforestation rate implies an increase in the forested area compared with the previous year (i.e. "reforestation"). Deforestation rates for Afghanistan, Brunei Darussalam, the Cook Islands, Georgia, Kazakhstan, Kiribati, Maldives, the Marshall Islands, Nepal, Palau, Samoa, Singapore, Tonga, Turkmenistan, Tuvalu, and Vanuatu are zero.

Source: Table 2.7.2, Key Indicators for Asia and the Pacific 2020.

Click here for figure data

---

[5]   For more information about the role of forests in the Earth's environment, go to https://www.un-redd.org/forest-facts.

Carbon dioxide emissions per capita increased in more than four-fifths of Asia and Pacific economies between 2000 and 2016

Asia and the Pacific's rising aggregate CO_2 emissions are the result of increased power generation and use of energy-consuming technologies such as cars and air conditioning units (ADB 2013). From 2000 to 2016, the region's total CO_2 emissions more than doubled from 7.98 billion metric tons to 17.14 billion metric tons (Table 2.7.2).

From 2000 to 2016, only 8 of 47 regional economies with available data were successful in reducing CO_2 emissions on a per capita basis (Figure 2.7.2).

Reductions of more than 1,000 metric tons of CO_2 emissions per capita were achieved in Singapore (5,473 metric tons), Nauru (4,003 metric tons), Uzbekistan (2,059 metric tons), Australia (1,774 metric tons), and New Zealand (1,200 metric tons).

During the review period, the largest increases in CO_2 emissions per capita occurred in Kazakhstan (5,958 metric tons), Mongolia (5,056 metric tons), and the PRC (4,468 metric tons).

Data Issues and Comparability

Data on greenhouse gases (GHGs) have been compiled from the Emissions Database for Global Atmospheric Research, a joint project of the European Commission Joint Research Centre and the Netherlands Environmental Assessment Agency. This database applies a technology-based emissions factor approach consistently for all economies. It utilizes a consistent set of activity data for calculating various substances, GHGs, and air pollutants; and relies on the spatial allocation of emissions on a 0.1-degree by 0.1-degree grid.

Figure 2.7.2: Change in Carbon Dioxide Emissions in Select Economies of Asia and the Pacific, 2000–2016
(t'000 per capita)

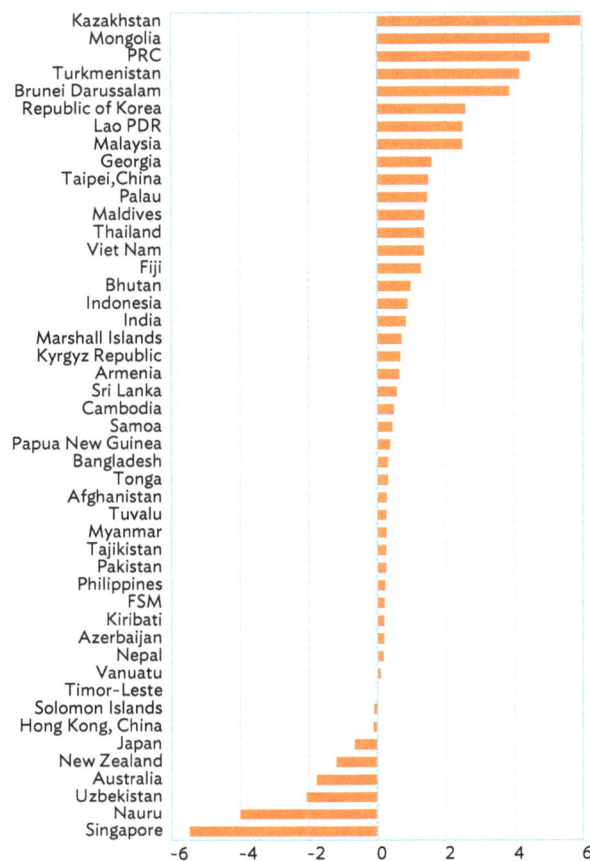

t = metric ton, FSM = Federated States of Micronesia, Lao PDR = Lao People's Democratic Republic, PRC = People's Republic of China.

Notes: Only economies with available data for both 2000 and 2016 are included. For Taipei,China, data refer to 2001 and 2016. For Timor-Leste, data refer to 2002 and 2016.

Source: ADB estimates using Table 2.7.2 and Table 2.1.1, Key Indicators for Asia and the Pacific 2020.

Click here for figure data

There may be substantial uncertainty in economy-level data—especially for methane, nitrous oxide, and other GHGs—due to the limited accuracy of international activity data and the emission factors selected for calculating emissions on an economy level. However, since Intergovernmental Panel on Climate Change methodologies are consistently used, and data are based on international information sources, there is sound basis for comparability.[6]

---

[6]   For more information on the methodologies of the Emissions Database for Global Atmospheric Research, go to https://edgar.jrc.ec.europa.eu/methodology.php.

The Food and Agricultural Organization of the UN monitors land use and forestry data using its own expert sources, country reports, satellite imagery, and official data reported on through questionnaires conducted by the organization.

Table 2.7.1:   Agriculture Land Use
(% of total land area)

ADB Regional Member	Agricultural Land				Arable Land				Permanent Cropland			
	2000	2005	2010	2017	2000	2005	2010	2017	2000	2005	2010	2017
Developing ADB Member Economies												
Central and West Asia[a]	**68.2**	**67.2**	**67.7**	**67.9**	**14.6**	**14.1**	**13.9**	**14.3**	**0.4**	**0.4**	**0.4**	**0.4**
Afghanistan	57.8	58.1	58.1	58.1	11.8	12.0	11.9	11.8	0.1	0.2	0.2	0.3
Armenia	46.5	56.4	60.9	58.9	15.8	16.0	15.8	15.7	1.3	1.8	1.9	2.1
Azerbaijan	57.4	57.6	57.7	57.8	22.1	22.3	22.8	25.3	2.9	2.7	2.8	3.0
Georgia	43.2	36.3	35.4	34.3	11.4	6.8	5.7	4.7	3.9	1.6	1.8	1.7
Kazakhstan	79.8	78.6	80.4	80.4	11.2	10.6	10.6	10.9	0.1	0.0	0.0	0.0
Kyrgyz Republic	55.9	56.0	55.3	55.0	7.1	6.7	6.7	6.7	0.3	0.4	0.4	0.4
Pakistan	47.6	46.7	45.7	48.0	40.3	39.1	38.1	40.5	0.9	1.0	1.1	1.0
Tajikistan	32.7	33.4	34.0	34.2	5.6	5.4	5.3	5.2	0.7	0.8	1.0	1.1
Turkmenistan	75.5	74.2	72.4	72.0	4.1	4.3	4.1	4.1	0.1	0.1	0.1	0.1
Uzbekistan	64.2	62.3	60.2	60.0	10.5	10.3	9.8	9.5	0.8	0.8	0.8	0.9
East Asia[a]	**59.2**	**57.2**	**56.9**	**57.9**	**11.0**	**10.4**	**9.9**	**11.0**	**1.0**	**1.2**	**1.3**	**1.5**
China, People's Republic of	55.6	55.1	54.8	56.2	12.6	12.0	11.4	12.7	1.2	1.3	1.5	1.7
Hong Kong, China	6.7	6.7	5.2	4.9	4.8	4.8	3.3	3.0	1.0	1.0	1.0	1.0
Korea, Republic of	20.5	19.4	18.2	17.2	17.8	17.0	15.5	14.3	2.1	1.9	2.1	2.3
Mongolia	84.0	73.0	73.1	71.3	0.8	0.4	0.4	0.4	0.0	0.0	0.0	0.0
Taipei,China	24.0	23.5	23.0	22.4	17.5	17.0	16.9	16.6	6.5	6.5	6.1	5.8
South Asia[a]	**59.0**	**58.8**	**58.6**	**58.6**	**51.5**	**51.0**	**50.3**	**50.1**	**3.2**	**3.6**	**4.2**	**4.5**
Bangladesh	72.2	71.5	71.0	70.6	64.1	60.8	59.9	59.1	3.5	6.1	6.5	6.8
Bhutan	13.3	15.6	13.6	13.6	2.7	4.4	2.6	2.6	0.5	0.5	0.3	0.1
India	60.9	60.6	60.4	60.4	54.1	53.6	52.8	52.6	3.1	3.4	4.1	4.4
Maldives	30.0	30.0	26.3	26.3	10.0	10.0	13.0	13.0	16.7	16.7	10.0	10.0
Nepal	29.6	29.3	28.8	28.7	16.4	15.9	15.2	14.7	0.8	0.9	1.1	1.5
Sri Lanka	37.5	40.0	41.8	43.7	14.6	17.5	19.1	20.7	15.9	15.5	15.6	15.9
Southeast Asia[a]	**25.7**	**27.4**	**29.4**	**31.5**	**14.5**	**15.1**	**15.7**	**16.6**	**7.4**	**8.4**	**9.8**	**11.1**
Brunei Darussalam	1.9	2.1	2.5	2.7	0.4	0.4	0.8	0.9	0.8	0.9	1.1	1.1
Cambodia	27.0	30.3	30.9	31.5	21.0	21.0	21.5	22.2	0.8	0.9	0.9	0.9
Indonesia	26.0	28.6	30.7	33.2	11.3	12.7	13.0	14.0	8.6	9.9	11.6	13.3
Lao People's Democratic Republic	7.8	8.6	9.6	10.4	4.0	5.0	6.1	6.7	0.4	0.4	0.6	0.7
Malaysia	21.1	21.7	22.5	26.1	2.6	2.9	2.6	2.6	17.6	18.0	19.0	22.7
Myanmar	16.5	17.2	19.2	19.7	15.2	15.4	16.5	16.9	0.9	1.4	2.2	2.3
Philippines	37.7	38.1	40.6	41.7	16.9	16.8	17.8	18.7	15.8	16.3	17.8	17.9
Singapore	1.8	1.1	1.1	0.9	1.5	1.0	0.9	0.8	0.3	0.1	0.1	0.1
Thailand	38.8	38.4	41.2	43.3	30.6	29.8	30.8	32.9	6.6	7.1	8.8	8.8
Timor-Leste	22.7	25.9	25.0	25.6	8.1	11.4	10.1	10.4	4.5	4.4	4.8	5.0
Viet Nam	28.2	32.4	34.7	39.2	19.9	20.5	20.8	22.5	6.2	9.8	11.9	14.6
The Pacific[a]	**3.6**	**3.6**	**4.0**	**4.0**	**0.9**	**0.9**	**1.0**	**1.0**	**1.9**	**1.9**	**2.1**	**2.1**
Cook Islands	20.0	11.4	5.6	6.3	7.5	5.2	2.9	4.2	12.5	6.2	2.7	2.1
Fiji	23.4	23.4	23.3	23.3	9.3	9.3	9.0	9.0	4.5	4.5	4.7	4.7
Kiribati	42.0	42.0	42.0	42.0	2.5	2.5	2.5	2.5	39.5	39.5	39.5	39.5
Marshall Islands	66.7	72.2	72.2	62.8	5.6	11.1	11.1	11.1	44.4	44.4	44.4	35.0
Micronesia, Federated States of	32.1	32.1	31.4	31.4	3.6	3.6	2.9	2.9	24.3	24.3	24.3	24.3
Nauru	20.0	20.0	20.0	20.0	–	–	–	–	20.0	20.0	20.0	20.0
Niue	18.5	18.5	19.2	19.2	3.8	3.8	3.8	3.8	10.8	10.8	11.5	11.5
Palau	10.9	10.9	10.9	10.9	2.2	2.2	2.2	2.2	4.3	4.3	4.3	4.3
Papua New Guinea	2.2	2.3	2.6	2.6	0.5	0.5	0.7	0.7	1.4	1.3	1.5	1.5
Samoa	17.0	14.8	12.4	12.4	4.9	3.9	2.8	2.8	11.0	9.5	7.8	7.8
Solomon Islands	2.7	3.2	3.8	3.9	0.5	0.6	0.7	0.7	2.0	2.3	2.9	2.9
Tonga	41.7	41.7	44.4	45.8	20.8	20.8	23.6	25.0	15.3	15.3	15.3	15.3
Tuvalu	66.7	56.7	60.0	60.0	–	–	–	–	66.7	56.7	60.0	60.0
Vanuatu	14.4	15.0	15.3	15.3	1.6	1.6	1.6	1.6	9.3	9.9	10.3	10.3
Developed ADB Member Economies[a]	**57.3**	**51.3**	**47.2**	**46.5**	**3.5**	**3.8**	**3.6**	**4.3**	**0.1**	**0.1**	**0.1**	**0.1**
Australia	59.3	53.4	49.0	48.3	3.1	3.4	3.3	4.0	0.0	0.0	0.1	0.0
Japan	14.4	12.9	12.6	12.2	12.3	12.0	11.7	11.4	1.0	0.9	0.9	0.8
New Zealand	58.5	44.5	43.3	40.5	5.7	1.6	1.9	2.2	0.2	0.2	0.3	0.3
DEVELOPING ADB MEMBER ECONOMIES[a]	**54.1**	**53.3**	**53.6**	**54.4**	**17.7**	**17.3**	**17.1**	**17.8**	**2.3**	**2.6**	**3.0**	**3.4**
ALL ADB REGIONAL MEMBERS[a]	**54.9**	**52.8**	**52.0**	**52.4**	**14.1**	**13.9**	**13.7**	**14.4**	**1.8**	**2.0**	**2.3**	**2.5**
WORLD[a]	**37.8**	**37.4**	**37.2**	**37.1**	**10.5**	**10.4**	**10.4**	**10.7**	**1.0**	**1.1**	**1.2**	**1.3**

– = magnitude equals zero, 0.0 = magnitude is less than half of unit employed, ADB = Asian Development Bank.

a Aggregates are weighted averages estimated using total land area for the respective year headings.

Source: Food and Agriculture Organization of the United Nations. FAOSTAT Database. http://www.fao.org/faostat/en/#data/RL (accessed 1 July 2020).

Table 2.7.2: Deforestation and Pollution

ADB Regional Member	Deforestation Rate[a,b] (average % change)		Carbon Dioxide Emissions[c] (t '000)		Nitrous Oxide Emissions (t '000 CO$_2$ equivalent)	
	2000	2017[e]	2000	2016	2000	2012
Developing ADB Member Economies						
Central and West Asia	**0.13**	**0.19**	**429,061**	**687,471**	**64,678**	**79,475**
Afghanistan	–	–	774	8,672	3,317	3,424
Armenia	0.06	-0.06	3,465	5,156	462	1,023
Azerbaijan	-0.23	-2.36	29,508	37,620	2,030	2,673
Georgia	-0.03	–	4,536	10,128	2,437	2,352
Kazakhstan	0.17	–	118,099	247,207	14,865	17,822
Kyrgyz Republic	-0.26	1.24	4,635	9,787	1,452	1,567
Pakistan	1.91	2.84	106,449	201,150	26,350	30,651
Tajikistan	-0.05	-0.10	2,237	5,310	1,110	1,848
Turkmenistan	–	–	37,539	70,630	3,046	4,924
Uzbekistan	-0.52	0.34	121,818	91,811	9,610	13,192
East Asia[f]	**-0.97**	**-0.67**	**4,130,776**	**10,861,569**	**442,145**	**610,871**
China, People's Republic of	-1.13	-0.75	3,405,180	9,893,038	414,138	587,166
Hong Kong, China	...	...	40,440	43,645	513	476
Korea, Republic of	0.13	0.12	447,561	620,302	18,576	14,979
Mongolia	0.69	0.77	7,506	25,368	5,058	3,548
Taipei,China	–	-4.54	230,089 (2001)	279,216	3,860 (2001)	4,701 (2016)
South Asia	**-0.07**	**-0.22**	**1,073,635**	**2,527,091**	**235,040**	**273,793**
Bangladesh	0.18	0.18	27,627	84,246	20,770	26,683
Bhutan	-0.38	-0.36	396	1,261	281	555
India	-0.22	-0.25	1,031,853	2,407,672	207,700	239,755
Maldives	–	–	451	1,445	12	27
Nepal	2.30	–	3,069	9,105	4,232	4,598
Sri Lanka	0.42	0.32	10,238	23,362	2,044	2,174
Southeast Asia[f]	**0.94**	**0.36**	**755,714**	**1,508,989**	**204,597**	**241,470**
Brunei Darussalam	0.40	–	4,712	7,664	395	342
Cambodia	1.20	1.33	1,977	9,919	3,295	16,685
Indonesia	1.89	0.75	263,419	563,325	94,933	93,139
Lao People's Democratic Republic	0.67	-1.02	968	17,763	3,265	8,987
Malaysia	0.36	-0.06	125,734	248,289	13,822	15,310
Myanmar	1.23	1.85	10,088	25,280	31,300	26,783
Philippines	-0.68	-3.08	73,307	122,287	12,365	12,762
Singapore	–	–	49,006	37,535	6,635	1,909
Thailand	-1.80	-0.18	172,697	283,763	18,677	30,833
Timor-Leste	1.29	1.61	161 (2002)	495	164	226
Viet Nam	-2.06	-0.88	53,645	192,668	19,746	34,494
The Pacific[f]	**0.00**	**0.01**	**4,543**	**10,906**	**4,574**	**4,422**
Cook Islands	-0.47	–	...	...	...	...
Fiji	-0.28	-0.48	843	2,046	343	344
Kiribati	–	–	33	66	3	4
Marshall Islands	–	–	99	143	0	0
Micronesia, Federated States of	-0.04	-0.04	125	143	11	11
Nauru	...	...	84	48	0	0
Niue	0.51	0.55	...	...	...	...
Palau	-0.36	–	209	224	0	0
Papua New Guinea	0.01	0.01	2,666	7,536	1,613	1,234
Samoa	-2.46	–	143	246	37	40
Solomon Islands	0.25	0.26	154	169	2,425	2,656
Tonga	–	–	95	128	22	22
Tuvalu	–	–	7	11	1	1
Vanuatu	–	–	84	147	118	109
Developed ADB Member Economies	**-0.04**	**-0.19**	**1,581,705**	**1,546,176**	**117,542**	**91,039**
Australia	-0.02	-0.25	329,443	375,908	75,581	54,247
Japan	0.03	0.01	1,219,281	1,135,886	30,411	24,911
New Zealand	-0.48	-0.00	32,981	34,382	11,549	11,880
DEVELOPING ADB MEMBER ECONOMIES[f]	**0.03**	**-0.16**	**6,393,729**	**15,596,026**	**951,034**	**1,210,030**
ALL ADB REGIONAL MEMBERS[f]	**0.02**	**-0.16**	**7,975,435**	**17,142,202**	**1,068,576**	**1,301,069**

continued on next page

Table 2.7.2:   Deforestation and Pollution (*continued*)

ADB Regional Member	Methane Emissions (t '000 CO_2 equivalent)		Other Greenhouse Gases[d] (t '000 CO_2 equivalent)	
	2000	**2012**	**2000**	**2012**
Developing ADB Member Economies				
Central and West Asia	**247,209**	**350,891**	**20,645**	**61,304**
Afghanistan	9,384	13,763	-1,596	-6,529
Armenia	2,565	3,426	290	3,155
Azerbaijan	9,955	19,955	2,810	4,672
Georgia	4,137	5,019	-222	222
Kazakhstan	38,779	71,350	21,926	29,301
Kyrgyz Republic	3,486	4,291	296	638
Pakistan	117,125	158,337	-4,421	28,977
Tajikistan	3,304	5,408	2,940	4,515
Turkmenistan	21,241	22,009	-155	-3,906
Uzbekistan	37,233	47,333	-1,222	258
East Asia[f]	**1,098,575**	**1,799,956**	**5,721**	**169,888**
China, People's Republic of	1,043,400	1,752,290	-13,867	141,901
Hong Kong, China	2,695	3,147	-49	7,583
Korea, Republic of	30,916	32,625	-15,104	15,096
Mongolia	9,218	6,257	28,437	2,178 (2010)
Taipei,China	12,346 (2001)	5,637 (2016)	6,304 (2001)	3,130 (2016)
South Asia	**682,859**	**779,205**	**54,475**	**37,139**
Bangladesh	89,247	105,142	-75	-9,406
Bhutan	1,032	1,770	384	-393
India	561,733	636,396	51,325	39,956
Maldives	34	52	…	…
Nepal	21,206	23,982	2,473	5,994
Sri Lanka	9,606	11,864	368	988
Southeast Asia[f]	**503,408**	**674,039**	**200,182**	**714,564**
Brunei Darussalam	3,882	4,539	538	2,808
Cambodia	14,985	35,915	21,857	70,139
Indonesia	170,032	223,316	63,007	21,192
Lao People's Democratic Republic	7,219	15,011	12,865	134,458
Malaysia	29,309	34,271	3,637	14,128
Myanmar	66,942	80,637	76,980	412,033
Philippines	49,911	57,170	13,268	10,485
Singapore	1,684	2,386	-8,889 (2001)	6,773
Thailand	83,564	106,499	11,347	45,142
Timor-Leste	450	732	-268	-556
Viet Nam	75,430	113,564	5,840	-2,038
The Pacific[f]	**4,594**	**4,818**		
Cook Islands	…	…	…	…
Fiji	705	715	-4	-97
Kiribati	13	16	-2	…
Marshall Islands	6	8	…	…
Micronesia, Federated States of	28	30	…	…
Nauru	3	3	…	…
Niue	…	…	…	…
Palau	1	1	…	…
Papua New Guinea	2,001	2,143	1,730	806
Samoa	116	133	36	55
Solomon Islands	1,394	1,449	127	229
Tonga	58	61	-88	-116 (2011)
Tuvalu	3	3	-0	0
Vanuatu	267	254	16	-20
Developed ADB Member Economies	**202,213**	**193,202**	**592,126**	**282,885**
Australia	128,133	125,588	520,957	164,077
Japan	47,496	38,957	68,010	114,664
New Zealand	26,584	28,658	3,158	4,144
DEVELOPING ADB MEMBER ECONOMIES[f]	**2,536,645**	**3,608,909**	**282,836**	**983,750**
ALL ADB REGIONAL MEMBERS[f]	**2,738,858**	**3,802,112**	**874,962**	**1,266,635**

… = data not available, – = magnitude equals zero, -0 or 0 = magnitude is less than half of unit employed, ADB = Asian Development Bank, CO_2 = carbon dioxide, t = metric ton.

a Rate refers to percentage change over previous year. A negative value indicates that the deforestation rate is decreasing (i.e., reforestation).
b Aggregates are calculated as the percent change of the sum of forested land area of the reporting economies.
c Data from the World Bank are expressed in kilotons (kt), while data provided in the table are expressed in thousands of metric tons (t), using a conversion factor of 1 kt = 1000 metric tons.
d Other greenhouse gas emissions refer to hydrofluorocarbons, perfluorocarbons, and sulphur hexafluoride.
e Estimates are calculated by taking the difference of the average of 2015–2017 and 2014 data.
f For estimating aggregates, imputation was done for economies with missing data by substituting available data from the nearest years.

Sources: Food and Agriculture Organization of the United Nations. FAOSTAT Database. http://www.fao.org/faostat/en/#data/RL (accessed 3 July 2020); and World Bank. World Development Indicators. http://data.worldbank.org/indicator (accessed 3 July 2020). For Taipei,China: Government of Taipei,China, Directorate General of Budget, Accounting and Statistics. Statistical Yearbook 2018. https://eng.dgbas.gov.tw/public/data/dgbas03/bs2/yearbook_eng/Yearbook2018.pdf (accessed 3 July 2020).

Click on the indictor name in the table header to access the time series in the Key Indicators Database.

Table 2.7.3: Freshwater Resources

ADB Regional Member	Internal Renewable Freshwater Resources		Annual Freshwater Withdrawals	Water Productivity[a]
	(m³ billion per year)	(m³ per inhabitant per year)		
	2017[b]	2017[c]	(m³ billion)	(constant 2010 $ per m³)
Developing ADB Member Economies				
Central and West Asia	**370**	**1,155**		
Afghanistan	47	1,327	20 (2000)	...
Armenia	7	2,341	3 (2017)	3.5 (2015)
Azerbaijan	8	826	13 (2017)	4.4 (2012)
Georgia	58	14,859	2 (2008)	6.6 (2008)
Kazakhstan	64	3,535	22 (2017)	7.4 (2010)
Kyrgyz Republic	49	8,094	8 (2006)	0.5 (2006)
Pakistan	55	279	200 (2017)	0.9 (2008)
Tajikistan	63	7,114	11 (2006)	0.4 (2006)
Turkmenistan	1	244	28 (2004)	0.4 (2004)
Uzbekistan	16	512	59 (2017)	0.6 (2005)
East Asia[d]	**2,913**	**1,948**		
China, People's Republic of	2,813	1,952	594 (2015)	15.0 (2015)
Hong Kong, China	...	...	...	...
Korea, Republic of	65	1,272	29 (2005)	31.9 (2005)
Mongolia	35	11,313	0 (2016)	12.3 (2009)
Taipei,China	...	...	...	...
South Asia	**1,880**	**1,209**		
Bangladesh	105	638	36 (2008)	2.9 (2008)
Bhutan	78	96,582	0 (2008)	3.8 (2008)
India	1,446	1,080	648 (2010)	2.6 (2010)
Maldives	0	69	0 (2008)	553.4 (2008)
Nepal	198	6,763	9 (2006)	1.4 (2006)
Sri Lanka	53	2,529	13 (2005)	3.2 (2005)
Southeast Asia	**4,993**	**7,696**		
Brunei Darussalam	9	19,827	...	...
Cambodia	121	7,535	2 (2006)	4.1 (2006)
Indonesia	2,019	7,648	223 (2016)	4.0 (2000)
Lao People's Democratic Republic	190	27,763	3 (2005)	1.4 (2005)
Malaysia	580	18,341	7 (2017)	18.3 (2005)
Myanmar	1,003	18,793	33 (2000)	0.5 (2000)
Philippines	479	4,565	93 (2017)	2.4 (2009)
Singapore	1	105	0 (2017)	...
Thailand	225	3,252	57 (2007)	5.5 (2007)
Timor-Leste	8	6,339	1 (2004)	0.5 (2004)
Viet Nam	359	3,762	82 (2005)	1.0 (2005)
The Pacific				
Cook Islands	...	...	...	...
Fiji	29	31,530	0 (2005)	35.7 (2005)
Kiribati	...	...	...	...
Marshall Islands	...	...	...	...
Micronesia, Federated States of	...	...	...	...
Nauru	...	...	...	...
Niue	...	...	...	...
Palau	...	...	...	...
Papua New Guinea	801	97,079	0 (2005)	27.3 (2005)
Samoa	...	...	...	...
Solomon Islands	45	73,123	...	...
Tonga	...	...	...	...
Tuvalu	...	...	...	...
Vanuatu	10	36,206	...	...
Developed ADB Member Economies	**1,249**	**7,974**		
Australia	492	20,123	16 (2017)	78.3 (2015)
Japan	430	3,373	81 (2009)	67.4 (2009)
New Zealand	327	69,486	10 (2014)	28.2 (2010)
DEVELOPING ADB MEMBER ECONOMIES[d]	**11,040**	**2,740**		
ALL ADB REGIONAL MEMBERS[d]	**12,289**	**2,936**		

... = data not available, 0 = magnitude is less than half of unit employed, $ = United States dollars, ADB = Asian Development Bank, m³ = cubic meter.

a   Gross domestic product in constant 2010 United States dollars per cubic meter of total freshwater withdrawal.
b   Aggregates are calculated as the sum of the economies.
c   Aggregates are weighted averages estimated using population.
d   For reporting economies only.

Sources: Food and Agriculture Organization of the United Nations. AQUASTAT Database. http://www.fao.org/nr/water/aquastat/data/query/index.html (accessed 4 July 2020); and World Bank. World Development Indicators. http://data.worldbank.org/indicator (accessed 4 July 2020).

VIII.   Government and Governance

Government and Governance presents statistics on the revenues and expenditures of governments across Asia and the Pacific; their fiscal balances; their expenditures on health and education services, and their financial commitments to social security and welfare. The theme's discussion focuses on government taxes as a proportion of GDP and the number of days required to start a business. The statistical tables also include the latest global rankings for Transparency International's Corruption Perceptions Index.

Government taxes represented one-fifth or more of GDP in almost half of all reporting economies

Government taxes include value-added tax, sales tax, import duties, income tax, profit tax, property tax, capital gains tax, and compulsory social security charges, among others. In 2019, government taxes were equal to or exceeded 20.0% of GDP in 12 of the 26 economies with available data (Table 2.8.2).

Comparing 2018 to 2019, the government taxes-to-GDP ratio rose in 11 of the 26 reporting economies between (Figure 2.8.1). The largest increases were observed in Nauru (2.8 percentage points), Cambodia (2.6 percentage points), and Armenia and New Zealand (1.4 percentage points each). In 15 economies, there was a decrease in government taxes as a percentage of GDP. The largest decreases were observed in the Solomon Islands (–3.5 percentage points), Pakistan (–1.4 percentage points), and Bhutan and Palau (1.2 percentage points each).

Between 2005 and 2019, more than four-fifths of economies in Asia and the Pacific reduced the number of days required to start a business

Simplifying registration procedures and restricting opportunities for bribes can reduce the amount of time required to start a business, which can facilitate entrepreneurial activity (World Bank 2019).

Figure 2.8.1: Government Taxes as a Proportion of Gross Domestic Product in Select Economies of Asia and the Pacific
(%)

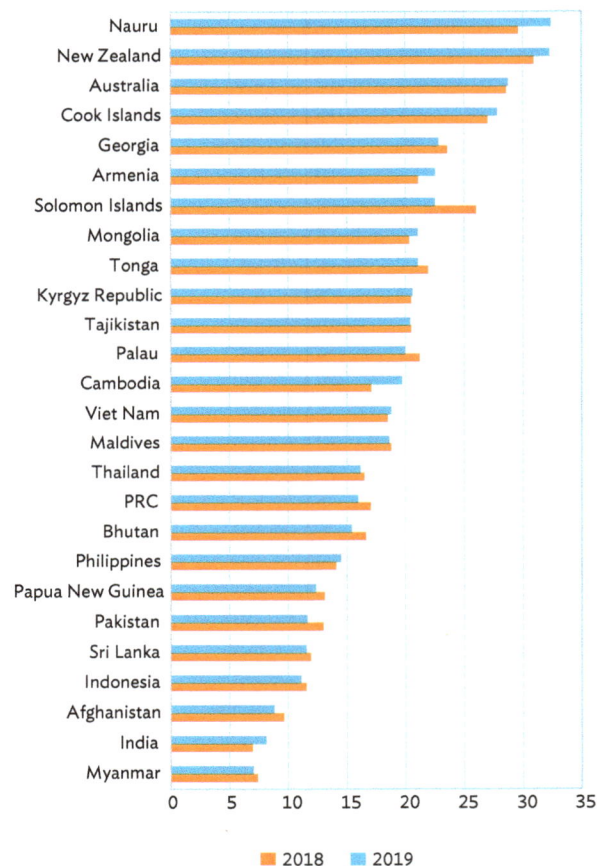

PRC = People's Republic of China.
Note: Only economies with data for both 2018 and 2019 are included in the chart. Data refer to general government, except for Bhutan; Cambodia; India; Maldives; Nauru; Palau; the Philippines; Solomon Islands; Sri Lanka; Tonga; and Viet Nam, where data refer to central government.
Source: Table 2.8.2, Key Indicators for Asia and the Pacific 2020.

Click here for figure data

From 2005 to 2019, 30 economies throughout Asia and the Pacific reduced the number of days required to start a business (Figure 2.8.2). During the same period, four economies experienced an increase in the number of days required, while three had no change. The largest reductions among individual economies were achieved by Timor-Leste (154.0 days), Brunei Darussalam (116.0 days), and Azerbaijan (109.5 days).

As demonstrated in Table 2.8.6 for 2005–2019, the average reduction in the number of days required to start a business varied by subregion as follows: Central and West Asia (33.6 days), Southeast Asia (33.0 days), South Asia (21.8 days), East Asia (19.5 days), and the Pacific (12.8 days). For the developed member economies, the average reduction was only 3.0 days.

Economies in which starting a business required 2 days or fewer in 2019 included New Zealand (0.5 days); Georgia (1.0 day); Hong Kong, China (1.5 days); Singapore (1.5 days); and Australia (2.0 days). The longest delays in starting a business in 2019 were observed in the Lao PDR (173.0 days), Cambodia (99.0 days), and Papua New Guinea (41.0 days).

Data Issues and Comparability

Most economies generally follow the IMF's Government Finance Statistics (GFS) guidelines: some still use the 1986 version, while others have switched to the 2001 or 2014 versions. The comparability of the data is limited by variations in the concepts and definitions used in different versions of the GFS framework. Furthermore, there is no single framework for an extended time series available in most economies that are using the 2014 guidelines, with most economies recording their transactions on a cash basis (and a few on an accrual basis).

Data on government expenditures and revenue are derived from economy sources and are therefore not standard throughout Asia and the Pacific. Data

Figure 2.8.2: Time Required to Start a Business in Select Economies of Asia and the Pacific
(days)

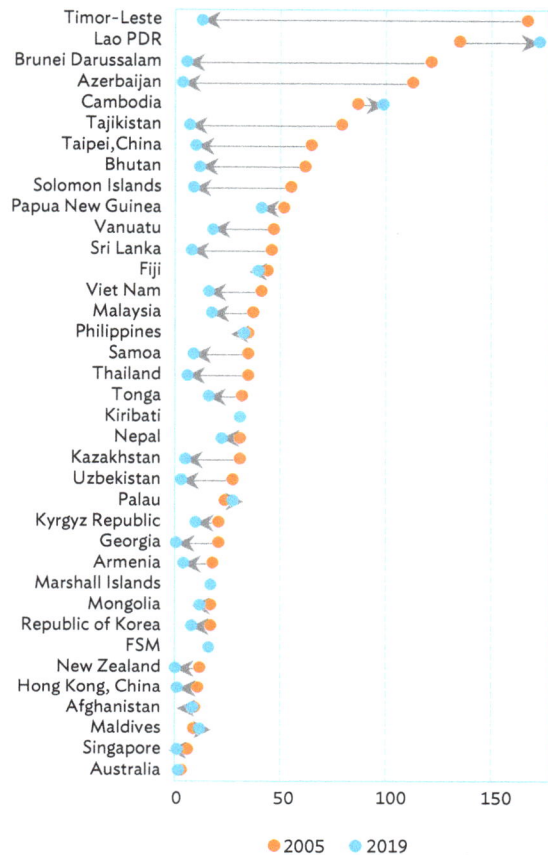

FSM = Federated States of Micronesia, Lao PDR = Lao People's Democratic Republic.
Note: Only economies with data for both years 2005 and 2019 are included. Initial year for Brunei Darussalam is 2006.
Source: Table 2.8.6, Key Indicators for Asia and the Pacific 2020.

Click here for figure data

refer to general government for some economies, and central government for other economies.

Statistics on the time, score, and rank for registering new businesses, and on perceived corruption, are taken from nonofficial sources. Common procedures are used in all economies and the researchers producing these data have refined their procedures over several surveys. However, because of the subjective nature of many of the data, they can only be used to give a broad idea of trends, levels, and rankings, so small changes from one year to the next should be interpreted with caution.

Table 2.8.1: Government Net Lending/Net Borrowing[a]
(% of GDP)

ADB Regional Member	2010	2011	2012	2013	2014	2015	2016	2017	2018	2019
Developing ADB Member Economies										
Central and West Asia										
Afghanistan[b]	2.4	-0.5	-0.6	3.6	-1.7	-1.4	0.2	-0.4	0.8	-2.0
Armenia	-5.0	-2.8	-1.5	-1.5	-1.9	-4.8	-5.5	-4.8	-1.6	-0.8
Azerbaijan	15.4	12.9	5.7	4.4	4.5	-2.8	2.4	1.9	9.6	...
Georgia	-4.3	-0.8	-0.6	-1.1	-1.9	-1.0	-1.3	-0.8	-0.7	-2.7
Kazakhstan	5.0	8.3	6.0	5.0	3.5	-2.2	-2.8	-3.0	1.4	...
Kyrgyz Republic	-4.9	-4.8	-6.5	-0.7	-0.5	-1.4	-4.4	-3.1	-1.1	-0.1
Pakistan[c]	-6.0	-6.4	-8.6	-8.1	-4.7	-5.2	-4.5	-5.8	-6.5	-8.8
Tajikistan	-9.2	-6.9	-3.5	-5.5	-3.8	-7.4	-10.1	-11.8	-10.6	-7.8
Turkmenistan	2.0	3.5	6.4	1.5	0.9	-0.7	-2.4	-2.8	-0.2	-0.2
Uzbekistan	...	...	...	8.4	7.8	6.8	4.0	1.5	3.2	...
East Asia										
China, People's Republic of	-1.6	-1.1	-1.6	-1.9	-1.8	-3.4	-3.8	-3.7	-4.1	-4.9
Hong Kong, China[d]	4.1	3.8	3.5	0.7	4.2	1.4	4.7	6.3	3.5	...
Korea, Republic of	...	...	1.1	1.4	1.3	1.2	2.5	2.6	3.1	...
Mongolia	-3.2	-11.8	-15.5	-8.3	-11.5	-10.9	-23.0	-11.1	-4.1	-8.2
Taipei,China	-2.6	-1.5	-2.8	-1.0	-0.8	0.2	-0.3	-0.1	0.1	...
South Asia										
Bangladesh[c]	-1.7	-0.9	-0.5	-1.3	-2.3	-2.2	-2.7	-3.0	-1.9	...
Bhutan[c]	1.5	-2.2	-1.2	-4.3	3.9	1.5	-1.1	-3.5	-0.3	-0.8
India[d]	-4.9	-5.9	-4.9	-4.5	-4.1	-3.9	-3.5	-3.5	-3.4	-3.5
Maldives[e]	-12.9	-5.8	-6.7	-3.5	-2.4	-6.5	-10.0	-3.1	-5.5	-4.2
Nepal[f]	-1.4	-1.0	-0.6	1.7	1.8	1.1	1.4	-3.1	...	...
Sri Lanka	-6.3	-5.8	-5.3	-5.3	-5.6	-7.6	-5.3	-5.5	-5.4	-6.8
Southeast Asia										
Brunei Darussalam[g]	15.1	24.7	18.0	7.6	-1.0	-14.8	-16.7	-13.2	0.2	-5.0
Cambodia	-4.5	-5.4	-4.4	-2.7	-1.3	-0.9	-0.4	-1.0	0.4	2.4
Indonesia	-0.6	-0.7	-1.5	-1.8	-2.6	-3.0	-1.9	-2.0	-1.7	-2.1
Lao People's Democratic Republic[h]	-0.9	-0.9	-0.7	-4.9	-3.3	-3.7	-4.9	-4.4	-6.0	...
Malaysia	-5.0	-4.6	-4.4	-3.8	-3.3	-3.1	-3.0	-2.9	-3.6	...
Myanmar[i]	...	...	-4.4	-3.2	-2.5	-4.4	-3.3	-3.7	-5.9	-4.0
Philippines	-3.3	-1.7	-1.9	-1.2	-0.5	-1.3	-2.2	-2.1	-3.1	-3.3
Singapore[d]	7.5	9.1	8.5	8.1	7.1	4.2	5.0	7.6	4.8	...
Thailand[h]	-0.7	-0.6	-0.8	0.6	-0.7	0.2	0.4	-0.4	0.1	0.4
Timor-Leste	...	...	...	-13.3	-33.0	7.3	-10.4	8.5	5.0	...
Viet Nam[j]	-2.1	-0.5	-3.4	-5.0	-4.7	-4.3	-4.0	-3.4	-3.5	-3.4
The Pacific										
Cook Islands[c]	2.9	9.6	0.8	14.2	-2.9	-7.8	1.4	8.7	5.2	5.0
Fiji	-2.6	-1.7	-1.4	-0.9	-2.4	-2.0	-0.8	-0.9	-4.4	...
Kiribati[c]	...	-6.9	3.5	20.3	44.7	56.1	21.6	16.8	51.9	...
Marshall Islands[h]	3.5	2.1	-0.8	-0.2	3.2	2.8	3.9	4.4	2.5	...
Micronesia, Federated States of[h]	0.5	-0.6	0.9	2.9	11.1	10.3	7.3	14.2	24.2	...
Nauru[c]	0.1	...	7.9	1.5	25.0	10.5	21.4	21.4	32.5	16.1
Niue	...	...	...	...	...	...	...	...	...	...
Palau[h]	-1.0	1.3	1.0	0.7	3.6	5.2	3.6	4.8	6.2	0.3
Papua New Guinea	...	...	...	...	...	...	...	-2.4	-2.6	-4.1
Samoa[c]	...	...	-8.1	-3.9	-4.8	-3.7	0.7	-0.6	1.3	...
Solomon Islands	5.6	6.1	4.6	3.6	2.1	0.8	-3.2	-2.2	1.5	-1.5
Tonga[c]	...	...	...	...	...	...	1.5	3.6	2.9	1.3
Tuvalu	...	...	11.5	26.6	29.0	40.0	4.8	...	...	...
Vanuatu	...	...	-1.6	-0.2	1.2	6.9	-0.3	2.2	...	...
Developed ADB Member Economies										
Australia[c]	-5.5	-4.8	-4.3	-2.7	-2.9	-2.9	-2.6	-2.2	-1.3	-1.2
Japan[d]	-8.9	-9.0	-8.2	-7.2	-5.0	-3.4	-3.4	-2.7	-2.2	...
New Zealand[c]	-3.4	-7.4	-2.6	-1.8	-0.8	-0.1	0.7	1.4	1.2	1.6

... = data not available, ADB = Asian Development Bank, GDP = gross domestic product.

a In general, economies follow the guidelines of the International Monetary Fund on Government Finance Statistics (GFS). Some economies still use the 1986 version of the GFS guidelines, while others have switched to the 2001 or 2014 guidelines. The comparability of the data in this table is limited by variations in the concepts and definitions used in different versions of the GFS framework. Data refer to government net lending/net borrowing as classified in the GFS 2001 or GFS 2014 framework, except for Bhutan; Brunei Darussalam; India; the Kyrgyz Republic; Maldives; Nauru; Pakistan; the People's Republic of China; Taipei,China; Tajikistan; Turkmenistan; and Viet Nam, where data refer to overall budgetary surplus/deficit as classified in the GFS 1986 framework. Data refer to general government, except for Bangladesh; Bhutan; Brunei Darussalam; Cambodia; the Federated States of Micronesia; Fiji; India; the Lao People's Democratic Republic; Malaysia; Maldives; the Marshall Islands; Nauru; Nepal; Palau; the Philippines; Solomon Islands; Sri Lanka; Taipei,China; Timor-Leste; Tonga; Tuvalu; Vanuatu; and Viet Nam, where data refer to central government. For Azerbaijan, data for 2000–2007 are based on the state budget. For Cambodia, data refer to central government excluding extra budgetary central government. For Pakistan, data refer to the consolidated federal and provincial governments. For the People's Republic of China, data refer to consolidated central and local governments. For Turkmenistan, data prior to 2011 refer to central government.
b For 2005–2011, GFS data are based on fiscal year beginning 21 March. For 2012, GFS data cover 9 months from 21 March to 20 December. For 2013 onward, GFS data are based on fiscal year ending 20 December. For 2005–2015, national accounts data are based on fiscal year beginning 21 March. For 2016 onward, national accounts data are based on fiscal year ending 20 December.
c Data are based on fiscal year ending 30 June.
d Data are based on fiscal year beginning 1 April.
e For 2013 onward, data are calculated excluding net lending.
f Data are based on fiscal year ending 15 July.
g For 2005 onward, data are based on fiscal year beginning 1 April. Data are derived as the excess of revenue over expenditure (ordinary plus charged) less the sum of contribution to a development fund, contribution to a government trust fund, and capital and currency adjustments.
h Data are based on fiscal year ending 30 September.
i For 2012–2018, GFS data are based on fiscal year beginning 1 April. For 2019, GFS data are based on fiscal year beginning 1 October. For 2012–2015, national accounts data are based on fiscal year beginning 1 April. For 2016 onward, national accounts data are based on fiscal year beginning 1 October.
j Taxes include local government taxes.

Sources: Economy sources. For Azerbaijan (2008–2018); Fiji; Hong Kong, China; Nepal, Sri Lanka (2000–2003); and Timor-Leste: International Monetary Fund. Government Finance Statistics. https://data.imf.org/ (accessed May–June 2020). For Nauru (2012–2019): International Monetary Fund. Staff Country Reports. Republic of Nauru: 2017 Article IV. http://www.imf.org/en/Publications/CR/Issues/2017/04/03/Republic-of-Nauru-2017-Article-IV-Consultation-Press-Release-Staff-Report-and-Statement-by-44794 (accessed 6 May 2020); and Republic of Nauru: 2019 Article IV. https://www.imf.org/en/Publications/CR/Issues/2020/01/29/Republic-of-Nauru-2019-Article-IV-Consultation-Press-Release-Staff-Report-and-Statement-by-49001 (accessed 6 May 2020).

Click on the indictor name in the table header to access the time series in the Key Indicators Database.

Table 2.8.2: Government Taxes[a]
(% of GDP)

ADB Regional Member	2010	2011	2012	2013	2014	2015	2016	2017	2018	2019
Developing ADB Member Economies										
Central and West Asia										
Afghanistan[b]	8.8	8.4	5.4	6.7	6.4	7.1	8.2	8.8	9.6	8.8
Armenia	17.7	17.8	19.2	22.0	22.2	21.3	21.5	21.0	21.1	22.5
Azerbaijan	12.3	12.3	12.9	13.5	14.3	15.7	14.7	13.3	13.1	...
Georgia	22.3	24.1	24.5	23.3	23.3	23.6	24.5	24.0	23.6	22.8
Kazakhstan	19.6	21.7	16.9	19.5	17.8	13.6	12.4	13.8	15.1	...
Kyrgyz Republic	17.9	18.5	20.6	20.5	20.6	19.7	19.7	19.5	20.5	20.6
Pakistan[c]	10.0	9.4	10.2	9.8	10.2	11.0	12.4	12.5	13.0	11.6
Tajikistan	18.0	19.5	19.6	20.8	22.7	20.8	20.4	20.3	20.5	20.4
Turkmenistan	...	17.5	20.2	17.7	17.0	15.6	...	...	...	...
Uzbekistan	...	...	...	21.1	20.4	20.3	20.0	17.3	19.7	...
East Asia										
China, People's Republic of	17.8	18.4	18.7	18.6	18.5	18.1	17.5	17.4	17.0	15.9
Hong Kong, China[d]	13.5	14.2	13.7	13.4	15.5	14.4	13.6	14.3	13.8	...
Korea, Republic of	...	...	18.0	17.3	17.3	17.6	18.4	19.0	20.1	...
Mongolia	24.2	24.3	21.1	21.9	19.1	17.7	16.0	17.9	20.3	21.1
Taipei,China	7.7	8.4	8.3	8.0	8.3	8.6	8.7	8.6	8.9	...
South Asia										
Bangladesh[c]	10.2	10.6	10.3	9.7	9.6	8.9	8.8	9.1	7.4	...
Bhutan[c]	13.3	15.1	16.5	15.6	14.8	15.0	14.5	14.2	16.6	15.4
India[d]	7.5	7.2	7.5	7.3	7.2	6.9	7.2	7.3	6.9	8.1
Maldives	8.8	12.1	15.5	17.5	19.1	19.4	19.8	20.2	18.7	18.6
Nepal[e]	13.4	13.3	13.9	15.3	15.9	16.7	18.7	21.0	...	...
Sri Lanka	11.3	11.3	10.4	10.5	10.1	12.4	12.2	12.5	11.9	11.6
Southeast Asia										
Brunei Darussalam[f]	...	...	...	...	...	...	...	...	...	...
Cambodia	7.3	7.6	11.6	12.1	14.6	14.6	14.8	15.8	17.1	19.7
Indonesia	12.1	12.2	12.5	12.5	12.1	12.0	11.6	11.2	11.5	11.1
Lao People's Democratic Republic[g]	13.8	14.3	13.6	13.7	13.8	13.5	12.9	11.1	11.5	...
Malaysia	13.3	14.8	15.6	15.3	14.8	14.1	13.6	13.0	12.0	...
Myanmar[h]	...	...	6.6	7.3	7.8	7.5	8.4	7.9	7.4	7.0
Philippines	11.6	11.8	12.3	12.7	13.0	13.0	13.1	13.6	14.0	14.5
Singapore[d]	12.8	13.1	13.6	13.3	13.6	13.1	13.3	14.0	13.1	...
Thailand[g]	16.1	17.7	16.8	18.4	17.3	17.6	16.8	16.3	16.5	16.1
Timor-Leste	...	...	...	7.6	8.7	7.8	9.5	8.7	8.5	...
Viet Nam[i]	22.4	22.3	19.0	19.1	18.2	18.0	17.9	18.3	18.5	18.8
The Pacific										
Cook Islands[c]	27.0	26.4	23.8	28.1	25.3	23.5	26.3	26.0	27.0	27.8
Fiji	21.8	23.0	23.2	23.6	22.7	23.7	23.5	24.7	24.2	...
Kiribati[c]	...	18.3	19.0	18.6	18.4	22.7	25.5	22.6	21.7	...
Marshall Islands[g]	15.8	14.7	14.0	14.2	13.4	14.0	14.4	14.3	14.5	...
Micronesia, Federated States of[g]	12.0	12.0	11.6	12.1	18.9	12.3	12.9	17.5	32.2	...
Nauru[c]	...	...	8.1	15.3	14.9	21.7	23.0	21.2	29.6	32.4
Niue	...	...	...	...	...	...	...	...	...	...
Palau[g]	17.0	17.9	18.4	18.5	19.3	20.3	19.9	19.8	21.2	20.0
Papua New Guinea	...	...	...	...	...	...	...	12.3	13.1	12.4
Samoa[c]	...	...	20.9	23.5	24.9	23.6	24.3	25.0	25.5	...
Solomon Islands	21.9	25.0	26.0	26.6	25.6	25.8	24.0	24.6	26.0	22.5
Tonga[c]	...	...	...	...	...	...	19.8	21.0	21.9	21.1
Tuvalu	...	...	28.5	34.7	30.1	33.1	28.0	...	...	...
Vanuatu	...	...	16.5	17.2	17.3	16.3	15.3	17.1	...	...
Developed ADB Member Economies										
Australia[c]	25.6	25.3	26.0	27.0	27.1	27.3	27.9	27.6	28.6	28.7
Japan[d]	15.7	16.4	16.7	17.4	18.7	18.8	18.6	19.0	19.4	...
New Zealand[c]	29.2	28.7	29.4	30.6	29.7	30.8	31.0	31.1	30.9	32.3

... = data not available, ADB = Asian Development Bank, GDP = gross domestic product.

a   In general, economies follow the guidelines of the International Monetary Fund on Government Finance Statistics (GFS). Some economies still use the 1986 version of the GFS guidelines, while others have switched to the 2001 or 2014 guidelines. The comparability of the data in this table is limited by variations in the concepts and definitions used in different versions of the GFS framework. Data refer to government taxes as classified in the GFS 2001 or GFS 2014 framework, except for Bhutan; Brunei Darussalam; India; the Kyrgyz Republic; Maldives; Nauru; Pakistan; the People's Republic of China; Taipei,China; Tajikistan; Turkmenistan; and Viet Nam, where data refer to tax revenue as classified in the GFS 1986 framework. Data refer to general government, except for Bangladesh; Bhutan; Brunei Darussalam; Cambodia; the Federated States of Micronesia; Fiji; India; the Lao People's Democratic Republic; Malaysia; Maldives; the Marshall Islands; Nauru; Nepal; Palau; the Philippines; Solomon Islands; Sri Lanka; Taipei,China; Timor-Leste; Tonga; Tuvalu; Vanuatu; and Viet Nam, where data refer to central government. For Armenia, data prior to 2010 refer to central government. For Azerbaijan, data for 2000–2007 are based on the state budget. For Cambodia, data refer to central government excluding extra budgetary central government. For Pakistan, data refer to the consolidated federal and provincial governments. For the People's Republic of China, data refer to consolidated central and local governments. For Turkmenistan, data prior to 2011 refer to central government.

b   For 2005–2011, GFS data are based on fiscal year beginning 21 March. For 2012, GFS data cover 9 months from 21 March to 20 December. For 2013 onward, GFS data are based on fiscal year ending 20 December. For 2005–2015, national accounts data are based on fiscal year beginning 21 March. For 2016 onward, national accounts data are based on fiscal year ending 20 December.

c   Data are based on fiscal year ending 30 June.

d   Data are based on fiscal year beginning 1 April.

e   Data are based on fiscal year ending 15 July.

f   For 2005 onward, data are based on fiscal year beginning 1 April. Data includes duties, taxes, and licenses.

g   Data are based on fiscal year ending 30 September.

h   For 2012–2018, GFS data are based on fiscal year beginning 1 April. For 2019, GFS data are based on fiscal year beginning 1 October. For 2012–2015, national accounts data are based on fiscal year beginning 1 April. For 2016 onward, national accounts data are based on fiscal year beginning 1 October.

i   Taxes include local government taxes.

Sources: Economy sources. For Azerbaijan (2008–2018); Fiji; Hong Kong, China; Nepal; Sri Lanka (2000–2003); and Timor-Leste: International Monetary Fund. Government Finance Statistics. https://data.imf.org/ (accessed May–June 2020). For Nauru (2012–2019): International Monetary Fund. Staff Country Reports. Republic of Nauru: 2017 Article IV. http://www.imf.org/en/Publications/CR/Issues/2017/04/03/Republic-of-Nauru-2017-Article-IV-Consultation-Press-Release-Staff-Report-and-Statement-by-44794 (accessed 6 May 2020); and Republic of Nauru: 2019 Article IV. https://www.imf.org/en/Publications/CR/Issues/2020/01/29/Republic-of-Nauru-2019-Article-IV-Consultation-Press-Release-Staff-Report-and-Statement-by-49001 (accessed 6 May 2020).

Click on the indictor name in the table header to access the time series in the Key Indicators Database.

Government Finance

Table 2.8.3:   Government Revenue[a]
(% of GDP)

ADB Regional Member	2010	2011	2012	2013	2014	2015	2016	2017	2018	2019
Developing ADB Member Economies										
Central and West Asia										
Afghanistan[b]	23.0	22.0	16.8	26.8	23.0	23.9	29.2	27.7	30.5	28.5
Armenia	23.2	24.0	24.4	24.2	24.4	23.8	23.8	22.9	23.1	24.6
Azerbaijan	47.0	45.6	41.4	40.5	40.1	34.4	35.3	35.3	39.9	…
Georgia	26.9	27.0	27.8	26.0	26.1	26.4	27.0	26.8	26.5	25.8
Kazakhstan	25.5	27.6	26.3	24.2	23.2	17.6	17.6	19.9	19.6	…
Kyrgyz Republic	23.1	24.2	26.2	26.1	27.3	27.7	25.3	25.2	25.0	26.1
Pakistan[c]	14.2	12.5	12.8	13.3	14.5	14.4	15.0	15.5	15.2	12.7
Tajikistan	19.3	21.1	21.5	22.7	25.1	23.7	23.3	22.5	23.3	23.0
Turkmenistan	15.8	18.1	21.0	18.4	17.9	16.6	11.7	14.9	13.5	13.0
Uzbekistan	…	…	…	30.3	29.0	27.6	27.5	24.3	27.8	…
East Asia										
China, People's Republic of	20.2	21.3	21.8	21.8	21.8	22.1	21.4	20.7	19.9	19.2
Hong Kong, China[d]	22.3	23.8	23.5	21.5	23.6	21.7	24.6	25.8	23.8	…
Korea, Republic of	…	…	33.3	32.3	32.3	32.2	32.6	33.2	33.5	…
Mongolia	32.0	32.2	29.3	31.0	28.2	25.8	24.4	26.1	28.5	29.3
Taipei,China	10.7	11.8	11.0	11.5	10.8	11.4	10.8	10.8	11.2	…
South Asia										
Bangladesh[c]	13.0	13.9	13.7	12.9	11.5	10.6	10.2	10.5	8.3	…
Bhutan[c]	27.4	23.0	22.6	21.3	21.5	21.4	19.8	19.5	22.8	17.9
India[d]	10.8	9.0	9.3	9.4	9.2	9.1	9.4	9.1	8.8	10.2
Maldives	19.3	22.6	22.0	23.3	26.4	26.4	27.2	27.3	25.3	24.8
Nepal[e]	18.1	18.5	18.7	19.5	20.6	21.1	23.3	24.4	…	…
Sri Lanka	13.0	13.2	12.2	12.0	11.5	13.3	14.1	13.8	13.5	12.6
Southeast Asia										
Brunei Darussalam[f]	49.0	55.5	49.4	41.2	32.7	20.9	23.0	23.1	32.9	26.1
Cambodia	13.8	12.5	16.3	17.9	19.1	18.5	19.8	20.4	22.1	23.9
Indonesia	16.6	16.8	17.0	16.9	16.8	15.1	14.4	14.1	14.8	14.3
Lao People's Democratic Republic[g]	21.7	21.5	20.8	20.9	20.9	20.3	16.2	13.9	15.0	…
Malaysia	19.4	20.3	21.4	20.9	19.9	18.6	17.0	16.1	16.1	…
Myanmar[h]	…	…	9.8	11.2	13.9	11.8	12.5	11.8	10.9	10.2
Philippines	12.9	13.4	13.8	14.2	14.4	14.7	14.5	14.9	15.5	16.1
Singapore[d]	16.8	17.0	17.5	17.2	18.0	18.0	18.5	20.3	18.4	…
Thailand[g]	20.6	21.3	20.4	22.2	21.3	22.2	21.4	20.8	21.2	20.9
Timor-Leste	…	…	…	63.0	59.4	91.0	87.8	80.9	85.8	…
Viet Nam[i]	26.7	25.5	22.3	22.8	22.0	23.5	24.4	25.7	25.6	25.6
The Pacific										
Cook Islands[c]	38.3	40.6	39.0	42.2	38.8	39.7	39.2	38.8	42.3	39.2
Fiji	24.3	25.6	25.6	26.1	25.9	27.4	26.1	27.5	27.0	…
Kiribati[c]	…	64.4	77.9	92.2	112.1	127.8	99.9	103.4	131.0	…
Marshall Islands[g]	62.3	57.4	51.8	54.4	52.8	58.8	61.0	68.3	62.6	…
Micronesia, Federated States of[g]	67.7	64.7	66.0	62.4	65.4	66.0	68.9	78.2	79.7	…
Nauru[c]	39.2	…	31.9	39.1	60.0	74.5	91.6	100.6	108.5	126.6
Niue	…	…	…	…	…	…	…	…	…	…
Palau[g]	46.7	45.1	44.9	41.1	43.7	41.2	42.0	40.0	44.4	43.5
Papua New Guinea	…	…	…	…	…	…	…	15.5	17.6	15.4
Samoa[c]	…	…	30.2	31.7	36.0	32.0	32.6	34.0	36.0	…
Solomon Islands	28.1	32.7	33.8	35.3	33.4	35.1	30.8	30.6	32.2	27.8
Tonga[c]	…	…	…	…	…	…	38.7	43.2	42.6	44.2
Tuvalu	…	…	105.3	123.3	140.4	184.0	161.5	…	…	…
Vanuatu	…	…	21.8	21.4	23.4	31.1	24.8	31.3	…	…
Developed ADB Member Economies										
Australia[c]	32.3	31.7	32.3	33.7	33.7	34.2	34.8	34.6	35.5	35.8
Japan[d]	30.2	31.5	32.0	33.1	34.9	35.6	35.4	35.7	36.3	…
New Zealand[c]	37.0	38.3	36.8	37.9	36.8	37.6	37.6	37.5	37.0	38.5

… = data not available, ADB = Asian Development Bank, GDP = gross domestic product.

a   In general, economies follow the guidelines of the International Monetary Fund on Government Finance Statistics (GFS). Some economies still use the 1986 version of the GFS guidelines, while others have switched to the 2001 or 2014 guidelines. The comparability of the data in this table is limited by variations in the concepts and definitions used in different versions of the GFS framework. Data refer to government revenue as classified in the GFS 2001 or GFS 2014 framework, except for Bhutan; Brunei Darussalam; India; the Kyrgyz Republic; Maldives; Nauru; Pakistan; the People's Republic of China; Taipei,China; Tajikistan; Turkmenistan; and Viet Nam, where data refer to total government revenue as classified in the GFS 1986 framework. Data refer to general government, except for Bangladesh; Bhutan; Brunei Darussalam; Cambodia; the Federated States of Micronesia; Fiji; India; the Lao People's Democratic Republic; Malaysia; Maldives; the Marshall Islands; Nauru; Nepal; Palau; the Philippines; Solomon Islands; Sri Lanka; Taipei,China; Timor-Leste; Tonga; Tuvalu; Vanuatu; and Viet Nam, where data refer to central government. For Cambodia, data refer to central government excluding extra budgetary central government. For Pakistan, data refer to the consolidated federal and provincial governments. For the People's Republic of China, data refer to consolidated central and local governments. For Turkmenistan, data prior to 2011 refer to central government.
b   For 2005–2011, GFS data are based on fiscal year beginning 21 March. For 2012, GFS data cover 9 months from 21 March to 20 December. For 2013 onward, GFS data are based on fiscal year ending 20 December. For 2005–2015, national accounts data are based on fiscal year beginning 21 March. For 2016 onward, national accounts data are based on fiscal year ending 20 December.
c   Data are based on fiscal year ending 30 June.
d   Data are based on fiscal year beginning 1 April.
e   Data are based on fiscal year ending 15 July.
f   For 2005 onward, data are based on fiscal year beginning 1 April. Data are derived as the excess of revenue over expenditure (ordinary plus charged) less the sum of contribution to a development fund, contribution to a government trust fund, and capital and currency adjustments.
g   Data are based on fiscal year ending 30 September.
h   For 2012–2018, GFS data are based on fiscal year beginning 1 April. For 2019, GFS data are based on fiscal year beginning 1 October. For 2012–2015, national accounts data are based on fiscal year beginning 1 April. For 2016 onward, national accounts data are based on fiscal year beginning 1 October.
i   Taxes include local government taxes.

Sources: Economy sources. For Azerbaijan (2008–2018); Fiji; Hong Kong, China; Nepal, Sri Lanka (2000–2003); and Timor-Leste: International Monetary Fund. Government Finance Statistics. https://data.imf.org/ (accessed May–June 2020). For Nauru (2012–2019): International Monetary Fund. Staff Country Reports. Republic of Nauru: 2017 Article IV. http://www.imf.org/en/Publications/CR/Issues/2017/04/03/Republic-of-Nauru-2017-Article-IV-Consultation-Press-Release-Staff-Report-and-Statement-by-44794 (accessed 6 May 2020); and Republic of Nauru: 2019 Article IV. https://www.imf.org/en/Publications/CR/Issues/2020/01/29/Republic-of-Nauru-2019-Article-IV-Consultation-Press-Release-Staff-Report-and-Statement-by-49001 (accessed 6 May 2020).

Click on the indictor name in the table header to access the time series in the Key Indicators Database.

Table 2.8.4: **Government Expenditure**[a]
(% of GDP)

ADB Regional Member	2010	2011	2012	2013	2014	2015	2016	2017	2018	2019
Developing ADB Member Economies										
Central and West Asia										
Afghanistan[b]	20.6	22.5	17.4	23.2	24.6	25.2	28.9	28.1	29.7	30.5
Armenia	28.2	26.8	25.9	25.7	26.3	28.6	29.3	27.7	24.7	25.4
Azerbaijan	31.6	32.8	35.7	36.1	35.6	37.2	32.8	33.5	30.3	...
Georgia	31.2	27.8	28.3	27.1	27.9	27.4	28.3	27.6	27.2	28.5
Kazakhstan	20.4	19.3	20.3	19.1	19.8	19.8	20.5	22.9	18.2	...
Kyrgyz Republic	31.2	32.0	34.5	29.3	30.3	31.3	31.8	31.3	27.7	28.4
Pakistan[c]	20.4	18.9	21.2	19.8	20.4	20.2	20.3	21.6	21.6	21.5
Tajikistan	27.2	28.5	25.2	28.6	28.9	31.9	33.4	34.6	34.0	30.8
Turkmenistan	13.8	14.6	14.7	16.9	17.0	17.3	14.1	17.8	13.7	13.3
Uzbekistan	...	...	...	25.4	24.7	24.3	23.6	22.8	24.6	...
East Asia										
China, People's Republic of	21.8	22.4	23.4	23.6	23.6	25.5	25.2	24.4	24.0	24.1
Hong Kong, China[d]	18.1	20.0	20.0	20.8	19.3	20.3	19.9	19.5	20.3	...
Korea, Republic of	...	...	32.2	30.9	31.0	31.1	30.2	30.7	30.4	...
Mongolia	35.2	44.0	44.8	39.3	39.8	36.8	47.3	37.1	32.6	37.5
Taipei,China	13.4	13.3	13.7	12.5	11.6	11.2	11.2	10.9	11.1	...
South Asia										
Bangladesh[c]	14.8	14.8	14.2	14.2	13.7	12.7	12.9	13.4	10.2	...
Bhutan[c]	35.6	38.4	39.1	36.9	31.6	29.8	32.6	32.8	34.5	25.0
India[d]	15.7	14.9	14.2	13.9	13.3	13.0	12.8	12.5	12.2	13.7
Maldives	33.2	31.3	29.8	27.0	29.1	34.0	37.6	30.9	31.5	30.1
Nepal[e]	19.5	19.5	19.3	17.8	18.8	20.1	21.9	27.5	...	...
Sri Lanka	19.3	19.0	17.5	17.3	17.0	20.9	19.5	19.3	18.8	19.4
Southeast Asia										
Brunei Darussalam[f]	34.0	30.8	31.4	33.6	33.6	35.7	39.7	36.3	32.8	31.1
Cambodia	18.3	17.9	20.7	20.6	20.5	19.4	20.2	21.4	21.7	21.5
Indonesia	17.2	17.5	18.4	18.7	18.5	17.8	16.9	16.5	16.5	16.3
Lao People's Democratic Republic[g]	22.7	22.4	21.5	25.7	24.2	24.1	21.1	18.3	21.0	...
Malaysia	24.4	25.0	25.8	24.7	23.2	21.7	20.0	19.0	19.7	...
Myanmar[h]	...	...	14.2	14.4	16.4	16.2	15.8	15.5	16.8	14.2
Philippines	16.2	15.1	15.7	15.4	14.9	16.0	16.7	17.0	18.6	19.4
Singapore[d]	9.3	7.9	9.0	9.2	10.9	13.8	13.4	12.7	13.5	...
Thailand[g]	21.3	21.9	21.2	21.6	22.0	22.0	21.0	21.2	21.1	20.5
Timor-Leste	...	...	...	76.3	92.4	83.6	98.2	72.4	80.8	...
Viet Nam[i]	27.2	25.4	28.2	28.8	26.4	28.2	26.8	27.1	29.2	29.1
The Pacific										
Cook Islands[c]	35.5	31.0	35.7	28.0	41.7	47.5	37.8	30.1	37.1	26.1
Fiji	27.0	27.3	27.0	26.9	28.4	29.4	26.9	28.4	31.4	...
Kiribati[c]	...	71.3	74.4	71.9	67.4	71.7	78.3	86.6	79.2	...
Marshall Islands[g]	58.8	55.3	52.6	54.6	49.6	56.0	57.1	64.0	60.1	...
Micronesia, Federated States of[g]	67.2	65.3	65.1	59.6	54.2	55.7	61.7	64.0	55.5	...
Nauru[c]	83.6	...	44.7	57.4	51.8	83.1	93.4	100.5	96.8	125.6
Niue	...	...	...	...	...	...	...	...	...	...
Palau[g]	25.8	28.8	27.4	31.6	31.1	26.4	27.1	29.3	33.5	34.3
Papua New Guinea	...	...	...	...	...	...	...	17.9	20.1	19.5
Samoa[c]	...	...	38.3	35.7	40.8	35.7	31.9	34.7	34.7	...
Solomon Islands	22.5	26.6	29.2	31.8	31.3	34.3	34.0	32.8	30.7	29.3
Tonga[c]	...	...	...	...	...	...	37.2	39.6	39.7	42.9
Tuvalu	...	...	93.8	96.7	111.4	144.0	156.7	...	...	...
Vanuatu	...	...	23.4	21.6	22.2	24.2	25.2	29.1	...	...
Developed ADB Member Economies										
Australia[c]	37.8	36.5	36.7	36.4	36.6	37.1	37.4	36.7	36.8	37.0
Japan[d]	39.1	40.4	40.2	40.4	39.8	39.0	38.8	38.4	38.5	...
New Zealand[c]	40.3	45.7	39.4	39.7	37.7	37.6	36.9	36.1	35.8	36.9

... = data not available, ADB = Asian Development Bank, GDP = gross domestic product.

a   In general, economies follow the guidelines of the International Monetary Fund on Government Finance Statistics (GFS). Some economies still use the 1986 version of the GFS guidelines, while others have switched to the 2001 or 2014 guidelines. The comparability of the data in this table is limited by variations in the concepts and definitions used in different versions of the GFS framework. Data refer to government expenditure as classified in the GFS 2001 or GFS 2014 framework, except for Bhutan; Brunei Darussalam; India; the Kyrgyz Republic; Maldives; Nauru; Pakistan; the People's Republic of China; Taipei,China; Tajikistan; Turkmenistan; and Viet Nam, where data refer to total government expenditure as classified in the GFS 1986 framework. Data refer to general government, except for Bangladesh; Bhutan; Brunei Darussalam; Cambodia; the Federated States of Micronesia; Fiji; India; the Lao People's Democratic Republic; Malaysia; Maldives; the Marshall Islands; Nauru; Nepal; Palau; the Philippines; Solomon Islands; Sri Lanka; Taipei,China; Timor-Leste; Tonga; Tuvalu; Vanuatu; and Viet Nam, where data refer to central government. For Cambodia: Data refer to central government excluding extra budgetary central government. For Pakistan, data refer to the consolidated federal and provincial governments. For the People's Republic of China, data refer to consolidated central and local governments. For Turkmenistan, data prior to 2011 refer to central government.
b   For 2005–2011, GFS data are based on fiscal year beginning 21 March. For 2012, GFS data cover 9 months from 21 March to 20 December. For 2013 onward, GFS data are based on fiscal year ending 20 December. For 2005–2015, national accounts data are based on fiscal year beginning 21 March. For 2016 onward, national accounts data are based on fiscal year ending 20 December.
c   Data are based on fiscal year ending 30 June.
d   Data are based on fiscal year beginning 1 April.
e   Data are based on fiscal year ending 15 July.
f   For 2003 onward, data are based on fiscal year beginning 1 April.
g   Data are based on fiscal year ending 30 September.
h   For 2012–2018, GFS data are based on fiscal year beginning 1 April. For 2019, GFS data are based on fiscal year beginning 1 October. For 2012–2015, national accounts data are based on fiscal year beginning 1 April. For 2016 onward, national accounts data are based on fiscal year beginning 1 October.
i   Includes local government expenditure.

Sources: Economy sources. For Azerbaijan (2008–2018); Fiji; Hong Kong, China; Nepal, Sri Lanka (2000–2003); and Timor-Leste: International Monetary Fund. Government Finance Statistics. https://data.imf.org/ (accessed May–June 2020). For Nauru (2012–2019): International Monetary Fund. Staff Country Reports. Republic of Nauru: 2017 Article IV. http://www.imf.org/en/Publications/CR/Issues/2017/04/03/Republic-of-Nauru-2017-Article-IV-Consultation-Press-Release-Staff-Report-and-Statement-by-44794 (accessed 6 May 2020); and Republic of Nauru: 2019 Article IV. https://www.imf.org/en/Publications/CR/Issues/2020/01/29/Republic-of-Nauru-2019-Article-IV-Consultation-Press-Release-Staff-Report-and-Statement-by-49001 (accessed 6 May 2020).

Click on the indictor name in the table header to access the time series in the Key Indicators Database.

Government Finance

Table 2.8.5:   Government Expenditure by Economic Activity[a]
(% of GDP)

ADB Regional Member	Health 2010	Health 2015	Health 2019	Education 2010	Education 2015	Education 2019	Social Protection 2010	Social Protection 2015	Social Protection 2019
Developing ADB Member Economies									
Central and West Asia									
Afghanistan[b]	0.9	1.2	1.5	3.6	3.6	3.4	0.5	1.4	1.3
Armenia	1.6	1.7	1.5	3.2	2.9	2.4	7.1	7.7	7.0
Azerbaijan	1.0	1.3	0.9 (2018)	2.9	3.1	2.6 (2018)	6.8	6.8	6.0 (2018)
Georgia	2.1	2.7	2.7	2.8	3.2	3.8	6.5	7.3	6.7
Kazakhstan	2.5	2.1	2.0 (2018)	3.5	3.3	3.3 (2018)	4.5	4.5	4.9 (2018)
Kyrgyz Republic	2.9	3.0	2.4	5.4	5.9	6.1	5.0	5.8	5.5
Pakistan	...	...	...	...	...	...	...	...	
Tajikistan	1.4	2.0	2.3	4.0	5.0	5.7	3.5	5.2	4.5
Turkmenistan	...			...			...		
Uzbekistan	...	2.5	2.3 (2018)	...	6.0	5.4 (2018)	...	7.4	6.3 (2018)
East Asia									
China, People's Republic of	1.2	1.7	1.7	3.0	3.8	3.5	2.2	2.8	3.0
Hong Kong, China[c]	2.4	3.2	3.0 (2018)	3.5	3.4	4.0 (2018)	2.4	2.9	3.4 (2018)
Korea, Republic of	0.2	0.3	0.2 (2018)	2.8	3.0	3.4 (2018)	4.3	5.3	5.7 (2018)
Mongolia	2.5	2.5	2.4	5.1	3.0	3.7	11.1	7.6	7.5
Taipei,China	0.2	0.1	0.1 (2018)	1.7	1.4	1.5 (2018)	3.1	3.3	3.2 (2018)
South Asia									
Bangladesh[d]	0.8	0.7	0.3 (2017)	2.0	2.0	2.5 (2017)	0.9	0.7	0.8 (2017)
Bhutan[d]	3.0	2.8	2.8	6.7	6.0	5.4	3.1	3.2	2.4
India[c]	1.0 (2011)	1.2	1.3 (2018)	4.4 (2011)	4.4	4.6 (2018)	1.4 (2011)	1.8	1.9 (2018)
Maldives	2.9	4.0	3.4	5.3	4.6	3.7	1.7	5.1	4.3
Nepal[e]	1.5	1.4	1.7 (2017)	3.9	3.7	4.1 (2017)	0.8	0.7	1.4 (2017)
Sri Lanka	1.2	1.6	1.6	1.6	2.1	1.9	1.7	5.0	...
Southeast Asia									
Brunei Darussalam[c]	1.8	2.3	2.0	3.6	4.1	3.6	0.8	0.8	0.7
Cambodia	1.3	1.3	1.3	1.6	2.0	2.7	0.5	0.8	0.9
Indonesia	1.0	1.1	1.5	3.4	3.3	3.1	0.1	0.3	1.3
Lao People's Democratic Republic	...	...	...	...	...	...	...	...	...
Malaysia	2.0	2.0	1.9 (2018)	6.1	4.8	4.3 (2018)	...	...	...
Myanmar[f]	0.7 (2012)	1.0	0.8	1.5 (2012)	2.1	2.0	0.4 (2012)	0.8	0.9
Philippines[g]	0.3	0.8	0.9	2.4	2.8	3.5	1.6	1.3	2.2
Singapore[c]	1.2	2.1	2.1 (2018)	3.0	2.9	2.6 (2018)	1.1	1.8	0.9 (2018)
Thailand[h]	...	1.1	1.3	...	3.8	3.0	...	2.5	3.1
Timor-Leste	4.0	3.7	3.4 (2018)	7.8	6.5	4.7 (2018)	16.3	11.7	8.6 (2018)
Viet Nam	...	...	...	...	...	...	...	...	...
The Pacific									
Cook Islands[d]	4.0	3.0	0.7	3.9	3.5	2.1	3.9	4.2	3.8
Fiji	...	...		...	...		...	...	
Kiribati[d]	...	9.9	12.2 (2018)	...	9.9	12.0 (2018)	...	1.4	1.2 (2018)
Marshall Islands[h]	7.8	7.6	12.0 (2017)	19.6	16.7	15.5 (2017)	–	–	3.6 (2017)
Micronesia, Federated States of	...	...	...	...	...	...	...	...	...
Nauru	...	...	...	...	...	...	...	...	...
Niue	...	...	...	...	...	...	...	...	...
Palau	...	...	...	...	...	...	...	...	...
Papua New Guinea	...	...	...	...	...	...	...	...	...
Samoa[d]	3.6	5.4	5.0	5.8	4.5	4.5	1.1	2.1	1.2
Solomon Islands	...	...	...	...	...	...	...	...	...
Tonga	...	...		...	...		...	...	
Tuvalu	8.5 (2012)	9.4	...	16.0 (2012)	23.2	...	6.1 (2012)	18.3	...
Vanuatu	2.9 (2011)	2.4	2.1 (2017)	6.2 (2011)	5.4	5.6 (2017)	0.0 (2011)	0.1	0.0 (2017)
Developed ADB Member Economies									
Australia[d]	6.7	6.8	7.1	5.9	5.4	5.4	9.9	10.4	9.7
Japan[c]	6.9	7.4	7.4 (2018)	2.8	2.6	2.5 (2018)	2.2	2.5	2.6 (2018)
New Zealand[d]	7.0	6.9	6.9	6.8	6.3	5.9	12.5	11.5	10.8

... = data not available, – = magnitude equals zero, 0.0 = magnitude is less than half of unit employed, ADB = Asian Development Bank, GDP = gross domestic product.

a   In general, economies follow the guidelines of the International Monetary Fund on Government Finance Statistics (GFS). Some economies still use the 1986 version of the GFS guidelines, while others have switched to the 2001 or 2014 guidelines. The comparability of the data in this table is limited by variations in the concepts and definitions used in different versions of the GFS framework. The table refers to government expenditure by economic activity as classified in the GFS 2001 or GFS 2014 framework, except for Bhutan; Brunei Darussalam; India; the Kyrgyz Republic; Maldives; the People's Republic of China; and Taipei,China, where data refer to health, education, and social security and welfare, as classified in the GFS 1986 framework. Data refer to general government, except for Bangladesh; Bhutan; Brunei Darussalam; Cambodia; India; Malaysia; Maldives; the Marshall Islands; Nepal; the Philippines; Samoa; Sri Lanka; Taipei,China; Timor-Leste; Tuvalu; and Vanuatu, where data refer to central government. For Cambodia, data refer to central government excluding extra budgetary central government. For the People's Republic of China, data refer to consolidated central and local governments.

b   For 2005–2011, GFS data are based on fiscal year beginning 21 March. For 2012, GFS data cover 9 months from 21 March to 20 December. For 2013 onward, GFS data are based on fiscal year ending 20 December. For 2005–2015, national accounts data are based on fiscal year beginning 21 March. For 2016 onward, national accounts data are based on fiscal year ending 20 December.

c   Data are based on fiscal year beginning 1 April.

d   Data are based on fiscal year ending 30 June.

e   Data are based on fiscal year ending 15 July.

f   For 2012–2018, GFS data are based on fiscal year beginning 1 April. For 2019, GFS data are based on fiscal year beginning 1 October. For 2012–2015, national accounts data are based on fiscal year beginning 1 April. For 2016 onward, national accounts data are based on fiscal year beginning 1 October.

g   For 2000–2013, data on education include expenditure on recreation, culture, and religion.

h   Data are based on fiscal year ending 30 September.

Sources: Economy sources.

Click on the indictor name in the table header to access the time series in the Key Indicators Database.

Table 2.8.6:   Indicators for Business Startups

ADB Regional Member	Time Required to Start a Business (days)			Score (Starting a Business)[a]			Rank[b]
	2005	2010	2019	2005	2010	2019	2019
Developing ADB Member Economies							
Central and West Asia[c]	**40.1**	**12.9**	**6.5**				
Afghanistan	9.5	9.5	8.5	83.2	87.8	92.0	52
Armenia	18.0	14.0	4.0	81.3	88.9	96.1	10
Azerbaijan	113.0	8.0	3.5	55.8	90.4	96.2	9
Georgia	21.0	3.0	1.0	79.9	95.8	99.6	2
Kazakhstan	31.0	25.0	5.0	77.6	83.9	94.4	22
Kyrgyz Republic	21.0	14.0	10.0	81.8	91.7	93.0	42
Pakistan	...	...	16.5	...	...	89.3	72
Tajikistan	79.0	16.0	7.0	25.5	80.7	93.2	36
Turkmenistan	...	...	...	...	...	...	...
Uzbekistan	28.0	14.0	3.0	77.1	81.5	96.2	8
East Asia[c]	**27.5**	**13.0**	**8.0**				
China, People's Republic of	...	...	8.5	...	...	94.1	27
Hong Kong, China	11.0	6.0	1.5	91.1	95.4	98.2	5
Korea, Republic of	17.0	14.0	8.0	61.4	84.5	93.4	33
Mongolia	17.0	17.0	12.0	75.6	82.2	86.7	100
Taipei,China	65.0	15.0	10.0	60.9	88.5	94.4	21
South Asia[c]	**37.0**	**31.8**	**15.3**				
Bangladesh	...	...	19.5	...	...	82.4	131
Bhutan	62.0	46.0	12.0	69.2	77.5	86.4	103
India	...	...	17.5	...	...	81.6	136
Maldives	9.0	12.0	12.0	89.8	88.3	89.2	74
Nepal	31.0	31.0	22.5	74.8	77.7	81.7	135
Sri Lanka	46.0	38.0	8.0	70.5	74.6	88.2	85
Southeast Asia[c]	**67.9**	**58.4**	**34.9**				
Brunei Darussalam	121.5 (2006)	108.5	5.5	48.9 (2006)	48.3	94.9	16
Cambodia	87.0	102.0	99.0	35.0	35.1	52.4	187
Indonesia	...	...	12.6	...	...	81.2	140
Lao People's Democratic Republic	135.0	86.0	173.0	57.1	62.1	62.7	181
Malaysia	37.5	17.5	17.5	73.4	81.0	83.3	126
Myanmar	...	77.0 (2012)	7.0	...	15.5 (2012)	89.3	70
Philippines	35.0	29.0	33.0	63.5	63.8	71.3	171
Singapore	6.0	2.5	1.5	91.2	96.5	98.2	4
Thailand	35.0	34.0	6.0	75.9	78.9	92.4	47
Timor-Leste	167.0	110.0	13.0	19.6	45.6	89.4	68
Viet Nam	41.0	36.0	16.0	73.1	77.8	85.1	115
The Pacific[c]	**35.3**	**32.4**	**22.5**				
Cook Islands	...	...	...	...	...	...	...
Fiji	44.0	44.0	40.0	75.2	75.8	73.6	163
Kiribati	31.0	31.0	31.0	76.1	76.3	78.4	149
Marshall Islands	17.0	17.0	17.0	87.2	87.8	88.4	83
Micronesia, Federated States of	16.0	16.0	16.0	68.2	70.1	69.6	174
Nauru	...	...	...	...	...	...	...
Niue	...	...	...	...	...	...	...
Palau	24.0	28.0	28.0	83.8	81.1	82.1	132
Papua New Guinea	52.0	52.0	41.0	76.2	76.3	80.1	142
Samoa	35.0	9.0	9.0	75.2	92.2	92.6	46
Solomon Islands	55.0	55.0	9.0	60.5	67.7	85.6	110
Tonga	32.0	25.0	16.0	86.2	88.6	90.9	62
Tuvalu	...	...	...	...	...	...	...
Vanuatu	47.0	47.0	18.0	67.6	72.0	81.5	137
Developed ADB Member Economies[c]	**7.5**	**1.5**	**4.5**				
Australia	3.0	2.5	2.0	96.2	96.5	96.6	7
Japan	...	...	11.1	...	...	86.1	106
New Zealand	12.0	0.5	0.5	95.6	100.0	100.0	1
DEVELOPING ADB MEMBER ECONOMIES[c]	**43.4**	**32.3**	**19.5**				
ALL ADB REGIONAL MEMBERS[c]	**41.4**	**30.7**	**18.5**				
WORLD	**50.7**	**35.9**	**19.6**				

... = data not available, ADB = Asian Development Bank.

a The score for ease of starting a business is the simple average of the scores for four component indicators: procedures, time and cost for an entrepreneur to start and formally operate a business, and the paid-in minimum capital requirement. The score is reflected on a scale from 0 to 100, where 0 represents the lowest and 100 represents the best performance.

b Rank among the 190 economies as presented in the World Bank's Doing Business 2020. The rank is determined by each economy's scores for starting a business.

c Aggregates are ADB estimates using data from Doing Business 2020. Estimates were calculated as the arithmetic average for reporting economies with data corresponding to the year heading.

Source: World Bank. Doing Business 2020. https://www.doingbusiness.org/ (accessed 20 July 2020).

Table 2.8.7: Corruption Perceptions Index[a]

ADB Regional Member	2000	2005	2010	2013	2014	2015	2016	2017	2018	2019	Rank in 2018[b]	Rank in 2019[b]
Developing ADB Member Economies												
Central and West Asia												
Afghanistan	...	2.5	1.4 |	8.0	12.0	11.0	15.0	15.0	16.0	16.0	172	173
Armenia	2.5	2.9	2.6 |	36.0	37.0	35.0	33.0	35.0	35.0	42.0	105	77
Azerbaijan	1.5	2.2	2.4 |	28.0	29.0	29.0	30.0	31.0	25.0	30.0	152	126
Georgia	2.4 (2002)	2.3	3.8 |	49.0	52.0	52.0	57.0	56.0	58.0	56.0	41	44
Kazakhstan	3.0	2.6	2.9 |	26.0	29.0	28.0	29.0	31.0	31.0	34.0	124	113
Kyrgyz Republic	...	2.3	2.0 |	24.0	27.0	28.0	28.0	29.0	29.0	30.0	132	126
Pakistan	2.3 (2001)	2.1	2.3 |	28.0	29.0	30.0	32.0	32.0	33.0	32.0	117	120
Tajikistan	...	2.1	2.1 |	22.0	23.0	26.0	25.0	21.0	25.0	25.0	152	153
Turkmenistan	...	1.8	1.6 |	17.0	17.0	18.0	22.0	19.0	20.0	19.0	161	165
Uzbekistan	2.4	2.2	1.6 |	17.0	18.0	19.0	21.0	22.0	23.0	25.0	158	153
East Asia												
China, People's Republic of	3.1	3.2	3.5 |	40.0	36.0	37.0	40.0	41.0	39.0	41.0	87	80
Hong Kong, China	7.7	8.3	8.4 |	75.0	74.0	75.0	77.0	77.0	76.0	76.0	14	16
Korea, Republic of	4.0	5.0	5.4 |	55.0	55.0	56.0	53.0	54.0	57.0	59.0	45	39
Mongolia	...	3.0	2.7 |	38.0	39.0	39.0	38.0	36.0	37.0	35.0	93	106
Taipei,China	5.5	5.9	5.8 |	61.0	61.0	62.0	61.0	63.0	63.0	65.0	31	28
South Asia												
Bangladesh	0.4 (2001)	1.7	2.4 |	27.0	25.0	25.0	26.0	28.0	26.0	26.0	149	146
Bhutan	...	6.0 (2006)	5.7 |	63.0	65.0	65.0	65.0	67.0	68.0	68.0	25	25
India	2.8	2.9	3.3 |	36.0	38.0	38.0	40.0	40.0	41.0	41.0	78	80
Maldives	...	3.3 (2007)	2.3 |	...	...	...	36.0	33.0	31.0	29.0	124	130
Nepal	...	2.5	2.2 |	31.0	29.0	27.0	29.0	31.0	31.0	34.0	124	113
Sri Lanka	3.7 (2002)	3.2	3.2 |	37.0	38.0	37.0	36.0	38.0	38.0	38.0	89	93
Southeast Asia												
Brunei Darussalam	...	...	5.5 |	60.0	...	21.0	58.0	62.0	63.0	60.0	31	35
Cambodia	...	2.3	2.1 |	20.0	21.0	21.0	21.0	21.0	20.0	20.0	161	162
Indonesia	1.7	2.2	2.8 |	32.0	34.0	36.0	37.0	37.0	38.0	40.0	89	85
Lao People's Democratic Republic	...	3.3	2.1 |	26.0	25.0	25.0	30.0	29.0	29.0	29.0	132	130
Malaysia	4.8	5.1	4.4 |	50.0	52.0	50.0	49.0	47.0	47.0	53.0	61	51
Myanmar	...	1.8	1.4 |	21.0	21.0	22.0	28.0	30.0	29.0	29.0	132	130
Philippines	2.8	2.5	2.4 |	36.0	38.0	35.0	35.0	34.0	36.0	34.0	99	113
Singapore	9.1	9.4	9.3 |	86.0	84.0	85.0	84.0	84.0	85.0	85.0	3	4
Thailand	3.2	3.8	3.5 |	35.0	38.0	38.0	35.0	37.0	36.0	36.0	99	101
Timor-Leste	...	2.6 (2006)	2.5 |	30.0	28.0	28.0	35.0	38.0	35.0	38.0	105	93
Viet Nam	2.5	2.6	2.7 |	31.0	31.0	31.0	33.0	35.0	33.0	37.0	117	96
The Pacific												
Cook Islands	...	...	...	...	...	...	...	...	...	...	...	...
Fiji	...	4.0	...	...	...	...	...	...	...	...	...	...
Kiribati	...	3.3 (2007)	3.2 |	...	...	...	...	...	...	...	...	...
Marshall Islands	...	...	...	...	...	...	...	...	...	...	...	...
Micronesia, Federated States of	...	...	...	...	...	...	...	...	...	...	...	...
Nauru	...	...	...	...	...	...	...	...	...	...	...	...
Niue	...	...	...	...	...	...	...	...	...	...	...	...
Palau	...	...	...	...	...	...	...	...	...	...	...	...
Papua New Guinea	...	2.3	2.1 |	25.0	25.0	25.0	28.0	29.0	28.0	28.0	138	137
Samoa	...	4.5 (2007)	4.1 |	...	52.0	...	...	...	...	...	...	...
Solomon Islands	...	2.8 (2007)	2.8 |	...	...	...	42.0	39.0	44.0	42.0	70	77
Tonga	...	1.7 (2007)	3.0 |	...	...	...	...	...	...	...	...	...
Tuvalu	...	...	...	...	...	...	...	...	...	...	...	...
Vanuatu	...	3.1 (2007)	3.6 |	...	...	...	...	43.0	46.0	46.0	64	64
Developed ADB Member Economies												
Australia	8.3	8.8	8.7 |	81.0	80.0	79.0	79.0	77.0	77.0	77.0	13	12
Japan	6.4	7.3	7.8 |	74.0	76.0	75.0	72.0	73.0	73.0	73.0	18	20
New Zealand	9.4	9.6	9.3 |	91.0	91.0	88.0	90.0	89.0	87.0	87.0	2	1

... = data not available, | = marks break in the series, ADB = Asian Development Bank.

a   For 2000–2011, scores relate to perceptions of the degree of corruption as seen by business people and country analysts, and are not comparable over time; scores range from 0 (highly corrupt) to 10 (very clean). From 2012 onward, an updated methodology was used to calculate scores, and these are presented on a scale from 0 (highly corrupt) to 100 (very clean). Due to the differences in methodology, scores prior to 2012 should not be compared with scores from 2012 onward.

b   Based on the Transparency International Index, an economy's rank indicates its position relative to the Corruption Perceptions Index of other economies of the world; 2018 and 2019 rankings compare 180 economies.

Source: Transparency International. Corruption Perceptions Index. https://www.transparency.org/cpi (accessed 8 July 2020).

Click on the indictor name in the table header to access the time series in the Key Indicators Database.

References

ADB. 2013. Asian Development Outlook 2013. Manila.

ADB. 2020. Asian Development Outlook 2020. Manila.

International Civil Aviation Organization (ICAO). 2018. Annual Report 2018: The World of Air Transport 2018. https://www.icao.int/annual-report-2018/Pages/the-world-of-air-transport-in-2018.aspx (accessed 4 August 2020).

International Civil Aviation Organization (ICAO). 2019. Annual Report 2019: The World of Air Transport 2019. https://www.icao.int/annual-report-2019/Pages/default.aspx (accessed 4 August 2020).

C. Y. Park and K. Shin. 2020. The Impact of Nonperforming Loans on Cross-Border Bank Lending. ADB Policy Briefs. No. 136. Manila: ADB.

U. Poudel. 2019. 10 More National Pride Projects in the Pipeline. Himalayan Times. 19 November.

A. Takenaka, J. Villafuerte, R. Gaspar, and B. Narayanan. 2020. COVID-19 Impact on International Migration, Remittances, and Recipient Households in Developing Asia. ADB Policy Briefs. No. 148. Manila: ADB.

UN. 2016. Energy Statistics Compilers Manual. New York.

UN. 2019. World Population Prospects 2019. https://population.un.org/wpp/ (accessed 5 August 2020).

UN. 2020. Conference on Trade and Development. World Investment Report 2020. Geneva.

UN-REDD Programme. 2020. Forest Facts. https://www.un-redd.org/forest-facts (accessed 6 August 2020).

World Health Organization (WHO). 2020. Investing In and Building Longer Term Health Emergency Preparedness During the COVID-19 Pandemic. Geneva.

World Bank. 2019. Doing Business 2019: Training for Reform. https://www.worldbank.org/content/dam/doingBusiness/media/Annual-Reports/English/DB2019-report_web-version.pdf.

PART III

Global Value Chains

The Evolving Comparative Advantages of Asian Economies

Snapshot

- The revealed comparative advantage (RCA) index, a classic measure in studies of trade, is recalculated to adjust for GVC activity, thereby providing a more accurate picture of competitiveness among economies in Asia and the Pacific.

- The RCA rankings in Asia for two GVC-linked sectors, electricals and business services, reveal both stability and change. From 2000 to 2019, Taipei,China maintained its place as the most competitive economy for electricals, having an unchanged RCA of 3.1. Meanwhile, Viet Nam registered a notable increase in its NRCA, from 0.1 to 0.6, while that of the People's Republic of China climbed from 1.1 to 2.3.

- Results affirm the potential of "servicification", especially in business services. Among the outstanding performers here was the Philippines, whose increase in RCA from 0.6 in 2000 to 1.0 in 2019 catapulted it to fifth place among the Asian economies. This is driven by its business process outsourcing sector.

- While increasing the space for international competition, GVCs also expose economies to greater uncertainties. On average, an increase in GVC participation of 10 percentage points is associated with a 0.06-increase in the standard deviation of the RCA index. This points to the need for a strong policy framework that maximizes benefits while minimizing risks.

The years since the 1990s have been a time of global value chain (GVC) revolution—the rise of internationally linked production processes that are fragmented across economies. The world we live in is no longer one where trade consists only of final goods for consumption: much of developing Asia's trade is in intermediate inputs that are used for further production in other economies. A product may contain value-added inputs from various economies around the world. In 2019, global exports of goods and services reached $25.7 trillion at current prices. However, about 15% of this was value that did not originate from the exporting economy.

GVC statistics were first included in *Key Indicators for Asia and the Pacific* (*Key Indicators*) in 2015. That report had focused on the exponential growth of intermediates trade for 11 Asian economies in 2000, 2005, and 2011. Data and analytical tools have steadily accumulated since then. In *Key Indicators 2019*, a decomposition of exports and final goods production was used to trace the flow of value-added to and from Asian economies. This covered 25 Asian economies for 2000 and 2007–2018.

In 2020, *Key Indicators* uses the same methodology of decomposing gross exports to recalculate the revealed comparative advantage

(RCA) index of Balassa (1965), a measure used to examine the competitiveness of Asian economies and identify the sectors they specialize in. Using gross exports paints a misleading picture of comparative advantage because, as mentioned above, not all exported value originates domestically. The foreign share of exports ranges from 10% for Japan, an economy with a large domestic economy, to 44% for the small, highly open Singapore. To account for GVCs, the new revealed comparative advantage (NRCA) is value-added adjusted—that is, it corrects the traditional measure of comparative advantage (TRCA), which relies on gross exports by reflecting only the domestic value-added via forward linkages (DVA_F)—the amount of domestic value-added that is generated from the production of total exports (Wang, Wei, and Zhu, 2018). The data are sourced from the latest release of the Asian Development Bank's Multi-Regional Input–Output Tables (MRIOTs), which extends the coverage of 25 Asian economies to 14 years (2000 and 2007–2019)[1]. The

---

[1]   The data presented in this Part III are not official statistics. Production and trade data from various sources were integrated into the input–output economic analysis framework and adjusted as required to conform to specific macroeconomic concepts. As such, data and statistics presented here could differ from relevant official statistics.

MRIOTs provide a 35-sector breakdown for each economy. However, for simplicity, some sections in this chapter aggregate results into the five-sector level.

How Revealed Comparative Advantage Changes Amid Global Value Chains

Underpinning all modern theories of trade is comparative advantage, the idea that economies will export that which they are relatively more efficient at producing and import that which they are less efficient at producing. However, because it is difficult to identify beforehand where economies have a comparative advantage, Balassa's insight was to allow the prevailing flows of trade to "reveal" such information. The RCA index is the ratio between the share of a sector in an economy's exports and the share of that sector in global exports. If this ratio is over 1, then the economy must have a comparative advantage in that sector (Box 1). This simple measure points to the sectors an economy is specializing in, or, put differently, the sectors that are relatively competitive in international markets. This information can then guide policy.

Box 1: Calculating Measures of Revealed Comparative Advantage

The traditional measure of revealed comparative advantage (TRCA) follows Balassa (1965). The measure is obtained by dividing the share of an economy–sector's gross exports with the sector's gross exports from all economies as a share of world total gross exports. More formally, TRCA can be expressed as

$$TRCA_i^r = \left(\frac{e_i^r}{\sum_{i=1}^{N} e_i^r}\right) \Bigg/ \left(\frac{\sum_{k=1}^{G} e_i^k}{\sum_{i}^{N} \sum_{k=1}^{G} e_i^k}\right)$$

where e_i^{r*} is economy r's exports of products from sector i, N is the number of products (or industries in the input–output setting), and G is the number of economies in the world economy. Economy r is said to have a comparative advantage (with respect to the world) in the production of product i if $TRCA_i^r > 1$. Otherwise, it is said to have a comparative disadvantage in product i.

Balassa's index more accurately reflects cross-economy differences in comparative advantage in a world that exclusively trades finished products. As argued in literature, TRCA may not be the most appropriate measure of comparative advantage in a global value chain world characterized by intensive and extensive networks of trade in intermediates. There are at least two reasons for this. First, TRCA ignores the fact that an economy–sector's value-added may be exported indirectly via the economy's exports in other sectors. Hence, a more conceptually correct measure should be able to account for value-added exported indirectly across economy–sectors. Second, TRCA neglects the fact that an economy–sector's gross exports may at least partly carry foreign value-added. Therefore, a conceptually correct measure should exclude foreign value-added embedded in exports.

The abovementioned empirical complications may be evaded by using forward-linkage based domestic value-added in exports (DVA_F) in lieu of gross exports, as proposed by Wang, Wei, and Zhu (2018). An economy-sector's DVA_F refers to the domestic value-added that is originated from that economy-sector and ultimately embodied in exports regardless of where these exports are finally consumed. Intuitively, DVA_F may be interpreted as a measure of an economy-sector's significance as a supplier of value-added in exports. Rewriting Balassa's index by replacing gross exports with DVA_F yields a new revealed comparative advantage measure that more accurately depicts patterns of specialization. Here, new revealed comparative advantage of economy r in product i is obtained using the following formula:

$$NRCA_i^r = \left(\frac{DVA\_F_i^r}{\sum_{i=1}^{N} DVA\_F_i^r}\right) \Bigg/ \left(\frac{\sum_{k=1}^{G} DVA\_F_i^k}{\sum_{i}^{N} \sum_{k=1}^{G} DVA\_F_i^k}\right)$$

As in TRCA, economy r is said to have a comparative advantage (with respect to the world) in the production of good i if $NRCA_i^r > 1$. Otherwise, it is said to have a comparative disadvantage in product i.

References

B. Balassa. 1965. Trade Liberalisation and "Revealed" Comparative Advantage. *The Manchester School.* 33(2). pp. 99–123.

Z. Wang, S. Wei, and K. Zhu. 2018. Quantifying International Production Sharing at the Bilateral and Sector Levels. NBER Working Paper No. 19677. Cambridge, MA: National Bureau of Economic Research.

To illustrate how accounting for GVCs yields differences in the RCA index that sometimes reveal diverging pictures of comparative advantage, Figure 3.1.1 plots TRCA and NRCA ratios against each other for each of the five broad sectors in 2000 and 2019. While they are highly correlated, there are multiple cases where an economy notches a comparative advantage under one but not the other. For instance, in both 2000 and 2019, Bhutan, Cambodia, and Nepal had RCA indices of over 1 for business services using the traditional method, but less than 1 using the new method. This suggests that their exports in the business services sector contain much foreign value-added. These findings often show in industry sectors where fragmentation of production processes is pervasive, such as in the metals, automotive, and electronics sectors. Correcting for the double counting of imported intermediates in gross trade provides a more accurate picture of domestic production because it traces where the value-added originally comes from—not from the exporting developing economy where low value-added activities, such as processing and assembly activities, are based, but from developed economies where parent firms retain high value-added activities.

Conversely, Bangladesh, India, and Pakistan's comparative *dis*advantages in the primary sector are reversed under the NRCA in 2000. As developing economies, their agriculture and mining exports have more domestic content than those of the more industrialized economies, boosting their export shares once foreign content is netted out. By 2019 however, only Pakistan had a comparative advantage; both TRCA and NRCA for Bangladesh and India had fallen below 1.

The scatterplots in Figure 3.1.1 are color-coded by income category. Looking at the TRCA and NRCA ratios by income category shows that lower-income economies in Asia tend to specialize more in the primary and low-technology manufacturing sectors, where capital and knowledge requirements are less demanding. The income divide in the services sectors, meanwhile, is more ambiguous, with economies across income groups specializing in the export of business, public, and personal services. As pointed out in recent literature (Mercer-Blackman and Ablaza 2018), there is a global trend of "servicification" of manufacturing—the phenomenon whereby manufacturing processes are increasingly becoming service-oriented, which is particularly pervasive in business services. This could explain why the comparative advantage of services in some high-income economies improves when value-added is adjusted, as value-added in business services in some high-income economies are often exported indirectly by being embedded in their manufacturing exports, and thus, are double counted in the exports of middle-income economies. Correcting for the double counting of the indirect value-added in services exports and tracing where these sectors' value-added in exports originated, the shares of value-added in the services exports of some developing economies become much less impressive, while those of high-income economies improve.

Figure 3.1.1: Revealed Comparative Advantage (Traditional and New) Indices for Asian Economies, 2000 and 2019

(a) Primary

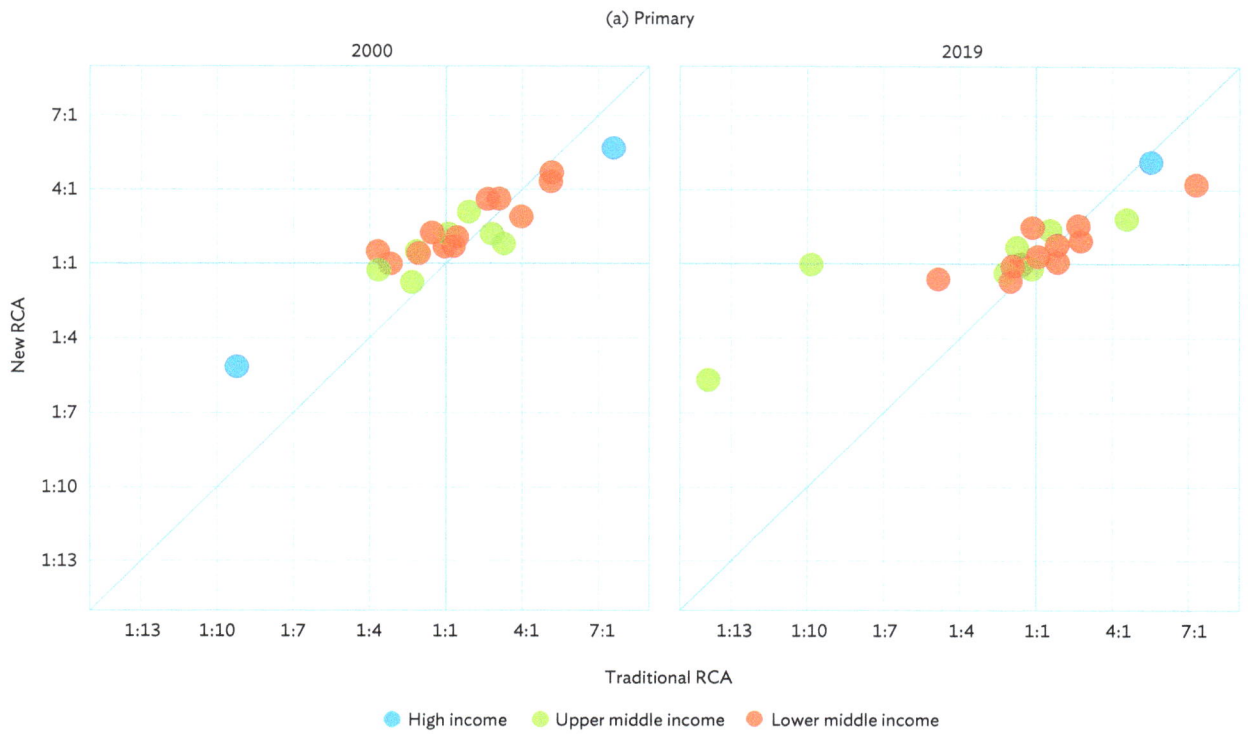

High income   Upper middle income   Lower middle income

Click here for figure data

(b) Low-Technology Manufacturing

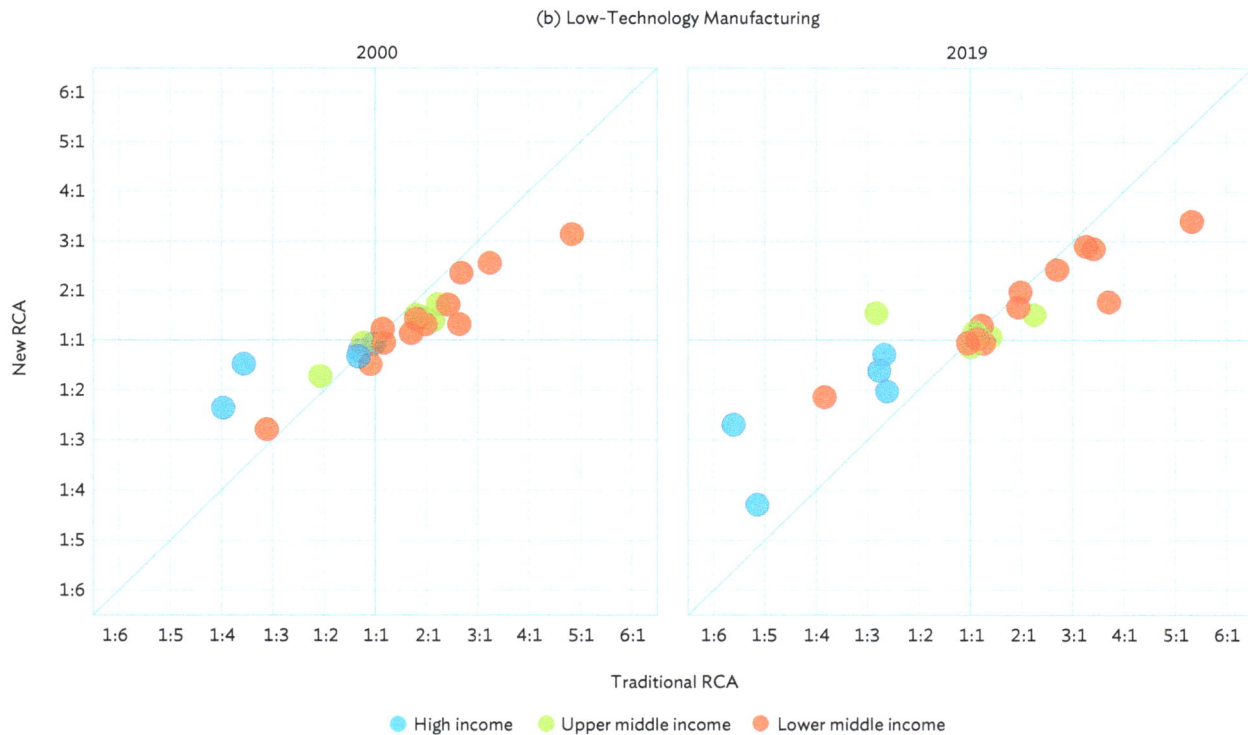

High income   Upper middle income   Lower middle income

continued on next page

Click here for figure data

Figure 3.1.1: continued

(c) Medium- and High-Technology Manufacturing

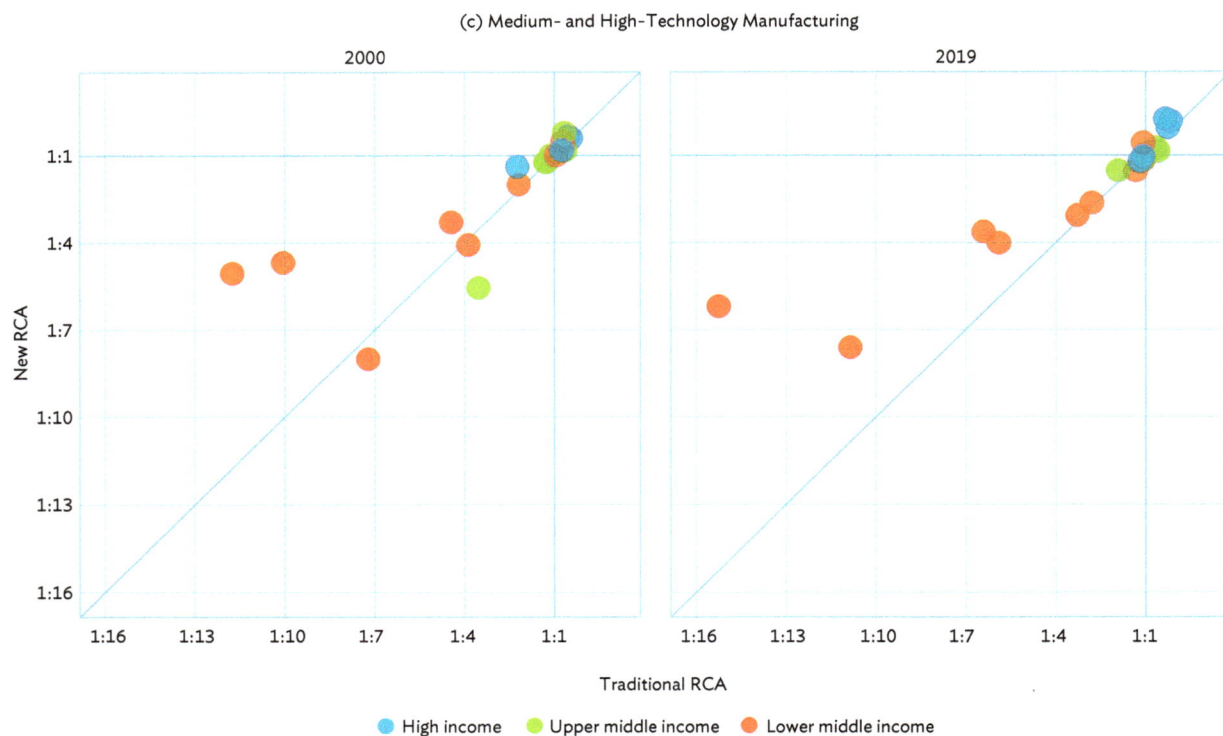

2000 · 2019

New RCA / Traditional RCA

● High income   ● Upper middle income   ● Lower middle income

Click here for figure data

(d) Business Services

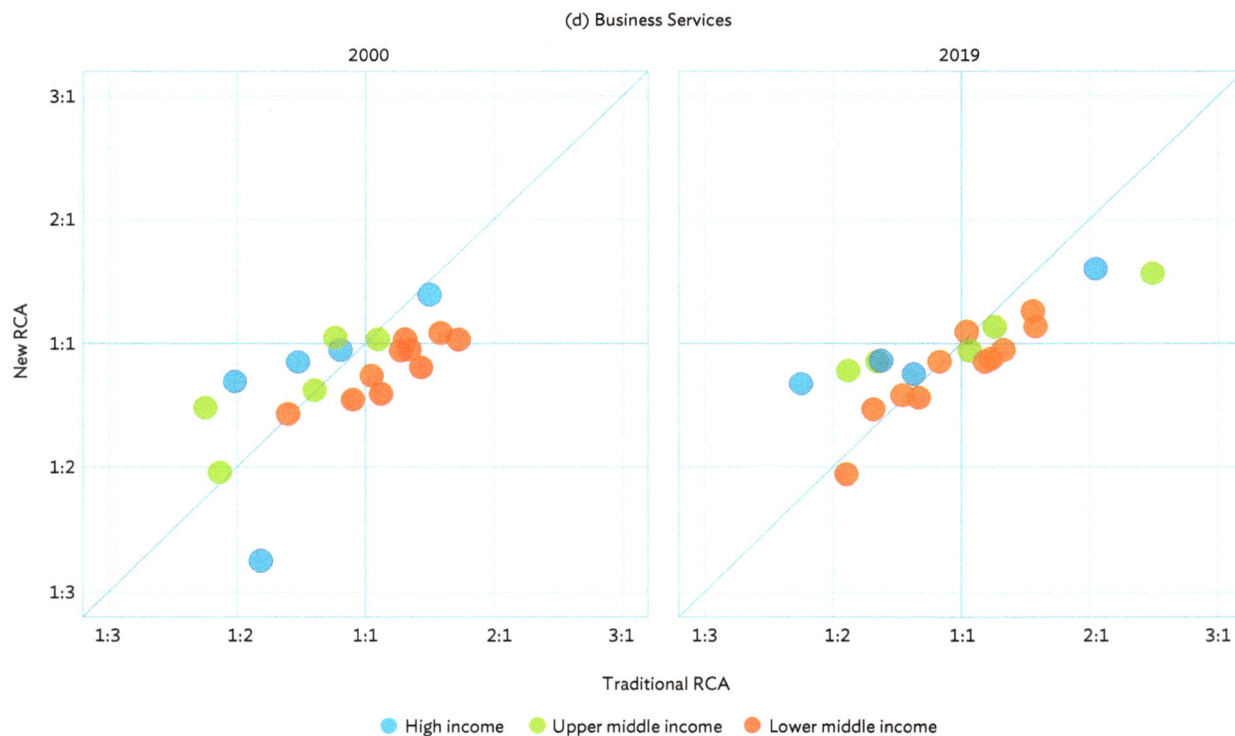

2000 · 2019

New RCA / Traditional RCA

● High income   ● Upper middle income   ● Lower middle income

continued on next page

Click here for figure data

Figure 3.1.1: continued

(e) Personal and Public Services

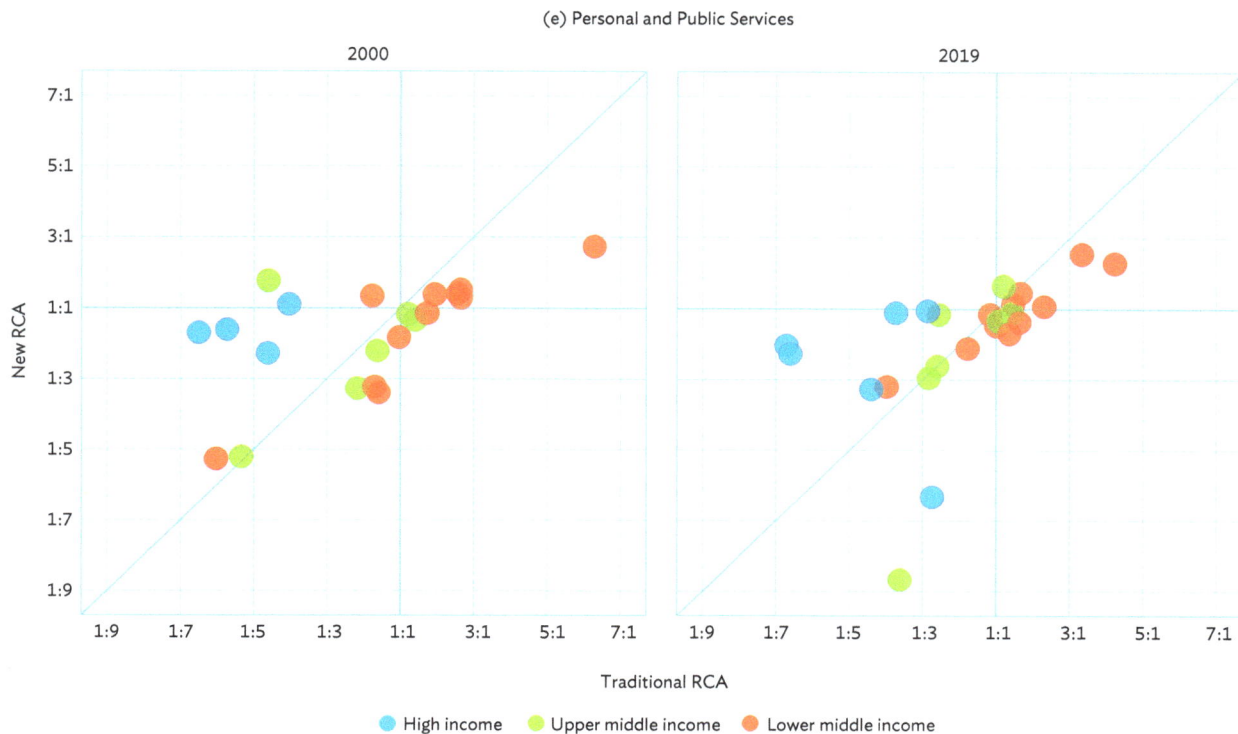

2000   2019

RCA = revealed comparative advantage.
Note: Income categories were sourced from the World Bank. Outliers were excluded to improve readability of figure.
Source: Asian Development Bank estimates based on the methodology of Balassa (1965) and Wang, Wei, and Zhu (2018) using Asian Development
           Bank Multi-Regional Input-Output Tables (2000 and 2019).

Click here for figure data

The Evolution of Comparative Advantage in Asia

Figure 3.1.2, which plots the evolution of the NRCA for Asian economies and regions[2], shows that competitiveness tends to be stable over time, though key events do sometimes cause sharp but temporary movements. Following the global financial crisis, for instance, the primary sector NRCAs of those near the threshold of 1 declined steeply, then recovered quickly in 2009. Central and West Asia remained the most competitive subregion in primary sectors, with exports of unprocessed and semi processed commodities such as crude oil for Kazakhstan, cotton for Uzbekistan, and briquettes from coal for Mongolia. Central and West Asia was followed by Southeast Asia (including

Fiji), although there was a steady decline in the latter subregion's NRCA, from 1.5 in 2007 to 1.2 in 2019.

Southeast Asia + Fiji was most competitive in the low-technology manufacturing sector. Some of the subregion's main exports are rubber articles and animal and vegetable fats and oil. South Asia also specializes in low-technology manufactures, particularly textile products such as garments and linen.

The more developed economies of East Asia, including Japan and the People's Republic of China (PRC), displayed a comparative advantage in technology- and capital-intensive sectors. The subregion is known as a manufacturing hub for highly specialized electronic components used in motor vehicles, machinery, and other equipment, and its NRCA reflects this specialization, rising steadily from 1.6 in 2007 to 1.8 in 2019. For most of

[2]   For the purposes of this analysis, Central and West Asia includes Mongolia and South Asia includes Pakistan. Fiji is grouped with South East Asian economies.

the period under consideration, no other subregions had a comparative advantage in medium- to high-technology manufacturing.

South Asia, home to a formidable business process outsourcing (BPO) industry, stayed at the top of NRCA rankings for the business service sector. Just below it was Southeast Asia, which overtook Central and West Asia after 2009. Such switches in rankings are more apparent at the economy level, which Figure 3.1.3 shows for two key sectors in GVCs: electricals and business services.

Figure 3.1.2: New Revealed Comparative Advantage Indices for Asian Economies, 2007–2019

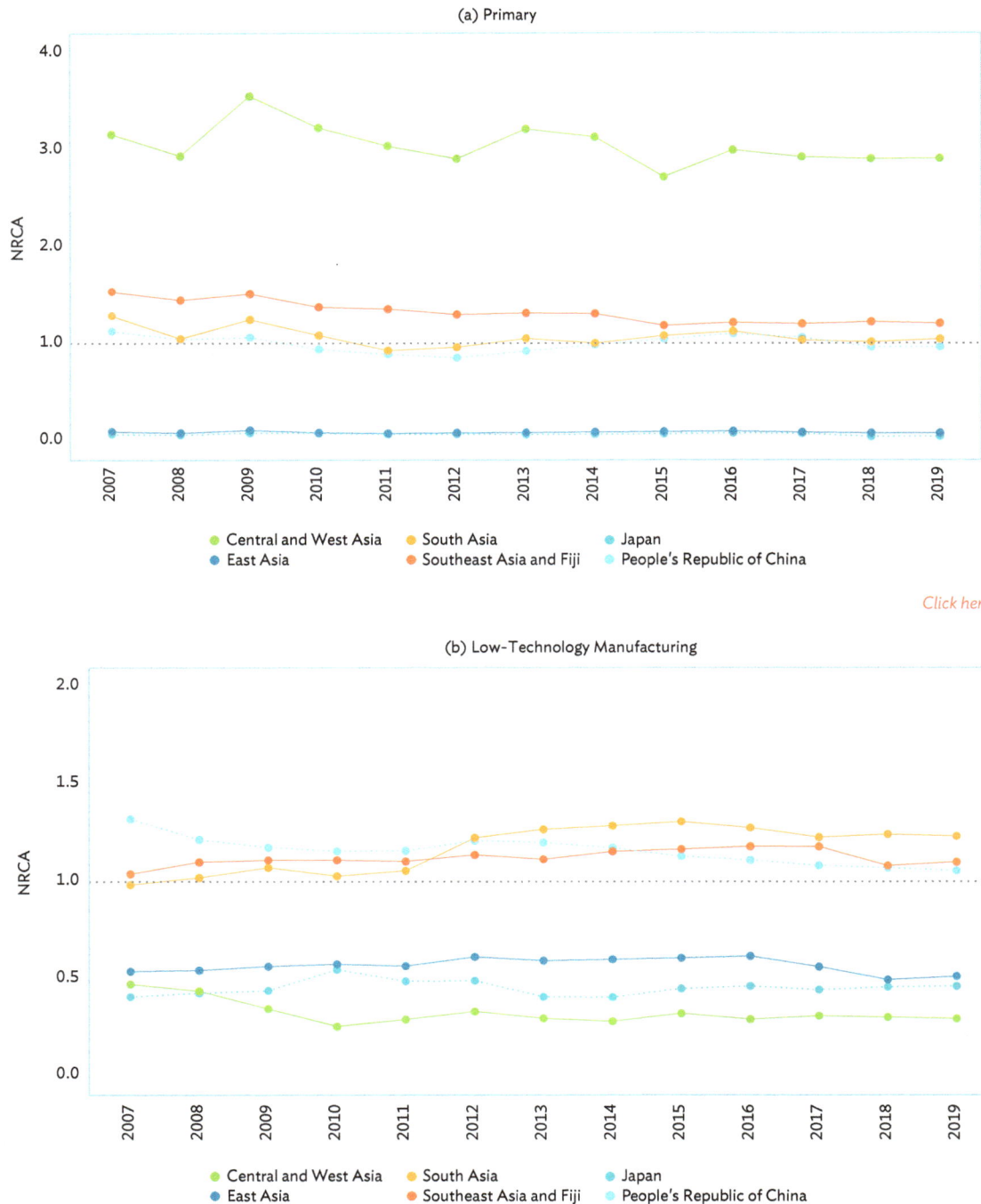

(a) Primary

Click here for figure data

(b) Low-Technology Manufacturing

continued on next page

Click here for figure data

Figure 3.1.2: continued

(c) Medium- and High-Technology Manufacturing

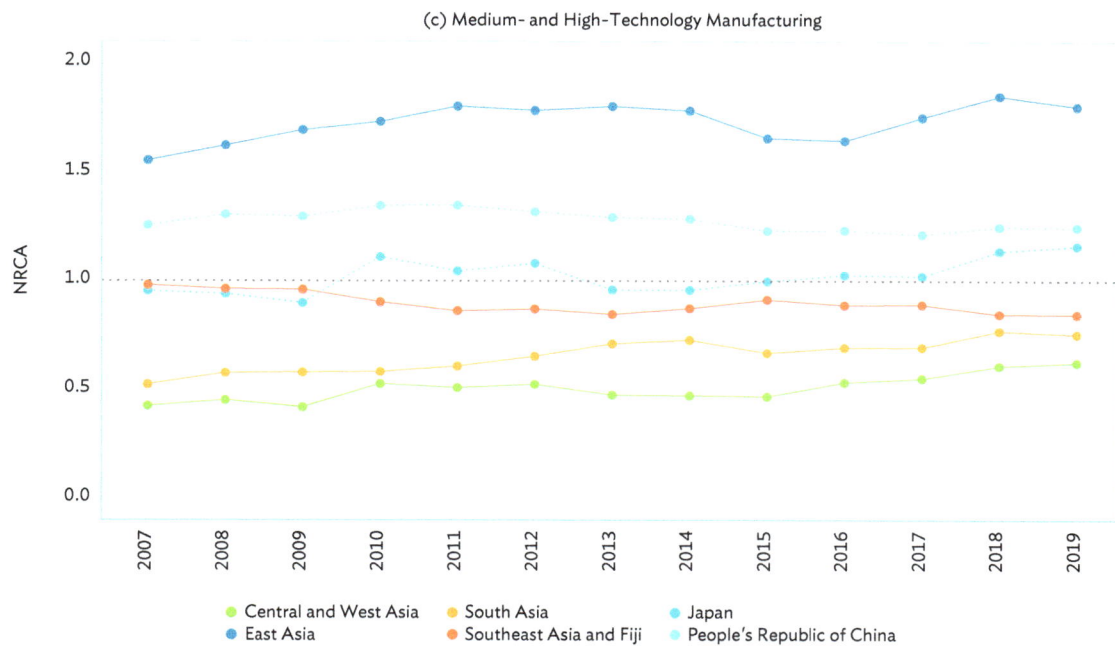

Click here for figure data

(d) Business Services

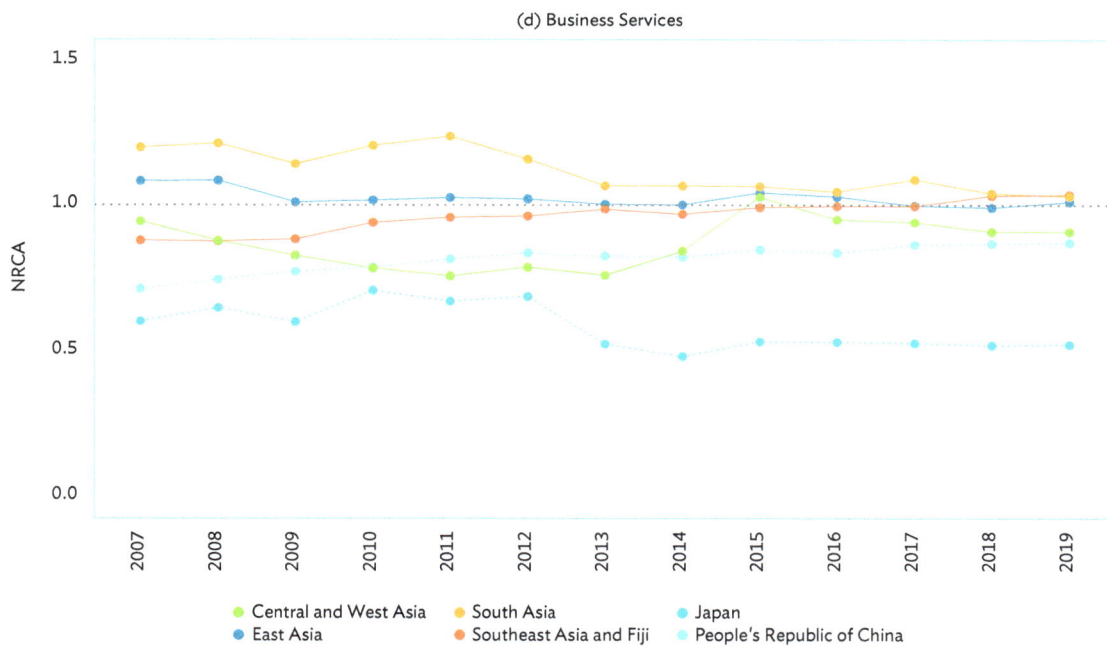

Click here for figure data

Figure 3.1.2: continued

(e) Personal and Public Services

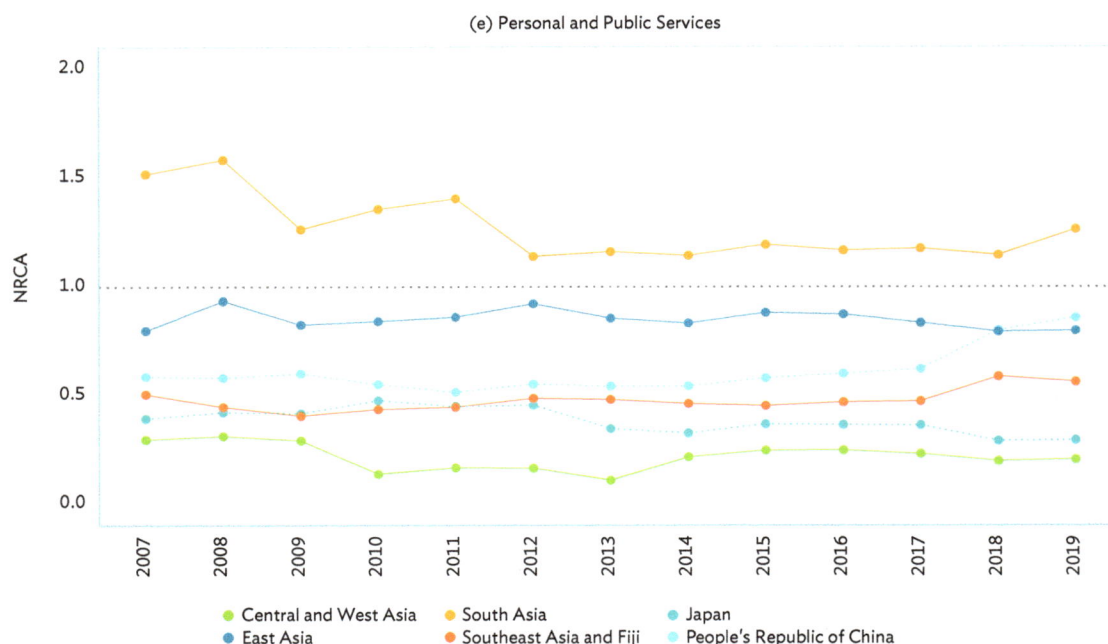

NRCA = new revealed comparative advantage.

Note: Central and West Asia = Kazakhstan, Kyrgyz Republic, and Mongolia. East Asia = Hong Kong, China; Republic of Korea; and Taipei,China. South Asia = Bangladesh, Bhutan, India, Maldives, Nepal, Pakistan, and Sri Lanka. Southeast Asia and Fiji = Brunei Darussalam, Cambodia, Indonesia, Fiji, Lao People's Democratic Republic, Malaysia, Philippines, Singapore, Thailand, Viet Nam.

Source: Asian Development Bank estimates based on the methodology of Balassa (1965) and Wang, Wei, and Zhu (2018) using Asian Development Bank Multi-Regional Input-Output Tables (2007-2019).

Click here for figure data

Varying levels of competitiveness can be observed when the analysis is extended to the comparative advantage of Asian economies in the electrical and optical equipment sector. From 2000 to 2019, Taipei,China maintained its place as the most competitive economy for the electricals and optical equipment sector, having an unchanged NRCA of 3.1. Meanwhile, Viet Nam registered a notable increase in its NRCA, from 0.1 to 0.6. While still not technically holding a comparative advantage, it did rise several places to overtake such manufacturing hubs as India, Indonesia, and Thailand. This reflects how Viet Nam is increasingly becoming a destination for businesses relocating from the PRC. Nevertheless, over the same period the PRC's index rose to become comparable to Japan's. Among those whose ranking worsened was the Philippines, whose NRCA declined from 2.8 in 2000 to 1.4 in 2019, corresponding to a fall from second of 25 economies to seventh.

Meanwhile, the Philippines more than made up for its decline in electrical and optical equipment with its steep ascent in the business services sector, mostly through renting of machinery and equipment and other business services. Its NRCA here, which rose from 0.6 to 1.0, catapulted it to sixth place in 2019, driven by the expansion of its BPO industry since the 2000s. More importantly, this indicates that the success of the BPO industry in the Philippines meant not only a growth in the gross exports of low-level BPO services, but also a rise in high-value-added BPO services. This finding is distinct compared to the competitiveness of the BPO industry in India, which is a BPO giant. India's BPO sector registered a stagnant NRCA of 1.0, causing it to move down in the NRCA rankings. Elsewhere, Pakistan experienced a tremendous decline in NRCA, falling from fourth place in 2000 to the bottom 10 in 2019.

Figure 3.1.3: New Revealed Comparative Advantage of Asian Economies, 2000, 2010, and 2019

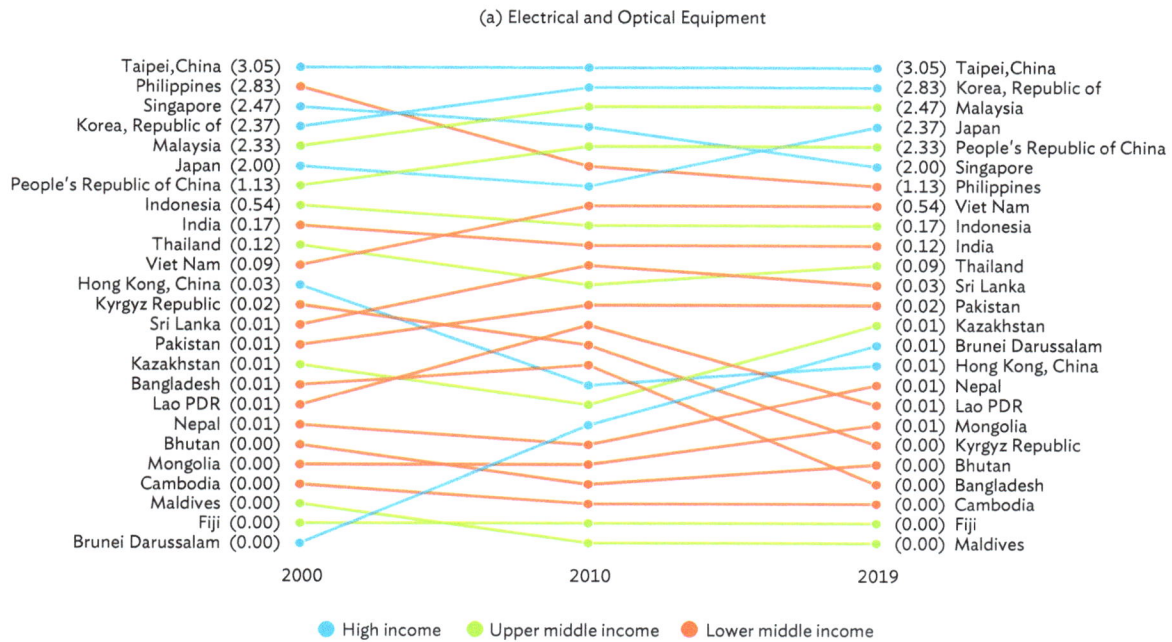

(a) Electrical and Optical Equipment

2000		2019
Taipei,China (3.05)		(3.05) Taipei,China
Philippines (2.83)		(2.83) Korea, Republic of
Singapore (2.47)		(2.47) Malaysia
Korea, Republic of (2.37)		(2.37) Japan
Malaysia (2.33)		(2.33) People's Republic of China
Japan (2.00)		(2.00) Singapore
People's Republic of China (1.13)		(1.13) Philippines
Indonesia (0.54)		(0.54) Viet Nam
India (0.17)		(0.17) Indonesia
Thailand (0.12)		(0.12) India
Viet Nam (0.09)		(0.09) Thailand
Hong Kong, China (0.03)		(0.03) Sri Lanka
Kyrgyz Republic (0.02)		(0.02) Pakistan
Sri Lanka (0.01)		(0.01) Kazakhstan
Pakistan (0.01)		(0.01) Brunei Darussalam
Kazakhstan (0.01)		(0.01) Hong Kong, China
Bangladesh (0.01)		(0.01) Nepal
Lao PDR (0.01)		(0.01) Lao PDR
Nepal (0.01)		(0.01) Mongolia
Bhutan (0.00)		(0.00) Kyrgyz Republic
Mongolia (0.00)		(0.00) Bhutan
Cambodia (0.00)		(0.00) Bangladesh
Maldives (0.00)		(0.00) Cambodia
Fiji (0.00)		(0.00) Fiji
Brunei Darussalam (0.00)		(0.00) Maldives

● High income ● Upper middle income ● Lower middle income

Click here for figure data

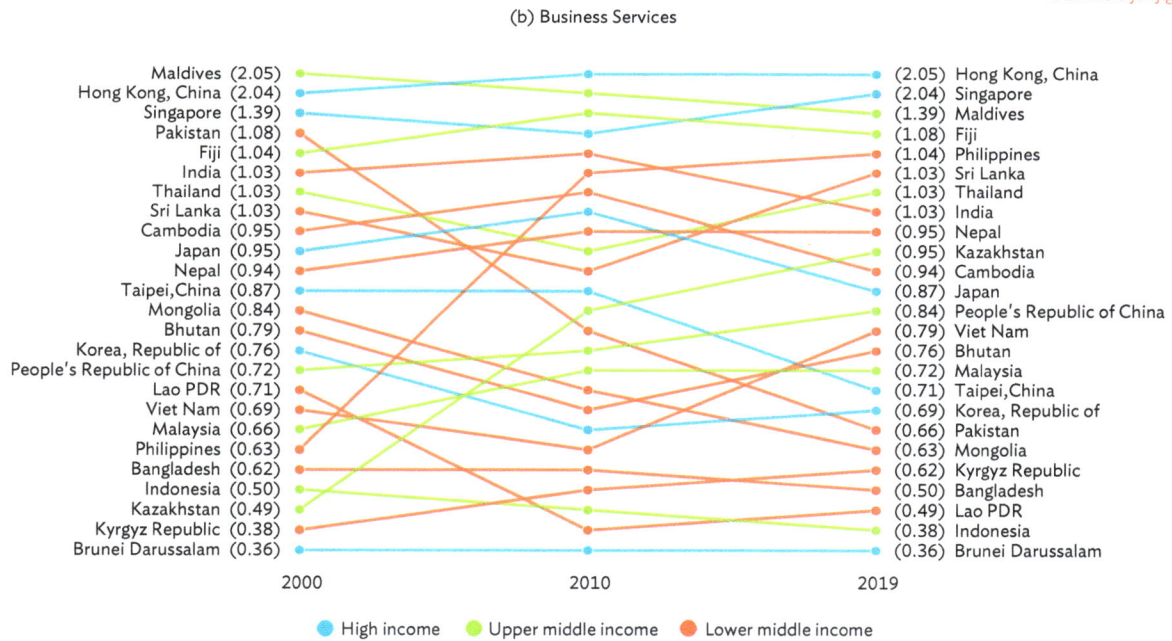

(b) Business Services

2000		2019
Maldives (2.05)		(2.05) Hong Kong, China
Hong Kong, China (2.04)		(2.04) Singapore
Singapore (1.39)		(1.39) Maldives
Pakistan (1.08)		(1.08) Fiji
Fiji (1.04)		(1.04) Philippines
India (1.03)		(1.03) Sri Lanka
Thailand (1.03)		(1.03) Thailand
Sri Lanka (1.03)		(1.03) India
Cambodia (0.95)		(0.95) Nepal
Japan (0.95)		(0.95) Kazakhstan
Nepal (0.94)		(0.94) Cambodia
Taipei,China (0.87)		(0.87) Japan
Mongolia (0.84)		(0.84) People's Republic of China
Bhutan (0.79)		(0.79) Viet Nam
Korea, Republic of (0.76)		(0.76) Bhutan
People's Republic of China (0.72)		(0.72) Malaysia
Lao PDR (0.71)		(0.71) Taipei,China
Viet Nam (0.69)		(0.69) Korea, Republic of
Malaysia (0.66)		(0.66) Pakistan
Philippines (0.63)		(0.63) Mongolia
Bangladesh (0.62)		(0.62) Kyrgyz Republic
Indonesia (0.50)		(0.50) Bangladesh
Kazakhstan (0.49)		(0.49) Lao PDR
Kyrgyz Republic (0.38)		(0.38) Indonesia
Brunei Darussalam (0.36)		(0.36) Brunei Darussalam

● High income ● Upper middle income ● Lower middle income

Lao PDR = Lao People's Democratic Republic.
Note: New revealed comparative advantage indices are in parentheses. Income categories were sourced from the World Bank.
Source: Asian Development Bank estimates based on the methodology of Balassa (1965) and Wang, Wei, and Zhu (2018) using Asian Development Bank Multi-Regional Input-Output Tables (2000, 2010, and 2019).

Click here for figure data

Competitiveness Under Global Value Chains: Opportunities and Challenges

By slicing up the production process so that economies can specialize in particular stages, GVCs have allowed more space for competition. Economies such as the PRC and Viet Nam have gained from serving as assembly hubs for global manufacturing, whereas others such as India and the Philippines have dominated the more service-oriented parts of production through BPOs. These would not be possible without the intensified trade in intermediate inputs seen under GVCs.

However, extended supply chains pose risks of their own. Financial crises, international trade tensions, and the COVID-19 pandemic all show that GVC participation, while holding many opportunities, also brings with it the potential for increased uncertainty. This is borne out by the robust positive correlation between GVC participation—measured as the share of output engaged in GVCs according to the framework of Wang, Wei, Yu, and Zhu (2017)—and volatility in the NRCA. That is, the more an economy–sector engages in GVCs relative to its economic size, the more its competitiveness tends to fluctuate. On average, a 10 percentage-point increase in GVC participation is associated with a 0.06-point increase in the NRCA's standard deviation.

This relationship is displayed in Figure 3.1.4 for two sectors. Electricals and optical equipment, being the classic GVC-linked sector, is again shown, along with water transport, a subsector under business services with high rates of GVC involvement. Both panels of the figure exhibit the positive relationship between GVC participation and NRCA volatility.

In the electricals and optical equipment sector, the highest NRCA volatilities were seen in Taipei,China and the Philippines at 0.35 and 0.39, respectively. Both of these had average GVC participation rates of over 50%. In water transport, the port-city of Singapore was at the extreme: its RCA volatility was 1.1 while its GVC participation was 82%. These are average relationships, however, and cases exist that go against them. For instance, Hong Kong, China, whose electricals and optical equipment sector participates in GVCs at the rate of 68%, registered negligible RCA volatility. Similarly, Viet Nam's water transport sector, participating at the rate of 40%, had volatility of just 0.04.

While it is premature to treat the relationship as causal in either direction, it is safe to say that exposure to GVCs does tend to involve greater fluctuations in trading patterns, especially for smaller economies. It would therefore do well for policymakers to consider strategies to mitigate such uncertainty. For example, diversifying trading partners means that one's economy will not rise and fall with the fortunes of a single export destination or import source.

Figure 3.1.4: Global Value Chain Participation and Volatility in the Revealed Comparative Advantage Index, 2007–2019

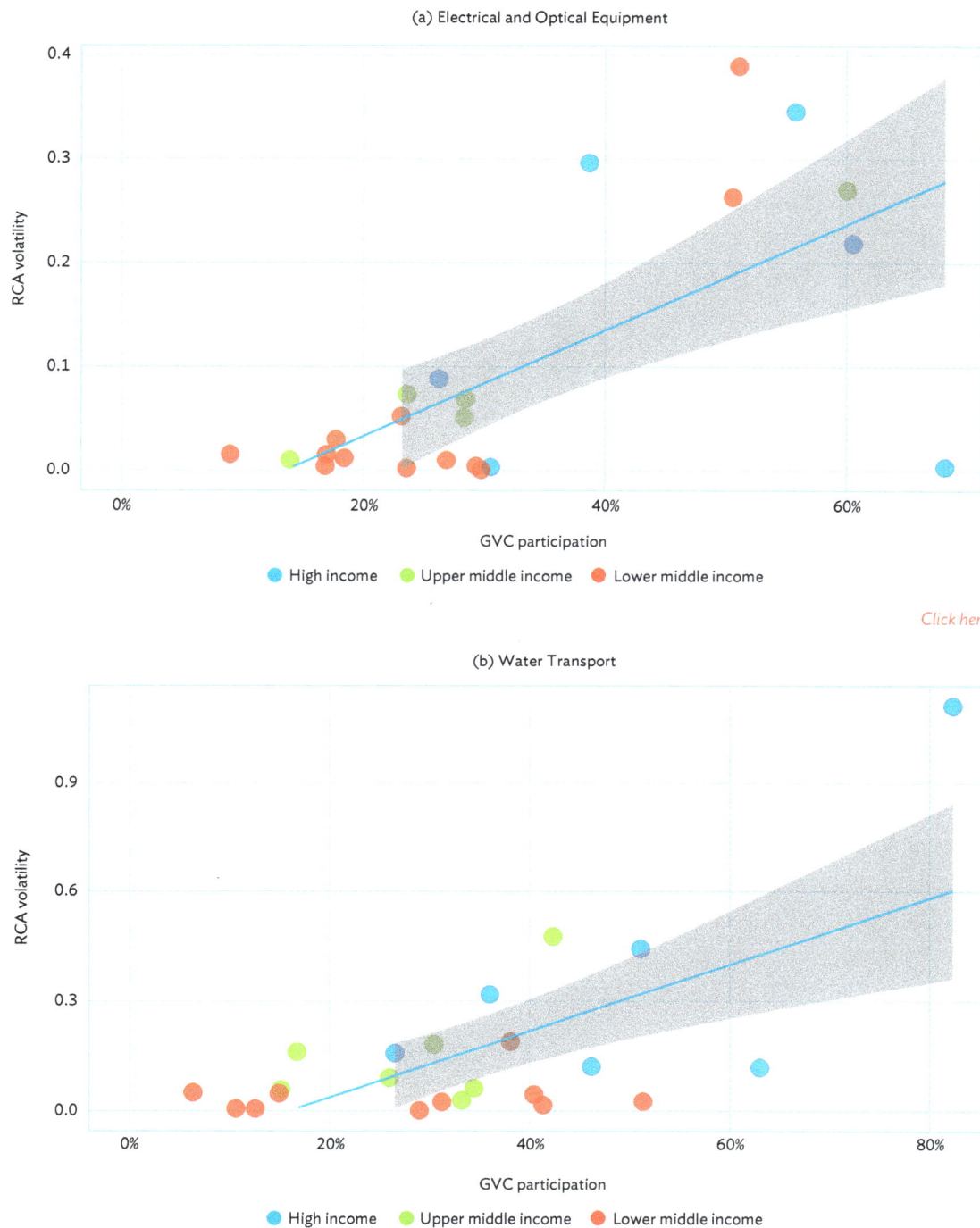

(a) Electrical and Optical Equipment

Click here for figure data

(b) Water Transport

GVC = global value chain, RCA = revealed comparative advantage.
Notes: Income categories were from the World Bank. RCA volatility is the standard deviation of the New RCA index over 2007–2019.
         GVC participation is the average of the forward and backward rates over 2007–2019.
Source: Asian Development Bank estimates based on the methodology of Balassa (1965) and Wang, Wei, and Zhu (2018) using Asian Development
         Bank Multi-Regional Input-Output Tables (2007–2019).

Click here for figure data

Conclusion

While GVCs remain as entrenched as ever, they are undergoing profound changes. Global trade is already showing signs of dismantling following the international trade tensions that arose at the beginning of 2018. This occurred 10 years after another trade-destabilizing event, the 2008 financial crisis. The COVID-19 pandemic is expected to further disrupt and shorten many supply chains. Nevertheless, this chapter has shown that Asia and the Pacific has come a long way in linking its economies to GVCs since 2000. The region is learning to produce goods, not just assemble them, and to participate in GVCs so that economies can specialize in those activities where they have comparative advantage, thereby augmenting their income and allowing them to upgrade their production. Recognizing this as crucial to economic growth, a key strategy of developing economies is to invest in their comparative advantages, or areas where they produce relatively more efficiently than other economies. However, these economies must keep in mind that GVCs—and globalization in general—can create both opportunities and risks. Not all economies benefit in GVCs and participating in such chains can create vulnerabilities to the volatile global trade environment.

References

B. Balassa. 1965. Trade Liberalisation and "Revealed" Comparative Advantage. *The Manchester School*. 33(2). pp. 99–123.

V. Mercer-Blackman and C. Ablaza. 2018. The Servicification of Manufacturing in Asia: Redefining the Sources of Labor Productivity. *ADBI Working Paper Series No. 902*. Tokyo, Japan: Asian Development Bank Institute.

Z. Wang, S. Wei, X. Yu, and K. Zhu. 2017. Measures of Participation in Global Value Chains and Global Business Cycles. *NBER Working Paper No. 23222*. Cambridge, MA: National Bureau of Economic Research.

Z. Wang, S. Wei, and K. Zhu. 2018. Quantifying International Production Sharing at the Bilateral and Sector Levels. *NBER Working Paper No. 19677*. Cambridge, MA: National Bureau of Economic Research.

Global Value Chain Tables for Economies of Asia and the Pacific

ADB Regional Member	Table 3.2.1.a: Value-Added Decomposition of Exports—Primary Sector				
	Exports	VAX_G	RDV_B	FVA	PDC
	($ million)	(% share in exports)			
Bangladesh					
2009	361.74	93.70	0.07	4.97	1.26
2019	654.15	90.99	0.07	8.00	0.94
Bhutan					
2009	108.93	94.29	0.02	5.04	0.66
2019	133.13	95.23	0.02	4.07	0.68
Brunei Darussalam					
2009	3,659.50	91.46	0.01	5.38	3.14
2019	4,231.58	85.84	0.02	7.91	6.23
Cambodia					
2009	232.53	90.46	0.14	6.98	2.42
2019	1,324.66	86.40	0.07	10.91	2.62
China, People's Republic of					
2009	19,586.92	88.55	2.75	5.89	2.82
2019	25,848.57	89.35	3.95	4.48	2.23
Fiji					
2009	125.67	80.27	0.00	16.97	2.75
2019	204.67	78.64	0.00	17.66	3.70
Hong Kong, China					
2009	84.55	55.47	0.08	34.63	9.82
2019	100.41	56.68	0.11	30.52	12.69
India					
2009	18,740.98	95.58	0.80	2.59	1.03
2019	28,348.22	94.99	0.93	2.98	1.10
Indonesia					
2009	36,377.02	94.75	0.63	2.65	1.96
2019	31,567.29	95.53	0.61	2.30	1.56
Japan					
2009	2,356.48	83.13	1.82	10.47	4.58
2019	1,611.23	86.23	1.30	9.10	3.38
Kazakhstan					
2009	25,743.65	89.25	0.20	6.09	4.46
2019	27,670.46	85.89	0.10	7.80	6.21
Korea, Republic of					
2009	637.96	84.34	0.26	13.18	2.23
2019	746.91	84.10	0.49	12.03	3.38
Kyrgyz Republic					
2009	371.74	74.19	0.01	19.74	6.06
2019	441.73	81.72	0.03	14.55	3.70
Lao People's Democratic Republic					
2009	561.34	93.54	0.01	4.72	1.73
2019	1,637.05	92.32	0.07	4.46	3.15

continued on next page

Table 3.2.1.a: continued

Table 3.2.1.a: Value-Added Decomposition of Exports—Primary Sector					
ADB Regional Member	**Exports**	**VAX_G**	**RDV_B**	**FVA**	**PDC**
	($ million)	(% share in exports)			
Malaysia					
2009	18,625.49	85.39	0.40	8.80	5.41
2019	13,348.32	88.11	0.60	5.96	5.33
Maldives					
2009	38.48	53.95	0.01	38.94	7.10
2019	24.78	63.64	0.01	30.46	5.88
Mongolia					
2009	1,358.81	80.46	0.01	13.55	5.98
2019	6,094.31	78.30	0.02	16.38	5.30
Nepal					
2009	136.87	91.53	0.03	7.96	0.48
2019	81.21	90.38	0.07	8.84	0.71
Pakistan					
2009	1,727.14	96.05	0.06	3.06	0.83
2019	2,146.36	94.97	0.04	4.10	0.90
Philippines					
2009	973.80	91.68	0.18	6.24	1.90
2019	2,189.60	86.97	0.18	10.50	2.35
Singapore					
2009	47.71	71.83	0.03	22.31	5.84
2019	59.36	64.35	0.12	25.67	9.86
Sri Lanka					
2009	688.54	89.70	0.05	8.48	1.78
2019	624.53	90.55	0.03	7.51	1.91
Taipei,China					
2009	1,215.17	77.14	0.09	19.92	2.86
2019	1,601.03	77.05	0.08	19.59	3.28
Thailand					
2009	2,974.08	84.36	0.20	12.21	3.23
2019	11,987.94	87.96	0.14	9.71	2.18
Viet Nam					
2009	8,342.62	68.81	0.23	21.30	9.66
2019	29,740.65	77.01	0.37	16.62	6.00

0.00 = magnitude is less than half of unit employed, $ = United States dollars, FVA = foreign value-added, ADB = Asian Development Bank, PDC = pure double counted terms, RDV_B =domestic value-added first exported then returned home, VAX_G = domestic value-added absorbed abroad.

Source: Asian Development Bank. Multi-Regional Input–Output Tables Database. https://mrio.adbx.online/ (accessed 1 August 2020).

Click here to download the table.

ADB Regional Member	Exports	VAX_G	RDV_B	FVA	PDC
	($ million)	(% share in exports)			

Table 3.2.1.b: Value-Added Decomposition of Exports—Low-Technology Manufacturing Sector

ADB Regional Member	Exports ($ million)	VAX_G	RDV_B	FVA	PDC
Bangladesh					
2009	14,073.48	84.48	0.01	14.71	0.81
2019	38,841.44	79.25	0.03	18.56	2.16
Bhutan					
2009	223.23	80.05	0.00	14.21	5.74
2019	240.36	75.07	0.00	15.69	9.24
Brunei Darussalam					
2009	33.43	56.17	0.00	37.69	6.14
2019	129.10	47.29	0.01	42.17	10.54
Cambodia					
2009	1,934.42	68.74	0.00	29.21	2.05
2019	6,651.78	62.50	0.00	35.01	2.49
China, People's Republic of					
2009	312,667.79	86.07	0.60	12.22	1.11
2019	591,144.59	88.30	1.46	8.93	1.30
Fiji					
2009	296.75	70.70	0.00	25.77	3.53
2019	454.93	69.38	0.00	26.49	4.13
Hong Kong, China					
2009	6,314.96	65.66	0.06	29.43	4.84
2019	6,465.05	56.91	0.07	36.02	7.00
India					
2009	42,679.73	83.56	0.27	14.46	1.71
2019	93,715.13	82.67	0.31	14.74	2.28
Indonesia					
2009	49,516.69	84.78	0.18	12.57	2.47
2019	76,165.22	85.00	0.14	12.49	2.37
Japan					
2009	39,964.75	87.82	1.47	7.79	2.93
2019	54,330.61	84.08	0.92	11.27	3.72
Kazakhstan					
2009	1,006.48	83.55	0.14	12.84	3.48
2019	1,479.83	79.22	0.20	16.58	4.00
Korea, Republic of					
2009	30,463.69	72.74	0.27	22.33	4.66
2019	38,665.17	73.53	0.36	21.19	4.92
Kyrgyz Republic					
2009	251.69	66.22	0.01	29.03	4.74
2019	382.56	68.61	0.02	28.42	2.95
Lao People's Democratic Republic					
2009	382.87	80.13	0.00	16.13	3.73
2019	3,491.33	78.22	0.01	15.57	6.20
Malaysia					
2009	47,892.74	65.53	0.12	29.38	4.96
2019	39,252.36	73.41	0.22	19.71	6.67

continued on next page

Table 3.2.1.b: continued

Table 3.2.1.b: Value-Added Decomposition of Exports—Low-Technology Manufacturing Sector					
ADB Regional Member	Exports	VAX_G	RDV_B	FVA	PDC
	($ million)	(% share in exports)			
Maldives					
2009	145.01	51.04	0.00	41.93	7.03
2019	203.00	59.22	0.00	35.23	5.55
Mongolia					
2009	153.35	72.77	0.01	23.21	4.01
2019	362.40	67.55	0.02	27.19	5.24
Nepal					
2009	328.75	76.53	0.01	21.17	2.28
2019	297.72	72.87	0.03	23.74	3.36
Pakistan					
2009	18,302.05	86.47	0.03	11.72	1.78
2019	15,097.64	83.02	0.03	14.65	2.30
Philippines					
2009	8,666.30	85.19	0.05	12.42	2.34
2019	21,564.94	76.50	0.08	20.22	3.19
Singapore					
2009	6,871.04	57.46	0.06	35.83	6.66
2019	13,753.14	52.19	0.08	38.92	8.81
Sri Lanka					
2009	5,176.48	80.26	0.02	17.57	2.15
2019	5,618.05	84.57	0.01	13.89	1.53
Taipei,China					
2009	18,093.26	63.84	0.11	29.74	6.31
2019	24,491.09	59.50	0.10	32.84	7.57
Thailand					
2009	28,435.94	72.08	0.11	23.36	4.45
2019	47,678.96	77.89	0.11	17.93	4.07
Viet Nam					
2009	25,226.70	66.08	0.03	30.90	2.99
2019	130,942.32	66.89	0.12	28.97	4.03

0.00 = magnitude is less than half of unit employed, $ = United States dollars, FVA = foreign value-added, ADB = Asian Development Bank, PDC = pure double counted terms, RDV_B =domestic value-added first exported then returned home, VAX_G = domestic value-added absorbed abroad.

Source: Asian Development Bank. Multi-Regional Input–Output Tables Database. https://mrio.adbx.online/ (accessed 1 August 2020).

Click here to download the table.

Table 3.2.1.c: Value-Added Decomposition of Exports—Medium- and High-Technology Manufacturing Sector

ADB Regional Member	Exports ($ million)	VAX_G	RDV_B	FVA	PDC
			(% share in exports)		
Bangladesh					
2009	467.70	84.82	0.07	12.41	2.69
2019	827.59	87.10	0.07	11.15	1.68
Bhutan					
2009	78.51	76.99	0.01	21.42	1.58
2019	99.74	74.79	0.01	22.93	2.26
Brunei Darussalam					
2009	2,680.71	88.59	0.01	8.64	2.76
2019	2,885.49	86.31	0.01	9.64	4.04
Cambodia					
2009	22.04	72.56	0.01	23.47	3.96
2019	122.94	65.81	0.03	29.05	5.11
China, People's Republic of					
2009	738,733.23	79.26	1.65	15.31	3.78
2019	1,522,122.85	82.03	2.98	11.08	3.92
Fiji					
2009	43.31	61.65	0.01	33.28	5.06
2019	53.49	61.99	0.00	34.54	3.47
Hong Kong, China					
2009	6,719.50	24.59	0.04	54.59	20.79
2019	10,889.83	13.05	0.02	61.35	25.57
India					
2009	69,501.64	68.02	0.57	21.44	9.97
2019	187,077.09	70.08	0.57	20.82	8.53
Indonesia					
2009	43,911.43	81.45	0.40	13.00	5.16
2019	87,780.20	81.53	0.40	12.26	5.81
Japan					
2009	443,265.16	81.03	1.22	13.11	4.63
2019	679,745.02	76.08	0.81	17.12	5.99
Kazakhstan					
2009	8,206.43	85.00	0.24	8.60	6.16
2019	14,258.37	85.42	0.17	7.10	7.31
Korea, Republic of					
2009	344,984.88	62.73	0.29	29.45	7.53
2019	530,279.01	65.33	0.38	25.57	8.72
Kyrgyz Republic					
2009	667.25	71.15	0.01	20.86	7.98
2019	986.85	77.00	0.02	13.56	9.42
Lao People's Democratic Republic					
2009	19.42	70.62	0.01	24.24	5.13
2019	38.61	78.13	0.07	14.58	7.22
Malaysia					
2009	90,839.02	45.64	0.16	41.05	13.16
2019	149,181.14	58.36	0.33	26.50	14.80

continued on next page

Table 3.2.1.c: continued

Table 3.2.1.c: Value-Added Decomposition of Exports—Medium- and High-Technology Manufacturing Sector					
ADB Regional Member	**Exports**	**VAX_G**	**RDV_B**	**FVA**	**PDC**
	($ million)	(% share in exports)			
Maldives					
2009	11.20	52.83	0.00	43.79	3.39
2019	3.56	63.61	0.00	31.37	5.01
Mongolia					
2009	44.10	65.27	0.01	24.69	10.02
2019	246.42	71.17	0.01	21.52	7.30
Nepal					
2009	97.70	62.39	0.09	32.60	4.92
2019	119.31	58.80	0.18	34.69	6.33
Pakistan					
2009	1,630.18	72.99	0.05	21.21	5.75
2019	1,717.46	71.20	0.05	22.55	6.20
Philippines					
2009	18,770.65	60.22	0.15	24.38	15.26
2019	35,891.66	43.88	0.17	36.84	19.12
Singapore					
2009	116,221.04	38.16	0.07	45.86	15.91
2019	191,393.99	41.04	0.14	43.75	15.07
Sri Lanka					
2009	1,065.70	64.57	0.02	27.97	7.43
2019	517.63	55.44	0.03	35.55	8.98
Taipei,China					
2009	178,433.50	54.69	0.17	32.45	12.68
2019	286,377.50	53.45	0.19	31.78	14.58
Thailand					
2009	74,769.53	57.31	0.19	30.63	11.88
2019	108,159.37	61.73	0.18	27.41	10.67
Viet Nam					
2009	8,401.61	55.21	0.14	31.18	13.48
2019	57,319.87	46.55	0.24	36.60	16.61

0.00 = magnitude is less than half of unit employed, $ = United States dollars, FVA = foreign value-added, ADB = Asian Development Bank, PDC = pure double counted terms, RDV_B =domestic value-added first exported then returned home, VAX_G = domestic value-added absorbed abroad.

Source: Asian Development Bank. Multi-Regional Input–Output Tables Database. https://mrio.adbx.online/ (accessed 1 August 2020).

Click here to download the table.

ADB Regional Member	Exports	VAX_G	RDV_B	FVA	PDC
	($ million)	(% share in exports)			
Bangladesh					
2009	2,053.95	94.71	0.02	4.61	0.65
2019	2,916.65	94.08	0.07	4.99	0.86
Bhutan					
2009	51.85	80.55	0.00	15.96	3.49
2019	240.10	81.28	0.01	13.94	4.77
Brunei Darussalam					
2009	484.36	77.06	0.00	19.78	3.15
2019	496.80	73.79	0.01	20.94	5.26
Cambodia					
2009	1,219.88	81.76	0.01	15.13	3.11
2019	4,204.31	79.43	0.01	16.16	4.40
China, People's Republic of					
2009	222,237.60	90.70	2.01	5.47	1.82
2019	428,627.28	90.29	4.54	3.52	1.65
Fiji					
2009	954.99	72.94	0.01	22.93	4.13
2019	1,645.14	75.92	0.01	20.11	3.96
Hong Kong, China					
2009	111,358.09	80.35	0.10	16.97	2.59
2019	184,827.04	78.90	0.11	17.98	3.01
India					
2009	85,126.30	92.36	0.62	5.66	1.36
2019	129,071.07	87.50	0.55	9.67	2.29
Indonesia					
2009	7,819.28	91.26	0.22	6.99	1.53
2019	8,781.69	89.03	0.19	9.01	1.76
Japan					
2009	152,194.79	95.23	1.09	2.90	0.78
2019	149,660.49	94.31	0.91	3.63	1.16
Kazakhstan					
2009	12,384.87	87.95	0.50	9.04	2.51
2019	18,034.81	88.00	0.53	8.25	3.21
Korea, Republic of					
2009	36,479.80	88.83	0.40	8.39	2.37
2019	79,734.76	86.16	0.45	10.40	3.00
Kyrgyz Republic					
2009	309.89	77.34	0.02	17.77	4.87
2019	394.75	78.31	0.03	16.60	5.07
Lao People's Democratic Republic					
2009	178.84	84.38	0.01	12.27	3.35
2019	904.53	88.69	0.02	8.51	2.78
Malaysia					
2009	23,765.36	79.04	0.19	16.78	3.99
2019	34,688.54	82.31	0.22	12.83	4.64

Table 3.2.1.d: Value-Added Decomposition of Exports—Business Services Sector

continued on next page

.

:

Now.

Table 3.2.1.d: continued

Table 3.2.1.d: Value-Added Decomposition of Exports—Business Services Sector					
ADB Regional Member	Exports ($ million)	VAX_G	RDV_B	FVA	PDC
		(% share in exports)			
Maldives					
2009	1,695.95	65.01	0.00	28.55	6.44
2019	3,181.35	67.44	0.00	25.03	7.53
Mongolia					
2009	496.58	79.29	0.01	16.14	4.56
2019	1,747.62	73.13	0.03	19.57	7.27
Nepal					
2009	542.93	84.55	0.01	12.50	2.93
2019	578.07	86.16	0.07	10.80	2.97
Pakistan					
2009	4,394.01	90.85	0.07	7.11	1.97
2019	4,669.95	90.98	0.07	6.67	2.27
Philippines					
2009	14,566.86	91.80	0.08	6.36	1.76
2019	46,022.05	87.70	0.14	9.34	2.82
Singapore					
2009	102,316.26	66.71	0.07	25.98	7.24
2019	264,358.39	62.09	0.17	27.87	9.87
Sri Lanka					
2009	4,185.65	84.49	0.02	12.29	3.20
2019	5,486.56	91.27	0.02	6.65	2.06
Taipei,China					
2009	37,516.29	88.32	0.23	8.89	2.56
2019	78,299.67	85.42	0.27	10.93	3.39
Thailand					
2009	16,010.23	82.13	0.12	14.84	2.91
2019	92,825.96	87.98	0.13	9.67	2.21
Viet Nam					
2009	8,107.19	77.18	0.05	19.31	3.46
2019	40,944.88	83.37	0.18	13.16	3.29

0.00 = magnitude is less than half of unit employed, $ = United States dollars, FVA = foreign value-added, ADB = Asian Development Bank, PDC = pure double counted terms, RDV_B =domestic value-added first exported then returned home, VAX_G = domestic value-added absorbed abroad.

Source: Asian Development Bank. Multi-Regional Input–Output Tables Database. https://mrio.adbx.online/ (accessed 1 August 2020).

Click here to download the table.

Table 3.2.1.e: Value-Added Decomposition of Exports—Personal Services Sector					
ADB Regional Member	**Exports**	**VAX_G**	**RDV_B**	**FVA**	**PDC**
	($ million)	(% share in exports)			
Bangladesh					
2009	343.55	95.72	0.03	3.02	1.23
2019	2,892.91	94.35	0.12	3.26	2.26
Bhutan					
2009	5.09	87.14	0.00	10.85	2.02
2019	26.33	86.47	0.00	11.18	2.35
Brunei Darussalam					
2009	60.42	83.70	0.00	15.06	1.24
2019	61.91	75.65	0.00	21.33	3.01
Cambodia					
2009	77.31	87.79	0.01	9.85	2.36
2019	152.38	82.48	0.01	14.11	3.40
China, People's Republic of					
2009	10,283.39	90.78	0.71	7.28	1.23
2019	21,995.37	91.79	2.02	5.12	1.06
Fiji					
2009	82.81	80.10	0.00	18.17	1.73
2019	56.00	86.27	0.00	12.82	0.91
Hong Kong, China					
2009	989.45	88.08	0.14	9.75	2.04
2019	1,187.35	87.47	0.12	10.19	2.22
India					
2009	6,982.95	97.31	0.00	2.67	0.01
2019	14,388.48	97.69	0.01	2.30	0.01
Indonesia					
2009	1,607.74	90.55	0.13	8.07	1.24
2019	1,720.81	91.65	0.24	6.70	1.41
Japan					
2009	3,589.61	94.99	0.59	3.70	0.72
2019	2,876.63	93.20	0.36	5.57	0.87
Kazakhstan					
2009	491.57	85.54	0.02	13.63	0.81
2019	371.73	82.34	0.04	16.65	0.98
Korea, Republic of					
2009	2,783.24	88.84	0.36	8.98	1.82
2019	4,970.12	87.44	0.33	10.20	2.03
Kyrgyz Republic					
2009	99.73	84.24	0.00	13.05	2.71
2019	223.27	87.57	0.01	9.52	2.91
Lao People's Democratic Republic					
2009	7.71	85.63	0.00	12.14	2.24
2019	185.48	90.56	0.01	7.95	1.48
Malaysia					
2009	2,310.77	78.70	0.13	18.39	2.78
2019	1,828.55	83.15	0.04	15.81	1.01

continued on next page

Table 3.2.1.e: continued

Table 3.2.1.e: Value-Added Decomposition of Exports—Personal Services Sector					
ADB Regional Member	**Exports**	**VAX_G**	**RDV_B**	**FVA**	**PDC**
	($ million)	(% share in exports)			
Maldives					
2009	176.74	81.31	0.00	16.93	1.76
2019	91.67	85.75	0.01	10.40	3.85
Mongolia					
2009	32.78	82.17	0.00	14.57	3.25
2019	46.49	75.19	0.01	22.28	2.52
Nepal					
2009	357.93	88.41	0.03	9.49	2.07
2019	514.44	90.03	0.09	7.84	2.04
Pakistan					
2009	1,533.96	85.11	0.02	13.85	1.02
2019	1,249.83	88.31	0.02	10.73	0.94
Philippines					
2009	579.84	91.98	0.05	6.42	1.55
2019	2,348.87	88.60	0.15	8.52	2.73
Singapore					
2009	834.53	74.79	0.10	18.65	6.46
2019	2,330.69	74.06	0.14	19.37	6.43
Sri Lanka					
2009	468.75	88.16	0.01	10.67	1.16
2019	460.79	93.63	0.01	5.69	0.66
Taipei,China					
2009	970.62	89.42	0.07	9.79	0.73
2019	1,289.72	87.76	0.08	11.30	0.87
Thailand					
2009	1,998.12	84.61	0.08	14.14	1.16
2019	8,385.20	88.75	0.07	10.20	0.98
Viet Nam					
2009	340.14	84.03	0.02	15.28	0.68
2019	2,879.97	88.32	0.22	9.68	1.78

0.00 = magnitude is less than half of unit employed, $ = United States dollars, FVA = foreign value-added, ADB = Asian Development Bank, PDC = pure double counted terms, RDV_B =domestic value-added first exported then returned home, VAX_G = domestic value-added absorbed abroad.

Source: Asian Development Bank. Multi-Regional Input–Output Tables Database. https://mrio.adbx.online/ (accessed 1 August 2020).

Click here to download the table.

ADB Regional Member	Exports	VAX_G	RDV_B	FVA	PDC
	($ million)	(% share in exports)			
Bangladesh					
2009	17,300.42	85.82	0.01	13.26	0.90
2019	46,132.73	81.15	0.04	16.71	2.09
Bhutan					
2009	467.60	82.98	0.01	13.44	3.57
2019	739.66	81.08	0.01	13.85	5.06
Brunei Darussalam					
2009	6,918.43	89.11	0.01	7.89	2.99
2019	7,804.89	84.53	0.01	10.05	5.40
Cambodia					
2009	3,486.17	75.19	0.01	22.33	2.46
2019	12,456.08	71.04	0.01	25.77	3.18
China, People's Republic of					
2009	1,303,508.93	83.07	1.47	12.69	2.77
2019	2,589,738.66	84.98	2.89	9.22	2.90
Fiji					
2009	1,503.53	73.18	0.01	23.03	3.79
2019	2,414.23	74.85	0.01	21.26	3.89
Hong Kong, China					
2009	125,466.55	76.67	0.09	19.56	3.68
2019	203,469.68	74.72	0.10	20.84	4.34
India					
2009	223,031.61	83.52	0.53	11.91	4.04
2019	452,599.99	80.09	0.51	14.67	4.72
Indonesia					
2009	139,232.17	86.76	0.37	9.75	3.12
2019	206,015.22	85.36	0.33	10.63	3.68
Japan					
2009	641,370.79	84.91	1.20	10.29	3.59
2019	888,223.99	79.72	0.83	14.43	5.02
Kazakhstan					
2009	47,833.01	88.03	0.28	7.50	4.19
2019	61,815.20	86.22	0.25	8.03	5.50
Korea, Republic of					
2009	415,349.57	65.96	0.30	26.92	6.82
2019	654,395.96	68.54	0.39	23.33	7.74
Kyrgyz Republic					
2009	1,700.29	72.98	0.01	20.80	6.21
2019	2,429.17	77.72	0.02	16.20	6.05
Lao People's Democratic Republic					
2009	1,150.17	87.21	0.01	10.07	2.71
2019	6,257.01	83.79	0.03	11.41	4.77
Malaysia					
2009	183,433.38	59.62	0.18	31.30	8.91
2019	238,298.90	66.18	0.31	22.16	11.35

Table 3.2.1.f: Value-Added Decomposition of Exports—All Sectors

continued on next page

Table 3.2.1.f: continued

ADB Regional Member	Exports ($ million)	VAX_G	RDV_B	FVA	PDC
		(% share in exports)			
Maldives					
2009	2,067.38	65.15	0.00	28.77	6.08
2019	3,504.36	67.41	0.00	25.28	7.30
Mongolia					
2009	2,085.63	79.32	0.01	15.13	5.54
2019	8,497.25	76.56	0.02	17.68	5.74
Nepal					
2009	1,464.17	82.87	0.02	14.63	2.48
2019	1,590.75	83.09	0.08	13.96	2.88
Pakistan					
2009	27,587.35	87.95	0.05	9.97	2.03
2019	24,881.24	84.99	0.04	12.59	2.37
Philippines					
2009	43,557.44	76.88	0.10	15.33	7.69
2019	108,017.12	70.91	0.14	20.65	8.30
Singapore					
2009	226,290.59	51.80	0.07	36.46	11.67
2019	471,895.58	53.32	0.15	34.59	11.93
Sri Lanka					
2009	11,585.11	81.22	0.02	15.80	2.96
2019	12,707.57	86.90	0.01	11.04	2.05
Taipei,China					
2009	236,228.84	60.99	0.18	28.34	10.49
2019	392,059.00	60.42	0.20	27.57	11.81
Thailand					
2009	124,187.91	64.98	0.16	26.22	8.64
2019	269,037.43	75.66	0.15	18.29	5.90
Viet Nam					
2009	50,418.26	66.63	0.08	27.39	5.90
2019	261,827.69	70.67	0.22	22.76	6.34

0.00 = magnitude is less than half of unit employed, $ = United States dollars, FVA = foreign value-added, ADB = Asian Development Bank, PDC = pure double counted terms, RDV_B =domestic value-added first exported then returned home, VAX_G = domestic value-added absorbed abroad.

Source: Asian Development Bank. Multi-Regional Input–Output Tables Database. https://mrio.adbx.online/ (accessed 1 August 2020).

Click here to download the table.

ADB Regional Member	VAX_G	DVA_B	DVA_F	VAX_B	VAX_F
			Value-Added Export Measure to Gross Exports Ratio (%)		
Bangladesh					
2009	93.70	93.77	580.06	93.70	579.95
2019	90.99	91.07	618.31	90.99	618.06
Bhutan					
2009	94.29	94.30	102.18	94.29	102.16
2019	95.23	95.25	108.61	95.23	108.59
Brunei Darussalam					
2009	91.46	91.48	117.68	91.46	117.67
2019	85.84	85.86	109.98	85.84	109.97
Cambodia					
2009	90.46	90.61	215.42	90.46	215.29
2019	86.40	86.49	118.97	86.40	118.90
China, People's Republic of					
2009	88.55	91.67	812.54	88.55	798.53
2019	89.35	93.51	1,165.75	89.35	1,129.62
Fiji					
2009	80.27	80.28	101.15	80.27	101.15
2019	78.64	78.64	99.54	78.64	99.53
Hong Kong, China					
2009	55.47	55.55	57.07	55.47	56.99
2019	56.68	56.80	65.07	56.68	64.95
India					
2009	95.58	96.41	160.23	95.58	159.08
2019	94.99	95.99	176.14	94.99	174.76
Indonesia					
2009	94.75	95.42	133.67	94.75	132.94
2019	95.53	96.17	181.60	95.53	180.73
Japan					
2009	83.13	85.06	424.96	83.13	418.39
2019	86.23	87.60	413.84	86.23	409.25
Kazakhstan					
2009	89.25	89.46	79.57	89.25	79.38
2019	85.89	85.98	74.77	85.89	74.67
Korea, Republic of					
2009	84.34	84.63	815.56	84.34	812.06
2019	84.10	84.63	787.59	84.10	783.27
Kyrgyz Republic					
2009	74.19	74.19	82.13	74.19	82.12
2019	81.72	81.75	61.76	81.72	61.74
Lao People's Democratic Republic					
2009	93.54	93.56	105.06	93.54	105.05
2019	92.32	92.39	112.25	92.32	112.18
Malaysia					
2009	85.39	85.89	159.74	85.39	159.18
2019	88.11	88.87	271.97	88.11	270.54

Table 3.2.2.a: Value-Added Exports by Various Measures—Primary Sector

continued on next page

Table 3.2.2.a: continued

Table 3.2.2.a: Value-Added Exports by Various Measures—Primary Sector					
ADB Regional Member	**VAX_G**	**DVA_B**	**DVA_F**	**VAX_B**	**VAX_F**
	Value-Added Export Measure to Gross Exports Ratio (%)				
Maldives					
2009	53.95	53.97	211.32	53.95	211.31
2019	63.64	63.65	230.46	63.64	230.44
Mongolia					
2009	80.46	80.48	73.67	80.46	73.66
2019	78.30	78.32	61.84	78.30	61.83
Nepal					
2009	91.53	91.56	154.18	91.53	154.13
2019	90.38	90.45	203.66	90.38	203.49
Pakistan					
2009	96.05	96.11	351.93	96.05	351.76
2019	94.97	95.01	334.93	94.97	334.80
Philippines					
2009	91.68	91.87	427.23	91.68	426.61
2019	86.97	87.15	297.83	86.97	297.27
Singapore					
2009	71.83	71.85	114.67	71.83	114.57
2019	64.35	64.50	108.82	64.35	108.57
Sri Lanka					
2009	89.70	89.75	174.05	89.70	173.98
2019	90.55	90.58	142.18	90.55	142.14
Taipei,China					
2009	77.14	77.20	175.38	77.14	175.02
2019	77.05	77.08	171.72	77.05	171.37
Thailand					
2009	84.36	84.58	268.76	84.36	268.13
2019	87.96	88.12	168.77	87.96	168.46
Viet Nam					
2009	68.81	69.08	94.26	68.81	94.06
2019	77.01	77.42	68.97	77.01	68.67

ADB = Asian Development Bank, DVA_B = domestic value-added exports by backward industrial linkages, DVA_F = domestic value-added exports by forward industrial linkages, VAX_B = value-added exports by backward industrial linkages, VAX_F = value-added exports by forward industrial linkages, VAX_G = domestic value-added absorbed abroad.

Source: Asian Development Bank. Multi-Regional Input–Output Tables Database. https://mrio.adbx.online/ (accessed 1 August 2020).

Click here to download the table.

Table 3.2.2.b: Value-Added Exports by Various Measures—Low-Technology Manufacturing Sector

ADB Regional Member	VAX_G	DVA_B	DVA_F	VAX_B	VAX_F
	Value-Added Export Measure to Gross Exports Ratio (%)				
Bangladesh					
2009	84.48	84.49	42.48	84.48	42.48
2019	79.25	79.28	43.17	79.25	43.15
Bhutan					
2009	80.05	80.05	75.50	80.05	75.50
2019	75.07	75.07	66.93	75.07	66.93
Brunei Darussalam					
2009	56.17	56.17	101.40	56.17	101.39
2019	47.29	47.29	37.34	47.29	37.33
Cambodia					
2009	68.74	68.74	48.34	68.74	48.34
2019	62.50	62.50	52.55	62.50	52.55
China, People's Republic of					
2009	86.07	86.53	57.35	86.07	56.66
2019	88.30	89.62	55.50	88.30	54.18
Fiji					
2009	70.70	70.70	54.13	70.70	54.13
2019	69.38	69.38	59.03	69.38	59.02
Hong Kong, China					
2009	65.66	65.72	74.96	65.66	74.88
2019	56.91	56.96	74.97	56.91	74.87
India					
2009	83.56	83.80	51.44	83.56	51.22
2019	82.67	82.95	49.77	82.67	49.54
Indonesia					
2009	84.78	84.93	47.80	84.78	47.68
2019	85.00	85.12	47.57	85.00	47.48
Japan					
2009	87.82	89.35	145.11	87.82	142.94
2019	84.08	85.04	139.85	84.08	138.37
Kazakhstan					
2009	83.55	83.66	190.30	83.55	189.74
2019	79.22	79.38	122.39	79.22	122.04
Korea, Republic of					
2009	72.74	73.04	80.12	72.74	79.78
2019	73.53	73.87	98.52	73.53	97.99
Kyrgyz Republic					
2009	66.22	66.23	56.33	66.22	56.32
2019	68.61	68.63	63.52	68.61	63.50
Lao People's Democratic Republic					
2009	80.13	80.13	45.66	80.13	45.65
2019	78.22	78.24	58.28	78.22	58.27
Malaysia					
2009	65.53	65.64	32.02	65.53	31.96
2019	73.41	73.64	48.33	73.41	48.15

continued on next page

Table 3.2.2.b: continued

Table 3.2.2.b: Value-Added Exports by Various Measures—Low-Technology Manufacturing Sector					
ADB Regional Member	**VAX_G**	**DVA_B**	**DVA_F**	**VAX_B**	**VAX_F**
	Value-Added Export Measure to Gross Exports Ratio (%)				
Maldives					
2009	51.04	51.04	74.99	51.04	74.98
2019	59.22	59.22	244.95	59.22	244.94
Mongolia					
2009	72.77	72.78	57.61	72.77	57.60
2019	67.55	67.57	114.30	67.55	114.27
Nepal					
2009	76.53	76.55	55.78	76.53	55.77
2019	72.87	72.90	61.78	72.87	61.75
Pakistan					
2009	86.47	86.50	34.19	86.47	34.17
2019	83.02	83.05	33.69	83.02	33.67
Philippines					
2009	85.19	85.24	65.94	85.19	65.88
2019	76.50	76.58	62.57	76.50	62.49
Singapore					
2009	57.46	57.47	86.47	57.46	86.37
2019	52.19	52.20	92.83	52.19	92.61
Sri Lanka					
2009	80.26	80.27	56.23	80.26	56.22
2019	84.57	84.58	64.94	84.57	64.93
Taipei,China					
2009	63.84	63.93	61.65	63.84	61.52
2019	59.50	59.55	65.20	59.50	65.04
Thailand					
2009	72.08	72.18	53.19	72.08	53.09
2019	77.89	77.99	67.29	77.89	67.18
Viet Nam					
2009	66.08	66.09	42.88	66.08	42.85
2019	66.89	66.97	50.52	66.89	50.40

ADB = Asian Development Bank, DVA_B = domestic value-added exports by backward industrial linkages, DVA_F = domestic value-added exports by forward industrial linkages, VAX_B = value-added exports by backward industrial linkages, VAX_F = value-added exports by forward industrial linkages, VAX_G = domestic value-added absorbed abroad.

Source: Asian Development Bank. Multi-Regional Input–Output Tables Database. https://mrio.adbx.online/ (accessed 1 August 2020).

Click here to download the table.

ADB Regional Member	VAX_G	DVA_B	DVA_F	VAX_B	VAX_F
	Value-Added Export Measure to Gross Exports Ratio (%)				
Bangladesh					
2009	84.82	84.90	198.46	84.82	198.40
2019	87.10	87.18	3,623.39	87.10	3,621.76
Bhutan					
2009	76.99	77.00	46.67	76.99	46.66
2019	74.79	74.80	47.85	74.79	47.84
Brunei Darussalam					
2009	88.59	88.60	47.83	88.59	47.82
2019	86.31	86.32	46.45	86.31	46.44
Cambodia					
2009	72.56	72.58	205.30	72.56	205.27
2019	65.81	65.84	121.45	65.81	121.42
China, People's Republic of					
2009	79.26	80.88	51.43	79.26	50.47
2019	82.03	84.98	45.68	82.03	44.17
Fiji					
2009	61.65	61.66	64.72	61.65	64.72
2019	61.99	61.99	76.92	61.99	76.92
Hong Kong, China					
2009	24.59	24.60	7.43	24.59	7.42
2019	13.05	13.02	4.49	13.05	4.48
India					
2009	68.02	68.57	47.79	68.02	47.42
2019	70.08	70.64	40.80	70.08	40.49
Indonesia					
2009	81.45	81.84	59.36	81.45	59.10
2019	81.53	81.93	51.84	81.53	51.60
Japan					
2009	81.03	82.22	51.36	81.03	50.60
2019	76.08	76.87	50.35	76.08	49.82
Kazakhstan					
2009	85.00	85.24	55.74	85.00	55.58
2019	85.42	85.59	59.81	85.42	59.68
Korea, Republic of					
2009	62.73	63.00	44.22	62.73	44.02
2019	65.33	65.70	45.31	65.33	45.05
Kyrgyz Republic					
2009	71.15	71.16	58.76	71.15	58.75
2019	77.00	77.02	66.69	77.00	66.67
Lao People's Democratic Republic					
2009	70.62	70.63	151.10	70.62	151.09
2019	78.13	78.20	325.57	78.13	325.46
Malaysia					
2009	45.64	45.76	30.39	45.64	30.29
2019	58.36	58.67	29.49	58.36	29.33

Table 3.2.2.c: Value-Added Exports by Various Measures—Medium- and High-Technology Manufacturing Sector

continued on next page

Table 3.2.2.c: continued

Table 3.2.2.c: Value-Added Exports by Various Measures—Medium- and High-Technology Manufacturing Sector					
ADB Regional Member	**VAX_G**	**DVA_B**	**DVA_F**	**VAX_B**	**VAX_F**
	Value-Added Export Measure to Gross Exports Ratio (%)				
Maldives					
2009	52.83	52.83	82.35	52.83	82.34
2019	63.61	63.61	241.00	63.61	240.98
Mongolia					
2009	65.27	65.28	71.58	65.27	71.57
2019	71.17	71.17	104.21	71.17	104.19
Nepal					
2009	62.39	62.48	59.57	62.39	59.51
2019	58.80	58.98	67.53	58.80	67.38
Pakistan					
2009	72.99	73.04	75.21	72.99	75.16
2019	71.20	71.25	83.07	71.20	83.02
Philippines					
2009	60.22	60.37	38.12	60.22	38.03
2019	43.88	44.03	34.08	43.88	33.96
Singapore					
2009	38.16	38.20	29.53	38.16	29.48
2019	41.04	41.14	30.78	41.04	30.68
Sri Lanka					
2009	64.57	64.60	71.33	64.57	71.31
2019	55.44	55.47	68.66	55.44	68.64
Taipei,China					
2009	54.69	54.86	44.37	54.69	44.23
2019	53.45	53.63	45.67	53.45	45.51
Thailand					
2009	57.31	57.50	36.72	57.31	36.60
2019	61.73	61.91	39.77	61.73	39.66
Viet Nam					
2009	55.21	55.36	61.88	55.21	61.77
2019	46.55	46.80	41.38	46.55	41.19

ADB = Asian Development Bank, DVA_B = domestic value-added exports by backward industrial linkages, DVA_F = domestic value-added exports by forward industrial linkages, VAX_B = value-added exports by backward industrial linkages, VAX_F = value-added exports by forward industrial linkages, VAX_G = domestic value-added absorbed abroad.

Source: Asian Development Bank. Multi-Regional Input–Output Tables Database. https://mrio.adbx.online/ (accessed 1 August 2020).

Click here to download the table.

Table 3.2.2.d: Value-Added Exports by Various Measures—Business Services Sector					
ADB Regional Member	VAX_G	DVA_B	DVA_F	VAX_B	VAX_F
	Value-Added Export Measure to Gross Exports Ratio (%)				
Bangladesh					
2009	94.71	94.74	587.33	94.71	587.24
2019	94.08	94.16	378.95	94.08	378.75
Bhutan					
2009	80.55	80.55	127.72	80.55	127.71
2019	81.28	81.29	95.41	81.28	95.40
Brunei Darussalam					
2009	77.06	77.07	95.90	77.06	95.89
2019	73.79	73.80	103.37	73.79	103.36
Cambodia					
2009	81.76	81.76	86.45	81.76	86.44
2019	79.43	79.44	82.30	79.43	82.29
China, People's Republic of					
2009	90.70	92.97	161.22	90.70	158.18
2019	90.29	95.09	203.44	90.29	195.93
Fiji					
2009	72.94	72.95	75.30	72.94	75.30
2019	75.92	75.93	75.32	75.92	75.32
Hong Kong, China					
2009	80.35	80.45	78.34	80.35	78.25
2019	78.90	79.01	76.44	78.90	76.34
India					
2009	92.36	93.00	110.38	92.36	109.66
2019	87.50	88.06	135.71	87.50	134.85
Indonesia					
2009	91.26	91.48	268.01	91.26	267.11
2019	89.03	89.22	395.63	89.03	394.40
Japan					
2009	95.23	96.38	158.62	95.23	156.56
2019	94.31	95.30	184.62	94.31	182.77
Kazakhstan					
2009	87.95	88.46	120.09	87.95	119.55
2019	88.00	88.56	122.93	88.00	122.37
Korea, Republic of					
2009	88.83	89.36	229.92	88.83	228.88
2019	86.16	86.68	187.47	86.16	186.45
Kyrgyz Republic					
2009	77.34	77.36	107.68	77.34	107.66
2019	78.31	78.33	137.04	78.31	137.00
Lao People's Democratic Republic					
2009	84.38	84.39	114.14	84.38	114.14
2019	88.69	88.71	124.02	88.69	124.00
Malaysia					
2009	79.04	79.31	148.11	79.04	147.72
2019	82.31	82.56	164.37	82.31	163.71

continued on next page

Table 3.2.2.d: continued

Table 3.2.2.d: Value-Added Exports by Various Measures—Business Services Sector					
ADB Regional Member	**VAX_G**	**DVA_B**	**DVA_F**	**VAX_B**	**VAX_F**
	Value-Added Export Measure to Gross Exports Ratio (%)				
Maldives					
2009	65.01	65.01	59.13	65.01	59.12
2019	67.44	67.44	51.64	67.44	51.63
Mongolia					
2009	79.29	79.30	99.75	79.29	99.73
2019	73.13	73.16	113.58	73.13	113.54
Nepal					
2009	84.55	84.56	95.71	84.55	95.69
2019	86.16	86.23	95.30	86.16	95.22
Pakistan					
2009	90.85	90.92	103.27	90.85	103.20
2019	90.98	91.06	140.16	90.98	140.07
Philippines					
2009	91.80	91.89	108.99	91.80	108.87
2019	87.70	87.85	92.14	87.70	91.98
Singapore					
2009	66.71	66.82	74.26	66.71	74.18
2019	62.09	62.29	67.13	62.09	66.95
Sri Lanka					
2009	84.49	84.51	96.07	84.49	96.05
2019	91.27	91.28	100.40	91.27	100.39
Taipei,China					
2009	88.32	88.59	129.71	88.32	129.36
2019	85.42	85.73	107.19	85.42	106.85
Thailand					
2009	82.13	82.25	178.28	82.13	177.89
2019	87.98	88.12	109.11	87.98	108.92
Viet Nam					
2009	77.18	77.24	115.92	77.18	115.82
2019	83.37	83.55	115.75	83.37	115.45

ADB = Asian Development Bank, DVA_B = domestic value-added exports by backward industrial linkages, DVA_F = domestic value-added exports by forward industrial linkages, VAX_B = value-added exports by backward industrial linkages, VAX_F = value-added exports by forward industrial linkages, VAX_G = domestic value-added absorbed abroad.

Source: Asian Development Bank. Multi-Regional Input–Output Tables Database. https://mrio.adbx.online/ (accessed 1 August 2020).

Click here to download the table.

ADB Regional Member	VAX_G	DVA_B	DVA_F	VAX_B	VAX_F
			Value-Added Export Measure to Gross Exports Ratio (%)		

Table 3.2.2.e: Value-Added Exports by Various Measures—Personal Services Sector

ADB Regional Member	VAX_G	DVA_B	DVA_F	VAX_B	VAX_F
Value-Added Export Measure to Gross Exports Ratio (%)					
Bangladesh					
2009	95.72	95.75	148.19	95.72	148.16
2019	94.35	94.49	114.68	94.35	114.56
Bhutan					
2009	87.14	87.14	105.43	87.14	105.43
2019	86.47	86.47	66.61	86.47	66.61
Brunei Darussalam					
2009	83.70	83.70	129.75	83.70	129.74
2019	75.65	75.66	68.26	75.65	68.25
Cambodia					
2009	87.79	87.80	111.01	87.79	111.00
2019	82.48	82.49	110.73	82.48	110.71
China, People's Republic of					
2009	90.78	91.51	246.26	90.78	242.46
2019	91.79	93.85	358.85	91.79	347.78
Fiji					
2009	80.10	80.11	78.98	80.10	78.98
2019	86.27	86.27	97.45	86.27	97.44
Hong Kong, China					
2009	88.08	88.24	382.65	88.08	382.16
2019	87.47	87.61	467.11	87.47	466.47
India					
2009	97.31	97.30	118.75	97.31	118.57
2019	97.69	97.68	116.40	97.69	116.23
Indonesia					
2009	90.55	90.67	124.50	90.55	124.18
2019	91.65	91.89	158.20	91.65	157.72
Japan					
2009	94.99	95.58	423.83	94.99	418.45
2019	93.20	93.55	495.11	93.20	490.40
Kazakhstan					
2009	85.54	85.53	80.42	85.54	80.31
2019	82.34	82.33	67.05	82.34	66.98
Korea, Republic of					
2009	88.84	89.32	329.54	88.84	328.06
2019	87.44	87.81	349.13	87.44	347.29
Kyrgyz Republic					
2009	84.24	84.24	68.39	84.24	68.38
2019	87.57	87.57	77.77	87.57	77.76
Lao People's Democratic Republic					
2009	85.63	85.63	67.25	85.63	67.25
2019	90.56	90.57	67.19	90.56	67.18
Malaysia					
2009	78.70	78.83	77.06	78.70	76.92
2019	83.15	83.13	118.38	83.15	118.07

continued on next page

Table 3.2.2.e: continued

Table 3.2.2.e: Value-Added Exports by Various Measures—Personal Services Sector					
ADB Regional Member	**VAX_G**	**DVA_B**	**DVA_F**	**VAX_B**	**VAX_F**
	Value-Added Export Measure to Gross Exports Ratio (%)				
Maldives					
2009	81.31	81.31	81.98	81.31	81.97
2019	85.75	85.75	170.86	85.75	170.85
Mongolia					
2009	82.17	82.17	116.89	82.17	116.88
2019	75.19	75.19	176.62	75.19	176.59
Nepal					
2009	88.41	88.44	67.45	88.41	67.43
2019	90.03	90.11	66.50	90.03	66.44
Pakistan					
2009	85.11	85.13	73.12	85.11	73.10
2019	88.31	88.33	72.89	88.31	72.87
Philippines					
2009	91.98	92.03	107.67	91.98	107.59
2019	88.60	88.76	89.01	88.60	88.86
Singapore					
2009	74.79	74.93	128.62	74.79	128.45
2019	74.06	74.24	133.85	74.06	133.53
Sri Lanka					
2009	88.16	88.17	111.33	88.16	111.32
2019	93.63	93.64	139.83	93.63	139.81
Taipei,China					
2009	89.42	89.47	347.54	89.42	346.69
2019	87.76	87.81	327.54	87.76	326.64
Thailand					
2009	84.61	84.69	89.02	84.61	88.90
2019	88.75	88.82	87.58	88.75	87.49
Viet Nam					
2009	84.03	84.04	104.59	84.03	104.53
2019	88.32	88.55	132.90	88.32	132.54

ADB = Asian Development Bank, DVA_B = domestic value-added exports by backward industrial linkages, DVA_F = domestic value-added exports by forward industrial linkages, VAX_B = value-added exports by backward industrial linkages, VAX_F = value-added exports by forward industrial linkages, VAX_G = domestic value-added absorbed abroad.

Source: Asian Development Bank. Multi-Regional Input–Output Tables Database. https://mrio.adbx.online/ (accessed 1 August 2020).

Click here to download the table.

Table 3.2.2.f: Value-Added Exports by Various Measures—All Sectors					
ADB Regional Member	**VAX_G**	**DVA_B**	**DVA_F**	**VAX_B**	**VAX_F**
	Value-Added Export Measure to Gross Exports Ratio (%)				
Bangladesh					
2009	85.82	85.84	85.84	85.82	85.82
2019	81.15	81.19	81.19	81.15	81.15
Bhutan					
2009	82.98	82.99	82.99	82.98	82.98
2019	81.08	81.09	81.09	81.08	81.08
Brunei Darussalam					
2009	89.11	89.12	89.12	89.11	89.11
2019	84.53	84.54	84.54	84.53	84.53
Cambodia					
2009	75.19	75.20	75.20	75.19	75.19
2019	71.04	71.05	71.05	71.04	71.04
China, People's Republic of					
2009	83.07	84.54	84.54	83.07	83.07
2019	84.98	87.87	87.87	84.98	84.98
Fiji					
2009	73.18	73.18	73.18	73.18	73.18
2019	74.85	74.85	74.85	74.85	74.85
Hong Kong, China					
2009	76.67	76.76	76.76	76.67	76.67
2019	74.72	74.82	74.82	74.72	74.72
India					
2009	83.52	84.05	84.05	83.52	83.52
2019	80.09	80.61	80.61	80.09	80.09
Indonesia					
2009	86.76	87.13	87.13	86.76	86.76
2019	85.36	85.69	85.69	85.36	85.36
Japan					
2009	84.91	86.11	86.11	84.91	84.91
2019	79.72	80.55	80.55	79.72	79.72
Kazakhstan					
2009	88.03	88.31	88.31	88.03	88.03
2019	86.22	86.46	86.46	86.22	86.22
Korea, Republic of					
2009	65.96	66.26	66.26	65.96	65.96
2019	68.54	68.93	68.93	68.54	68.54
Kyrgyz Republic					
2009	72.98	72.99	72.99	72.98	72.98
2019	77.72	77.74	77.74	77.72	77.72
Lao People's Democratic Republic					
2009	87.21	87.22	87.22	87.21	87.21
2019	83.79	83.82	83.82	83.79	83.79
Malaysia					
2009	59.62	59.79	59.79	59.62	59.62
2019	66.18	66.49	66.49	66.18	66.18

continued on next page

Table 3.2.2.f: continued

ADB Regional Member	VAX_G	DVA_B	DVA_F	VAX_B	VAX_F
	Value-Added Export Measure to Gross Exports Ratio (%)				
Maldives					
2009	65.15	65.15	65.15	65.15	65.15
2019	67.41	67.41	67.41	67.41	67.41
Mongolia					
2009	79.32	79.33	79.33	79.32	79.32
2019	76.56	76.58	76.58	76.56	76.56
Nepal					
2009	82.87	82.89	82.89	82.87	82.87
2019	83.09	83.16	83.16	83.09	83.09
Pakistan					
2009	87.95	88.00	88.00	87.95	87.95
2019	84.99	85.04	85.04	84.99	84.99
Philippines					
2009	76.88	76.98	76.98	76.88	76.88
2019	70.91	71.05	71.05	70.91	70.91
Singapore					
2009	51.80	51.87	51.87	51.80	51.80
2019	53.32	53.47	53.47	53.32	53.32
Sri Lanka					
2009	81.22	81.24	81.24	81.22	81.22
2019	86.90	86.91	86.91	86.90	86.90
Taipei,China					
2009	60.99	61.17	61.17	60.99	60.99
2019	60.42	60.62	60.62	60.42	60.42
Thailand					
2009	64.98	65.14	65.14	64.98	64.98
2019	75.66	75.81	75.81	75.66	75.66
Viet Nam					
2009	66.63	66.71	66.71	66.63	66.63
2019	70.67	70.90	70.90	70.67	70.67

ADB = Asian Development Bank, DVA_B = domestic value-added exports by backward industrial linkages, DVA_F = domestic value-added exports by forward industrial linkages, VAX_B = value-added exports by backward industrial linkages, VAX_F = value-added exports by forward industrial linkages, VAX_G = domestic value-added absorbed abroad.

Source: Asian Development Bank. Multi-Regional Input–Output Tables Database. https://mrio.adbx.online/ (accessed 1 August 2020).

Click here to download the table.

Table 3.2.3.a: Revealed Comparative Advantage by Aggregate Sector (Traditional Method)		
ADB Regional Member	**2009**	**2019**
	(ratio)	
Bangladesh		
Business Services Sector	0.13	0.19
Low-Technology Manufacturing Sector	5.11	5.33
Medium- and High-Technology Manufacturing Sector	0.07	0.00
Personal Services Sector	3.41	3.33
Primary Sector	0.23	0.01
Bhutan		
Business Services Sector	0.44	1.18
Low-Technology Manufacturing Sector	2.90	1.99
Medium- and High-Technology Manufacturing Sector	0.37	0.30
Personal Services Sector	0.54	1.64
Primary Sector	2.28	1.83
Brunei Darussalam		
Business Services Sector	0.27	0.23
Low-Technology Manufacturing Sector	0.03	0.10
Medium- and High-Technology Manufacturing Sector	0.85	0.84
Personal Services Sector	0.44	0.36
Primary Sector	5.17	5.52
Cambodia		
Business Services Sector	1.37	1.23
Low-Technology Manufacturing Sector	3.37	3.26
Medium- and High-Technology Manufacturing Sector	0.01	0.02
Personal Services Sector	1.11	0.56
Primary Sector	0.65	1.08
China, People's Republic of		
Business Services Sector	0.67	0.60
Low-Technology Manufacturing Sector	1.46	1.39
Medium- and High-Technology Manufacturing Sector	1.24	1.33
Personal Services Sector	0.39	0.39
Primary Sector	0.15	0.10
Fiji		
Business Services Sector	2.49	2.49
Low-Technology Manufacturing Sector	1.20	1.15
Medium- and High-Technology Manufacturing Sector	0.06	0.05
Personal Services Sector	2.75	1.07
Primary Sector	0.82	0.86
Hong Kong, China		
Business Services Sector	3.48	3.32
Low-Technology Manufacturing Sector	0.31	0.19
Medium- and High-Technology Manufacturing Sector	0.12	0.12
Personal Services Sector	0.39	0.27
Primary Sector	0.01	0.01
India		
Business Services Sector	1.50	1.04
Low-Technology Manufacturing Sector	1.16	1.27
Medium- and High-Technology Manufacturing Sector	0.68	0.93
Personal Services Sector	1.56	1.46
Primary Sector	0.82	0.64
Indonesia		
Business Services Sector	0.22	0.16
Low-Technology Manufacturing Sector	2.16	2.26
Medium- and High-Technology Manufacturing Sector	0.69	0.96
Personal Services Sector	0.58	0.38
Primary Sector	2.55	1.56

continued on next page

Table 3.2.3.a: continued

Table 3.2.3.a: Revealed Comparative Advantage by Aggregate Sector (Traditional Method)		
ADB Regional Member	**2009**	**2019**
	(ratio)	
Japan		
Business Services Sector	0.93	0.61
Low-Technology Manufacturing Sector	0.38	0.37
Medium- and High-Technology Manufacturing Sector	1.51	1.73
Personal Services Sector	0.28	0.15
Primary Sector	0.04	0.02
Kazakhstan		
Business Services Sector	1.02	1.06
Low-Technology Manufacturing Sector	0.13	0.15
Medium- and High-Technology Manufacturing Sector	0.37	0.52
Personal Services Sector	0.51	0.28
Primary Sector	5.26	4.56
Korea, Republic of		
Business Services Sector	0.34	0.44
Low-Technology Manufacturing Sector	0.45	0.36
Medium- and High-Technology Manufacturing Sector	1.81	1.83
Personal Services Sector	0.33	0.35
Primary Sector	0.02	0.01
Kyrgyz Republic		
Business Services Sector	0.72	0.59
Low-Technology Manufacturing Sector	0.90	0.96
Medium- and High-Technology Manufacturing Sector	0.86	0.92
Personal Services Sector	2.92	4.23
Primary Sector	2.14	1.85
Lao People's Democratic Republic		
Business Services Sector	0.61	0.53
Low-Technology Manufacturing Sector	2.02	3.41
Medium- and High-Technology Manufacturing Sector	0.04	0.01
Personal Services Sector	0.33	1.36
Primary Sector	4.77	2.66
Malaysia		
Business Services Sector	0.51	0.53
Low-Technology Manufacturing Sector	1.58	1.01
Medium- and High-Technology Manufacturing Sector	1.08	1.42
Personal Services Sector	0.63	0.35
Primary Sector	0.99	0.57
Maldives		
Business Services Sector	3.22	3.31
Low-Technology Manufacturing Sector	0.43	0.35
Medium- and High-Technology Manufacturing Sector	0.01	0.00
Personal Services Sector	0.62	1.20
Primary Sector	0.18	0.07
Mongolia		
Business Services Sector	0.93	0.75
Low-Technology Manufacturing Sector	0.45	0.26
Medium- and High-Technology Manufacturing Sector	0.05	0.07
Personal Services Sector	0.78	0.25
Primary Sector	6.37	7.30
Nepal		
Business Services Sector	1.46	1.33
Low-Technology Manufacturing Sector	1.36	1.14
Medium- and High-Technology Manufacturing Sector	0.15	0.17
Personal Services Sector	12.19	14.88
Primary Sector	0.91	0.52

continued on next page

Table 3.2.3.a: continued

Table 3.2.3.a: Revealed Comparative Advantage by Aggregate Sector (Traditional Method)		
ADB Regional Member	**2009**	**2019**
	(ratio)	
Pakistan		
Business Services Sector	1.63	0.68
Low-Technology Manufacturing Sector	2.51	3.71
Medium- and High-Technology Manufacturing Sector	0.15	0.16
Personal Services Sector	1.96	2.31
Primary Sector	0.64	0.88
Philippines		
Business Services Sector	1.31	1.55
Low-Technology Manufacturing Sector	1.21	1.22
Medium- and High-Technology Manufacturing Sector	0.94	0.75
Personal Services Sector	0.66	1.00
Primary Sector	0.22	0.21
Singapore		
Business Services Sector	1.77	2.04
Low-Technology Manufacturing Sector	0.18	0.18
Medium- and High-Technology Manufacturing Sector	1.12	0.92
Personal Services Sector	0.18	0.23
Primary Sector	0.00	0.00
Sri Lanka		
Business Services Sector	1.42	1.58
Low-Technology Manufacturing Sector	2.71	2.70
Medium- and High-Technology Manufacturing Sector	0.20	0.09
Personal Services Sector	2.02	1.67
Primary Sector	0.58	0.50
Taipei,China		
Business Services Sector	0.62	0.73
Low-Technology Manufacturing Sector	0.46	0.38
Medium- and High-Technology Manufacturing Sector	1.65	1.65
Personal Services Sector	0.20	0.15
Primary Sector	0.05	0.04
Thailand		
Business Services Sector	0.51	1.26
Low-Technology Manufacturing Sector	1.39	1.08
Medium- and High-Technology Manufacturing Sector	1.31	0.91
Personal Services Sector	0.80	1.43
Primary Sector	0.23	0.45
Viet Nam		
Business Services Sector	0.63	0.86
Low-Technology Manufacturing Sector	3.04	1.94
Medium- and High-Technology Manufacturing Sector	0.36	0.36
Personal Services Sector	0.34	0.86
Primary Sector	1.62	2.76

0.00 = magnitude is less than half of unit employed, ADB = Asian Development Bank.

Source: Asian Development Bank. Multi-Regional Input–Output Tables Database. https://mrio.adbx.online/ (accessed 1 August 2020).

Click here to download the table.

Table 3.2.3.b: Revealed Comparative Advantage by Aggregate Sector (Value-Added Method)		
ADB Regional Member	**2009**	**2019**
	(ratio)	
Bangladesh		
Business Services Sector	0.55	0.56
Low-Technology Manufacturing Sector	3.01	3.40
Medium- and High-Technology Manufacturing Sector	0.28	0.28
Personal Services Sector	3.08	2.53
Primary Sector	1.18	0.85
Bhutan		
Business Services Sector	0.40	0.87
Low-Technology Manufacturing Sector	3.14	1.96
Medium- and High-Technology Manufacturing Sector	0.36	0.32
Personal Services Sector	0.36	0.72
Primary Sector	2.11	1.75
Brunei Darussalam		
Business Services Sector	0.18	0.18
Low-Technology Manufacturing Sector	0.04	0.05
Medium- and High-Technology Manufacturing Sector	0.78	0.83
Personal Services Sector	0.33	0.16
Primary Sector	5.14	5.13
Cambodia		
Business Services Sector	0.95	0.89
Low-Technology Manufacturing Sector	2.58	2.89
Medium- and High-Technology Manufacturing Sector	0.06	0.07
Personal Services Sector	0.85	0.47
Primary Sector	1.41	1.29
China, People's Republic of		
Business Services Sector	0.77	0.87
Low-Technology Manufacturing Sector	1.17	1.06
Medium- and High-Technology Manufacturing Sector	1.30	1.25
Personal Services Sector	0.60	0.86
Primary Sector	1.06	0.96
Fiji		
Business Services Sector	1.55	1.56
Low-Technology Manufacturing Sector	1.05	1.09
Medium- and High-Technology Manufacturing Sector	0.10	0.09
Personal Services Sector	1.55	0.75
Primary Sector	0.85	0.82
Hong Kong, China		
Business Services Sector	2.15	2.11
Low-Technology Manufacturing Sector	0.35	0.23
Medium- and High-Technology Manufacturing Sector	0.02	0.01
Personal Services Sector	1.02	0.90
Primary Sector	0.00	0.00
India		
Business Services Sector	1.19	1.09
Low-Technology Manufacturing Sector	0.85	0.94
Medium- and High-Technology Manufacturing Sector	0.67	0.85
Personal Services Sector	1.15	1.13
Primary Sector	1.18	0.99
Indonesia		
Business Services Sector	0.41	0.45
Low-Technology Manufacturing Sector	1.41	1.50
Medium- and High-Technology Manufacturing Sector	0.81	1.05
Personal Services Sector	0.43	0.38
Primary Sector	2.95	2.36

continued on next page

Table 3.2.3.b: continued

Table 3.2.3.b: Revealed Comparative Advantage by Aggregate Sector (Value-Added Method)		
ADB Regional Member	**2009**	**2019**
	(ratio)	
Japan		
Business Services Sector	1.04	0.88
Low-Technology Manufacturing Sector	0.76	0.78
Medium- and High-Technology Manufacturing Sector	1.55	1.95
Personal Services Sector	0.72	0.49
Primary Sector	0.13	0.07
Kazakhstan		
Business Services Sector	0.84	0.94
Low-Technology Manufacturing Sector	0.33	0.25
Medium- and High-Technology Manufacturing Sector	0.41	0.65
Personal Services Sector	0.24	0.12
Primary Sector	3.57	2.81
Korea, Republic of		
Business Services Sector	0.72	0.75
Low-Technology Manufacturing Sector	0.64	0.62
Medium- and High-Technology Manufacturing Sector	2.09	2.17
Personal Services Sector	0.87	0.95
Primary Sector	0.14	0.09
Kyrgyz Republic		
Business Services Sector	0.64	0.65
Low-Technology Manufacturing Sector	0.82	0.94
Medium- and High-Technology Manufacturing Sector	1.19	1.42
Personal Services Sector	1.43	2.27
Primary Sector	1.81	1.05
Lao People's Democratic Republic		
Business Services Sector	0.48	0.49
Low-Technology Manufacturing Sector	1.26	2.84
Medium- and High-Technology Manufacturing Sector	0.11	0.10
Personal Services Sector	0.13	0.59
Primary Sector	4.32	2.55
Malaysia		
Business Services Sector	0.76	0.82
Low-Technology Manufacturing Sector	1.01	0.88
Medium- and High-Technology Manufacturing Sector	0.95	1.13
Personal Services Sector	0.42	0.34
Primary Sector	2.00	1.67
Maldives		
Business Services Sector	1.77	1.58
Low-Technology Manufacturing Sector	0.58	1.54
Medium- and High-Technology Manufacturing Sector	0.03	0.01
Personal Services Sector	0.63	1.64
Primary Sector	0.44	0.18
Mongolia		
Business Services Sector	0.71	0.69
Low-Technology Manufacturing Sector	0.39	0.47
Medium- and High-Technology Manufacturing Sector	0.07	0.16
Personal Services Sector	0.60	0.31
Primary Sector	4.45	4.21
Nepal		
Business Services Sector	1.02	0.95
Low-Technology Manufacturing Sector	1.09	1.02
Medium- and High-Technology Manufacturing Sector	0.18	0.25
Personal Services Sector	5.18	6.39
Primary Sector	1.28	0.91

continued on next page

Table 3.2.3.b: continued

Table 3.2.3.b: Revealed Comparative Advantage by Aggregate Sector (Value-Added Method)		
ADB Regional Member	2009	2019
	(ratio)	
Pakistan		
Business Services Sector	1.15	0.70
Low-Technology Manufacturing Sector	1.16	1.76
Medium- and High-Technology Manufacturing Sector	0.22	0.28
Personal Services Sector	0.85	1.06
Primary Sector	1.93	2.47
Philippines		
Business Services Sector	1.12	1.25
Low-Technology Manufacturing Sector	1.23	1.29
Medium- and High-Technology Manufacturing Sector	0.80	0.65
Personal Services Sector	0.48	0.67
Primary Sector	0.91	0.62
Singapore		
Business Services Sector	1.54	1.60
Low-Technology Manufacturing Sector	0.37	0.37
Medium- and High-Technology Manufacturing Sector	1.10	0.95
Personal Services Sector	0.24	0.31
Primary Sector	0.00	0.00
Sri Lanka		
Business Services Sector	1.01	1.13
Low-Technology Manufacturing Sector	2.23	2.42
Medium- and High-Technology Manufacturing Sector	0.30	0.13
Personal Services Sector	1.44	1.44
Primary Sector	0.94	0.58
Taipei,China		
Business Services Sector	0.80	0.80
Low-Technology Manufacturing Sector	0.56	0.49
Medium- and High-Technology Manufacturing Sector	2.06	2.25
Personal Services Sector	0.61	0.44
Primary Sector	0.11	0.08
Thailand		
Business Services Sector	0.84	1.13
Low-Technology Manufacturing Sector	1.35	1.15
Medium- and High-Technology Manufacturing Sector	1.28	0.86
Personal Services Sector	0.57	0.89
Primary Sector	0.73	0.72
Viet Nam		
Business Services Sector	0.66	0.87
Low-Technology Manufacturing Sector	2.32	1.66
Medium- and High-Technology Manufacturing Sector	0.58	0.38
Personal Services Sector	0.28	0.86
Primary Sector	1.72	1.92

0.00 = magnitude is less than half of unit employed, ADB = Asian Development Bank.

Source: Asian Development Bank. Multi-Regional Input–Output Tables Database. https://mrio.adbx.online/ (accessed 1 August 2020).

Click here to download the table.

Table 3.2.4.a: Vertical Specialization, Disaggregated—Bangladesh

	Exports	VS	FVA_FIN	FVA_INT	DDC	FDC
	($ million)	(% of gross exports)	(% of VS)			
Leather, Leather Products, and Footwear						
2009	375.55	10.29	82.54	10.77	0.01	6.67
2019	131.18	11.51	77.86	10.84	0.06	11.25
Public Administration and Defense; Compulsory Social Security						
2009	1,179.54	4.69	8.46	58.38	0.05	33.12
2019	3,284.66	6.01	1.91	50.51	0.87	46.71
Textiles and Textile Products						
2009	13,190.63	16.52	78.34	12.12	0.06	9.47
2019	38,365.45	27.74	69.25	12.90	0.49	17.35

$ = United States dollars, DDC = domestic value-added double counted in exports, FDC = foreign value-added double counted in exports, FVA_FIN = foreign value-added in exports for final consumption, FVA_INT = foreign value-added in intermediate exports, VS = vertical specialization.

Source: Asian Development Bank. Multi-Regional Input–Output Tables Database. https://mrio.adbx.online/ (accessed 1 August 2020).

Table 3.2.4.b: Vertical Specialization, Disaggregated—Bhutan

	Exports	VS	FVA_FIN	FVA_INT	DDC	FDC
	($ million)	(% of gross exports)	(% of VS)			
Agriculture, Hunting, Forestry, and Fishing						
2009	84.02	4.71	31.17	55.53	0.01	13.28
2019	50.64	1.97	24.36	62.94	0.02	12.68
Electricity, Gas, and Water Supply						
2009	194.96	9.98	1.43	65.18	0.01	33.38
2019	208.38	13.11	2.28	54.68	0.01	43.03
Inland Transport						
2009	16.24	27.18	52.35	36.26	0.00	11.38
2019	65.12	34.17	22.51	52.68	0.01	24.80

0.00 = magnitude is less than half of unit employed, $ = United States dollars, DDC = domestic value-added double counted in exports, FDC = foreign value-added double counted in exports, FVA_FIN = foreign value-added in exports for final consumption, FVA_INT = foreign value-added in intermediate exports, VS = vertical specialization.

Source: Asian Development Bank. Multi-Regional Input–Output Tables Database. https://mrio.adbx.online/ (accessed 1 August 2020).

Table 3.2.4.c: Vertical Specialization, Disaggregated—Brunei Darussalam

	Exports	VS	FVA_FIN	FVA_INT	DDC	FDC
	($ million)	(% of gross exports)	(% of VS)			
Coke, Refined Petroleum, and Nuclear Fuel						
2009	2,601.05	9.90	11.91	60.10	0.02	27.97
2019	2,804.19	11.59	8.75	58.61	0.01	32.62
Mining and Quarrying						
2009	3,656.94	7.96	0.32	69.76	0.03	29.89
2019	4,205.13	13.77	3.37	55.27	0.01	41.34
Water Transport						
2009	123.40	20.20	24.21	34.95	0.02	40.82
2019	103.04	22.59	22.53	38.92	0.02	38.53

$ = United States dollars, DDC = domestic value-added double counted in exports, FDC = foreign value-added double counted in exports, FVA_FIN = foreign value-added in exports for final consumption, FVA_INT = foreign value-added in intermediate exports, VS = vertical specialization.

Source: Asian Development Bank. Multi-Regional Input–Output Tables Database. https://mrio.adbx.online/ (accessed 1 August 2020).

Table 3.2.4.d: Vertical Specialization, Disaggregated—Cambodia

	Exports	VS	FVA_FIN	FVA_INT	DDC	FDC
	($ million)	(% of gross exports)	(% of VS)			
Hotels and Restaurants						
2009	662.93	15.67	61.31	25.79	0.01	12.89
2019	1,747.61	19.46	60.38	23.25	0.01	16.36
Textiles and Textile Products						
2009	1,771.17	34.17	76.88	12.09	0.00	11.02
2019	5,950.21	44.15	83.99	7.75	0.00	8.26
Wholesale Trade and Commission Trade, Except of Motor Vehicles and Motorcycles						
2009	310.88	21.11	29.61	41.22	0.01	29.16
2019	1,448.79	23.64	37.50	30.74	0.02	31.74

0.00 = magnitude is less than half of unit employed, $ = United States dollars, DDC = domestic value-added double counted in exports, FDC = foreign value-added double counted in exports, FVA_FIN = foreign value-added in exports for final consumption, FVA_INT = foreign value-added in intermediate exports, VS = vertical specialization.

Source: Asian Development Bank. Multi-Regional Input–Output Tables Database. https://mrio.adbx.online/ (accessed 1 August 2020).

Table 3.2.4.e: Vertical Specialization, Disaggregated—China, People's Republic of

	Exports	VS	FVA_FIN	FVA_INT	DDC	FDC
	($ million)	(% of gross exports)	(% of VS)			
Electrical and Optical Equipment						
2009	409,678.08	26.19	64.80	15.78	2.97	16.45
2019	817,180.35	19.53	53.80	19.02	4.98	22.20
Machinery, Nec						
2009	103,889.31	17.86	66.05	19.05	2.06	12.84
2019	197,172.89	13.62	60.03	20.99	2.69	16.29
Textiles and Textile Products						
2009	143,666.75	11.03	80.20	10.84	1.17	7.79
2019	253,250.96	7.80	74.71	11.58	1.77	11.94

$ = United States dollars, DDC = domestic value-added double counted in exports, FDC = foreign value-added double counted in exports, FVA_FIN = foreign value-added in exports for final consumption, FVA_INT = foreign value-added in intermediate exports, VS = vertical specialization.

Source: Asian Development Bank. Multi-Regional Input–Output Tables Database. https://mrio.adbx.online/ (accessed 1 August 2020).

Table 3.2.4.f: Vertical Specialization, Disaggregated—Fiji

	Exports	VS	FVA_FIN	FVA_INT	DDC	FDC
	($ million)	(% of gross exports)	(% of VS)			
Air Transport						
2009	188.58	54.55	25.59	59.43	0.00	14.98
2019	273.36	62.62	23.93	60.75	0.00	15.32
Food, Beverages, and Tobacco						
2009	181.14	26.17	45.11	41.28	0.01	13.61
2019	316.39	28.45	50.39	32.35	0.01	17.26
Hotels and Restaurants						
2009	266.71	22.29	58.55	29.76	0.01	11.68
2019	646.73	24.63	57.48	26.17	0.01	16.34

0.00 = magnitude is less than half of unit employed, $ = United States dollars, DDC = domestic value-added double counted in exports, FDC = foreign value-added double counted in exports, FVA_FIN = foreign value-added in exports for final consumption, FVA_INT = foreign value-added in intermediate exports, VS = vertical specialization.

Source: Asian Development Bank. Multi-Regional Input–Output Tables Database. https://mrio.adbx.online/ (accessed 1 August 2020).

Table 3.2.4.g: Vertical Specialization, Disaggregated—Hong Kong, China

	Exports	VS	FVA_FIN	FVA_INT	DDC	FDC
	($ million)	(% of gross exports)	(% of VS)			
Financial Intermediation						
2009	11,195.35	9.60	25.77	51.60	0.96	21.67
2019	21,641.34	8.75	28.08	51.69	0.67	19.56
Retail Trade, Except of Motor Vehicles and Motorcycles; Repair of Household Goods						
2009	13,034.34	9.57	64.12	26.87	0.21	8.80
2019	19,565.62	10.36	67.69	21.99	0.48	9.84
Wholesale Trade and Commission Trade, Except of Motor Vehicles and Motorcycles						
2009	64,992.37	25.81	53.93	33.35	0.16	12.56
2019	110,614.88	28.58	53.96	30.28	0.32	15.43

$ = United States dollars, DDC = domestic value-added double counted in exports, FDC = foreign value-added double counted in exports, FVA_FIN = foreign value-added in exports for final consumption, FVA_INT = foreign value-added in intermediate exports, VS = vertical specialization.

Source: Asian Development Bank. Multi-Regional Input–Output Tables Database. https://mrio.adbx.online/ (accessed 1 August 2020).

Table 3.2.4.h: Vertical Specialization, Disaggregated—India

	Exports	VS	FVA_FIN	FVA_INT	DDC	FDC
	($ million)	(% of gross exports)	(% of VS)			
Coke, Refined Petroleum, and Nuclear Fuel						
2009	16,618.55	50.16	15.85	28.10	0.49	55.57
2019	56,724.91	40.16	27.98	37.91	0.50	33.61
Renting of M&Eq and Other Business Activities						
2009	53,733.40	10.18	33.41	44.60	0.75	21.23
2019	82,230.37	4.80	53.18	27.76	1.16	17.90
Textiles and Textile Products						
2009	17,413.28	13.39	73.60	14.51	0.22	11.67
2019	35,480.52	13.27	65.49	16.40	0.33	17.78

$ = United States dollars, DDC = domestic value-added double counted in exports, FDC = foreign value-added double counted in exports, FVA_FIN = foreign value-added in exports for final consumption, FVA_INT = foreign value-added in intermediate exports, VS = vertical specialization.

Source: Asian Development Bank. Multi-Regional Input–Output Tables Database. https://mrio.adbx.online/ (accessed 1 August 2020).

Table 3.2.4.i: Vertical Specialization, Disaggregated—Indonesia

	Exports	VS	FVA_FIN	FVA_INT	DDC	FDC
	($ million)	(% of gross exports)	(% of VS)			
Coke, Refined Petroleum, and Nuclear Fuel						
2009	9,656.11	10.01	23.33	46.60	0.81	29.26
2019	41,122.06	8.72	28.28	40.97	0.76	29.99
Food, Beverages, and Tobacco						
2009	17,843.96	8.61	26.02	54.89	0.52	18.57
2019	33,913.11	9.07	34.36	51.09	0.32	14.23
Mining and Quarrying						
2009	32,613.53	5.88	1.80	55.37	1.47	41.36
2019	27,087.48	5.02	0.40	60.54	1.31	37.75

$ = United States dollars, DDC = domestic value-added double counted in exports, FDC = foreign value-added double counted in exports, FVA_FIN = foreign value-added in exports for final consumption, FVA_INT = foreign value-added in intermediate exports, VS = vertical specialization.

Source: Asian Development Bank. Multi-Regional Input–Output Tables Database. https://mrio.adbx.online/ (accessed 1 August 2020).

Table 3.2.4.j: Vertical Specialization, Disaggregated—Japan

	Exports	VS	FVA_FIN	FVA_INT	DDC	FDC
	($ million)	(% of gross exports)	(% of VS)			
Basic Metals and Fabricated Metal						
2009	75,790.05	20.82	8.36	51.15	2.51	37.98
2019	111,529.52	28.11	9.26	52.34	1.47	36.93
Electrical and Optical Equipment						
2009	135,472.89	14.98	36.93	29.76	2.92	30.39
2019	172,890.10	18.13	37.02	30.18	2.09	30.71
Transport Equipment						
2009	126,721.31	12.87	73.32	17.08	0.87	8.74
2019	209,056.49	17.15	68.85	19.82	0.64	10.68

$ = United States dollars, DDC = domestic value-added double counted in exports, FDC = foreign value-added double counted in exports, FVA_FIN = foreign value-added in exports for final consumption, FVA_INT = foreign value-added in intermediate exports, VS = vertical specialization.

Source: Asian Development Bank. Multi-Regional Input–Output Tables Database. https://mrio.adbx.online/ (accessed 1 August 2020).

Table 3.2.4.k: Vertical Specialization, Disaggregated—Kazakhstan

	Exports	VS	FVA_FIN	FVA_INT	DDC	FDC
	($ million)	(% of gross exports)	(% of VS)			
Basic Metals and Fabricated Metal						
2009	4,755.21	11.02	3.22	47.54	0.69	48.56
2019	10,958.50	12.22	4.68	40.16	0.57	54.59
Mining and Quarrying						
2009	24,743.45	11.81	5.03	60.04	0.51	34.42
2019	26,407.59	13.92	20.39	41.90	0.45	37.25
Wholesale Trade and Commission Trade, Except of Motor Vehicles and Motorcycles						
2009	5,639.39	8.88	11.63	62.86	0.52	24.99
2019	13,765.71	9.65	3.24	66.23	0.80	29.73

$ = United States dollars, DDC = domestic value-added double counted in exports, FDC = foreign value-added double counted in exports, FVA_FIN = foreign value-added in exports for final consumption, FVA_INT = foreign value-added in intermediate exports, VS = vertical specialization.

Source: Asian Development Bank. Multi-Regional Input–Output Tables Database. https://mrio.adbx.online/ (accessed 1 August 2020).

Table 3.2.4.l: Vertical Specialization, Disaggregated—Korea, Republic of

	Exports	VS	FVA_FIN	FVA_INT	DDC	FDC
	($ million)	(% of gross exports)	(% of VS)			
Chemicals and Chemical Products						
2009	38,938.51	38.33	4.97	60.48	0.94	33.62
2019	74,475.98	37.18	8.04	55.22	0.88	35.86
Electrical and Optical Equipment						
2009	135,546.62	33.56	48.19	23.94	1.08	26.79
2019	206,587.02	29.29	40.40	28.36	1.28	29.96
Transport Equipment						
2009	82,053.59	30.75	86.19	9.27	0.15	4.39
2019	89,175.22	30.62	65.66	21.46	0.35	12.52

$ = United States dollars, DDC = domestic value-added double counted in exports, FDC = foreign value-added double counted in exports, FVA_FIN = foreign value-added in exports for final consumption, FVA_INT = foreign value-added in intermediate exports, VS = vertical specialization.

Source: Asian Development Bank. Multi-Regional Input–Output Tables Database. https://mrio.adbx.online/ (accessed 1 August 2020).

Table 3.2.4.m: Vertical Specialization, Disaggregated—Kyrgyz Republic

	Exports	VS	FVA_FIN	FVA_INT	DDC	FDC
	($ million)	(% of gross exports)	(% of VS)			
Agriculture, Hunting, Forestry, and Fishing						
2009	365.78	25.37	36.34	40.11	0.01	23.55
2019	253.32	17.25	46.52	32.66	0.06	20.76
Basic Metals and Fabricated Metal						
2009	582.53	27.15	24.79	44.09	0.01	31.11
2019	881.53	20.73	19.06	40.94	0.01	39.99
Public Administration and Defense; Compulsory Social Security						
2009	96.32	17.42	39.01	41.64	0.01	19.34
2019	218.09	12.74	35.30	38.97	0.02	25.71

$ = United States dollars, DDC = domestic value-added double counted in exports, FDC = foreign value-added double counted in exports, FVA_FIN = foreign value-added in exports for final consumption, FVA_INT = foreign value-added in intermediate exports, VS = vertical specialization.

Source: Asian Development Bank. Multi-Regional Input–Output Tables Database. https://mrio.adbx.online/ (accessed 1 August 2020).

Table 3.2.4.n: Vertical Specialization, Disaggregated—Lao People's Democratic Republic

	Exports	VS	FVA_FIN	FVA_INT	DDC	FDC
	($ million)	(% of gross exports)	(% of VS)			
Agriculture, Hunting, Forestry, and Fishing						
2009	72.78	3.62	7.85	63.19	0.02	28.94
2019	570.57	3.70	13.14	33.36	0.08	53.43
Electricity, Gas, and Water Supply						
2009	93.35	8.14	19.74	52.11	0.01	28.14
2019	2,262.10	7.60	17.02	47.62	0.02	35.34
Mining and Quarrying						
2009	488.55	15.36	10.70	63.08	0.01	26.21
2019	1,066.49	15.70	14.63	54.63	0.02	30.72

$ = United States dollars, DDC = domestic value-added double counted in exports, FDC = foreign value-added double counted in exports, FVA_FIN = foreign value-added in exports for final consumption, FVA_INT = foreign value-added in intermediate exports, VS = vertical specialization.

Source: Asian Development Bank. Multi-Regional Input–Output Tables Database. https://mrio.adbx.online/ (accessed 1 August 2020).

Table 3.2.4.o: Vertical Specialization, Disaggregated—Malaysia

	Exports	VS	FVA_FIN	FVA_INT	DDC	FDC
	($ million)	(% of gross exports)	(% of VS)			
Coke, Refined Petroleum, and Nuclear Fuel						
2009	14,274.68	29.47	54.60	15.61	0.40	29.39
2019	13,015.25	19.74	35.67	19.62	0.81	43.90
Electrical and Optical Equipment						
2009	43,519.52	65.93	50.74	18.73	0.60	29.94
2019	99,299.98	49.56	33.67	16.80	1.56	47.98
Food, Beverages, and Tobacco						
2009	24,788.22	28.65	57.23	30.05	0.36	12.36
2019	17,658.47	21.14	62.36	16.71	0.24	20.69

$ = United States dollars, DDC = domestic value-added double counted in exports, FDC = foreign value-added double counted in exports, FVA_FIN = foreign value-added in exports for final consumption, FVA_INT = foreign value-added in intermediate exports, VS = vertical specialization.

Source: Asian Development Bank. Multi-Regional Input–Output Tables Database. https://mrio.adbx.online/ (accessed 1 August 2020).

Table 3.2.4.p: Vertical Specialization, Disaggregated—Maldives

	Exports	VS	FVA_FIN	FVA_INT	DDC	FDC
	($ million)	(% of gross exports)	(% of VS)			
Air Transport						
2009	46.12	48.93	31.66	54.60	0.00	13.74
2019	94.85	30.53	34.49	57.63	0.01	7.87
Food, Beverages, and Tobacco						
2009	15.42	46.31	60.70	30.80	0.00	8.50
2019	85.90	42.25	83.27	9.25	0.00	7.48
Hotels and Restaurants						
2009	1,330.24	35.61	42.15	36.70	0.00	21.14
2019	2,850.85	36.53	40.81	32.77	0.01	26.42

0.00 = magnitude is less than half of unit employed, $ = United States dollars, DDC = domestic value-added double counted in exports, FDC = foreign value-added double counted in exports, FVA_FIN = foreign value-added in exports for final consumption, FVA_INT = foreign value-added in intermediate exports, VS = vertical specialization.

Source: Asian Development Bank. Multi-Regional Input–Output Tables Database. https://mrio.adbx.online/ (accessed 1 August 2020).

Table 3.2.4.q: Vertical Specialization, Disaggregated—Mongolia

	Exports	VS	FVA_FIN	FVA_INT	DDC	FDC
	($ million)	(% of gross exports)		(% of VS)		
Agriculture, Hunting, Forestry, and Fishing						
2009	157.06	10.82	35.96	49.01	0.01	15.02
2019	475.14	15.04	65.13	22.93	0.01	11.93
Mining and Quarrying						
2009	1,201.75	25.84	1.64	69.35	0.01	29.00
2019	5,619.17	24.63	14.83	61.05	0.02	24.10
Wholesale Trade and Commission Trade, Except of Motor Vehicles and Motorcycles						
2009	94.56	20.69	10.75	60.77	0.01	28.47
2019	437.68	26.03	10.62	58.47	0.02	30.89

$ = United States dollars, DDC = domestic value-added double counted in exports, FDC = foreign value-added double counted in exports, FVA_FIN = foreign value-added in exports for final consumption, FVA_INT = foreign value-added in intermediate exports, VS = vertical specialization.

Source: Asian Development Bank. Multi-Regional Input–Output Tables Database. https://mrio.adbx.online/ (accessed 1 August 2020).

Table 3.2.4.r: Vertical Specialization, Disaggregated—Nepal

	Exports	VS	FVA_FIN	FVA_INT	DDC	FDC
	($ million)	(% of gross exports)		(% of VS)		
Inland Transport						
2009	126.24	30.90	27.05	51.80	0.01	21.15
2019	149.04	35.11	16.59	65.72	0.01	17.68
Other Community, Social, and Personal Services						
2009	237.41	7.79	12.35	68.78	0.02	18.85
2019	334.37	9.46	12.84	71.14	0.02	16.01
Public Administration and Defense; Compulsory Social Security						
2009	99.87	22.15	22.88	51.32	0.01	25.79
2019	175.12	11.42	24.37	42.96	0.01	32.66

$ = United States dollars, DDC = domestic value-added double counted in exports, FDC = foreign value-added double counted in exports, FVA_FIN = foreign value-added in exports for final consumption, FVA_INT = foreign value-added in intermediate exports, VS = vertical specialization.

Source: Asian Development Bank. Multi-Regional Input–Output Tables Database. https://mrio.adbx.online/ (accessed 1 August 2020).

Table 3.2.4.s: Vertical Specialization, Disaggregated—Pakistan

	Exports	VS	FVA_FIN	FVA_INT	DDC	FDC
	($ million)	(% of gross exports)		(% of VS)		
Food, Beverages, and Tobacco						
2009	1,939.90	6.89	47.49	36.39	0.04	16.08
2019	2,704.71	9.07	54.53	27.90	0.02	17.54
Retail Trade, Except of Motor Vehicles and Motorcycles; Repair of Household Goods						
2009	1,149.79	5.53	36.61	43.49	0.07	19.84
2019	1,436.97	6.73	46.52	33.93	0.05	19.50
Textiles and Textile Products						
2009	7,893.52	8.75	49.31	26.27	0.04	24.37
2019	11,245.40	11.39	54.25	21.85	0.02	23.89

$ = United States dollars, DDC = domestic value-added double counted in exports, FDC = foreign value-added double counted in exports, FVA_FIN = foreign value-added in exports for final consumption, FVA_INT = foreign value-added in intermediate exports, VS = vertical specialization.

Source: Asian Development Bank. Multi-Regional Input–Output Tables Database. https://mrio.adbx.online/ (accessed 1 August 2020).

Table 3.2.4.t: Vertical Specialization, Disaggregated—Philippines

	Exports	VS	FVA_FIN	FVA_INT	DDC	FDC
	($ million)	(% of gross exports)		(% of VS)		
Electrical and Optical Equipment						
2009	13,207.39	45.33	18.56	31.86	0.48	49.10
2019	22,713.72	64.10	30.36	22.96	0.27	46.41
Food, Beverages, and Tobacco						
2009	6,143.06	9.58	42.59	37.04	0.08	20.29
2019	17,201.08	17.35	58.57	25.80	0.09	15.54
Renting of M&Eq and Other Business Activities						
2009	8,658.29	6.40	10.03	60.92	0.31	28.73
2019	25,760.97	8.98	10.73	56.77	0.38	32.11

$ = United States dollars, DDC = domestic value-added double counted in exports, FDC = foreign value-added double counted in exports, FVA_FIN = foreign value-added in exports for final consumption, FVA_INT = foreign value-added in intermediate exports, VS = vertical specialization.

Source: Asian Development Bank. Multi-Regional Input–Output Tables Database. https://mrio.adbx.online/ (accessed 1 August 2020).

Table 3.2.4.u: Vertical Specialization, Disaggregated—Singapore

	Exports	VS	FVA_FIN	FVA_INT	DDC	FDC
	($ million)	(% of gross exports)		(% of VS)		
Coke, Refined Petroleum, and Nuclear Fuel						
2009	27,939.88	78.26	38.13	37.33	0.18	24.37
2019	36,639.34	68.11	39.46	31.00	0.63	28.91
Electrical and Optical Equipment						
2009	53,834.74	63.38	36.02	28.05	0.67	35.26
2019	98,400.56	61.45	44.35	24.40	0.67	30.58
Wholesale Trade and Commission Trade, Except of Motor Vehicles and Motorcycles						
2009	45,920.47	31.54	15.43	62.77	0.43	21.36
2019	112,187.04	38.43	22.81	51.21	0.67	25.30

$ = United States dollars, DDC = domestic value-added double counted in exports, FDC = foreign value-added double counted in exports, FVA_FIN = foreign value-added in exports for final consumption, FVA_INT = foreign value-added in intermediate exports, VS = vertical specialization.

Source: Asian Development Bank. Multi-Regional Input–Output Tables Database. https://mrio.adbx.online/ (accessed 1 August 2020).

Table 3.2.4.v: Vertical Specialization, Disaggregated—Sri Lanka

	Exports	VS	FVA_FIN	FVA_INT	DDC	FDC
	($ million)	(% of gross exports)		(% of VS)		
Food, Beverages, and Tobacco						
2009	1,298.39	14.18	69.40	20.69	0.01	9.89
2019	1,887.64	10.38	59.49	27.16	0.01	13.34
Inland Transport						
2009	1,268.90	18.53	38.38	46.65	0.02	14.95
2019	2,195.87	12.54	31.93	51.96	0.01	16.09
Textiles and Textile Products						
2009	2,502.55	28.35	75.60	13.28	0.03	11.09
2019	2,861.96	16.03	75.07	15.40	0.01	9.52

$ = United States dollars, DDC = domestic value-added double counted in exports, FDC = foreign value-added double counted in exports, FVA_FIN = foreign value-added in exports for final consumption, FVA_INT = foreign value-added in intermediate exports, VS = vertical specialization.

Source: Asian Development Bank. Multi-Regional Input–Output Tables Database. https://mrio.adbx.online/ (accessed 1 August 2020).

Table 3.2.4.w: Vertical Specialization, Disaggregated—Taipei,China

	Exports	VS	FVA_FIN	FVA_INT	DDC	FDC
	($ million)	(% of gross exports)		(% of VS)		
Chemicals and Chemical Products						
2009	25,884.70	57.07	3.06	63.55	0.39	33.00
2019	32,228.17	56.07	9.48	57.19	0.38	32.95
Electrical and Optical Equipment						
2009	97,928.25	40.08	27.04	35.81	1.14	36.01
2019	175,042.81	41.79	20.50	38.33	1.34	39.82
Wholesale Trade and Commission Trade, Except of Motor Vehicles and Motorcycles						
2009	20,560.81	10.47	30.55	43.79	0.99	24.67
2019	39,357.15	12.10	31.26	39.42	0.91	28.40

$ = United States dollars, DDC = domestic value-added double counted in exports, FDC = foreign value-added double counted in exports, FVA_FIN = foreign value-added in exports for final consumption, FVA_INT = foreign value-added in intermediate exports, VS = vertical specialization.

Source: Asian Development Bank. Multi-Regional Input–Output Tables Database. https://mrio.adbx.online/ (accessed 1 August 2020).

Table 3.2.4.x: Vertical Specialization, Disaggregated—Thailand

	Exports	VS	FVA_FIN	FVA_INT	DDC	FDC
	($ million)	(% of gross exports)		(% of VS)		
Basic Metals and Fabricated Metal						
2009	37,192.55	47.12	18.48	53.08	0.37	28.07
2019	51,760.59	39.55	17.19	52.29	0.47	30.05
Food, Beverages, and Tobacco						
2009	12,962.54	26.03	56.01	32.23	0.18	11.58
2019	21,717.67	17.59	66.87	21.54	0.20	11.39
Wholesale Trade and Commission Trade, Except of Motor Vehicles and Motorcycles						
2009	6,214.60	15.13	32.44	43.66	0.41	23.48
2019	32,975.03	10.68	25.64	41.27	0.61	32.47

$ = United States dollars, DDC = domestic value-added double counted in exports, FDC = foreign value-added double counted in exports, FVA_FIN = foreign value-added in exports for final consumption, FVA_INT = foreign value-added in intermediate exports, VS = vertical specialization.

Source: Asian Development Bank. Multi-Regional Input–Output Tables Database. https://mrio.adbx.online/ (accessed 1 August 2020).

Table 3.2.4.y: Vertical Specialization, Disaggregated—Viet Nam						
	Exports	VS	FVA_FIN	FVA_INT	DDC	FDC
	($ million)	(% of gross exports)	(% of VS)			
Agriculture, Hunting, Forestry, and Fishing						
2009	1,923.91	27.55	30.83	53.14	0.15	15.88
2019	19,950.58	21.70	43.25	32.85	0.34	23.55
Food, Beverages, and Tobacco						
2009	10,505.64	33.14	62.04	29.24	0.05	8.67
2019	38,157.76	32.28	60.96	21.83	0.18	17.03
Mining and Quarrying						
2009	6,418.71	38.66	0.45	75.33	0.31	23.92
2019	9,372.97	20.65	19.52	51.59	0.83	28.06

$ = United States dollars, DDC = domestic value-added double counted in exports, FDC = foreign value-added double counted in exports, FVA_FIN = foreign value-added in exports for final consumption, FVA_INT = foreign value-added in intermediate exports, VS = vertical specialization.

Source: Asian Development Bank. Multi-Regional Input–Output Tables Database. https://mrio.adbx.online/ (accessed 1 August 2020).

Click here to download the table.

Definitions

This section contains the definitions of statistical indicators that are covered in Part I – Sustainable Development Goals (SDGs), Part II – Regional Trends and Tables, and Part III – Global Value Chains (GVCs). The definitions are taken mostly from the Asian Development Bank's Development Indicators Reference Manual, including websites and publications of international and private organizations such as the Food and Agriculture Organization of the United Nations (FAO); International Labour Organization (ILO); International Monetary Fund (IMF); International Telecommunication Union (ITU); Organisation for Economic Co-operation and Development (OECD); Transparency International; United Nations Children's Fund (UNICEF); United Nations Educational, Scientific and Cultural Organization (UNESCO); United Nations Population Division (UNPD); United Nations Statistics Division (UNSD); World Bank; World Health Organization (WHO); and United Nations World Tourism Organization (UNWTO). The definitions for GVCs are taken from ADB's Key Indicators for Asia and the Pacific 2015. The SDG indicators are arranged according to their respective goals and targets before they are defined, while the indicators for the Regional Trends and Tables are grouped according to their themes and subtopics before they are defined. In many instances, the indicators themselves, rather than their growth rates or ratios to another indicator, are defined.

Sustainable Development Goals

Goals and Targets	Statistical Indicators	Definition
Goal 1. End poverty in all its forms everywhere		
Target 1.1: By 2030, eradicate extreme poverty (currently measured as people living on less than $1.90 a day) for all people everywhere.	1.1.1.a: Proportion of the population living below the international poverty line, by sex, age, employment status, and geographical location (urban or rural)	Proportion of the population living on less than $1.90 a day, measured at 2011 international prices, adjusted for purchasing power parity (PPP). Note: The PPP conversion factor for private consumption is the number of units of a country's currency required to buy the same amount of goods and/or services in the domestic market as a United States (US) dollar would buy in the US.
	1.1.1.b: Proportion of the employed population living below the international poverty line, by sex	Proportion of the employed population living in households with per capita consumption or income below the international poverty line of $1.90 a day. Note: The proportion of working poor in total employment (also known as the working poverty rate) combines data on household income or consumption with labor force framework variables measured at the individual level, and sheds light on the relationship between household poverty and employment. The numbers are International Labour Organization modeled estimates. Employed persons refer to all persons of working age who, during a short reference period such as a day or a week, performed work for others in exchange for pay or profit.

(continued on next page)

Goals and Targets	Statistical Indicators	Definition
Target 1.2: By 2030, reduce at least by half the proportion of men, women, and children of all ages living in poverty in all its dimensions, according to national definitions.	1.2.1: Proportion of the population living below the national poverty line, by sex, age, and geographical location (urban or rural)	Percentage of the total population living below the national poverty line. Note: National poverty rates are defined at country-specific poverty lines in local currencies, which are different in real terms across countries and different from the international poverty line of $1.90 a day. Thus, national poverty rates cannot be compared across countries or with the poverty rate of $1.90 a day.
Target 1.3: Implement nationally appropriate social protection systems and measures for all, including floors, and by 2030 achieve substantial coverage of the poor and the vulnerable	1.3.1: Proportion of population covered by social protection floors/systems, by sex, distinguishing children, unemployed persons, older persons, persons with disabilities, pregnant women, newborns, work-injury victims and the poor and the vulnerable.	Percentage of the population effectively covered by a social protection system, including social protection floors, which provide old age pensions, social security, and health insurance benefits. Effective coverage of social protection is measured by the number of people who are either actively contributing to a social insurance scheme or receiving benefits (contributory or noncontributory). Coverage is expressed as a share of the respective population. (i) Population covered by at least one social protection benefit (effective coverage): proportion of the total population receiving at least one contributory or noncontributory cash benefit, or actively contributing to at least one social security scheme. (ii) Older persons: ratio of persons above statutory retirement age receiving an old-age pension to the number of persons above statutory retirement age (including contributory and noncontributory). (iii) Vulnerable persons covered by social assistance: ratio of social assistance recipients to the total number of vulnerable persons (defined as all children plus adults not covered by contributory benefits and persons above retirement age not receiving contributory benefits, i.e., pensions). (iv) Children: ratio of children or households receiving child or family cash benefits to the total number of children or households with children.
Goal 2. End hunger, achieve food security and improved nutrition, and promote sustainable agriculture		
Target 2.1: By 2030, end hunger and ensure access by all people, in particular the poor and people in vulnerable situations, including infants, to safe, nutritious, and sufficient food all year round.	2.1.1: Prevalence of undernourishment	Proportion of the population whose habitual food consumption is insufficient to provide the dietary energy levels that are required to maintain a normal active and healthy life. Note: Undernourishment is defined as the condition by which a person has access, on a regular basis, to amounts of food that are insufficient to provide the energy required for conducting a normal, healthy, and active life, given his or her own dietary energy requirements.
Target 2.2: By 2030, end all forms of malnutrition, including achieving, by 2025, the internationally agreed targets on stunting and wasting in children under 5 years of age, and address the nutritional needs of adolescent girls, pregnant and lactating women, and older persons.	2.2.1: Prevalence of stunting—height for age <-2 standard deviation from the median of the World Health Organization (WHO) Child Growth Standards—among children under 5 years of age	Prevalence of stunting—height-for-age <-2 standard deviation from the median of WHO Child Growth Standards—among children under 5 years of age. Note: Stunting refers to the impaired growth and development that children experience from poor nutrition, repeated infection, and inadequate psychosocial stimulation.

(continued on next page)

Goals and Targets	Statistical Indicators	Definition
	2.2.2.b: Prevalence of malnutrition—weight for height <-2 standard deviation from the median of the WHO Child Growth Standards—among children under 5 years of age (wasting)	Prevalence of wasting—weight for height <-2 standard deviation from the median of WHO Child Growth Standards—among children under 5 years of age. Note: Child wasting refers to a child who is too thin for his or her height and is the result of recent rapid weight loss or the failure to gain weight.
	2.2.2.a: Prevalence of malnutrition—weight for height >+2 standard deviation from the median of the WHO Child Growth Standards—among children under 5 years of age (overweight)	Prevalence of overweight—weight for height >+2 standard deviation from the median of WHO Child Growth Standards—among children under 5 years of age. Note: Child overweight refers to a child who is too heavy for his or her height.
Target 2.a: Increase investment, including through enhanced international cooperation, in rural infrastructure, agricultural research and extension services, technology development, and plant and livestock gene banks in order to enhance agricultural productive capacity in developing countries, in particular least developed countries.	2.a.1: The agriculture orientation index for government expenditures	The Agriculture Orientation Index for Government Expenditures is defined as the Agriculture share of government expenditure, divided by the Agriculture value added share of gross domestic product (GDP), where agriculture refers to the agriculture, forestry, fishing, and hunting sector. The measure is a currency-free index, calculated as the ratio of these two shares. National governments are requested to compile government expenditures according to the Government Finance Statistics system and the Classification of Functions of Government, and agriculture value-added share of GDP according to the System of National Accounts. Note: Government Expenditure are all expenses and acquisition of nonfinancial assets associated with supporting a particular sector, as defined in the Government Finance Statistics Manual 2014 developed by the International Monetary Fund (IMF).
	2.a.2: Total official flows (official development assistance plus other official flows) to the agriculture sector	Gross disbursements of total official development assistance (ODA) and other official flows from all donors to the agriculture sector. Note: The Development Assistance Committee defines ODA as those flows to countries and territories on the committee's List of ODA Recipients and to multilateral institutions which are (i) provided by official agencies, including state and local governments, or by their executive agencies; and (ii) each transaction is administered with the promotion of the economic development and welfare of developing countries as its main objective; and (iii) is concessional in character and conveys a grant element of at least 25% (calculated at a rate of discount of 10%). Other Official Flows are defined as transactions by the official sector which do not meet the conditions for eligibility as ODA, either because they are not primarily aimed at development, or because they are not sufficiently concessional. They also exclude officially supported export credits.

(continued on next page)

Goals and Targets	Statistical Indicators	Definition
Goal 3. Ensure healthy lives and promote well-being for all at all ages		
Target 3.1: By 2030, reduce the global maternal mortality ratio to less than 70 per 100,000 live births.	3.1.1: Maternal mortality ratio	Number of maternal deaths during a given time period per 100,000 live births during the same time period. Note: The term maternal deaths refers to the annual number of female deaths from any cause related to, or aggravated by, pregnancy or its management (excluding accidental or incidental causes) during pregnancy and childbirth or within 42 days of termination of pregnancy, irrespective of the duration and site of the pregnancy, expressed per 100,000 live births, for a specified time period.
	3.1.2: Proportion of births attended by skilled health personnel	Percentage of childbirths attended by professional health personnel. These are competent maternal and newborn health professionals educated, trained, and regulated to national and international standards. They are competent to: (i) provide and promote evidence-based, human-rights based, quality, socioculturally sensitive, and dignified care to women and newborns; (ii) facilitate physiological processes during labor and delivery to ensure a clean and positive childbirth experience; and (iii) identify and manage or refer women and/or newborns with complications. Traditional birth attendants, even if they receive a short training course, are not included. Note: Having a skilled attendant at the time of delivery is an important lifesaving intervention for both mothers and babies. Not having access to this key assistance is detrimental to women's health and gender empowerment because it could cause the death of the mother or long-lasting disability, especially in marginalized settings.
Target 3.2: By 2030, end preventable deaths of newborns and children under 5 years of age, with all countries aiming to reduce neonatal mortality to at least as low as 12 per 1,000 live births and under-5 mortality to at least as low as 25 per 1,000 live births.	3.2.1: Under-5 mortality rate	The probability of a child born in a specific year or period dying before reaching the age of 5 years, if subject to age specific mortality rates of that period, expressed per 1,000 live births. Note: The under-5 mortality rate as defined here is, strictly speaking, not a rate (i.e., the number of deaths divided by the number of population at risk during a certain period of time) but a probability of death derived from a life table and expressed as a rate per 1,000 live births.
	3.2.2: Neonatal mortality rate	Probability that a child born in a specific year or period will die during the first 28 completed days of life, if subject to age-specific mortality rates of that period, expressed per 1,000 live births. Note: Neonatal deaths (deaths among live births during the first 28 completed days of life) may be subdivided into early neonatal deaths, occurring during the first 7 days of life, and late neonatal deaths, occurring after the seventh day but before the 28th completed day of life.
Target 3.3: By 2030, end the epidemics of AIDS, tuberculosis, malaria, and neglected tropical diseases; and combat hepatitis, water-borne diseases, and other communicable diseases.	3.3.1: Number of new HIV infections per 1,000 uninfected population, by sex, age, and key populations	Number of new HIV infections per 1,000 person-years among the uninfected population.
	3.3.2: Tuberculosis incidence per 100,000 population	Estimated number of new and relapse tuberculosis cases (all forms of tuberculosis, including cases in people living with HIV) arising in a given year, expressed as a rate per 100,000 population.
	3.3.3: Malaria incidence per 1,000 population	The number of new cases of malaria per 1,000 people at risk each year.

(continued on next page)

Goals and Targets	Statistical Indicators	Definition
Target 3.4: By 2030, reduce by one third premature mortality from noncommunicable diseases through prevention and treatment, and promote mental health and well-being.	3.4.1: Mortality rate attributed to cardiovascular disease, cancer, diabetes, or chronic respiratory disease	Probability of dying between the ages of 30 and 70 years from cardiovascular diseases, cancer, diabetes, or chronic respiratory diseases, defined as the percentage of 30-year-old people who would die before their 70th birthday from cardiovascular disease, cancer, diabetes, or chronic respiratory disease, assuming that a person would experience current mortality rates at every age and he or she would not die from any other cause of death (e.g., injuries or HIV/AIDS). Note: Probability of dying refers to the likelihood that an individual would die between two ages given current mortality rates at each age, calculated using life table methods. The probability of death between two ages may be called a mortality rate.
	3.4.2: Suicide mortality rate	The number of suicide deaths in a year, divided by the population and multiplied by 100,000. Note: The number of suicide deaths refers to crude suicide rates (per 100,000 population).
Target 3.6: By 2020, halve the number of global deaths and injuries from road traffic accidents.	3.6.1: Death rate due to road traffic injuries	Number of road traffic fatal injury deaths per 100,000 population.
Target 3.7: By 2030, ensure universal access to sexual and reproductive health care services, including for family planning, information and education, and the integration of reproductive health into national strategies and programme	3.7.1: Proportion of women of reproductive age (15–49 years) who have their need for family planning satisfied by modern methods	The percentage of women of reproductive age (15–49 years) who desire either to have no (additional) children or to postpone the next child, and who are currently using a modern method of contraception. . The indicator is also referred to as the demand for family planning satisfied with modern methods.
	3.7.2: Adolescent birth rate (15–19 years) per 1,000 women in that age group	Annual number of births to females aged 15–19 years per 1,000 females in the respective age group.
Target 3.8: Achieve universal health coverage, including financial risk protection, access to quality essential healthcare services and access to safe, effective, quality and affordable essential medicines and vaccines for all	3.8.1 Coverage of essential health services (defined as the average coverage of essential services based on tracer interventions that include reproductive, maternal, newborn and child heath, infectious diseases, non-communicable diseases and service capacity and access, among the general and the most disadvantaged population)	The indicator is an index reported on a unitless scale of 0 to 100, which is calculated as the geometric mean of 14 tracer indicators of health service coverage. Note: The index of health service coverage is calculated as the geometric means of tracer indicators. The tracer indicators are organized by four broad categories of service coverage: (i) reproductive, maternal, newborn, and child health; (ii) infectious diseases; (iii) noncommunicable diseases; and (iv) service capacity and access.

(continued on next page)

Goals and Targets	Statistical Indicators	Definition
Target 3.9: By 2030, substantially reduce the number of deaths and illnesses from hazardous chemicals and air, water, and soil pollution and contamination.	3.9.1: Mortality rate attributed to household and ambient air pollution	Expressed as the number of deaths and death rate. Death rates are calculated by dividing the number of deaths by the total population (or indicated if a different population group is used, e.g., children under 5 years). Note: Evidence from epidemiological studies has shown that exposure to air pollution is linked to, among others, the important diseases taken into account in this estimate: - acute respiratory infections in young children (estimated under 5 years of age); - cerebrovascular diseases (stroke) in adults (estimated above 25 years of age); - ischemic heart diseases in adults (estimated above 25 years of age); - chronic obstructive pulmonary disease in adults (estimated above 25 years of age); and - lung cancer in adults (estimated above 25 years of age).
	3.9.2: Mortality rate attributed to unsafe water, unsafe sanitation, and lack of hygiene—exposure to unsafe water, sanitation, and hygiene for all (WASH) services	Number of deaths from unsafe water, unsafe sanitation, and lack of hygiene —exposure to unsafe water, sanitation and hygiene for all (WASH) services—in a year, divided by the population, and multiplied by 100,000.
Goal 4. Ensure inclusive and equitable quality education and promote lifelong learning opportunities for all		
Target 4.2: By 2030, ensure that all girls and boys have access to quality early childhood development, care, and preprimary education, so that they are ready for primary education.	4.2.2: Participation rate in organized learning (1 year before the official primary entry age), by sex	Percentage of children in the given age range who participate in one or more organized learning programs, including programs which offer a combination of education and care. Participation in early childhood and in primary education are both included. The age range will vary by country depending on the official age for entry to primary education. Note: An organized learning program is one that consists of a coherent set or sequence of educational activities designed with the intention of achieving predetermined learning outcomes or the accomplishment of a specific set of educational tasks. Early childhood and primary education programs are examples of organized learning programs. The official primary entry age is the age at which children are obliged to start primary education, according to national legislation or policies.
Target 4.c: By 2030, substantially increase the supply of qualified teachers, including through international cooperation for teacher training in developing countries, especially least developed countries and small island developing states.	4.c.1.a: Proportion of teachers in preprimary education who have received at least the minimum organized teacher training 4.c.1.b: Proportion of teachers in primary education who have received at least the minimum organized teacher training	Percentage of teachers by level of education taught (pre-primary, primary, lower secondary, and upper secondary education) who have received at least the minimum organized pedagogical teacher training pre-service and in-service required for teaching at the relevant level in a given country. Note: Number of teachers in a given level of education who are trained is expressed as a percentage of all teachers in that level of education.

(continued on next page)

Goals and Targets	Statistical Indicators	Definition
	4.c.1.c: Proportion of teachers in lower secondary education who have received at least the minimum organized teacher training 4.c.1.d: Proportion of teachers in upper secondary education who have received at least the minimum organized teacher training	A teacher is trained if they have received at least the minimum organized pedagogical teacher training pre-service and in-service required for teaching at the relevant level in each country.
Goal 5. Achieve gender equality and empower all women and girls		
Target 5.3: Eliminate all harmful practices, such as child, early, and forced marriage, and female genital mutilation.	5.3.1: Proportion of women aged 20–24 years who were married or in a union before age 15 and before age 18	Proportion of women aged 20–24 years who were married or in a union before age 15 years and before age 18 years. Note: Both formal (i.e., marriages) and informal unions are covered under this indicator. Informal unions are generally defined as those in which a couple lives together (i.e., cohabits) for some time, intends to have a lasting relationship, but for which there has been no formal civil or religious ceremony.
Target 5.5: Ensure women's full and effective participation in, and equal opportunities for leadership at, all levels of decision-making in political, economic, and public life.	5.5.1: Proportion of seats held by women in national parliaments	The proportion of seats held by women in national parliaments, as of 1 January of reporting year, is currently measured as the number of seats held by women members in single or lower chambers of national parliaments, expressed as a percentage of all occupied seats. Note: National parliaments can be bicameral or unicameral. This indicator covers the single chamber in unicameral parliaments and the lower chamber in bicameral parliaments. It does not cover the upper chamber of bicameral parliaments. Seats are usually won by members in general parliamentary elections. Seats may also be filled by nomination, appointment, indirect election, rotation of members, and by-election. Seats refer to the number of parliamentary mandates, or the number of members of parliament.
	5.5.2: Proportion of women in managerial positions	Proportion of females in the total number of persons employed in senior and middle management. Senior and middle management correspond to major group 1 in International Standard Classification of Occupations (ISCO)-08 and ISCO-88, minus category 14 in ISCO-08 (hospitality, retail, and other services managers) and minus category 13 in ISCO-88 (general managers), since these comprise mainly managers of small enterprises. Note: The indicator provides information on the proportion of women who are employed in decision-making and managerial roles in government, large enterprises, and institutions, thus providing some insight into women's power in decision-making and in the economy (especially compared to men's power in those areas).

(continued on next page)

Goals and Targets	Statistical Indicators	Definition
Goal 6. Ensure availability and sustainable management of water and sanitation for all		
Target 6.1: By 2030, achieve universal and equitable access to safe and affordable drinking water for all.	6.1.1: Proportion of population using safely managed drinking water services	Proportion of the population using safely managed drinking water services is currently being measured by the proportion of the population using an improved basic drinking water source that is located on premises, available when needed, and free of fecal (and priority chemical) contamination. Note: Improved drinking water sources include the following: piped water into a dwelling, yard, or plot; public taps or standpipes; boreholes or tubewells; protected dug wells; protected springs; packaged water; delivered water and rainwater. "Located on premises": a water source at the point of collection is within the dwelling, yard, or plot. "Available when needed": households are able to access sufficient quantities of water when needed. "Free from fecal (and priority chemical) contamination": water complies with relevant national or local standards. In the absence of such standards, reference is made to the WHO Guidelines for Drinking Water Quality http://www.who.int/water_sanitation_health/dwq/guidelines/en/). E. coli or thermotolerant coliforms are the preferred indicator for microbiological quality, and arsenic and fluoride are the priority chemicals for global reporting. The WHO/UNICEF Joint Monitoring Programme (JMP) for Water Supply, Sanitation, and Hygiene estimates access to basic services for each country, separately in urban and rural areas, by fitting a regression line to a series of data points from household surveys and censuses. This approach was used to report on use of 'improved water' sources for Millennium Development Goal monitoring. The JMP is evaluating the use of alternative statistical estimation methods as more data become available. The JMP 2017 update and SDG baselines report describes in more detail how data on availability and quality from different sources, can be combined with data on use of different types of supplies, as recorded in the current JMP database to compute the safely managed drinking water services indicator. https://washdata.org/report/jmp-2017-report-final.
Target 6.2: By 2030, achieve access to adequate and equitable sanitation and hygiene for all, and end open defecation, paying special attention to the needs of women and girls and those in vulnerable situations.	6.2.1.a: Proportion of population using safely managed sanitation services	The proportion of the population using a basic sanitation facility, including handwashing facility with soap and water, that is not shared with other households and where excreta is safely disposed in situ or treated off-site. Note: Improved sanitation facilities include flush or pour-flush toilets to sewer systems, septic tanks or pit latrines, ventilated improved pit latrines, pit latrines with a slab, and composting toilets.

(continued on next page)

Goals and Targets	Statistical Indicators	Definition
		"Safely disposed in situ": when pit latrines and septic tanks are not emptied, the excreta may still remain isolated from human contact and can be considered safely managed. For example, with the new SDG indicator, households that use twin pit latrines or safely abandon full pit latrines and dig new facilities, a common practice in rural areas, would be counted as using safely managed sanitation services.
		"Treated offsite": not all excreta from toilet facilities conveyed in sewers (as wastewater) or emptied from pit latrines and septic tanks (as faecal sludge) reaches a treatment site. For instance, a portion may leak from the sewer itself or, due to broken pumping installations, be discharged directly to the environment. Similarly, a portion of the faecal sludge emptied from containers may be discharged into open drains, to open ground or water bodies, rather than being transported to a treatment plant. And finally, even once the excreta reach a treatment plant a portion may remain untreated, due to dysfunctional treatment equipment or inadequate treatment capacity, and be discharged to the environment. For the purposes of SDG monitoring, adequacy of treatment will initially be assessed based on the reported level of treatment.
		"A handwashing facility with soap and water": a handwashing facility is a device to contain, transport or regulate the flow of water to facilitate handwashing.
Target 6.4: By 2030, substantially increase water-use efficiency across all sectors and ensure sustainable withdrawals and supply of freshwater to address water scarcity and substantially reduce the number of people suffering from water scarcity.	6.4.2: Level of water stress; freshwater withdrawal as a proportion of available freshwater resources	The level of water stress: freshwater withdrawal as a proportion of available freshwater resources is the ratio between total freshwater withdrawn by all major sectors and total renewable freshwater resources, after taking into account environmental water requirements. Note: Total freshwater withdrawal is the volume of freshwater extracted from its source (rivers, lakes, aquifers) for agriculture, industries, and municipalities. Freshwater withdrawal includes primary freshwater (not withdrawn before), secondary freshwater (previously withdrawn and returned to rivers and groundwater, such as discharged wastewater and agricultural drainage water) and fossil groundwater. Main sectors, as defined by International Standard Industrial Classification standards, include agriculture, forestry and fishing, manufacturing, electricity industry, and services. Environmental water requirements are the quantities of water required to sustain freshwater and estuarine ecosystems. This indicator is also known as water withdrawal intensity. Total renewable freshwater resources are expressed as the sum of internal and external renewable water resources. Internal renewable water resources are defined as the long-term average annual flow of rivers and recharge of groundwater, generated from endogenous precipitation, for a given country. External renewable water resources refer to the flows of water entering the country, taking into consideration the quantity of flows reserved to upstream and downstream countries through agreements or treaties.

(continued on next page)

Goals and Targets	Statistical Indicators	Definition
Target 6.a: By 2030, expand international cooperation and capacity-building support to developing countries in water- and sanitation-related activities and programs, including water harvesting, desalination, water efficiency, wastewater treatment, recycling, and reuse technologies.	6.a.1: Amount of water- and sanitation-related ODA that is part of a government-coordinated spending plan	Amount of water- and sanitation-related ODA that is part of a government-coordinated spending plan is defined as the proportion of total water- and sanitation-related ODA disbursements that are included in the government budget. Note: The amount of water- and sanitation-related ODA is a quantifiable measurement as a proxy for "international cooperation and capacity development support" in financial terms. A low value of this indicator (near 0%) would suggest that international donors are investing in water- and sanitation-related activities and programs in the country, outside the purview of the national government. A high value (near 100%) would indicate that donors are aligned with the national government and national policies and plans for water and sanitation.
Goal 7. Ensure access to affordable, reliable, sustainable, and modern energy for all		
Target 7.1: By 2030, ensure universal access to affordable, reliable, and modern energy services.	7.1.1: Proportion of population with access to electricity	Percentage of the population with access to electricity. Note: Access to electricity addresses major critical issues in all the dimensions of sustainable development. The target has a wide range of social and economic impacts, including facilitating development of household-based income-generating activities and lightening the burden of household tasks.
	7.1.2: Proportion of population with primary reliance on clean fuels and technology	Number of people using clean fuels and technologies for cooking, heating and lighting divided by total population reporting that any cooking, heating or lighting, expressed as percentage. "Clean" is defined by the emission rate targets and specific fuel recommendations (i.e. against unprocessed coal and kerosene) included in the normative guidance WHO guidelines for indoor air quality: household fuel combustion.
Target 7.2: By 2030, increase substantially the share of renewable energy in the global energy mix.	7.2.1: Renewable energy share in total final energy consumption	Percentage of final consumption of energy that is derived from renewable resources. Note: Renewable energy consumption includes consumption of energy derived from hydro, solid biofuels, wind, solar, liquid biofuels, biogas, geothermal, marine sources, and waste. Total final energy consumption is calculated from national balances and statistics as total final consumption minus nonenergy use.
Target 7.3: By 2030, double the global rate of improvement in energy efficiency.	7.3.1: Energy intensity measured in terms of primary energy and GDP	Energy supplied to the economy per unit value of economic output. Note: Total energy supply, as defined by the International Recommendations for Energy Statistics, is made up of production, plus net imports, minus international marine and aviation bunkers plus-stock changes. GDP is the measure of economic output. For international comparison purposes, GDP is measured in constant terms at PPP.
Goal 8. Promote sustained, inclusive, and sustainable economic growth, full and productive employment, and decent work for all		
Target 8.1: Sustain per-capita economic growth in accordance with national circumstances and, in particular, at least 7% GDP growth per annum in the least developed countries.	8.1.1: Annual growth rate of real GDP per capita	Percentage change in the real GDP per capita between 2 consecutive years. Note: Real GDP per capita is calculated by dividing GDP at constant prices by the population of a country or area. The data for real GDP is measured in constant US dollars to facilitate the calculation of country growth rates and aggregation of the country data.

(continued on next page)

Goals and Targets	Statistical Indicators	Definition
Target 8.2: Achieve higher levels of economic productivity through diversification, technological upgrading, and innovation, including through a focus on high-value-added and labor-intensive sectors.	8.2.1: Annual growth rate of real GDP per employed person	Annual percentage change in real GDP per employed person. Note: The real GDP per employed person being a measure of labor productivity, this indicator represents a measure of labor productivity growth, thus providing information on the evolution, efficiency and quality of human capital in the production process.
Target 8.5: By 2030, achieve full and productive employment and decent work for all women and men, including for young people and persons with disabilities, and equal pay for work of equal value.	8.5.2: Unemployment rate, by sex, age, and persons with disabilities	Percentage of persons in the labor force who are unemployed. Note: Unemployed persons are defined as all those of working age (usually persons aged 15 and above) who were not in employment, carried out activities to seek employment during a specified recent period, and were currently available to take up employment given a job opportunity, where: (i) "not in employment" is assessed with respect to the short reference period for the measurement of employment; (ii) to "seek employment" refers to any activity when carried out, during a specified recent period comprising the past 4 weeks or 1 month, for the purpose of finding a job or setting up a business or agricultural undertaking; (iii) the point when the enterprise starts to exist should be used to distinguish between search activities aimed at setting up a business and the work activity itself, as evidenced by the enterprise's registration to operate or by when financial resources become available, the necessary infrastructure or materials are in place, or the first client or order is received, depending on the context; and (iv) "currently available" serves as a test of readiness to start a job in the present, assessed with respect to a short reference period comprising that used to measure employment (depending on national circumstances, the reference period may be extended to include a short subsequent period not exceeding 2 weeks in total, so as to ensure adequate coverage of unemployment situations among different population groups).
Target 8.6: By 2020, substantially reduce the proportion of youth not in employment, education, or training.	8.6.1: Proportion of youth (aged 15–24 years) not in education, employment, or training	Proportion of youth (aged 15–24 years) who are not in education, employment, or training, also known as "the NEET rate". It conveys the number of young persons not in education, employment, or training as a percentage of the total youth population.
Target 8.7: Take immediate and effective measures to eradicate forced labor, end modern slavery and human trafficking, and secure the prohibition and elimination of the worst forms of child labor, including recruitment and use of child soldiers, and, by 2025, end child labor in all its forms.	8.7.1: Proportion of children aged 5–17 years engaged in child labor	The number of children aged 5–17 years reported to be in child labor during the reference period (usually the week prior to the survey). The proportion of children in child labor is calculated as the number of children in child labor, divided by the total number of children in the population.

(continued on next page)

Goals and Targets	Statistical Indicators	Definition
Target 8.10: Strengthen the capacity of domestic financial institutions to encourage and expand access to banking, insurance, and financial services for all.	8.10.1: Number of commercial bank branches and ATMs per 100,000 adults	The number of commercial bank branches per 100,000 adults refers to the number of commercial banks branches reported by the central bank or the main financial regulator of the country every year. To make it comparable, this number is presented as a reference per 100,000 adults in the respective country. The number of ATMs per 100,000 adults, refers to the number of ATMs in the country for all types of institutions, such as commercial banks, non-deposit-taking microfinance institutions, deposit-taking microfinance institutions, credit unions, financial cooperatives, and others. This information is reported every year by the central bank or the main financial regulator of the country. To make it comparable, this number is presented as a reference per 100,000 adults in the respective country.
	8.10.2: Proportion of adults (aged 15 years and older) with an account at a bank or other financial institution or with a mobile-money service provider	Percentage of adults (aged 15+) who report having an account (of their own or held with someone else) at a bank or another type of financial institution or have personally used a mobile-money service in the past 12 months.
Target 8.a: Increase Aid for Trade support for developing countries, in particular least developed countries, including through the Enhanced Integrated Framework for Traderelated Technical Assistance to Least Developed Countries	8.a.1 Aid for Trade commitments and disbursements	Aid for Trade is reported here by recipient, as well as by donor country. This is measured as total ODA allocated to aid for trade in 2015 US dollars.
Goal 9. Build resilient infrastructure, promote inclusive and sustainable industrialization, and foster innovation		
Target 9.1: Develop quality, reliable, sustainable, and resilient infrastructure, including regional and transborder infrastructure, to support economic development and human well-being, with a focus on affordable and equitable access for all.	9.1.a: Passenger volume by road transport, measured in millions of passenger-kilometers	Passenger and freight volumes are the sums of the passenger and freight volumes reported for the road and rail carriers in terms of number of people and metric tons of cargo, respectively. Note: The International Transport Forum collects data on transport (rail and road) statistics on annual basis from all its member countries. Data are collected from transport ministries, statistical offices, and other institutions designated as official data sources. Although there are clear definitions for all the terms used in this survey, countries might have different methodologies to calculate passenger-kilometers and ton-kilometers. Methods could be based on traffic or mobility surveys, using very different sampling methods and estimating techniques, which could affect the comparability of the statistics.
	9.1.b: Freight volume by road transport, measured in millions of ton-kilometers	
	9.1.c: Passenger volume by rail transport, measured in millions of passenger-kilometers	
	9.1.d: Freight volume by rail transport, measured in millions of ton-kilometers	
Target 9.2: Promote inclusive and sustainable industrialization and, by 2030, significantly raise industry's share of employment and GDP, in line with national circumstances, and double its share in least developed countries.	9.2.1: Manufacturing value added as a proportion of GDP and per capita	Manufacturing value added (MVA) as a proportion of GDP is a ratio between MVA and GDP, both reported in constant 2015 US dollars. MVA per capita is calculated by dividing MVA in constant 2015 US dollars by the population of a country or area.

(continued on next page)

Goals and Targets	Statistical Indicators	Definition
	9.2.2: Manufacturing employment as a proportion of total employment	Share of manufacturing employment in total employment.
Target 9.4: By 2030, upgrade infrastructure and retrofit industries to make them sustainable, with increased resource-use efficiency and greater adoption of clean and environmentally sound technologies and industrial processes, with all countries taking action in accordance with their respective capabilities.	9.4.1: Carbon dioxide (CO_2) emissions per unit of value-added	CO_2 emissions per unit value-added is an indicator calculated as ratio between CO_2 emissions from fuel combustion and the value added of associated economic activities. The indicator can be calculated for the whole economy (total CO_2 emissions to GDP) or for specific sectors, notably the manufacturing sector (CO_2 emissions from manufacturing industries per MVA). CO_2 emissions per unit of GDP are expressed in kilograms of CO_2 per constant 2010 US dollar PPP of GDP. CO_2 emissions from manufacturing industries per unit of MVA are measured in kilograms of CO_2 equivalent per unit of MVA in constant 2015 US dollars.
Target 9.5: Enhance scientific research and upgrade the technological capabilities of industrial sectors in all countries, in particular developing countries, including, by 2030, encouraging innovation and substantially increasing the number of research and development workers per 1 million people and public and private research and development spending.	9.5.1: Research and development expenditure as a proportion of GDP	Amount of research and development expenditure divided by the total output of the economy.
	9.5.2: Researchers (full-time equivalent) per million inhabitants	Number of research and development workers per 1 million people.
Target 9.a: Facilitate sustainable and resilient infrastructure development in developing countries through enhanced financial, technological, and technical support to African countries, least developed countries, landlocked developing countries, and small island developing states.	9.a.1: Total official international support (ODA plus other official flows) to infrastructure	Gross disbursements of total ODA and other official flows from all donors in support of infrastructure.
Target 9.b: Support domestic technology development, research, and innovation in developing countries, including by ensuring a conducive policy environment for, among other things, industrial diversification and value addition to commodities.	9.b.1: Proportion of medium- and high-tech industry value-added in total value-added	Ratio of the value added by medium- and high-tech (MHT) industry to total MVA. Note: Industrial development generally entails a structural transition from resource-based and low-tech activities to MHT activities. A modern, highly complex production structure offers better opportunities for skills development and technological innovation. MHT activities are also the high-value addition industries of manufacturing with higher technological intensity and labor productivity. Increasing the share of MHT sectors also reflects the impact of innovation.

(continued on next page)

Goals and Targets	Statistical Indicators	Definition
Target 9.c: Significantly increase access to information and communications technology and strive to provide universal and affordable access to the Internet in least developed countries by 2020.	9.c.1.a: Proportion of the population covered by narrowband (2G) mobile networks 9.c.1.b: Proportion of the population covered by 3G mobile networks 9.c.1.c: Proportion of the population covered by LTE mobile networks	Proportion of the population covered by a mobile network, broken down by technology, refers to the percentage of inhabitants living within range of a mobile-cellular signal, irrespective of whether or not they are mobile-phone subscribers or users. This is calculated by dividing the number of inhabitants within range of a mobile-cellular signal by the total population and multiplying by 100. Note: Coverage refers to Long-Term Evolution (LTE), broadband (3G), and narrowband (2G) mobile-cellular technologies: 2G mobile population coverage refers to the percentage of inhabitants within range of a mobile networks with access to data communications (e.g. Internet) at downstream speeds below 256 Kbit/s. This includes mobile-cellular technologies such as general packet radio service (GPRS), code division multiple access (CDMA) 2000 1x and most enhanced data for GSM (global system for mobile communications) evolution (EDGE) implementations. 3G population coverage refers to the percentage of inhabitants that are within range of at least a 3G mobile-cellular signal, irrespective of whether or not they are subscribers. Long-term evolution (LTE) population coverage refers to the percentage of inhabitants that live within range of LTE/LTE-Advanced, mobile WiMAX/WirelessMAN or other more advanced mobile-cellular networks, irrespective of whether or not they are subscribers.
Goal 10. Reduce inequality within and among countries		
Target 10.1: By 2030, progressively achieve and sustain income growth of the bottom 40% of the population at a rate higher than the national average.	10.1.1.a: Growth rates of household expenditure or income per capita among the bottom 40% of the population	The growth rate in the welfare aggregate of the bottom 40% of the population is calculated as the annualized average growth rate in per capita real consumption or income of the bottom 40% of the income distribution in a country from household surveys over a period of approximately 5 years.
	10.1.1.b: Growth rates of household expenditure or income per capita	The national average growth rate in the welfare aggregate is calculated as the annualized average growth rate in per capita real consumption or income of the total population in a country from household surveys over a period of approximately 5 years.
Goal 11. Make cities and human settlements inclusive, safe, resilient, and sustainable		
Target 11.1: By 2030, ensure access for all to adequate, safe, and affordable housing and basic services, and upgrade slums.	11.1.1: Proportion of the urban population living in slums, informal settlements, or inadequate housing	The proportion of the urban population living in slums, informal settlements, or inadequate housing to total urban population is currently being measured by the proportion of the urban population living in slums and informal settlements. This indicator has been monitored for the past 17 years by United Nations (UN)-Habitat in mostly developing countries with a new component—inadequate housing or affordability—that applies largely to the developed countries. By integrating these two components, the indicator is now universal and can be monitored in both developing and developed regions. The inadequate housing component allows capturing housing informality in more developed countries and wealthier urban contexts. Note: This indicator is expected to be a composite one, with the main components of slum/informal settlements' and the added component of affordability defining inadequate housing.

(continued on next page)

Goals and Targets	Statistical Indicators	Definition
Target 11.5: By 2030, significantly reduce the number of deaths and the number of people affected, and substantially decrease the direct economic losses relative to global GDP caused by disasters, including water-related disasters, with a focus on protecting the poor and people in vulnerable situations	11.5.2: Direct economic loss in relation to global GDP, damage to critical infrastructure, and number of disruptions to basic services, attributed to disasters	Direct economic loss is the monetary value of total or partial destruction of physical assets existing in the affected area. Direct economic loss is nearly equivalent to physical damage. Note: The original national disaster loss databases usually register physical damage value (housing unit loss, infrastructure loss, etc.), which needs conversion to a monetary value according to the United Nations International Strategy for Disaster Reduction methodology*. The converted global value is divided by global GDP (inflation adjusted, constant US dollars) calculated from the World Bank Development Indicators.
Target 11.6: By 2030, reduce the adverse per capita environmental impact of cities, including by paying special attention to air quality and municipal and other waste management.	11.6.2: Annual mean levels of fine particulate matter (PM), e.g., PM2.5 and PM10, in cities, measured in total (population weighted) micrograms per cubic meter	The mean annual concentration of fine suspended particles of less than 2.5 microns in diameters (PM2.5) is a common measure of air pollution. Note: The mean is a population-weighted average for urban population in a country and is expressed in micrograms per cubic meter
Goal 12. Ensure sustainable consumption and production patterns		
Target 12.2: By 2030, achieve the sustainable management and efficient use of natural resources	12.2.1: Material footprint, material footprint per capita, and material footprint per GDP	Material footprint is the attribution of global material extraction to domestic final demand of a country. The total material footprint is the sum of the material footprint for biomass, fossil fuels, metal ores, and nonmetal ores. This indicator is calculated as raw material equivalent of imports plus domestic extraction minus raw material equivalents of exports. For the attribution of the primary material needs of final demand, a global, multiregional input-output framework is employed.
	12.2.2: Domestic material consumption, domestic material consumption per capita, and domestic material consumption per GDP	Domestic material consumption (DMC) is a standard material flow accounting indicator and reports the apparent consumption of materials in a national economy. Note: DMC reports the amount of materials that are used in a national economy. DMC is a territorial (production side) indicator. DMC also presents the amount of material that needs to be handled within an economy, which is either added to material stocks of buildings and transport infrastructure or used to fuel the economy as material throughput. DMC describes the physical dimension of economic processes and interactions. It can also be interpreted as long-term waste equivalent. Per capita DMC describes the average level of material use in an economy – an environmental pressure indicator – and is also referred to as metabolic profile.

(continued on next page)

Goals and Targets	Statistical Indicators	Definition
Goal 13. Take urgent action to combat climate change and its impacts		
Target 13.1: Strengthen resilience and adaptive capacity to climate-related hazards and natural disasters in all countries.	13.1.1.a: Number of persons affected by disasters	Number of people who were directly affected by disasters per 100,000 population. Note: Directly affected means people who have suffered injury, illness, or other health effects; who were evacuated, displaced, or relocated; or have suffered direct damage to their livelihoods, economic, physical, social, cultural, and/or environmental assets.
	13.1.1.b: Number of deaths due to disasters	The number of people who died during disaster, or directly after, as a direct result of the hazardous event.
	13.1.2: Number of countries that adopt and implement national disaster risk reduction strategies in line the Sendai Framework for Disaster Risk Reduction 2015–2030	Number of countries that adopt and implement local disaster risk reduction strategies in line with national disaster risk reduction strategies. Note: The score of adoption and implementation of national disaster risk reduction strategies in line with the Sendai Framework (Index) was developed to monitor progress and achievement against Indicator 13.1.2. The score of an economy indicates its compliance of alignment of national strategies with the Sendai Framework based on self-assessments of the economy using 10 criteria for monitoring the progress of national disaster risk reduction strategies.
Goal 14. Conserve and sustainably use the oceans, seas, and marine resources for sustainable development		
Target 14.5: By 2020, conserve at least 10% of coastal and marine areas, consistent with national and international law and based on the best available scientific information.	14.5.1: Coverage of protected areas in relation to marine areas	The indicator measures the coverage of protected areas in relation to marine areas and shows temporal trends in the mean percentage of important sites for marine biodiversity (i.e., those that contribute significantly to the global persistence of biodiversity or key biodiversity areas) that are wholly covered by designated protected areas. Note: The International Union for Conservation of Nature (IUCN) defines a protected area as "a clearly defined geographical space, recognized, dedicated and managed, through legal or other effective means, to achieve the long-term conservation of nature with associated ecosystem services and cultural values."
Goal 15. Protect, restore, and promote sustainable use of terrestrial ecosystems, sustainably manage forests, combat desertification, halt and reverse land degradation, and halt biodiversity loss		
Target 15.1: By 2020, ensure the conservation, restoration, and sustainable use of terrestrial and inland freshwater ecosystems and their services, in particular forests, wetlands, mountains, and drylands, in line with obligations under international agreements.	15.1.1: Forest area as a proportion of total land area	Size of forest cover in relation to total land area. Note: Forest is defined as "land spanning more than 0.5 hectares with trees higher than 5 meters and a canopy cover of more than 10%, or trees able to reach these thresholds in situ. It does not include land that is predominantly under agricultural or urban land use". Total land area is the total surface area of a country less the area covered by inland waters, such as major rivers and lakes.
	15.1.2: Proportion of important sites for terrestrial and freshwater biodiversity that are covered by protected areas, by ecosystem type	Proportion of important sites for terrestrial and freshwater biodiversity that are covered by protected areas shows temporal trends in the mean percentage of each important site for terrestrial and freshwater biodiversity (i.e., those that contribute significantly to the global persistence of biodiversity) that is covered by designated protected areas.

(continued on next page)

Goals and Targets	Statistical Indicators	Definition
Target 15.4: By 2030, ensure the conservation of mountain ecosystems, including their biodiversity, in order to enhance their capacity to provide benefits that are essential for sustainable development	15.4.1: Coverage by protected areas of important sites for mountain biodiversity	Coverage by protected areas of important sites for mountain biodiversity shows temporal trends in the mean percentage of each important site for mountain biodiversity (i.e., those that contribute significantly to the global persistence of biodiversity) that is covered by designated protected areas. Note: Protected areas, as defined by the IUCN (IUCN; Dudley 2008), are clearly defined geographical spaces, recognized, dedicated, and managed, through legal or other effective means, to achieve the long-term conservation of nature with associated ecosystem services and cultural values. Importantly, a variety of specific management objectives are recognized within this definition, spanning conservation, restoration, and sustainable use: "(i) Category Ia: Strict nature reserve; (ii) Category Ib: Wilderness area; (iii) Category II: National park; (iv) Category III: Natural monument or feature; (v) Category IV: Habitat/species management area; (vi) Category V: Protected landscape/seascape; (vii) Category VI: Protected area with sustainable use of natural resources."
Target 15.5: Take urgent and significant action to reduce the degradation of natural habitats, halt the loss of biodiversity and, by 2020, protect and prevent the extinction of threatened species.	15.5.1: Red List Index	The Red List Index measures changes in aggregate extinction risk across groups of species. It is based on genuine changes in the number of species in each category of extinction risk on the IUCN Red List of Threatened Species (IUCN 2015), which is expressed as changes in an index ranging from 0 to 1. Note: The Red List Index value ranges from 1 (all species are categorized as "Least Concern") to 0 (all species are categorized as "Extinct"), indicating how far the set of species has moved overall toward extinction. Threatened species are those listed on The IUCN Red List of Threatened Species in the categories Vulnerable, Endangered, or Critically Endangered (i.e., species that are facing a high, very high, or extremely high risk of extinction in the wild in the medium-term future).
Goal 16. Promote peaceful and inclusive societies for sustainable development; provide access to justice for all; and build effective, accountable, and inclusive institutions at all levels		
Target 16.1: Significantly reduce all forms of violence and related death rates everywhere.	16.1.1: Number of victims of intentional homicide per 100,000 population, by sex and age	Total count of victims of intentional homicide divided by the total population, expressed per 100,000 population. Intentional homicide is defined as the unlawful death inflicted upon a person with the intent to cause death or serious injury (International Classification of Crime for Statistical Purposes, ICCS 2015). Population refers to total resident population in a given country in a given year. Note: This indicator is widely used at national and international levels to measure the most extreme form of violent crime, providing a direct indication of lack of security.
Target 16.3: Promote the rule of law at the national and international levels, and ensure equal access to justice for all.	16.3.2: Unsentenced detainees as a proportion of the overall prison population	Total number of persons held in detention who have not yet been sentenced, as a percentage of the total number of persons held in detention, on a specified date.

Goals and Targets	Statistical Indicators	Definition
Target 16.5: Substantially reduce corruption and bribery in all their forms.	16.5.2: Proportion of businesses that had at least one contact with a public official and that paid a bribe to a public official, or were asked for a bribe by those public officials during the previous 12 months	Proportion of firms that were asked for a gift or informal payment when meeting with tax officials. Note: This indicator aims to ascertain whether or not firms have been solicited for gifts or informal payments (i.e., bribes) when meeting with tax officials. Paying taxes are required of formal forms in most countries, and the rationale for this indicator is to measure the incidence of corruption during this routine interaction.
Target 16.9: By 2030, provide legal identity, including birth registration, for all.	16.9.1: Proportion of children under 5 years of age whose births have been registered with a civil authority, by age	Proportion of children under 5 years of age whose births have been registered with a civil authority.
Goal 17. Strengthen the means of implementation and revitalize the Global Partnership for Sustainable Development		
Target 17.3: Mobilize additional financial resources for developing countries from multiple sources	17.3.2: Volume of remittances (in US dollars) as a proportion of total GDP	Personal remittances comprise personal transfers and compensation of employees. Personal transfers consist of all current transfers in cash or in kind made or received by resident households to or from nonresident households. Compensation of employees refers to the income of (i) border, seasonal, and other short-term workers who are employed in an economy where they are not resident; and (ii) residents employed by nonresident entities.
Target 17.4: Assist developing countries in attaining long-term debt sustainability through coordinated policies aimed at fostering debt financing, debt relief, and debt restructuring, as appropriate, and address the external debt of highly indebted poor countries to reduce debt distress	17.4.1: Debt service as a proportion of exports of goods and services	Percentage of debt services (principle and interest payments) to the exports of goods and services. Debt services covered in this indicator refer only to public and publicly guaranteed debt.
Target 17.9: Enhance international support for implementing effective and targeted capacity-building in developing countries to support national plans to implement all the Sustainable Development Goals, including through North-South, South-South, and triangular cooperation.	17.9.1: Dollar value of financial and technical assistance (including through North-South, South-South, and triangular cooperation) committed to developing countries	Gross disbursements of total ODA and other official flows from all donors for capacity-building and national planning. Note: ODA refers to "those flows to countries and territories on the Development Assistance Committee List of ODA Recipients and to multilateral institutions which are (i) provided by official agencies, including state and local governments, or by their executive agencies; and (ii) each transaction is administered with the promotion of the economic development and welfare of developing countries as its main objective; and is concessional in character and conveys a grant element of at least 25% (calculated at a rate of discount of 10%). Other official flows (excluding officially supported export credits) are defined as transactions by the official sector that do not meet the conditions for eligibility as ODA, either because they are not primarily aimed at development or because they are not sufficiently concessional.

Goals and Targets	Statistical Indicators	Definition
Target 17.18: By 2020, enhance capacity-building support to developing countries, including for least developed countries and small island developing states, to increase significantly the availability of high-quality, timely, and reliable data disaggregated by income, gender, age, race, ethnicity, migratory status, disability, geographic location, and other characteristics relevant in national contexts.	17.18.3: Number of countries with a national statistical plan that is fully funded and under implementation, by source of funding	Count of countries that are either (i) implementing a strategy, (ii) designing a strategy, or (iii) awaiting adoption of a strategy in the current year. Note: The indicator is based on the annual Status Report on National Strategies for the Development of Statistics. In collaboration with its partners, PARIS21 reports on country progress in designing and implementing national statistical plans. This indicator can be disaggregated by geographical area. Regional-level aggregates are based on the total count of national strategies.
Target 17.19: By 2030, build on existing initiatives to develop measurements of progress on sustainable development that complement GDP, and support statistical capacity-building in developing countries.	17.19.1: Dollar value of all resources made available to strengthen statistical capacity in developing countries	US dollar value of ongoing statistical support in developing countries. Note: The indictor is based on the Partner Report on Support to Statistics, which is designed and administered by PARIS21 to provide a snapshot of the US dollar value of ongoing statistical support in developing countries.
	17.19.2: Number of countries that have conducted at least one population and housing census in the past 10 years	Countries that have conducted at least one population and housing census in the past 10 years. This includes countries that compile their detailed population and housing statistics from population registers, administrative records, sample surveys, other sources, or a combination of those sources.

Regional Trends and Tables

Indicator	Definition
PEOPLE	
Population	
Midyear Population	Estimates of the midyear de facto population. De facto population includes all persons physically present in the country during the census day, including foreign, military, and diplomatic personnel and their accompanying household members; and transient foreign visitors in the country or in harbors. Note: Some economies have population data referenced to different period end points (e.g., 1 January for the Kyrgyz Republic, 31 December for the People's Republic of China, and 1 October for India).
Growth Rates in Population	Number of people added to (or subtracted from) a population over a given period of time because of natural increase and net migration, expressed as a percentage of the population at the given period of time.
Net International Migration Rate	Number of immigrants minus the number of emigrants over a period, divided by the person-years lived by the population of the receiving country over that period. It is expressed as net number of migrants per 1,000 population.
Urban Population (as % of total population)	Population living in urban areas, defined in accordance with the national definition or as used in the most recent population census. Because of national differences in the characteristics that distinguish urban from rural areas, the distinction between urban and rural populations is not amenable to a single definition that would be applicable to all countries. National definitions are most commonly based on size of locality. Population that is not urban is considered rural. The estimated population living in urban areas at midyear as a percentage of the total midyear population in a country.
Age Dependency Ratio	Ratio of the nonworking-age population to the working-age population. Since countries define working age differently, a straightforward application of the definition will lead to noncomparable data. The Asian Development Bank therefore uses the following United Nations definition that can be calculated directly from an age distribution: $$\frac{\text{Population aged } (0-14) + (65 \text{ and over}) \text{ years}}{\text{Population aged } (15-64) \text{ years}} \times 100$$
Labor Force and Employment	
Labor Force Participation Rate	Percentage of the labor force to the working-age population. The labor force is the sum of those employed and unemployed but seeking work. The labor force participation rate measures the extent of the economically active working-age population in an economy. It provides an indication of the relative size of the supply of labor available for the production of goods and services in the economy. It must be noted that the definition of working-age population varies across countries. Note: Recommendations from the 19th International Conference of Labour Statisticians have been adopted by some economies, and hence these economies may not have comparable data across years. The conference provides the statistical concept of work for reference purposes; and the operational concepts, definitions, and guidelines for (i) three distinct subsets of work activities, referred to as forms of work, which include own-use production work, employment work, and volunteer work; (ii) related classifications of the population according to their labor force status and main work status; and (iii) measures of labor underutilization. The concept of employment has also been refined to refer to work for pay or profit.
Employment in Agriculture	Employment in agriculture, including forestry and fishing, that corresponds to division 1 (International Standard of Industrial Classification [ISIC] revision 2), tabulation categories A and B (ISIC revision 3), and category A of ISIC revision 4.

(continued on next page)

Indicator	Definition
Employment in Industry	Employment in industry includes mining and quarrying; manufacturing; electricity, gas, steam, and air-conditioning supply; water supply; sewage, waste management, and remediation activities; and construction.
Employment in Mining and Quarrying	Employment in mining and quarrying that corresponds to division 2 (ISIC revision 2), tabulation category C (ISIC revision 3), and category B of ISIC revision 4.
Employment in Manufacturing	Employment in manufacturing that corresponds to division 3 (ISIC revision 2), tabulation category D (ISIC revision 3), and category C of ISIC revision 4.
Employment in Electricity, Gas, Steam, and Air-Conditioning Supply; Water Supply; Sewerage, Waste Management and Remediation Activities	Employment in electricity, gas, steam, and air-conditioning supply; water supply; sewerage, waste management, and remediation activities that corresponds to division 4 (ISIC revision 2), tabulation category E (ISIC revision 3), and categories D and E of ISIC revision 4.
Employment in Construction	Employment in construction that corresponds to division 5 (ISIC revision 2), tabulation category F (ISIC revisions 3), and category F of ISIC revision 4.
Employment in Service	Employment in service includes wholesale and retail trade; repair of motor vehicles and motorcycles; accommodation and food service activities; transportation and storage; information and communication; financial and insurance activities; real estate activities; and other services.
Employment in Wholesale and Retail Trade; Repair of Motor Vehicles and Motorcycles	Employment in wholesale and retail trade; repair of motor vehicles and motorcycles that corresponds to division 6 (subdivisions 61 and 62, ISIC revision 2); tabulation category G (ISIC revision 3); and category G of ISIC revision 4.
Employment in Accommodation and Food Service Activities	Employment in accommodation and food service activities that corresponds to division 6 (subdivision 63, ISIC revision 2); tabulation category H (ISIC revision 3); and category I of ISIC revision 4.
Employment in Transportation and Storage	Employment in transport and storage that corresponds to division 7 (subdivision 71, ISIC revision 2); tabulation category I (sub-categories 60–63, ISIC revision 3); and category H of ISIC revision 4.
Employment in Information and Communication	Employment in information and communication that corresponds to division 7 (subdivision 72, ISIC revision 2); tabulation category I (subcategory 64, ISIC revision 3); and category J of ISIC revision 4.
Employment in Financial and Insurance Activities	Employment in financial and insurance activities that corresponds to division 8 (subdivisions 81–82, ISIC revision 2), tabulation category J (ISIC revision 3), and category K of ISIC revision 4.
Employment in Real Estate Activities	Employment in real estate activities that corresponds to division 8 (subdivision 83, ISIC revision 2); tabulation category K (subcategory 70, ISIC revision 3); and category L of ISIC revision 4.
Employment in Other Services	Employment in other services that corresponds to divisions 9 and 0 (ISIC revision 2), tabulation categories L to Q (ISIC revision 3), and categories M to U of ISIC revision 4.
Poverty Indicators	
Proportion of Population below $1.90 a Day (2011 PPP)	Percentage of the population living on less than $1.90 a day at 2011 purchasing power parity (PPP).
Proportion of Population below $3.20 a Day (2011 PPP)	Percentage of the population living on less than $3.20 a day at 2011 PPP.
Income Ratio of Highest 20% to Lowest 20%	Income or consumption share that accrues to the richest 20% of the population, divided by the income or consumption share of the lowest 20% of the population.
Gini Coefficient or Index	Measure of the degree to which an economy's income distribution diverges from perfect equal distribution. A value of zero (0) implies perfect equality while a value of one (1) implies perfect inequality.
Human Development Index	Composite index of long and healthy life (measured by life expectancy at birth), knowledge (measured by expected years of schooling and mean years of schooling), and decent standard of living (measured by gross national income per capita in United States [US] PPP dollars).

(continued on next page)

Indicator	Definition
Social Indicators	
Life Expectancy at Birth	Number of years that a newborn is expected to live if prevailing patterns of mortality at the time of his or her birth are to stay the same throughout his or her life.
Crude Birth Rate	Ratio of the total number of live births in a given period to the midyear total population of the same period, expressed per 1,000 people.
Crude Death Rate	Ratio of the number of deaths occurring within a given period to the midyear total population of the same period, expressed per 1,000 people.
Total Fertility Rate	Number of children that would be born to a woman if she were to live to the end of her childbearing years and bear children in accordance with current age-specific fertility rates.
Primary Education Completion Rate	Total number of new entrants in the last grade of primary education, regardless of age, expressed as a percentage of the total population at the theoretical entrance age to the last grade of primary education. This indicator is also known as "gross intake ratio to the last grade of primary." The ratio can exceed 100% due to overaged and underaged children who enter primary school late, early, and/or repeat grades.
Adult Literacy Rate	The percentage of the population aged 15 years and older who can both read and write (with understanding) a short simple statement on his or her everyday life. Generally, literacy also encompasses numeracy, i.e., the ability to make simple arithmetic calculations.
Expected years of schooling, primary to tertiary	Number of years a person of school entrance age can expect to spend within the specified level of education (from primary to tertiary level).
Mean years of schooling	Average number of completed years of education of a country's population aged 25 years and older, excluding years spent repeating individual grades.
Primary Pupil–Teacher Ratio	Average number of pupils (students) per teacher at the primary level of education in a given school year. This indicator is used to measure the level of human resources input in terms of number of teachers in relation to the size of the primary pupil population.
Secondary Pupil–Teacher Ratio	Average number of pupils (students) per teacher at the secondary level of education in a given school year. This indicator is used to measure the level of human resources input in terms of number of teachers in relation to the size of the secondary pupil population.
Physicians	Physicians, including general and specialist medical practitioners, expressed in terms of the number per 1,000 people.
Hospital Beds	In-patient beds for both acute and chronic care available in public, private, general, and specialized hospitals and rehabilitation centers expressed in terms of the number per 1,000 people.
Number of Adults Living with HIV	All adults, defined as men and women aged 15 years and older, with HIV infection, whether or not they have developed symptoms of AIDS, estimated to be alive at the end of a specific year.
ECONOMY AND OUTPUT	
National Accounts	
Gross Domestic Product	Unduplicated market value of the total production activity of all resident producer units within the economic territory of a country during a given period. It is calculated without making deductions for depreciation of fabricated assets or for depletion and degradation of natural resources. Transfer payments are excluded from the calculation of gross domestic product (GDP). GDP can be calculated using the production, expenditure, and income approaches. Production-based GDP is the sum of the gross value added by all resident producers in the economy, plus any taxes and minus any subsidies not included in the value of the products. Gross value added is the net output of an industry after adding up all outputs and subtracting intermediate inputs. Income-based GDP is the sum of the compensation of employees, mixed income, operating surplus, consumption of fixed capital, and taxes, less subsidies on production and imports.

(continued on next page)

Indicator	Definition
	Expenditure-based GDP is the sum of final consumption expenditure of households, nonprofit institutions serving households, and the government; gross capital formation; and exports minus imports of goods and services. GDP can be measured at current prices (the prices of the current reporting period), and constant prices (obtained by expressing values in terms of a base period and chain volume measure).
GDP at PPP	Measures obtained by using PPP to convert the GDP into a common currency, and by valuing them at a uniform price level. They are the spatial equivalent of a time series of GDP for a single country expressed at constant prices. At the level of GDP, they are used to compare the economic size of countries.
GDP at Current US Dollar	GDP at local currency units are obtained from the economy sources and are converted to US dollars using the official exchange rates from the International Monetary Fund (IMF). The exchange rates used are expressed as the average rate for a period of time (average of period), calculated as annual averages based on the monthly averages (local currency units relative to the US dollar).
GDP per Capita at PPP	GDP at PPP, divided by the midyear population.
GNI per Capita, Atlas Method	The gross national income (GNI) converted to US dollars using the World Bank Atlas method, divided by the midyear population. GNI is the sum of value added by all resident producers, plus any product taxes (less subsidies) not included in the valuation of output, plus net receipts of primary income (compensation of employees and property income) from abroad. GNI, calculated in national currency, is usually converted to US dollars at official exchange rates for comparisons across economies, although an alternative rate is used when the official exchange rate is judged to diverge by an exceptionally large margin from the rate actually applied in international transactions. To smooth fluctuations in prices and exchange rates, a special Atlas method of conversion is used by the World Bank. This applies a conversion factor that averages the exchange rate for a given year and the 2 preceding years, adjusted for differences in rates of inflation between the country, and through 2000, the G-5 countries (France, Germany, Japan, the United Kingdom, and the US). From 2001, these countries include the Euro area, Japan, the United Kingdom, and the US.
GDP per Capita at Current US Dollar	GDP at current US dollar value, divided by the midyear population.
Agriculture Value Added	The gross output of the agriculture sector, less the corresponding value of intermediate consumption. The industrial origin of value added is determined by ISIC revision 4, where agriculture corresponds to ISIC Section A and includes agriculture, forestry, and fishing.
Industry Value Added	The gross output of industry sectors, less the corresponding value of intermediate consumption. The industrial origin of value added is determined by ISIC revision 4, where industry corresponds to ISIC Sections B–F and includes mining and quarrying (B); manufacturing (C); electricity, gas, steam, and air-conditioning supply (D); water supply; sewerage, waste management, and remediation activities (E); and construction (F).
Services Value Added	The gross output of services sectors, less the corresponding value of intermediate consumption. The industrial origin of value added is determined by ISIC revision 4, where services corresponds to ISIC Sections G–U and includes wholesale and retail trade; repair of motor vehicles and motorcycles (G); transport and storage (H); accommodation and food service activities (I); information and communication (J); financial and insurance activities (K); real estate activities (L); professional, scientific, and technical activities (M); administrative and support service activities (N); public administration and defense; compulsory social security (O); education (P); human health and social work activities (Q); arts, entertainment, and recreation (R); other service activities (S); activities of households as employers; undifferentiated goods- and services-producing activities of households for own use (T); and activities of extraterritorial organizations and bodies (U).

(continued on next page)

Indicator	Definition
Household Consumption Expenditure	Market value of all goods and services, including durable products (such as cars, washing machines, and home computers), purchased or received as income in kind by households. It excludes purchases of dwellings but includes imputed rent for owner-occupied dwellings. It also includes payments and fees to governments to obtain permits and licenses. The expenditure of nonprofit institutions serving households is generally included for most economies.
Government Consumption Expenditure	Includes all current outlays on purchases of goods and services (including wages and salaries of government employees). It also includes most expenditure on national defense and security but excludes government military expenditures that are part of public investment.
Gross Capital Formation	Total value of gross fixed capital formation, changes in inventories, and acquisitions less disposals of valuables. Gross fixed capital formation is the total value of a producer's acquisitions, less disposals, of tangible goods (such as buildings) and intangible goods (such as computer software) that are intended for use in production during several accounting periods, plus certain specified expenditure on services that adds to the value of non-produced assets. Changes in inventories are changes in stocks of produced goods and goods for intermediate consumption, and the net increase in the value of work in progress. Valuables are goods (such as precious metals and works of art) that are not used up in production but are acquired as stores of value in the expectation that they will retain or increase their value over time.
Exports of Goods and Services	Consist of sales, bartering, or gifts or grants of goods and services from residents to nonresidents. The treatment of exports in the System of National Accounts is generally identical with that in the balance of payments accounts as described in the IMF's Balance of Payments Manual.
Imports of Goods and Services	Consist of purchases, bartering, or receipts of gifts or grants of goods and services by residents from nonresidents. The treatment of imports in the System of National Accounts is generally identical with that in the balance of payments accounts as described in the IMF's Balance of Payments Manual.
Gross Domestic Saving	Difference between GDP and final consumption expenditure, where final consumption expenditure is the sum of the final consumption of household, nonprofit institutions serving households, and the government.
Production	
Agriculture Production Index	Relative level of the aggregate volume of agricultural production for each year in comparison with the base period. It is based on the sum of price-weighted quantities of different agricultural commodities produced after deductions of quantities used as seed and feed weighted in a similar manner. The resulting aggregate therefore represents disposable production for any use, except as seed and feed.
Manufacturing Production Index	An index covering production in manufacturing. The exact coverage, the weighting system, and the methods of calculation vary from country to country, but the divergences are less important than, for example, in the case of price and wage indexes.
MONEY, FINANCE, AND PRICES	
Prices	
Consumer Price Index	An index that measures changes in prices against a reference period of a basket of goods and services purchased by households. Based on the purpose of the consumer price index, different baskets of goods and services can be selected. For macroeconomic purposes, a broad-based basket is used to represent the relative price movement of household final consumption expenditure.
Food and Nonalcoholic Beverages Price Index	An index that covers food and nonalcoholic beverages purchased by the household mainly for consumption or preparation at home including services for food processing for own consumption. The index corresponds to Classification of Individual Consumption by Purpose (COICOP) Version 1999 division 01. Excluded are food and nonalcoholic beverages that are provided as part of a food-serving service under hotels and restaurants (COICOP division 11).

(continued on next page)

Indicator	Definition
Alcoholic Beverages, Tobacco, and Narcotics Price Index	An index that covers the purchase of alcoholic beverages, tobacco, and narcotics, regardless of where these are consumed, but not provided as part of a food-and-beverage-serving service under hotels and restaurants. Services for the production of alcohol for own consumption are also included. The index corresponds to COICOP division 02. Excluded are alcoholic beverages purchased for immediate consumption in hotels, restaurants, cafes, bars, kiosks, street vendors, automatic vending machines, etc. classified under restaurants, cafes, and the like (COICOP Group 11.1.1).
Clothing and Footwear Price Index	An index that covers all clothing materials, garments, articles and accessories, footwear and related services, including cleaning, repair, and hire of clothing and footwear, and the purchase of secondhand clothing and footwear. The index corresponds to COICOP division 03.
Housing, Water, Electricity, Gas, and Other Fuels Price Index	An index that covers goods and services for the use of the house or dwelling and its maintenance and repair; the supply of water and miscellaneous services related to the dwelling; and energy used for heating or cooling. The index corresponds to COICOP division 04.
Furnishings, Household Equipment, and Routine Household Maintenance Price Index	An index that covers a wide range of products to equip the house or dwelling and the household durables, semidurables, and nondurables as well as some household services. Includes all kinds of furniture (including lightning equipment, household textiles, glassware, tableware and household utensils), major and smaller electric household appliances, tools and equipment for house and garden, and goods for routine household maintenance. The index also includes the repair, installation, and rental services of the goods. Domestic services by paid staff in private service, supplied by enterprises or self-employed persons, window-cleaning and disinfecting services, as well as dry-cleaning and laundering of household textiles and carpets, are also included. The index corresponds to COICOP division 05.
Health Price Index	An index that covers health services provided during an overnight stay, services that do not require an overnight stay, diagnostic imaging services, medical laboratory services, patient emergency transportation, and emergency rescue services. The index also includes medicines and health products, covering all products that are separately invoiced from health services, except when administered under the direct supervision of a health care professional during an overnight stay. The index corresponds to COICOP division 06.
Transport Price Index	An index that covers four main categories of goods and services for transportation: (i) purchase of vehicles covers motor cars, motor cycles, bicycles, and animal-drawn vehicles; (ii) goods and services for the operation of the personal transport equipment cover parts and accessories for personal transport equipment, fuels and lubricants, and the repair and maintenance of personal transport equipment including expenditures for parking spaces in garages or in public places, expenditures for tolls, and expenditures to acquire a driving certificate; (iii) transport services provided by the market, structured by the mode of transport; and (iv) transport services of goods covers postal and courier services, removal and storage services, and the delivery of any kinds of goods when charged separately. The index corresponds to COICOP division 07. It excludes purchases of recreational vehicles such as camper vans, caravans, trailers, aeroplanes, and boats that are classified under the Recreation and Culture Price Index.
Communication Price Index	An index that covers three main groups of goods and services: (i) information and communication equipment, including equipment for the capture, recording, and reproduction of sound and vision; software; and information and communication services; (ii) information and communication services, including telephones and other communication services; internet access services; television and radio licenses; fee and subscription services, including streaming services of films and music; and (iii) repair, maintenance, and rental of information and communication equipment. The index corresponds to COICOP division 08.

(continued on next page)

Indicator	Definition
Recreation and Culture Price Index	An index that covers a wide range of goods and services for recreation, sport, and culture and is structured into eight groups: (i) recreation durables such as photographic equipment, other major durables for recreation, such as camper vans, boats, yachts, aeroplanes, and the like; (ii) nonmajor durable recreational goods such as games and toys, including video game computers, celebration articles, equipment for sport, camping, and open-air recreation; (iii) garden products and plants and flowers and purchases of pets and expenditures for pets, excluding veterinary services; (iv) recreational services cover rental, maintenance, and repair of goods, veterinary and other services for pets, recreational and leisure services, such as amusement parks, games of chance and expenditures for sporting services, both expenditures for practicing sports as well as expenditures for attendance of sport events; (v) cultural goods such as musical instruments and audio-visual media; (vi) cultural services such as cinemas, theatres, concerts, museums, and other cultural sites, and photographic services; (vii) newspapers, all kinds of books, stationery and drawing materials; and (viii) package holidays that include transportation, accommodation, food provision, or tour guide. The index corresponds to COICOP division 09.
Education Price Index	An index that covers educational services only. It includes: (i) education by radio or television broadcasting as well as e-learning and correspondence courses; (ii) admission and registration fees as well as tuition fees; and (iii) other education-related fees such as camps and/or field trips, course fees, diploma fees, examination fees, graduation fees, laboratory fees, physical education fees, etc. The index corresponds to COICOP division 10. It excludes expenditures on other education-related goods and services such as school uniforms, education support services, such as health-care services, transport services (except in the case of excursions that are part of the normal school program), text books and academic journals, stationery, catering services, and accommodation services.
Restaurants and Hotels Price Index	An index that covers services provided by restaurants, cafes, and similar facilities, either with full or limited- or self-service, or by canteens, cafeterias, or refectories at work or at school and other educational establishment's premises. It also includes catering services and accommodation services. The index corresponds to COICOP division 11.
Miscellaneous Goods and Services Price Index	An index that covers insurance and financial services. It also includes personal care, prostitution, personal effects not elsewhere classified, social protection, financial services not elsewhere classified, and other services not elsewhere classified. The index corresponds to COICOP division 12.
Wholesale Price Index	A measure that reflects changes in the prices paid for goods at various stages of distribution up to the point of retail. It can include prices of raw materials for intermediate and final consumption, prices of intermediate or unfinished goods, and prices of finished goods. The goods are usually valued at purchasers' prices.
Producer Price Index	A measure of the change in the prices of goods and services, either as they leave their place of production or as they enter the production process. A measure of the change in the prices received by domestic producers for their outputs or of the change in the prices paid by domestic producers for their intermediate inputs.
GDP Deflator	A measure of the annual rate of price change in the economy as a whole for the period shown, obtained by dividing GDP at current prices by GDP at constant prices.
Money and Finance	
Money Supply	Refers to the total amount of money in circulation in a specific country. Money supply can be measured in different ways: M1 (Narrow Money) is a measure of money supply that includes all coins and notes (M0) as well as personal money in current accounts. M2 (Intermediate Money) is the sum of M1 and personal money in deposit accounts. M3 (Broad Money) is the sum of M2 and government and other deposits. According to the Organization for Economic Co-operation and Development, M3 includes currency, deposits with an agreed maturity of up to 2 years, deposits redeemable at notice of up to 3 months and repurchase agreements, money market fund shares or units, and debt securities up to 2 years.

(continued on next page)

Indicator	Definition
	Not all countries publish the same types of aggregates, and even when aggregates are the same name (e.g., M1, M2, M3, etc.), their asset composition often differs significantly. Cross-country differences in national definitions of lowered-ordered aggregates also arise from differences in the maturity categories of nontransferable deposits included in a particular money aggregate. For example, the definition of M2 in one country may include time deposits with maturities of 1 year or less, whereas another country's M2 definition may include time deposits with maturities of 2 years or less. When the monetary policy strategy consists of monetary aggregate targeting, the choice of the definition of the targeted aggregate is guided mainly by two considerations. The aggregate should be sufficiently sensitive to interest rate changes for the central bank to be able to control it and display a stable relationship over time to the movement of the overall price level.
Interest Rate on Savings Deposits	Rate paid by commercial and similar banks for savings deposits.
Interest Rate on Time Deposits	Rate paid by commercial and similar banks for time deposits.
Lending Interest Rate	Bank rate that usually meets the short- and medium-term financing needs of the private sector. This rate is normally differentiated according to creditworthiness of borrowers and objectives of financing.
Yield on Short-Term Treasury Bills	Rate at which short-term securities are issued or traded in the market.
Domestic Credit Provided by Banking Sector	Includes all credits to various sectors on a gross basis, except credit to the central government, which is net. The banking sector includes monetary authorities, deposit money banks, and other banking institutions for which data are available (including institutions that do not accept transferable deposits but do incur such liabilities as time and savings deposits). Examples of other banking institutions are savings and mortgage loan institutions and building and loan associations.
Ratio of Bank Nonperforming Loans to Total Gross Loans	Value of nonperforming loans divided by the total value of the loan portfolio (including nonperforming loans before the deduction of loan loss provisions). The amount recorded as nonperforming should be the gross value of the loan as recorded in the balance sheet, not just the amount that is overdue.
Stock Market Price Index	Index that measures changes in the prices of stocks traded in the stock exchange. The price changes of the stocks are usually weighted by their market capitalization.
Stock Market Capitalization	The share price times the number of shares outstanding (including their several classes) for listed domestic companies. Investment funds, unit trusts, and companies whose only business goal is to hold shares of other listed companies are excluded. Data are end of year values converted to US dollars using corresponding year-end foreign exchange rates. Also known as market value.
Exchange Rates	
Official Exchange Rate	The exchange rate determined by national authorities or the rate determined in the legally sanctioned exchange market. It is calculated as an annual average based on the monthly averages (local currency units relative to the US dollar).
Purchasing Power Parity Conversion Factor	Number of units of country B's currency that are needed in country B to purchase the same quantity of an individual good or service, which one unit of country A's currency can purchase in country A.
Price Level Index	Ratio of the relevant PPP to the exchange rate. It is expressed as an index on a base of 100. A price level index (PLI) greater than 100 means that, when the national average prices are converted at exchange rates, the resulting prices tend to be higher on average than prices in the base country (or countries) of the region (and vice versa). At the level of GDP, PLIs provide a measure of the differences in the general price levels of countries. PLIs are also referred to as comparative price levels.
GLOBALIZATION	
Balance of Payments	
Trade in Goods Balance	Difference between exports and imports of goods.
Trade in Services Balance	Difference between exports and imports of services.
Current Account Balance	Sum of net exports of goods, services, net income, and net current transfers.

(continued on next page)

Indicator	Definition
Total Remittances	Sum of personal remittances and social benefits. Personal remittances include personal transfers (part of current transfers); compensation of employees less taxes, social contributions, transport, and travel; and capital transfers between households. Social benefits include benefits payable under social security funds and pension funds: they may be in cash or in kind. Includes income from individuals working abroad for short periods, income from individuals residing abroad, and social benefits from abroad.
Foreign Direct Investment	Refers to net inflows of investment to acquire a lasting management interest (10% or more of voting stock) in an enterprise operating in an economy other than that of the investor. It is the sum of equity capital, reinvestment of earnings, other long-term capital, and short-term capital as shown in the balance of payments.
External Trade	
Merchandise Exports or Imports	Covering all movable goods, with a few specified exceptions, the ownership of which changes between a resident and a foreigner. For merchandise exports, it represents the value of the goods and related distributive services at the customs frontier of the exporting economy, i.e., the free on board (FOB) value. Merchandise imports, on the other hand, are reported in cost, insurance, and freight (CIF) values.
Trade in Goods	Sum of merchandise exports and merchandise imports.
Direction of Trade	
Direction of Trade: Merchandise Exports and Imports	The direction of trade represents the value of merchandise exports and imports disaggregated according to a country's primary trading partners. Imports are reported on a CIF basis and exports are reported on a FOB basis, with the exception of a few countries for which imports are also available in FOB. Time series data includes estimates derived from reports of partner economies for nonreporting and slow-reporting economies.
International Reserves	
International Reserves	External assets that are readily available to, and controlled by, monetary authorities for meeting balance-of-payments financing needs, for intervention in exchange markets to affect the currency exchange rate, and for other related purposes (such as maintaining confidence in the currency and the economy, and serving as a basis for foreign borrowing). Consist of monetary gold, special drawing rights holdings, reserve position in the IMF, currency and deposits, securities (including debt and equity securities), financial derivatives, and other claims (loans and other financial instruments).
Ratio of International Reserves to Imports	International reserves outstanding at the end of the year as a proportion of imports of goods from the balance of payments during the year, where imports of goods are expressed in terms of a monthly average. It is a useful measure for reserve needs of countries with limited access to capital markets.
Capital Flows	
Net Official Development Assistance	Concessional flows to developing economies and multilateral institutions provided by official agencies, including state and local governments, or by their executing agencies, administered with the objective of promoting the economic development and welfare of developing economies, and containing a grant element of at least 25%. Net flow takes into account principal repayments for loans, offsetting entries for forgiven debt, and recoveries made on grants.
Net Other Official Flows	Official sector transactions with countries on the Development Assistance Committee List of Official Development Assistance Recipients, which do not meet the conditions for eligibility as official development assistance, either because they are not primarily aimed at development, or because they have a grant element of less than 25%. Net flow takes into account principal repayments for loans, offsetting entries for forgiven debt, and recoveries made on grants.

(continued on next page)

Indicator	Definition
Net Private Flows	Sum of direct investment and portfolio investment. Direct investment is a category of international investment made by a resident entity in one economy (direct investor) with the objective of establishing a lasting interest in an enterprise that is resident in an economy other than that of the investor (direct investment enterprise). "Lasting interest" implies the existence of a long-term relationship between the direct investor and the enterprise and a significant degree of influence by the direct investor on the management of the direct investment enterprise. Direct investment involves both the initial transaction between the two entities and all subsequent capital transactions between them and among affiliated enterprises, both incorporated and unincorporated. Portfolio investment is the category of international investment that covers investment in equity and debt securities, excluding any such instruments that are classified as direct investment or reserve assets.
Aggregate Net Resource Flows	Sum of net official development assistance, net other official flows, and net private flows.
External Indebtedness	
Total External Debt	Debt owed to nonresidents repayable in currency, goods, or services. It is the sum of public, publicly guaranteed, and private nonguaranteed long-term debt, use of IMF credit, and short-term debt. Short-term debt includes all debt having an original maturity of 1 year or less and interest in arrears on long-term debt.
Public and Publicly Guaranteed Debt	Comprises long-term external obligations of public debtors, including the national government, political subdivisions (or an agency of either), and autonomous public bodies, and external obligations of private debtors that are guaranteed for repayment by a public entity.
External Debt as a Percentage of GNI	Total external debt as a percentage of GNI. GNI is the sum of value added by all resident producers plus any product taxes (less subsidies) not included in the valuation of output, plus net receipts of primary income (compensation of employees and property income) from abroad.
External Debt as a Percentage of Exports of Goods and Services and Primary Income	Total external debt as a percentage of exports of goods, services, and primary income. Exports of goods, services, and primary income constitute the total value of exports of goods and services, receipts of compensation of nonresident workers, and investment income from abroad.
Total Debt Service Paid	The sum of principal repayments and interest actually paid in currency, goods, or services on long-term debt, interest paid on short-term debt, and repayments (repurchases and charges) to the IMF.
Total Debt Service Paid as a Percentage of Exports of Goods and Services and Primary Income	Total debt service paid as a percentage of exports of goods, services, and primary income.
Tourism	
International Tourist Arrivals	The number of tourists (overnight visitors) who travel to a country other than that in which they usually reside, and outside their usual environment, for a period not exceeding 12 months, and whose main purpose of visit is other than the activity remunerated from within the country visited. In some cases, data may also include same-day visitors when data on overnight visitors are not available separately. Data refer to the number of arrivals and not to the number of people.
International Tourism, Receipts	The receipts earned by a destination country from inbound tourism and covering all tourism receipts resulting from expenditures made by visitors from abroad. These include lodging, food and drinks, fuel, transport in the country, entertainment, shopping, etc. This concept includes receipts generated by overnight visits as well as by same-day trips. It does, however, exclude the receipts related to international transport by contracted residents of the other countries (for instance ticket receipts from foreigners travelling with a national company).

(continued on next page)

Indicator	Definition
TRANSPORT AND COMMUNICATIONS	
Transport	
Road Traffic Deaths	Death caused by a road traffic crash and occurring within 24 hours (Kiribati, the Federated States of Micronesia, Solomon Islands, Timor-Leste, Tonga); 7 days (Azerbaijan, Bhutan, the People's Republic of China, Tajikistan, Turkmenistan, Viet Nam); 30 days (Armenia, Australia, Cambodia, Fiji, India, Indonesia, Japan, Kazakhstan, the Republic of Korea, Lao PDR , Malaysia, Mongolia, Myanmar, Nepal, New Zealand, Papua New Guinea, Singapore, Sri Lanka, Uzbekistan); unlimited time period (Afghanistan, the Cook Islands, Georgia, Maldives, the Philippines, Samoa, Thailand); within a year (the Kyrgyz Republic); no definition for other countries.
Road Network	Refers to the Asian Highway that consists of highway routes of international importance within Asia, including highway routes substantially crossing more than one subregion; highway routes within subregions that connect neighboring subregions; and highway routes located within member states that provide access to: (i) capital cities; (ii) main industrial and agricultural centers; (iii) major air, sea, and river ports; (iv) major container terminals and depots; and (v) major tourist attractions.
Motor Vehicles	Include cars, buses, freight vehicles, and two- and three-wheeled vehicles.
Container Port Traffic	Measures the flow of containers from land to sea transport modes, and vice versa, in 20-foot equivalent units, a standard-size container. Data refer to coastal shipping as well as international journeys. Transshipment traffic is counted as two lifts at the intermediate port (once to offload and again as an outbound lift) and includes empty units.
Air Transport, Passengers Carried	Air passengers carried include both domestic and international aircraft passengers of air carriers registered in the country.
Air Transport, Carrier Departures Worldwide	Registered carrier departures worldwide are domestic takeoffs and takeoffs abroad of air carriers registered in the country.
Air Transport, Freight	Air freight is the volume of freight, express, and diplomatic bags carried on each flight stage (operation of an aircraft from takeoff to its next landing), measured in metric tons multiplied by kilometers traveled.
Rail Lines	Rail lines are the length of railway route available for train service, irrespective of the number of parallel tracks.
Rail Network	Length of rail lines divided by the land area.
Railways, Passengers Carried	Passengers carried by railway are the number of passengers transported by rail multiplied by kilometers traveled.
Railways, Goods Transported	Goods transported by railway are the volume of goods transported by railway, measured in metric tons multiplied by kilometers traveled.
Communications	
Telephone Subscribers	Fixed-telephone subscriptions refer to the sum of active number of analogue fixed telephone lines, voice-over-IP subscriptions, fixed wireless local loop subscriptions, ISDN voice-channel equivalents, and fixed public payphones.
Mobile Phone Subscribers	The proportion of individuals who used a mobile telephone in the 3 months prior to data collection. A mobile (cellular) telephone refers to a portable telephone subscribing to a public mobile telephone service using cellular technology, which provides access to the PSTN. This includes analogue and digital cellular systems and technologies such as IMT-2000 (3G) and IMT- Advanced. Users of both postpaid subscriptions and prepaid accounts are included.
Fixed-Broadband Subscribers	Fixed-broadband subscriptions refer to fixed subscriptions to high-speed access to the public internet (a TCP/IP connection), at downstream speeds equal to, or greater than, 256 kilobits per second. This includes cable modem, DSL, fiber-to-the-home/building, other fixed (wired)- broadband subscriptions, satellite broadband and terrestrial fixed wireless broadband. This total is measured irrespective of the method of payment. It excludes subscriptions that have access to data communications (including the Internet) via mobile-cellular networks. It should include fixed WiMAX and any other fixed wireless technologies. It includes both residential subscriptions and subscriptions for organizations.

(continued on next page)

Indicator	Definition
Internet Users	The frequency of internet use by individuals who used the internet from any location in the 3 months prior to data collection. Internet can be used via a computer, mobile, phone, personal digital assistant, games machine, digital TV etc.

ENERGY AND ELECTRICITY

Energy

Indicator	Definition
GDP per Unit of Energy Use	The ratio of GDP to total energy use (measured per petajoule) with GDP converted to 2017 constant international dollars using PPP rates. An international dollar has the same purchasing power over GDP as a US dollar has in the US.
Energy Production	Primary energy production that is the capture or extraction of fuels or energy from natural energy flows, the biosphere, and natural reserves of fossil fuels within the national territory in a form suitable for use. Inert matter removed from the extracted fuels and quantities reinjected, flared, or vented are not included. The resulting products are referred to as primary products.
Energy Use	Energy production plus imports minus exports, minus international marine bunkers, minus international aviation bunkers, minus stock changes. Also referred to as energy supply.
Energy Imports, Net	Energy imports, net estimated as energy use less production, both measured in petajoules.

Electricity

Indicator	Definition
Electricity Production	Gross production, which is the sum of the electrical energy production by all the generating units and/or installations concerned (including pumped storage), measured at the output terminals of the main generators. Also referred to as electricity generation.
Sources of Electricity	Refers to the different types of technology and/or processes for the generation or production of electricity, including: (i) electricity from combustible fuels, which refers to the production of electricity from the combustion of fuels that are capable of igniting or burning, i.e., reacting with oxygen to produce a significant rise in temperature; (ii) hydroelectricity, which refers to electricity produced from devices driven by fresh, flowing, or falling water; (iii) nuclear electricity, which refers to electricity generated by nuclear plants; and (iv) other electricity, which includes solar, wind, wave, tidal, other marine electricity, geothermal, electricity generated from chemical heat, and electricity from other sources not elsewhere specified.
Electric Power Consumption Per Capita	Total electricity consumption divided by midyear population, where consumption refers to energy-industries-own-use and final consumption. Energy-industries-own-use refers to the consumption of electricity for the direct support of the production and preparation for use of fuels and energy. Final consumption refers to the consumption of electricity by manufacturing, construction and nonfuel mining, transport, and households and other consumers (nonenergy use being irrelevant for electricity).
Household Electrification Rate	Percentage of households with an electricity connection.

ENVIRONMENT

Land

Indicator	Definition
Agricultural Land or Area	Land area that is arable, under permanent crops, and/or under permanent meadows and pastures.
Arable Land	Land under temporary agricultural crops (double-cropped areas are counted only once), temporary meadows for mowing or pasture, land under market, and kitchen gardens and land temporarily fallow (less than 5 years). The abandoned land resulting from shifting cultivation is not included. Data for arable land are not meant to indicate the amount of land that are potentially cultivable.

(continued on next page)

Indicator	Definition
Permanent Cropland	Land cultivated with long-term crops that do not have to be replanted for several years (such as cocoa and coffee); land under trees and shrubs producing flowers, such as roses and jasmine; and nurseries (except those for forest trees, which should be classified under "forestry"). Permanent meadows and pastures are excluded from land under permanent crops.
Deforestation Rate	Rate of permanent conversion of natural forest area into other uses, including shifting cultivation, permanent agriculture, ranching, settlements, and infrastructure development. Deforested areas do not include areas logged but intended for regeneration or areas degraded by fuel-wood gathering, acid precipitation, or forest fires. A negative rate indicates reforestation or increase in forest area.
Pollution	
Carbon Dioxide Emissions	Carbon dioxide emissions, largely by-products of energy production and use, account for the largest share of greenhouse gases, which are associated with global warming. Anthropogenic carbon dioxide emissions result primarily from fossil fuel combustion and cement manufacturing. In combustion, different fossil fuels release different amounts of carbon dioxide for the same level of energy used: oil releases about 50% more carbon dioxide than natural gas, while coal releases about twice as much. Cement manufacturing releases about half a metric ton of carbon dioxide for each metric ton of cement produced. Data for carbon dioxide emissions include gases from the burning of fossil fuels and cement manufacture but excludes emissions from land use such as deforestation.
Nitrous Oxide Emissions	Nitrous oxide emissions are mainly from fossil fuel combustion, fertilizers, rainforest fires, and animal waste. Nitrous oxide is a powerful greenhouse gas, with an estimated atmospheric lifetime of 114 years, compared with 12 years for methane. The per-kilogram global warming potential of nitrous oxide is nearly 310 times that of carbon dioxide within 100 years.
Methane Emissions	Methane emissions are those stemming from human activities such as agriculture and from industrial methane production. A kilogram of methane is 21 times as effective at trapping heat in the earth's atmosphere as a kilogram of carbon dioxide within 100 years.
Other Greenhouse Gases	By-product emissions of hydrofluorocarbons, perfluorocarbons, and sulfur hexafluoride. Although emissions of these artificial gases are small, they are more powerful greenhouse gases than carbon dioxide, with much higher atmospheric lifetimes and high global warming potential.
Freshwater	
Internal Renewable Water Resources	Internal renewable water resources (IRWR) refer to the long-term average annual flow of rivers and recharge of aquifers generated from endogenous precipitation. Double-counting of surface water and groundwater resources is avoided by deducting the overlap from the sum of the surface water and groundwater resources. IRWR in billion cubic meters per year refers to surface water produced internally, plus groundwater produced internally deducted by the overlap between surface water and groundwater. IRWR in cubic meters per inhabitant per year is calculated as total annual IRWR divided by total population.
Annual Freshwater Withdrawals	Sum of surface water withdrawal and groundwater withdrawal. Total water withdrawal summed by sector deducted by: desalinated water produced, direct use of treated wastewater, and direct use of agricultural drainage water.
Water Productivity	Water productivity is the ratio of the net benefits from crop, forestry, fishery, livestock, and mixed agricultural systems to the amount of water used to produce those benefits. It is calculated as GDP in constant US dollar prices, divided by annual total water withdrawal.

(continued on next page)

Indicator	Definition
GOVERNMENT AND GOVERNANCE	
Government Finance	
Government Net lending/Net borrowing	Net lending (+) / net borrowing (–) is a summary measure indicating the extent to which government is either putting financial resources at the disposal of other sectors in the economy or abroad, or utilizing the financial resources generated by other sectors in the economy or from abroad. It may be viewed as an indicator of the financial impact of government activity on the rest of the economy and the rest of the world. Net lending (+) / net borrowing (–) is a balancing item calculated as the net operating balance (revenue minus expense) minus the net investment in nonfinancial assets. Net lending/net borrowing is also equal to the net acquisition of all financial assets minus the net incurrence of all liabilities from transactions. For economies following the IMF's Government Finance Statistics 1986 framework, the indicator refers to the overall budgetary surplus / deficit measured as the difference between total revenue (including grants) and total expenditure (including net lending).
Government Taxes	Taxes are compulsory, unrequited amounts receivable by government units from institutional units. Certain compulsory receivables, such as fines, penalties, and most social security contributions are not considered taxes. For economies following the IMF's Government Finance Statistics 1986 framework, tax revenue are compulsory transfers to the central government for public purposes, which includes social security contributions.
Government Revenue	Government revenue is an increase in net worth resulting from a transaction. Revenue transactions have counterpart entries either in an increase in assets or in a decrease in liabilities - thereby increasing net worth. General government units have four types of revenue: (i) compulsory levies in the form of taxes and certain types of social contributions; (ii) property income derived from the ownership of assets; (iii) sales of goods and services; and (iv) other transfers receivable from other units. For economies following the IMF's Government Finance Statistics 1986 framework, the total revenue (including grants) consists of current and capital revenues. Current revenue is the revenue accruing from taxes as well as all current nontax revenues, except transfers received from foreign governments and international institutions. Capital revenue constitutes the proceeds from the sale of nonfinancial capital assets.
Government Expenditure	Government expenditure is the sum of expense and the net investment in nonfinancial assets. Expense is a decrease in net worth resulting from a transaction. The major types of expense are compensation of employees, use of goods and services subsidies, grants, social benefits, and other expense. The acquisition of a nonfinancial asset by purchase or barter is not an expense because it has no effect on net worth. Similarly, amounts payable on loans extended and repayments on loans incurred are not classified as expense. Nonfinancial assets are economic assets other than financial assets. Nonfinancial assets are stores of value and provide benefits either through their use in the production of goods and services or in the form of property income and holding gains. These assets are classified as fixed assets, inventories, valuables, and nonproduced assets. For economies following the IMF's Government Finance Statistics 1986 framework, total expenditure (including net lending) consists of current and capital expenditures. Current expenditure comprises purchases of goods and services by the central government, transfers to noncentral government units and to households, subsidies to producers, and interest on public debt. Capital expenditure covers outlays for the acquisition or construction of capital assets and for the purchase of intangible assets, as well as capital transfers to domestic and foreign recipients. Loans and advances for capital purposes are also included.

(continued on next page)

Indicator	Definition
Government Expenditure on Education	Government expenditure on education includes expenditure on services provided to individual pupils and students and expenditure on services provided on a collective basis. Expenditure on education is allocated to pre-primary and primary education, secondary education, post-secondary nontertiary education, tertiary education, subsidiary services to education, education not definable by level, and research and development (R&D) education. For economies following the IMF's Government Finance Statistics 1986 framework, the indicator refers to government expenditure on education affairs and services.
Government Expenditure on Health	Government expenditure on health includes expenditure on services provided to individual persons and services provided on a collective basis. Expenditure on health is allocated to medical products, appliances, and equipment; outpatient services; hospital services; public health services; R&D health; and health not elsewhere classified. For economies following the IMF's Government Finance Statistics 1986 framework, the indicator refers to government expenditure on health affairs and services.
Government Expenditure on Social Protection	Government expenditure on social protection includes expenditure on services and transfers provided to individual persons and households and expenditure on services provided on a collective basis. Expenditure on social protection is allocated to sickness and disability, old age, survivors, family and children, unemployment, housing, social exclusion not elsewhere classified, and R&D social protection. For economies following the IMF's Government Finance Statistics 1986 framework, the indicator refers to government expenditure on social security and welfare affairs and services.
Governance	
Time Required to Start Up a Business	Number of calendar days needed to complete the procedures to legally operate a business. If a procedure can be accelerated at additional cost, the fastest procedure, independent of cost, is chosen.
Score (Starting a Business)	The score for starting a business is the simple average of the scores for each of the component indicators: the procedures, time and cost for an entrepreneur to start and formally operate a business, and the paid-in minimum capital requirement.
Rank (Starting a Business)	The ranking of economies on the ease of starting a business is determined by sorting their scores for starting a business.
Corruption Perceptions Index	Ranks countries and territories based on how corrupt or otherwise their public sector is perceived to be. It is a composite index—a combination of polls—drawing on corruption-related data collected by a variety of reputable institutions. The index reflects the views of observers from around the world, including experts living and working in the countries and territories evaluated. From 2000 to 2011, scores ranged from 10 (highly clean) to 0 (highly corrupt). From 2012 onward, calculation of the score has used an updated methodology and is now presented on a 100 (very clean) to 0 (highly corrupt) scale. Due to this difference in methodology, scores from years prior to and including 2011 should not be compared with scores from 2012 onward. A country's rank indicates its position relative to the other countries or territories included in the index. It is important to keep in mind that a country's rank can change simply because new countries enter the index or others drop out.

Global Value Chains

Indicator	Definition
Business Services Sector	Consists of the sectors: Sale, Maintenance, and Repair of Motor Vehicles and Motorcycles; Retail Trade, Except of Motor Vehicles and Motorcycles; Repair of Household Goods; Hotels and Restaurants; Inland Transport; Water Transport; Air Transport; Other Supporting and Auxiliary Transport Activities; Activities of Travel Agencies; Post and Telecommunications; Financial Intermediation; Real Estate Activities; Renting of Machinery and Equipment; and Other Business Activities.
Domestic Value-Added via Backward Linkages (DVA_B)	Value-added that is originated from all domestic sectors that are embedded in the exports of a particular sector in the source economy, regardless of where it is ultimately absorbed.
Domestic Value-Added via Forward Linkages (DVA_F)	Domestic value-added that is exported via all forward linkages, regardless of where it is ultimately absorbed. Alternatively, this refers to domestic value-added that is originated from a particular sector and ultimately embodied in exports (regardless of where these exports are finally consumed).
Domestic Value-Added Absorbed Abroad (VAX_G)	All domestic value-added embodied in gross exports and ultimately absorbed abroad.
Domestic Value-Added First Exported then Returned Home (RDV_B)	Domestic value-added that is first exported, but then returned to the home economy for domestic consumption. This would happen, for example, when the Philippines exports electronic parts to the People's Republic of China for the final assembly of laptops, which are then returned to the Philippines for consumer purchase.
Foreign Value-Added (FVA)	Imported inputs of goods and services in the overall exports of an economy.
Global Value Chains (GVCs)	A network of interlinked stages of production for goods and services that straddles international borders. Typically, a GVC involves combining imported and domestically produced goods and services into products that are then exported for use as intermediates in the subsequent stage of production or as final consumption products.
GVC Participation	There are various ways to measure the participation of economies in GVCs. A simple metric is the share of foreign value-added in total exports. It reflects the extent to which an economy uses foreign inputs in producing exports. A more rigorous measure is vertical specialization.
Low-Technology Industrial Sector	Consists of the sectors: Food, Beverages, and Tobacco; Textiles and Textile Products; Leather, Leather Products, and Footwear; Wood and Products of Wood and Cork; Pulp, Paper, Paper Products, Printing, and Publishing; Rubber and Plastics; Manufacturing, NEC; Recycling; Electricity, Gas, and Water Supply; and Construction.
Medium- and High-Technology Industrial Sector	Consists of the sectors: Coke, Refined Petroleum, and Nuclear Fuel; Chemicals and Chemical Products; Other Nonmetallic Minerals; Basic Metals and Fabricated Metals; Machinery, NEC; Electrical and Optical Equipment; and Transport Equipment.
Personal and Public Services Sector	Consists of the sectors: Public Administration and Defense; Compulsory Social Security; Education; Health and Social Work; Other Community, Social, and Personal Services; and Private Households with Employed persons.
Primary Sector	Consists of the sectors: Agriculture, Hunting, Forestry, and Fishing; and Mining and Quarrying.
Pure Double-Counted Terms (PDC)	In a GVC, some goods or services may cross the same national border on three or more occasions.
Revealed Comparative Advantage (RCA)	Traditional method: Introduced by Bela Balassa, this index represents the relative advantage an economy has in the export of any given good or service. An economy is said to have an RCA in a product if it exports more than its "fair share", or a share that is equal to or greater than the share of the product to total world trade. Value-added method: Based on Wang, Wei and Zhu (2018), this measure is similar to the traditional RCA method, except that it is based on DVA_F rather than gross exports. An economy is said to have an RCA in a product if its DVA_F matches or exceeds the share of the product's DVA_F in total global value-added in exports.
Value-Added Exports via Backward Linkages (VAX_B)	Value-added that is originated from all domestic sectors and ultimately absorbed abroad via the exports of a particular sector in the source economy. For example, the domestic value-added of Japanese automobile exports includes that of all Japanese sectors (e.g., business services, computers) used as inputs.

(continued on next page)

Indicator	Definition
Value-Added Exports via Forward Linkages (VAX_F)	Domestic value-added that is originated from a particular sector and ultimately absorbed abroad via the exports of all sectors in the source economy. For example, besides direct export, the value-added of the Japanese business services sector may be exported as an input to Japanese automobiles. This indicator is useful in understanding the contribution of a given sector to the economy's aggregate exports.